Praise for The Debt Trap

"Private equity plays a crucial role in modern economies. What Sebastien Canderle explains is that the sector's performance depends on a very specific set of value triggers, first among them the optimal use of leverage. Get the mix wrong, however, and as the book's well-researched case studies demonstrate, even the most experienced fund managers can come to regret their foray into leveraged buyouts. *The Debt Trap* is filled with grounded analysis and is an authoritative book for PE practitioners and scholars alike."

Franklin Allen, Nippon Life Professor of Finance and Economics at the Wharton School of the University of Pennsylvania, and Brevan Howard Centre director at Imperial College in London

"Written for an audience with a working knowledge of finance, *The Debt Trap* dissects the dealmaking that undergirds leveraged buyouts and provides an essential road map to the many ways that this has changed since the 2008 financial crisis. Detailed examinations of high-profile buyouts demystify the excessively risky and opaque means – new and old – that private equity firms use to acquire companies. *The Debt Trap* should be required reading for the staff and trustees of institutional investors, and for professionals working at lending institutions, but the clear writing and compelling case studies make it appealing to a much wider audience."

Eileen Appelbaum, Senior Economist at the Center for Economic and Policy Research, and author of *Private Equity at Work*

"Private equity has thrived on debt. Excessive debt can harm companies. This important book shows how and why thanks to a rich set of in-depth case studies. It is essential reading for practitioners and students of private equity."

François Degeorge, Senior Chair of the Swiss Finance Institute and Professor of Finance at the Università della Svizzera italiana

"Sebastien Canderle has written a genuinely compelling book that raises crucial questions about modern-day PE investment practices. *The Debt Trap* is a thoughtful and stimulating work that helps to frame the debate on value creation in the world of alternative finance."

Pablo Fernández, Professor of Financial Management and PricewaterhouseCoopers Chair of Corporate Finance at IESE Business School

"Not only does *The Debt Trap* offer plenty of warning for private investors about investing in IPOs where the company floating is backed by a Private Equity house, but also offers institutional investors plenty of evidence of what can go wrong with companies saddled with the exorbitant debt an LBO can bring. We're also taken on a tour of the most favoured practices of PE owners when trying to extract the maximum return on their investment... What I most like about this book is its broad scope in explaining the social effects of this kind of financial engineering."

Owen Jones, *Fidelity*

"Sebastien Canderle's book should be at the top of recommended reading lists for every finance course. It is a skilful critique of the fast-paced private equity industry. Drawing on a vast amount of research, *The Debt Trap* gives fascinating insights into some of the most illustrious leveraged buyouts, which will help to improve our teaching of finance and contribute to a sounder financial industry. For that reason it deserves to be read."

Jacques Régniez, Professor of Economics and Finance at the State University of New York

"*The Debt Trap* is a very valuable addition to the inordinately small body of literature on the subject of private equity... By breaking down the asset class's methods through relatable examples, Canderle has opened the door for further investigation into the opaque world of private equity."

Darragh Riordan, Real Deals

"Call it 'the art of the leveraged buyout'... Canderle explores some of the more controversial business strategies such as quick flips, repeat dividend recaps, heavy cost cutting, and asset stripping as related to leveraged buyouts...the author brings these investment strategies to life through real-world application - offering an up-close view of private equity deal-making. The text is a great resource for PE fund managers and business people alike."

Wharton Magazine

"A valuable contribution to the literature on private equity, *The Debt Trap* is an absorbing study of why leverage is a two-edged sword and should be used with utmost caution. The book is an important read for anyone involved in the private equity world or even the finance world at large."

Jacob Wolinsky, CEO of ValueWalk

THE DEBT TRAP

ALSO BY SEBASTIEN CANDERLE

Private Equity's Public Distress

THE DEBT TRAP

How leverage impacts
private-equity performance

SEBASTIEN CANDERLE

HARRIMAN HOUSE

HARRIMAN HOUSE LTD

18 College Street

Petersfield

Hampshire

GU31 4AD

GREAT BRITAIN

Tel: +44 (0)1730 233870

Email: enquiries@harriman-house.com

Website: www.harriman-house.com

First published in Great Britain in 2016

This reprint 2017

Copyright © Sebastien Canderle

Print ISBN: 978-0-85719-540-1

eBook ISBN: 978-0-85719-541-8

British Library Cataloguing in Publication Data

A CIP catalogue record for this book can be obtained from the British Library.

Contents

PREFACE

In the fall of 2014, I gave a series of lectures on private equity to a group of graduate business students. As part of the process, we discussed actual transactions, delving into the intricacies of leveraged buyout financing and structuring. Soon, I realised that the students were far more interested in the business stories than in the theory. And the reason – at least the one they gave me – is that they could readily understand how the concepts were applied in the real world. Almost immediately, I started working on writing full case studies, a version of which is now in your hands.

This book describes how the principles of private equity dealmaking work out in practice. It does so by describing LBOs that took place in recent years, focusing on fundamental aspects of debt-fuelled transactions. In that, it is fairly unique. Few publications offer an inside view of the effects of leverage on PE-backed companies. Throughout, the reader will apprehend how the application of value triggers, introduced in Chapter 1, impacts the performance of fund managers and their investee businesses. In dividing the case studies between various themes, the primary goal has been to provide the reader with a critical analysis of the main techniques applied by buyout sponsors.

Yet, each section should not be considered in isolation, but very much as part of the industry's process of constant development and reinvention. Unlike certain other disciplines that are subject to limited change, such as accounting and corporate finance, the area of private equity is one that is continually evolving. Financial innovation, new tax systems, political influences, refreshed regulatory regimes and powerful lobbying render the descriptions of particular PE topics dated almost before they are printed.

In a sense, this volume integrates and expands on a number of ideas covered in my first book *Private Equity's Public Distress*. Where it differs is in the depth and breadth of its analysis of specific transactions. The latter are not just covered at the outset but during the life of the company under PE ownership and post-exit. This is an important nuance, for many PE-backed businesses frequently struggle to recover from their LBO adventure.

The book is intended for all PE practitioners, investors, corporate managers, academics and business students who are keen to master the art of leveraged buyouts while bearing in mind the lessons and pitfalls highlighted in each case study. This knowledge will, hopefully, enable significant improvement in the sector's ability to create value, while preserving the interests of all stakeholders, the sanity of the corporate world and the stability of financial markets.

September 2016

ABBREVIATIONS AND LEXICON

A&E Amend and Extend process whereby lenders to a leveraged company consent to the amendment of the credit agreement and an extension of the debt maturities to avoid a default. In exchange, lenders are typically granted a higher margin on their loans and a consent fee.

Basis point (bp) One hundredth of one percentage point.

Bullet loan Loan where the repayment of the entire principal, and sometimes of the principal and interest, is due on the maturity date.

Carried interest Or carry. The share of capital gains assigned to the general partner.

CLO Collateralised loan obligation. A security comprised of a pool of loans with different maturities, seniorities, coupons and risk profiles.

Coupon The interest rate paid on a bond (as a percentage of the bond's par value).

Debt exchange Transaction by which the issuer/borrower exchanges new securities for existing ones in order to extend loan maturities, reduce the total amount of debt outstanding, and/or convert debt into equity.

Debt-for-equity swap Whereby debt is turned into equity.

Debt push-down Process by which LBO loans are lowered in the group structure in order to obtain a tax-effective interest deduction on the LBO loans.

Debt-to-Equity ratio Or leverage ratio. A stricter definition of leverage is the debt-to-capital ratio, where capital = debt + equity.

EBITDA Earnings before interest, tax, depreciation and amortisation.

Equitisation Debt-for-equity swap.

Euribor Euro InterBank Offered Rate. A key benchmark interest rate for LBO loans.

EV Enterprise value. The combination of equity (market capitalisation for listed companies) and debt, net of cash.

First lien   First-lien loans give their holders priority rights, in case of default or liquidation, over the assets used as collateral for the loan. Because of the security they benefit from, first-lien loans are lower-yielding than other loans.

First-loss facility   The most junior tranche in a structured finance transaction. The part of the debt structure that will suffer losses first in case of default.

GP (general partner)   Company that manages capital invested as equity in leveraged transactions, a.k.a. PE fund manager, LBO firm or financial sponsor.

High-yield bond   Or junk bond. Generally, the most junior/subordinated debt instrument.

IRR   Internal rate of return. The annualised compound return rate on an investment and the key performance yardstick of PE fund managers. IRR is reported net or gross of fees charged by the fund manager.

Junior debt   Subordinated loans, such as mezzanine and high-yield bonds, that are not always secured on assets.

Libor   London InterBank Offered Rate. A key benchmark interest rate for LBO loans.

LP (limited partner)   Institutional or wealthy individual investor committing funds to a GP.

OPM   Other people's money. In PE jargon, it is money GPs can afford to lose.

PIK (payment-in-kind)   PIK instruments give the right to the issuer to pay accrued interest at the time that the principal is repaid.

To PIK a loan   To stop paying cash interest on a loan and convert it instead into a bullet payment.

Price flex   A change in the spread or margin on a syndicated loan. If demand is lower than anticipated, the margin on the loan is increased (or flexed upward) to encourage demand. A reverse flex occurs when a loan is oversubscribed.

PTP   Public-to-private. Delisting of a publicly traded company.

RBO   Relapse buyout. The purchase by a PE firm of a former portfolio company.

Recap(italisation)   Restructuring of the balance sheet where equity is replaced with debt, or vice versa.

Revolver   Or revolving credit facility; working capital facility. Instrument used to finance short-term cash requirements.

SBO   Secondary buyout. By extension, includes tertiaries, quaternaries, quintenaries and other follow-on sponsor-to-sponsor deals.

Second lien   Second-lien loans give rights on the assets used as collateral that are subordinated to those of first-lien noteholders.

Senior debt   Higher lien loans that must be repaid first in case of default by, or liquidation of, the issuer.

Toggle PIK note   Bond where the issuer has the option to defer an interest payment by agreeing to pay an increased coupon in the future.

Warranted mezzanine   A mezzanine loan that gives right to warrants. A warrant is a security that gives the holder the right to buy shares in a company.

Yield   Interest rate earned on a loan (as a percentage of its market value). If a loan trades at a discount, its yield will be higher than the coupon, and conversely if a loan trades at a premium, its yield will be lower than the coupon.

Zombie company   A portfolio company that is unable to meet its debt commitments but remains under PE ownership, often for a protracted period.

Zombie fund   A GP unable to raise a follow-on fund and staying alive in order for its employees to keep earning management fees (and, incidentally, for the remaining portfolio assets to be exited).

INTRODUCTION

"Those who cannot remember the past are condemned to repeat it."[1]

George Santayana

Debt is one of the most lethal of financial weapons. If you wish to annihilate a business, a brutal means of ensuring that it will not outlive the next economic cycle is by breezily stuffing its balance sheet with expensive loans.

It is not just the cost of the debt (the interest expense) that is the problem – it is generally pegged to the interbank rate and therefore somewhat benefits from the loosening of monetary policy that normally accompanies a recession. Rather, it is the absolute quantum of debt, meaning the size of principal repayments, and the maturity of this liability that can strangle even the most frugal company. Revenues tend to drop off during an economic slowdown, and profitability and cash flows follow the same path, whilst debt obligations – scheduled reimbursements and accruing interest charges – do not. As the case studies will highlight, this is when leveraged businesses can get in trouble. Long-term debt binds the borrower to a series of future cash payments. The penalty for failing to meet such obligations can be severe.

Equally, debt is an extremely effective instrument of value creation. By minimising their initial equity commitment and levering up their position, investors can yield returns that far exceed those of fast-moving technology firms or businesses operating in strong-growth emerging markets. Cost of debt is usually much lower than the cost of equity. Thus, the higher the amount of loans raised, the lower the weighted cost of capital. Since returns on equity rise as financial gearing increases, there is no question that, in private equity, the use of debt is critical to success. The easiest and quickest way to outperform your peers is to borrow heavily, whereas it is a lot more strenuous to boost underlying investment performance through operational improvements. Hence the tendency by the vast majority of leveraged buyout (LBO) funds to maximise rather than optimise leverage. As one general partner (GP) puts it:

1

"Our philosophy is to lever our deals as much as we can, to give the highest returns to our limited partners."[2]

This manual contains a description of transactions as varied as listings, public-to-privates (PTPs), repurchases, private investments in public equity (PIPEs), quick flips, recapitalisations and secondary buyouts (SBOs). All 14 buyouts have one thing in common: they owe their performance primarily to the vast amount of capital borrowed from third parties. Whether they generated a prodigious rate of return for their private equity (PE) backers or ended up in the arms of their creditors is essentially due to how they dealt with their indebtedness.

Some managed to boost their internal rate of return (IRR) on invested capital through early exits and/or refinancings (Celanese, Debenhams, Hertz), others rescheduled their loans whenever it became clear that they would fail to repay them (witnessing numerous loan extensions or restructuring processes). Others again were saved from the bailiffs thanks to a resurgent market or the helpful support of central bankers or governments (Foxtons), while the unlucky ones fell into the arms of less understanding lenders (EMI, Frans Bonhomme, Gala Coral, PagesJaunes, Seat Pagine Gialle), or filed for bankruptcy (TXU, Caesars Entertainment). These businesses usually spent years trying to recover from their LBO experience. All, without exception, greatly suffered – either during or post-LBO – from their huge level of debt, hence the title of this book.

Fusion of the debt and equity worlds

Although to some readers this might come across as just semantics, the term 'private equity' is fast becoming a misnomer. What makes the analysis of leveraged transactions all the more tricky is the sector's recent transformation. In the summer of 2007 the financial markets across the globe froze. While the trigger of this lending crisis was the inflated American property market – and more specifically its bloated, low-quality, built-on-quicksand subprime segment – the Credit Crunch had an immediate impact on the world of buyouts, which are reliant on a well-functioning banking system.

With the stated goal of avoiding a repeat of the 2008 financial crisis, governments, central bankers and regulators introduced tougher lending rules for 'too-big-to-fail' institutions, in particular large commercial banks. As a consequence, the latter significantly scaled down their lending activities, reinforced their risk-management procedures and introduced stricter lending conditions.

In parallel, the largest PE participants launched initiatives to mitigate the many mistakes made during the bubble of 2004 to 2007. Handling over $4 trillion of capital by the end of 2015,[3] the PE sector has sought to diversify, almost on an industrial scale, into equally lucrative (at least for fund managers) fee-earning public-market and real-estate funds. Many PE fund managers are also active private-debt providers, and increasingly so. As several of the case studies show, it is in part thanks to the strong desire of non-banking lenders, among them a number of traditional PE investors like Apollo, Blackstone and Kohlberg Kravis Roberts (KKR), to take advantage of the fact that they are not subject to the new banking rules, that many leveraged companies remained afloat.

This was reinforced by the central banks' concerted decisions to keep interest rates at historical lows from 2009 onwards, and by the strong preference expressed by conventional lenders to agree to reschedule LBO loans in order not to have to recognise them as losses on their books. As several of our case stories will emphasise, many traditional lenders willingly passed on their LBO loan positions to private-debt managers, also known as shadow lenders for their ability to operate outside the remit of regulation.

Eager to dilute the fallout of their overextended LBO activities, PE firms sought to retain control by taking positions on the debt side of transactions. Yet it would be wrong to underplay the continued influence of these players on mainstream mergers and acquisitions (M&As). Through their LBO divisions, the most powerful PE fund managers own companies generating billions of dollars in revenues and employing millions of people worldwide. The sector accounts for a large proportion of M&A activity and initial public offerings (IPOs) in a given year. In view of its growing sway over our financial markets and economies, clearly PE is an industry worth getting to know.

Good or evil?

While in the first three decades of its history PE had been able to fob its critics off by headlining high-profile success stories and strong returns, the post-financial crisis years have reopened the eternal debate about whether the buyout sector actually adds value. Put another way: once returns are adjusted for the profligate use of debt and the various economic and social spillovers such as layoffs, asset disposals and plant closures, does PE create macroeconomic wealth for the long term? Or are LBOs simply a vehicle for fund managers to divert a significant proportion of capital gains into their coffers to the detriment of the portfolio companies' employees and society at large?[4]

Unfortunately the only way to fully answer this question would be to review the entire portfolio of LBOs carried out globally in the last 40 years and to determine whether, on a net basis, PE investments created jobs, generated economic benefits, and improved the well-being of all stakeholders above and beyond what corporations would have achieved without PE's contribution. Such a task is virtually impossible.

For one thing, with the exception of a few investment trusts and holdings that are publicly listed and fully report the audited performance of their underlying portfolio, the vast majority of PE fund managers are private partnerships that operate under a code of silence and do not have, and certainly do not seek, to disclose information to the public. Not surprisingly, when they do so they are extraordinarily cautious, selectively using the services of a very powerful PR machine to advertise investments that have proved successful – where success is defined as having yielded strong returns on investment for their fund providers, known as limited partners or LPs – or that can enhance the profile of the PE firm due to the transaction's size or image.

Several reports have been issued in the past to underscore the undisputable merits of leveraged buyouts in terms of job creation, revenue growth and R&D initiatives. Such studies have, almost without exception, been released by trade associations (such as the National Venture Capital Association in the US), or by industry-sponsored research bodies (e.g., the Private Equity Growth Capital Council), if not by corporations with a strong vested interest in stressing the virtues of PE because they derive a significant portion of their revenues from LBO firms – naturally the big four accountancy firms and several strategy consultancies frequently release laudatory notes on the sector. One could be forgiven for viewing these as slightly biased.

In any case, there have now been quite a few research papers issued by university professors and consultants that articulate many of private equity's shortcomings, with insufficient or inadequate reporting, financial and credit risk exposure, and labour market considerations top of the list.[5] Tellingly, in its *Global Private Equity Report 2014*, management consultancy Bain & Company analysed nearly 2,700 deals globally and noted that the worst-performing PE firms (those yielding a net fund IRR of less than 5%) lost money on approximately half of their deals. But Bain's analysis is all the more striking for the fact that the best-performers (with a net fund IRR exceeding 15%) failed to break even on over a quarter of their transactions. Not such a great record coming from so-called sophisticated investors.

No matter which side of the argument you sit on, the buyout sector was part of, and a strong contributor to, the hostile takeover/junk bond mania of the late 1980s as well as the debt orgy of the mid-noughties. No industry can be implicated in two bubbles within a 20-year period without standing guilty of some sort of misconduct.

Real cases as analytical tools

Because of its pathologically compulsive quest for secrecy and the diverse and complex features of its dealmaking, private equity cannot be conceived in its entirety. To proclaim at a stroke that the whole sector is evil or a force for good is meaningless – and beside the point, since it cannot be proven due to the lack of reliable, unbiased and independently verifiable evidence. A number of experts have admitted that there is no consistent and complete set of performance data to properly benchmark PE funds' returns against those of other alternative funds and the public markets. Anyway, no one entity or industry is either all good or bad, and the world of unlisted stocks is too complex to be reduced to glib categorisation. Rather, I believe that it is more intuitive to underline the sector's failings and fortunes by relaying the intricacies of real transactions.

Unwilling to debate the merits of one side against the other, I have therefore chosen a different approach – the case study method – to describe the main tricks of the trade as well as, in some instances, flaws and misdeeds propagated by LBOs in recent years. The present compilation of actual transactions paints the industry's performance-maximising techniques in all their nuances.

Through 14 real-life deals, this work should help the reader to understand how PE makes money and what is occasionally wrong with some of the practices implemented by LBO fund managers. The protagonists are authentic, the stories genuine. I have also included suggestions for tackling and eliminating the worst behaviours and, unlike the standard case study approach, I provide personal views to better apprehend the full range of colours that are part of the familiar LBO patchwork.

I must declare one caveat. The perceptive reader will note that most of the examples cover companies that were, at some point in their history, either quoted on a stock exchange (before and/or after their leveraged transaction), or partly financed with high-yield bonds or other form of listed securities. There is a very simple explanation for that. Again, LBO fund managers are private partnerships – often established in tax havens for obvious reasons – that do not have to reveal information on their dealings and financial performance. To write up a case study on these firms and their unquoted investee companies would require relying exclusively on second-hand accounts and press releases. But these are far from neutral. To show the shortcomings of such an approach I have included the story of Frans Bonhomme (Chapter 8), a business that remained private throughout its LBO experience and on which limited information was freely and willingly made available.

Consequently, the most desirable way to gather crucial deal-related information is by looking at public, ideally independently audited or regulated, disclosures.

Only companies with shares or bonds listed on an exchange must make such disclosures, hence their overwhelming presence in the following case histories.

Naturally, I am fully aware of the risk of producing general rules and recommendations on the back of a short list of anecdotal illustrations. By doing so I am exposing my views to much criticism, and I am providing the industry's stalwarts with the excuse that these flawed or failed deals do not in any way discredit the entire sector, but are rather isolated, unintended and unpredictable accidents. I concede that all investors have at some point in their life made mistakes and no one can be expected to be right all the time. Because 14 debt-laden transactions bombed miserably or harmed the underlying business should not mean that PE activity is unsound. However, as you are about to read, because of the errors described in these examples and due to their increasing frequency in the total volume of deals, they can to a great extent be considered representative of wider issues for the sector.

One of the implicit aims of this book is to help investors stay clear of deals that have a high likelihood of failure, either because of the intrinsic risks of the target or the industry it participates in, or because a fund manager's investment methodology does not follow best practice.

Outline of the book

The roots of this book lie in the realisation that a growing proportion of the investment activities of our modern economy take place outside the remit of regulation. This lack of transparency, coupled with fairly obscure terminology, makes private equity baffling, not to mention that the industry is prone to coining new words with eerie regularity.

Every day brings its share of financial news. If the omnipresence of economic and financial information in today's world is easily noticeable, deciphering how and why particular events happen, and their consequences, is much more tortuous. Beyond the mastery of the relevant jargon, the intricacy of leveraged transactions makes knowledge of market theories and financial instruments essential to understanding the effects of LBOs on our market economy.

My purpose here is to apply the case method to draw attention to the most salient failings and excesses of leveraged buyouts; it is not to provide a crash course on private equity. Accordingly, the book presumes good knowledge and understanding of key industry-specific terms, principles and practices nowadays in use. In this respect, those readers not familiar with PE's sometimes unfathomable idiom should find the lexicon at the front of this book handy, and should refer to it when needed. At times, performance data and other financial information, including debt multiples and equity returns, were deliberately rounded off or simplified to avoid swamping the debate with unnecessary detail. I trust this will not distract the reader from the core message.

After a brief introduction to the current approaches and methodologies of PE investing, the book is divided into nine parts. Each section focuses on a particular practice frequently adopted by LBO firms during the credit boom of the noughties and, despite everybody's best intentions, perpetuated ever since. Detailed case studies illustrate the main shortcomings and risks that these industry practices embody. Through the story of Gala Coral, Part One tackles the overused and abused secondary buyout, including its derivatives: tertiary, quaternary and subsequent LBOs.

Part Two covers a trend that has seen LBO investors, traditionally so keen to emphasise their fundamental value-enhancing expertise and long-term perspective, push for early realisations of their investments through quick flips and periodic recapitalisations – the Hertz and Celanese scenarios provide fitting, if somewhat brief, enlightenment.

Part Three will press home a point raised with persistence by journalists and academics: the use of financial engineering with the objective of boosting returns, notwithstanding the market changes affecting the target. It would be difficult to come up with two cases more telling than bankrupt energy giant TXU and defunct music major EMI. These deals help to articulate the concept of the 'risks pyramid', where financial risk (leverage) is piled on top of business-specific issues, operational transformation, market transitions and/or technological shifts, turning this hierarchy of risks into a house of cards.

Part Four introduces a concept that has emanated from the increasing maturity of the sector, where PE managers buy back companies that they previously owned and had disposed of. I call these transactions relapse buyouts (RBOs).

Part Five deals with several factors related to the sector's maturity and its long-term imprint on the leveraged businesses. Two case studies, Debenhams and DX, will help depict the trend of listings, delistings and relistings that has been so prevalent since the early noughties.

Part Six relates another interaction between the realm of private equity and that of public markets through the practice of leveraged private investments in public equity, or PIPEs. In that respect, our cases PagesJaunes and Seat Pagine Gialle will raise issues around corporate governance and social responsibility.

Part Seven will close the topic of PE's relationship with stock markets through the illustration of two troubled PE-backed IPOs. Both eDreams and Foxtons will demonstrate with little room for doubt that it is, at times, wiser to stay clear of companies being introduced to the stock exchange by their PE owners.

The company detailed in Part Eight will highlight the techniques and strong-arm tactics used by modern-day asset-strippers. Casino operator Harrah's/Caesars is the ideal candidate to throw this matter into sharp relief. The final section of the book offers concluding remarks, recommendations and personal views about the future.

The designations used to introduce the case studies can appear at first quite arbitrary. However, my point is to explain the whys and wherefores of PE transactions and the case studies that best reflect them. Yes, Debenhams and DX could have been included in the section on PE-backed IPOs, but the aim of Part Five is to describe the impact that a series of frequent corporate transitions, including a leveraged take-private and a relisting, can have on the underlying business. It is true that Celanese could have been placed among the delisting-relisting case studies, but its quick flip depicts the concept of time value of money in all its splendour. Similarly, Gala Coral qualified for inclusion in the financial engineering and risks pyramid section, but it is such a classic case of quaternary buyout that it justly belonged to Part One.

I hope that this book provides a deeper understanding of how financial, operational and strategic decisions upset the well-being of leveraged investee companies, and how the implementation of better practices can help industry professionals achieve superior performance for their investors.

In the past, the industry's resolute supporters have spared no effort to stress private equity's unrivalled track record in terms of job creation and operational achievements, while its detractors have vigorously portrayed buyout firms as bottom feeders and senseless capitalist locusts. My view, after more than 12 years working for and with PE investors, is that the reality lies somewhere in the middle. Both sides make some good arguments, though undoubtedly what the following cases underline is that, on occasions, LBO professionals could stand accused of incompetence, dereliction of duty, or malice. PE fund managers would argue that their failures owe much to bad luck. It's a moot point. I let you, the reader, be the judge of that.

CHAPTER 1
Tricks of the Trade

"We're not talking about brain surgery here.
This is finance – add, subtract, multiply and divide."[1]

Stephen Schwarzman, Chairman of The Blackstone Group

FOR THOSE ACQUAINTED WITH GENERAL CORPORATE finance principles, what follows will simply serve as a refresher course to frame the case studies in their appropriate context. For readers not *au fait* with the remarkable world of finance, this chapter should give a better understanding of why PE fund managers do the things they do.

The ultimate goal of all LBO operators – referred to as financial sponsors, general partners or GPs throughout this book – is to maximise the performance of the capital they manage on behalf of their institutional investors, the previously mentioned LPs. It is where their duty of care lies. And based on the evidence of the case studies presented hereinafter, not much can distract them from reaching that goal.

The reason behind this compulsive objective is competitive pressure. PE firms wrestle with a swarm of similar expert investors. There is indeed very little differentiation between the various GPs: their staff members are all former bankers or management consultants, many are chartered accountants or MBA graduates, they raise money from the same LPs, and all apply the same financial wizardry aiming to deliver performance. To put it very briefly, this means that they must achieve superior returns, often regardless of the consequences, in order to beat the competition.

Note that, in theory, absolute returns are meaningless since, in corporate finance parlance, an investor should always aim for a risk-adjusted return. If an LBO firm yields the highest returns amongst its peer group, it might be because it has acquired or honed superior skills in selecting acquisition targets, managing them and finding the most value-maximising exit opportunities; or it might be due to the fact that its investment executives are taking much greater risk than their peers are. In practice, it is literally impossible to determine which is the case. And GPs know it. Hence their sole, self-confessed goal of targeting the highest IRR, without making much disclosure about how this was achieved.

Boosting the IRR

In order to achieve their target returns, LBO fund managers have several tools, and they often use a combination of them to deliver the most awe-inspiring performance. The following drivers represent the five pillars of value creation (or value triggers) from a GP's standpoint:

1. **Maximising leverage at inception and frequently refinancing the capital structure** (a.k.a. recapitalisations) by raising further debt in order to pay out dividends (hence the term 'dividend recap'). It enables the PE house to partially realise its investment. It is this 'first pillar' that created the most controversy in the period leading to the Credit Crunch and afterwards, as excessive indebtedness and frequent recapitalisations often left the underlying companies with a stretched balance sheet, unable to meet their loan obligations or fund their growth going forward.

2. **Add-on acquisitions** completed at a lower entry multiple than the one originally paid to buy the portfolio company. That makes them value accretive. Value can also be gleaned through synergistic benefits achieved by merging the acquirer and the target(s). This 'second pillar' is often the main value-driver of buy-and-build strategies for small and mid-market LBOs, in the $50 million to $500 million enterprise-value (EV) range.

3. **Underlying performance improvements and cash-flow maximisation**. This third value trigger has traditionally been a vital tool used by LBO investors during the ownership period, and these operational gains can be achieved by:

   - increasing margins through better cost management (e.g., relocating production facilities to lower-cost countries) and economies of scale via volume growth;

   - lifting cash generation, via reductions in working-capital requirements, cuts in capital expenditure, minimised cash leakage, and sale and leaseback arrangements;

   - discontinuing or disposing of loss-making or low-margin activities. This practice earned some of the early LBO players the moniker 'asset-stripper'. It was common place in the 1970s and 1980s when conglomerates were being taken apart and many of their divisions were an amalgamation of unrelated, underperforming activities. Nowadays few companies suffer from the same lack of focus. We will see with the Caesars case study (Chapter 15) that this has forced financial sponsors to get more creative;

- growing sales, for instance through a refined price point strategy or new product launches.

4. **Multiple-arbitrage**, or 'fourth pillar', meaning exiting a portfolio company at a higher earnings multiple than the one paid at the time of the initial investment. This arbitrage rests on the economic cycle and cannot be relied upon at the outset. It is a nice freebie if it occurs. Many PE investors are quick in claiming some sort of skill involved in achieving any upswing while begrudging poor market conditions when such arbitrage turns negative. Frankly, multiple-arbitrage is heavily cycle-dependent.

5. The last, but arguably most important, factor is the **duration of the investment holding period**. Because of the concept of time value of money, of which more later, most GPs aim to partially or completely get out of an investment as early as possible. This 'fifth value trigger' is not just at the root of the Hertz and Celanese cases; it explains many of financial sponsors' most neurotic obsessions around dividend recaps. While all experienced PE firms place this factor at the core of their investment strategy by aiming to get out of an investment as soon as possible, because the approach is hugely controversial – how can they claim to be long-term value creators if they seek a quick exit? – no LBO manager will ever admit to being short-term focused. The following section, however, will demonstrate why an early exit (full or partial) goes a long way towards explaining superior investment returns.

The essence of IRR maximisation lies in the total amount of leverage contracted. The less equity a buyout firm has to fork out in order to gain majority ownership of an asset, the higher its potential return on investment. Before they even think of boosting their IRR through the other pillars aforementioned, PE executives aim to negotiate the largest and cheapest debt package and minimise their equity ticket.

To better understand why PE investors operate that way, and to help bring out the key reasons behind the odd behaviours described in this book's case studies, a few illustrations will help the reader understand how IRR gets shaped by leverage and the timing of cash flows. The following sets of tables delineate a range of returns that an LBO might achieve. Let us consider eight scenarios with three variables:

- Variable 1 = the amount of leverage (i.e., debt/equity ratio) at inception. We use two different scenarios: 60% or 90% debt.

- Variable 2 = the timing of dividend recaps during the life of the LBO. Again, we review two possibilities: achieving a dividend recap in year 2 or in year 4, while leaving all the other cash flows unchanged.

- Variable 3 = the timing of the exit. We assume a full disposal in year 5 or year 6.

One of the assumptions made in all these scenarios is that none of the debt is repaid during the life of the transaction, but obviously in reality some of it could have been repaid. Assuming no repayment makes the scenarios more easily comparable.

The first couple of scenarios (Table 1.1) look at dividend recapitalisations in years 3 and 4 and an exit of the PE investor in year 6. Both scenarios have the same entry and exit enterprise values. These two scenarios only differ in one way: scenario A uses 90% debt whereas scenario B only uses 60%.

Table 1.1: Year 6 exit with dividend payouts in years 3 and 4

	Scenario A			Scenario B		
	Debt/Equity = 9/1			Debt/Equity = 3/2		
	Equity	**Debt**	**EV**	**Equity**	**Debt**	**EV**
year 0	100	900	1,000	400	600	1,000
year 1	0	0		0	0	
year 2	0	0		0	0	
year 3	50	50		50	50	
year 4	150	150		150	150	
year 5	0	0		0	0	
year 6	100	1,100	1,200	400	800	1,200
IRR	**29%**			**8%**		

The next two scenarios (Table 1.2) look at dividend recapitalisations in years 2 and 3 and an exit of the PE investor in year 6. Both have the same entry and exit enterprise values. These two scenarios only differ in one way: scenario C uses 90% debt whereas scenario D only uses 60%.

Table 1.2: Year 6 exit with dividend payouts in years 2 and 3

	Scenario C			Scenario D		
	Debt/Equity = 9/1			Debt/Equity = 3/2		
	Equity	**Debt**	**EV**	**Equity**	**Debt**	**EV**
year 0	-100	900	1,000	-400	600	1,000
year 1	0	0		0	0	
year 2	150	150		150	150	
year 3	50	50		50	50	
year 4	0	0		0	0	
year 5	0	0		0	0	
year 6	100	1,100	1,200	400	800	1,200
IRR	**44%**			**9%**		

Table 1.3 shows dividend recaps in years 3 and 4 and an exit of the PE investor in year 5. The entry and exit EVs are the same for both. Again, these two scenarios only differ in one way: scenario E uses 90% debt whereas scenario F only uses 60%.

Table 1.3: Year 5 exit with dividend payouts in years 3 and 4

	Scenario E			Scenario F		
	Debt/Equity = 9/1			Debt/Equity = 3/2		
	Equity	**Debt**	**EV**	**Equity**	**Debt**	**EV**
year 0	-100	900	1,000	-400	600	1,000
year 1	0	0		0	0	
year 2	0	0		0	0	
year 3	50	50		50	50	
year 4	150	150		150	150	
year 5	100	1,100	1,200	400	800	1,200
IRR	**31%**			**9%**		

The last set of scenarios (Table 1.4) looks at dividend recaps in years 2 and 3 and an exit of the PE investor in year 5. Both have the same entry and exit enterprise values. The only difference between them is the leverage they use.

Table 1.4: Year 5 exit with dividend payouts in years 2 and 3

	Scenario G			Scenario H		
	Debt/Equity = 9/1			Debt/Equity = 3/2		
	Equity	**Debt**	**EV**	**Equity**	**Debt**	**EV**
year 0	-100	900	1,000	-400	600	1,000
year 1	0	0		0	0	
year 2	150	150		150	150	
year 3	50	50		50	50	
year 4	0	0		0	0	
year 5	100	1,100	1,200	400	800	1,200
IRR	**47%**			**11%**		

Several conclusions can be drawn from these examples:

i. It is better to leverage the balance sheet as much as operationally possible since – assuming all other parameters remain constant – a capital structure with 90% of debt yields significantly higher IRRs for the equity holders than a 60/40 debt-to-equity ratio: scenario A beats B, C beats D, E beats F, and G beats H.

ii. It is more advantageous to do a dividend recap as early as possible in the life of the LBO – a dividend payout in year 2 generates higher average annual returns than one in year 4: example C beats A, D beats B, G beats E, and H beats F.

iii. It is also more profitable to exit as early as possible – although we assume here a constant enterprise value between year 5 and year 6, therefore no value creation during the extra year (which clearly might not be a very accurate reflection of all LBO situations). Still, scenarios exhibiting an exit in year 5 help obtain higher returns than those with an exit a year later – as we shall see, this is the main reason behind the popularity of 'quick flips': scenario E beats A, F beats B, G beats C, and H beats D.

The first point (i) of our conclusion underlines the effect of leverage and why PE investors might want to limit their equity injection to the strict minimum. But it is important to note two other benefits related to debt financing:

- Let us first deal with the principle of weighted average cost of capital. It is because the cost of debt is typically much lower than the cost of equity that it is beneficial for PE firms to finance at least a portion of their investments with loans. A word of caution, which many industry professionals will be quick to disregard: debt is an addictive drug. The aim is to optimise leverage, not to maximise it. At the risk of flogging this idea to death, many of our case studies duly reveal that, at times, the risk of default or distress exceeds any gain derived from the lower cost of debt.

- The second benefit relates to tax. In most countries, debt interest repayments are tax-deductible, whereas dividend payouts are not. Borrowing helps a company to reduce its tax liability. Instead of paying the government and see cash leak out to be used for general purposes such as infrastructure, schools or healthcare, it makes more sense to pay the lenders and improve the investee company's financial position. A PE fund manager's sole duty is to its LPs, not to any other stakeholders, be they society at large or the tax authorities – at least, this is how many financial sponsors see it.

Points (ii) and (iii) drawn from the foregoing eight scenarios introduce the concept of time value of money. What we mean when we state that time holds value is that a dollar today is more valuable than a dollar a year from now. Essentially, it is because you can put your money to work over the next 12 months, implying that the dollar you receive today would have earned interest and grown into more than one dollar a year from now.

Despite their vehement protestations to the contrary, PE investors prefer to get their money back as soon as possible, which often creates a welter of conflicting interests between the financial sponsor (for whom an early exit means a higher IRR) and the investee company's ongoing management and employees (for whom the long-term viability of the business is more important than any other consideration). That being said, financial sponsors can easily sway the view held by senior corporate executives (and key employees) by providing them with a carrot in the form of a life-changing equity stake in the leveraged business.

Fuzzy reporting

For those not abreast of the way IRRs are reported, it is important to keep in mind that unless a fund has been fully realised – meaning that all portfolio companies have been disposed of – the reported number is what is called an interim IRR. That number includes actual yields on realised and partially realised assets as well as expected returns on unrealised assets.

Actual rates of return are easy enough to compute: the typical LBO will see cash-outs take place at the inception of the transaction whereas cash inflows occur via dividend recaps, partial exits (typical in IPOs where the financial sponsor cannot always sell its entire stake in one go) or a full realisation (the standard format for a trade sale or secondary buyout, although some SBOs see the selling PE firm roll over part of its investment, in which case it is treated as a partial realisation). The actual IRR is simply the time-adjusted annualised rate of return of all cash outflows and cash inflows.

Where the calculation becomes more art than science is when you throw into the pot the unrealised portion of the portfolio. Since all the cash flows have not occurred yet, the GP only knows for sure the value of the original investment (cash outflow). In order to estimate an IRR for the unrealised element, a comparables valuation approach is used.

Comparable earnings multiples are applied to each relevant portfolio company's earnings with an approximate exit date, and an expected rate of return is measured. While there are guidelines issued by the relevant trade bodies, that's all they are: guidelines. Using comps to determine an expected rate of return for a portfolio company is only appropriate if the portfolio company can ever be sold. In addition, as explained above, this number is extremely time-sensitive. If for instance a business is facing a lawsuit because of environmental issues, who knows what its value is and when it will become disposable. It is not just the investee company that could be the problem. Another unknown relates to the health of the economy. If the stock market or the economy is in freefall, then the timing of an IPO, a trade sale or an SBO can be difficult to control.

In short, it is dangerous to rely on interim IRR figures since they have been prepared by the same fund managers who completed that deal in the first place. They have a vested interest in painting a rosy picture and in picking favourable comps as well as a timely asset sale. Though fund managers bring in accountancy firms to audit the methodology and output of IRR reports on an annual basis, external auditors themselves rely on assumptions which, by definition, are impossible to corroborate. Who would have known in late 2006 that the Credit Crunch was months away and that the financial crisis would disturb exit timings for several years. Whatever comparables were used at the peak of the bubble proved somewhat optimistic.

The trick of relying on ill-defined IRR reporting standards is widely applied by GPs eager to publicise their exploits. So next time you read quarterly reports issued by limited partners or annual reviews published by trade associations, bear in mind that the IRR numbers they quote are often interim data that include unrealised asset returns. A lot can change between the interim and the final stage. And there is limited consistency in the methodology these expert financiers adopt.

> **IMPORTANT**
>
> Several case studies offer a comparison between the performance achieved by some PE fund vintages and the returns provided by key public stock indices over the same period. These returns are not strictly comparable because PE firms can optimise their investments' capital structure by maximising debt funding and are able to time their exit. Also, the IRRs they achieve become crystallised once individual portfolio companies are realised. By contrast, the compound annual growth rate of returns reported by public markets assume that all funds are unlevered and remain invested throughout the period covered. As such, due to the impact of the time value of money as well as the lack of leverage and value triggers, returns achieved by public market investors should be markedly inferior to those achieved by financial sponsors. And yet, it is instructive to see how major PE investment vehicles frequently underperform stock markets.

Full-scale addiction

What you will notice when going through the book is that the not-so-secret sauce that enables LBO houses to cook up fantastic returns for themselves and their LPs is termed 'leverage', one of the fundamental factors discussed above to boost IRRs. That explains why, between 2001 and 2007, debt-to-earnings before interest, tax, depreciation and amortisation (EBITDA) multiples in the American mid-market LBO sector rose from 3.4 times to 5.6 times. Over the same period, leverage had increased from 57% to 63% of LBO funding.

In 2009, following the financial crisis, leverage was down to 3.3 times EBITDA and accounted for only half of total enterprise value. Because debt is so central to the ability of PE firms to beat public stock markets, it did not take long for leverage parameters to edge up, and by 2014 debt-to-EBITDA multiples in the US stood at 5.7 times, whereas leverage was at 60% to 65% depending on what research paper you believe.[2]

Europe was not left out. In 2001 the average leverage ratio sat at 4.3 times EBITDA. By 2007 loans accounted for more than 60% of total LBO values, reaching 5.85 to 6.6 times EBITDA according to various sources. As in the US, leverage ratios dropped (to four times) in 2009. But when median EV multiples in Europe reached ten times EBITDA in 2014 (on par or slightly higher than during the peak of 2007-08), debt also represented 5.5 times earnings. The share of debt in deals is likely to keep increasing as the economy strengthens and credit markets regain confidence.[3] Without debt, the private equity magic vanishes.

The imitation game

One of the easiest tricks in any PE firm's toolkit is to mimic its peers' strategies. When they see one of their rivals buy a company in a sector, financial sponsors usually waste little time – that sector instantly becomes 'flavour of the moment' among LBO shops.

In October 1997, Japanese bank Nomura's private equity unit acquired British bookmaker William Hill from Brent Walker, a conglomerate that was being carved out piecemeal. Immediately, the UK gambling sector became a key target for LBO investors, with Prudential's PE division acquiring bingo club owner Gala in December of the same year, and Deutsche Bank's Morgan Grenfell Private Equity buying out betting shop chain Coral 12 months later. We will analyse this scenario in Chapter 2. A few years later, the entire (or so it felt) European business-directory publishing sector went through a series of LBOs that involved no less than ten PE houses.

The copycat policy embraced by most, if not all, financial sponsors indicates that their skills are not so much based on identifying unique assets on which to apply their industry and operational know-how, but rather on following what their peers are doing and trying to implement the same sorts of tricks. If dividend recaps worked for Thomson Directories and Yellow Brick Road, they were bound to work on PagesJaunes (see Chapter 11) and Seat Pagine Gialle (see Chapter 12), irrespective of the market context. Or so the thinking went.

*   *   *

Over the years, these tricks of the trade helped PE fund managers to preserve a reputation as savvy investors. As I explain in Part Nine, their success owes a lot to a combination of factors that may not have long to live: exclusive access to cheap and loosely-covenanted debt, self-regulation, limited disclosure requirements, and weak corporate governance. But before going into this, let us pore over a few case studies.

PART ONE
Asset-Shifting: Secondary Buyouts and their Offspring

THE TERM SECONDARY BUYOUT (SBO) DESCRIBES THE completion by a financial sponsor of the leveraged buyout of a business owned by another PE firm. The more disparaging observers often refer to them as 'pass-the-parcel' transactions. Quite rare in the 1990s, sponsor-to-sponsor deals are a direct product of the credit boom that occurred in the US and in Europe during the first half of the noughties, and a sure sign that the industry has reached maturity (some would say senility) in these geographies. The motivations behind such deals depend on whether you are a buyer or a seller.

- On the buy-side: running out of targets to acquire, because corporations do not want to sell or lenders are not prepared to offer attractive terms, PE firms are sometimes left with little alternative but to go after companies that have already undergone a buyout. An SBO often only requires a recapitalisation, a much more straightforward process than the full-blown underwriting and syndication process of a loan package for a business that the debt markets are not familiar with.

- On the sell-side: struggling to exit an aging portfolio, unable to find corporate buyers willing to pay their demanding valuations, or facing volatile stock markets that do not guarantee an orderly IPO process, PE fund managers can turn to their peers to help them take a cumbersome investee business off their hands.

Back in 2001, less than 5% of buyouts were SBOs. A decade later, in some countries these deals were ten times more prevalent. According to public records, on a global basis SBOs accounted for 40% of exits by PE firms in 2014. In fact, with the exception of the year 2009, when the proportion was closer to 30%, on the sell-side (portfolio realisations) the data has been quite consistent since 2006, accounting for two out of five transactions.[1] In terms of acquisitions (buy-side), SBOs account for at least a quarter of buyout transactions worldwide.[2] Nicknamed asset-strippers in the days of hostile corporate carve-outs and pugnacious restructurings in the 1980s, the once-mighty dealmakers have turned into dull, fly-by-night asset-sharers and swappers.

Upon selling out of bingo operator Gala and passing the baton to Candover and Cinven in January 2003, Matthew Turner, then director of exiting shareholder PPM Ventures, had matter-of-factly explained: "This is the era of the tertiary buyout."[3] But secondaries and tertiaries are now so *last decade*. A noticeable number of portfolio companies are already on their quaternary buyouts, while others have reached the fanciful stage of quintenary buyout.

You will find supporters of this sort of deal, explaining with all the rationality of a drug addict that each stage has brought to the underlying portfolio company a fresh cash infusion that will transform it into the national or international champion it is craving to become. Undoubtedly, they will cite anecdotal evidence to prove their point. Most operators in the industry have come across excellent small to medium-sized businesses that have successfully completed several back-to-back buyouts. Companies following buy-and-build strategies are great candidates for SBOs since they require a longer-term approach to growth, in conflict with PE firms' typical four-to-five-year investment horizon.

But to be most effective, these transactions demand that the founder or senior executive team remain the majority owner or a significant minority shareholder. This situation enables corporate executives to keep the business focused on long-term expansion rather than just on speedy returns for the financial sponsors. Being able to control the agenda and make sure that the company is not overleveraged is a way to avoid the worst excesses of SBOs.

Founder-owners with meaningful voting rights or contractual protections can make sure that their PE backers do not get carried away by raising expensive high-yield bonds, paying themselves dividends on a yearly basis, or increasing the company's gearing ratio regardless of the consequences. Our first case study shows that corporate managers with a small stake in the business, like Gala Coral's John Kelly and Neil Goulden, can quickly become peons in a game of chess that they cannot influence.

As a general rule, the succession of SBOs, morphing into tertiaries and beyond, and the numerous recapitalisations that come with them, are unhealthy for the underlying assets. They are the equivalent of overexploiting farmland without letting it lie fallow once in a while. Sucking out any spare cash to pay out dividends to the sponsors and repay loans to the lenders (instead of re-injecting it into the business) and maintaining a high gearing ratio on a permanent basis can have traumatic long-term consequences as far as job creation, competitive position, and strategic focus are concerned.

Two scenarios covered in other parts of this casebook fit the bill. Frans Bonhomme (Chapter 8) was a quaternary buyout while eDreams (Chapter 13) was a secondary preceded by a VC round. I use these two cases to emphasise other issues related to PE practices later in the book; neither embodies the shortcomings of SBOs as well as the series of transactions portrayed in the next chapter.

Business lore has it that the first generation of family entrepreneurs creates and builds the company, the second consolidates it, while subsequent ones destroy it. Could it be that the same rule applies to leveraged buyouts? What is it like when a company operates with high leverage not for a short period but continuously, year after year, LBO after LBO? Let us consider the Gala Coral story.

CHAPTER 2
Gala Coral – Game on!

O N SATURDAY 19 NOVEMBER 1994, THE BRITISH PUBLIC WAS exposed to a new game of chance. Over the years, the UK Government had taken an increasingly tolerant view on gambling. In this instance, though, the game's sponsor was the government itself. That evening the first National Lottery draw in the country since 1826 took place live on TV, with 25 million viewers tuning in to BBC One. Fifteen million people were reported to have purchased a total of 35 million £1 tickets.[1]

The lucky winning-ticket holders were not the only benefitting parties. A significant share of the tickets' face value was to be distributed to support good causes, including arts, heritage and sports. For the government, earning lottery duty levied on each ticket's face value was also an easy way to raise money through a stealth tax. But there was one clear set of losers: gambling and betting venue operators. Bass PLC was one of them.

At that time, Bass was an awkwardly sprouting conglomerate whose genesis reached as far back as the late 18th century. Born as a single brewery, it had grown into a major beer maker and distributor with a £7.5 billion market capitalisation and interests in the leisure sector, including hotels, pubs, casinos, bingo clubs and betting shops. Bass's bingo activities, managed under the Gala brand, were badly scarred by the launch of the National Lottery, with admissions in its clubs falling in the two years that followed. Over that period UK bingo operators suffered a 16% drop in admissions as a result of the lottery.[2]

Trying to fortify its position in the gambling market, in early 1997 Bass attempted to acquire the second largest betting shop operator William Hill from its owners Brent Walker, but it had been outbid by Japanese bank Nomura's Principal Finance unit. Frustrated in its strategy to build a dominant gaming business, Bass decided that it was better off exiting the sector.

In December 1997 industry veteran John Kelly – who had run rival Mecca's bingo business for over five years until its acquisition in 1990 by another leisure conglomerate, Rank Organisation – led a management buy-in (MBI) of Gala, paying £235 million for the chain of 130 bingo clubs with the support of PPM

Ventures, the PE arm of global insurer Prudential. Desperate to get out of a declining business unit, Bass had apparently accepted a bid £200 million below Gala's book value.[3] On the other hand, the conglomerate was now able to focus its attention on its brewery and hotel management operations. It was prepared to incur a write-down for the privilege.

Coral's story

Joseph Kagarlitsky was born in Warsaw on 11 December 1904.[4] At the time there was no such thing as a Polish state; Warsaw was part of the Russian empire. While Poland would eventually gain its independence at the end of the First World War, Kagarlitsky had already left the country with his mother and brother (Joseph's father had passed away by then), moving to Britain in 1912. Shortly after arriving to London the family changed its name to Coral to facilitate its social integration. Growing up in Britain as a Polish-Russian immigrant at such a young age no doubt made Joseph independent-minded and probably explains his later 'entrepreneurial' ventures.

After dropping out of school at the age of 14, Joseph (by then Joe) worked as a clerk in a lamp-making company while on the side acting as a runner, an illegal occupation taking bets on behalf of bookmakers. This side activity cost him his job. He ended up joining an advertising agency but still maintained his interest in betting. In 1927 he set up his first pitches at the White City greyhound tracks, northwest London.[5] The first ever modern greyhound race in the country had taken place the year before at Belle Vue Stadium, in Manchester. Given the enthusiasm expressed by the public, in late 1926 the Greyhound Racing Association (GRA) had gained ownership of White City Stadium, an arena that had been built for the 1908 London Olympics. GRA moved in and started running weekly greyhound races in White City from 1927 onwards.[6]

Joe Coral had a number of jobs before finally becoming a bookmaker at greyhound races in 1936. While this activity has today become niche, back then greyhound races could draw huge audiences. In 1939 a record 92,000 spectators attended the English Greyhound Derby final. Aside from his legitimate business at these races, Coral is believed to have run illegal street betting and financed gambling clubs without declaring the income.

He prospered during the Second World War, when he was unable to take up military service because of childhood paralysis in both arms.[7] As the racing calendar was reduced during the war, Coral developed sports-betting activities. After the conflict he was one of several bookmakers advertising 'betting by post' in major sporting newspapers, including *Sporting Life* and the *Sporting Chronicle*. He remained active in greyhound racing and credit betting with cheques (where no ready money changed hands) until cash betting was legalised in 1960 with the introduction of the Betting and Gambling Act.

This act legalised off-course cash betting and allowed licensed betting shops, bingo halls and casinos. One stated aim of the government in adopting this new law was to take gambling off the streets and end the practice of bookmakers sending runners to collect from punters, which had been Coral's very first introduction to the trade.

Betting shops were allowed to open in May of the following year and Coral launched his first shop shortly thereafter. Any new betting office needed to show 'unstimulated demand' before being granted a licence. One way was to convert existing business premises into a licensed betting office. Coral paid to have the sweetshop of one of his agents turned into a betting shop. By 1962 Coral had 23 sites, and nine years later the company merged with its rival Mark Lane to total 589 shops. The fast-expanding business became a public limited company in 1974 and rebranded as Coral Leisure, quickly diversifying into casinos, bingo halls and hotels. By 1977 Coral's estate was the fourth largest in the country.[8]

As a publicly listed company Coral Leisure failed to inspire, its diversification strategy having yielded little for its shareholders. An easy prey for larger conglomerates, in 1980 the group became the subject of a bidding battle between catering-to-brewery Grand Metropolitan and pub manager Bass PLC. Having grown into an operation with £15 million in annual profit, in October 1980 Coral was acquired for £82.5 million by Bass, although the latter ended up disposing of Coral's underperforming casino operations.[9] Staying on as life president of the bookmaking operations, Joe Coral oversaw the expansion of the betting-shop activities. Elsewhere in the group, in May 1991 Gala Bingo was formed when Bass purchased Granada Theatre's bingo clubs and merged them with the existing Coral Social Clubs. Gala was officially launched in October of that year.

Like most conglomerates, Bass spent most of the late 1990s undoing its past gluttony by disposing of non-core activities. For a quoted company trying to deliver predictability to its shareholders, the gaming sector had always been somewhat erratic, with trading affected one day by the weather, the other by the introduction of new games (think the National Lottery), and the following week by unexpected wins by punters or new regulations.

The rational type often wonders why people bother gambling. After all, it is common knowledge that the casino or betting shop always wins in the end. But the whole point of making a bet resides in the quixotic view that, in life, anything is possible. As a case in point, during its 1996 financial year, Coral's profits sustained a £4 million hit related to a freakish sport result: superstar horse racing jockey Frankie Dettori riding all seven winners on British Champions' Day at Ascot that year. Now, what were the odds of that happening? 25,095 to 1.[10]

That kind of volatility was never going to suit a publicly-listed concern. Just like it had spun off its bingo clubs via the MBI of Gala, that same month of December 1997 the conglomerate found a buyer for its betting activities. Ladbrokes, the largest betting-shop chain in Britain, had tabled a £375.5 million bid to gobble up Coral's 900 shops.[11]

Unfortunately, nine months later the Monopolies and Mergers Commission and the Trade Secretary ruled that the transaction was against the public's interest, so Ladbrokes had to undo it.[12] In December 1998 the group reluctantly flogged Coral for £390 million via a management buyout backed by Morgan Grenfell Private Equity, Deutsche Bank's investment arm.[13] Almost two years to the day after the death of Joe Coral, the business was regaining its independence.

Primary to secondary

Under the leadership of John Kelly and the financial backing of PPM, bingo operator Gala spent the late 1990s consolidating its number two position in the sector, behind leader Rank's Mecca. In the summer of 1998 Gala acquired the Ritz clubs in exchange for equity, giving Ritz's financial owners Duke Street Capital a 25% stake in the combined entity.[14] By September 1999 the group had 149 bingo halls, annual sales of £190 million, and £37 million in earnings before interest and tax (EBIT) versus £24 million the year it was acquired from Bass. The quick performance improvement enacted by Kelly and the rest of management meant that the business was in need of further cash injection if external expansion was to continue.

While there were rumours that the business could float, instead it ended up being flipped for £400 million in March 2000 to another financial sponsor: Credit Suisse First Boston Private Equity. This secondary buyout was meant to scale up Gala even further. PPM liked the idea so much that it retained a 20% holding. In a sign that the financial community was getting more comfortable with the usually unreliable gaming industry, this SBO was being funded with £200 million of senior debt and £100 million of high-yield bonds. The three-quarters of leverage represented eight times prior-year EBIT. As CSFB's investment executives put it:

> "The bingo industry is growing strongly and further deregulation offers considerable potential. In a highly fragmented industry Gala can further consolidate its position as the market leader and we're excited by the prospects."[15]

Within a month of its secondary Gala was back on the shopping trail, logging the £90 million acquisition of Riva's 27 clubs and becoming the leading bingo operator in the country. Eight months later, the group was adding 29 casinos to its tally by paying their owners, hotel group Hilton, £253 million for them. That year Gala made its first online move by launching *bingo.co.uk*.

Unfortunately, out of the blue, Credit Suisse First Boston took the decision in late 2001 that it no longer wanted to do deals out of Europe, electing to limit its PE activities to the New York office. Consequently, it let its senior European team go. While Kelly and the rest of the Gala management team had received assurances that CSFB would continue to fully support them, by the end of 2002 it was apparent that further expansion would need to be funded by another party.[16] And it was a matter of urgency. The British Government was in the process of drafting new gambling laws that would introduce further deregulation to the sector. The proposed relaxation could potentially allow the creation of Las Vegas-type casinos. Kelly himself publicly suggested that he could bring some of Gala's 166 bingo clubs and 28 casinos under one roof.[17]

Some of the new laws rumoured to be under consideration by the British Government included a relaxation of opening hours and the 24-hour 'cooling-off' period before new members can be admitted to a casino. They would also allow operators to offer a wider range of gambling activities alongside slot machines, or even unlimited stakes and prizes. Kelly was campaigning for the restrictions on advertising to be addressed and was broadcasting the idea of a 'gambling shed', combining a casino, bingo hall, betting shop and other gaming activities, set around a food court.[18] The opportunities seemed boundless.

In July 2002, acknowledging that it could no longer play an active role in the development of Gala, CSFB Private Equity appointed investment bankers Deutsche Bank and Credit Suisse to examine all strategic options, including a sale of the business or an IPO.[19] Following CSFB's decision to wind up its European LBO operations, Gala had not made any acquisitions in either 2001 or 2002, so management was certainly keen to find more supportive backers.

One of the most frequent negotiation techniques used by PE sellers and their advisers is publicly to state, usually via a richly-paid PR agency, an enterprise value at which the business will be floated. It sends a strong message to the market that buyers need not apply if they are not prepared to bid at least that minimum price. Strangely, this method works wonders as bidders tend to forget the most basic of negotiation skills, like setting a walk-away price, for instance.

Sure enough, Gala's owners made it clear from the outset that they were considering an IPO at £1 billion or above. Then, they started a dual-track process, calling all interested parties to submit indicative bids while also meeting asset managers likely to want to participate in a flotation. The upside potential that an abatement of gambling laws represented was certainly the main driver behind the lofty valuation expectations. As one observer noted at the time:

"Gala would be one of the main beneficiaries of the government's planned gaming deregulation and any bid must reflect that. If the bids aren't high enough then a flotation is still very much an option."[20]

Given the dotcom crash and its impression on the world's stock exchanges, few people took the listing route as a credible alternative to an outright sale. Either a corporate rival or a financial sponsor would offer more certainty. Even though Gala's advisers kept feeding the specialist press with indications that they were prepared to go through an IPO, those were the days when no one, certainly not the still-shaken stock markets, could outbid cash-rich PE investors. For the year 2002, PE's share of mergers and acquisitions in the UK had been 45%, so financial sponsors were hot favourites to take Gala away.[21] A market analyst commented:

"A cash business like Gala is one of the few you could get away in these markets. But it's hard to see the market placing as high a valuation on the business as a private equity buyer paying cash."[22]

The usual suspects showed up at the door, with PE titans KKR (managing a $3 billion European fund), Permira (who had raised €3.5 billion in 2000) and BC Partners (putting to work its €4.3 billion 2001 vintage) all rumoured to be vying for the asset. It was a heated battle. But after four months, in January 2003, via a tertiary buyout much in tune with the emerging LBO bubble, British duo Candover and Cinven contrived a means of outbidding Permira, the last remaining obstacle between them and the winning prize.[23]

Completed at an EV of £1.25 billion, or 11.8 times earnings before interest, tax and amortisation (EBITA), the deal was financed with less than half a billion pounds in equity. Although they were reported to have partially cashed out, management were reinvesting part of their £90 million-plus proceeds to retain a 10% stake in the business.[24] Kelly himself had crystallised a fortune of £20 million.[25] CSFB sold its 70% and PPM its remaining 15% holding, leaving management and the new PE consortium to push the casino-cum-bingo operator through its next stage of development.

Tertiary

By 2003 Candover and Cinven were two of the most distinguished PE houses in Europe. Headquartered in London, they had contributed in their own ways to the emergence and establishment of LBOs in Britain throughout the 1980s and 1990s. Most of their investment activity had taken place in the UK, although they had occasionally taken a pop at the European continental markets, in particular the two major economies of France and Germany. Still, their expertise lay in Britain, and they were keen to defend their turf against incoming US rivals like KKR and direct home competitors like Permira and BC Partners.

Candover, founded in 1980, and Cinven, born three years earlier, were not only pioneers; they were collaborators too. In the past they had frequently worked in partnership. Throughout the 1990s they had invested alongside each other in at least half a dozen buyouts. Their close tie was partly explained by the fact that one of Candover's consummate deal doers and now chairman, Stephen Curran, had worked at Cinven before joining Candover in May 1981. After a few years of going their separate ways and vying for the European dealmaking crown, they were once again joining forces to pick up the premier bingo operator in the country.

The timing was perfect. Both fund managers had closed large funds in the previous 12 months and were at that stage concentrating on closing large transactions, in the £500 million-to-£1 billion category. Candover's 2001 fund, closed in May 2002, had raised €2.7 billion and could, in principle, put to work in a single transaction 15% of that capital, or €400 million. Candover's accomplice on the Gala bid had received €4.4 billion for its fund Cinven III, which implied some firepower in excess of €600 million per deal. Both LBO houses were just starting to invest their latest vintage.

For Gala's management it was good news as it indicated that the new financial sponsors would be prepared to support the business for several years. All PE funds typically raise capital for a ten-year period, meaning that they must invest and return the cash commitments to their LPs within that time. Ten years was certainly plenty enough for the Gala deal.

*   *   *

Almost as soon as it closed, the Gala transaction – the largest tertiary ever completed in Europe – raised questions about what enhancements the new owners could possibly produce that the two previous buyouts had not already delivered. The target was already market leader in bingo, with a 40% market share, and accounted for a fifth of the casino segment. Extracting any further value would be laborious. On the positive front there was plenty of upside to be derived from the highly anticipated gambling liberalisation. Marek Gumienny, Candover's Managing Director leading the transaction, commented that the target's "organic growth record, robust cash flows and recent expansion into casinos would ensure it was well placed to exploit any further deregulation in the gaming industry."[26]

Ignoring the cynics, within six months of its third LBO Gala's management signed an agreement with Harrah's Entertainment, the largest casino operator in the US (see Chapter 15), to invest up to $1 billion in order to open vast new gaming complexes up to eight times bigger than the casinos Gala operated. We were months if not years away from the adoption of new gambling legislation so the move seemed a bit precipitate, but as Kelly himself publicly explained, the group wanted to be up and running once the deregulated landscape was approved. The size of these mega-casinos would reach up to 100,000 square feet each. Potential sites included Birmingham, Blackpool, Leeds and Newcastle. Lobbyists made claims regarding knock-on impacts in terms of job creation (as high as 100,000 direct and 250,000 indirect jobs), local economic value (£1.7 billion inward investments) and tax income (up to £1.5 billion per annum) that were appealing even if unsubstantiated.[27]

A more realistic and understated objective was for the upcoming liberalisation to make visiting casinos and betting shops a more pleasant experience, with food, drink and live entertainment. Legislation needed to change anyhow, if only to take into account the changes that had occurred since the prevalent gambling laws had been set out in the 1960s. For instance, the internet, interactive TV and mobile phones were increasingly being used for gambling, but were not covered by the current regulatory framework. In the meantime, gambling activity was benefitting from a strong economy, with Gala recording a 6.5% revenue growth in the financial year to 30 September 2003; operating earnings were up a solid 7.5%.

It was in June of the following year that the British Government announced a much stricter set of policies which, though still keeping the door open to the launch of Las Vegas-style leisure and gaming resorts, introduced measures to protect youngsters and vulnerable gamblers by setting limits on prizes and slot machines, and to give new powers to local authorities to prevent casinos from opening in their area. Justifying this turnabout, a spokesman explained:

> "We are slowing down the pace of reform because we had a lot of concerns.
> We looked at Australia where deregulation was introduced too quickly
> and led to a higher proportion of people with gambling problems."[28]

To add insult to injury, in December the government presented a key amendment to its controversial gaming bill by preventing existing casino operators from increasing the number of slot machines in their premises once the bill had become law in 2005.[29]

The market's reaction to the new proposals was unmistakable. On the publication of each amendment all the major publicly listed gambling groups in the country saw their shares tumble. It was bad news for the sector, and it was a blow to Candover and Cinven's interests. The success of their Gala investment was predicated on deregulation. Still, Gala was a cash machine. With cash margins (read EBITDA) of 27%, the group could easily service its debt. While it had not made any significant acquisition since Candover and Cinven's tertiary, the high-volume, low-ticket gambling company was still a growth story. Its annual EBITDA had climbed from £36 million at the time of the December 1997 MBI to £146 million in the 2004 financial year. The number of bingo halls had gone from 130 to 166 over that period, and the group now owned 30 casinos.[30]

Despite its desire to protect the public against the worst effects of full-scale gambling liberalisation, throughout the fall of 2004 the British Government repeated its intention to allow the construction of 20 to 40 'super-casinos'. All the major US gambling groups, from Caesars to MGM to Las Vegas Sands and of course Harrah's, were signing deals across the country to build casino and hotel complexes. Some industry experts questioned whether so many new venues could ever be commercially viable and what impact they would have on the existing operators. A commonly-held view was that the government was railroading the bill, eager to generate additional tax income from these new gambling activities.[31]

With a decision still hanging in midair, in early 2005 Candover and Cinven launched a £1.025 billion recap to pay themselves a dividend, returning £275 million, not far from half their original investments, to their LPs. At seven times EBITDA, the total debt ratio was up from less than six at the time of the tertiary two years earlier. The senior debt multiple was increased from 4.3 to 5.4 times. In spite of the unresolved regulatory situation, the credit markets were placing a premium on an asset that was hugely cash generative and considered recession-proof.

Not only was Gala's leverage up, conveying the market's generosity, but the structure and cost of that debt had improved significantly: the mezzanine portion had been reduced from £190 million back in 2003 to £120 million two years later, and its cash and PIK (i.e., rolled up) elements had each lost 100 basis points (meaning that their interest rate had dropped by 1%). Complementing the reduced mezzanine tranche, a much cheaper (though six months shorter) £40 million second-lien loan had been underwritten.[32]

In parallel, an exit for Gala was being considered. The company had hived off its loss-making, high-end Maxims casino the previous year and was now a much more focused high-volume, low-stake gaming business. Discussions with investment bankers had determined that an IPO would likely assign a £1.8 billion valuation to the business. At such a price tag, Candover and Cinven could hope to make two times their money. It would be a reasonable result, especially since the two PE houses had failed to implement any real change during their two years of ownership.

But an exit at this stage would fail to factor in any potential upside from an upcoming liberalisation. If they sold now, they both took the risk of leaving money on the table, especially because the casino activities appeared affected by the dicey environment: sales had risen 5% but came with a 14% fall in operating profit in the 2005 fiscal year. Luckily for them, a hybrid solution presented itself, offering them the option of partially cashing out while positioning themselves to participate in any future upside.

Looking at the Gala transaction from the outside, pan-European LBO powerhouse Permira had continued to express a firm interest in taking part in this success story. Managing a €5.1 billion fund raised two years earlier, the buyout shop was targeting the larger end of the M&A spectrum. At times it was a head-splitting exercise to put so much money to work. There were few businesses in the UK and across Europe where one could invest €300 million to €600 million of equity in one go. Gala was one of them.

Permira had fallen at the last hurdle back in 2003. This time, though, it had an ace up its sleeve: one of its investment partners, Martin Clarke, had joined the firm in the summer of 2002 straight from PPM Ventures, the very first backers of the Gala purchase from Bass in December 1997. Clarke knew the asset well, and his connection with Kelly was likely to be a clincher. Permira wanted in on the deal and was prepared to pay richly for it. It would have been churlish not to accept.

In August 2005, less than a month before Gala's float was due to go ahead, in a move that even took their IPO advisers by surprise, Candover and Cinven sold Permira a 30% stake in the bingo and casino operator in exchange for £200 million. The implied enterprise value of £1.89 billion translated into a lavish 15.1 times EBITA multiple. Total debt was reaching a cool 9.75 times based on EBITA for the 2005 financial year. Multiples were getting punchy.

Following this quaternary transaction, Gala had now returned Candover and Cinven 1.3 times their equity investments.[33] But in order to boost their IRR further, they needed to make a drastic move. The challenge was that organic expansion had run its course. Without full-scale liberalisation and several super-casino projects Gala would not deliver the obligatory upside and adequate returns. Going through a series of dividend recapitalisations was never going to make this deal one to remember.

With Permira on board they had gathered the necessary equity ammunition to go on a shopping spree. One particular target was in fact being publicly marketed during that summer, and it was one that all parties, Gala's management and investors, knew very well indeed: bookmaker Coral. The Gala investment troika wanted Coral and were prepared to pay up. The question wasn't if, it wasn't even when; it was how much. But first, a little stage setting: Coral had itself recently gone through radical change.

Coral's secondary

Recall that our earlier brief historic overview of Coral left the company in the hands of Morgan Grenfell Private Equity, the backers in late 1998 of a management buyout of the business from Ladbrokes. Coral was then the UK's third largest betting shop owner with a chain of 827 outlets. Like all the country's bookmakers, it was withstanding a sluggish period, partly due to the tax environment.

To spur a revival, within a year of the buyout Morgan Grenfell had financed the acquisition of Eurobet, an online betting business based in gambling tax haven Gibraltar. After having considered the purchase of a licence to run a business from there, Coral took a shortcut by buying Eurobet. The target's predominantly football (read soccer) orientated site had flourished to become one of the biggest betting websites in Europe. These offshore operations allowed British punters to place bets without having to pay the 9% duty applied in the UK. Market numbers one and two, Ladbrokes and William Hill, were also making plans to expand overseas.

Immediately after closing this acquisition, MGPE retained advisers Lehman to help it flip the business via an initial public offer. After 14 months of ownership, in February 2000 a tentative £1 billion valuation was placed on Coral Eurobet, due in no small part to the internet hype surrounding the Eurobet deal. At that price the PE owners were well placed to make a killing. But then, as had been predicted on many occasions, the world's stock markets tanked. The dotcom bubble had finally landed and was about to run out of runway. By May the Coral float was on hold. Against its will, and despite Coral's strong financial performance – EBITDA had jumped 39% in the first 16 weeks of the year – Morgan Grenfell needed to stay the course a little longer.[34]

Later in the year, trouble hit again; this time in the shape of an exceptional loss at the Eurobet unit, which MGPE had until then valued at £500 million. While its owners certainly would have preferred to keep such a matter under wraps, because it was partly funded with bonds listed in New York Coral had to disclose in January 2001 that Eurobet had incurred a £12 million loss – almost half the group's annual profits – on online bets related to the 2000 European football tournament.[35] Despite such a blow, in the year to September 2000 the Coral Group had seen turnover rise by over 50% to £1.33 billion while gross profits were still up 10% to £162 million.

And yet this level of profitability was not sufficient to prevent a breach of banking covenants. The Eurobet exceptional loss and an increase in marketing expenses for the online platform contributed to a group operating loss of over £4 million. The £500 million loan book translated into £50 million in annual interest charges. In October 2000, shortly after the end of Coral's financial year, MGPE was forced to inject a further £10 million in order to stay in control of the business.[36]

Things then went from bad to worse for Coral and its PE owner. Trading deteriorated in the early part of 2001: in the first 16 weeks of the year revenue fell 13% while gross profit was flat. Following a series of bad news stories at the portfolio level (the need to inject a total of £45 million to fund Eurobet's marketing expenses and avoid breaching banking covenants was just one of them), MGPE's parent Deutsche Bank lost patience with the unit's leadership style and removed Chief Executive Graham Hutton.[37]

Watching the saga evolve, Coral's competitors kept making approaches to try to buy the business on the cheap. The public equity markets remained in the doldrums so were no longer a viable exit option for MGPE. Coral's rivals knew that much. In the summer of 2001, bookmaker Stanley Leisure's senior executives considered bidding, but financing the acquisition of a group worth twice as much as theirs was proving nigh on impossible. Casino operator Rank also looked into the matter. For MGPE, however, there was a major hurdle to any agreement: following the collapse in stock valuations and the respective comparable multiples, its Coral holding was now worth half as much as when it had planned a flotation in early 2000. Sale plans were put on hold, only to be revived six months later.

By April 2002, Coral Eurobet had turned a corner. Its half-year interim results indicated that EBITDA had leapt 90% to £39 million on turnover of £820 million, up a fifth despite Eurobet's decision to discontinue low-margin businesses in Asia.[38] The chief reason behind such a sharp improvement in trading was the decision by the British Government to scrap the betting tax. Since 6 October 2001 bookmakers were being taxed on their gross profits at a rate of 15%, meaning that punters no longer had to pay the 9% betting tax previously levied in shops. This new regulation, aimed at stopping offshore gambling tax avoidance, had directly benefitted betting-shop owners.

Sensing the opening of a unique, and certainly welcome, window of opportunity, MGPE relaunched the Coral sale process. The M&A landscape remained uncertain. The year 2001 had seen total LBO transaction values decline by 12% across Europe. Financing deals was still proving tricky in the first half of 2002. And yet, even though the FTSE 100 index was pursuing its free fall (it would hit an eight-year low in early March 2003), with all of Coral's main competitors expressing interest in buying the bookmaker, in August 2002 British PE firm Charterhouse Development Capital (CDC) went all out in order to pip everyone to the post – 15 parties were reported to have submitted a bid, including runner-up casino owner Rank.

At £860 million, or approximately ten times annualised EBITDA, Charterhouse's headline price significantly exceeded expectations. CDC's bid did not present the kind of synergistic benefits that Rank would have achieved. Coral's finance director Mick Mariscotti, who was reported to have made £5 million by partly cashing out, admitted that Charterhouse and management's offer "was a full price."[39] MGPE had patiently waited for trading to recover before flogging the asset in a secondary buyout. It was a lower valuation than the £1 billion hailed at the peak of early 2000, but it still allowed Morgan Grenfell to make a rumoured two-times return on equity. It was Charterhouse's turn to try to make money on this bet.

At the time CDC took the helm, Coral Eurobet was managing 870 betting shops across Britain, the Eurobet internet bookmaking division, two greyhound tracks and a small telephone-betting operation. The plan was to expand organically and through acquisitions of local betting shops that did not have Coral's economies of scale and brand power.

Activity at the betting shop operator and all its British rivals soon felt the effect of the introduction in 2001 of new electromechanical devices called fixed-odds betting terminals (FOBTs). These machines allowed UK players to bet on the outcome of various games and events with fixed odds. Roulette, bingo, horseracing and greyhound racing as well as slot machines were now readily available by the touch of a few buttons. Eventually, due to their highly addictive nature, these FOBTs would come to be known as the crack cocaine of betting. In the meantime, they were a boon for Coral and its owners.

In its 2003 financial year, the company made operating profit of £85 million, but the big news came from the top line: amounts wagered had risen from £2 billion the previous year to £3.8 billion, all mostly thanks to the emergence of these previously uneconomic low-margin, small-stake betting machines. The betting tax abolition, which had already helped Morgan Grenfell secure a great exit, had likewise contributed to this surge in volumes, helping Coral to double the size of its telephone-betting operation.[40] Before 2001 bookmakers' sales had been taxed at 6.75%, meaning that it was uneconomic to offer any bet with a margin smaller than that tax rate. Now that bookmakers' gross profits were taxed rather than customers' stakes, FOBT bets were profitable.

As could be expected, in February 2004 Charterhouse set up a £830 million refinancing to help repay a £160 million shareholder loan. The PE firm got back more than 60% of the capital it had spent buying Coral Eurobet 16 months earlier.[41] This quick recap had been made possible by the underlying asset's solid financial performance. Coral's revenue had also been driven by the acquisition and opening of new outlets in a bid to gain market share over competitors Ladbrokes and William Hill. Having expanded the chain with 150 new shops since Charterhouse's SBO, in November 2003 the group had acquired the 34 stores controlled by the Joyce family in the northeast of England. By early 2004 Coral operated more than 1,100 betting shops.[42]

Growth continued unabated as the group opened another 100 outlets or so in the 2004 financial year. Sales received further uplift from the change in taxation and the popularity of the fixed-odds terminals. In the 12 months to September 2004 Coral Eurobet employed over 6,700 employees, its EBITDA had doubled to £180 million, and with total amounts waged up more than two-fifths to £5.4 billion the group was crowned the country's biggest private company by revenue (gross revenue rather than the net commissions earned by the group).[43]

Taking advantage of Coral's brisk trading and the receptive debt markets, in keeping with the much-rehashed policy of maximising returns, Charterhouse decided to launch yet another recapitalisation process. In December 2004 a £1.25 billion refinancing returned a further £400 million of capital. It was the equivalent of a good day at the races: Charterhouse had by now fully recouped its original £278 million equity and still held a 75% stake in the business. With an EV of £1.6 billion, or nine times EBITDA, total net debt sat at £1.15 billion, or 6.4 times EBITDA.[44] As sure as night follows day and spring follows winter, after spending three years in the saddle Charterhouse celebrated its second dividend recap by planning an exit.

By the summer of 2005 Coral Eurobet was preparing its IPO. Lehman was advising, just as it had advised Morgan Grenfell on a possible flotation three years earlier. By now the bookmaker was running 1,260 shops, up 44% over three years.[45] There were early indications that the phenomenal growth related to FOBTs was slowing down. But the booming stock markets (major indices were up 20% over the previous 12 months), expanding LBO transaction values (up more than a quarter across Europe since January 2004) as well as the strong appetite for gambling stocks (online gambling site PartyGaming had recently listed and immediately joined the FTSE 100 index, while the online marketplace for punters Betfair was also eyeing a float) created the perfect setting for Charterhouse to cash out.[46] It was time for Gala and its trio of PE owners to get into the picture.

The merger

Given its sensational performance under Charterhouse's ownership, the Coral group was considered a prized asset. Its main listed competitor, William Hill, traded at ten times EBITDA. That was the benchmark. With Eurobet's internet angle and exposure to foreign markets – three-quarters of the group's internet revenue came from abroad – the growth was set to continue and needed to be factored into any valuation.[47] Despite serious interest from several parties, this race had only one real contender; one able to pay a full price due to the expected synergies it could derive from the acquisition.

After just two months of negotiations, in October 2005 Gala purchased Coral Eurobet in a tertiary buyout worth £2.18 billion, representing slightly more than ten times EBITDA, or 13 times EBITA. Usually, add-on acquisitions are meant to represent an incremental build-up on the original investment. Thanks to its recent financial track record, Coral Eurobet was worth more than the initial £1.2 billion Gala transaction.

When winning the Coral auction back in December 1998, MGPE had in fact beaten one key rival financial sponsor: its £390 million bid had convincingly exceeded Cinven's £375 million.[48] The third highest bid had come from none other than Candover. Then, in 2002, the latter had been outbid by Charterhouse whereas Cinven had not shown much interest at the time, for the simple fact that between March 1999 and June 2002 it was, alongside buyout fund manager CVC, the co-owner of William Hill, a business acquired in an SBO from Nomura's PE arm.

To say that in the past ten years major PE firms had nursed a passion for the gambling sector would be stating the obvious. Maybe they could relate to the principle according to which, no matter how you cut the numbers, the odds are always stacked in favour of the house. But Candover and Cinven had been on the losing side too often. Coral Eurobet was never going to get away this time. With a combined EV of £4.2 billion funded with £2.8 billion of loan facilities, Gala Coral would be the UK's biggest PE-owned business in 2005. Upon their merger Gala and Coral Eurobet were the country's largest private company, with £7.4 billion in gross revenues.[49] Had it been listed on the London Stock Exchange, its market cap would have made it a constituent of the large-cap FTSE 100 index. And to think that eight years earlier John Kelly had taken ownership of Bass's bingo operation for a mere £235 million!

The move was as much defensive as offensive. Just three months earlier William Hill had consolidated its number two position by paying more than £500 million for the fourth largest bookmaker, Stanley Leisure, and its 624 betting shops. Only Gala and its earnest financial owners had the arsenal capable of neutralising the competition, but also to make the most of the upcoming deregulation. By creating the largest gambling and betting group in the country, they seemed unassailable.

For now, Coral Eurobet's outgoing senior executives were the real winners: Chief Executive Vaughn Ashdown had scooped a £40 million fortune and Finance Director Mick Mariscotti had made his own £30 million on the tertiary sale. Both Ashdown and Mariscotti were said to have already shared £15 million in the 2004 refinancing after having taken home £7 million and £5 million respectively from the 2002 SBO.[50]

Hurdle running

John Kelly and the rest of the Gala Coral management team did not waste time patting themselves on the back. In January 2006 the group closed the acquisition of the County Clubs Bingo chain in Scotland. But despite their best efforts to build a national champion, they were about to face some headwind. The UK Government's plans to create one or even several super-casinos kept being pushed back and the upcoming smoking ban in public places – to take place on 1 July 2007 – promised to be a disaster for a company whose client demographics included many smokers. While detractors and supporters traded blows regarding the ban's likely impact on public health, there was no possible argument about its likely fallout on trading. Following their introduction on 29 March 2004 in neighbouring Ireland and on 26 March 2006 in Scotland, smoking bans had had devastating commercial effects on pubs, bars and restaurants.

Still, the restriction in England and Wales was yet to come so management's strategic focus was very much on growth. In its first 12 months of activity (to September 2006), the newly-formed Gala Coral Group's number of betting shops increased from 1,260 to 1,488, its casinos went from 20 to 32 and its bingo estate rose from 166 to 173 halls following the County Clubs transaction.[51] The following year the number of Coral betting outlets reached nearly 1,600, but the group chose to stabilise its casino and bingo estates, focusing most of management's efforts on online and international expansion. The platform *galabingo.com*, launched in February 2006, became the largest online bingo site in the UK. In the year to 29 September 2007 group turnover was up 7% on the prior year to £1.3 billion, while EBITDA exceeded £400 million.[52] It is at that point that the group's destiny tipped over.

Having gone before a pre-legislative scrutiny committee made up of members from both Houses of Parliament, the 2005 Gambling Act was stripped of the most ambitious commercial goals set in the draft bill submitted by Tony Blair's administration in early 2004. Under the proposed terms of the draft bill, bingo operators could have installed more slot machines while casino operators could have, for the first time, advertised their products. They could theoretically have stayed open for longer. While lobbying had been relentless, at times forceful, in the end the usual pitfalls associated with gambling – money-laundering and punters' addiction – played against further deregulation.

Past studies had shown that casino resorts, such as those in Las Vegas and Atlantic City in America, generated wealth for councils and towns but could also cause problems like spiralling local gambling addiction and an increased sex trade. While proponents of relaxation had suggested incorporating financial commitment from the gambling industry to pay for research and treatment for people whose gambling became a habit, instead the government chose to walk away in the face of unyielding public opposition.

Having previously considered the introduction of the group to the London Stock Exchange, management had to call the flotation off. Stock markets were shaken by the Credit Crunch. Gala's trading was also flagging. In January 2008 the business disclosed that it was shutting five of its bingo venues, maintaining at the time that it was part of a regular portfolio review. But the truth eventually came out that, due to significant underperformance against the management business plan (EBITDA had only risen by 1.8% in the fiscal year 2007), the company's leverage sat at a demanding seven times EBITDA. The group's senior debt was even trading at a discount on the secondary market.[53]

Management had waited for the uncertainty related to the smoking ban to clear before launching the IPO roadshow, but the financial crisis was now jeopardising this plan indefinitely. In February there were rumours that US gambling group Harrah's had considered a bid for Gala, though the latter's capital structure would have seemed too stretched to make any offer attractive to its PE owners.[54] In March, SVG (ex-Schroder Ventures Group), one of Permira's main limited partners, revealed that it had halved Gala Coral's carrying value in its books to reflect lower market comparable earnings multiples.

To reassure its trading partners and customers, Gala Coral felt compelled to announce in December 2007: "The group is comfortable with the current level of debt",[55] only to add three months later:

> "The group constantly reviews its capital structure to ensure both a prudent level of debt and sufficient headroom to allow ongoing investment in the continued development of the business, both in the UK and internationally."[56]

These words immediately proved misplaced and idealistic. Because of its underperformance against budget, the gambling company was expected to breach its debt covenants throughout 2008. Threatening to take over the business, Gala Coral's lenders had requested new funding from equity houses Candover, Cinven and Permira. After haggling for months with the banks, on 4 April 2008 the PE trio was strong-armed into injecting £125 million of new money to keep control of the company. It was revealed that the performance had deteriorated further due to the introduction of new regulation in the second half of 2007, which had obligated the group to remove jackpot machines from bingo halls. As expected, the institution of the smoking ban had sapped attendance in bingo halls across the country: Gala's activities in that segment sustained a 25% drop in revenue and a 14% contraction in operating profit in the financial year to September 2008. And casinos had been impacted too, seeing turnover and operating earnings fall 16% and 50% respectively.

The only piece of good news came from the Coral Eurobet side of the business where sales and profit growth continued, even if that failed to compensate for the casino and bingo reversal. The group's turnover had pulled back 3%, and with EBITDA down 10% the company's already unreasonable financial gearing ratio shot up to 7.4 times earnings. Post-exceptionals, the total-net-debt-to-EBITDA ratio reached 12.8 times.[57] The company's normal covenants allowed for a net-debt-to-EBITDA ratio of no more than 6.2 times.[58] However you cut it, Gala Coral was in breach.

In its June 2008 interim report, Candover Investments Plc, the general partner's eponymous publicly listed parent company, and one of its key investors, had followed SVG's example and written down Gala Coral's equity value by 50%. By December Gala was valued at zero in SVG's and Candover's full-year financial accounts: a complete write-off, months after a fresh capital injection and less than two years after the owners had contemplated a £5 billion-plus IPO. Putting an end to this bleak chapter of the gambling group's existence, in September 2008 Chairman John Kelly had announced his retirement. He had spent 11 years at the wheel, but since the business was no longer in growth mode and was entering a reorganisation phase, Kelly had elected Chief Executive Neil Goulden to the top spot, effective 1 January 2009.

Things did not improve; far from it. The year 2008 witnessed significant erosions for the group's gambling divisions, leading management to book a £140 million impairment of the casinos and bingo clubs. For the following 12-month period to September 2009 the bingo unit suffered further goodwill impairment of £289 million, almost a quarter of the group's net book value. The adjustment had been made necessary by the government's shock rise in bingo duty from 15% to 22% earlier that year.

Then came restructuring costs: after a £40 million hit on the income statement in 2008, another £72 million related to redundancies and casino and bingo club closures was booked in the year to September 2009. Six of the group's remaining 156 bingo halls were earmarked for closure. While consolidated revenue was down less than 1% in 2009, Gala Coral recorded a post-exceptionals operating loss of £150 million.[59] The same worthless equity value was maintained in Candover's and SVG's 2009 financial statements. Luck was no longer on the bookie's side.

From PE-backed to lender-led

Gala's troubles had not gone unnoticed. American distressed debt specialist Apollo Global Management had started buying up debt in the group in late 2008, purchasing some pieces in the secondary market for 60 pence on the pound. Reviewing its strategic options on the advice of investment bank Lazard, Gala had considered selling off up to a third of its bingo venues or even spinning off a division in order to generate some welcome cash and repay part of its expensive debt.[60] No one had risen to the bait.

Other alternatives were being considered to save the company, including a debt-for-equity swap as well as a proposal tabled by the group's main lender Royal Bank of Scotland to break the company apart. As part of its debt commitments, Gala Coral faced an £80 million loan repayment due by September 2009 and another one twice as large the following year.[61] Time was running out.

When the business was in sight of breaching its loan covenants in the third quarter of 2009, the PE owners were impelled to start negotiations with the main mezzanine holders Park Square and Intermediate Capital Group (ICG). Both were well-known lenders and had nurtured long-term relationships with the three British private equity firms. In fact, Candover Investments Plc had been an investor in several of ICG's funds, including its two latest vintages: the €387 million ICG Mezzanine Fund 2000 and the €1.5 billion ICG Mezzanine Fund 2003.

So conversations remained amicable and the few details that emerged in the financial columns in the fall of 2009 indicate that in exchange for writing off £540 million of debt, the mezz holders' equitisation would only grant them a 50% holding in Gala. It would still enable Candover, Cinven and Permira to retain half their equity stake.[62] But this gentlemen's club approach was the legacy of a foregone era. The Americans were about to crash the party.

First, desperate to avoid seeing its equity investment getting completely obliterated in a debt-for-equity exchange, Permira partnered with US buyout group Blackstone. The latter had initially offered to inject £300 million alone in exchange for 75% of the company, leaving the junior lenders with 25%. Permira and its new best friend proposed to make a fresh equity injection in order to gain control of the group. But in early December their contemptible offer was rejected by 80% of the mezz holders. Because the latter also held 40% of the company's senior debt, they were aiming to gain support from the rest of the lenders to block Permira and Blackstone's move.[63] If you think that this is all getting a bit bewildering to follow, multiparty bargaining was about to get even more fiendishly complicated.

You will recall that Apollo had already expressed some interest in Gala's loans when those were quoted at a serious discount; at some point the gambling group's mezzanine was quoted at 22 pence on the pound. On 20 December 2009 the American distressed-debt manager suggested putting in £250 million for 50% of the shares, and the junior lenders would be granted 50% in exchange for converting their mezzanine loans into equity. As everyone was getting ready for the Christmas holiday, Gala Coral and its management were contemplating three options: a simple debt-for-equity swap from the junior lenders in exchange for half the company's shares; a Permira-Blackstone bid for 75% of the leveraged business; and Apollo's cash injection for 50% in the group. The battle for Gala Coral was raging.

The New Year saw a decisive move by Apollo and two of its fellow American credit institutions – hedge fund manager Cerberus and global bank Goldman Sachs – when the three of them acquired £130 million of the gambling group's mezzanine debt from ICG at a 31% discount. Then, in March 2010, after more than nine months of intense negotiations, the mezzanine lenders took control of the casino operator through a debt-for-equity swap – with Apollo holding 25% of the business alongside Cerberus, Goldman Sachs, special situation fund manager York Capital and mezz specialist Park Square.[64]

Although newspaper articles declared that the junior lenders had agreed to waive their claim on the entire mezz notes, the exact terms of the transaction would eventually transpire when Gala Coral published its 2009 financial accounts in the summer of 2010. The accounts divulged that the deal was a lot sweeter for Apollo and its acolytes than press reports had suggested. The mezzanine debt of £570 million had been in fact divided into £450 million of 'sustainable' mezz repayable in October 2020 and accruing interest at a rate exceeding 15%, and £120 million of 'unsustainable' mezz released, that is written-off, by the junior lenders. The latter had made a £210 million equity injection while the senior debt facilities had also been amended.[65] Shortly after the restructuring, rating agency Moody's started its coverage of Gala Coral with a speculative grade. Although the equitisation of part of the LBO loans had brought some relief, the group remained heavily geared up with a debt-to-EBITDA ratio of 6.8-to-1.[66]

Just two years after forking out an additional £125 million equity ticket in exchange for resetting covenants, the PE trio was losing ownership of the business. Candover and Cinven had each recorded a 40% loss on the transaction, representing approximately €200 million worth of equity. It could have been worse, were it not for Permira's generous offer to buy a third of their stake in 2005, allowing them to partially cash out at that stage. Permira had joined the party a bit late and lost its entire investment, more than half a billion euros.

Over the last 18 months Gala Coral had become a zombie company, unable to meet its debt burden. Destitute, the group had no alternative but to assent to the terms set by its lenders. In its financial year ended 25 September 2010 it recorded £122 million of asset impairment for its bingo unit due to club closures and an additional £54 million in restructuring costs.[67] The bleeding was relentless. Management had terminated underperforming venues, bringing its number of bingo clubs and casinos to 145 and 26 respectively, down from 173 and 32 four years earlier. But scaling down had not been sufficient.

By the time its reorganisation had been finalised and it was taken over by its lenders, Gala Coral had become the nation's biggest LBO restructuring ever. Its internet-based betting activities had held up well in the recession, but the bingo halls and casinos had never recovered from the increasing popularity of online bingo, the introduction of a smoking ban and the stricter gambling regulation and tax regime implemented in recent years. The financial crisis and the ensuing Great Recession had finished the job. Management had done its best to protect EBITDA margins between 2008 and 2010 (they had only fallen from 30.7% to 29.2%), but the 11% decline in turnover over that period had hurt profitability and prevented the business from meeting its debt obligations. If computed after taking into account the exceptional goodwill impairment adjustments, EBITDA in the 2009 financial year had turned into a heavy loss.

Bad news had piled up and pressure had surfaced in unusual places. In January 2009, for instance, credit insurers had abruptly withdrawn cover against unpaid bills to Gala Coral's suppliers, sending signals to the market that the gambling group's high leverage raised questions about its solvency.[68] There were also a few signs that John Kelly's 'retirement' in December 2008 might not be final: in October 2009 it was reported that the mezz lenders had briefly considered bringing him back as chairman, only nine months after his departure. Worse still, on 1 September 2010, in a move that could be construed as a sure indication that Kelly's interests were no longer aligned with Gala Coral's, he had resurfaced as a member of the board of directors of Ladbrokes, his former employer's main rival. When Gala's restructuring had occurred four months earlier, Kelly's remaining stake in the group had being wiped out alongside those of Candover, Cinven and Permira. He was free to move on.

As for his successor Neil Goulden, he stepped down as chairman of the board on 8 November 2010, five months after formalising the change in ownership, in a move that bore all the hallmarks of burnout. He had spent ten years at Gala, including four as chief executive. His two years in the chair had seen him run back-to-back financial and operational reorganisation plans and despite all this hard work he had lost a non-negligible £10 million during the debt-for-equity swap. When announcing that deal, he had summed up his mood pretty well, publicly stating: "It's been the year from hell. I'm going to write a book about it."[69] His CEO, Dominic Harrison, had himself stepped down in July and resigned from the board on 30 September 2010. The new American shareholders had completed their par-for-the-course management reshuffle.

Deconglomeration

The new board, led by chairman Rob Templeman, previously chief executive of fashion retailer Debenhams (see Chapter 10), got cracking in implementing a complete overhaul. Friday 27 May 2011 was a red-letter day marking Gala Coral's new beginnings. That day the group refinanced £1.6 billion of debt and paid down £150 million of pre-existing senior debt. A distinction was made between covenant net debt and gross net debt so that covenant breaches would be less likely. Crucially, the maturity date of the group's borrowings was extended, with a significant proportion of the senior debt and the mezzanine falling due far enough in the future to give Gala Coral's management sufficient time to plan an exit.

The 2011 annual report revealed that management had opted to record a major adjustment to the business: £550 million in impairments (£300 million related to Coral, the rest to online activities) coupled with a fourth restructuring round worth £40 million in exceptional costs. The betting and remote-gambling activities' exceptional adjustments were the realisation that the 2005 tertiary buyout of Coral Eurobet had been closed at a full multiple, one that no longer reflected the post-Lehman reality. Templeman and the rest of the management team could start with a clean slate.

Over the previous four years, the group had booked roughly £1.2 billion of impairment-related expenses. In a written statement submitted to the UK's Culture, Media and Sport Parliamentary Committee in June 2011, Gala Coral's management disclosed that the combined cost of the Act (removal of machines), the smoking ban and increased taxation amounted to £120 million per annum in EBITDA, the equivalent of a 30% negative blow on profitability.[70] Because of the group's weak performance and the expectation that leverage would exceed seven times EBITDA for the year to September 2012, on 2 December 2011 credit experts Moody's downgraded Gala's corporate family rating, highlighting that the risk of default was substantial. The near-term outlook remained uncertain following soft consumer demand and, according to the rating agency, delivering on the business plan was now unlikely.[71]

In 2012 the group focused on growing in areas identified by Goulden the year before as needing immediate attention. Management launched new online platforms for the UK market through *Coral.co.uk, Galabingo.com* and *Galacasino.com*, operated out of Gibraltar. Internationally, Italy saw its EBITDA expand 23%. Bookmaker Coral grew turnover and earnings by more than 5%; it remained the third largest retail-betting business in the UK, with a market share of 20%, an estate of more than 1,750 shops, and a workforce of 10,000.[72] Because casinos kept underperforming, in 2013 the group completed their disposal: in May of that year, it sold 19 of its UK casinos to Rank for £179 million, recording a £60 million loss on disposal, which showed that, despite the impairment adjustments booked in the previous five years, some of Gala's assets remained overvalued. Double Diamond Gaming would end up buying the remaining four casinos in December.[73]

The rumour mill went into overdrive about a possible IPO but it was a bit premature; the company was still in the process of rationalising its activities. The press had reported in the summer of 2013 that the group was trying to flog its 140 bingo halls. A year later, in the first public acknowledgement that the combination of Gala and Coral had been a step too far in empire-building, the group publicly announced that it had retained advisers Lazard to auction off its Gala Retail division, the one containing the bingo business.

Although management claimed to be pleased with the turnaround of that unit, in truth its number of admissions, revenues and gross profit had been flat or down for three years on the trot. Only a savage cut in operating costs had delivered value. However, the timing was great. The bingo activities had been boosted in the spring when the British Government's Budget had decided to halve duty on bingo profits to 10%, giving a much-needed impetus to Gala's sale process.[74] After spending the best part of 2014 in negotiations, on 22 December 2014 the lender-led group managed to sell 47 bingo properties – or 40% of its estate – to fund manager M&G Investments for a deal estimated to be worth £173 million.[75] The rest of the bingo clubs kept looking for a home.

Two businesses – Gala and Coral – that had been disposed of separately by Bass PLC in December 1997, within days of each other, and that had been reunited eight years later by ever-zealous PE deal doers, were once again to go their separate ways. PE's process of creative destruction had gone full circle. Reports emerged that a Gala flotation was lined up for the summer. Its lender-led quintenary buyout was finally reaching a denouement.

In July 2015 it was confirmed that the rudderless gambling group was indeed going public, not via an IPO but by merging with its publicly traded rival Ladbrokes; the same Ladbrokes that, on competition grounds, had been forced by the British Trade Secretary in 1998 to sell off Coral. Should the merger receive competition clearance this time around, combining the UK's number two and number three betting shop operators to control 45% of the overall market, it would value Gala Coral – still given a highly speculative grade by rating agency Moody's – just above £2 billion, including £900 million of outstanding bank debt. A far cry from the £4.2 billion price tag Candover, Cinven and Permira had come up with ten years earlier, the bid nevertheless granted the business a cool 9.5 times EV-to-EBITDA multiple. Under the proposal, Gala Coral's shareholders were to hold 48.25% of the newly formed Ladbrokes Coral – an immediate constituent of the FTSE 100 index – no doubt with the intention of gradually disposing of their stake in the near future. As for the identity of the chairman who would be heading Ladbrokes Coral, it was none other than Ladbrokes's Senior Independent Non-Executive Director John Kelly.[76] As I said: full circle.

After nearly 18 years under LBO status, was the gambling company finally about to be rid of PE investors once and for all? Only a brave person would bet on it.[77] While the two groups were waiting for competition clearance, and shortly before Ladbrokes's shareholders overwhelmingly approved the merger, in October 2015 Gala Coral decided to sell its remaining 130-strong bingo chain to that division's senior executives, in a £241 million management buyout backed by financial sponsor Caledonia Investments. Despite the bingo clubs' downtrend in admissions and the fact that the growing internet operation *Galabingo.com* was not part of the transaction, Caledonia was reported to be attracted to the chain's reliable revenue streams.[78]

Making the wrong bets

It took ten years for the Gala Coral Eurobet mishmash to be broken up after a painful indigestion. But what verdict can we draw from this 'pass-the-parcel' account?

1. The corporate world seems eager to forget lessons from the past. It would be simple to explain away Gala Coral's LBO mishap as the result of unfortunate circumstances. Who could have foreseen the change of heart from the British Government regarding gambling deregulation and the introduction of the smoking ban? But the history of the gambling industry is packed with that sort of unfortunate turns of events:

    *   In 1990 Mecca Leisure, the company for which John Kelly used to work, had surrendered its independence and been taken over by Rank Organisation after a series of poorly conceived acquisition moves, funded with too much borrowing.[79]

- Bass PLC had offloaded its Coral betting shops and Gala bingo halls in 1997 because trading had suffered from ferocious competition from the National Lottery. The bingo industry had lost about 100 clubs and 3,200 jobs in the ensuing two years. In its 1995-96 fiscal year, Gala's operating profits had tallied £31 million; the following year, the business had recorded only £24 million, leading Bass PLC to book a £177 million asset write-down.[80] Wasn't this proof enough that gambling is a fluky industry?

2. It is best not to use too much leverage when operating in a highly regulated sector of the economy. The smoking ban had been discussed many years before the Coral add-on. Its impact on neighbouring Ireland since 2004 was already clear, so the debt structure should have reflected the predictable drop in bingo club and casino attendance that was certain to follow. Arguably, the regulatory onslaught was unusually fierce: the sector had to face a smoking ban in 2007 (July), the Gambling Act enacted in 2007 (September) and highly negative tax hikes in consecutive budgets (FOBTs in 2006, casinos in 2007 and bingo in 2008). The Credit Crunch was the killer blow, forcing governments to seek new fiscal revenues. In its April 2014 Budget, the British Government announced a surprise tax increase on betting machines (FOBTs again) from 20% to 25%, and granted greater powers to local authorities for them to limit the number of betting shops on their high streets. The tax change prodded all the industry's players into planning shop closures for those that were only marginally profitable. William Hill announced more than 100 closures and Gala's expected shrinkage was believed to number 80. Should that sort of business be quaffing expensive loans and facing stringent loan covenants that offer limited flexibility when the next downturn, credit contraction or change in legislation presents itself?

3. When leverage effects go into reverse, events can unfold very swiftly – a theme that we will visit in several of the following chapters. In a recession, covenant breaches give creditors significant bargaining power. Even if loan documentation grants the PE investors certain rights, including the right to cure via a fresh equity injection, slower growth means that ambitious business plan projections become impossible to meet. Miss one loan-related payment and the principal creditor can take control practically overnight. In March 2009, even though Candover had just elected to chalk the book value of its equity in Gala Coral down to zero, the firm's Senior Managing Director Marek Gumienny confidently explained: "Why would you sell it today? You will sell it when multiples recover. This business,

I can guarantee it, will generate substantial equity profits for all our investors."[81] Just 12 months later, Candover and its co-investors Cinven and Permira had lost all their equity in the business when the junior lenders had grabbed control. For businesses like Gala Coral with strong underlying fundamentals, it only takes a few enterprising distressed debt investors to recognise that buying discounted loans on the secondary market can help them to gain control of a good quality asset (the largest gambling operator in the country) at a temporarily deflated valuation.

4. Once in charge, lenders can be a lot more patient and lenient towards corporate zombies. For alternative investment firms, a new strategy emerged during the financial crisis, one that allows them to tighten their hold on a portfolio business by positioning themselves on both the equity and debt sides. What is striking from the Apollo club's debt-for-equity swap is that the total leverage borne by Gala Coral actually increased after the financial restructuring. As shown in Figure 2.1, based on pre-exceptionals EBITDA, under the previous ownership the gearing ratio was always below eight times. After the restructuring, it exceeded that multiple for each year from 2011 onwards, which partly explains why management had been at pains to lead a turnaround. But investing £210 million in fresh capital enabled the new owners to reset covenants and redefine what debt portion counted towards the 'covenant net debt' calculation. It is only because of this charitable covenant reset that Gala Coral was able to operate despite its continued underperformance against budget and the deterioration of its net-debt-to-EBITDA ratio.

5. To state the obvious, what brought Gala Coral to the brink of bankruptcy is not the change in regulation, the smoking ban or even the economic recession and its impact on gambling products consumption – in fact the gambling sector proved more resilient than experts had anticipated. No, Gala Coral was taken over by its lenders because it was absurdly overleveraged compared to its peers. As Gala's competitors demonstrated, without that much debt laden on the balance sheet the business would not have needed a financial restructuring. Publicly listed betting chains Ladbrokes and William Hill suffered like many in the Great Recession, but their healthier capital structure meant that there were never talks of default or administration.

Figure 2.1: Gala Coral's EBITDA margin and net-debt-to-EBITDA ratio (2006-14)

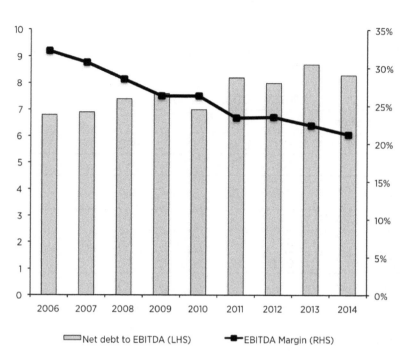

Source: Company accounts and author's analysis

Over half of UK adults participate in some form of gambling – excluding the National Lottery, which would bring the proportion to almost three-quarters. The majority of this activity takes place through a combination of bricks and mortar and remote web-based services. So the group was ideally positioned to benefit from such demand. All of Gala Coral's rivals – Mecca bingo clubs and Grosvenor casinos' owner Rank Group, as well as bookmakers Ladbrokes and William Hill – faced the same market conditions. All three were publicly listed and saw their stocks tumble 70% to 80% from their 2007 peak to their nadir in late 2008. All were indebted, as can be seen from Table 2.1, but none were carrying the sort of toxic debt levels loaded on Gala Coral's balance sheet. In their annual reports all three stated 3 to 3.5 times as their long-term target net-debt-to-EBITDA ratio. Theirs were in fact closer to two times during the financial crisis, as exhibited in Table 2.1. William Hill was even able to complete a rights issue in 2009. Consequently, none of Gala's rivals ended up in the hands of their creditors.

Table 2.1: Financials for Ladbrokes, Rank and William Hill – 2007-12 (£millions except for ratios)

	2007	2008	2009	2010	2011	2012
Ladbrokes						
Revenue	1,235.0	1,178.7	1032.2	980.1	976.1	1084.4
EBITDA	470.7	376.8	283.7	251.7	230.5	287.4
Net Debt / EBITDA	1.9x	2.6x	2.4x	2.0x	2.0x	1.3x
Rank Group						
Revenue	534.4	522.2	540	533.9	580.7	600.5
EBITDA	98.9	86.6	83.9	84.3	97	104.4
Net Debt / EBITDA	3.2x	2.6x	2.2x	1.6x	Net Cash	Net Cash
William Hill						
Revenue	940.4	963.7	997.9	1071.8	1136.7	1278.9
EBITDA	325.2	318.6	300.8	314.3	285.4	339.2
Net Debt / EBITDA	3.3x	3.2x	2.0x	1.6x	1.5x	1.0x

Source: Company accounts and author's analysis

Gala Coral was the only UK business to operate in all three high-street gambling categories – bingo halls, casinos and betting shops – all of which had been hit by regulatory and tax changes in recent years. Nevertheless, if its PE owners had behaved like their counterparts at Ladbrokes, Rank and William Hill, they would have retained ownership of the business. This last point of our verdict is common to many other stories related throughout this book: buyout fund managers can afford to take more risks because their personal exposure to a potential collapse of a company is limited – or so they thought until the financial crisis – to bruised egos.

Gambling with other people's money, also known as OPM in private equity jargon, has always been more enjoyable than risking one's own. This is the main driver behind Gala Coral's ever increasing debt ratios as the group kept being subjected to SBOs and dividend recaps. As explained in Chapter 1, putting in as little equity as possible ideally positions PE investors for a potentially huge payday and the equivalent IRR. That is, if all goes according to plan.

Capital punishment

After their loss of control of the gambling group, the company's three backers endured mixed fortunes, but none of them managed to yield returns high enough to beat the industry-standard 8% hurdle rate (the minimum return ordinarily guaranteed to limited partners before GPs receive a share of the gains).

Candover had a few bad years post-financial crisis, as the DX buyout in Chapter 9 will further exhibit. Eventually, after losing control of several high-profile portfolio companies and turning into a zombie fund by failing to raise a new investment vehicle in 2008, the firm went into wind-down mode in December 2010. Its assets and management company were sold off to a subset of its senior executives, but the entire transaction team behind the Gala Coral tertiary-quaternary had already left or, in the case of deal leader Gumienny, would be gone within a year.[*]

Cinven had a tough time dealing with the disappearance of Gala Coral from its portfolio. At least, that is how it looks from reading the PE firm's 2010 annual review. Gala Coral had been taken over by its lenders, but there is no reference to this fact in the document. Still, credit given where credit is due: despite losing control of a few investee companies during the financial crisis (see Chapter 8 on Frans Bonhomme), Cinven came out of it with the reputation of a resilient investor capable of adapting to the less hospitable landscape.

This goes a long way toward explaining its success in closing a fifth fund at €5.3 billion in June 2013. So does the fact that the firm achieved a net IRR of 8% for investors in its 2006 vintage fund (Cinven IV) as at 31 December 2012.[82] It was better than the unlevered returns achieved on the FTSE 100 over the period (+4.5% with dividends reinvested over the same seven years) and as good as the

---

*. For further information on Candover, refer to *Private Equity's Public Distress*, Sebastien Canderle (2011).

FTSE 250's performance (+8%). While smaller than the 2006 vehicle (Cinven IV had raised €6.5 billion), the 2013 vintage was perhaps a sign that LPs trusted that the LBO firm had learned a great deal from the downturn.

As for former mega-buyout investor Permira, after more than two years on the road it closed a fund in June 2014. With €5.3 billion, the new vintage was less than half the size of its predecessor raised eight years earlier and in line with Cinven's quantum, settling Permira back in the large mid-cap buyout segment. It is understandable: as of 31 December 2013 Permira's limited partners had received a modest IRR of 7.5% for investing in the 2006 vintage fund.[83] On an unlevered basis, LPs could have earned 6.2% on the FTSE 100 or 10.7% a year by sticking their capital into the FTSE 250 mid-cap index in January 2006 and leaving it there for the next eight years.

Permira chose to turn the Gala Coral page in a fairly unique way. Don't look for any mention of the casino operator in its website's investment section (at least Cinven had the decency to refer to it). Don't try to identify who led the transaction at its end. The original deal team has left, and none of its remaining professionals, including those who at some point sat on Gala Coral's board of directors, take claim for it. As we will see with the Seat Pagine Gialle PIPE in Chapter 12, Permira's website does not include a comprehensive record of all its past deals.[*]

Irrespective of all the above, the key determinant behind the success of the primary buy-in completed by PPM Ventures in 1997 and the discomfort felt by the threesome that took part in the tertiary/quaternary buyout years later is 'value'. PPM took ownership of Gala for less than ten times EBIT, or about 6.5 times EBITDA. Ten years later, Candover, Cinven and Permira were valuing the combined Gala Coral at 15 times EBIT and 10.6 times EBITDA, using debt multiples of ten and seven respectively – the debt multiples for the quaternary transaction were the same as the total EV multiples of the first buyout.[84]

You could presume that this multiple upgrade was driven by consequential improvement in underlying performance, in particular in terms of profit margins and growth. But you'd be wrong. Organically (ignoring acquisitions), Gala and its subsequent incarnation Gala Coral recorded single-digit annual earnings growth at best and no meaningful uplift in margins other than one-off synergistic benefits (in fact between 2006 and 2007 EBITDA only grew by 1.8% and margin fell from 32.2% to 30.7%). When the recession hit, the company was hemmed in as the leverage ratio began working its way up. By 2008, on a

---

*. Permira website 31 December 2015 – the disastrous buyout of Italian directories group Seat Pagine Gialle is not listed either among Permira's past transactions.

post-exceptionals basis, multiples exceeded 11 times EBITDA for senior and 2.4 times for mezzanine. A bit of a shift from the respective 4.25 and 1.4 subscribed at the time of Candover and Cinven's tertiary in 2003.

As the Gala Coral story displays, just because a business has grown in the past does not mean that it will do so in the future. Under its first and second buyouts Gala had benefitted from robust market fundamentals. The principal reasons for the growth were the abolition of individual tax on betting in September 2001, the green light given to consuming alcohol on casino gaming floors, and the use of credit cards for gambling.[85] The tertiary and quaternary transactions did not get assistance from such tailwind, and when the much-anticipated deregulation failed to materialise the growth story had vanished with it.

Primary and secondary buyouts, especially those of small and mid-cap businesses, often generate value through buy-and-build strategies. Tertiary and quaternary acquisitions of large companies cannot take advantage of operational inefficiencies and so will usually depend on a major move such as a large acquisition. If the vaunted synergies or market liberalisation fail to deliver, as Gala Coral's numerous closures of bingo halls and casinos between 2010 and 2013 indicate, layoffs are more likely.

Having endured five and four buyout transactions respectively, including one lender-led, Gala and Coral saw their capital structure evolve so much that it is worth doing a quick recap(itulation):

1997	Gala goes through a £235 million MBI with an EV of 6.5 times EBITDA and ten times EBIT.
1998	Coral is subject to a £390 million MBO. EV is on approximately ten times EBIT.[86]
2000	Gala undergoes an SBO worth £400 million. Debt-to-equity ratio is 75/25, with corresponding leverage of eight times EBIT, and EV of 10.7 times EBIT.
	Coral submits to a forced equity cure in order not to breach covenants.
2002	Charterhouse buys Coral in an £860 million SBO, or ten times EBITDA.
2003	Candover and Cinven complete a tertiary of Gala at £1.24 billion EV, or 8.6 times EBITDA. Total debt ratio is 5.8 times, senior debt ratio is 4.25 times EBITDA.

2004   Coral endures two refinancings and returns £560 million to Charterhouse, a good example of the industry's first and fifth pillars of value creation (re-leveraging and accelerated partial realisation respectively).

2005   Candover and Cinven lead a £1.025 billion dividend recap at Gala to pay themselves £275 million. Total debt ratio reaches seven times EBITDA, senior debt multiple is 5.4 times EBITDA.

Permira buys 30% of Gala in a quaternary valuing the business at £1.89 billion, a 15.1 times EBITA multiple. Total debt equates to 9.75 times EBITA.

Coral is sold to Gala in a tertiary worth £2.2 billion, ten times EBITDA, 13 times EBITA.

The combined Gala Coral is valued at £4.2 billion (over 10.6 times EBITDA) funded with a £2.8 billion debt package equivalent to two-thirds of EV, 7.1 times EBITDA.

2008   Because of poor trading, Gala Coral's total net debt rises to 7.4 times EBITDA. Post-exceptionals, the ratio reaches 12.8 times EBITDA.

2010   A lending consortium led by Apollo takes control of Gala Coral in a quintenary. Total net debt of £2.2 billion sits at seven times EBITDA (pre-exceptional items).

2011   As Gala Coral's performance worsens, seeing its EBITDA drop 15% year on year, its new owners lead a financial restructuring that introduces a distinction between covenant net debt (at 5.1x EBITDA) and total net debt (at 8.2x EBITDA).

2015   Lender-owners agree a deal with Ladbrokes, valuing Gala Coral at 9.5 times EBITDA and net debt at 4.1 times.

Over a period of 18 years the abuse that both Gala and Coral were subjected to gives a new meaning to the phrase *capital punishment*.

PART TWO
Asset-Flipping: Recaps and Quick Flips, or the Art of Making a Quick Buck

THE MAIN CRITICISM ADDRESSED TOWARDS THE PUBLIC markets is their short-termism. The endless list of rules prescribed upon quoted companies by stock market regulators, starting with the need to report on a quarterly basis for the largest businesses, half-yearly for the smaller ones, has been claimed as one of the main reasons behind the growing popularity of private equity. Financial sponsors are said to have a longer investment horizon than public investors. There is just one problem with this view. In many instances it does not reflect reality.

Many LBOs completed during the noughties faced the same level of short-term abuse as many public companies. For reasons that will become clear when you read the two following chapters, PE investors' obsession with IRR maximisation led them to focus their attention on speedy cash-flow improvements, cost savings, dividend recapitalisations and accelerated exits. While there are significant advantages associated with PE transactions – limited disclosures, weak regulatory oversight compared to that of the public markets, and prodigious fee-earning potential, to name a few – the biggest frustration of doing such deals is the lack of liquidity.

Over the years the industry has produced an array of methods to provoke liquidity events. Quick flips and recapitalisations are prime examples. In a dividend recap, a portfolio company takes on additional debt in order to distribute the proceeds to its PE owners. For financial sponsors it is an easy way to increase an investment's returns without having to give away any part of the ownership – they receive cash but do not cash out.

There is no clear definition of what constitutes a quick flip, but most commentators agree that the partial or full disposal of an asset within two years of an LBO qualifies. In spite of this fuzzy definition, there is significant research material on the practice as it is certainly not a new phenomenon, even if the recent LBO bubble (pre-financial crisis) witnessed a surge in its frequency, justifying the PE sector's new appellation of 'fast money'.

Many specialists and academics behind such research have spent a great deal of effort analysing the performance of quick flips, in particular when the information was available publicly because the PE backer had chosen to float the business. What this work has demonstrated, perhaps predictably, is that holding a portfolio company for a short period has a marked positive impact on returns for the PE investor, but a poor result for the buying public and institutional shareholders in those cases when quick flips occur via an IPO.[1]

However, it is not just these transactions' financial performance that should be of concern, for the employees of these flipped and recapitalised businesses seem to suffer most particularly. According to research, listings of quick flips lead to a higher probability of financial distress.[2] This, in turn, hurts the company's market position and its employees' well-being.

Accelerated exits will always depend on market demand, so they should logically be more prevalent in bullish times. Unsurprisingly, our two case studies Hertz and Celanese come from the noughties bubble. They will not shake off the perception that LBO firms that choose to exit an asset shortly after having acquired it do not add much value to the underlying business.

The obvious reason is that the investors do not stay long enough to have a meaningful influence in terms of performance upswing and corporate strategy. Blackstone's nine-month holding period in Celanese before relisting the business demonstrates this point clearly. So does Hertz's 11-month period between its LBO and its IPO, even if its owners ended up being stuck far longer than expected.

CHAPTER 3
Hertz – The Need for Speed

Disclaimer: The author used to work at Carlyle. In order not to breach contractual obligations, no personal opinions are expressed in this chapter regarding Carlyle's actions or the firm itself.

THE HERTZ CORPORATION IS THE WORLD'S LARGEST CAR rental operator with a presence in nearly 8,400 locations in approximately 150 countries. It is the second biggest operator in the US behind Enterprise Holdings in terms of revenues, locations and the number of cars in service.[1] But it is the number one airport car rental brand in America and at more than 100 major airports in Europe. It also rents out trucks and vans, and runs a very large equipment-rental business. Hertz Equipment Rental Corporation offers construction and industrial equipment, power generation and industrial pump services to industrial companies, government and local contractors and consumers from over 300 branches in North America, Europe and China.[*] The entertainment services division combines rental of vehicles and specialised equipment for movie studios and large event organisers.

The group's history started in 1918 when Walter L. Jacobs, a Chicago native, launched the first rent-a-car business in America with a fleet of 12 Model-T Fords. Calling the business Rent-a-Car Inc, he sold it only five years later to John Hertz, president of Yellow Cab and Yellow Truck and Coach Manufacturing Company. Although he renamed the business Hertz Drive-Ur-Self System, John Hertz did not hold onto the company all that long either, selling it instead to car manufacturer General Motors (GM) in 1926.

Jacobs stayed involved as president of the rental company under GM's leadership, introducing one of the industry's main innovations – airport locations – and taking the opportunity to buy the business back from GM in 1953. A year later the Hertz Corporation was listed on the New York Stock Exchange. Although

---

[*]. In early 2016 Hertz Corporation was in the process of spinning off its equipment-rental business.

he retired from the corporate presidency in 1960, Jacobs remained director of the company until 1968, by which stage he had introduced another of the rental industry's crucial innovations: credit card use.[2]

Flip-flopping

The company was not spared the effects of the frenzy that surrounded conglomerates in the 1960s, and in 1967 it fell into the hands of RCA Corporation, a giant communications-to-electronics group that had decided to diversify into whatever took its managers' fancy. Then, Hertz was passed on from one corporate owner to another, leaving RCA's remit in 1985 when UAL Inc., the parent holding of United Airlines, gobbled it up for $587 million.[3]

Only two years later, with Hertz now the world's largest car rental company, management bought the business back from UAL for $1.3 billion after forming an acquisition vehicle, Park Ridge, alongside automotive manufacturer Ford. Management held 20% of Hertz. Ford owned the remaining 80% until 1988 when Swedish car maker Volvo decided to acquire a quarter of Ford's stake. By May 1989 Volvo had taken an additional 6% to bring its holding to 26%.[4] Over the ensuing five years Ford diluted its stake further and only held 49% of the business by early 1994. That year Ford management made a U-turn and bought the other minority shareholders out.[5]

Despite all these seemingly disruptive changes at the shareholding level Hertz performed well operationally, expanding into more overseas markets and introducing new services such as quicker computerised driving directions and faster reservation and return policies. The company continued as a wholly-owned subsidiary of Ford until April 1997, at which point Hertz completed a public offering of 50.6% of its class A common stock – the rental operator was back on the stock exchange.

But then, Ford's senior executives changed their mind again and took the view that it was better to own all of Hertz's shares. As the dotcom bubble had run out of steam in 2000, the public markets had tanked indiscriminately. Stocks were being hammered irrespective of whether the listed company was an internet start-up or the global leader in car rentals. In March 2001 Ford acquired all of Hertz's outstanding class A shares that it did not already own. As a result Hertz's shares ceased to be traded on the New York Stock Exchange.[6]

By now anyone could have guessed that Ford was likely to have another change of heart not too far in the future. If there is one category of opportunistic buyers who know how to take advantage of corporate owners unsure of what treasure they hold in their coffers, it is PE fund managers. Indeed, it only took four years for Ford's management to flip-flop and put Hertz under strategic review.

In April 2005, Ford announced that the rental business was up for grabs.[7] After experiencing years of lacklustre performance in its mainstream car division (in 2004 Ford's car volumes had dropped 4.5%, and they would fall a further 5% in 2005),[8] Ford had decided that it did not need to be part of the car hire sector after all.

One of the major issues that Ford encountered by being the owner of the largest car rental company in America is that it was able to sell cars to replenish Hertz's fleet but Hertz's rivals were not keen on purchasing Ford models. Once the car hire unit was carved out, the automotive maker would be free to market its vehicles to the entire rental industry. Ford also made no secret of the fact that a sale of the business would let it raise the price of vehicles sold to the third-party owner of Hertz. All in all, the spin-off seemed like a straightforward corporate decision.

The year 2005 was propitious for leveraged buyouts. Whereas the collapse of the internet bubble had initially tempered the enthusiasm of corporate M&A and debt markets, the year 2004 had seen a marked resurgence of PE dealmaking. In the US the number of LBOs had gone from about 440 in 2003 to 630 the following year. Since 2001 the total value of buyout deals had grown steadily from $23 billion to $137 billion in 2004, or a compound annual growth rate exceeding 80%. During the same four years the share of M&A activity accounted for by buyouts had grown from 8% to 21%.[9]

So to claim that financial sponsors were prime candidates for Hertz's acquisition is a fair reflection of the deal environment at the time. Especially once you factor in the car rental company's business model fundamentals, such as predictable cash-flow generation (indispensable to meet monthly interest repayments) and 38%-plus EBITDA margins (ideal to pile on debt).

There was no question that Hertz was a quality asset. Its top line had increased from $5.6 billion in 2001 to $6.7 billion three years later. Over the same period EBITDA had jumped from $2.06 billion to $2.54 billion. For Ford the benefit of owning Hertz had been obvious. In the financial year 2004 over half of the cars acquired by Hertz for its US car rental fleet and a bit less than 30% of those acquired for the international fleet were manufactured by Ford and its subsidiaries.[10] Yet because of the sorry state of the US car market, where sluggish demand was creating excess production capacity, Ford was seen as a distressed seller, a view that was reinforced in May 2005 when rating agency Standard & Poor's dropped the bonds of Ford and its financial services arm Ford Motor Credit one rung to a BB+ rating, bringing the debt of the two corporations to high-yield (i.e., junk) status.[11] This is not a great position to be in when trying to get the best price for an asset.

Making things even harder was the fact that other automotive sector deals were on the market at the same time: Visteon Corporation and Delphi Corporation, former car parts units of Ford and General Motors respectively, had separately hired JPMorgan Chase to conduct reviews of their businesses. Thus, although a sale was the preferred option, Ford was playing it safe by also considering a flotation, if only to keep the bidders honest. By the summer the auction process had turned into a two-horse race. On one side was a PE consortium bringing together Texas Pacific Group, Blackstone, Thomas H. Lee, and Bain Capital. On the other was a PE triumvirate, assembling equally prominent Clayton, Dubilier & Rice (CD&R), The Carlyle Group, and investment bank Merrill Lynch's private equity division.[12] For such celebrated investors to be vying for Hertz was a sure sign that the latter was a world-class asset.

In September 2005, in what was the largest leveraged buyout since Kohlberg Kravis Roberts had paid $31 billion for RJR Nabisco 16 years earlier, the consortium led by Clayton Dubilier came to an agreement with Hertz's owner to purchase the car rental group for $15 billion, including over $11 billion of existing debt.[13] Completed in an era when all mega-buyout funds were trying to outdo each other by signing multibillion-dollar-deals, Hertz was one of 2005's biggest specimens.

The transaction closed on 21 December 2005, with CD&R, Carlyle and Merrill Lynch Global Private Equity ultimately paying 5.3 times consolidated EBITDA and 13.15 times corporate EBITDA (not adjusted for depreciation related to the car rental fleet and interest expense relating to certain car rental fleet financing). Despite the lack of competition from trade buyers during the auction, the financial sponsors certainly were not getting a bargain price.

* * *

Clayton, Dubilier & Rice could claim to be one of the oldest players in the PE arena, having been around since 1978. Although the group was headquartered in the Mecca of finance, New York City, its model differed from that of some of its rivals in that its team was very operational, getting deeply involved in the running of portfolio companies. Bolstering the firm's reputation was the presence on its leadership team of senior adviser Jack Welch, the legendary former head of America's largest conglomerate GE, known as 'Neutron Jack' due to his reputation for eliminating employees while leaving the office buildings intact.

Hertz certainly met CD&R's investment criteria, which focused on industries exhibiting favourable long-term trends and with limited exposure to technological obsolescence, government regulation or commodity pricing – as we will see in Part Three, it is a set of guidelines some of its peers could be well advised to follow. Clayton Dubilier's share of the equity ticket – $800 million – on the Hertz acquisition represented a big chunk of the PE group's $3.5 billion latest fund. Accordingly, it needed to find co-investors.

The Carlyle Group was not as time-honoured as CD&R but it was equally prestigious. Formed in 1987 after its five founders – a bunch of lawyers and public company finance directors – met to discuss their plans at the Carlyle Hotel in New York, the firm's head office is in Washington, D.C., close to America's political elite. Carlyle started life as a PE investor with a strong focus on the defence industry. Over the years it had expanded at such a fast pace that by 2005 it ranked as the world's second largest alternative investment group by assets under management (AUM), behind Blackstone. It had diversified into other sectors of the economy, and by the time the Hertz deal came on its radar, private equity represented less than three-quarters of Carlyle's $30 billion AUMs, with real estate, distressed opportunities and credit funds accounting for the rest.[14]

As a division of a mammoth financial group, Merrill Lynch Global Private Equity had nothing to envy its two co-investors. Established in New York in the mid-1990s, it frequently benefitted from its parent company's network of clients and the existence of an in-house leveraged finance division. Frequently, in a strategy not too dissimilar to that of its illustrious rival Goldman Sachs, Merrill Lynch GPE partnered with the most sizeable buyout groups in North America and Europe in order to offer a packaged solution of debt-plus-equity to multibillion-dollar buyouts. In March 2005, the group had already teamed up with CD&R alongside investment firm Eurazeo to purchase French electrical supplies distributor Rexel for €3.7 billion. Merrill's PE division had also completed a very high-profile LBO in Britain two years earlier by delisting fashion retailer Debenhams (see Chapter 10). Fundamentally, Merrill Lynch was a great deal partner for financial sponsors keen to access a whopping amount of cheap debt.

Contributing $2.3 billion in equity towards the total consideration, the three new owners were using more than $12 billion of loans – that gave leverage just shy of 85%. Approximately half of the LBO loans were to be financed via asset-backed securities (ABS), which is an ideal way to raise cheap debt since the lower cost of funding using ABS can be as much as 400 to 500 basis points vs. the high-yield market. However, it is rarely offered by lenders as a source of M&A funding. Only well-versed asset managers like CD&R, Carlyle and Merrill Lynch could have coerced lenders into such a sweet deal.

In addition, although ABS instruments are common in the equipment rental industry – rental-car receivables lend themselves readily to securitisation – the magnitude of the proposed tranche was unprecedented. Normally ABS rental-car transactions total $1 billion at best. Here, as if to underscore the agreeable nature of lenders in those days, the financial sponsors raised $4.3 billion issued by a special purpose vehicle and backed by Hertz's American car rental fleet, and an additional $1.78 billion tranche issued by some of the group's foreign subsidiaries under asset-based revolving loan facilities worth $2.93 billion related to rental equipment and vehicles.

The rest of the LBO loans were more ordinary, with a $2 billion senior secured term loan facility, the second biggest high-yield bond issuance in the US that year, totalling $2.7 billion, and including $1.8 billion of 8.875% senior notes due 2014, $225 million of 7.875% senior notes due 2014, and $600 million of 10.5% senior subordinated notes due 2016.[15] The group also went through the refinancing of existing senior notes for a total $3.7 billion, a $1.185 billion intercompany note, and a $1.935 million interim credit facility, among others. Leading the underwriting of these debt instruments were Lehman Brothers, Deutsche Bank, Goldman Sachs, JPMorgan and, naturally, Merrill Lynch.[16] It was a big undertaking.

Strip and flip

The PE threesome was thinking of doing a BIMBO (that's not me being rude – it's a hybrid of management buy-in and buyout where the leadership team of the target comes from both outside and within the business). They were happy with the CFO in place, a chap called Paul Siracusa who had worked at Hertz for 36 years, so it is fair to say that he knew the business well and would be ideal to quarterback the financial sponsors' ambitious cost-cutting programme. However, the current chairman and CEO Craig Koch, who had been with the group since 1971, had announced his retirement on 7 November 2005 due to a family medical issue, and the press release indicated that he would stay in place until 1 January 2007.[17] Thus, the PE consortium was on the lookout for an experienced chief exec.

The first six months following the LBO went smoothly. So much so that on 30 June 2006 Hertz entered into a fresh debt facility with Deutsche Bank, Lehman, Goldman, Morgan Stanley, JPMorgan Chase and Merrill Lynch (it was important to distribute arrangement fees as widely as possible across Wall Street to secure these banks' ongoing loyalty). Hertz issued a loan in order to pay the three financial sponsors a $1 billion dividend, returning to them more than two-fifths of the money they had invested only eight months earlier.[18]

Then, within two weeks of these first half-year results, the rental company announced that it was preparing to float on the New York Stock Exchange.[19]

It was surprising that the PE owners, especially Clayton Dubilier given its reputation as a business builder, were content to flip Hertz so soon. But the public markets were red hot, so it made sense to take advantage of the situation. Only two days later, on 19 July 2006, the PE owners brought in Mark Frissora, until that point CEO of automotive component manufacturer Tenneco, to be Hertz's new boss. In order to minimise disruption, Frissora initially joined as chief executive and board director before taking over the chairman position from Koch on 1 January 2007.

On Wednesday 15 November 2006, 11 months after undergoing an LBO, Hertz completed its initial public offering at a per-share price of $15. The listing of the business so soon after the buyout had made the markets wary, so pricing had occurred just below the expected range of $16-to-$18. The group used the proceeds of $1.3 billion to repay borrowings that were outstanding under a loan facility, and to pay related transaction fees and expenses. The proceeds were also used to pay special cash dividends of $1.12 per share on 21 November to stockholders on record prior to the IPO – in a nutshell, the three financial sponsors were cashing in another $425.5 million cheque.[20] After the stock public offering, the trio's combined holding had been brought down from 99% to less than 72%.[21] The year 2006 had been a great one for public markets. American companies had raised the highest amount of money for six years through IPOs.[22] This partial exit by Hertz's financial owners was timed perfectly.

For unclear reasons, though, Hertz's flip faced a barrage of abuse from all corners. First, in August, shortly after Hertz had filed its listing prospectus, *BusinessWeek* ran a story condemning the financial sponsors' eagerness to partially cash out so early and warned public investors that, based on recent performance of other PE-backed floats, Hertz was unlikely to do well in the aftermarket.[23] Then, at the time of Hertz's pricing in November 2006, Jim Cramer, a host for TV broadcaster CNBC with a fiery personality, told viewers not to bother with the stock, adding that in his opinion the car hire sector was not attractive and Hertz's stock would not hit the $20 mark any time soon.[24] If by that he meant that it would take 54 trading days for the share price to reach that target, then he was correct.

But most of the abuse came a bit later, from observers who questioned the ethical aspect of quick flips and watched in horror as Hertz went on a cost-slashing campaign over the ensuing few months. The issue was that, although the group had experienced strong revenue growth since its buyout, the cost base had risen even faster.[25] Under an LBO model, this sort of trend is not sustainable.

The best way to silence the critics was to deliver good results. For the whole of 2006 Hertz expanded its top line by 8%. Not as good as the 12% recorded the year before, but much better than the 5.4% registered by key rival Avis Budget. Encouragingly, Hertz's corporate EBITDA had risen by a fifth.[26]

As noticed by the most vocal commentators, under PE ownership the group was actively looking for ways to ramp up operating efficiency, informing the markets that, as part of its effort to implement cost savings, management was making adjustments, including headcount reductions and process improvements to optimise workflow at rental locations and maintenance facilities, as well as streamlining back-office operations. This could be construed as a nod to the good slash-and-burn strategies of yesteryear. On 5 January and 28 February 2007, Hertz announced job reductions involving 1,550 employees, primarily in its US car rental operations, but also in the equipment rental operations, the corporate headquarters in New Jersey, the Oklahoma City service centre, as well as in foreign markets.[27] The reorganisation exercise had started.

This aggressive approach to cost management was not winning the PE owners many friends. In April the Service Employees International Union (SEIU) issued a report on the private equity industry with a profile section dedicated to the Hertz buyout. As you would expect from a trade union, the SEIU's report on the car rental company's case study was not entirely positive. Entitled *Hertz so good: the hidden costs of a "quick flip"*, the exposé summarised several of the findings reported in newspaper articles and Hertz's filings since the LBO, and denounced the financial sponsors' tactics such as the high leverage used for the buyout, the dividend recapitalisation of early 2006, the special dividend paid out of part of the IPO proceeds, as well as the 5% headcount reduction implemented in the first quarter of 2007.[28] CD&R, Carlyle and Merrill Lynch were getting some unwelcome publicity, and their next step was not going to make the pill easier to swallow for those furious detractors.

In June 2007, the three investors completed a secondary public offering at a price of $22.25 a share, generating $1.15 billion. Hertz did not receive any of the proceeds but paid $2 million in expenses. After the secondary offering, the combined ownership percentage of the financial sponsors decreased to 55%.[29] More importantly, only 18 months into the buyout, they had recouped their original equity and zoomed to a capital gain of $200 million-plus. The timing of this second placing was flawless. Days later, two hedge funds managed by American bank Bear Stearns collapsed, formally announcing the start of the Credit Crunch that would give jitters to the debt and equity markets. But these were early days yet and few could have foreseen what was coming.

Given the strong economy, in August the vehicle rental industry was once again front-page news when family-owned Enterprise Rent-A-Car acquired its two rivals Alamo and National, which had been under the control of hedge fund manager Cerberus since October 2003. The combined group was to have a fleet of over 1 million vehicles.[30] Three months later it was Zipcar's turn to go on the acquisition trail. The seven-year-old Boston-headquartered car-sharing company, which included VC firms Greylock Partners and Benchmark Capital among its investors, took control of its closest rival in the United States, Seattle-based Flexcar. The combined group would instantly cover 50 cities in 23 states.[31] The car hire sector was in vogue.

While its rivals were leading a consolidation phase, Hertz intensified its efficiency programme. During the fourth quarter of 2007 management finalised or substantially completed contract terms with service providers to outsource select functions relating to real estate facilities management and construction, procurement, and information technology. The move resulted in a decrease in headcount.[32] And yet, despite all these value-maximising efforts, Hertz's stock ended the year at $15.89 a share, up less than 6% on its IPO price 13 months earlier and down more than two-fifths from its all-time high of $26.99 recorded on 29 June 2007. The first few months of the Credit Crunch had led the car rental company's stock to stall out and go into reverse. For now, it looked like an overreaction. Hertz had performed beautifully throughout the year, recording another year of strong top-line expansion – revenues were up 8% – and solid profitability, with both consolidated and corporate EBITDA up 12% as 2,000 employees had been let go.[33]

* * *

Delivering a good set of quarterly figures, on 28 May 2008, during an analyst meeting, CEO Frissora revealed that the group had generated $640 million in revenue initiatives. But the most important slide was allotted to the progress made in management's projected cost improvements. In 2007 alone, $187 million of the cost base had been shaved, including through 'delayering' (meaning staff reductions), business process outsourcing and reengineering, and the restructuring of the European operations. The goal was for all these initiatives to reduce costs by more than $800 million within three years.

The same presentation showed that the group was on a run-rate of $3.55 billion at the EBITDA line, which gave it a very reasonable net-debt-to-EBITDA ratio of three times. Group leverage stood at 78.4% and corporate leverage (excluding fleet-related debt and capital) at 62%. The maturity schedule of the corporate debt showed that $1.9 billion of it was due by 2012 and another $2.2 billion by 2014, but other than that it was very manageable. Fleet debt maturities required more caution since $1 billion was due for repayment in 2009 and another $5 billion the year after.[34] As Frissora went through the presentation, the group's financial position seemed sound. The road ahead, alas, was about to get slippery.

The Credit Crunch had significantly impaired the availability of financing for most sectors of the economy. Naturally, the first nine months of 2008 saw US GDP growth wobble. A third quarter GDP correction was provoked by the collapse of Lehman Brothers, the fifth largest bank on Wall Street at the time of filing for Chapter 11. It was bad news for Hertz since the rental company derived two-thirds of its activity from America. Although the Lehman bankruptcy had taken place on 15 September, therefore two weeks before the end of the quarter, Hertz's results for the three months ended 30 September showed a marked slowdown: revenues from car rentals were flat year-on-year while equipment-rental revenues had suffered a 7% fall stemming from the slump in the US housing and construction industry. Unfortunately, during the same period expenses had edged up 9%.[35] Further cost reduction was needed, especially because in the last three months of the year the American economy tanked 2.1% as the banking sector went through one bail-out after another.[36] One thing was certain: any lingering scarcity of financing would have devastating consequences on the vehicle rental industry.

As the year 2008 ended Hertz's stock stood at $5.07 a share, two-thirds below its IPO price. But its management had nothing to be ashamed of. The group's main listed competitor, Avis Budget, had seen its share price go from a high of $13.74 a share in the first quarter of 2008 to an all-time low of $0.38 in the fourth quarter.[37] Hertz's stock had hit its nadir at $1.55 on 21 November 2008 before managing to regain some composure by year end, but by that stage the market cap erosion had driven leverage to 86% of enterprise value. When he reported full-year 2008 results, Chief Exec Frissora must have been relieved that revenues were only down 2%. Consolidated EBITDA, on the other hand, had slipped by 46% to $1.9 billion after nearly $1.2 billion of goodwill and other asset impairment charges. Net debt, which had proudly reached three times earnings back in May, had shot up to 5.5 times EBITDA. Almost two-thirds of the impairment was related to the equipment-rental division, which was badly affected by the housing crash. In May and June the division had initiated the closure of 22 branches to gain further operating efficiencies. More closures in the US and Europe had been announced during the third quarter. As for the exceptional write-offs related to vehicle rental, they covered the closure of 48 off-airport locations initiated also in the third quarter.

Eager to maintain its cost base in line with revenues, the PE-backed company had laid off 4,500 employees.[38] All industry operators had been compelled to align the size of their fleet and workforce with demand. Avis Budget had joined Hertz's cost-saving model by shrinking its headcount by 13% that year, but the move had not prevented its corporate EBITDA from tumbling two-thirds. By the same token, Avis had also recorded a $1.26 billion write-off for goodwill and brand impairment, primarily as a result of reduced market valuations.[39] The two rivals were matching each other's strategy.

Long trip

It turns out that the hullabaloo about Hertz's financial sponsors' quick flip had been a little premature. The Great Recession was about to remodel the LBO experience into a slow getaway. In the first quarter of 2009 Hertz's management watched year-on-year car rental revenues drop by more than a fifth and equipment rental activity contract by a third.[40] Following Lehman Brothers's bankruptcy, the financial markets had all but shut down. The business of renting cars is dependent on permanent financing; in order to renew the fleet of vehicles, it is essential that access to debt be readily available. The largest car rental operators, Avis Budget and Hertz among them, spent the first months of 2009 testing the waters for new loan issuances. Little by little the debt markets seemed to be opening up, but one event was about to shake the sector's confidence further.

On 1 June 2009, General Motors, America's largest car company, declared itself bankrupt. For months the 101-year-old car maker had teetered because of the financial crisis. The auto industry, heavily dependent on consumer credit, had seen sales fall off a cliff. From over 16 million vehicles sold in the US each year between 2002 and 2007, the run-rate had got closer to 10 million in the second half of 2008 and the first months of 2009, the worst number of auto sales in America since 1992, the country's last recession. General Motors had tried to hold its own, seeing its market share shrink modestly from 23.8% to 22.6%. The real issue was that the collapse in volumes had made the car giant's cost structure unsustainable. GM needed to get in shape and filing for Chapter 11 would give management the means to do just that. In exchange for giving the US Government 60% of its equity in a hugely controversial multibillion-dollar bail-out, the publicly-listed auto group was to be removed from the Dow Jones Industrial Average, an index it had joined in 1925.[41] GM's troubles were bad news for the rental industry, which relied on America's largest car manufacturer to refresh its fleet periodically. But Hertz was working hard on revitalising its own capital structure.

At the time when GM sought bankruptcy protection, Hertz was in the process of completing a follow-on public offering at a price of $6.50 per share. Furthermore, in May the car rental specialist entered into subscription agreements with CD&R and Carlyle to purchase an additional 32.1 million shares (or about 10% of its common stock) at a price of $6.23 per share, generating proceeds to the rental group of $200 million – more or less the net gains that they had generated so far through two special dividends in 2006 and the secondary stock offering the following year. Through this private offering, closed on 7 July, the two financial sponsors bought stock at a 58.5% discount to the $15-per-share IPO price. Giving effect to both the public and the private offerings, the two sponsors' ownership percentage now stood at 51%. It was unfortunate that the rental operator's third PE owner was in the midst of a corporate integration, having seen its parent Merrill Lynch salvaged by Bank of America earlier in the year due to overexposure to the US subprime lending sector. Hertz could no longer count on Merrill Lynch GPE as a backer. All the same, between the follow-on public offering and the private offering, Hertz had raised $529 million of cash.

It was quite a feat and a welcome source of funding in such an uncertain climate. But what was even more outstanding was that, in parallel, Hertz completed a $475 million offering of 5.25% convertible senior notes due 2014. For investors, such convertibles gave the chance to take part in any future price recovery of the company's stock. For Hertz, the goal was to strengthen its credit metrics as it explored options for refinancing $9.7 billion of loans, including $5 billion coming due in the second half of 2010.[42] Hertz used the net proceeds from the stock public offering, the PE firms' private offering and the convertible debt issuance to increase its liquidity and towards the repayment of fleet financing facilities.[43]

Hertz's efforts to prop up its balance sheet were rightly rewarded by the markets, with the group seeing its stock rise from less than $2 a share in March to $8 by the end of June 2009. The additional capital gave management comfort that it could weather the storm. No one knew how long the recession would last, and trading certainly continued to be dire. In the second quarter of the year, Hertz recorded a 19% year-on-year decrease in vehicle rental revenues. Because operating expenses had not been cut as radically and speedily, the group recorded a net loss of $150 million for the first six months of the year.[44]

The second half of the year only brought marginal relief. The vehicle rental business got better in the third quarter but was still down 11.5% on the prior year. As for the equipment rental unit, it fared worse in the third quarter than in the first half of the year. Thanks to slight improvements in car rentals and solid cost control, however, the group generated a net income. Hertz was already back in profit. Although the American economy had started to pick up in the last quarter, for the whole of 2009 US GDP had shrunk 2.8%.[45] The airline industry – a major contributor to car hire since operators like Hertz and Avis Budget derived about three-quarters of revenues from their on-airport fleet – was in agony. Air traffic worldwide had recorded its worst demand decline in history, falling 3.5% year-on-year.[46]

The effects of the Great Recession on trading were very visible when Hertz released full-year numbers. In 2009 management had watched revenues crash to $7.1 billion, $1.4 billion below 2008. The good news was that management's cost-saving initiatives had paid off, helping corporate EBITDA to fall by just

$120 million to $980 million. Because management had managed to reduce net debt by $1 billion on the prior year, the leverage ratio had fallen back to 3.5 times EBITDA. The group had also scaled down in the face of the slowdown in demand. Direct operating expenses had fallen 17% to $4.1 billion and selling, general and administrative expenses had been similarly reduced to $641 million.[47] No further asset impairment had been necessary.

In spite of the GM bankruptcy and the recession the debt markets had started opening up to the car industry, enabling Hertz to complete a $2.14 billion ABS offering in September. In the same vein, its peer Avis Budget had rebuilt its capital structure by placing ABS notes of $550 million and $450 million in July and September respectively, and by raising a $300 million convertible bond in October.[48] Investors had been reassured by these operators' efficiency improvements. In the past three years, Hertz had terminated 8,500 positions, bringing its headcount to 23,050 by the end of 2009. Its rival Avis had been even more drastic. Having taken a more laid-back approach to cost management in the years leading up to the crisis, Avis Budget had fiercely reacted to the economic slowdown by shrinking its workforce by 8,000 between 2008 and the first quarter of 2010, which partly helped it record a 50% jump in EBITDA for 2009.[49]

M&A pile-up

Having sent the right message by refilling its coffers in the first half of the year, Hertz had benefitted from a 135% jump in its share price during 2009. Equally, the year had brought acquisition opportunities. In April the group had bought its troubled rival Advantage Rent-A-Car for $33 million. Advantage was much smaller and generated just $146 million in revenues in 2008, but it enabled Hertz to add 20 locations.[50] That same month Hertz had gobbled up Rent One, a provider of power to event and media companies in Spain, while in August it had added to its stable Automoti Group, an online marketplace for consumers to directly purchase used cars at discounted prices.[51] And then the next few months delivered an even bigger opportunity.

Revived by its $1 billion equity-cum-debt hoard raised in the spring, since November 2009 Hertz had been in discussions with low-cost rental operator Dollar Thrifty. In April 2010, the former made a $1.27 billion bid for its rival. It was a gutsy move. Hertz was now on a much firmer footing – its first-quarter trading for 2010 had seen car rental revenues increase by more than 10% – but it remained loss-making despite its relatively low fixed-cost base: its business model operated with two-thirds of variable costs, according to management.[52] However, the bid was a typical manoeuvre from a PE-owned business. A combination with Dollar Thrifty would enable the group to sit down with its creditors and rework the capital structure, a move that would become indispensable if profitability did not shape up soon. With over $10 billion of debt on its balance sheet, of which 57% was related to its fleet of vehicles, Hertz was facing several maturities in the coming years. A refinancing would be desirable.

Gradually, though, trading picked up. In the quarter ended 30 June 2010, the group was even back in positive territory, posting a $5 million profit before tax. It was gratifying. Performance improvement could come in handy to help pursue external growth. Especially because, in July, Hertz's approach to Dollar Thrifty prompted Avis Budget to counterbid with a suggested $1.33 billion. Dollar Thrifty's management was pressed to consider the proposal and it was bound to render the target more expensive to whichever party won the prize.

An industry that was running out of options a year earlier was now in the midst of a consolidation battle. Avis and Hertz spent the summer locking horns, until 30 September when the bidding war seemed to have ended as Dollar Thrifty's shareholders rejected Hertz's $1.44 billion offer. Shortly before that, Avis had added a break-up fee to its higher $1.53 billion bid. In October Avis Budget and Dollar Thrifty started working together to get antitrust approval for the merger.[53] The chase was over.

In 2010 the US economy had confirmed the positive swing recorded in the last quarter of 2009: GDP was up 2.5%. Throughout the year Hertz's recovering home market, still its largest revenue-generator by far, had played a major part in boosting the group's top line, up for the first time since 2007. And the efficiency gains made since the buyout had enhanced profitability. Between March 2006 and December 2010 management had used the sharpest of blades to slash through the group's fattest morsels: headcount had shrunk from 32,200 to 22,900, a pretty astonishing 29% reduction. In the US, labour cuts had been even more severe, reaching a third of the workforce. This radical delayering was paying dividends: with sales up 6.5% in 2010, consolidated EBITDA and corporate EBITDA had increased 7.1% and 12.4% respectively.[54] The group's leverage had fallen below 60% for the first time since the LBO, and the net-debt-to-EBITDA ratio was also at its lowest point: 3.1 times. Despite the disappointment of missing out on Dollar Thrifty, the group was in rude health.

Slow drip

The Great Recession and the financial crisis had sabotaged the group's expansion plans, and the high indebtedness required constant monitoring by management. Refinancing was practically an ongoing exercise anyway for a rental business since a significant proportion of the fleet debt was of a short-term nature. With $5 billion of loans due for repayment in 2011, management could ill afford to stay idle. Between September 2010 and February 2011, Hertz issued $1.7 billion worth of senior notes. It used the proceeds to redeem existing shorter-dated loans.[55]

Ever since January 2008, Hertz's stock had stubbornly sat below its introductory price. After three long years during which the financial sponsors' patience was fully tested, in February 2011 the stock hit the $15-mark. Not wasting any time, a month later the PE backers sold 50 million shares of their Hertz stock (a bit less than 24% of their combined holding) to Goldman Sachs as the sole underwriter.[56] Although their proceeds were undisclosed, with the stock trading at around $15 the trio had collected something in the region of $750 million. With the growth story firmly back on – consolidated revenues were up 7% in the first quarter of 2011 – Hertz's management went back to the important topic of external expansion.[57]

Avis Budget had been working with the antitrust authorities to get its acquisition of Dollar Thrifty cleared. By the spring, with no approval yet in sight, Hertz took the impudent step of tabling a revised offer in excess of $2 billion for Dollar Thrifty.[58] Because it was taking so long for Avis to get the go-ahead and there were justified concerns about the dominant position a merged Avis Budget-Dollar Thrifty would hold in the lower-priced segment of the market, Avis's management started looking at other M&A options. In June it was reported that the group was finalising the purchase of Avis Europe to consolidate international operations. Facing few regulatory hurdles, the deal was sealed by September. That same month Avis officially ended talks with Dollar Thrifty, considering that the share price was getting expensive.[59] The road was now wide open for Hertz to proceed.

While in discussions with Dollar Thrifty's management, in July Hertz purchased fleet leasing company Donlen for $250 million in cash plus $680 million of existing fleet debt.[60] What explained the PE-backed group's sudden burst of activity was the fact that 2011 had seen strong recovery. Revenues from car rentals were up 9% and equipment-rental activity had jumped 12%. The vehicle rental division had finally exceeded its record of 2007, although equipment hire remained a third below the previous peak. EBITDA had recorded double-digit growth and was on par with the performance of 2006. It was taking a while but traces of the Great Recession were slowly being erased.

When the PE trio had decided to list Hertz in November 2006, many had suggested that Ford had left money on the table by selling out the year before. Yet as the year 2011 drew to a close Hertz's enterprise value was $15 billion, the same Ford had received six years earlier. It now looked like the car manufacturer had made the right call. The truth was that the financial sponsors' attempted quick flip was rather dependent on financial engineering. And the latter required debt markets to play ball, something they had not done since the Credit Crunch. Without the ability to comprehensively refinance the LBO debt, Clayton Dubilier, Carlyle and Bank of America Merrill Lynch were at the mercy of the markets.

But things had started to brighten up recently and the first six months of 2012 brought further improvement in trading. Both divisions grew at the fastest pace since the Credit Crunch. The group's profitability, at the pre-tax and net income levels, was firmly positive; the same period of 2011 had registered losses.[61] Solid trading was the best way for management to convince the markets that the company was a good credit risk: in March 2012 Hertz easily placed a $250 million add-on to its 6.75% senior notes due 2019.[62]

Inspired by this performance, in August, after more than two years of on-and-off negotiations, Hertz confirmed that it was acquiring its leisure- and value-focused rival Dollar Thrifty for $2.6 billion in cash, on multiples of 3.63 times EBITDA and 8.6 times corporate EBITDA. These were attractive multiples compared to the ones applied to Hertz at the time of its late 2005 LBO, although Dollar Thrifty had shown no revenue growth between 2009 and 2011, so it was hardly a dynamic business. Since the bidding war with Avis had started in early 2010 Dollar Thrifty's stock had more than doubled, but Hertz had finally bagged the deal. In America the combined Hertz Dollar Thrifty would hold a 24% market share, not as large as Enterprise's 38%, but much greater than Avis Budget's 18.5%.[63]

Closing on 19 November 2012, the acquisition provided impetus to the stock, with the public markets eager as often to back a growth story. After hovering in the $12-to-$14-a-share range for most of the year, in December Hertz's stock edged back up past $15. The financial sponsors leaped at the chance to sell a further 50 million shares, or 31% of their remaining stake, to JPMorgan as sole underwriter.[64] Based on the prevailing share price, they had pocketed $800 million.

By now, the effects of the Great Recession were almost fully offset. The number of airline passengers in the US had reverted to the level reached in 2008.[65] America's GDP was firmly above its 2008 peak and had grown 2.3% in 2012.[66] The car and equipment rental group was ready to make the most of the recovery. At year end, the combined Hertz Dollar Thrifty employed 30,000, turned over $9 billion and made $3.4 billion in consolidated EBITDA.[67] Net debt stood at 4.4 times EBITDA, and leverage had climbed back up to 68.5% thanks to a $7.3 billion refinancing exercise. Thanks to the purchase of Dollar Thrifty, the group had consolidated its number two market position and offered the promise of significant post-merger synergies.

Understandably, the markets loved the growth-and-profit story, pushing the Hertz stock up more than 50% to $25 a share between 31 December 2012 and early May 2013. It was the signal the financial sponsors had been waiting for. First, in March they brought their stake down from 26% to 12.5%. Given the price of $20 the stock was trading at, the three financial sponsors had collectively taken home $1.2 billion.[68] And on 9 May, CD&R announced publicly that it had sold its remaining stake in the rental group. Together with Carlyle and Bank of America Merrill Lynch, it had sold 49.8 million shares. The share price had raced to $24.96 beforehand, granting the consortium another $1.24 billion.

After eight years and a series of dividends, a secondary offering and four block sales, the financial sponsors had finally exited.[69] Shortly before their final bow, in April, Hertz had made a strategic investment in C.A.R. Inc., formerly operating as China Auto Rental, the largest car rental company in China with revenues of $250 million. Via a 20% investment and joint venture, Hertz was strengthening its position in the world's fastest-growing market.[70] Its management had proved that it is possible to be under PE ownership as well as publicly listed and to still expand through acquisitions.

The year 2013 had been a huge success for the group. Its stock shot up 76%, revenues soared by a fifth and corporate EBITDA increased 29% – although most of the gain was due to the first full-year integration of Dollar Thrifty, including $160 million of revenue synergies.[71] Significant benefits were predicted to be derived from running distinctive brands and targeting different industry segments while sharing the same fleet, maintenance facilities, systems, technology and administrative infrastructure. And the combined group would enjoy complementary demand patterns with mid-week commercial demand balanced by weekend leisure demand. It was promising.

A showcase for the PE showroom

In the eight years under PE ownership, it could be rightly argued that the group had undergone a profound reorganisation. Even before completing the transformative Dollar Thrifty acquisition, management had introduced initiatives aimed at preserving margins. As we saw, the number of employees had decreased from 32,200 in May 2006 to less than 24,000 by the time the Dollar Thrifty deal was being finalised.

In a sense, one could assign the operational resilience of Hertz to the fortunate timing of its efficiency programme. By cutting headcount and implementing business process reengineering throughout 2006-08 the group was lean enough to sustain the Great Recession. As can be seen on Figure 3.1, the acquisitions of Donlen in 2011 and Dollar Thrifty the following year contributed to the reversal of the aggressive headcount reduction exercise, but a group turning over $11 billion in 2014 had the same number of employees as the one making $7.5 billion nine years earlier. The group had increased productivity for 29 consecutive quarters, up 34.5% between 2006 and 2013. Over the same period, it had made $3 billion in cumulative savings.[72]

Figure 3.1: Hertz's total number of employees from 2003 to 2014

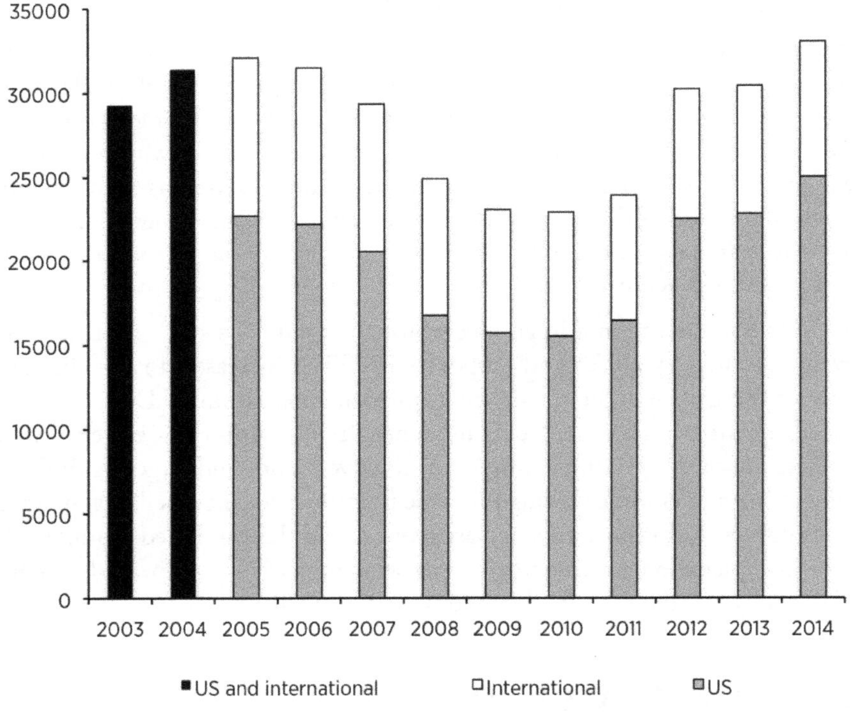

Source: Company accounts and author's analysis

Irrespective of the quick flip, which by the time the PE backers had completely sold out looked more like a slow drip, Hertz's management had taken the opportunity of its spin-off from the Ford group to reduce its ties with the car maker. Hertz had not wasted time diversifying its fleet of vehicles. From top vehicle supplier in 2004 – you will recall that the Ford Corporation's brands accounted for more than half of Hertz's American fleet and a third of its international vehicles – ten years later Ford was ranked fifth behind GM (24% of Hertz's fleet worldwide), Fiat Chrysler, Nissan and Toyota. Accounting for only a tenth of Hertz's global fleet, Ford was well behind its rivals.[73] The LBO had given Hertz more bargaining power to shop around. And the acquisition of Dollar Thrifty – an operator with a vast fleet of brands from the Chrysler Group – had also contributed to the fleet's diversification.

With the exception of the year 2008, Hertz's revenue and profitability proved very resilient, as illustrated in Figure 3.2. That explains why the company was a strong candidate for an LBO. In fact, excluding the $1.2 billion of impairment charges booked in 2008, Hertz's EBITDA margin that year would have been 36%, only marginally lower than the 37%-to-39% recorded in other years. As revealed in the company's 2011 annual filing, revenues had grown at a compound annual growth rate of 5.2% over the previous 20 years, with year-over-year growth in 17 of those 20 years.[74] The explanation lies in the industry structure.

Figure 3.2: Hertz's revenue growth and EBITDA margin from 2003 to 2014

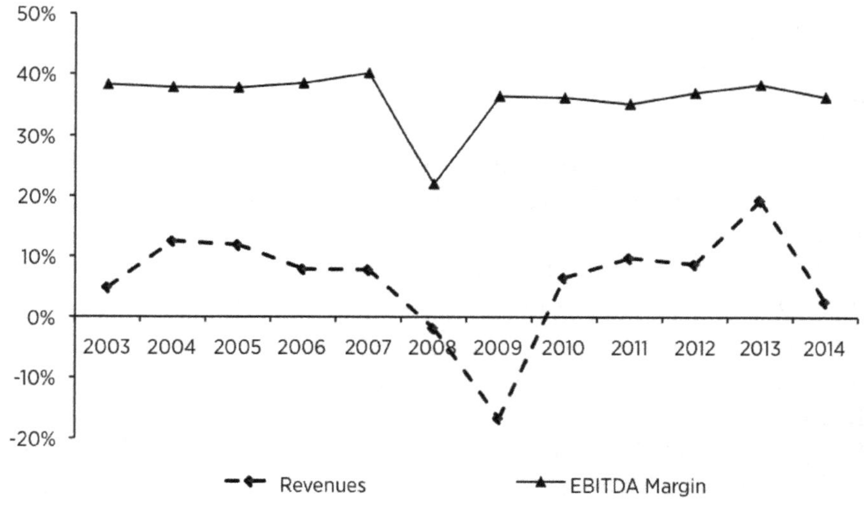

Source: Company accounts and author's analysis

The nature of the car hire market can best be described as oligopolistic. A handful of players control the market, which is never a great thing for consumers but works admirably for shareholders. It allows the operators to take advantage of their bargaining power. In fact, Hertz and its rivals were frequently being taken to court by consumers for failing to clearly disclose the various fees they levied for their services.[75] Regularly, the European Commission for consumer protection looked into sharp practices in this mostly self-regulated industry.[76] In the same vein, a report by the British Government's Competition and Markets Authority published in July 2015 identified the usual concerns with oligopolistic markets: a lack of transparency about the total price when making a booking, rental contract terms and conditions, fuel policies, how vehicle damage was assessed and charged for, and how disputes were dealt with. The list goes on.

In America the dominance of the three largest operators was undeniable. After Hertz's acquisition of Dollar Thrifty in late 2012, the three largest car rental operators – Enterprise, Hertz and Avis Budget – controlled four-fifths of the US market.[77] After Avis acquired car-sharing company Zipcar in early 2013, market concentration was reinforced even further.[78]

It might seem odd that an industry so dependent on economic growth managed to recover so quickly after the Great Recession. However, there are reasons why it was possible. First, commercial contracts with corporate clients are very sticky. The renewal rate of car hire contracts is usually above 90% and frequently exceeds 95%. Second, with the introduction of frequent-user rewards cards, leisure customers had also become a lot more loyal than in the past. Although they might have deserted Hertz and its rivals in 2008 and 2009, they came back to the same operator as soon as the economy had bounced back and they were ready to travel again. Third, in order to preserve cash, all operators decided to postpone the upgrade of their fleet, using vehicles longer before renewing them. While risky – using a car longer increases repair costs and decreases its resale value – this technique helped maintain positive cash flows. Although 45% below their 2007 level, operating cash flows still amounted to $1.7 billion in 2009.[79]

It is this resilience that explains why the same investment strategy was followed by French investment firm Eurazeo less than six months after the Hertz buyout. In March 2006, Eurazeo agreed to acquire European car rental operator Europcar for €3.1 billion from its owner, German car manufacturer Volkswagen, outbidding a long list of PE peers that comprised Apax, Blackstone, Cerberus (which at the time still owned Alamo and National), Cinven and even Carlyle and Merrill Lynch GPE.[80]

Unfortunately the French investment group did not get a chance to flip Europcar as efficiently as its American peers had done with Hertz. Instead, Eurazeo got stuck with its portfolio company until June 2015 (for more than nine years), at which point it listed the business on the Euronext Paris bourse at a €3.5 billion enterprise value.[81] The headline price did not look like a great improvement on the price paid by Eurazeo. It was actually worse than it appears since, in late 2006, Europcar had purchased Alamo's and National's European operations. Therefore, the group listed in 2015 was a bigger business than in 2006.[82]

A spoiled legacy

Ten years after going through an LBO, operationally Hertz was a strong business. It had consolidated its number two position in the American market. In 2008 the group had entered the car-sharing market, operating in cities, universities and corporate campuses worldwide. In 2009 the group had launched Rent2Buy, a service to buy a used rental car that operated in select parts of the United States. It had diversified its revenue stream by entering the low-cost segment in 2012 through Dollar Thrifty. And it had consolidated its position in the fast-growing Chinese market by taking a stake in C.A.R.

But in other ways, the group did not seem to have changed much. In 2004 three-quarters of its car rental revenues originated from rentals at airport locations; ten years later 72% of these revenues in America came from airport locations.[83] The odd thing is that despite the significant headcount reduction implemented under PE ownership, EBITDA margins had not got better either. In 2005 they sat at 38%; so did they six years later.

It could be argued that the economic crisis sapped operating performance but, as explained, a major proportion of the group's costs were variable, which somewhat preserved margins in the downturn. By 2011 Hertz was generating $8.3 billion in revenues compared to less than $7.5 billion in 2005, so with one-third of costs being fixed, this should have translated into higher margins. Economies of scale had not materialised.

If operating efficiency did not translate into bottom-line gains, it also failed to benefit public shareholders. Certain aspects of the transaction should be borne in mind by outside parties coming across the PE industry in their future dealings. For a start, although Hertz was listed in November 2006, it failed to distribute a cash dividend in any of the following nine years. That's a troubling story for public investors who helped the PE threesome cash out.

Management summed up the reason for such skimpy behaviour by explaining "agreements governing our indebtedness restrict our ability to pay dividends". The group never attempted to shrink its debt pile. Instead, it refinanced, amended and extended its LBO loans. The indentures of the senior notes and the senior subordinated notes also contained covenants restricting the ability to redeem stock. Other than $555 million spent on purchasing treasury shares in 2013, Hertz's management never wasted a cent on redeeming common stock between 2007 and 2014.[84] There wasn't much support offered to the share price.

The group's capital structure had remained heavily debt-soaked. While it was normal for fleet debt to rise in line with trading, corporate debt had also increased, from $4.8 billion in 2007 to $6.4 billion in 2014 after the purchase of Dollar Thrifty. Debt was not sustainably scaled down, possibly because market capitalisation had gone up steadily since 2011, so there was enough of an equity cushion, as seen in Figure 3.3. After the mid-2014 stock correction discussed further below, by late 2015 net debt accounted for 70% of the capital structure.

Figure 3.3: Hertz's enterprise value broken out between net debt and equity

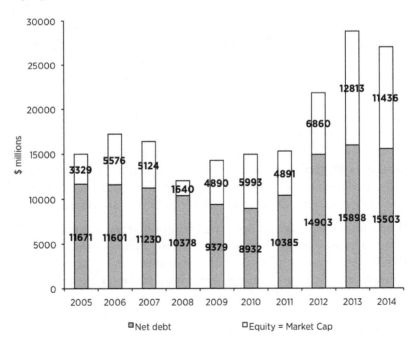

Source: Company accounts and author's analysis

Keeping a lot of debt on the balance sheet is never healthy. For one thing, it fails to give the business flexibility. And it prevents public shareholders from getting a well-deserved dividend yield. Maybe this is why, in March 2014, the group announced that it would spin off its equipment rental business with the aim of raising $2.5 billion to reduce debt and fund a $1 billion share buyback.[85]

The main reason why the PE's legacy will remain tarnished is not because of the quick flip or the dividend recaps orchestrated within one year of the LBO. And it won't be because of the lack of dividend distribution to the public either. Within months of the financial sponsors' final exit from the business, Hertz's management announced the unfortunate discovery of accounting errors. The 2011, 2012 and 2013 accounts had to be restated and the filing of the 2014 financial statements would eventually be delayed. The June 2014 bombshell led to the resignation of the PE-backed chairman and CEO Mark Frissora in early September, after activist investor Carl Icahn, holding an 8.5% stake in Hertz by then, had called for his head.[86]

Much to the chagrin of public shareholders, these accounting inaccuracies led to a postponement of the equipment rental division's carve-out and, together with the limited gains derived from the Dollar Thrifty acquisition, forced a significant re-rating of the Hertz stock, as can be seen in Figure 3.4. By late December 2015 the price was driven below the introductory $15 per share. Not the best result for patient shareholders.

Between 2009 and 2014, Hertz performed in line with the mid-cap Russell 1000 Index, but its stock only doubled in value during that period whereas the Rental & Leasing Services benchmark tripled.[87] Since Hertz didn't pay dividends, its stockholders were truly out of pocket.

Sector experts would point out that Avis Budget did not pay dividends either between 2007 and 2013, so it would be unfair to claim that PE-owned Hertz treated its shareholders any worse than the Avis senior execs treated theirs. But as Figure 3.5 shows, there is one major difference between the two companies. Between 30 December 2010 (the date when Avis Budget Group switched from the NYSE to the Nasdaq exchange) and the second quarter of 2013 (when CD&R, Carlyle and Bank of America Merrill Lynch fully exited from Hertz), the two stocks had not shown the same sort of equity returns for shareholders. Hertz's stock had risen 80% during that period while Avis Budget's had increased by 117%.

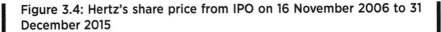

Figure 3.4: Hertz's share price from IPO on 16 November 2006 to 31 December 2015

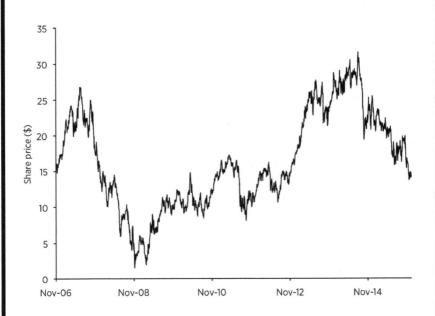

What is most striking about Figure 3.5 is that the differential between the two operators widened dramatically as soon as the PE backers vanished. The poor performance of the Hertz stock is not just due to the accounting restatement of the 2011, 2012, 2013 and 2014 quarterly and annual accounts – although that clearly did not send the right message to public investors. The Dollar Thrifty integration also failed to buoy up trading: in 2014 revenues only advanced 2.4% while corporate EBITDA collapsed by a third. In the first nine months of 2015 trading got worse, with worldwide car rental and equipment rental revenues falling 5% and 2% respectively year-on-year.[88]

Despite all the management talk about operational improvements, Hertz had failed to deliver efficiency between 2010 and 2014. Over that period, Hertz's EBITDA increased by 1.5 times, in line with revenues. By contrast, Avis Budget's EBITDA more than quadrupled when revenues had risen by a factor of 1.65.[89] In addition, Hertz issued an extra 10% of common stock during the period, thereby diluting shareholders' ownership and earnings per share, whereas Avis's number of outstanding stock remained stable. The Hertz stock's underperformance relative to its peers had been one of Carl Icahn's major gripes.

Figure 3.5: Avis Budget's vs. Hertz's stock performances (index 100 on 30 December 2010)

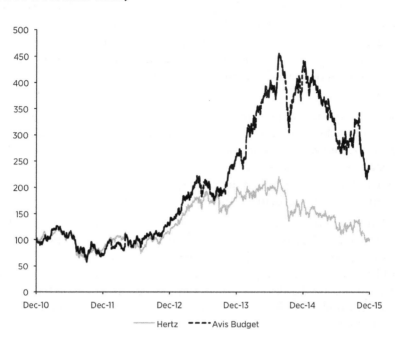

Another factor that partly explains why Hertz's stock performed less well than Avis Budget's and the rest of the Rental & Leasing Services benchmark is that, despite weaker earnings delivery, it had generally traded at a premium. In 2010 Hertz was trading on an enterprise value-to-EBITDA ratio of 5.26 times compared to Avis's 3.8 times. In 2012, when Avis was trading on an EV multiple of 4.5 times EBITDA, Hertz was on 6.4 times. By 2014 even though Avis Budget's multiple had risen to 5.8 times, Hertz's had reached 6.7 times. Hertz offered a superior product to its users so the market felt that its stock ought to be quoted at a premium. By December 2015 Hertz's EV multiple had reverted to the mean, trading at 5.7 times earnings vs. Avis's 5.6.

The big jump in stock performance between late 2012 and the first half of 2014 was primarily due to the widely hyped synergistic and strategic benefits to be gained from the purchase of Dollar Thrifty. The accounting restatements and poor 2014 results destroyed all prospects of value enhancement. By that stage, the three PE backers had returned the keys and made a dash for the hills.

Driving returns

Clayton Dubilier and its two deal partners had made a combined $6.3 billion in proceeds (split almost equally between the three of them), or 2.5 times their investment in Hertz.[90] This is definitely a better record than the American Government's performance on the bail-out of General Motors: apparently over $11 billion of taxpayers' money was lost in this lukewarm experience with socialism.[91]

And yet, without the government stepping in, who knows what would have happened to the wider economy, the car industry, highly levered companies like Hertz, and private equity more specifically. To a certain extent, Hertz's PE backers owed their salvation and the fantastic returns achieved on the transaction to the determination expressed by government officials and central bankers not to let the financial and car industries go under.

As of 31 December 2014, Clayton Dubilier had generated a net IRR of 10.5% out of its CD&R Fund VII, the 2005 vintage used to invest in Hertz.[92] The latter had greatly contributed to the performance, since the entire CD&R VII fund had only returned 1.4 times LPs' capital compared to Hertz's 2.5 times. But given that total unlevered returns (with dividends reinvested) for the Dow Jones Industrial Average and the S&P 500 over the same period had been 8%, Clayton Dubilier's returns on that fund were not stellar.

As for Carlyle Partners IV, the vehicle used by the other sponsor to back the Hertz buyout, it had generated 2.2 times its LPs' commitments by the end of 2014. As of 31 December of that year, the net IRR recorded by the US-focused 2005 vintage fund was 14.6%.[93] Again, Hertz was partly responsible for that achievement.

Merrill Lynch Global Private Equity had the misfortune of being a captive fund dependent on the healthy balance sheet of its parent company. Sadly, global investment bank Merrill Lynch had not been managed with what could be termed best-practice corporate governance, so in January 2009 it was coaxed into the arms of Bank of America, an institution run out of Charlotte, North Carolina, a world apart from unforgiving Wall Street. For Merrill's PE division, it put at once a stop on further investments as its activities were absorbed by Bank of America Capital Investors. The PE activities would be spun off by the banking group a year later, as part of an industry-wide clean-up effort to separate universal lending activities from casino banking.

* * *

As mentioned, the fury surrounding the PE firms' swift evacuation was overdone. Why should the Hertz flip get such bad press when so many other LBOs closed at the time received the same treatment, on occasion with much more zest?

Other examples of equally precipitate, if not speedier, exits include the flotation of satellite service provider PanAmSat in March 2005, just seven months after owners KKR, Carlyle and Providence Equity had taken control – they had reportedly made a three-fold return at the time.[94] In fact, the trio had already pulled out almost its entire equity in the company in October 2004, just one month after making the investment.[95]

The satellite sector seemed favourable for that sort of abuse since, in February 2005, an investment vehicle called Zeus Holdings and comprising luminaries Apollo, Madison Dearborn, Apax and Permira, had pulled a dividend out of Intelsat just six days after its buyout of the satellite company had closed, extracting 60% of its initial $515 million equity investment.[96] Accelerated exits are so frequent in private equity that if we labelled the Hertz case extreme, what would we make of the PanAmSat and Intelsat scenarios?

As we are about to see, while the financial sponsors of satellite operators were reaping huge profits, via its buyout of chemical company Celanese, PE titan Blackstone was in the process of writing the textbook on quick flips, showing what sort of returns can be achieved by taking full advantage of the time value of money without being rudely interrupted by a down cycle.

CHAPTER 4
Celanese – Rich Chemistry

O N 16 DECEMBER 2003, THE BLACKSTONE GROUP announced its intention to take over German chemicals company Celanese. By the time the announcement was made, Blackstone had already secured commitment from the target's main minority shareholder Kuwait Petroleum Corporation (KPC). The latter held 29% of the stock. The €32.5-a-share bid, a miserable 13% premium over the three-month average share price, gave the target a market value of €1.6 billion. The enterprise value – including the assumption of €446 million in debt and €1 billion in pension liabilities – totalled €3.1 billion ($3.8 billion), the largest LBO ever orchestrated in Germany at the time. It was also the largest public-to-private (PTP) ever in the country.[1] Quickly, the transaction would break other records.

In truth, Celanese was not your typical German company: less than half of its revenues were generated in Europe and two-thirds of its assets resided in North America. To understand why, let's backtrack a little.

The specialty chemicals group started trading way back in the 1910s. In December 1912, Swiss brothers Drs Camille and Henri Dreyfus – the latter having worked until that point at chemical company Hoffmann La Roche – set up a new venture called Cellonit Gesellschaft Dreyfus & Co. to produce fireproof celluloid out of cellulose acetate. Established in Basel, Switzerland, the business developed compounds for film materials and paints for airplanes. Invited by the British Government to produce its new airplane paint, from 1916 Henri ran the British Cellulose & Chemical Manufacturing Co.

Two years later, as the First World War was coming to an end and contracts for airplane paint dried up, Camille incorporated The American Cellulose & Chemical Manufacturing Company in New York and commenced the construction of a factory in Maryland to make cellulose acetate. Reinventing both the British and American entities as producers of yarns and fibres, the two brothers ensured their survival.

Renamed Celanese Corporation of America in 1927, the US business listed on the New York Stock Exchange three years later. The British and American operations remained a family affair and, following Henri's death, Camille led both until he passed away in 1956. The company remained independent until its takeover in February 1987 by German rival Hoechst, a leader in fibre, organic and specialty chemicals. Over time the group developed strong market positions in both chemicals and pharmaceuticals.[2]

The most recent incarnation of Celanese, with over €4 billion in sales, had been formed from the chemical activities of Hoechst. When Hoescht had agreed to merge its life-sciences unit with French pharmaceutical company Rhône-Poulenc, it had combined its industrial chemical operations in a new company called Celanese and elected, in July 1999, to demerge by offering its own investors shares in the new entity. Celanese had traded on the Frankfurt and New York Stock Exchanges since its introduction at €16 on 25 October 1999. The stock was twice as valuable when Blackstone tabled its offer four years later.[3]

The German group's activities were run out of four divisions: chemical products, acetate products, the technical polymers unit Ticona, and performance products. To explain what each of these encompassed, it is best to define them by their end-user markets. The company's chemicals were developed for major applications in paints, coatings, adhesives, lubricants and detergents. Given the size of these product segments, it is not surprising that the Chemical Products division accounted for two-thirds of the group's sales, with the automotive industry a mainstream customer segment. Acetate products, about 12% of group sales, were used in conveyor belts, seat belts and electronic components. Ticona was used in filters, whereas the rest of the group's revenue came from performance products like sweeteners employed by the beverage, confectionery, baked goods and dairy product sectors.

To say that the capital structure of the LBO promised to be complex would be a mild understatement. The €3.1 billion buyout of Celanese had been supported with €2.58 billion of debt, of which €1.28 billion was a subordinated bridge to a bond, itself split between a €681 million bridge to sub debt and a €601 million bridge to junior sub debt. In short, that was a split high-yield bond. The deal also comprised a €250 million five-year revolver and a €150 million five-year letter of credit, both at 250 basis points over Libor, whereas the €500 million seven-year term loan B – denominated in euros and US dollars – was at 275 bps over Libor.

It was far from plain-vanilla borrowing, so to reflect the excessive and convoluted structure of the transaction, rating agencies Moody's and Standard & Poor's were giving the debt package a speculative grade, a notch or two into subprime territory. Assuming it received approval from all Celanese shareholders, Blackstone's total equity exposure on the deal would be slightly less than €700 million. Led by Morgan Stanley on the bond side and by Deutsche Bank for senior loans, the debt syndication process went into motion in the early months of 2004.[4]

Blackstone's alchemic tricks

The Blackstone Group was a very powerful alternative asset manager, initially set up as a financial advisory boutique in 1985 by former Lehman Brothers investment bankers Peter Peterson and Stephen Schwarzman. Peterson was Lehman's former chairman – having being ousted by CEO Lew Glucksman in the summer of 1983 – and Schwarzman had been one of the bank's lead M&A partners. The latter, a friend of US President George W. Bush and, like him, a Yale and Harvard Business School alumnus, had been the main force behind Blackstone's ascendance in the private equity firmament. On the basis of his energy and contacts, the firm had grown its assets under management from $3 billion in 1995 to $27 billion eight years later. Though PE activities still accounted for over half of the group's AUMs, Blackstone had started diversifying as a matter of course since the 1990s and now managed funds of hedge funds, real estate and credit funds.[5]

The Celanese bid was important for Blackstone's ambitions in Europe. The firm had opened its first German office in Hamburg three months earlier, so acquiring the chemicals company so soon after would send a strong message. A few days before announcing the bid, Blackstone had partnered with European peer Apax to target another German business, waste-handler SULO Group, in a €500 million buyout.

The firm's equity was originating from its Blackstone Capital Partners IV, at the time the largest institutional PE fund ever raised at $6.45 billion. Completed in July 2002, this investment vehicle had been pretty active, helping the firm to claim the world's largest buyout of 2002: the $4.7 billion buyout of TRW's automotive systems division. The stars were aligned for the Celanese transaction to take place.[6]

*　*　*

Realising that its far-from-generous offer was not winning over the crowds – despite support from both Celanese's management and minority shareholder KPC – in March 2004 Blackstone decided to lower the minimum acceptance threshold the firm deemed necessary to go ahead with its takeover bid from 85% to 75%. A few weeks later, it became clear why. In the face of resistance from some activists, by early April the offer had been endorsed by investors accounting for only 83.6% of outstanding Celanese shares.

Regardless, the American PE group declared its intention to take the business off the exchanges.[7] Having marketed the debt facilities in the US to maximise liquidity, the lead banks had seen the term loan B oversubscribed. There was real appetite for that debt portion secured on Celanese's assets. The $1.57 billion high-yield bond issuance, which had to wait until the transaction had been okayed by enough shareholders to be certain to go through, was launched in May.[8]

Unfortunately, because it had not achieved the 95% acceptance rate required in Germany to delist a company, Blackstone was facing a delayed minority squeeze-out procedure. In Germany, the Takeover Act calls for a bidder to hold at least 95% of a target's share capital in order to impel minority shareholders to accept an offer. In July the Celanese shares were delisted from the NYSE but remained listed on the German börse. That same month Blackstone issued what is termed a domination and profit and loss transfer agreement to instruct Celanese's management board that it wished to acquire the German minority shareholders. The agreement was approved at the extraordinary general meeting on 30/31 July 2004.

While relatively clear-cut, this procedure was somewhat onerous, with the bidder having to guarantee a certain minimum dividend to the minority shareholders choosing not to sell. As part of the agreement, the American PE group agreed to pay each shareholder wishing to retain Celanese shares a dividend in the form of a cash payment of €2.89 per share for each full year under effectiveness of the domination and profit and loss transfer agreement. Blackstone was also offering cash compensation to stockholders to purchase their shares for €41.92 each. The new price tag had been determined via a valuation exercise done by accountants Ernst & Young. That offer was open until 1 October, giving shareholders three months to agree to it.[9]

Still, the PE investor's rapacious methods failed to secure unanimous support. In August some of the remaining minority shareholders sued to overturn the domination vote. Nevertheless, Celanese's new owner was keen to boost its returns on investment, so time was of the essence. Now that it (sort of) controlled the chemicals group's destiny and could influence its management, Blackstone requested that Celanese issue another tranche of junk bonds and pass on the proceeds to the PE owner.

The syndication of the original dual-currency high-yield note supporting the LBO had been so successful, thanks to great appetite from the US debt markets, that it was vital for Blackstone to take advantage of this, perhaps temporary, strong demand by leveraging the target even further and pulling a dividend out. The cash payout took place in late June 2004 and was in the form of a $225 million add-on to the $1 billion tranche of 9.625% senior subordinated notes that had priced at par earlier that month. Proceeds were used to repay €165 million of PIK notes at the holding company level (HoldCo) and allowed the PE firm to partly repay its LPs in record time.

The aggressive move pushed the debt-to-EBITDA ratio to 5.4 times for the 12 months ended 31 March 2004, prompting Moody's to downgrade the company's junk bond by one notch to B3, firmly set in the 'highly speculative' category. To justify the sudden downgrade, Moody's analysts explained that they had previously been naïve in believing that the chemicals company and its owner would aim to be more circumspect in their use of leverage:

> "Moody's prior analysis had recognised BCP's [Celanese's holding company] ability to add additional debt, but had anticipated that the company would exercise restraint and focus on improving credit metrics."[10]

At the same time that it downgraded the Celanese debt, Moody's warned that the covenants in the chemicals group's senior sub-notes allowed Celanese to take on more than $500 million of additional debt without being subject to the two-times fixed-charge coverage ratio.* On that hint, Blackstone was more than happy to oblige. In September 2004, Celanese sold a two-part senior discount note, including $163 million face value ($100 million proceeds) of ten-year non-call five series A notes priced at 61.275 to yield 10% and $690 million face value ($413 million proceeds) of ten-year non-call five series B notes priced at 59.829 to yield 10.50%.

For those not familiar with the phraseology, a 'ten-year non-call five' means that the debt instrument had a ten-year maturity and could not be called (i.e., redeemed) in the first five years without the issuer incurring severe penalties (meaning, high prepayment fees). As for the discounted pricing, its purpose is to offer a certain yield to the bonds. Therefore, a $163 million face value note priced at a 61.275% discount yields 10% to investors who only have to pay $100 million for the privilege.

This new issue did nothing to enhance Celanese's financial ratios. Never mind: just three months after completing its buyout of the company, Blackstone had completely cashed out, taking $225 million off the table in June and another $500 million this time around, returning to its LPs more than the $650 million invested. The short timetable was certain to beef up its IRR.[11]

---

*. A fixed-charge coverage ratio measures a firm's ability to pay its fixed financing expenses with its earnings.

Celanese's management team also got busy rationalising the acetate business and looking for targets. In October, on the advice of Lehman Brothers, the chemicals group decided to buy Acetex, a Canadian producer of various organic compounds and technical polymers, for $492 million. And the following month it bid $208 million for Vinamul Polymers, the emulsion polymer business of chemical producer ICI.[12] Neither transaction was transformative, though the moves showed willingness to lift underlying performance. But it all was very much secondary. Blackstone's exclusive focus was on delivering further value for its own investors; swiftly, it goes without saying.

Blackstone's disappearing trick

Shortly after Blackstone had announced its intention to buy Celanese in December 2003, James Behre, a sector specialist with Trusco Capital, had complained in the unmistakably bitter tone of the outraged analyst:

> "It's ridiculous. We're in the beginning of an upturn in the business cycle for this company, and I'm sure two years from now we're going to be asked to buy this back at a much higher price in an IPO."[13]

But Blackstone was not willing to wait that long. In early November 2004, the PE firm filed with the Securities and Exchange Commission (SEC) an application for a partial IPO of Celanese, four months after the chemicals group's delisting from the New York Stock Exchange.[14] After hurriedly completing two dividend recaps, Blackstone was ready for a quick flip.

Two months later, on 21 January 2005, it conducted a relisting and Celanese became a public corporation traded on the same NYSE. Demand had been moderate, in part due to the chemicals company's high leverage, so pricing had been cut from the original range of $19-$21 per share to $16. About $803 million of the $1.08 billion proceeds were used to pay Blackstone a dividend rather than cut Celanese's debt.[15]

When Blackstone had announced its intention to take the company private in late 2003, the buyout group's chairman, Stephen Schwarzman, had explained the rationale for the move: "taking Celanese private will provide the company with increased flexibility to more actively pursue its strategic objectives."[16] Yet, by relisting the business six months after having officially taken ownership, Blackstone completed one of the largest and quickest flips in PE history. Like so many of its peers at the time, the financial sponsor had become a short-term speculator.

The debt markets had seen demand increase steadily in recent months. These were the early days of the credit bubble. But it was unclear how long this sudden burst in LBO loans demand would last. The upside potential from an IRR viewpoint was too great to miss. Which is why, in parallel to launching its relisting, Celanese was marketing a $240 million perpetual convertible preferred share, sort of a convertible bond with a fixed dividend instead of fixed interest. The coupon was set at 4.25%. The company also borrowed an additional $1.14 billion to refinance some of its existing instruments, and used $200 million of the proceeds to fund the completion of its Vinamul acquisition.[17] The debt markets seemed insatiable and the limits of Celanese's balance sheet were being tested.

Funnily enough, while Blackstone was putting Celanese shares back into American public hands, over in Germany the PE owner had not yet managed to gain consent from the minority shareholders. On 3 January 2005, Celanese extended the acceptance period of its mandatory offer. The deadline was pushed back to 1 April 2005 and still stood at €41.92 per share.[18]

Facing approximately 16% of recalcitrant shareholders, Blackstone combined Celanese AG – including the European and Asian operations – and Celanese Americas, the North American operations, into Celanese Corp (HoldCo), headquartered in the US. With the unalloyed conviction of the largest PE firm in the world, Blackstone then issued shares through HoldCo in order to force a liquidity event across the Atlantic and give itself a fat dividend. What was blocking the Frankfurt Stock Exchange delisting, however, was the fact that one party in particular had gathered a large chunk of the still listed minority stake in order to push for a higher offer from Blackstone.

In view of the negative reaction that the Celanese take-private had received in Germany, it would not have been that surprising if the rebellious investor had been German. In fact, it was American activist hedge fund Paulson & Co. Run by its founder and president John Paulson, the special situations firm was controlling 11.4% of Celanese's shares and demanding a higher price from Blackstone. Having taken the view very early on that Ernst & Young's €41.92-a-share valuation was inadequate, Paulson had retained its own valuation advisers, Susat & Partners, who stated that a fair value of the Celanese shares was more than €65, or double Blackstone's December 2003 bid.

At Celanese's annual general meeting that took place in Frankfurt on 19 and 20 May 2005, shareholders gathered to make their feelings known. A Paulson representative expressed the view that the company's sale process had been "riddled with conflicts of interest and failures of corporate governance", which explained the "grossly insufficient" offer tabled by Blackstone. Now that Celanese had been relisted, the activist firm argued that the equivalent value of the old Celanese AG shares was in fact €72.86 a piece, or 74% higher than the revised €41.92 offered by Blackstone. Until the two sides' disagreement could be resolved, Celanese was in the unusual situation of having a dual listing at differing values. Understandably, its German shares started trading above the €41.92 Blackstone offer, reaching almost €49 in late May 2005.[19]

Twenty-seven minority shareholders filed lawsuits in late May and June of 2005 in the Frankfurt District Court contesting the shareholder resolutions passed at the 19-20 May annual general meeting.[20] The most headstrong of them eventually settled: in August, after a legal skirmish that had seen one of the world's most aggressive hedge funds battle it out with the largest private equity group, Paulson and Blackstone came to an agreement. Like all other public shareholders who had held out for over a year, Paulson had been granted €51 per share, 57% more than Blackstone's very first proposal in late 2003. The arbitrageur had also received €2 per share to settle pending claims.[21]

Now that exuberant financial shareholders had worked out their differences, Celanese could have been expected to focus on operational matters and growth strategy with the full support of Blackstone. Instead, over the next two years, the latter methodically executed its exit plan. In December 2005 it sold 5 million shares at $18 a share with Credit Suisse First Boston acting as sole book-runner and underwriter. Blackstone had tried to dispose of 20 million shares in early November but had pulled its proposed offering after an 8.2% sell-off in Celanese shares. It had eventually sold 12 million shares – about 12% of its holding – later that month. Just as the IPO at the start of the year had proved difficult, Blackstone was finding it tough to cast off its overleveraged investee.

Interestingly, ahead of the December stock sale, Celanese had increased its earnings guidance for 2005 and projected significant growth in 2006. This could only help in stabilising the share price and facilitate Blackstone's secondary offering.[22] Six months later, on 15 May 2006, the PE group monetised a further 35 million shares – roughly one-third of its stake – through an overnight block public offering underwritten by Goldman Sachs. Although all the proceeds, $744 million, went to Blackstone, Celanese incurred $2 million of fees.[23] And on 7 November the financial sponsor sold an additional 30 million shares. Underwritten by Morgan Stanley, the offering netted Blackstone a further $603 million and helped it reduce its stake in the chemicals company to about 14.1%.[24]

Apparently undisturbed by its backer's doggedness to head for the door, management pursued its own agenda. In line with its strategy to divest non-core operations, Celanese announced in December 2006 that it had agreed to sell its Acetyl Intermediates segment's oxo products and derivatives businesses to PE firm Advent International, for a purchase price of €480 million ($636 million).[25]

The following month the chemical group finally undertook a squeeze-out of the remaining 2% of Celanese AG shares. Celanese Corporation had owned 98% of the German company's shares since November 2005 but, due to ongoing legal disputes, it had taken that long for the German delisting finally to occur. Celanese Corporation had to pay a full (some would say, fair) price for it: €66.99 per share. Maybe Paulson & Co had been right after all.[26]

Bringing its quick flip to a fruitful end, in May 2007 Blackstone cleaned out the last of its holdings in the chemicals group through another block sale. Closing the Celanese chapter, the financial sponsor received a final $784.8 million gift for its 22.1 million shares. The relative ease with which underwriter Morgan Stanley managed to offload that many shares was partly helped by the fact that Celanese had recently initiated a $400 million stock repurchase programme. If the portfolio company could help its previous owner get out, then why not try.[27]

Blackstone's magic

When Blackstone sold the last of its shares in 2007, it had recouped six times what it had invested (not including post-IPO dividends and monitoring fees). Within three years of its investment the buyout group had collected a total of $4 billion in proceeds, netting a windfall of $3.4 billion, again excluding dividends and fees earned over the period.

How did Blackstone achieve such returns?

First and foremost, the American buyout firm only paid 7.1 times EBITDA to take the chemicals group private.[28] Its intention to buy Celanese as cheaply as possible was demonstrated in its decision, in March 2004, to lower from 85% to 75% the acceptance rate at which it would choose to go ahead with the takeover. It is common for bidders to increase their offer when facing resistance from a target's shareholders, but Blackstone preferred to maintain its low-ball offer and wear existing shareholders out by sticking to its guns.

With the exception of hedge fund Paulson & Co and a few renegades, the strategy worked to perfection as Blackstone managed to convince institutions and individuals holding about 84% of the stock that €32.5 a share was acceptable. Paulson contended Blackstone had got Celanese on the cheap owing to a cosy relationship with investment bank Goldman Sachs, Celanese's adviser as well as an investor in two Blackstone funds. As was the case for so many M&A bankers then and now, Goldman was also a regular adviser to Blackstone on other transactions, so its relationship with the PE group had been described as somewhat conflicted.[29]

But getting in on a low EBITDA multiple means nothing if you can't get out at a higher one – multiple-arbitrage is one of the key value

---

triggers. In January 2005, Celanese was relisted for an enterprise value of $7.5 billion, or more than nine times trailing EBITDA. The positive difference was derived from better operating performance but also, in a textbook arbitrage move, by a rerating due to higher US comparables, meaning that Celanese's American peers – DuPont and Dow Chemical for instance – traditionally warranted higher earnings multiples than their European counterparts, the category to which Frankfurt-based Celanese AG had previously belonged. Thus, Celanese's EV had gone up 97% in just 13 months simply on a change of venue – the higher valuation did not even take into account the $500 million Acetex acquisition announced in October of the previous year since it would take the European Commission until July 2005 to ratify it.[30]

Second, when it delisted Celanese, Blackstone only had to deploy $650 million of equity out of the total $3.8 billion enterprise value.[31] That's a rather splendid leverage ratio of 83%. Needless to say, Blackstone had learned to master the first pillar of PE value creation, or the art of minimising its equity ticket in exchange for a bigger chunk of cheap debt. The PE house consistently and repeatedly optimised leverage by testing the debt markets' appetite.

Above all, Blackstone and its underwriters adapted their debt offer to prevailing market conditions. For instance, while their intention at the time of the LBO had been to issue $1.57 billion of high-yield bonds, realising that they could get away with a cheaper debt package, they reduced the bond deal by $250 million in favour of launching a US dollar-denominated, 425 basis points over Libor, second-lien loan of equal size. The junk bond was priced at 9.625%, so with US dollar Libor interest rates sitting at 2%, senior lien was indeed a lot cheaper (by more than 330 basis points).[32]

Third, and this is what pushed the rate of return to stratospheric levels, Blackstone got back its original equity very quickly. As a result of the time-value-of-money concept described in Chapter 1, the fact that the PE owner received over $700 million in the first six months of ownership – a total of $1.5 billion in the first year – contributed to its unusually robust returns. Remember that IRR is not only the industry's performance yardstick, it is also what enables a PE firm to exceed the 8% hurdle rate and grant carried interest to its own employees. As we saw, a good chunk of the $1.08 billion raised during the January 2005 IPO went to Blackstone.

The massive upside was also driven by several refinancings shortly after completing the buyout, one in June, the other in September 2004, when the $500 million proceeds of a junk bond offering had gone into the PE group's pockets. In addition, the portfolio company had paid $111 million in advisory fees to its owner, all within a year.[33] As Kathleen Smith of Renaissance Capital put it at the time of the relisting:

> "Celanese did not use a penny of the money raised in the IPO to pay down Celanese's debt. Obviously, that's not good for the shareholders, but then it's apparent that the private equity group Blackstone was looking out for themselves. By our standards, that's an example of poor corporate governance."[34]

Fourth, makers of chemical products operate in a cyclical sector. Blackstone bought Celanese after years of sector underperformance due to slowing demand in the face of rising natural gas prices, the industry's main raw material. The PE firm was buying the German company at the bottom of the cycle. At the time of the Blackstone bid, Celanese was undergoing a restructuring of its loss-making acetate and technical polymers divisions, so that had not been fully reflected in the chemicals group's share price. But the full-year results to 2004 were due to record significant gains, as explained by Celanese's CEO Claudio Sonder in February 2004. Ahead of its January 2005 IPO, Celanese recorded its highest operating income in more than five years.[35]

Fifth, as is the norm among financial sponsors, Blackstone did everything to minimise cash outflows, a.k.a. cash leakage, and that includes tax-related payments. One of the first decisions enacted by the PE firm upon taking ownership of Celanese was to move Celanese's headquarters away from tax-hungry Germany – where the corporate levy at the time could reach 39% of worldwide income – to Delaware, an American state applying a flat rate of 8.7%.

The LBO structure was also optimised from a fiscal standpoint, with the group's ultimate holding company Blackstone Crystal Holdings Capital Partners based in the Cayman Islands and its European equivalent BCP Caylux Holdings (BCP) headquartered in tax conduit Luxembourg. Simply changing its corporate address from Germany to America had also benefited operating results due to the weaker dollar – 60% of the group's revenue came from international markets denominated in the US currency. Every little helps.

Sixth, although observers speculated that Blackstone had ruthlessly cut costs at Celanese (the third pillar of value creation), in reality the PE firm reaped the benefits of reorganisation efforts championed by the target's management ahead of the take-private. Although Blackstone was certainly in a position to impose its agenda (five of its own employees sat on Celanese's board of directors until stock disposals were completed in 2007),[36] the chemical group's executives had already restructured parts of the group, incurring special charges of $416 million in severance costs, plant closure costs and goodwill impairment in 2001 alone, for instance, and reducing headcount from 10,600 in December 2001 to 9,500 two years later.

Naturally under Blackstone's guidance staff numbers fell further but the period of ownership had been too short for the financial sponsor to dictate operational improvements.[37] As shown in Figure 4.1, between 2004 and 2007 profitability progressed steadily, testifying to the dramatic impact of global economic growth and the company's headcount reductions alongside broader reorganisation efforts led by management.

Figure 4.1: Number of employees and operating profit (2002-10)

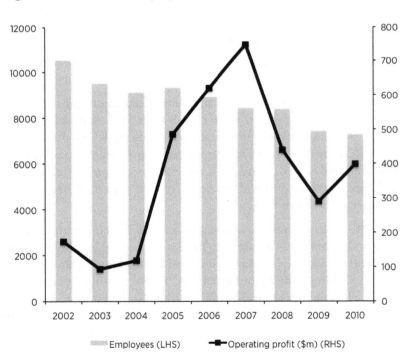

Source: Company accounts

Blackstone's sidereal gains on the Celanese transaction were in part thanks to the chemicals company's financial recovery – between 2003 and 2007 Celanese's gross margins climbed by 700 basis points. This fortunate timing was compounded by the emergence of the Credit Crunch in May 2007, the same month that the PE investor had fully cashed out. Unremarkably, gross margin was crippled by the financial crisis and the ensuing economic slowdown, falling from over 22% in 2007 to the high teens a year later. But by then Blackstone had taken its ball and gone home.

Importantly, the Celanese transaction highlights the growing influence that global buyout groups like Blackstone had on Wall Street before (and since) the LBO bubble. We saw that to ensure the full backing of major investment banks, Blackstone did not hesitate to spread its riches far and wide, successively involving different financial advisers and underwriters to back its buyout-delisting of Celanese and the subsequent refinancings, relisting and secondary stock offerings.

Morgan Stanley and Lehman Brothers – the latter being the Blackstone co-founders' former employer – had co-sponsored the January 2005 relisting. Lehman had also advised on the Acetex acquisition and Morgan Stanley had managed the secondary stock offerings in November 2006 and May of the following year. Credit Suisse had led the secondary offerings in late 2005. And Goldman Sachs had underwritten the May 2006 placement. On the debt front, Deutsche Bank had managed the senior loan syndication and Morgan Stanley had led the bond syndication effort. By securing the goodwill of so many Wall Street banks, Blackstone was getting support for the orderly execution of its LBO and subsequent exits.

A look at Paulson & Co's counter-resolution issued ahead of the May 2005 meeting of Celanese shareholders is equally very instructive. In particular, the hedge fund manager points out an interesting discrepancy between the numbers used by Blackstone on the buy-side in late 2003 and those used in early 2005 when the PE group was launching Celanese Corporation's IPO and had therefore become a seller looking for a higher valuation. Paulson states that the full year:

"2003 EBITDA taken from the Celanese AG financial reports and the Ernst & Young report is US$415 million [the number used by Blackstone when bidding $3.8 billion in December 2003]. However, the Celanese Corp. IPO prospectus tells prospective U.S. investors that FY 2003 EBITDA was $502 million, 21% more [the number used by Blackstone on the sell-side, in the listing prospectus issued

> in January 2005]. The offering documents for Blackstone's debt offerings for Celanese give FY 2003 pro forma adjusted EBITDA of US$681 million, 64% more than the Celanese AG shareholder figures [the number used in a junk-bond offering]."[38]
>
> Nobody said that accounting was an exact science.

Celanese's tricky situation

How did Celanese, the largest LBO and public-to-private in German history at the time, perform during and after the very short period of PE-ownership? Under Blackstone's ownership, Celanese's senior execs no longer worked exclusively to ensure the long-term development of their chemicals business. They had to help the company's new owner cash out as quickly as feasible in order to lift its IRR. Operating cash flows and debt issues were not reinvested in long-term projects (except via the use of specific acquisition, capex and revolver facilities) – they were siphoned out to pay dividends. As we saw, over $700 million was paid out to the PE house between June and September 2004.

During and immediately after Blackstone's short stay, Celanese's finances were pretty ropey. The chemicals group had become trapped in listless dependence. It needed a regular fix of freshly deferred loans in order to keep going. In November 2005, the company retained underwriter Deutsche Bank to lead a refinancing of its $1.4 billion term loan B, looking to make it cheaper by cutting the spread to 175 basis points from 225 bps.[39] In April 2007 it refinanced, amended and extended (A&E) its credit facility, which consisted of $1.6 billion term loans due 2011, a $600 million revolving credit facility terminating in 2009 and an approximate $228 million credit-linked revolver also terminating in 2009. Total debt remained stubbornly high at the $3.5 billion mark until 2009, a year when the financial crisis made life arduous for overleveraged companies.

There was a risk that the business might not be able to meet all its loan commitments, so on 29 September 2010 it entered into another amend-and-extend agreement with its lenders to restate the senior secured credit agreement arranged in April 2007, reducing the term loan facility from $2.7 billion to $2.5 billion and staggering maturities in 2014, 2016 and 2018 instead of the initial maturity date of 2014. Thereafter, thanks to decent operating cash flows during the economic recovery, the company managed to reduce its debt level to $3 billion between 2011 and 2013. But its loans proved once again too much to bear and, on 14 September 2014, manifestly on a roll, Celanese agreed a third A&E to grant a portion of its term C loan and its revolving facility a new maturity of 2018.

One of the particularities of Celanese's operations is that the company frequently committed itself to 'commercial debt'; what the sector calls 'unconditional purchase obligations'. These liabilities are take-or-pay provisions included in certain long-term purchase agreements. To aggressively leverage businesses facing such contractual obligations is unwise. These commercial commitments are dependent on the level of activity and thus closely follow the economic cycle. In the case of Celanese, purchase obligations amounted to $2.2 billion in 2006, $3.1 billion in 2007, $1.6 billion in 2009 when the world economy was in recession, and $3.4 billion in both 2011 and 2014. For that reason, to use traditional bank debt-to-earnings ratios is sort of irrelevant. As can be seen in Figure 4.2, Celanese's total 'fixed contractual debt obligations', both financial and commercial, were in the $7 billion to $10 billion range. It is easy to understand why senior managers at Celanese felt the need to request A&E procedures in order to give themselves room to manoeuvre. They did not want bank loans to restrain their day-to-day running of the company.

It is important to specify that Celanese never defaulted on its bank debt in the years after its relisting. However, it would not be an exaggeration to remark that its directors spent considerable efforts trying to manage the business around its loan commitments. Take the example of its aforementioned April 2007 refinancing and A&E transaction: while entering into a new credit agreement consisting of $2.28 billion and €400 million of new term loans due 2014, and thereby retiring its existing $2.45 billion credit facility dated as of 6 April 2004, the chemicals company had also commenced a tender offer to repurchase some of its common stock – a scheme from which Blackstone benefitted, naturally. As part of this refinancing the company had used $200 million of its own cash to repay part of the credit facility. Again, management was playing a skilful juggling act. It was tough sledding.

Given the debt straightjacket Celanese was wearing post-LBO, it is not surprising that the dividend yield on its common stock stayed below 1% until 2013, a full eight years after its relisting. As management also explained in the company's annual reports, even as late as the 2014 financial statements, the amount available to them to pay cash dividends was restricted by the existing senior credit facility and the indentures governing the senior unsecured notes. In addition, because the *Fortune 500* company had issued convertible perpetual preferred stock (a security with no maturity date) upon its January 2005 IPO, until this instrument was redeemed in February 2010 Celanese was required to pay scheduled quarterly fixed dividends before it could pay any dividend to the common stockholders.

Figure 4.2: Celanese total fixed contractual debt obligations (2005-14)

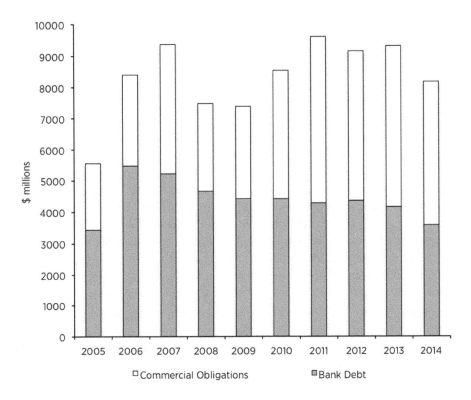

Source: Company accounts

So public shareholders acquiring common stock in Celanese were never going to be rightly compensated – unless you count receiving dividends in dribs and drabs as adequate – as long as the group remained heavily indebted. Their only hope was for the Celanese stock to keep appreciating, yielding capital gains rather than cash payouts. Thankfully for them, management had introduced an aggressive share-repurchase programme to support Celanese's stock. In 2008 alone, a year when its share price collapsed 70% in the midst of the financial crisis, the group acquired $378 million worth of common stock. From 2008 to 2012 the total dollar amount of this repurchase scheme totalled $501 million. And as just observed, once in a while the group used its operating cash flows to repay debt.[40] That is cash that could probably have found better use in R&D, capex or expansion projects. Management probably felt that it was necessary to prop up the share price and market cap in order to keep the company's leverage ratio bearable.

In spite of its loan obligations and regular capital restructurings, the chemicals group performed rather well, all things considered. Credit must be given to its senior executives who carried out a thorough operational restructuring exercise – the realignment of the manufacturing footprint leading to the significant headcount reductions already mentioned – alongside a strategic shift towards emerging markets, including a well-timed expansion into fast-growing China. Thanks to its discipline in cost management, the company was able to sustain a 25% revenue drop during the 2009 global recession.

Still, the Celanese saga certainly did not help private equity to project a positive image in continental Europe. With an increasing number of German companies falling into the hands of financial sponsors, the industry became the object of rapt attention in national media in the years leading up to the financial crisis. Naturally, the fact that Blackstone generated an unusually high bonanza from the Celanese transaction did not escape the German press, notably weekly news magazine *Der Spiegel*.[41]

Worse, while Blackstone was busy extracting cash out of its portfolio company, politicians also began to take notice of the industry's unconventional practices. In November 2004 the chairman of Germany's ruling Social Democratic Party, Franz Müntefering, referred to PE funds as "locusts", declaring: "We must help companies acting in the interest of their future and the future of their employees against irresponsible locust swarms, who measure success in quarterly intervals, suck off substance and let companies die once they have eaten them bare."[42] Müntefering carried a lot of weight in national matters, even joining Angela Merkel's Government the following year as Minister of Labour and Social Affairs. He was not specifically talking about Celanese – other LBOs in the country had raised concerns among the political elite – but the evidence in this case study cannot help to build an argument against his view.

Blackstone ended up closing its German office in 2007, not because the group felt embarrassed by its poor reputation in the country – it certainly viewed its six-time return performance on Celanese with a sense of pride – but because it had decided to consolidate its European activities out of London. Yet three years later it reopened an office there, this time in Düsseldorf.

Perhaps in a fitting tribute to the gods of prudence, and as fair retribution to the Celanese episode, in the summer of 2012 the American investment firm handed control of investee Klöckner Pentaplast, a German packaging producer, to its junior lenders. Trying to offer reasons behind Blackstone's €220 million equity loss on a transaction completed at the peak of the buyout bubble in 2007, some conjectured that the PE house had paid too much and compounded the mistake by putting in only a sliver of its own money and loading its acquisition with debt, at 7.3 times EBITDA.

However, the main reason why the packaging company had turned into a zombie was not just because of disproportionate leverage, a common feature in most LBOs. The debt binge had ended with the Credit Crunch shortly after the deal had closed, contrasting with the Celanese buyout not in its style but in its timing within the debt cycle. Had Pentaplast been acquired in 2004 rather than 2007, it would have turned into another home run. Blackstone Capital Partners IV, the fund used to finance the Celanese PTP, had generated an IRR of nearly 37%. Blackstone Capital Partners V, raised in 2006 and used to fund the Pentaplast acquisition, had generated a net yield of 7.6%,[43] below the 8% hurdle rate benchmark. PE investing is cycle-dependent.

PART THREE
Financial Engineering and the Risks Pyramid

T HE FOLLOWING STATEMENT MIGHT COME AS A SURPRISE to some readers: private equity investors do not use risk-management tools. They perform sensitivity analyses on valuations and relevant due diligence, but their financial models are subject to biases, some related to subjectivity, others to ignorance.

The biggest weakness of PE investment decision-making systems, however, lies in the lack of risk-adjusted investment procedures. Information is gathered on an ad hoc basis; data input and analyses are not automated and are subject to individual judgements. As a consequence, risk assessment is incomplete, often inaccurate.

Not only do PE firms fail to gauge risk appropriately, but few seem to bother to draw from experience. Like the airline industry, private equity works through trial and error. But, unlike airlines, LBO fund managers do not bother to recover 'black boxes' to identify the causes of errors. It is a shame, because failures are great learning opportunities. In 1974 the number of onboard fatalities per million plane departures was close to 300. Forty years later, the fatality rate has dropped below 50 per million departures. That's the power of learning from mistakes.[1]

Most LBO fund managers would be incapable of pointing out where their investments have gone bad or, before investing their capital, where the key uncertainties of a transaction lie: is it technological innovation (EMI), a change in regulation (Gala Coral), a sudden influx of substitutive supply (TXU)? If they could identify these risks, they would not know how to factor them into their decision making. Because they make bets on the future, buyout managers need to ascribe themselves to scenario planning, an investment method common in project financing due to the vast array of uncertainties inherent in infrastructure and exploration projects. This comprehensive tool offers a systematic analysis of an investment's risk profile.

By bringing in discipline at the investment committee level, fund managers would avoid the sorts of bets that our next two case studies expose all too well. The risks pyramid on the next page summarises the various layers of risks typical to a buyout, with the leverage sitting atop, ready to make the edifice cave in should the gamble be excessive.

What I term *risks pyramid* is the amalgamation of all uncertainties inherent to any investment. A company will always face unpredictability, whether related to its level of fixed costs, market positioning, exposure to the economic cycle, poor management skills, technological innovation, the regulatory environment, or any other factor (as illustrated in the diagram below). No company represents a risk-free investment opportunity. If an investor fails to properly carry out due diligence on a target, its market and a long list of uncontrollable factors, the chance that its LBO will unravel is very real. Without a proper analytical framework to assess exposure to a variety of parameters, there is no way to determine whether a 70% or 80% leverage ratio is even remotely reasonable.

LBO failures are clearly not uncommon, but they should be. Many GPs fail to take into consideration risks specific to a target, being too absorbed in their own financial ingenuity. Since its inception the LBO industry has constantly tried to push the envelope of what is morally acceptable in terms of capital structuring.

Our next two case studies demonstrate what happens when a financial sponsor decides to add financial risk (leverage) to an already sky-scraping and unstable risks pyramid. At the time of their buyouts, energy giant TXU operated in the partly deregulated, hugely cyclical electricity sector, whereas record label EMI was one of the music majors facing an onslaught from digital substitution. We will see that their PE investors significantly underestimated the uncertainties these companies were exposed to. To financial gurus, risk management matters a lot less than dealmaking prowess. Hopefully, the following two chapters will serve as black boxes to avoid similar mistakes in the future.

CHAPTER 5
TXU – Power Struggles

O N 29 APRIL 2014, ONE OF THE LARGEST COMPANIES OF the state of Texas collapsed into Chapter 11 bankruptcy protection, sitting on $40 billion of expensive loans, a significant proportion of them coming due within months. Dallas-headquartered Energy Future, formerly known as TXU, was the tenth biggest bankruptcy case in the history of the United States – the second biggest for Texas, behind scandal-struck Enron. On at least one count, however, the company was number one: it was the largest ever bankrupt leveraged buyout.

Energy Future's purposeful beginnings dated back to 1882, shortly after the invention of the incandescent light bulb by Thomas Edison. That year North Texas was introduced to electric lights by the Dallas Electric Lighting Company. Three years later, neighbouring city Fort Worth was granted the same privilege by the Fort Worth Electric Light and Power Company. In 1912 the North Central and East Texas electricity markets saw the creation of the Texas Power & Light Company, the aggregation of 13 electric companies brought together by Electric Bond and Share Company, a subsidiary of General Electric Company. It is the Electric Bond and Share that, over the following three decades, played the role of builder and consolidator of the electricity supply network across the state of Texas. In 1929 it formed Texas Electric Service Company to serve the Fort Worth area, before merging it shortly after the end of the Second World War with its Dallas operations and the Texas Power & Light Company. The combined entity was renamed Texas Utilities Company.

Over the next half century, the latter introduced several solutions that made it a pioneer in the state, including the installation of the industry's first outdoor generator in 1948, the use of lignite (i.e., coal) to provide electricity for aluminium production, and the first 345-kilovolt transmission interconnection between Dallas and Houston in 1963. In December 1974 Texas Utilities also started the construction of the state's first nuclear plant.

While in the 1990s the group expanded overseas, its core activities remained Texas-centric. Following the acquisition of activities in the gas sector, the group was renamed TXU in 1999, shortly before separating its regulated delivery activities (variably named Oncor or TXU Electric Delivery over the years) from the competitive energy generation and transmission businesses, in line with new regional regulation. The latter required that, from 1 January 2002, previously integrated electricity operators should be unbundled, separating power generators, retail electricity providers and transmission and distribution (T&D) companies.

As one of the largest incumbents, TXU was logically impacted when the markets were deregulated. With its hands full trying to tackle new competitors, senior management chose to divest non-core and loss-making operations, or 'value-disadvantaged businesses' to use its own jargon. In quick succession TXU Europe, TXU Australia and the gas activities were disposed of. After the restructuring, and despite the significant loss of customers due to competitive activity, the years 2004 to 2006 saw steady growth in operating revenues, thanks to higher natural gas prices and external expansion.

No matter how you sliced the data, by the end of 2006 TXU was an imposing organisation, posting nearly $11 billion in revenues and $5 billion of operating cash flows, managing 19 power plants, including one of only two nuclear plants operating in Texas. It ran three of the state's ten largest plants by generating capacity and accounted for 18% of its total electric power capacity. TXU's retail division, the second largest in Texas, provided 23% of the state's residential consumption and 13% of its industrial consumption.[1]

What could have led a corporation with this enviable market position to file for Chapter 11 in the spring of 2014? To answer this question, we need to travel ten years back, to the days of easy money and LBO madness.

When egos collide

When it comes to dealmaking, as in so many things in America, size matters. Throughout the first half of the noughties, the magnitude of leveraged buyouts had resolutely gone up. The phenomenon had gathered momentum as the first decade of the new millennium reached its mid-point. All the major participants wanted to earn bragging rights in the hall of fame of mega-buyouts.

The year 2005 had seen deals like Hertz (reviewed in Chapter 3), and Capmark Financial – the latter done by KKR – exceed the $15 billion mark in enterprise value. They were just part of a warm-up session. January 2006 saw the announcement by Cerberus of its intention to acquire retailer Albertson's for over $17 billion. Once the year was firmly afoot, the industry's hotshots started competing amongst themselves to get out the most outlandish predictions. On 26 January, while attending the World Economic Forum in Davos, Switzerland,

Martin Halusa, Chairman of PE group Apax, declared that he could envisage the creation of a $100 billion fundraise within ten years.[2] With Blackstone about to close the industry's largest fund on record, a $13 billion vintage, it was difficult to see how any LBO manager could sponsor a vehicle 7.7 times larger within a decade. But fact-based statements were never a forte of impassioned financiers. The point was to warn the world that no one was safe.

Even if fundraisers were getting ahead of themselves, deal-doers were not to be surpassed. By May, Carlyle and Goldman Sachs were closing the $21.6 billion purchase of oil producer Kinder Morgan. Now that the $20 billion threshold had been reached, it was hardly worth getting out of bed for deals valued at less than that. In quick succession, the LBOs of Hospital Corporation of America ($32.7 billion), casino operator Harrah's Entertainment (over $27.5 billion, see Chapter 15), and communications conglomerate ClearChannel ($25.7 billion) were announced in July, October and November 2006 respectively. What was needed, though, was a killer blow; a deal so large that others would seem puny by comparison. If someone was going to give it a go, it had to be record-breaker supremo Henry Kravis.

KKR had long being the trailblazer of private equity and its co-founder Henry Kravis the sector's most celebrated nabob. Launched in 1976 by three former Bear Stearns investment bankers, Kohlberg Kravis Roberts & Co. had defined multibillion-dollar LBOs as its legitimate market niche. The firm had held, since December 1988 and until 2006, the title of biggest LBO sponsor following its $31 billion acquisition of food and tobacco conglomerate RJR Nabisco. Though the lacklustre performance of that deal had convinced KKR and other financial sponsors to stay clear of jumbo deals, PE firms had recently been tempted back, if only to latch on to the mega-buyout crown. These lofty buyouts were not just highly visible, which was helpful in a sector that craves for bragging rights but whose success and aggressive techniques depend on the actors' ability to operate out of the public eye; they were also hugely lucrative.

The only way the KKR executives could complete multibillion-dollar transactions was by raising multibillion-dollar funds. By March 2007, the firm's AUMs exceeded $53 billion, up from $17 billion in December 2003. What had underscored KKR's and its executives' success over the years was the ability to levy ongoing fees for providing managerial and other services to their LPs, as well as transaction and monitoring commissions in connection with the underlying investments. For fees to rack up nicely, asset size was of the essence.

So, as the firm had grown its asset base, its fee income had been multiplied by eight between 2003 and 2006. Its recent fundraising drive had been stunning. The KKR 2006 Fund was not yet closed but had already collected more than $16.6 billion, already 2.8 times larger than the 2002 vintage. By early 2007, the firm employed nearly 400 people, had raised 16 individual funds and deployed over $30 billion of its LPs' capital across 31 years. It could claim in its IPO prospectus that same year that it had completed the largest buyouts in the United States, the Netherlands, Denmark, India, Australia, Singapore and France. It did not fail to point out in the same prospectus that, in mid-2007, it held 40 companies in portfolio, together generating more than $100 billion of annual revenues.

If size was such a core determinant of KKR's investment strategy, the firm could not possibly let rivals claim the biggest deal of the bubble. Not known for exercising much restraint during competitive auctions, thanks to its incomparable network of contacts built since the 1970s KKR was equally adept at sourcing proprietary deals.

For a while, investor speculation had pointed to potential takeovers of US energy groups. But few believed that an LBO was possible in the regulated distribution segment. KKR was not known for caring for conventional wisdom. Importantly, the recent deregulation of the sector's generation and transmission activities in several parts of the US made the sector attractive. What was needed was a political approach to alleviate regulatory concerns.

But first, KKR had to find a target sizeable enough to warrant its involvement. Its deal team eventually found one so big that even mighty KKR could not go it alone. In November 2006, the New York-headquartered investment firm, guided by its energy and natural resources specialist Marc Lipschultz, joined forces with its peer Texas Pacific Group to make an approach to TXU. A utility company with integrated generation and distribution capabilities, the target was not the ideal candidate as it was likely to require a lengthy regulatory clearance procedure. TXU's management welcomed the unsolicited approach by the two PE firms,[3] acknowledging their sector credentials – the duo had partnered together with Blackstone only three years earlier when buying power plant operator Texas Genco for $3.65 billion. They had flipped the business 15 months later for $8.3 billion, earning a six-fold return on their investment.[4]

With TXU, Texas Pacific Group was not just playing on home turf; it was putting money to work in a sector it knew inside out. Being based in Fort Worth, its executives had deep connections in the energy space. Better still, two of its co-founders, David Bonderman and James Coulter, had worked for Robert Bass, an investor whose father and great uncle had made a fortune in the oil industry as wildcatters in the first half of the 20th century. Bonderman had been COO of the Robert M. Bass Group before setting up TPG in 1993. TXU was an obvious target, and Bonderman himself was set to become a board director. In need of significant firepower, KKR had not chosen to partner with a weakling: TPG had just raised $15 billion from its LPs and was ready to put the committed capital to good use.

KKR and TPG were eager to bring in another party to co-invest alongside them. Thankfully, they knew one that was not only a world-class institution, like them, but also an influential LBO debt provider. The transaction was to request complex credit products that only a handful of players were capable of structuring; the co-investor they were going to invite was one of them. Better still, the party could not strictly be considered a rival since it frequently invested its own capital alongside lead PE investors. This potential ally was investment bank Goldman Sachs. With Goldman at their side, KKR and TPG knew that they could not be outgunned. The bank employed 30,000 people worldwide, had multiplied net revenues by a factor of six in the past ten years, and had grown its asset base from $150 billion to $1 trillion over the same period.[5] It was big, clearly meeting KKR's stringent size criteria.

What was determinant in choosing Goldman as deal partner was its presence in asset management, M&A, research and, naturally, leveraged finance (Goldman had arranged the debt financing for KKR and TPG's GenCo deal three years earlier, for instance).[6] Through a division called the Principal Investment Area, the full-service bank had become a member of the exclusive club of financial sponsors by taking equity positions in corporations, which enabled it to cross-sell other products such as loans and M&A advisory services to portfolio companies and co-investors. Goldman's PE arm had collaborated with KKR and TPG remarkably often, investing alongside them and four other firms in the $11.8 billion purchase of SunGard Data Systems in 2005, and in association with Blackstone in the $10.8 billion acquisition of medical device manufacturer Biomet the following year.

One way or another, due to its formidable balance sheet and deal-sourcing capabilities, Goldman had taken part in most of the largest LBO transactions. Not one to be outclassed by PE groups, the bank was in the process of raising its latest private-equity investment vehicle, GS Capital Partners VI, with committed capital in excess of $20 billion.

A supersized punt on high gas prices

After weeks of negotiations with the target's management, in late February 2007 KKR, TPG and Goldman bid $69.25 a share, giving TXU a market capitalisation of $32 billion. It was 15% more than the previous close and a 25% premium to the average closing price in the previous 20 days. Over $12 billion of existing debt – 2.2 times EBITDA – was to be assumed.

According to public records, KKR and TPG were rumoured to be considering putting up $5 billion and Goldman Sachs $1.5 billion. American banks Lehman, Citigroup and Morgan Stanley were also investing, providing what was called an 'equity bridge', a recently introduced trend for financial sponsors to spread the risk among a larger group of investors by reducing individual equity tickets while still retaining control of the asset and making sure that debt arrangers stayed on side in the eventuality that liquidity problems should occur in the future. It was smart thinking, almost prescient.

The headlines spoke of a total deal value of $43 billion to $46 billion, marking the largest LBO transaction ever.[7] The target was the most important energy producer in Texas, itself the biggest natural gas producing state in the US.[8] Ranked 228th by revenues in the 2006 *Fortune 500* annual listing of America's biggest corporations, TXU could justly be classified as a corporate elephant. Its market capitalisation also made it the world's 273rd and America's 111th largest publicly listed company according to *Forbes* magazine. The bid valuation helped the company to enter America's top 100 market cap standing for 2007.

The rationale for the deal was quite straightforward: the price of natural gas had gone up steadily for several years and, along with that of other commodities, was widely predicted to keep going up for several more.

In order to help with the regulatory clearance, the bidders secured the services of eminences like former Secretary of State James Baker (to act as Advisory Chairman), former US Environmental Protection Agency Administrator and Chairman Emeritus of the World Wildlife Fund William Reilly (it cannot hurt to appear 'green' when buying an energy company), and former Secretary of Commerce Donald Evans. All would sit on the board of directors alongside a few local politicos. In addition, TXU was to create an independent Sustainable Energy Advisory Board and agreed to ditch plans to build eight of its proposed 11 coal plants in the face of opposition by environmentalists, replacing them with 'cleaner' nuclear plants instead. It was left to the Public Utility Commission of Texas (PUCT), the Federal Energy Regulatory Commission and the Governmental Nuclear Regulatory Commission to determine whether the leveraged buyout of one of the largest energy companies in the country was prudent from an energy policy standpoint, in the interest of the consumer, or even safe for the long-term viability of TXU's various divisions.

There was a 50-day 'go-shop' period until 16 April. Advised by investment bank Lazard, TXU's independent directors had solicited interest from over 70 parties.[9] Apparently, a consortium including Blackstone and Carlyle had contemplated bidding before realising that they were simply too far behind to ever be able to package anything remotely as palatable to TXU's management, the regulators and public shareholders.[10]

Unexpectedly, on 24 July TXU's chairman and CEO John Wilder announced his decision to leave as the group was going through the final hurdles of regulatory clearance and shareholder approval. Looking at the small print, it appeared that Wilder, who had only joined the energy giant three years earlier, was entitled to a $280 million change-of-control compensation if the LBO went ahead.[11] Enough to retire on.

Requiring the endorsement of two-thirds of shareholders, the deal was enthusiastically backed by more than 95% of them on Friday 7 September 2007 as the Credit Crunch was unfolding. That same month, regulators cleared the buyout, with the target agreeing to ring-fence its distribution operation Oncor, limiting in particular that division's leverage to 60% and all annual dividend payout to net income. With no further hurdle, the deal closed in October.

The financial sponsors and their co-investing banks controlled TXU, renamed Energy Future Holdings (EFH) Corp., through a company called Texas Holdings, as shown in Figure 5.1. The group was being set up as three different operating divisions. The group's cash cow, TXU Electric Delivery, was renamed Oncor Electric Delivery and would contain the group's regulated activities.

TXU Energy Company would become Texas Competitive Electric Holdings (from then on referred to as Texas Competitive or TCEH), representing three-quarters of the group's assets for over 80% of its revenues, and including all the subsidiaries engaged in competitive electricity market activities split into two main divisions: TXU Energy, servicing over 2 million residential and industrial customers, and the group's largest unit, Luminant, responsible for electricity generation, development and the construction of new facilities. EFH and Oncor had implemented certain structural and operational ring-fencing measures based on guarantees given by Texas Holdings to the state's Public Utility Commission. Energy Future was ready to roll.

Recent turmoil in the credit markets was making the debt syndicate nervous, but three of these banks were also investing on the equity side, so it was an easier sell than other deals trying to close at the time. Termination fees were $1 billion for any party that chose to walk away from the deal, be it the bidders, the debt providers or the company itself. It was an added incentive to stay the course. With most of Wall Street involved on the financing arrangement one way or another, the loans were being sliced and diced, securitised and repackaged into readily tradable collateralised loan obligations (CLOs).[12] The banks even managed to place a three-part $7.5 billion bond, the largest high-yield note in history – another landmark for the buyout of all records.[13] The bubble hadn't popped just yet.

Figure 5.1: Energy Future's group structure at the time of LBO in October 2007

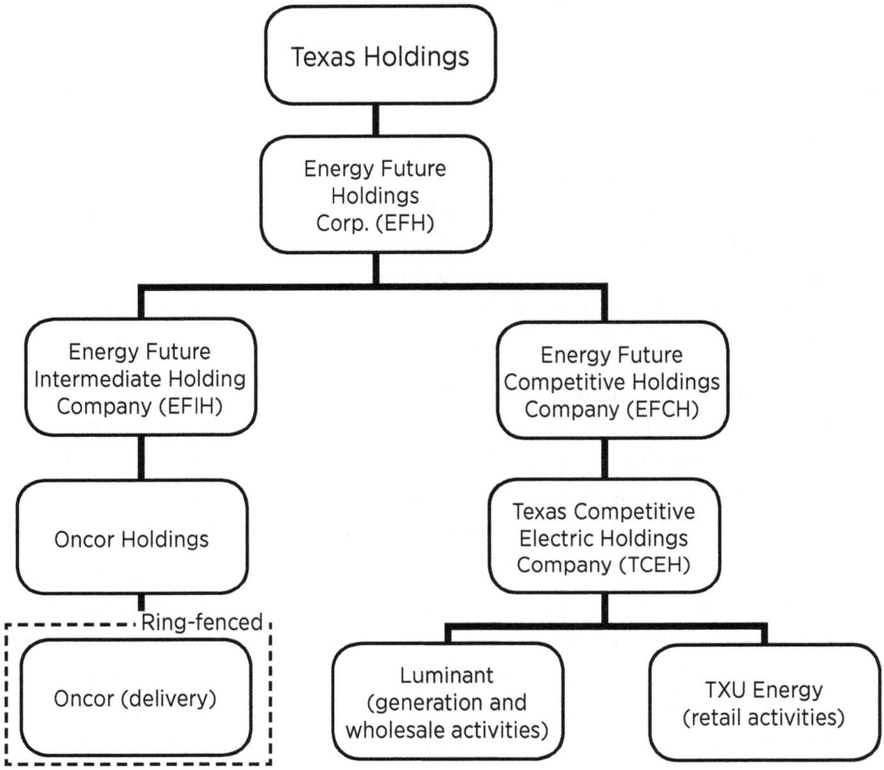

Source: Energy Future Holdings

In the end, the debt syndication went so well that the issuers managed to catch the biggest fish of all. In early December it transpired that Omaha, Nebraska-based investment guru Warren Buffett had purchased, from none other than Goldman Sachs, $1.1 billion of TXU's 10.25% cash-pay notes at a 5% discount and $1.1 billion of the 10.5% PIK toggle notes[*] at 93 cents on the dollar – two of the energy group's junk bonds.[14] If Goldman was a seller of these bonds, what was Buffett seeing in them? Time would eventually tell who was on the right side of the trade.

---

[*]. Toggle notes – see Abbreviations and Lexicon.

When the year ended, the total enterprise value of TXU came to $40.1 billion (including $5.3 billion of existing debt), dwarfing any previous LBO. The target's EBITDA for the year was $3.9 billion, implying an entry multiple north of ten times, compared to sector benchmarks of eight-to-nine times.[15] The financial investors' equity contributions had totalled $8.3 billion, leaving leverage a tad over 79% of the capital structure, or eight times EBITDA for debt covenant purposes.[16] Both Moody's and Standard & Poor's gave the debt package a speculative grade.

Leverage was certainly high, but it was structured in an uncannily clear-cut way, at least by PE standards. The bulk of the debt, $28.6 billion or so, sat within TCEH (and its parent EFC Holdings), which represented the vast majority of the group's activities. That unit only had to respect one covenant – a maximum secured leverage ratio of 7.25 times EBITDA starting in the quarter ended 30 September 2008. At the group holding level, Energy Future held onto $6.5 billion of loans. As for Oncor, because of regulatory requirements, it only had debt of $3.8 billion (via its parent EFIH).

It was a much civilised affair. What was less civilised was the repayment schedule of all that debt: over $20 billion of it was due in 2014, creating a maturity wall of a magnitude rarely seen in corporate history.[17] At this stage, the issuer's owners and lenders probably assumed that TXU was to be exited or refinanced before maturity, as is customary. This deal, it turns out, would be anything but customary.

* * *

Operationally, under the leadership of new Chief Executive and industry veteran John Young, the initial period of ownership went relatively smoothly, with group revenues up 11% year-on-year for the first two quarters of 2008. The three months ended 30 June, in particular, saw strong revenue growth in all three divisions: retail, wholesale and regulated delivery. Due to increasing forward natural gas prices during the first half of the year, however, the company incurred $6.1 billion in unrealised mark-to-market losses, a figure that had no cash implication but still demonstrated the sector's volatility.[18]

Nonetheless, things looked very promising for shareholders as commodity prices, including oil and gas, were forecast to keep their unremitting climb. Oil had reached $122 a barrel on 6 May 2008, on the day when Goldman Sachs's sector specialists had issued a report that would have warmed the hearts of the energy group's owners. According to Goldman's experts, the price of crude oil was to reach $150 to $200 a barrel within the following two years as supply was expected to fail to keep pace with demand from emerging markets.[19] The US economy was experiencing a sharp slowdown as the Credit Crunch was gaining momentum, so it wasn't clear whether Energy Future would fully benefit from the 'super spike' in the oil price, but other commodities, and in particular natural gas, were predicted to follow oil's lead.

With interest charges of $4.94 billion for the full year 2008, the group certainly was not in an enviable position. The leverage ratio at EFC Holdings (the competitive sector unit) shot up from 8.5 times at the end of 2007 to 10.1 times in December 2008.[20] In order not to run out of liquidity in a world experiencing the worst financial crisis in recent memory, the group had drawn on its credit facilities and exercised the payment-in-kind (PIK) option on certain of its debt securities – an election that both Energy Future and Texas Competitive could make every six months until November 2012. This is how flexible credit terms had become at the peak of the debt bubble.[21] The PIK option meant that the group could delay and accrue interest instead of paying it in cash.

Thanks in part to the $1.25 billion generated from the sale of a minority stake in Oncor, Energy Future's liquidity position had only fallen marginally from a cash position of $4.9 billion at the end of 2007 to less than $4.5 billion a year later. But with the now well-entrenched economic recession the group was likely to need all the spare cash it could catch hold of. The second half of 2008 had sustained demand weakness, with all divisions recording year-on-year revenue declines in the fourth quarter. The group's results were in synch with the rest of the economy: the US had seen GDP growth gradually fade from 3% in the first quarter of 2008 to minus 0.9% in the last three months of the year.[22]

Disappointingly, Goldman's rosy scenario of an oil spike had not panned out. Instead, crude oil had seen its price collapse 71% between July and December, shedding $100 to end the year at $40 a barrel due to weak demand fundamentals. Over the same period, natural gas prices had sunk by 57%, reaching $5.71 per Henry Hub MMBtu by year end.[23]

The notation MMBtu, or one million British thermal units, is commonly used as a measure of the energy content in natural gas. In America, natural gas futures contracts are traded on the New York Mercantile Exchange (NYMEX) under the Henry Hub appellation, borrowed from the eponymous distribution hub in Louisiana, a pivot of 13 major pipeline systems, and the most liquid trading point in the North American gas distribution system. The Henry Hub spot price is the benchmark against which generators determine whether to increase production from their plants or to keep the least efficient facilities idle until a higher marginal price makes it compelling to reopen them. As for most commodities, however, natural gas prices are mainly a function of market supply and demand, and recently the latter had fallen. For the whole of 2008, electricity consumption in the country had contracted by 1.6%.

In line with the accounting principle of prudence, Energy Future had to report a goodwill impairment charge of $8.86 billion at the end of the year, placing in full view the impact that market conditions were having on its activities. Having recognised $23 billion of goodwill upon its LBO a year earlier, the group had reversed two-fifths of it. On the secondary markets, even Texas Competitive's term loans – normally the safest part of the capital structure given the security they held on the underlying assets – had been hit by the market correction following the mid-September Lehman Brothers bankruptcy. By late October these loans traded in the mid-70s, or at a 25% discount to face value.[24] The equity and parts, if not most, of the junior debt were now worthless. They only had an option value.

Power failure

The first full year of operation had demonstrated how capricious energy markets could be, and the recession promised to make 2009 equally interesting. In the first three months of the year, the American economy shrank 1.9%. Energy Future saw operating revenues fall 9% that quarter, with the underperformance the result of an 11% contraction in the TCEH division. The financial crisis continued unabated, an inescapable correction to years of credit feast. In the quarter ended 30 June 2009, national GDP yielded further ground, losing 3.2%. EFH duly recorded another reduction in revenues: 22% down on the same period of 2008. Again, the poor results were derived from the competitive activities, with TCEH's revenues losing 24% while the regulated unit's were up 4%. Alarmingly, the group's cash burn in the quarter had reached half a billion dollars.

With natural gas trading below $6 per MMBtu all year due to further contraction in per-capita electricity demand, the company had benefitted from trading gains, but it was not helping the LBO's fundamentals. A crucial point at issue, it soon developed, was that such low gas prices, though helpful to calculate EBITDA-related covenants with the inclusion of unexpected hedging profits, did nothing for revenue growth and led to low operating income and poor cash generation. Partly for that reason, in the summer of 2009 rating agency Moody's downgraded several tranches of Texas Competitive's debt further into the highly speculative category.[25]

To boost its liquidity, reduce its outstanding debt and extend the weighted average maturity of its loans, the group launched a $4.9 billion refinancing in October, trying to get lenders to swap their existing debt for $3 billion in new secured notes in EFH (it was a 40% haircut on the existing face value, and some of the series were reportedly accorded less than 50 cents on the dollar).

Only $357 million of old notes were tendered. The coercive amend-and-extend (A&E) exercise was a bleak failure.

If the group was only to generate $1.5 billion to $1.7 billion in operating cash a year as it had done in the previous two years, it definitely needed to sort out its debt commitments by any means available, even if it left lenders stranded. Unsurprisingly, TCEH made the PIK election for both interest payments on its toggle notes in 2009, saving itself another cash outlay of $500 million or so, but thereby accruing debt to be repaid at a later date.

The situation was a real concern for bondholders. Some of them would likely have preferred to get out by selling their notes, even at a deep discount. Unfortunately, there was little demand for their distressed instruments and EFH had no cash to spare so could ill-afford to buy back their cheaply valued positions: the group had burned a further half a billion dollars of cash in the last quarter of 2009. As had been the case during the 1980s, the high-yield notes were earning their moniker 'junk bonds'. If there was any comfort for bondholders, it was that KKR had already recognised in its books, two years after the LBO, a significant loss in relation to its Energy Future investment.[26]

* * *

The beginning of 2010 confirmed that the US economy was on firmer ground. That could explain why the company was able to raise $500 million of new senior secured debt in January, somewhat cancelling out its cash burn of the previous quarter. Having failed to exchange and reschedule the existing debt, the company only had one option left to solve its liquidity crisis: issue more loans to its already gigantic pile. At this stage, the markets were still prepared to lend at a reasonable rate to support the PE owners in their attempt to retain control: the January issue had been completed at a very affordable – considering the distressed state of Energy Future – 10% coupon rate with a ten-year maturity.

The improving economy had a positive impact on trading, with both the competitive units and Oncor reporting double-digit revenue growth in the first three months of 2010. Profitability was up, but leverage ratios continued to deteriorate due to the recent debt issuance and the fact that interest payments were being rolled forward by exercising the PIK option. More of a concern was the fact that operating cash flows kept getting worse, down 80% on the prior year at TCEH in that first quarter. Duly protected by the ring-fencing mechanism and regulatory barriers to entry, Oncor kept delivering robust cash flows, but Energy Future was not allowed to access them, so it gave little comfort to the group's PE sponsors and lenders.

Keen to address its liquidity problems and remain solvent, the company then spent the rest of the year going from one debt issuance to another A&E process to more debt offering and A&E. Between April and July, it issued $527 million of 10% notes due 2020 in exchange for $684 million of existing senior notes due 2014. In a public debt exchange transaction in August, EFIH (Oncor's parent) issued $2.2 billion of 10% notes due 2020 and paid $500 million in cash in exchange for $3.6 billion of existing EFH senior notes. Still desperate for further runway in its maturity schedule, in October Texas Competitive issued $336 million of 15% senior secured second-lien notes due 2021 in exchange for $477 million of senior notes. That same month, TCEH again issued $350 million of 15% senior secured second-lien notes due 2021 and used the proceeds to repurchase $523 million of TCEH and EFH notes.

Moody's took this as its cue to downgrade the group's rating further into highly speculative territory with a Caa3 grade, two notches above rock-bottom default.[27] But management and the financial sponsors were not quite done yet. In November, TCEH issued another series of second-lien notes due 2021, this one worth $885 million, in exchange for $850 million of existing TCEH 10.25% notes and $420 million of toggle notes.

All this housekeeping only served to reinforce the fact that managing leverage had become a full-time occupation and Texas Holdings' equity remained worthless. In its SEC filings KKR continued to record a paper loss: the New York-based PE firm, rather optimistically, valued its equity at 30 cents on the dollar at the end of June 2010.[28]

Out of juice

The investors taking a punt on the newly issued high-coupon notes were attracted by the very generous yield on these unsecured tranches. Because some were trading in the secondary market at a significant discount, the actual yield was in the low 20s, meaning that for every dollar invested bondholders could receive an annual interest rate of 20%-plus. With the federal funds rate sitting near 0%, it was a magnificent premium. But it obviously was representative of the risk these noteholders were exposed to. If natural gas prices did not go up soon, it would affect Energy Future's performance and cash-flow potential, making leverage unsustainable. Sitting below $4 per MMBtu, natural gas had swooned to an eight-year low during 2010.

Thankfully, the second half of the year had seen a marked operational improvement. Oncor continued to perform admirably. Competitive unit TCEH had seen demand return, with volumes up 2% for the retail activities and up 21% for wholesale. If the group was still weakened by its stretched balance sheet, commercially the tide had finally turned positive. TCEH managed to meet its maintenance covenant thanks to $1 billion of hedging gains but also because it obtained agreement from its sympathetic lenders to exclude parts of its debt from the definition: as at 31 December 2010 the secured-debt-to-adjusted-EBITDA ratio stood at 5.19, well below its covenant of 6.75. Together with the numerous refinancing procedures enforced throughout the year, better financial results helped the total-debt-to-EBITDA ratio at Texas Competitive fall to 8.5 from the 9.5 registered a year earlier.

Because of significant underperformance against budget and lower than expected gas prices, there had been no alternative but for Energy Future to recognise further goodwill impairment at the end of 2010. This time around, the corporation's book value was reported to be $4.1 billion lower. All of the adjustment related to the group's competitive electric division. So it probably was not much of a surprise when, on Friday 25 February 2011, Aurelius Capital, a $50 million investor in one of Texas Competitive's term loans, asserted to the lead arranger Citibank that an event of default had occurred with respect to an intercompany loan not being in compliance with the credit agreement. Texas Competitive's 10.25% unsecured bonds due November 2015 duly tanked to the mid-50s, trading at a discount of more than 40%.[29] While Aurelius's claim was publicly denied by Energy Future's management and Citi itself, the leak highlighted that the underperforming company was likely facing an uphill struggle to keep its concerned lenders at bay.

The issue became irrelevant when, two months later, TCEH amended and extended $16.4 billion of its term loans from October 2014 to October 2017 and $1.4 billion of the revolver from October 2013 to October 2016. That same month of April, the competitive electric unit also issued $1.75 billion of 11.5% senior secured notes due 2020 to repay $770 million of existing term loans due between 2011 and 2014, $646 million of revolver and $188 million of letter of credit loans.[30] It was dull but unavoidable as performance was fast falling behind the management business plan's projections.

The first two trading quarters of 2011 only emphasised too well why management had been desperate to reschedule and trim a big chunk of the debt. Oncor's revenues had risen by 3% thanks to higher volumes, but TCEH's top line was down 16% year-on-year, a result of weak volumes, customer attrition and lower prices. That obviously fed straight to the EBITDA line, with Oncor's up 5% whereas the competitive division's had fallen 10%. The second half saw the regulated operation's revenues grow 8% while Texas Competitive's dived at a double-digit rate. The market shift away from the competitive segment was profound and understandable: the average price for natural gas had been 9.2% lower in 2011 than the year before, decreasing from $4.34 per MMBtu in 2010 to $3.94 in 2011.[31]

Several factors were driving this. First, whereas US GDP had risen by 2.5% in 2010, the year 2011 had seen a softening of the economy with only a 1.6% increase. In turn, electricity consumption per capita had declined by more than 1% that year. However, a more drastic cause was behind the persistent fall in natural gas prices. For more than five years now, a new source of energy had come on-stream and built production capacity on a major scale. Disrupting the supply chain, including in Energy Future's home state of Texas, US shale gas had seen its daily production go from less than 5 billion cubic feet in 2007 to 25 billion four years later.

Figure 5.2: US Dry Shale natural gas production (2002-11)

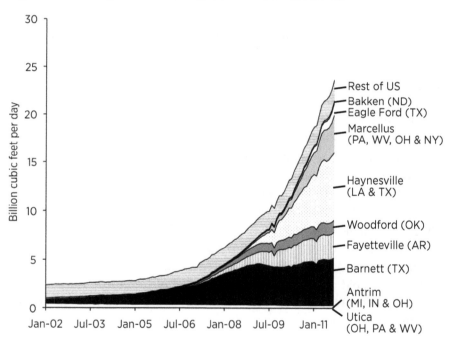

Source: United States Energy Information Administration (March 2012)

What had enabled energy companies to tap the huge shale gas reserves in the US at commercially sustainable rates was the adoption of two techniques that had until recently proved too costly and inefficient: horizontal drilling and hydraulic fracturing (a.k.a. fracking). As seen in Figure 5.2, it was in the Barnett play in north-central Texas that the widespread use of these techniques had first led to a hike in production. For that reason, in 2011 the US had seen natural-gas-derived energy production exceed coal-sourced production for the first time in 30 years.[32]

KKR recognised the potential that fracking offered, stating in one of its sector reports that growth in shale gas had resulted in a 27% increase in US natural gas production between 2005 and 2011.[33] Thus, while its Energy Future investment had lost its sparkle, the New York-based PE firm had started making fresh bets in the sector, this time backing the right horse – or so it hoped. In January 2011, it announced the purchase of Barnett Shale properties from energy group ConocoPhillips, and five months later it sold its 40% stake in shale developer Hilcorp, netting $1.1 billion for itself only one year after making the investment.[34]

Natural gas prices had fallen further than anticipated, and it was now driven by disequilibrium between supply and demand. Consumption and, therefore, volumes were up for the entire Texan energy market; however they were down for TCEH. What the latter's revenue shortfall indicated was that business was going elsewhere. Energy Future was no longer facing a demand shortage like it had during the Great Recession; it was facing an oversupply of cheaper fuel alternative, which pulled consumers away from Texas Competitive.

Energy Future's owners might have identified great opportunities to capitalise on this fracking revolution, but the year 2011 had been arrestingly dire for Energy Future, with TCEH recording a 14.5% contraction in operating revenues. EBITDA at that division had slipped by more than 7% over the last 12 months. The promising upswing of the second half of 2010 had been short-lived.

In anticipation, TCEH's sole maintenance covenant (the secured-debt-to-adjusted-EBITDA ratio) had been amended in April 2011. Instead of an original threshold of 6.50 to be met at the end of December, the company's very compassionate lenders agreed that the test be loosened to a far less exacting eight-to-one. The actual leverage ratio had shot up from 5.19 times adjusted EBITDA at the end of 2010 to 5.78 a year later, but the competitive electric division now benefitted from significant headroom. Including both secured and unsecured loans, the total-debt-to-EBITDA ratio, however, had soared from 8.5 to 9.3. In an SEC filing KKR admitted that, at the end of 2011, its equity holding was worth 10 cents on the dollar.[35]

* * *

Texas Competitive was due a breather, but the early months of 2012 proved that it would not be forthcoming. In the first quarter of the year, TCEH recorded further deterioration, losing 27% of its revenues year-on-year. Gas prices kept tumbling, which gave the division a chance to report more gains on its hedges – in April the Henry Hub natural gas price would in fact hit a 13-year low of $1.95 per MMBtu, in part due to an unusually warm winter in the US. As a result, less than 12 months after extending the maturities of its term loans, TCEH had seen operating cash flows halve. Its term loans, supposedly secured, were trading in the low 60s.[36] The real snag was that the business simply could not compete with cheaper supply alternatives. As a consequence, since the LBO the retail business had lost 17% of its customers.[37] Apparently trading in a parallel universe, Oncor kept delivering double-digit revenue and EBITDA growth.[38]

In the summer of 2012, Moody's downgraded Energy Future's debt to its second worst rating; ever closer to default. Concerned about the risk of contagion to the group's regulated activities, the agency even downgraded Oncor's debt to Baa2, still investment grade but only two notches above the speculative category.[39] Wall Street analysts seemed to have found a new pastime calling the date of Texas Competitive's default and concomitant bankruptcy petition.

So management spent the summer months and part of the fall getting Oncor's parent company EFIH to issue $1.3 billion of first-lien and second-lien debt in order to exchange $1.76 billion of old loans sitting at the group holding level. What was the purpose of this? It was threefold: first, a big chunk of old debt was being bought and retired at discounts of 20% to 40%. Second, the move enabled the debt held by EFH to be pushed down to group entities sitting closer to the cash-flow generative asset base of Oncor (it was a way to motivate lenders to hand over their old notes despite their earlier maturities) and not to sit between Texas Holdings (the group parent company where KKR and the other equity investors had staked out their position) and the soon-to-be-placed-under-bankruptcy-protection Texas Competitive. Some of the retired EFH loans had been guaranteed by EFCH (Texas Competitive's direct parent as illustrated by the group chart in Figure 5.1). In short, it meant that the equity investors wanted to avoid seeing strongly-performing Oncor get contaminated by diseased Texas Competitive, and to maximise their chances of retaining control of the regulated unit by removing intercompany loan guarantees.

Finally, the third reason for the move was to delay the inevitable event of default: over $300 million of EFH loans redeemed through the exchange were due for repayment by 2014.

By now you are likely to be confused by the seemingly helpless scenario: what was the point of repaying old debt (even at a discount) by issuing new loans if all parties agreed with the indisputable fact that Texas Competitive was heading for the wall? TXU kept tripping over the same rocks. Excess leverage and cheap natural gas prices were not going away, leaving the deadbeat company nowhere to hide. But KKR and TPG were buying themselves time, just in case gas prices finally went their way, which would enable them to negotiate in a stronger position against the group's lenders.

The surge in supply from unconventional sources, particularly shale, had driven the price of natural gas lower than worst-case scenarios had envisioned, reaching a permanent plateau of $2.5 to $3.5 per MMBtu in the second half of 2012. For the first time since the LBO, in the 2012 financial statements Texas Competitive's cash flows issued from operating activities had turned negative. The 20% collapse in operating revenues (after a fall of 15% the year before) coupled with the erosion of operating margins had transformed the previous cash cow into a cash drain.

Now playing catch-up, TCEH and its parent company EFCH acknowledged that the enterprise value had been further eroded and $1.2 billion of goodwill was erased in the 2012 annual report.[40] KKR had no alternative but to write down its investment further, pointing toward a 95% downward correction to the equity value as at 31 December 2012.[41]

To inform all relevant parties that the group's performance was in no way management's fault, the 2012 accounts disclosed that, "to provide a total executive compensation package comparable to the executive compensation packages" of executives with similar responsibilities at peer companies "and to maintain a strong alignment" between management and other stakeholders, CEO John Young would see his target cash bonus increase to 125% of its base salary from 2013 on. His salary would also rise from $1.2 million to $1.35 million, up 35% on the year 2009 figure. His 2012 performance-based cash bonus had earned him almost $2.3 million. But the real whopper was that in September Young had received $6 million of deferred compensation as part of a long-term incentive award.

The CFO, Paul Keglevic, was not to be left destitute, seeing a wage increase from $650,000 in 2012 to $735,000 from the following year onwards (up a more modest 22.5% since 2009). He bagged a bonus of $1.05 million in 2012 and more than $2.4 million as part of his deferred compensation.[42]

So much cash was getting out of the door that you could be forgiven for thinking that trading wasn't all that bad. The year 2012 had seen group revenues fall more than 10% year-on-year while EBITDA had shed 50%. PE owners certainly know how to keep management loyal.

Power shift

With operating revenues sitting one-third below their level of 2010, Texas Competitive had turned into a corporate zombie. Unable to meet its debt commitments, it relied on its management to PIK as much of its loan interest as possible, issue new notes with longer maturities and pursue further A&Es, in the hope of seeing natural gas prices turn around and permanently reach a steady state of $6 per MMBtu, at which point the group would be able to generate sufficient cash to pay back its debt. But time was running out as $4 billion of TCEH term loans were coming up for repayment in October 2014. Unless gas prices moved up quickly, there was only one way out.

Management did not have the luxury of waiting for this eventuality. In January 2013 the credit agreement governing TCEH's senior secured facilities was amended to extend $645 million due in October 2013 to October 2016, bringing the maturity date of loans totalling $2.05 billion to 2016. Fees in consideration for the extension were settled through the incurrence of $340 million of incremental term loans maturing in October 2017.

You are not misreading: for extending $645 million, lenders had been paid a $340 million fee.[43] This shows how desperate the PE trio was to delay an event of default. Sensing their strong negotiating position, the lenders were teaching the traditionally commission-hungry PE owners a thing or two about fee maximisation.

And it was getting messier by the day. In that same month of January, Oncor's parent company EFIH issued $1.3 billion of secured notes due 2020 in exchange for $1.3 billion of existing Energy Future Holdings and EFIH secured notes with earlier maturities. In connection with these debt exchanges, the group received consent from the noteholders for group entities EFCH and EFIH to become unrestricted subsidiaries, thereby further eliminating inter-company guarantees. In effect, it made each entity independent of one another; a crucial point should Texas Competitive file for bankruptcy and launch a restructuring, a scenario that had, in everyone's opinion, become a certainty.

Understandably, in view of so much capital restructuring, negotiations were starting to get interesting between the monolithic energy group's owners KKR, TPG and Goldman on one side and the lenders, including hedge fund managers and special-situation experts Franklin, Apollo, Oaktree and Blackstone's credit unit GSO, on the other. Some of the unsecured notes these credit investors held were trading at or below 30 cents on the dollar, implying an annual yield of 45% or more depending on the coupon rate – such a high-yield is the telltale characteristic of a junk bond, another indication that the group was close to an event of default.

The default was widely expected for the following year. All parties were preparing themselves. As is common at such advanced stage of distress, Energy Future, Oncor, the PE sponsors and the lenders had already appointed their respective restructuring advisers. Imperceptibly, but irrevocably, bargaining power was shifting towards the credit side of the group's capital structure, and other than carrying out feeble financial reengineering, there was very little that management and the owners could do about it. Continuing to trim debt through discounted deals was the act of a desperate party. There was no arguing that Energy Future's back was against the wall.

In the meantime, trading started picking up at Texas Competitive due to moderately buoyant natural gas prices. TCEH's operating income rose quarter after quarter throughout 2013. Unfortunately, the jump in gas prices had not been enough to compensate for Texas Competitive's customer attrition in both residential and business retail activities. Consumers had continued to prefer cheaper alternatives to TCEH's offer. Shale gas was making coal and nuclear uncompetitive. When TCEH posted its year-end figures, EBITDA had dropped by 18.5% year-on-year.[44] As a consequence, management booked another $1 billion of goodwill write-down, bringing total goodwill impairment since the LBO to $14.4 billion. The financial sponsors had somewhat got their prognosis wrong. With a balance sheet carrying over $32 billion of debt, that is 11.3 times EBITDA, the competitive electric unit was left with only one thing to do: prepare for bankruptcy.

Having entered into negotiations with its lenders to try to find a solution to its unmanageable capital structure, Energy Future decided to make a $270 million interest payment to its TCEH unsecured noteholders to buy itself and its PE owners more time. The move did not go down well with the company's first-lien creditors who were getting impatient to take control.[45] According to proposed preliminary term sheets by creditor Fidelity, with about $24.4 billion of claims these first-lien lenders were to wind up with 94.2% of the equity. The company's unsecured noteholders at the HoldCo level (EFH) would receive 3.8% of the company, while KKR, TPG, and Goldman would be left with just 2%. Other reorganisation plans emerged, all attempting to come up with a tax-free spinoff structure, but they failed to convince all the warring parties.[46]

Acknowledging that a bankruptcy of Energy Future would necessarily harm the regulated side of the group, in August credit specialist Moody's issued its now customary summertime – yet apocalyptic – missive, electing to downgrade Oncor's parent company (EFIH) to Caa1, mid-table in the speculative category. EFIH, it had determined, was no longer safe from contagion.[47] With over $7 billion of loans sitting on its balance sheet, whatever happened with the regulated unit would not benefit the financial sponsors; too many creditors had claims on the Oncor assets ahead of them. As a sign of capitulation, both KKR and TPG wrote down their equity one last time as 2013 ended: the New York juggernaut marked its $2.1 billion ticket down by 99% and Bonderman's Texan outfit valued its $1.5 billion investment at $68 million.[48] They just couldn't bring themselves to admit that their investment was totally worthless.

Unplugged

The price of natural gas ended 2013 above $4 per MMBtu and pursued its ascent in the early months of 2014, hovering near $6 by February. It was all very promising but the growing rivalry of shale plays meant that, even in the most upbeat scenario where prices would stay at $6, there was no longer any hope that Texas Competitive's retail activities could win back the customers lost over the preceding three years. Shale gas-fuelled electricity was henceforth a compelling alternative to Energy Future's coal and nuclear-based proposition.

In the first quarter of the year, as management was preparing to file for Chapter 11, Texas Competitive saw revenues climb 20% thanks to a surge in prices and volumes in the wholesale and residential segments. But it was too little, too late. The business could not generate sufficient cash to meet its growing loan commitments. For its regulated and competitive divisions combined, Energy Future had seen its debt balloon from $36.3 billion in 2011 to more than $40.2 billion two years later due to accruing interest, and despite the numerous A&E and discounted loan repurchases implemented by management.

The first quarter of 2014 was coming to an end when a *Financial Times* article suggested that the group was in breach of its first-lien debt-to-earnings covenant. If true, unless it was to be cured by fresh cash injection or waived by the relevant loan holders, the breach would make it impossible for auditors, who were going through their annual review of the 2013 fiscal year, to declare Energy Future a going concern, thereby triggering a technical default and allowing creditors to file for an involuntary bankruptcy petition.[49] Then, the group missed $109 million of interest payments due on 1 April. With a 30-day grace period to make amends, management extended a deadline to file the annual report and entered into last-minute negotiations with creditors.[50]

Dead drunk on debt, Energy Future finally folded on 29 April 2014, filing for bankruptcy protection in the state of Delaware, six-and-a-half years after undergoing its LBO. Ring-fenced Oncor was not part of the filing. Significant value erosion had occurred due to the impact of natural gas prices, down two-thirds since the buyout, on the group's performance. TCEH's operating cash flows had gone from an inflow of $1.66 billion in 2008 to outflows of $439 million and $174 million in 2012 and 2013 respectively.

For the division's bondholders, it was time to face the facts. Based on comparable multiples, it wasn't just on the equity side that value had evaporated; there was also little of it left in the high-yielding, unsecured notes. Using prevailing EV multiples of other energy companies, with EBITDA of $1.1 billion in 2013 TCEH could, at best, warrant a $10 billion valuation. Since the nominal value of Texas Competitive's term loans exceeded $15 billion, it meant that even the senior secured lenders stood to recover less than two-thirds of their capital while second-lien and unsecured noteholders – who opposed the filing – were left with nothing but the valuable lesson that trusting in the investment acumen of PE fund managers can be a very costly mistake.

With most of its loans sitting so much under water for the best part of the last four years, it was astonishing that it had taken so long for the group to collapse. The reason can be found in the type of covenant-lite transactions that lenders had allowed LBO investors to complete in the final months of the credit bubble. Without the right to trigger an event of default, and only too happy to kick the can down the road in exchange for fat fees, Texas Competitive's creditors had become accessories to the company's slow downfall. After years wasted away in routinely amending, extending and exchanging expensive loans, Energy Future – an ironic, doubly unfortunate misnomer given the group's lethargic cash generation and its lack of real prospects – was ready to join the private equity graveyard, the only part of the mega-buyout sector displaying any sign of growth.

For the past two years, debt-holding in Texas Competitive had become a waiting game as investors in unsecured notes trading at 30 to 70 cents on the dollar were sitting tight until an event of default materialised. Because several high-profile creditors, including Anchorage, Appaloosa, Bluecrest, JPMorgan, Morgan Stanley and Oak Hill, objected to the Chapter 11 filing, the targeted timeframe of exiting bankruptcy within 11 months looked hopeful. Launching an auction process in the summer of 2014 to dispose of Oncor, Energy Future's senior execs were undeterred. Hope was all they had.

* * *

For months after the bankruptcy filing, parties negotiated a demerger of the ailing company, which would see a separation of Oncor from the competitive businesses of Luminant and TXU Energy. The two sides had operated independently since regulated Oncor had been ring-fenced in 2007. It was fortunate since their respective performance post-LBO had been diametrically opposed to the expectations their PE backers had held at the outset. Under the prevailing workout resolution scenarios, Texas Competitive was due to fall into the arms of its first-lien lenders, among them the biggest names in distressed-debt land, with Apollo, Oaktree and Centerbridge leading the pack. Oncor's parent EFIH would see its creditors – including Avenue, York Capital and GSO Capital – swap their discounted debt for more promising equity.

Regardless of the bankruptcy judges' decision, it is instructive to review the performance of Energy Future's two main divisions. Figure 5.3 demonstrates that Texas Competitive's results were negatively impacted by the Great Recession, with revenues falling by a fifth in 2009.

Figure 5.3: Texas Competitive's (TCEH) operating revenues and EBITDA margins (2007-14)

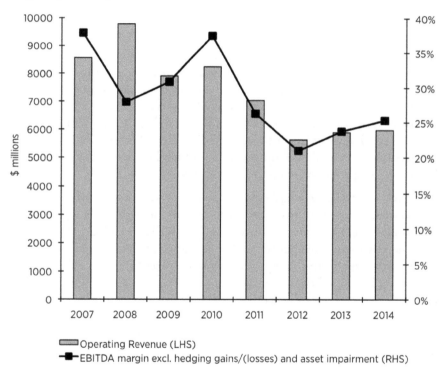

Source: Energy Future Competitive Holdings Company annual reports

Whereas the economic downturn was somewhat anticipated, the key scenario that KKR, TPG and Goldman had bet on – that natural gas prices would remain at their historical high – never materialised. Instead, prices reached a new equilibrium below $4 per MMBtu. This, in turn, had two effects: low spot prices brought down wholesale prices with them, a factor that was never fully compensated by concomitant volume increases due to the subdued economic recovery. As observed, the second effect of permanently low prices was to make lower-cost suppliers (mainly frackers) more competitive.

The customer attrition that Texas Competitive's retail unit had experienced since market deregulation in January 2002 had therefore persisted. Between 2002 and 2006 the number of retail customers served by TXU Energy had tumbled from 2.7 million to 2.2 million. By late 2013 that number had reached 1.7 million. Given that, in the ten years leading to 2012, Texas experienced population growth of 21%,[51] losing customers on such a scale meant a terrible erosion of market share for TXU. Consumers were shopping elsewhere.

But while the erosion during the LBO period may be attributable to the emergence of shale plays, the customer base attrition before the buyout indicates that the group's offering was not competitively-priced. As a consequence, total retail sales volumes had dipped 17%, 11% and 5% in 2005, 2006 and 2007. Pursuing that trend, by 2013 TXU's retail electricity revenues had fallen by almost a third from their 2008 level.[52] Presumably not the sort of downside scenario the financial sponsors had looked at. The full impact of lower market prices can be seen in Texas Competitive's profitability: between 2006 and 2012, EBITDA margin shrank from 42% to just 18%.

At times, TCEH's leverage was in excess of 30 times earnings, though the company reported year after year that its debt-to-EBITDA ratio was comfortably below its maintenance covenant. KKR and TPG had negotiated with the LBO loan providers (major banks that not only arranged the loans but also participated on the equity side, as we have seen) that the debt covenants should not be too tight and that they should also exclude certain loans and cost items – hence the term 'adjusted EBITDA'. As they went through several A&Es in the ensuing years, the financial sponsors continued to request that freshly issued loans be excluded from the covenant definition, meaning that they did not form part of the ratio calculations.

KKR et al. also took advantage of the coordinated effort of major central banks to keep interest rates at an historical low for an unprecedented lengthy period. If not for that, Energy Future would have faltered sooner. The excessively levered buyouts completed at the peak of the credit bubble only survived (or were allowed to plod along as lifeless entities) because of the ability to refinance and extend debt repayment schedules thanks to robust financial markets sustained by quantitative easing and low interest rates. That allowed PE investors to buy time in the hope that their LBOs' prospects would improve. Nevertheless, refinancing was an expensive tool. For each A&E process lenders had to be incentivised in the form of consent fees, some as high as 350 basis points (3.5%), plus meaningful margin increases in order to agree to reschedule or shrink the value of their debt. Despite Energy Future's risk profile, the higher coupons were attractive enough to convince investors looking for yield in a near-0% Fed rate environment.

Figure 5.4: Texas Competitive's (TCEH) leverage ratios and maintenance covenant (2008-13)

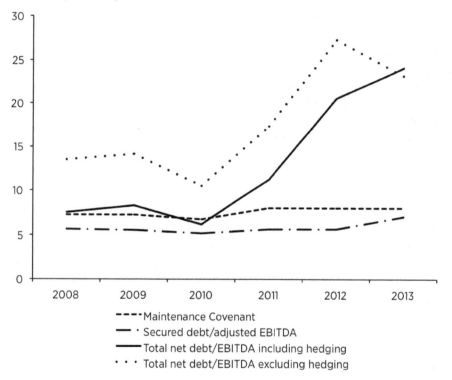

Source: Energy Future Competitive Holdings Company annual reports and author's analysis. Debt only includes TCEH loans, not EFCH or EFH loans

A key reason why lenders, whose sole form of control is to ensure that covenants are met as a way to assess whether a borrower can ever redeem its debt, would be willing to relinquish so much power to the benefit of financial sponsors is that they were making bountiful fees in (re-)arranging loans while also syndicating the same loans to a whole bunch of unsuspecting third parties (even Warren Buffett temporarily let his guard down). Still, Figure 5.4 illustrates the difference between leverage according to the PE-friendly maintenance covenant definition (only applicable to certain secured loans), and the total leverage including all LBO debt and without adjusting earnings. I use two sets of EBITDA figures, with and without hedging gains, to demonstrate that, if it wasn't for such non-operating gains, leverage ratios would have exceeded ten times EBITDA from the very first day of the LBO. As existing hedges began rolling off in 2013, the two sets of EBITDA figures converged, which explains why leverage ratios also did.

Energy Future benefitted from a covenant-lite structure. Within three years of the buyout, EBITDA was no longer sufficient to cover interest. In 2011, for instance, Texas Competitive was facing net interest expenses of $3.7 billion; its EBITDA (excluding hedging gains) sat at $1.4 billion, less than half the one recorded the year before. If the LBO had been signed in a normal credit environment, the fact that the interest cover (EBITDA-to-net interest) was below 1 would have triggered a breach. By December 2013 interest cover sat at 0.65 times. Not something your average banker witnesses every day. The unregulated division's performance reveals the full effect of LBO techniques as practiced ahead of the financial crisis.

* * *

In contrast, regulated and ring-fenced Oncor performed strongly, as Figure 5.5 shows. Between 2004 and 2014, the electricity distributor's revenues grew at a compound annual growth rate of 5.5%. Even at the worst point of the Great Recession, top-line growth remained positive. Spot gas prices had little repercussion on Oncor's growth and profitability, with EBITDA margin remaining at 50% to 52.5% throughout the period under review.

Because the financial sponsors had been forced to ring-fence Oncor, in the end the Energy Future saga was very much a tale of two halves. Texas Competitive's performance had been left exposed to a price war and oversupply (driven by the surge in shale gas) in its Texan markets; Oncor had flourished under the regulated model, lifting revenues from $2.6 billion in 2008 to $3.1 billion three years later and $3.8 billion in 2014, while annual operating cash flows had risen from $828 million in 2008 to $1.3 billion in the years 2011 to 2014.

Figure 5.5: Oncor's operating revenues and EBITDA margin (2007-14)

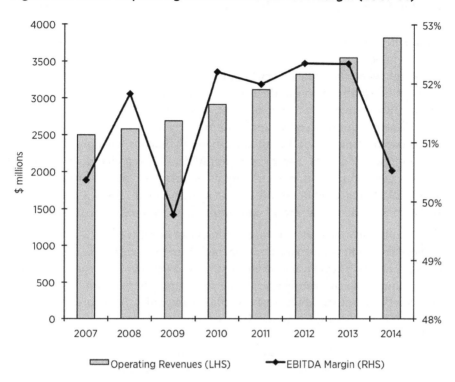

Source: Oncor Electric Delivery Company LLC annual reports and author's analysis

Oncor's ring-fencing also protected it from overleverage: from 2008 to 2014, the debt-to-capital ratio stayed within a very reasonable 40% to 43% range. At Texas Competitive, that figure exceeded 100% every year post-LBO, reaching 135% at the end of 2011, 152% the year after, and 188% by December 2013, at which stage it was high time to pull the plug. Behind Oncor's solid results lies the market structure under which the vast majority – about 85% – of the Texan electric transmission grid operated. Transmission and distribution companies like Oncor were responsible for offering non-discriminatory access to their network. All wholesale market participants, including Energy Future's Luminant, were granted access to the state's distribution grid. That explains why Luminant, one of Texas's largest electricity wholesalers and generators, represented a big chunk of Oncor's total revenues – 35% to 40% for the years 2008 to 2010; 25% to 30% between 2012 and 2014.[53]

The good thing for Oncor was that its activities were not affected by the spot price but by gas usage. Obviously, consumption depends to a certain extent on the cost of energy, but demand for T&D services is fairly sticky as residential customers still need to use air conditioners during hot summers and heaters in the winter, and to light their homes. Similarly, industrial clients consume less energy when their machinery lies idle, but unless they go under businesses still need to use energy to run their operations. Another positive factor is that a transmission system is customer-agnostic. It does not matter to Oncor whether it distributes gas produced by Luminant or by frackers; it gets paid for the use of its system. Thus, while Luminant's share of Oncor's revenues diminished between 2008 and 2014, Oncor was simply distributing electricity produced by other generators. That explains why its performance gained ground in line with GDP. Being the largest T&D system operator in Texas, Oncor reaped the benefits of increasing energy consumption as economic activity picked up.

The case of Oncor demonstrates why utilities can be great candidates for LBOs: predictable cash flows, regulated pricing, high barriers to entry. But what the case also proves is that regulators, when they wish to get involved, can have a very positive impact in protecting underlying assets from the excessive indebtedness to which PE investors subject their portfolio companies. As reported by Oncor in its annual reports, the ring-fencing measures had been taken to enhance its credit quality, but they were also introduced to reduce the risk that its assets and liabilities would get consolidated with those of TCEH in the event of a bankruptcy.[54] The ring-fencing fulfilled that role beautifully.

A supersized blunder

Berkshire Hathaway CEO Warren Buffett is reported to have said that owning utilities is not a way to get rich; it is a way to stay rich. While this mantra certainly still holds, what Buffett failed to keep in mind when he bought high-yield bonds in Energy Future is that he had also, on multiple occasions, declared that he preferred to stay clear of businesses under PE ownership. For that oversight, Berkshire Hathaway's investors ended up paying dearly. Buffett owned up to his mistake by humbly admitting, in his 2011 shareholder letter, that the purchase of those bonds had been 'a major unforced error'. Net net, Berkshire suffered a pre-tax loss of $873 million.[55]

KKR, TPG and Goldman Sachs didn't follow Buffett's example by publicly apologising. Yet it is apparent that three key factors played a central role in the failure of the TXU buyout and delisting:

1. After the good times, the bad times

The rationale behind the deal was that natural gas prices would keep on rising and help to generate cash to repay the LBO debt. The reasons why TXU had done well in the years leading up to its buyout-delisting are twofold:

1. The price of natural gas had increased steadily (in line with the price of crude oil, with which it had showed uncannily high correlation), which benefitted producers and distributors since wholesale electric rates in Texas were tied to natural gas spot prices.

2. TXU generated much of its power from efficient (meaning, cheaper than gas-fuelled) coal and nuclear plants.

First, let's look at the price of natural gas. Between September 2001 and the last quarter of 2005, the natural gas spot price at the Henry Hub terminal in Louisiana shot up from about $2 per million British thermal unit to more than $13 per MMBtu (see Figure 5.6). That's a whopping jump of six times, or an annual growth rate of over 65%. Another attribute of natural gas prices is that they are determined by the law of supply and demand, which is itself impacted by macro factors: trade agreements, natural disasters, GDP growth, governmental storage and export policies among others.

The conclusion of this argument is that natural gas prices are extremely unstable. In 2003, for instance, the Henry Hub spot price registered 119% volatility.[56] That year, America had chosen to invade Iraq and started unsettling the Middle East, the world's main producer of oil. What had driven the big push in natural gas prices between 2001 and 2005 were the September 11 terrorist attacks in America and the wars waged in Afghanistan and Iraq afterwards. The effect that these events had on energy prices worldwide cannot be overplayed; it was extreme, but also unusual, hence the spike in prices. Because of the all-powerful law of supply and demand, it was only a matter of time before new suppliers, including substitutes like shale-gas explorers, viewed the $13 per MMBtu as too enticing to ignore.

In the first quarter of 2007, as KKR, TPG and Goldman's menagerie of advisers and consultants were keeping themselves busy with forecast analyses and business plans, TXU incurred a quarterly mark-to-market loss of $697 million on hedging positions. Since October 2005 the group had initiated a long-term hedging programme to reduce exposure to future changes in the price of natural gas.[57] On that occasion the strategy backfired.

Figure 5.6: Henry Hub natural gas price in US$ per million Btu (January 1997-December 2015)

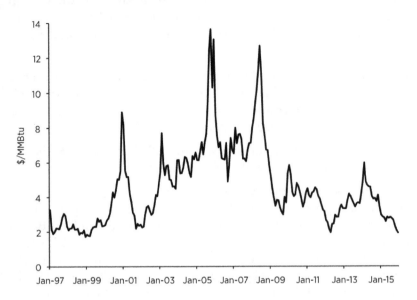

A read through TXU's August 2007 investor presentation at the time of the LBO process illustrates how wrong management and the PE consortium got it. Listing the numerous challenges that they assumed the group faced over the coming years, the presentation included the use of hedges as a limiting factor in Luminant's ability to benefit from expected gas price increases over the next five years.[58] The rationale for the deal was that natural gas prices (which set the cost of electricity) would rise or remain at their historical high. Instead, they plunged by more than 60% between 2008 and 2012, reverting to the $2-to-$4-per-MMBtu range seen in the late 1990s, and in 2001 and 2002. To grasp how much of an issue that was, consider that according to management a $1 move in the price of natural gas had a $2.4 billion impact on profits.[59] In the third quarter of 2008 the company generated $4 billion of after-tax unrealised mark-to-market gains from natural gas hedges.

The business was not so much an electricity producer and distributor as an energy trader. Since deregulation had been introduced in 2002, hedging had been a crucial mechanism to soften the force of natural gas price movements. As the company had reported in its 2003 annual report:

"Natural gas prices increased significantly in 2003, but historically the price has moved up and down due to the effects of weather, industrial demand, supply availability and other economic factors. Consequently, sales price management and hedging activities are critical in achieving targeted gross margins."[60]

In summary, prices of natural gas – as those of all commodities – are unpredictable. In 2008 the US Energy Information Administration had projected that America's natural-gas production would remain fairly flat for the following couple of decades. But their projections were, like any economist's forecast, completely unreliable. The sort of unreliability that makes energy producers and distributors poor candidates for LBOs. By dint of constantly aiming for the highest debt-to-equity ratio, the triumvirate of owners met their match in the unexpected drop in natural gas prices.

* * *

The second factor behind TXU's recent success was its ability to produce electricity cheaply from its own coal and nuclear plants. In industry argot, the decision made by suppliers to produce energy is defined by the market heat rate (calculated as the wholesale market price of electricity divided by the market price of natural gas). Also known as the 'break-even natural gas market heat rate', this ratio measures the efficiency at which a plant converts natural gas into electricity, as expressed in millions of British thermal units (MMBtu) per megawatt hour (MWh). This yardstick dictates whether a plant stays open or is retired. Only a natural-gas generator with an operating heat rate below market value can make money by burning natural gas to generate power.

Until the financial crisis, economic growth encouraged producers like TXU to invest in new plants to become more efficient (the almost endless availability of cheap debt back then was also a big stimulus to invest). As it was in discussions with KKR and TPG, management was planning to build 11 new coal plants. The company had plans to expand its generation capacity because natural gas prices were supposed to stay high. High natural gas prices implied an inversely low market heat rate.

The post-LBO environment changed all this. The combination of the Credit Crunch, the ensuing Great Recession, the growing adoption of renewable energy production, and the sudden economic viability of fracking technology forced a persistent collapse of the price of natural gas (due to both lower demand and increasing supply substitution).

Although it led to an increase in market heat rate, EFH chose to shelve a number of its natural gas-fuelled plants as they proved less effective than cheaper alternatives. Nineteen plants were retired and four mothballed in 2009 and 2010. By contrast, changes in natural gas prices had a limited effect on the cost of generating electricity from the group's nuclear and coal/lignite plants. Energy Future chose to invest in these production capabilities instead, using its natural gas-fuelled plants as peaking units that could be ramped up or down to balance electricity supply and demand.

Soon after the TXU buyout, the US oil and gas industry entered a period of sustained increase in supply (which in return led to the price of oil and that of natural gas to become uncorrelated). The brisk and sudden build-up in shale gas capabilities created disequilibrium between the supply of and the demand for energy products. Figure 5.7 brings home the point that the impact was localised. The fracking revolution mostly affected the US natural gas spot price (Henry Hub). Prices in Japan and Europe suffered during the Great Recession but gradually regained all or some of the lost ground.

Going back to our question: how likely were increases in natural gas and wholesale electricity prices to offset the rising cost of debt used to fund the LBO? It was impossible to know where prices would go during the period of PE ownership. You do not need to be an authority in commodities markets to know that spikes only exist because they follow troughs. What goes up must come down.

What is apparent when reading reports on the sector is that, partly because of its importance in fostering economic growth, the oil and gas industry has one of the most towering of risks pyramids. To grasp its complexity, you could do worse than to read *The Prize*, a very comprehensive book by oil expert Daniel Yergin. Prices of oil (and other commodities by extension) are dependent on so many political and economic factors (as just one example, think of the current push for renewables) that attempting to forecast them is the macroeconomic research equivalent of crystal-ball reading.

The energy and commodities sectors frequently and regularly go through seismic shifts due to wars or geopolitical tensions such as the Iranian revolution of 1979, changes in taxes and regulations, technological innovations, and substitution by new sources (the impact of shale gas is limited compared to what the discovery of rock oil did to support the United States' industrial development in the second half of the 19th century and the first half of the 20th century) that affect the supply and demand pricing model. What Yergin conveys extremely well is the sector's tendency to go through bubbles and crashes at sporadic intervals. If there is one constant, it is that energy prices go through haphazard trends dependent on so many variables that all we can predict is that prices will remain unpredictable.

Figure 5.7: Natural gas prices from October 2007 (TXU's buyout) to April 2014 (TCEH's Chapter 11)

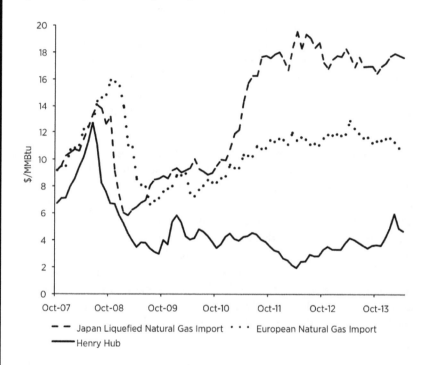

In summary, KKR, TPG and Goldman had no idea, back in 2007, where natural gas prices would be six months or five years down the line. They just took a supersized punt on the sector with their investors' money. Which also fits in rather well with another constant underscored by Yergin in his anthology: because of its central status in our economic and industrial development models (where would the car and plane industries and a variety of products like paint, fertilizers and plastic be today without oil discovery?), the energy industry attracts every generation's greedy speculators. But cyclical industries are not recommended hunting grounds for highly leveraged transactions.

2. Too complex a capital structure

It would be natural for the trio of PE investors to blame their failed LBO on the (unusually) low prices for natural gas in the seven years that followed their investment. To them, it was an unforeseeable phenomenon, but we have just explained that the history of hydrocarbons is filled with unpredictability.

Perhaps the biggest hurdle that the three PE investors faced when trying to salvage their investment was the complexity of the debt package, and the fact that each loan tranche had been syndicated and acquired on the secondary market by so many credit specialists with their own agenda that it was impossible for Energy Future to ever agree a financial restructuring that would please all the parties. The Texas Competitive loan syndicate was reported to include over 500 lenders.[61] With too many dissenting views to accommodate, in the end Energy Future came a cropper.

While handy when the PE owners were trying to keep sole ownership of the business and creditors were unable to obtain approval from at least 50% of the lender group to assert their rights, getting creditor acceptance remained impossible when management sought a pre-packaged administration procedure in 2013. I have already explained that many junior lenders opposed the Chapter 11 voluntary filing in April 2014; they had also requested a transfer of the bankruptcy case from Delaware to Dallas, where the group's operations resided. The same creditors had opposed a consensual pre-pack bankruptcy suggested by the company and its equity holders as early as April 2013 as a way to avoid a lengthy spell in Chapter 11 that would end up hurting the business.[62]

Each party to the negotiations appointed its own legal and financial advisers – with some noteholders even filing a lawsuit against the company weeks after its bankruptcy petition, claiming that management was colluding with the first-lien creditors to drive down the value of Texas Competitive in order to virtually wipe out the unsecured creditors.[63] At least lawyers were making a decent living out of this anarchy. The possible tax implications of a debt-for-equity swap – commonly provoked by changes of ownership – and the question of which party would be liable to pay such taxes had largely hampered any agreement ahead of the April 2014 voluntary filing.

It will surprise no one to learn that the company and some of its creditors ended up in court in the summer of 2014 after Energy Future's management had intended to take on a $2 billion debtor-in-possession

(DIP) loan to reorganise the capital structure at Oncor's parent EFIH level. To boot, the DIP loan would have given a group of hedge fund lenders 60% of the company at the expense of other creditors.[64] The fun these people were having!

This type of PE transaction bears a striking resemblance to the practices applied in the US mortgage industry during the credit boom of 2002-07. LBO loans were tranched into an almost infinite number of slices (TCEH had over 30 lines of loans with varying yields and maturities on its balance sheet) and the loan covenant definitions were frequently amended to avoid a technical default. They were syndicated by the underwriting banks via special purpose vehicles in order to distribute widely and covertly subcomponents of the various slices across the financial system – each subtranche was held by at least half a dozen debt investors, collateralised debt/loan obligation (the famous CDO and CLO acronyms) and hedge fund managers, hence the difficulty faced by senior management in communicating with creditors. The sheer quantum of debt loaded on the borrower left little room for divergence, if any, from the original repayment plan. No one could pretend to be surprised by Texas Competitive's ultimate messy outcome. I will not expand further on the provocative quantum of leverage Texas Competitive was exposed to – the case study speaks for itself.

3. The supercycle theory

In view of the importance that natural gas price levels would hold on the LBO's performance, in a presentation delivered in August 2007 management had considered that at a Henry Hub price of $9 per MMBtu, the PE backers' return on investment would reach 20%, whereas at $6 per MMBtu, returns would be negative 36%. Management had not even considered a scenario where gas would trade below $6, a threshold it breached in late 2008, never to recover.[65]

The chief driver behind the TXU buyout was the notion that it was inconceivable for natural gas to experience long-lasting pricing pressure in the immediate future. The three investment groups thought, and so did most commodities experts at the time, that we were in a decades-long 'supercycle'.

The idea that commodities such as oil, natural gas or other natural resources move steadily up or down over long periods according to an underlying pattern had often been supported by industry pundits. With the price of oil up from $10 in 1998 to a peak of $99 on 21 November

2007 and the generally-held belief that oil reserves were to run out by the middle of the 21st century in many parts of the world, shortages were due to emerge and consumption from emerging markets set to rise, maintaining the oil price at a permanently high level, or on an upward trajectory for decades to come.

You will recall that, historically, the natural gas spot price was correlated to the price of crude oil. All this led to the universal view – held by management, the financial sponsors and their advisers, and the lenders – that gas prices would remain high enough throughout the LBO period for Energy Future to be able to redeem its debt and for the investors to make a fortune.

It would be easy to blame the buyout investors for failing to foresee the importance that shale gas would play in the future of energy production in Texas and the wider United States. In fairness, in 2006 and 2007 not a single sector report predicted that fracking would have any meaningful share of the electricity market in the short or medium term. The US Energy Information Administration did not even include shale gas in its 2009 outlook. Yet by 2012, the same agency was reporting that more than one-quarter of US natural gas production was from shale. Could this be a 'Black Swan' event that KKR, TPG and Goldman could use as an excuse for their failed investment?

Economists and investors alike have always been fond of patterns, even noticing regularities where there is only haphazard fluctuation. Since the 1930s, chartists had used technical analysis to invest in stocks and commodities markets. It is in the 1990s that mathematical finance developed pattern-recognition algorithms to replace humans with automatic trading tools. Traders and arbitrageurs became avid users and believers of the idea that money could be made by betting on trends.

Long-Term Capital Management's (LTCM) use of quantitative finance, to make hedging bets such as the purchase of a 29.75-year bond and the (short) sale of a 30-year bond, because historically the market price spreads between the two bonds had *always* shown a tendency *eventually* to converge, earned its founders public coverage when the firm had blown up in September 1998 with leverage exceeding 30 times its capital (a ratio multiplied tenfold when taking into account off-balance-sheet activity). The hedge fund manager had built its positions on the assumption that volatility could be diversified away. But it turned out that algorithms could only make order out of chaos up to a point and that past trends could become irrelevant if market fundamentals remained out of whack for longer than expected. The aftermath of the 1997 Asian financial crisis and the default of the Russian Government on its domestic bonds in the summer of 1998 hurt LTCM's 'convergence' (a.k.a. spread arbitrage) positions because, instead of converging, spreads started widening.

Despite this early warning, by the start of the new millennium pattern theory had percolated the world of private equity. The success of the TXU buyout was predicated on the idea that negative price movements could be hedged against, smoothing out any impact on earnings, while any price increases would naturally feed down to the bottom line. Energy Future and LTCM had much in common, both in their investment rationale and the misconception that any trend irregularity could only be temporary. Neither of them accounted for any persistent deviation from the norm, in accordance with pattern theory.

It is obviously reassuring to postulate that financial markets follow a predetermined course, easily measurable and predictable. It certainly helps to make investment decisions that would otherwise appear too risky. However, as we saw earlier, equally compelling arguments can be offered to support the description of energy markets as random, affected by so many idiosyncratic factors, from military conflicts to reserve discoveries, that it is impossible to forecast the price of commodities several years out.

For instance, in *The Prize*, Yergin explains that shortly after the Second Oil Shock in 1979, which had seen crude oil prices double in less than a year, shale oil production had become economically viable and had enjoyed a brief period of euphoria in various regions of America. Within two years, though, production had all but stopped following the fall in oil prices.

Though it was very likely that *eventually* (when shale reserves dwindle to a point where they do not materially affect supply or when low spot prices make fracking unviable) Henry Hub natural gas prices would revert to a normalised pattern and become correlated to oil price movements once again, it was presumptuous to bet heavily that prices would remain high simply because they were following a recognised upward trend. In terms of leveraging a bet on a premise, or a hunch, think of TXU as the PE equivalent of LTCM.[66]

The great power reset

With $1.76 billion of EBITDA in 2013, Oncor's value was approximately $15 billion based on peer multiples in the utility sector (in mid-2014 it received a $17.5 billion bid – ultimately rejected – from rival NextEra). Adding Texas Competitive's EV to Oncor's would translate into a $25 billion total enterprise value for Energy Future on the day of the bankruptcy – down from $40 billion at the time of the TXU buyout. That is $15 billion of value devastation in seven short years.

Back in 2007, three-quarters (or $30 billion) of TXU's value was in its competitive electric units, while the regulated activities were worth $10 billion. After one of the fiercest market adjustments in the natural gas and electricity sectors, Texas Competitive had lost two-thirds of its value while the bland but reliable utility Oncor had seen its value increase by half.

The interesting dynamic of the bankruptcy process, as it casually exceeded the intended 11-month exit timeframe, was that the longer Energy Future waited to dispose of Oncor, the more value it was likely to get for it. Back in the 1990s, regulated utilities offering steady cash flows and reasonable returns would have been prime candidates for an LBO. In the first half of the noughties, PE professionals were no longer interested in playing it safe. In fact, it was reported on several occasions that KKR and TPG's intention was to spin off mundane Oncor, which explains their strenuous efforts to disentangle the utility from the rest of the group. Sometimes, the best way for PE investors to create value is to be kept away from the underlying assets.

Just like large corporate transactions often turn out to be disasters – Vodafone's $200 billion acquisition of Germany's Mannesmann in 1999 and America Online's $165 billion bid for Time Warner the following year had eventually seen both combinations broken up – the TXU buyout marked the result of ego-driven business dealings by our generation's M&A pros. Buyout managers have proven no better at acquisitions than your typical corporate executive. As noted, KKR had been responsible for the largest LBO of the 1980s mania: RJR Nabisco. It had turned out to be a very poor move, as KKR had made a loss despite splitting the target into more digestible parts for potential buyers.[67] TXU was KKR's mega-deal of the noughties acquisition frenzy, and it fared even worse. The bigger they are, the harder they fall.

KKR's returns for the funds that got involved at the peak of the late 1980s and mid-noughties bubbles were comparable. By December 2014, the KKR 2006 vintage exhibited a not-quite-supersized net IRR of 7% (admittedly with some portfolio assets still unrealised), compared to slightly less than 9% for the KKR

1987 fund.[68] The 2006 fund's performance was on par with the 7% annual return of the S&P 500 from January 2007 to December 2014.

Needless to say, the public markets' performance had been achieved without leverage. If we were to assume that a public investor had levered itself up 50% (a very reasonable ratio by PE standards), the S&P 500 annual returns would have exceeded 10%, after adjusting for the cost of borrowing. How did the KKR 1987 vehicle's annual yield fare against the same public benchmark? The S&P 500 returned 18% from 1988 to 1997 (again, without leverage).

TXU was the emblem of pre-financial crisis excess. KKR would have learnt a valuable lesson from the debacle, by staying clear of highly cyclical energy companies, for instance. Now, consider an investment that the same KKR made, post-Great Recession, in Samson, a company engaged in the exploration and production of oil and natural gas, including from very popular and promising shale plays. Headquartered in Tulsa, Oklahoma, incidentally the birthplace of KKR's Henry Kravis, Samson Resources was purchased for $7.2 billion in the largest LBO of the year 2011 anywhere in the world. When the Samson deal occurred, KKR had already written its equity in Energy Future down to 10 cents on the dollar. So its executive team, led by the same Marc Lipschultz, must have had some inkling that the sector was fraught with risks. Yet the PE group chose to borrow half of the Samson deal's value in the form of debt.

By now you have probably guessed what happened: Samson's margins were negatively impacted by the continuing fall in natural gas prices, with revenues remaining flat between 2012 and 2014, 10% below their 2011 level, operating cash flows a third of what they were pre-LBO (forcing repeat downgrades by credit rating agencies) and EBITDA down 15% in 2014 alone. Eventually Samson's management was forced to start a fire sale of its 'non-core' assets while in parallel running an all-too-common amend-and-extend process for the group's credit facilities. KKR had to write down its rumoured $2 billion equity ticket by 95% in December 2014. But it was all for nothing, and in August 2015 the shale gas explorer, crumbling under $4.1 billion of accruing loans, announced its intention to file for Chapter 11 bankruptcy protection in a TXU 2.0 type of scenario.[69] Talk about learning from your mistakes!

TPG Capital was co-lead on the highly speculative TXU transaction and deserves part of the blame, especially because one of the firm's co-founders, David Bonderman, was a board member of Energy Future. How could a local Texan investment firm, led by senior executives highly knowledgeable of the energy sector, fail to see the downside risks of the largest LBO in history? The investment firm's TPG Partners V fund, of the same 2006 vintage as the KKR vehicle invested in TXU, yielded a net IRR even lower than that of its New York-headquartered co-investor. At 3.5% as of 31 December 2014, annualised returns were half what TPG's limited partners could have earned had they invested their capital in the S&P 500. The Caesars case study (see Chapter 15), about another TPG bet that did not pay off, will shed further light on the Texan outfit's investment record.

As part of its TXU involvement, Goldman had served as financial adviser, led the largest corporate high-yield financing ever and created an innovative commodity risk management programme to support the acquisition. But Goldman never disclosed to what degree the TCEH bankruptcy affected its performance. In the intervening period, the financial crisis had forced the bulge-bracket investment bank to shrink its asset base by a quarter and its gross leverage by more than 60%.[70] These were humbling times.

CHAPTER 6
EMI – Out of Tune

T HE YEAR WAS 1931. THE ECONOMY WAS STILL REELING from the Great Crash and the banking crisis that had ensued. Yet two companies with roots reaching as far back as the origins of recorded sound were destined to play a major part in the future of the music industry.

In March of that year, the Gramophone Company – established by German-born American Emile Berliner in London in 1897 – and the Columbia Gramophone Company agreed to merge. The resulting combined entity, operating in the fields of sound recording, and recording and playback equipment, was christened Electric and Music Industries Ltd. After surviving the Great Depression, the company grew in stature in the 1950s and 1960s, representing a roster of prestigious artists, including Frank Sinatra, the Beach Boys, and Pink Floyd. Probably the best decision in its history came in 1962 when it signed the Beatles and released their first single *Love Me Do*. Eventually rebranded EMI to reflect its gradual move away from recording and broadcasting equipment, by the early 1970s the company had become indisputably the most iconic and sought-after independent record label in the world.

EMI's independent status lost some lustre after the group's acquisition by British conglomerate Thorn Electrical Industries in late 1979, when it was amalgamated with Thorn's Liberty Records and Imperial Records, and later with Chrysalis Records and Virgin Records following their acquisitions in 1989 and 1992 respectively. As it grew in size, inevitably the company came under criticism for being somewhat bureaucratic and unmanageable. Partly to address this handicap it regained its independence by listing on the stock exchange in 1996, the year when it signed the Spice Girls. Now demerged from Thorn, the recorded music and publishing activities were renamed EMI Group PLC. By then the industry was starting to experience the internet revolution, in particular the creation of online music stores, music e-tailers, digital jukeboxes, track downloads, peer-to-peer file-sharing, and their sidekick: online piracy.

Developments in digital technology were outpacing the ability of all copyright-based industries, including music, to protect their assets from unlawful downloads. Illegally copying CDs was already rife when Napster, an internet music-sharing website, was conceived in 1999 as one of the earliest peer-to-peer online platforms. Napster showed no respect for copyright and let its users freely copy and share music files. By the time the music majors had filed a lawsuit and obtained an injunction to close the site in 2001, cross-border piracy had started to considerably curtail shipments of sound carriers (cassettes, records and CDs) and to undermine the entire value chain of the music industry. A new generation of teenagers and 20-somethings had gotten into the habit of getting music online for free and viewed file-sharing as a given right. Between 2000 and 2005 shipment of CDs in America fell by more than a fifth to $10.5 billion. Then the trend accelerated, with physical shipment dropping by 11% in 2006 alone and by a distressing 19% the following year.[1] Record labels needed to act fast if they wanted to survive.

In 2003 the industry found an unlikely saviour in Steve Jobs, CEO of computer maker Apple. The latter had launched its iTunes online music store that year, helping the record labels to sell their catalogue digitally. In the same month EMI had taken the lead by making available over 140,000 tracks from over 3,000 of its artists for sale online.[2] But all these initiatives did not change the reality: between 1999 and 2007 shipments of physical music media in the US had halved. As for legal digital downloads, they had gone from a share of market revenue of 0.9% in 2004 to 11.2% three years later.[3]

In hindsight, by giving consumers convenience and reliability at a price-point they could accept, services like iTunes had only served to accelerate the progressive erosion of physical product sales and weaken the music majors' hold on the industry. By introducing a flat-rate model (of 79 cents or pence per single), Apple had not only taken away the record labels' ability to set pricing, a key characteristic of any product or service, but it had also unbundled digital albums, thereby removing a central piece of the music groups' traditional revenue generation: the physical sale of premium-priced albums.[4] Gradually losing their grip on the distribution process, record labels had limited options if they wanted their artists to feature on the largest online music platform in the world. In the face of so much market confusion, EMI's senior management was scrambling to find a way to bolster its position.

Booby prize

On 24 April 2007, the employees of British buyout firm Terra Firma were coming to terms with the decision to pull out of the fight for Alliance Boots, a very large healthcare wholesaler and retailer listed on the London Stock Exchange and a member of the FTSE 100 index. The transaction – the largest take-private in the UK and Europe ever to be orchestrated by a PE investor – had been a hard-fought battle. To clinch the prize, KKR had apparently outbid Terra Firma by a mere £100 million (in an £11 billion transaction).

It was all the more dispiriting because closing the deal would have given Terra Firma and its flamboyant majority owner, Chairman and CEO Guy Hands, the prestige they were craving. In a statement released that day, Terra Firma lamented:

> "Boots is a critically important national institution, and we are naturally disappointed not to be able to execute the bold vision we had for the company and its critical role in the provision of healthcare in the UK."[5]

But all was not lost. Hands and his team were already working around the clock on another public-to-private, that of record company EMI Group PLC, itself a pretty 'important national institution'. Terra Firma was determined not to let that one get away.

*   *   *

When potential suitors started looking at EMI's books in early 2007, there was no telling whether their due diligence process was going to lead to completion. The record company had been involved in so many on-and-off M&A discussions in recent years that no one dared speculate what the outcome would be this time around. In fact, the whole industry had been subject to consolidation mania since the start of the new millennium, as if clubbing together was ever going to help in the fight against the online threat.

In 2000, Warner Music had tried to acquire EMI but the deal had been scuppered by the regulatory backwash of Time Warner and AOL's $350 billion mega-merger, later designated 'the biggest mistake in corporate history' (that's saying something).[6] EMI and Germany's Bertelsmann Music Group (BMG) had then tried to merge, but their discussions had halted in May 2001 in the face of regulatory hurdles. In September 2003, Warner Music and Bertelsmann had been in merger talks. When the period of exclusivity had ended, EMI had wooed Warner once again with a $1.6 billion offer; to no avail.[7] BMG had finally elected to merge with Sony Music Entertainment in March 2004. That same year Warner Music had been acquired by former Polygram and Universal owner Edgar Bronfman Jr. in a $2.6 billion LBO backed by PE investors Thomas H. Lee, Providence Equity and Bain Capital.

After its partial listing in May 2005, Warner started to reveal public information regarding its performance. This naturally generated more interest from outsiders. A year later EMI was spurned in its $4.2 billion bid for Warner, only to see the latter turn back and attempt to buy EMI for 315p a share, at a 20% premium to the prevailing share price.[8] In truth, it made a lot of sense for the British company – the fourth largest record label in the world, with a 13% market share in 2006 – and Warner Music, ranked third with 14% of the global market, to combine their assets in order to match the might of leader Universal Music and runner-up Sony BMG. EMI had an enviable publishing catalogue and a strong European presence while its American counterpart had a more successful recorded music division and was the third biggest music group in the US, a crucial territory accounting for over 30% of the industry's global shipment.[9]

It seemed that only egos prevented the two from tying the knot. Both EMI's chairman Eric Nicoli and Warner Music's Bronfman wanted to head the combined entity. In late June 2006, after it had seen its increased $4.6 billion bid for Warner rebuffed, EMI rejected a £2.54 billion counteroffer. Eventually, the tit-for-tat bidding war between them ended in the face of renewed regulatory uncertainty.

These multiple rounds of bidding over such a protracted period were bound to create a loss of focus and significant uncertainty among employees. In the face of online piracy, EMI had underperformed since the start of the millennium and was always in danger of falling behind. It did not take long for management to disappoint. Half-year results to 31 October 2006 registered negative top-line growth of 6% due in part to delayed album releases. It also became clear that full-year performance would come way short of analysts' expectations.

To demonstrate initiative as the group was issuing a profit warning, on 11 January 2007 Nicoli announced that, as part of a widespread reorganisation, he would take over the reins of the recorded music division, firing in the process CEO Alain Levy and vice chairman David Munns, the two divisional executives he had hired six years earlier to turn things around. Within one month EMI had to release another profit warning, thereby admitting that management did not quite have a grip on the numbers. With its British peer on the ropes, in March Warner Music submitted a revised bid. Seemingly too proud to negotiate in such a blatant position of weakness, EMI's board of directors duly rejected Warner's new offer.[10]

While in normal circumstances a party that repeatedly fails to find a match tends to be spurned, oddly enough these numerous aborted bids became the cue for other prospectors to come forward. The usual opportunists emerged as potential bidders. Due to its slow growth and falling profitability, EMI was perceived as a basket case by many. Most of the investors volunteering to take a closer look had a knack for turnarounds and special situations. Hedge fund managers Cerberus and Fortress as well as distressed specialist Apollo were among the rumoured parties circling the target. All were American. All but one.[11]

The main problem that both the seller and interested buyers faced was that EMI had rejected Warner's 260p a share offer at a time when the company's financial performance was fast deteriorating, leading to two profit warnings in as many months and the suspension of dividend payments. In January and February 2007, rating agencies Moody's and Standard & Poor's both downgraded EMI's debt.

In the past, when facing a weakened prey, financial sponsors had acted as scavengers. But the prevailing credit bubble had enabled these bottom fishers to mend their ways by regularly outbidding corporate buyers. The availability of cheap, no-strings-attached debt and the sheer quantum of it had given LBO shops an unassailable advantage in any bidding war. On 21 May 2007, almost a month to the day after losing the Alliance Boots battle, acting through a newly established acquisition vehicle called Maltby Capital, Terra Firma made a 265p-a-share overture for EMI, translating into a £2.4 billion market capitalisation. The attraction to the music group's shareholders was that, like all leveraged buyouts, Terra Firma's proposal was a cash bid, whereas any consideration by Warner Music might have been made partly in shares. Importantly, Hands's offer would not face months of regulatory uncertainty since his firm owned no other music assets. Just short of a 2% premium to Warner's 'inadequate' bid rejected by EMI two months earlier, the proposal was at once recommended as 'fair and reasonable' by EMI's directors. Subsequent events would divulge that no other party had bothered to submit a binding offer.

Karaoke-loving Hands and his colleagues might have lost the battle to protect Alliance Boots against American predators, but they had succeeded in grabbing another national treasure. One hundred and ten years after the establishment of the Gramophone Company and the revolution of recorded sound, EMI remained British. Still, it needed to reinvent itself without delay.

Be careful what you wish for

Hands had a simple, though far from simplistic, plan in mind. In mid-April 2007, unquestionably feeling under pressure from the attention it had received from suitors, EMI's senior management appointed advisers to look into a potential securitisation of its music publishing assets in order to borrow against its back catalogue. Management was keen to reduce the cost of the company's debt burden, which sat at £910 million and 5.2 times EBITDA as of 31 March 2007.[12] Securitisation was one way to do it. And securitisation was something Guy Hands knew a great deal about.

A few years ago, it would have been laborious to explain this innovative product. But the financial crisis has given our generation the uncommon opportunity to experience the repercussions of the subprime bubble. Securitisation is the process of taking an illiquid asset or group of assets (say mortgages) and packaging them into a marketable security (think residential mortgage-backed security, or RMBS). That financial instrument can then be freely traded on a public exchange.[*] Hands had long been a keen advocate and user of this financial engineering technique. In fact, he was widely acknowledged as one of its pioneers in Europe.

Before joining Japanese bank Nomura in 1994, he had been a eurobond trader with Goldman Sachs. Since securitisation consists of raising money in the bond market and securing it against cash flows generated by tangible assets such as hotels or retail outlets, Hands was in his element. He had lost interest in selling bonds but was keen to launch a securitisation business. It is only because his employer Goldman had failed to see the potential that he set up shop at the Japanese bank. While in charge of Nomura's Principal Finance unit in the late 1990s, he had used securitisation to liquefy tangible assets in sectors heavy on the property front: rolling stock (Angel Trains for £672 million in 1995), residential homes (Annington for £1.6 billion in 1996), pubs (Inntrepreneur for £1.2 billion in 1997) and retail outlets like betting shops (William Hill for £700 million in 1997 – see Chapters 2 and 15 to gauge the obsessive interest of PE investors in the gambling sector).

It was during the £1.85 billion auction process of Le Meridien hotels in the first half of 2001 that both Hands and Nomura realised their interests were diverging. For Nomura, the Principal Finance arm was capital hungry, which is never a good thing for a bank. When he had joined in 1994, Hands had convinced Nomura that he should be allowed to use the bank's vast capital base to take assets onto its own books and then lay off that risk via securitisation, but the amount of tied-up capital had racked up nonetheless. For Hands, being part of a captive investment business was restrictive, and he was not the type of individual to set himself limits. Over seven years, both sides had made a mint in the securitisation business – a reported £1.5 billion. Now Hands wanted to fly solo.[13]

* * *

When the EMI opportunity came knocking, Hands had been running his outfit Terra Firma for five years. The record label had arguably the most sought-after music catalogue of the industry. While recording studios were

---

[*]. The Foxtons story (in Chapter 14) will offer further intelligence on the topic.

not great candidates for LBOs due to the unpredictability of physical sales and the heightened competitive threat of new online distribution channels, music publishing assets, with long-term copyright agreements and recurring loyalty payments, lent themselves well to Hands's favourite financial engineering technique. Securitisation, which Hands had reportedly dubbed the "crack cocaine of financial services",[14] was on the cards, and a lot more.

The deal emerged at the right time. Terra Firma had closed its latest fund, Terra Firma Capital Partners III, during that same month of May 2007. It had raised €5.4 billion, or 157% more than the previous vintage completed three years earlier.[15] Such a big jump in fund size was another sign that the sector was operating in a bubble, but for now it was great news for EMI's board of directors.

For a company trying to attract private equity buyers, the best time to convince them to part with their money comes twice: at the very beginning of the life of a fund – when the new equity must find a home and the investment team is keen to demonstrate that the huge commitments received from LPs were imperatively needed – and towards the end of a fund's life when the capital is almost completely deployed and the general partner intends to launch a new fundraising.

The EMI buyout was so large that it could enable Terra Firma to hit two birds with one stone: to fully commit the remainder of the uninvested capital from its 2004 vintage (the so-called TFCP II) and start investing a significant chunk of the recently closed TFCP III. Granting the target a total EV of £3.2 billion – a £2.4 billion market cap plus £800 million of loans sitting on EMI's books – Terra Firma had bid a mindboggling 18.4 times full-year 2007 EBITDA multiple (or 21.3 times EBITA) for a far-from-stellar business. In its last financial year to March 2007, EMI had recorded a 16% fall in revenue to £1.75 billion, while its EBITDA tumbled 37% to £174 million. EMI's recording unit had fallen off a cliff, with its profitability down two-thirds on the prior year. After restructuring charges, the group had lost £264 million.[16]

When reporting the acquisition in its 2007 annual review, Terra Firma proudly stated that it would allow its executives to draw fully on their expertise in strategically transforming businesses, repositioning assets and enhancing cash flows.[17] What Hands wanted to do is termed an institutional buyout (IBO), meaning a buyout without the incumbent management team, with the aim of selecting and bringing in new executives after the closing of the transaction. Following the announcement of the deal, he made various public statements condemning EMI's corporate culture and the sense of entitlement from sections of the company's staff. He needed to shake things up. The main issue was that few candidates had prior experience in reorganising a music major, and slashing costs in an industry reliant on human talent was always a sticky proposition. With a restructuring plan aiming to shrink the workforce by a third, Hands was facing criticism from executives, artists, and agents.[18]

He was right, of course, in thinking that the music group had been seriously mismanaged in the past. And in normal circumstances Terra Firma's widely advertised proficiency in turning around troubled companies might have paid off. However, a series of factors was to render this restructuring problematic and cause the former Goldman Sachs whizz to regret the bombastic comments uttered shortly after gaining control of the company.

When making a presentation before the Royal Television Society in September 2007, Hands described Terra Firma's investment strategy and proclaimed that he and his colleagues looked "for the worst business we can find in the most challenged sector and we get really happy if it's really, really bad," before adding "We're just hoping EMI is as bad as we think it is."[19] He was about to have his wish granted many times over.

*   *   *

As global credit markets buckled in the summer of 2007, Citi got stuck with the entire EMI loan package. Unsparing in its bleakness, the syndication environment had vanished, leaving the US bank with £2.6 billion of debt. Between the time of Terra Firma's bid submission in the third week of May and the deadline for acceptances to be received from EMI's shareholders on 1 August, credit conditions had seriously worsened. Citi was not alone in holding onto an unwieldy package; few lenders were able to bail out of their risky positions. More than $60 billion worth of deals had been pulled from the corporate credit markets in the month preceding the EMI buyout compared to none in the whole of 2006.[20] The Credit Crunch had emerged out of the defaults in the US subprime mortgage market.

For that reason, Citi had made the availability of its loans, struck on covenant-lite terms, dependent on Terra Firma's obtaining at least 90% consent from EMI's shareholders for its offer. Often, banks waive that condition and accept to provide financing even if a PE bidder does not reach the squeeze-out level, the threshold that enables a buyer to force hold-out minorities to tender their stock so that the listed company can be taken off the quote. Both sides can easily agree to push back the deadline with the agreement of the relevant market authorities. Rather hoping that Terra Firma would fail to reach the 90% threshold, giving the bank the right to walk away from the deal, Citi held its ground and demanded that the condition be met, as was stipulated in the financing agreement.

Because many EMI stockholders had counted on another party to outbid Terra Firma, they had withheld their support, even pushing the share price to 271p in the days following the takeover announcement. By 14 July, Terra Firma had only obtained shares from 3.8% of the public; by 20 July it had received support from 26%; and by 28 July only 80% of investors had handed over their shares. Regrettably for Citi, Hands and his advisers at Dresdner Kleinwort put on a spurt in the days preceding the deadline and eventually obtained the endorsement of 91.5% of stockholders.[21] Contractually obligated, Citi was on the hook for £2.6 billion. As the deal closed, the bank was the clear loser in this transaction. It would eventually have a chance to get even.

Until then, the total cash injection and the loan package were staggering. Citi had offered £1.18 billion in senior term loans, £1.41 billion in a securitised bridge-loan facility (to repay EMI's existing loans), and £155 million worth of mezzanine. Aside from £704 million of preference shares, Terra Firma had subscribed £1.05 billion in the form of a shareholder loan maturing in 2017 and accruing interest at a rate of 8% a year.[22] All in all, not far from £4.3 billion of fresh liquidity had been injected in the acquisition vehicle Maltby in order to give its music assets enough cash to undergo the type of restructuring Hands had in mind. The balance sheet was debt-heavy. The covenant-lite structure of the Citi loans also meant that there were few triggers that enabled the lender to step in if a default occurred. The main condition was that the debt had to stay within a certain multiple of earnings, tested every six months. If it did not, Terra Firma could inject new equity to cure the breach. It looked like a sweet deal for EMI and Terra Firma, less so for Citi.

From "really, really bad" to worse

Five days after announcing that it had gained acceptance from EMI's shareholders, Terra Firma received bad news from its portfolio company. In the first quarter of its new financial year EMI had recorded a 20% decline in CD sales and a 13% fall in turnover at its recorded music division. While the smaller publishing unit's revenues were up 12% and nascent digital sales had increased 26%, it was not enough to compensate: the group, with total turnover down 5%, was in need of some urgent remedy.[23]

All the non-executive board members had stepped down upon Terra Firma gaining control of the business.[24] About half of the senior execs were let go or quit within weeks. The group's 56-year-old boss Eric Nicoli and his finance director Martin Stewart did not even have to wait for the company to be delisted from the London Stock Exchange before leaving with generous 'golden goodbyes'.[25]

Hands nominated himself as chairman of the new supervisory board and elevated Chris Roling, one of Terra Firma's managing directors, to the top executive job as president and chief operating officer, with added responsibility for the finance function. An American national with an accomplished career in the US and Europe, Roling was a previous finance director at Imperial Chemical Industries, Getty Images and food manufacturer Kellogg. He had never operated in the music world. As head of business transformation, Hands also parachuted in another Terra Firma MD in the person of Ashley Unwin, a former Andersen and Deloitte consultant and the Head of Talent at the PE firm. Both Roling and Unwin had joined Terra Firma earlier that year.

One of Hands's top lieutenants who had previously worked at Nomura, Julie Williamson, took over as chief investment officer and oversaw the music publisher's relationships with outside parties. Lord Birt, a former Director-General of the BBC from 1992 to 2000 and an adviser to Terra Firma since 2005, was appointed to EMI's supervisory board alongside former Northern Foods CEO Patricia O'Driscoll, whose title of chief restructuring officer would leave no one perplexed. None of these newly appointed executives had any past relevant experience in the music business.[26]

And that was more or less the point. Turnaround aficionado Hands wanted to introduce a fresh approach to making money in the sector. His thinking was that EMI was by far the worst performer among the music majors and needed some tough love. In particular, the cost base had to be trimmed. Jobs were at risk. This wasn't news. In the year to March 2007 Nicoli and his team had already incurred over £150 million in restructuring costs on the back of several chapters of reorganisation. Terra Firma wanted to go much further.

Over the last three years, Warner Music had gone through a similar exercise under the guidance of its three private equity shareholders. The American music label was of similar size to EMI with $3.5 billion (£1.8 billion) of revenues in 2007, but employed 4,000 people, a third less than its British rival. In its recording business, EMI was making a 3.25% profit margin. Warner's margin on recorded music was three times higher. Warner had already realised that releasing new CDs was not the way to make money going forward. It was looking for new revenue streams from touring, merchandising and artist management. Since the turn of the millennium, the suits had equally taken control of strategic decision-making at the two largest music groups Sony BMG and Vivendi Universal and had spent years leading the consolidation game and shaving overheads. That was how Terra Firma aimed to lift performance: by changing the old-fashioned approach of doing business still prevalent at EMI.

The immediate aftermath of the buyout saw Hands trying to scale down Terra Firma's £1.5 billion equity ticket in EMI. Representing a third of the LBO group's total assets under management, it was the kind of overexposure Hands and his team were keen to rectify. Shopping the asset around to other PE groups, hedge funds and its own limited partners, Terra Firma wanted to offload £500 million, in a move that outsiders interpreted as a sign that the firm was disillusioned with the purchase. After months of effort, it found a few investors prepared to take the bait, injecting £250 million in exchange for a 16% stake in EMI.

To astute onlookers, EMI was an overleveraged, underperforming company operating in a sector undergoing a veritable revolution. Few were brave enough to predict where the music industry was heading or where EMI's valuation stood. And the credit squeeze that had ravaged the markets since the summer was also hampering the company's securitisation attempts to use its publishing catalogues as collateral with a view to refinance outstanding debt, pay a dividend or generate spare cash to reinvest in core operations. Despite the partial equity syndication, events were not going Terra Firma's way.[27]

Hands's disenchantment also led him to issue an internal memo to all EMI staff shortly after closing the transaction. In it, he indicated that the group should be prepared to axe artists who did not work hard enough in promoting their music and were instead paying more attention to advances EMI was willing to pay them. But what attracted the attention of commentators was the proposed strategic review, including the intention to shrink the workforce. Hands blamed previous management for wasting money in lavish corporate and entertainment expenses, as he publicly disclosed how EMI used to spend £200,000 a year on fruit and flowers at their West London offices or £20,000 on candles to decorate a Los Angeles apartment to entertain artists – the Terra Firma team quickly learned that fruit, flowers and candles are the industry's accounting euphemism for drugs, booze and prostitutes, which could explain the size of the expense account.

The newly appointed executives discovered that the situation was even worse than what they had imagined. Over the years EMI had built a reputation for its generosity towards departing managers: in 2001, as he was stepping down from his role as CEO of the recorded music unit, Ken Berry reportedly pocketed £5 million in compensation, while his successor Alain Levy, dismissed by Nicoli in January 2007, received a less kind-hearted £3 million pay-off (though some press articles spoke of £7 million). Nicoli's golden parachute upon Terra Firma's buyout totalled £3.3 million.

To curtail the corporate overheads, an initial £100 million of cost-cuts had been identified, but with so much bad news piling up as 2007 was coming to a close, even Hands must have wondered whether he could make the deal work.[28]

* * *

Following a disastrous performance in his geographies the previous year, the head of EMI UK & Ireland's recording division, veteran Tony Wadsworth, stepped down in January 2008, shortly after his chief operating officer and the group's CIO and the head of human resources departed. Wadsworth had worked at EMI for 26 years, ten of them as chairman and chief executive of its UK recorded music arm. He had helped bring on board big acts like Radiohead, Coldplay, Blur, and Gorillaz. For him to take the fall the year when the entire national market of physical album sales had dropped 13% seemed unfair. EMI's problems were on par with the rest of the sector. Wadsworth was a well-known and respected executive in the industry, so his departure was unlikely to go down well among artists and their managers.

Regardless, his operational duties were immediately assumed by Mike Clasper, educated at St John's College, Cambridge with a double first in engineering, and one of Terra Firma's operational managing directors as well as a member of EMI's supervisory board. The newly appointed executive had held various senior roles at fabric and homecare concern Procter & Gamble before heading the British Airports Authority but, it goes without saying, he had never worked in the music industry. That same month, newspapers headlined a plan by EMI and its new PE owners to axe 2,000 employees (including 400 middle managers), primarily in the recorded music division, although it was not clear over what period and in which territories.

Despite the fuzzy details of this £200 million annual savings exercise, Hands's plan was evidently going full steam ahead, with a swat team of 50 advisers tasked to rationalise the business. However, the lengthening list of senior departures was raising concerns among artists. Some of them, including stars like Robbie Williams and Coldplay, chose to go on strike in reaction to Terra Firma's ruthless asset-stripping tactics, arguing that some of these management changes added uncertainty around EMI's ability to efficiently market and distribute future albums. Hands's boorish comments, widely reported in the press, regarding the extravagant advances paid to certain acts, or his suggestion that artists & repertoire (A&R) personnel were somewhat lazy, had not been great PR either. Used to dealing with physical assets like pubs and hotels, Hands was learning that managing creative talent requires a softer touch.[29]

Maltby's accounts for the year to 31 March 2008 showed that pre-exceptionals EBITDA had edged up 5% year-on-year, but revenues had shed 17% to £1.46 billion. Terra Firma's shareholder loan had already been marked down 30% at the HoldCo level.[30] If the loan was impaired, then the PE firm's preference shares, which were subordinated, had to be worthless. It was not the best possible start for the group's ambitious reorganisation.

Because Hands had announced that no EMI employee would receive a bonus if the company did not generate underlying earnings in excess of £150 million for the 12 months to 30 June 2008, observers speculated that lenders Citi were owed a first interest repayment of that amount on that day. Things got worse when press articles later stipulated that the company had missed its June goal by £17 million, making the earnings target for the 12 months to 30 September even higher, at £180 million. All this exacerbated the feeling by artists and their agents that the business was now being run by bean counters rather than the commercial talent-scouting personnel of the group's A&R department. Still, it was difficult to quibble with the decision to rationalise the business: the record company had 14,000 artists on its roster, both dead and alive, most of them unprofitable. Hands claimed that less than 15% of artists turned a profit. Some 30% of artists who were paid an advance ended up never recording an album. According to him, such misuse of shareholders' money needed to stop.[31]

Meanwhile, Citi could have been forgiven for not paying too much attention to EMI's financial and operational woes. On 15 January 2008, the American lender reported a $9.8 billion loss for the last three months of 2007. It had also written down $18.1 billion in numbing subprime mortgage losses. Running out of liquidity, the bank received cash injections from the Singapore Government's investment agency GIC and the Kuwait Investment Authority totalling $10 billion in exchange for equity stakes. These followed a $7.5 billion investment from the Abu Dhabi Investment Authority. Instead of worrying about EMI's survival, Citi executives were concerned about keeping their own jobs.[32]

Shaking things up

It took until April 2008 for freshly levered EMI finally to announce some good news. Terra Firma had somehow managed to hire industry veteran Nick Gatfield (who had started his career at EMI years earlier) away from Universal's Island Records to take charge of the British major's A&R activities in North America and the UK, with all the labels in these territories reporting to him. A truly respected individual when it came to repertoire management and artist signings, Gatfield was credited with building soul singer Amy Winehouse's career at Universal. His enrolment was widely acclaimed by the specialist press. That same month, former Google CIO Douglas Merrill enlisted as president and COO of EMI New Music to lead the group's digital strategy and business development activities. Eight months after EMI's buyout, a senior executive with serious tech experience had finally joined the fray.[33] And in the summer, Terra Firma managed to convince someone to take over the reins of the recording division: Elio Leoni Sceti, a consumer goods expert, was hired as CEO of the operationally troubled EMI Music unit. Naturally, Leoni Sceti had never worked in the music business – apologies if I sound like a broken record.

By the end of 2008, most of the original team appointed by Hands had left and had been replaced. One of Hands's close lieutenants, however, was given further responsibilities. Stephen Alexander had done the operational due diligence on the EMI transaction and, with Hands trying to beef up EMI's senior team, he was appointed to the board of directors of Maltby on 20 January 2009, alongside Leoni Sceti.[34] That same month, the former boss of television broadcaster ITV, Charles Allen, took over Hands's role as EMI's non-executive chairman.[35]

The music group's first full year of activity under Terra Firma ownership, that is the 12 months ended 31 March 2009, delivered a strong message that the new owners were determined to reconstruct the business. EMI recorded an impairment charge of £1.04 billion and restructuring costs of £136 million. The strategic review had included significant headcount reductions, the outsourcing of certain non-core business areas, centralising back-office functions for the group's 40 or so music labels, and renegotiating contracts with suppliers. But the pain was only just starting. To boost the top line during the 2009 fiscal year, the approach to market was tweaked: a freshened-up partnership with artists was developed, and new income streams such as enhanced digital services and corporate sponsorship arrangements were generated.

In no small part thanks to the launch of a new album, *Viva la Vida*, by one of the company's true global artists, British band Coldplay, and the startling success of Katy Perry's single *I Kissed a Girl*, EMI could reveal that its revenue had risen 8%. Coldplay's new album – given away for free to fans attending the band's summer tour, in another sign that piracy and digital adoption were forcing artists to market their act inventively – had been a global success and a bestseller on iTunes, granting EMI and its backers a bit of a breather. But it was not enough to solve their problems.

The shakeup and exceptional write-offs impacted the financial accounts. It created a dilemma for the company's external auditors KPMG. While in 2008 they had somehow managed to get comfortable with the viability and sustainability of EMI's operations, this time they had no alternative but to insert an 'emphasis of matter' paragraph to their report. Because the fiscal year 2009 operating loss had mushroomed to £1 billion, KPMG issued a stark warning, explaining that "the ability of the Group to continue as a going concern is dependent upon the continued availability of existing banking facilities, which require the Group to comply with the covenants set out in those facilities." They added that shareholders needed to agree to an equity injection, but that at the time of issuing their opinion, such agreement was still not forthcoming. The audit firm also alluded to a matter that had been reported extensively in the media ever since Terra Firma's buyout: the pension trustees had been requesting a cash injection to fill a hole in the EMI Group Pension Fund. Yet the LBO owner had refused to make any payment, arguing that, according to its own calculations, the pension fund was showing a surplus. KPMG were simply pointing out that the disagreement between both parties put the group at risk of default if lenders and shareholders refused to bridge the gap.[36]

It was also in March 2009 that the founder of Terra Firma relinquished the title of CEO at his investment firm, taking on the dual role of chairman and chief investment officer. Though some observed that it was a gesture by Hands to appease his investors in the wake of the ill-judged EMI deal, the announcement stated that the change would enable him to focus on portfolio management and international development. In short, he was still very much in control. What soon transpired was that he had elected to step down from key executive positions in order to reduce his business ties with the United Kingdom and facilitate his move offshore. Unhappy with the Labour Government's decision to tax the rich, Hands was migrating to the tiny island of Guernsey, a tax haven that is part of the British Isles and lies only 75 miles off the coast of England. After having spent the best part of the previous 18 months complaining about EMI's overpaid executives, the move could only attract attention to Hands's own personal wealth.[37]

* * *

For EMI, further complication was created by its debt quantum. Pre-exceptionals, in March 2009 leverage stood at 9.5 times EBITDA and 16.6 times EBITA; ratios that could not hold in a post-Credit Crunch era. As highlighted in the audit report, the group's current liabilities exceeded current assets by over £400 million. Even though EBITDA before restructuring had risen from £183 million in fiscal year 2008 to £300 million the following year, that performance still fell short of the original plan. If cost cuts and the reorganisation were meant to tackle operating issues by lifting earnings, the balance-sheet side also needed dealing with.

The group's debt load was becoming burdensome, to say the least. In its 2008 annual review, investment firm Terra Firma had publicly admitted that EMI had lost half of its equity book value. Although the PE house had chosen not to disclose in its report the identities of two portfolio assets it had written down, the sheer size of the impairment (€1.4 billion) left no one in doubt that EMI represented the bulk of it.[38] The romance between Hands's Terra Firma and EMI had been short-lived. In the summer of 2009, a full two years after completing its EMI buyout, Terra Firma retained Blackstone's debt advisory team to provide guidance about how to solve EMI's gearing problem.

Discussions between Terra Firma and sole lender Citi were rumoured to have revolved around raising high-yield bonds to repay the existing loans or investing fresh equity in exchange for a partial debt write-down from the US bank. Some of the details leaked to the press made little sense. One story in particular referred to the use of cash proceeds from the bond issue to pay back the Citi loans at a 20% to 40% discount. It was difficult to see what Citi would have got out of such a deal other than instant liquidity, which it did not need since the American Government had bailed the bank out in late 2008 through a $45 billion stimulus package, subsequently becoming Citi's biggest shareholder and providing an almost unlimited credit line. Terra Firma would have to come up with something more palatable. Negotiations were expected to take months.[39]

As detailed in the EMI annual accounts, the sole covenant test that the company needed to meet was the debt-to-EBITDA ratio. Simply put, this ratio reveals how many years it would take a company to pay back its debt if both debt and EBITDA are held constant. Obviously neither of them is ever constant, and the covenant test itself is also variable. In the case of EMI, the test was tightening on a quarterly basis by rolling 12-month periods. What this means is that the covenant stepped down, sometimes significantly, each quarter end, making it progressively harder to achieve the required ratio and the respective solvency tests. Due to Terra Firma's commitment to significantly raise EBITDA post-acquisition, Citi would have expected (more like, demanded) that the leverage ratio reach a more manageable level.

As debt continued to expand – since a large chunk of the loans subscribed were of a bullet nature with accruing interest (meaning that principal and interest were repaid at the time of exit or at maturity, rather than according to a quarterly repayment timetable) – EMI's management was under pressure to grow earnings accordingly.

One technique used by LBO buffs is to inject further equity into the company (which the lenders allow them to treat as EBITDA for the purpose of covenant testing). Such cash injections are called 'equity cures', and EMI benefitted from them during the many periods when meeting its sole covenant proved difficult: £16 million of fresh equity was invested in the three months to 30 September 2008, £12.75 million the following quarter, £39.25 million in the period ended 31 March 2009, and £37 million the next quarter.

Of course, another way of boosting EBITDA is to remove overheads and drop loss-making artists. Staff numbers had been reduced by a further 2,000 between 2007 and early 2009 to reach 3,800. Another 400 would leave in the fiscal year to March 2010, most of them in the recording division. In the first three years of Terra Firma's ownership, despite a 40% reduction in headcount, EBITDA before restructuring costs had only seen marginal improvement. Terra Firma's reorganisation efforts were taking longer than planned.

The only way the British investment firm could now keep hold of EMI would be by securing significant additional equity funding. According to various estimates, it needed to raise some £500 million. To collect such a sum it required new investors or EMI would have to sell some of its labels or outsource its distribution networks in various territories. Only then would the music group no longer be threatened by future covenant breaches. For now Terra Firma could only acknowledge that it had written down the value of its EMI equity stake further. By late 2009, the haircut had reached 90% of the book value, although in its annual report the PE firm did not specifically name the asset for which it had recognised a further €256 million impairment.[40]

Blame game

As his portfolio company was slowly but surely falling out of his grasp and into that of lender Citi, Guy Hands turned belligerent. This time, however, the battle was not to be fought in the open-market arena. Instead, in a bizarre move that some interpreted as a negotiating ploy to force Citi to accept debt-forbearance, in December 2009 Hands filed a damage claim against the music company's lender.

The lawsuit aimed to prove that Terra Firma, a firm led by senior investment professionals with years of dealmaking experience and spending millions of pounds annually on due diligence advisory fees, had been tricked like a novice into overpaying for EMI when Citi had acted as sell-side adviser to the record company back in the spring of 2007. Oxford graduate Hands accused his one-time friend, Cambridge-educated David Wormsley – head of Citi's investment banking department at the time of the deal, and known by the endearing sobriquet 'The Worm' – of lying about another bidder, hedge fund Cerberus, being involved in the last round of the auction.

This misrepresentation, Hands alleged, led his firm to pay a "fraudulently inflated price" for EMI. The LBO-cum-securitisation guru wanted his money back, all £1.7 billion of it, including the original ticket and subsequent equity cures, plus damages. In total, he was seeking compensation for up to £5 billion. The suit also suggested that Citi was intent on driving the business to the brink of insolvency so that it could engineer a merger with its rival Warner Music.[41]

The court action was coming months after negotiations between the two parties had reached an impasse. At some stage Terra Firma and its investors were thought to have offered to put an additional £1 billion of equity into the business, but it was conditional on Citi forgiving the equivalent amount of its loans. Logically, the US bank had rejected the proposal since it was not offered any equity in exchange, suggesting instead a debt-for-equity swap that would dilute Terra Firma's stake and grant majority ownership to Citi. Unwilling to compromise, the PE house had tried to garner support from political allies by dramatically playing the patriotic card: in case it had been forgotten, EMI was a British company and Citi an American bank.

As if the music group was not facing enough uncertainty, reports revealed that Citi had approached potential buyers to push for a sale of EMI ahead of a likely default on interest payments. The record label and its owners had also contemplated selling off or leasing out assets including back catalogues, but splitting up the business would have given artists the right to terminate their contracts; not to mention that key lender Citi would have had a right of veto since its loans were partly secured on these assets. Thus, disposals were not much of an option. Perhaps it was not so surprising that talks had reached a dead-end.[42]

All wound-up, Hands had filed his suit in New York because of the nationality of the defendant, but also bearing in mind that the indemnities he would be granted – should he win – would be more generous if the case was tried by an American jury. But Citi was equally keen for the case to be heard in Britain, where the harm had allegedly been suffered. In the latter eventuality, however, the press speculated that because of his move to tax shelter Guernsey, Hands would find it tricky to appear as a witness since he needed to stay out of the UK for an indefinite period or face losing his non-resident tax status. Under the Labour Government of Prime Minister Gordon Brown, the UK authorities had started cracking down on tax exiles. Still, it would have been odd if Her Majesty's Revenue & Customs (HMRC) targeted Hands specifically. Its chairman since 2008 was none other than Mike Clasper, formerly on the supervisory board of EMI and an operational managing director of Terra Firma between 2006 and 2008. In the end, the courts agreed with Hands that the case should be heard in New York.

* * *

Although EBITDA reached £333 million in the 12 months to March 2010, the record company was facing more pressure. Despite improvements in operational performance, EMI's leverage stood at eight times EBITDA and 12.6 times EBITA. Independent auditors KPMG had little choice but to reiterate their concerns surrounding EMI's unsteady financial footing, both regarding the future availability of the bank facilities and the lack of agreement from EMI's owners about a much-needed equity injection further down the line. By March 2010 current liabilities exceeded current assets by a shocking £3.3 billion as a result of the reclassification of bank loans from long-term liabilities to short-term debt.[43]

In its attempt to redefine EMI's business model, management had incurred an operating loss of £480 million due to another impairment charge of £600 million and new initiatives like rationalising the property portfolio, further outsourcing and contract renegotiations that had cost £70 million.[44] As a consequence, EMI inevitably would have breached its loan covenant had Terra Firma and co-investors not injected £87.5 million in the last quarter of the financial year.

With the group clearing this covenant hurdle, it seemed like a convenient time to go through another management reshuffle. In March 2010, Leoni Sceti, 18 months or so into the job, departed and was replaced as head of the recorded music unit by the group's chairman and TV broadcasting veteran Charles Allen.[45] Allen's pressing mission was to demonstrate that the company's strategy offered a viable path through the maze of debt obligations and value erosion in the recorded business. The City's rumour mill maintained that Leoni Sceti had taken the view that there was no way through and opted out.

Bad news then piled on in quick succession: in the month of April alone, independent actuaries divulged that EMI's pension deficit had reached £250 million – a shortfall that the regulator officially asked Terra Firma to address; hundreds of additional layoffs were envisaged as part of Allen's five-year business plan; and singer Paul McCartney decided to regain control of his library of 50 post-Beatles albums released between 1970 and 2006 and move it to Californian label Concord Music, three years after pulling future recordings from EMI.[46]

Weeks before the company was to face its June quarter-end covenant test, a further £105 million was added to the equity pot in order to cure the expected breach. Terra Firma had apparently tried to raise a total of £360 million to plug the funding gap and see EMI through covenant tests until 2015, but that process had failed. One option considered had been a £200 million deal for licensing distribution rights of its back catalogue in the Americas to Universal or Sony. When these talks had collapsed, Terra Firma's investors had once more accepted to fork out the cash. Eventually, EMI's shareholders would get the point that they were merely putting good money after bad, but for now they remained blindly supportive.[47]

With the group clearing that covenant hurdle, it seemed like a convenient time to go through yet another management reshuffle (are you getting a sense of *déjà-vu?*). The month of June was to be as eventful as the previous three. Upon presenting his five-year business plan, Charles Allen stepped down from the executive chairmanship while restructuring architects Lord Birt and Pat

O'Driscoll resigned from the board of EMI's HoldCo, Maltby. Hands's preferred lieutenant, Stephen Alexander, was appointed chairman.

But the big news was that Roger Faxon, who had been running the music publishing division since 2007 and had also been EMI's finance director between 2001 and 2005, was promoted to group chief executive. For the first time since the buyout, the two divisions, recorded music and publishing, were being brought under common leadership and led by an industry veteran. It was a step in the right direction. The restructuring days seemed well and truly behind.[48]

And yet, in the summer of 2010, Terra Firma finally admitted that its portfolio company would continue to breach its banking covenants for the foreseeable future, and at least until 2015.[49] While the PE house and Citi were going through mediation before fighting it out in a New York court, their portfolio company was hurting with no end in sight. Still, a period of prosecution between the company's owner and lender seemed the perfect time for what else but a third management substitution in just nine months. Faxon, now firmly in charge as chief exec, chose to make his mark early: Nick Gatfield, head of EMI Music in North America, group COO Ronn Werre, and Billy Mann, president of new music, were let go in September.

After trading verbal blows in the run-up to the trial, EMI's owner and lender lined up their legal teams for the final showdown. On one side, Terra Firma had secured the services of law firm Boies, Schiller & Flexner, an East Coast dispute-resolution and litigation specialist. Hands had retained David Boies, one of the firm's co-founders, as counsel. To say that Boies was an eminent lawyer would not do him justice. After spending years at prestigious American law firm Cravath, the Yale Law School graduate had set up his own partnership in 1997. Of all the cases he had worked on during his illustrious career, it was his role as representative for Vice President Al Gore in *Bush v. Gore*, following the bungled 2000 US presidential election, that raised his public profile significantly.

On the defence side, Citi was represented by the no-less impressive Harvard Law School alumnus Ted Wells, a litigation partner at New York-headquartered law firm Paul, Weiss, Rifkind, Wharton & Garrison. Wells's various claims to fame included being part of the team defending former Drexel 'junk bond king' Michael Milken in his fraud trial back in 1989 and, more recently, successfully defending former New York Governor and Attorney General (and former employee of Wells's law firm) Eliot Spitzer, who was facing criminal charges for his involvement in a sex ring. Both Citi and Terra Firma had retained big hitters.

The trial started on 18 October 2010. Each side aimed to prove that its opponent was dishonest. Wells declared that the suit was brought only to save Guy Hands's fortune and reputation, and opined that the EMI transaction proved that Hands, an otherwise accomplished investor, had lost his 'golden touch'.

Boies emphasised that Citi had played conflicting roles by being advisers to the seller while at the same time offering Terra Firma, an old-time client, a very generous debt package. After three weeks of very public and bitter debates, on Thursday 4 November the eight-person New York jury determined that Terra Firma had failed to provide sufficient evidence that it had been booby-trapped by the bank. The fraud case was rejected. Guy Hands, who had waited two-and-a-half years to bring his claim against Citi, had failed to save face.[50]

Facing the music

Because of the sheer amount of debt sitting on its books, EMI's demise was quick and clinical. Since the July 2007 buyout, each ambitious cost-reduction exercise had been nullified by a comparable increase in debt commitments. Interest payments had promptly absorbed fresh cash flows and swelling pension obligations added to the group's already unmanageable liabilities. Plainly, future loan redemptions would duly negate bottom-line gains. During his skirmish with Citi over the past two years, Hands had been looking for a solution. He had held rescue talks with Warner Music, Bertelsmann, KKR, Universal, Sony, the Canada Pension Plan, frankly any party that could get him and EMI out of this mess. Nothing had been considered taboo. A break-up of the two divisions, a sale of distribution rights, a fresh equity injection, a debt refinancing. And yet, no solution seemed workable.

On 1 February 2011, EMI collapsed into administration and, via a debt/equity swap, Citi took sole ownership of the beleaguered record company. Throughout his negotiations and confrontations with the bank, Hands had hoped that Citi would be reluctant – as lenders usually are – to take control of the troubled company. His belief proved mistaken. The debt conversion saw EMI's loans hacked from £3.4 billion to £1.2 billion, making it the UK's largest pre-pack sale ever. Under that arrangement, administrators PricewaterhouseCoopers (PwC) had been appointed two weeks earlier and negotiated the sale to the main creditor.

For well over a year, Terra Firma and Citi had been arguing about EMI's financial stability. On carrying out a few balance-sheet and cash-flow tests shortly after their appointment, the PwC experts determined that a holding company had failed a solvency test triggered by the weight of its debts. Since under UK law a business is not allowed to trade once it has been established that it is insolvent, to minimise disruption the administrators sold Citi the business in exchange for booking a £2.2 billion loan impairment. This agreement had taken place between the company's management and Citi, without Terra Firma's knowledge or input. Guy Hands himself was holidaying in India at the time.

EMI's fate had been sealed when Hands admitted under oath, during the New York trial three months earlier, that the company's equity had no value. Eager to demonstrate Citi's conflicting buy-side and sell-side roles during the early 2007 auction, Hands disclosed to the court, and *a fortiori* to every reporter in attendance, a lot more about his portfolio company's financial position than otherwise necessary. He admitted that EMI's enterprise value had fallen to just £1.8 billion, less than the debt amount originally subscribed. In the end, his desire for revenge probably cost him control of EMI. Seeing a business in which he had sunk a third of Terra Firma's capital sold behind his back was Guy Hands's ultimate humiliation, not least because his team was still desperately looking for over £1 billion of fresh funds as the news broke. When issuing its 2010 annual review Terra Firma booked a final €1.13 billion value impairment – confirming a total loss of £1.75 billion for its investors – to close the EMI chapter, at least from an investment standpoint. His legal wrangle with Citi was just getting started.[51]

It had taken a bit more than two months for Terra Firma and its legal team to consider the Manhattan court ruling regarding their fraud claim against Citi. On 11 January 2011, Hands had resumed hostilities by launching an appeal to challenge the jury's decision. The appeal process, due to take several months, gave Hands enough time to prepare another lawsuit: in September, as Citi was planning to break up EMI and probably in an attempt to derail the auction process, Hands began a legal action to dispute Citi's rightful ownership and its seizure of EMI seven months earlier. Claims that the administrators were not validly appointed and that the sale undervalued the music group never won the judge over.[52] With its reputation in tatters, Terra Firma had little to lose from pursuing legal avenues.*

* * *

EMI's precarious financial situation had been detrimental to its operations. After the numerous departures of artists in the months preceding and following the LBO, more had ensued in 2010 and 2011. Given the frequent equity cures and warnings from auditors KPMG, the very public falling-out and legal feud between the company's owner and its lender, to say nothing of the painful reorganisations that had taken place under the various chairmen and CEOs since 2007, EMI needed a breather.

---

*. In June 2016, Guy Hands and Terra Firma finally decided to drop their ongoing lawsuit for fraudulent behaviour against Citi.

Citi's debt conversion brought debt-to-earnings multiples to more sustainable 6.1 times EBITA and 3.9 times EBITDA. Upon completing the swap, EMI's new owner started an orderly, deliberate search for a buyer, or more likely, several of them. Citi put the record company on the market in May 2011. That same month, EMI's American rival Warner Music had been sold by its PE backers after seven years of ownership. Warner had gone to Russian billionaire Len Blavatnik. The latter was the bookies' favourite to clinch the EMI prize. Independent labels and their trade associations were vocal in their opposition to seeing the British record label sold to another major. EMI Chief Exec Roger Faxon expressed his view that the group was better off operating as one entity. A sale to a rival would put him in the ejector seat.

Regardless, 80-year-old music pioneer EMI ended up being split three ways. On 12 November 2011, Universal outbid Warner to acquire the recorded music division for £1.2 billion, consolidating its leadership in Europe and North America. That same day Sony/ATV bested BMG Rights Management's bid to gain ownership of EMI's publishing activities alongside a PE consortium for £1.37 billion, instantly controlling a catalogue of over 2 million songs and a 31% share of the global market. Putting an end to one of the ugliest chapters of British business history, in July 2013 Warner took over renowned labels EMI Classics, Virgin Classics and Parlophone from Universal for £487 million following the regulators' request for the French major to sell them as a condition to its purchase of the recorded music arm.

While the combined proceeds of £2.6 billion from the three sales fell some way short of the loans' book value when the bank had yanked control nine months earlier (£3.4 billion, including compounded unpaid interest), it equalled more or less the value of the loans extended at the time of the LBO. Citi had, against all odds, managed to salvage something from this dire situation. But the trade-off was that, after years of mismanagement, the world's fourth largest music group had vanished, its name forever synonymous with corporate failure.[53]

A tricky track record

The legal wrangles between EMI's previous PE owner and its lender-turned-administrator Citi are of little relevance when considering the performance of the record company under LBO. At first glance, Terra Firma's turnaround credentials could be somewhat flattered by the underlying operating results. Figure 6.1 illustrates that, although EMI's revenue continued to fall during the LBO, its profitability reached levels that had not been seen under Nicoli's leadership period of 1999 to 2007. Under Nicoli's guidance, the group's EBITDA margin had never exceeded 15%. With Hands, it neared or topped 20% for the last three years of Terra Firma's ownership.

Figure 6.1: EMI Group's revenue and EBITDA margin (1999-2011)

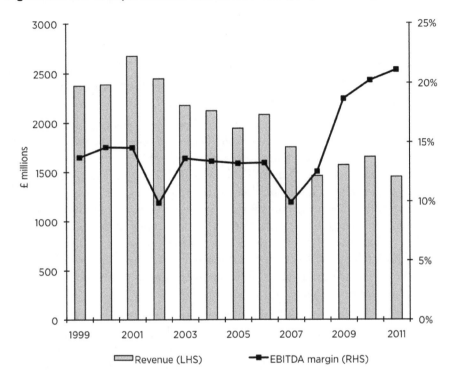

Source: Company accounts and author's analysis

However, there are some important caveats to this view. Top-line erosion was not just driven by the industry-wide aftershock of piracy and online migration of music consumption; it was also due to the flight of disillusioned or worried artists. The fact that EMI lost market share both at home and in international markets during its era under LBO suggests that Terra Firma's quirky leadership style was not quite suited to the singular world of recorded music.

To some industry experts, Hands's ambitious shakeup botched things up. He was at times guilty of micromanaging the business, asking at one point EMI executives to only ship CDs they expected to sell after discovering millions of pounds were being lost annually because of returns.[54] His remarks about the outrageous advances received by many artists and the laziness of some A&R personnel partly explained the defection of several top-name artists. Terra Firma's deal execs had probably been right to shave costs, but by taking the fat out, they had also cut into the muscle and hit the bone.

The aggressive restructuring had contrived to make matters worse for EMI, a business in the midst of the most ferocious technological upheaval in a generation. Between March 2007 and March 2010, the music group had seen its staff number go from more than 5,500 to just below 3,400.[55] With so much headcount reduction, the company had lost some of its senior talent and replaced it, as we saw, with operators rather than commercial and strategic experts. Many believed that the game plan had always been to focus efforts on the publishing arm and to quickly eliminate excesses like extravagant expense accounts and multi-year contracts with prima donna artists before offloading the recording unit. Whether that was indeed the aim, the financial crisis and the fast deteriorating business never gave the PE firm the chance to turn around a division that accounted for three-quarters of EMI's revenue.

At the time when Terra Firma vied for control of the record company, two facts were undisputable. First, the music industry was (and had always been) highly unpredictable. It was dependent on album releases by major artists in order to generate big winners. Bestsellers accounted for significant year-on-year revenue growth; more importantly they represented the bulk of profits for any record label. If, in a given year, fewer artists launched a new album or sold one-million-plus units, revenues in the recording unit suffered. Delays in new releases could seriously shake a label's results.

But the second and more fundamental point is that, since the late 1990s, the music market had suffered from the onslaught of online piracy. The effect on CD sales had been devastating: in the US, physical shipment had dropped 43% between 1999 and 2007.[56] Other territories suffered a similar fate. Piracy had reached a global scale that threatened the sector: in 2006 alone, 20 billion songs had been illegally downloaded.[57]

Due to its management's inability to act, EMI's performance had been in free fall. The group's enterprise value had fallen 60% between the time of its demerger from Thorn in 1996, which had granted the business an £8 billion valuation, and the delisting by Terra Firma 11 years later.[58] Because of its long history in pioneering the record industry, EMI had nurtured a fairly conservative culture. Its management was slow in acknowledging the threat from internet services.

The other majors and smaller independent labels had an equally hard time: between 2002 and 2007, Universal Music had seen its top line drop from €6.3 billion to €4.9 billion; a 29% correction for a company that had, during that period, spent hundreds of millions of dollars acquiring independent labels to further consolidate an ailing industry. And Warner Music's revenue had fallen from $3.4 billion in its 2003 fiscal year to $2.8 billion four years later.[59] Every participant was hurting.

As for EMI, despite booking over half a billion pounds of restructuring costs between 2001 and 2004, its financial and operating results had worsened. Over £240 million of exceptional costs related to the 2002 fiscal year alone, when the recently recruited boss of EMI Recorded Music, Alain Levy, had promised a 're-creation' of that division by announcing 1800 lay-offs and dropping a quarter of the group's artists due to poor performance – further evidence that Guy Hands's big restructuring plans were nothing new. Yet, throughout, group revenues had fallen from £2.67 billion in the financial year of 2001 to £1.75 billion in the 12-month period to 31 March 2007. In the face of digital migration, the traditional tools of corporate restructuring only provided short-term relief.

The uptick in profitability during the three years under LBO (2008-11) was driven by savage cost cuts. Similarly, a previous reorganisation implemented during Nicoli's chairmanship (2002-04) had led to a temporary improvement in profit margins (see Figure 6.1). But it was short-lived. And it failed to rectify the loss of revenues. On that basis, it was clear that EMI's recorded music unit was seriously sick. No business reporting such abysmal performance over more than half a decade of disruptive change across its value chain should have been considered a candidate for high financial gearing.[60]

During the quarter ended 30 December 2006, computer maker Apple had reported music-related revenues of $634 million. That's just for three months, and essentially for iTunes Store sales (i.e., that figure excludes the sale of iPod devices). All for a tech company that six years earlier had had no business in the music sector. EMI had made impressive progress in building online sales from £65 million in 2004-05 to £164 million (a bit less than 10% of group revenues) in the year ended 31 March 2007. Yet it was doing so by applying the old integrated model; that is by trying to reign over all production and distribution processes. This approach suited some artists, but others were ready to cut out the middleman, directly signing a contract with iTunes and other similar services in order to receive a much larger share of digital revenues derived from their art. The one-size-fits-all proposition no longer applied. For 2007, leading music group Universal had disclosed that only 14% of its revenues came from digital, or the equivalent of €680 million.[61] The music majors, even those professionally run like Universal Music – whose chairman and CEO until 2011, Doug Morris, had started his career as a songwriter, while his successor Lucian Grainge had left school to become a talent scout before working his way up – had struggled to adjust to the digital revolution and online piracy.

As Terra Firma was taking up the reins in the summer of 2007, the most salient question was: why should a PE firm and its interminable list of senior advisers and board members with no prior experience in the sector fare better than accomplished industry executives in turning around a global music group facing unrelenting competition from cash-rich innovators like Apple? What would they know about tackling fundamental market shifts like illegal downloads, mobile delivery and content distribution platforms? Under the chairmanship of Eric Nicoli, EMI had gone through three restructuring phases and reduced its headcount from 10,000 in the year ended 31 March 2001 to below 5,500 by mid-2007. Cutting another third of the staff was never going to have an impact on revenue. Which is not to say that there was no fat to remove, or that internal politics and vicious rivalry between the group's many labels did not need sorting out. But despite all the rhetoric about corporate excesses and overstaffing, the company had already reduced its workforce considerably. While it was correct that EMI and every major record company were known for being wasteful and for having adopted long ago a rock-and-roll attitude to entertainment expenses, the degree of technological innovation stirring the industry required a new business model, not just a leaner infrastructure. EMI was not so much a turnaround scenario as a corporate remodelling exercise.

Top-line expansion, above all in digital sales, was deemed to be more value accretive and would have generated higher margin uplift than one-off waste cuts. The problem with plans to boost sales is that they take time, a luxury EMI could ill-afford with a £3 billion loan package burning a hole in its balance sheet. Despite still receiving public acclaim for its music – winning 14 Grammy Awards in 2008 and 25 in 2009, as well as seven Brit Awards in each of these two years – EMI was stuck in a hamster wheel, its management and external advisers unable to deliver the sort of profitability gains necessary to keep up with the steepening financial covenant tests.

Technology disruption

After the emergence of the internet, the hideous economics of the music industry were glaring: online channels offered straightforward distribution and cheaper recording, without digital rights management (meaning that consumers could play the music they acquired on any portable device). Downloading and, later, streaming music cost a fraction of the price of traditional records or CDs. In fact, many streaming offerings were marketed on a 'freemium' basis, where only advanced features were chargeable and royalties paid to artists, songwriters and publishers.

As a consequence, between 2005 and 2013, the value of CD sales in the US dropped by a staggering 80% to $2 billion while digital sales quadrupled to $4.3 billion over the same period. The market had spoken. The recording industry initially refused to acknowledge that the internet had given consumers the freedom to select which tracks to download. What the majors needed to do was gradually discontinue the CD model and replace it with digital downloads of individual songs. That's what customers wanted and had wanted for years. And as the cliché goes: the customer is always right.

Yet some music labels underestimated the urgency of the matter – an easy mistake to make when you pay artists a measly $1 out of the $15-per-CD you charge consumers. Instead, they let start-ups with no credibility in the music space introduce the transition without much respect for digital rights. Eventually, the largest player in the sector, Universal Music, got its online strategy in order, becoming the most viewed channel on YouTube in 2007, creating MySpace Music in partnership with the eponymous social network a year later, and forming in December 2009 a joint venture with Google to launch the ad-based video-hosting service Vevo, which ranked as the number one online music destination in 2010. A decade after the creation of Napster and its promotion for music piracy, Universal was playing a leading role in online innovation.[62]

Consumers were not the only party keen to adopt the low-price web-based model. Some artists also eagerly embraced the new paradigm. In October 2007, while the Terra Firma crew still believed that it could reshape EMI, megastar Madonna had quit record label Warner Music to sign a ten-year, $120 million contract with concert promoter Live Nation to let the latter distribute her studio albums, sponsor her concert tours, and sell her merchandise. With this so-called '360 degree deal', she had rightly identified that concerts and merchandise were now worth more than records, and the agreement enabled her to retain a bigger share of the value she created.

That same month, in a move that underlined to what extent digitalisation was revolutionising music distribution, British rock band Radiohead – then just released from its EMI contract after refusing to sign a £3 million one-album deal with the record company because the band felt that new owner Guy Hands and his Terra Firma acolytes did not "understand the music industry" – chose to sell its latest album through its own website *radiohead.com*. Thereby retaining copyright ownership, Radiohead let fans decide what to pay for the album. The band had, as a matter of fact, received no payment for digital downloads under its previous EMI contract, so it surely found going direct to market compelling.

One key factor that music producers like EMI did not appreciate, or at any rate seriously overlooked when implementing their digital strategies, is that their traditional model, separating recording from delivery, had come to an end. The web enabled artists and start-ups to apply a one-stop-shop solution, with production and distribution blended seamlessly. Times were changing fast. The new environment seemed to be of benefit to lead acts like Radiohead and Madonna. Old-school recording groups were losing control of the production process.

On the brick-and-mortar front, UK music retailer Virgin Megastores lost £50 million in 2007 alone while its rival chain HMV – which started life in 1899 as EMI's second ever record label under the trademark His Master's Voice – saw its profits halve that year, in another sign that physical CD sales were in permanent decline. Product attributes valued by customers had shifted away from quality and physical ownership in favour of price and convenience. A copyrighted $20 CD containing 12 tracks – with perhaps only two or three of them genuinely of interest to the consumer – published by an official record label and distributed by a music retailer was deemed less valuable than a free pirated (or cheaper than $1) version of a single, downloaded within seconds from a peer-to-peer website or from the iTunes Store. The latter apparently accounted for 80% of the world's legal downloads by 2007, four years after its launch, no doubt because it gave its users the freedom to buy individual songs rather than the full 12-track opus.[63]

These changes in value appreciation by the music fan required a drastic change in cost structure, copyright management and organisational architecture. It necessitated a lean, innovative company willing to cannibalise or even discard its existing operations. The major international record companies were still running media outfits while the rest of the music world had morphed into a fast-growing technology-driven niche.

Hands and his senior executives were not just inexperienced in the music industry; they also had no relevant tech background. Newcomers, from Sean Parker at Napster to Steve Jobs at Apple, were fully immersed in internet culture. Terra Firma was certainly correct in its assessment that Eric Nicoli and the rest of the incumbent EMI executive team had failed to adapt to the new rules and needed to be replaced, but instead of appointing members of his own staff, Hands should have realised that what EMI needed was a complete cultural upheaval with the introduction of Silicon Valley techy types, not suits from London's financial district.

Had he read *The Innovator's Dilemma*, the seminal book published a decade earlier by Harvard professor and innovation expert Clayton Christensen, Hands would have realised that the internet represented a 'disruptive' technology that made preserving EMI as a traditional record label a doomed proposition. Previous advances, from the mechanical gramophone to electronic recording, from vinyl records to cassettes (the first vehicles of music piracy on a large scale) and CDs, could be characterised as 'sustaining' technologies, to use Christensen's terminology.

While it is beyond the scope of this case study to define in detail what separates sustaining technologies from disruptive ones, what we can say is that the latter introduce changes to the existing product or service's features that mainstream customers might not initially need or want, hence the difficulty for established operators to recognise the threat and adapt their offering.[*]

By revolutionising the music industry's value chain, internet start-ups and Apple introduced fundamental changes to the way music products and services were being marketed and distributed to the end user, thereby making it extremely challenging for established labels to maintain their market leadership unless they were prepared to redefine their business model. Record labels had capabilities, organisational structures and corporate cultures around values like sound quality, access to a wide choice of products and artists, and reliability. The internet was presenting consumers with a brand new set of values: low-price and convenience.

At first, the quality and speed of music-downloading platforms was abysmal, and a limited number of songs and artists were made available. In fact, internet penetration remained relatively low in most territories throughout the 1990s. In 1999 only 36% of Americans had internet access, and other developed countries were far behind the US. In the UK, Japan and Germany, only a fifth of the population had access that same year.[64] The vast majority of households were using slow dial-up connections. Broadband services like cable, fibre and DSL were first made available in businesses before being deliberately rolled out to homes. Five years later, as the internet penetration rate had reached two-thirds of the population in the US, Japan, Germany and the UK, web-based services were a compelling new way of delivering music to the end user, a way that was both a lot cheaper than CDs and extremely convenient. The compact disc, conceived in the early 1980s, had boosted demand thanks to significant improvement in listening quality. But it had done so for a hefty price hike. Despite slow web connections, digital downloads blossomed, eventually offering as good quality at a fraction of the cost. In just a decade, the internet revolution had crushed the music majors' oligopolistic position in production and distribution and rendered their model redundant, clunky, passé.[65]

It is correct that industry outsiders were more likely to succeed in reshaping EMI than old insiders like Nicoli – a thesis supported by Christensen's findings. The

---

[*]. Other experts speak of technological discontinuities to characterise disruptive innovation. Leaving aside consultant lingo, the terminology is not as important as the nature and impact of the technological change.

mistake that Hands made was to believe that any outsider would do. As stated, instead of recruiting finance pros or corporate experts, to solve the growth puzzle Hands should have targeted web specialists. Only they could put in place a new architecture to transform EMI into an internet-based music delivery platform and provide consumers a service that was in complete contrast to EMI's existing value network (low-price vs. quality, convenience vs. reliability). Instead, after months of looking for a new head for the group's recorded music arm, in July 2008 Terra Firma brought in Italian consumer goods executive Elio Leoni Sceti. What consumer sector was he an expert in? Health, hygiene and home products, after having spent 20 years at Procter & Gamble and Reckitt Benckiser.[66] How the new recruit, with no background in the media, music and internet sectors, was meant to lead the most audacious of corporate changeovers to meet the challenges of the digital age was not explained.

The fact that Hands had no prior experience in the tech world certainly helps to explain why he did not dare go that route. Instead, he used or considered using the only tricks that he and many a seasoned PE professional are accustomed to: cost cuts, asset disposals (reducing the roster of artists), contract renegotiations, refinancing, securitisation. All great financial and operating tools; all useless in the face of disruptive innovation.

Lost with all Hands

Contrary to popular belief, EMI's inability to adopt a web-based model was not a foregone conclusion. The company had experienced a similar threat to its records business and its very survival during the 1930s, not because of the economic depression, although it definitely had a marked impact on sales, but because of the emergence of radio broadcasting. As people started listening to music on the radio, the gramophone's ascendancy waned and record sales tanked. Luckily for its executives and employees, EMI was also a manufacturer of radio sets, so it managed to weather the storm. Sadly the business was not so well positioned in the late 1990s when internet adoption kicked in. But if its management had correctly identified the threat and opportunity that the web represented, the company could still have played a major role in online production and distribution.

With very few exceptions, the real success stories in the digital music space were all set up in the mid to late noughties – think iTunes (2003), YouTube (2005), Deezer (2006), and Spotify (2008). This tells us that EMI, along with the rest of the record industry, had a good five years after the emergence of internet music services to reconstruct its model around the new world of streaming and downloading. By 2004 digital downloads still only represented 1.5% of industry revenue in the US.[67] Rather than trying to invest early in loss-making but promising digital channels and platforms, the music majors were busy robbing each other's most profitable artists. It is unfortunate, as what Christensen has observed is that, when it comes to disruptive innovation, building a presence early on creates enormous competitive advantage, making it difficult for rivals to dislodge you. This compelling argument explains why in 2012, nine years after its conception, the iTunes Store's share of digital music sales in the US was still as high as 63%.[68]

Of course, the majors had not remained idle all those years: German media giant Bertelsmann had acquired Napster's assets out of bankruptcy in 2001, the same year that EMI, AOL, BMG and RealNetworks had launched subscription-based MusicNet. A year later Universal and Sony had created a joint venture (JV) called Pressplay to also provide music via subscription. But record companies had offered a small selection of artists on these platforms, without access to the catalogues of competing labels, and put too much emphasis on digital rights management to protect their legacy business. Spending fees on lawyers to take illegal file-sharers to court, the majors did not recognise that consumers primarily cared about price and convenience (how else to explain that piracy accounted for 40 billion worldwide downloads in 2008, meaning that 95% of all online music consumption was illegal?) and artists preferred to focus on concerts and merchandising in order to build a solid fanbase and drive music sales.[69]

Like radio broadcasting, the internet was a market discontinuity. Not only was it disruptive but it also replaced a key element of the record labels' core business: physical distribution of music. Record sales had initially fallen after the arrival of the radio. But after a while they had picked up again. Though it had appeared at first that radio broadcasting would supplant record playing, it turned out that both activities were complementary.

The internet offered more of a radical change: it aimed to disintermediate the record companies by substituting their existing distribution activities while still guaranteeing product ownership to the end-user. Digital downloading was a substitute to the physical distribution of CDs. To zero in on a problem of that magnitude, EMI needed to invest in internet delivery platforms, even if it meant losing money. And that was the issue.

For the music majors and independent labels alike, introducing their own internet solutions meant moving downmarket (to use Christensen's wording). Since all web-based digital download offerings were of lower-performance and generated lower margins than traditional recorded music activities – in the vast majority of cases, they were loss-making, and some, like Spotify, remained so, many years after their launch – how could the senior executives of publicly listed companies like EMI, Sony, Vivendi Universal and Warner Music explain such a move to their shareholders? The share prices of their companies would have suffered, and so would have these executives' stock options. Not ideal at a time when they were already under pressure to preserve margins due to the epidemic adoption of illegal peer-to-peer downloads.

Rather than reconfiguring their business model, the majors all chose the quick-fix route of cost-cutting. Also, it made more sense for incumbents to move upmarket, into the higher-margin segments of live performance and publishing. The latter activities (generating EBITDA margins of more than 30% at EMI against less than 10% in the recorded music business) had the added benefit of being highly recurrent, which brought consistency to cash flows – as remarked, that was the rationale behind Terra Firma's bid for EMI, and it was also the reason why in 2009 KKR had invested in BMG Rights Management, a publishing joint venture with media group Bertelsmann from which the American PE group had profitably exited four years later. How could a shift into unproven, loss-making internet activities get clearance at board level when very lucrative add-ons could be made elsewhere?

Unfortunately, such short-term decision-making is all too frequent in the face of disruptive technological change. While the cost structure had to be downsized in order to compete with leaner internet start-ups, the other side of the coin should have featured heavy investment in internet ventures that were likely to be money pits for years. With an excessive focus on short-term returns and under duress to quickly turn around EMI, Terra Firma was unlikely to have the patience for such a strenuous downmarket changeover. The brain drain among EMI veterans and the fast turnover of Terra Firma's appointees indicate that senior executives quickly became demotivated. Few outsiders who had initially bought into Hands's shakeup project hung around long enough to see it through: Mike Clasper stayed six months before becoming chairman of Her Majesty's Revenue & Customs; reorganisation architect Chris Roling stayed a bit more than a year as COO and finance director; COO for North America, Ronn Werre, made it 18 months in that role before leaving; head of A&R Nick Gatfield who had been pinched from Universal stayed two-and-a-half years; Leoni Sceti lasted less than two years as the recorded music division CEO; and Douglas Merrill lasted less than a year in his tech role.[70]

You can't always get what you want

EMI, one of the most colourful deals of the credit bubble, and sort of a consolation prize after Terra Firma had been outbid on Alliance Boots, turned out to be a crushing failure. Its much promised renaissance never occurred. As he was making his first incursion in the glamorous world of music, in 2007 Guy Hands promised that he would save EMI, mostly from itself. He was wrong.

His comment that EMI was the "worst company in the worst performing industry" might have been a slight exaggeration, even if many experienced music executives would have concurred.[71] However, after years of struggle marked by successive aborted or rejected merger talks with Warner, a handful of profit warnings, three restructuring plans, its impotence before the digital onslaught, and gradual market share erosion, EMI's ill-advised buyout only served to precipitate the venerable – but distinctly clapped-out – British company's demise.

In addition to the market trials to be expected for a business operating on a global stage and in a sector experiencing so much change, over the years EMI had also suffered from an unremitting exodus of world-class artists. Paul McCartney transferred his catalogue in the spring of 2010, as discussed earlier. Eighties band Queen left in late 2010 and Robbie Williams followed them to Universal a year later.[72] In March 2010, the company had even been successfully sued by Pink Floyd, one of its bestselling acts, over the unbundling of albums and the calculation of royalties for sales over the internet. EMI had failed to secure new artists capable of cracking the US market, the largest music market in the world. Its competitive position had inexorably petered out, to such an extent that, by the time it was broken up by Citi, EMI had lost its publishing leadership in the UK, its home market.

All this misfortune had reinforced the company's long-held moniker 'Every Mistake Imaginable', a tag often used and abused by journalists, rivals and employees alike, so long was the list of past corporate gaffes.[73] After becoming the largest failed LBO in European history, EMI's unflattering label is likely to stay in the record books. In a poetic way, the grand old institution that had been conceived out of economic necessity during the Great Depression – and had launched the careers of Elvis Presley and the Beatles among others – was taken apart against its will during the Great Recession as a symbol of our modern economy's taste for leverage. As records get gradually replaced by digital downloads, themselves gently supplanted by online and mobile streaming, maybe it is fitting that EMI, a vestige of the old music standard, should also disappear.

For Terra Firma, it proved a deal too far. EMI was not Guy Hands's first disastrous deal: back in 2003, Hands had just left Nomura when his £1.9 billion acquisition of hotel operator Le Meridien unravelled in the aftermath of the 11 September 2001 attacks. Terra Firma's chairman argued, after losing control of EMI in early 2011, that the reason behind EMI's blowing up in spectacularly public fashion was a timing issue, in reference to the sudden debacle in the credit and syndication markets. While this excuse can legitimately be used to explain Le Meridien's collapse – who could have foreseen the 9/11 terrorist attacks and their impact on hotel occupancy? – that was not the issue with the buyout of EMI. Having wagered a third of his LPs' money at or near the peak of the bubble into an industry he had never invested in before, Hands publicly stated his mea culpa in 2013 when declaring: "always ensure diversity in your wider portfolio".[74] Unable to raise a follow-on fund after knocking on LPs' doors for the best part of four years, in 2015 he reluctantly admitted that he would from now on invest his own fortune into future buyouts, on a deal-by-deal basis.

With his appetite for beaten-up companies no doubt less pronounced after the EMI adventure, Hands was left with the big task of rebuilding his reputation. Public records indicate that the performance of the Terra Firma Capital Partners III fund was very poor indeed. That vintage displayed a negative IRR of 11.5% as of 31 March 2015.[75] Between January 2007 and December 2014, limited partners could have earned 4.5% per annum, with dividends reinvested, by committing capital to the blue-chip FTSE 100.

The FTSE 250 index is also a good proxy. Sadly, this indicator does not soften the blow since total returns for mid-cap British listed companies averaged 7.6% a year over the same time period. Of course, these market returns are shown unlevered, so the picture for Terra Firma's investors is even bleaker than exposed here.

* * *

If we had to sum up where Hands and his troops got it wrong, the key points would be as follows:

1. They presumed – Hands himself publicly stated that he believed – that EMI was undervalued. As demonstrated in the TXU story and in the separate case studies on delistings (see Part Five), it is dangerous to assume that market experts who have been following a stock for several years are missing a trick by rating a company below

its true worth. Temporary mispricing can happen, especially after a crash, but it rarely occurs when markets are in a bubble, as they were in 2007. In reality, EMI's previous management (led by Nicoli) had not fully recognised the deterioration of value induced by the significant U-turn in market growth from 2001 onwards. Universal Music had booked €1.37 billion of impairment losses in 2003 'due to declining market conditions'; that same year EMI had only posted £12 million of goodwill impairment. The £1 billion asset impairment posted by EMI in March 2009 was a good six years behind the curve. At the time of its 2007 delisting, EMI was hugely overstating its asset value. It was overpriced, not a bargain as inferred by Terra Firma's post-buyout PR. It took two years for Hands to publicly admit that he had "paid too much".[76]

2. To state the obvious, to lever up any business at a double-digit EBITDA multiple is punchy; to do so with a company that has experienced revenue erosion for half a decade in the face of disruptive innovation is asking for trouble. Given its mediocre financial performance and its weak strategic positioning, EMI was not an LBO candidate. A business losing market share in a declining sector very much belonged to the old order of corporate mergers followed by an extensive reorganisation exercise of layoffs, product rationalisation, process synergies and business model rejuvenation. We saw that Terra Firma tried its luck at the game of reconstruction, but this is not to be attempted when the target is overloaded with expensive debt.

   Turnarounds are risky endeavours that require flexibility; something that high leverage cannot provide. The EMI buyout was effectively doomed from the start. A fact that experienced investors like Guy Hands and his colleagues should have known. But they seem to have found out the hard way: when filing his suit against Citi in late 2009, Hands admitted that EMI's potential was "being constrained by its debt".[77] With cash being diverted to meet interest payments, and with equity injections made necessary to cure impending covenant breaches, EMI was unable to invest in the sourcing of new artists, the nurturing of existing acts, or the development of digital solutions.

3. Instead of desperately trying to keep full control of EMI, including by launching a lawsuit against its lender, Terra Firma should have negotiated a partial but sizeable debt write-down with Citi in exchange for a meaningful stake in the company as soon as it realised that the turnaround would take longer than anticipated. By early 2009, after the restructuring team packed up and the board

of Maltby was revamped, there was no question that the only way forward was equitisation. Sharing ownership through a debt-for-equity swap would have provided the necessary breathing room. Had Terra Firma and Citi been on better terms they could have given EMI a second chance at securing solvency, remaining independent and seeing its transformation through.

4. None of the LBO's key participants – Hands, Terra Firma's employees appointed as interim operators, chief executive Leoni Sceti, or advisers in a supervisory or restructuring function – had prior experience in the music world. The issue wasn't just that Hands was not a music guy and had a limited grasp of talent management, though undeniably a basic appreciation of the sector's distinctive creativity would have helped. In addition, he and his associates knew little about the impact of the internet, the key driver behind music in the 21st century. The main strategic challenge facing record labels in 2007 was technological innovation. Digital piracy had become stubbornly entrenched, and neither the music industry nor regulatory bodies ever managed to formulate an effective solution to eradicate it. In 2012, illegal free music still represented half to two-thirds of digital downloads in most geographies, and 20% of fixed-line internet users worldwide regularly accessed services offering copyright-infringing music.[78]

Knowledge of the internet and all its possibilities in terms of music digitalisation would have been more valuable than fast-moving consumer goods expertise. The only senior operational hire in that space was former Google CIO, 37-year-old Douglas Merrill, who became head of EMI's online activities in the spring of 2008 and stayed less than a year. Without a senior exec sitting on the board and championing EMI's digital initiative, internet solutions were always going to play second fiddle to traditional recordings and physical distribution services.[79]

5. What Christensen's research tells us is that incumbents that successfully transition their business during a period of disruptive technological change do so by setting up separate entities acting independently from the main corporation. Instead of creating a new digital division controlled centrally, EMI needed to establish a brand new company, most likely operating from a US base since the rate of adoption of internet-based services was greater there. Staff expertise was also much advanced in America due to the many products introduced by promising early-stage ventures. Such a structure would

have been operationally and culturally different from the existing EMI group. It would also have operated according to a distinct value network, serving a separate set of consumers (keen to access music cheaply and conveniently, and not the least interested in building a collection of CDs). To try to make two different cultures with two distinct profit models coexist within a single organisation is extremely hard, if not impossible.[80]

6. Hands set up a complex, top-heavy, matrix-like organisation with global business units, just like he was used to doing for other portfolio assets. Members of the supervisory and restructuring boards as well as more junior staff were parachuted in for special missions (35 Terra Firma staff had reportedly been seconded to EMI in 2008), but their actions frequently alienated customer-facing employees and third parties like artist managers. In a presentation taking place in Munich, Germany, at the PE industry's annual gathering called SuperReturn, Hands had bluntly stated: "What we are doing is taking the power away from the A&R guys and putting it with the suits." This bureaucratic, hierarchical configuration generated tension between the acts and the straight-laced financial consultants. To reengineer tangible-asset-rich companies like pubs and hotels is very different from managing creative talent. Artists and their agents do not take lightly to being bossed around or to seeing the marketing budget for their new album release cut back in the interest of frugality.[81]

What is likely to have influenced Hands in his decision to buy EMI in the first place is the excellent short-term performance that the three backers of Warner Music's LBO had generated by the time the EMI auction was in full swing in May 2007. Three years into their investment, Bain Capital, Providence and TH Lee had already made $3.2 billion on their initial $1.3 billion equity outlay – receiving $350 million in dividends six months after their purchase and $680 million a couple of months later through the issuance of a junk bond, and selling some of their shares after the 2005 IPO. All this had been achieved in part by laying off 20% of Warner's workforce, and terminating contracts with nearly half of the artists on its roster.[82] Terra Firma's roadmap was not that imaginative, really, but it miscarried soon after the public-to-private.

Not so much a quick flip, more like a quick flop

There is an unwritten rule in the PE world: the success of a buyout is determined within the first six months of the transaction. If at the end of that inaugural period the investee company is on budget and meets its covenants, if its managers have delivered on the business plan prepared pre-buyout, then the LBO is likely to turn out well. Of course, a freak event can always happen, but barring such unexpected occurrence, the transaction should provide a decent return for its backers.

During the half-year following EMI's buyout and delisting:

- Terra Firma syndicated only a fraction of its £1.5 billion equity ticket;

- Citi remained the sole lender as no other institution wanted any part of the loans – mainly because of the sudden credit market deterioration, but also due to EMI's risk profile and the aggressive cov-lite nature of the debt;

- Preeminent acts like Radiohead, Paul McCartney and Rolling Stones walked to rival record labels. Pop singer Joss Stone launched a legal battle to try to free herself from a three-album contract she had with EMI;[83]

- The group had not made any add-on, failing to acquire in particular leading classical music publisher Boosey & Hawkes (representing the catalogues of Igor Stravinsky among others) when PE firm HgCapital had sold the business in April 2008. The same month EMI had seen UK publisher Chrysalis reject its £100 million-plus offer. Without a build-up strategy, it was difficult to see how the music group would grow significantly;[84]

- Hands had yet to attract a new CEO and no serious hire had been made to remodel the music company along a more tech-savvy framework;

- EMI's results were from day one prodigiously behind budget, leading to Terra Firma's £1.5 billion shareholder loan being valued at 70 pence on the pound on 31 March 2008, seven months after the PE group taking control of the music group.

Halfway through the first year of ownership, it was evident to experienced PE professionals that the EMI buyout was failing. Knowing what was coming, Terra Firma had tried to renegotiate the terms of the Citi loans from the outset. In view of the market mayhem and the chaotic internal shakeup, EMI could not operate with a tight covenant schedule. The general impression that Hands and his team had taken a punt when buying the record company was reinforced when details surfaced that they had code-named the LBO transaction process 'Project Dice' while an internal long-term plan to merge with rival Warner Music had been labelled 'Project Poker'.[85] It all seemed like a bit of a gamble, and maybe not just in retrospect.

The show must go on

While Terra Firma aims to survive the consequences of its messy foray into the world of music, it is not clear where the remaining three music majors will be in a decade or two. The evidence suggests that their catalogues – their cash cows for the last 20 years – will remain attractive enough to justify a securitisation and LBO transaction. The recorded music activities are a different story. In 2011, after years of a relentless decline, physical sales accounted for less than half of the music industry's revenues in the US, down from two-thirds three years earlier and 98% in 2001 (see Figure 6.2).

Figure 6.2: U.S. Recorded music revenues by format (1999-2011)

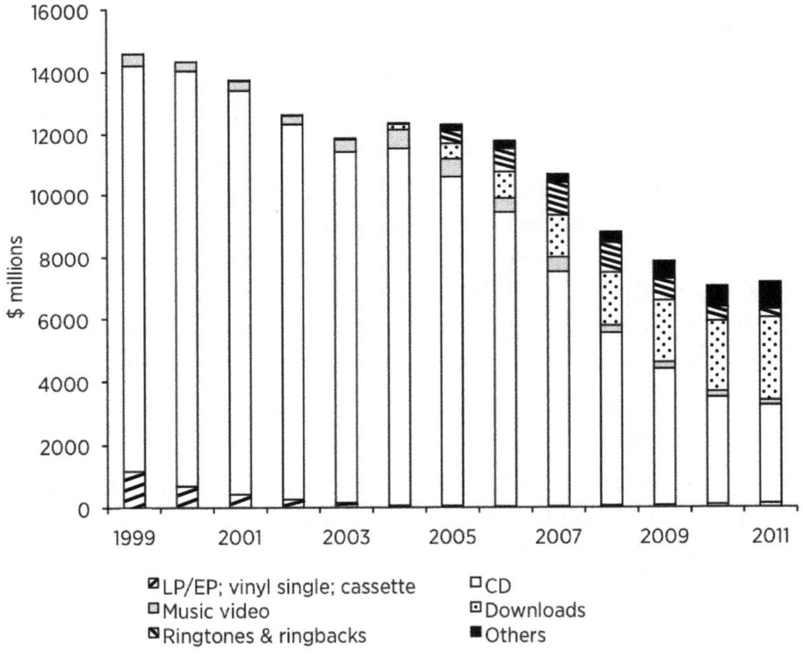

Source: Recording Industry Association of America (RIAA)

Music has always played a central part in human lives, not just as a form of communication or for its entertainment value, but also as a differentiating factor between cultures and civilisations, giving each of them a unique identity.

To say that it will always be part of society is stating the obvious. What is less permanent is the technique we use to broadcast it. Until late in the 19th century, music was a live art form. You had to be within hearing distance of the performer to capture it. Then, in 1877, the phonograph was devised by genius inventor Thomas Edison as the first instrument capable of recording sound. The gramophone introduced by Emile Berliner in the 1890s progressed from Edison's brainchild. The rest, as they say, is history.

The future of music as an art form is certain, and if anything its production and distribution will be amplified by the still nascent digital revolution. Artists now have more options to disseminate their creation, and the end consumer is keen to choose the cheapest access channel. The persistent, gradual erosion of the record labels' market share through the leakage of royalties indicates that the industry's value chain has switched over to new players like subscription service offerings Rhapsody, music-on-demand provider Deezer (partly funded by the three music majors and Len Blavatnik, and apparently worth more than $1 billion in 2015), streaming jukebox Spotify (valued at $8.5 billion in June 2015, despite losses of $200 million on $1.35 billion of sales in 2014), *à-la-carte* downloading platforms iTunes Store and Amazon MP3, and radio service provider Pandora (with a market valuation of $3.5 billion in April 2015). And in 2010 the world's largest concert promoter Live Nation and ticket-seller Ticketmaster merged to extend their hold over the live music sector. This new generation of producers and distributors, proposing a more affordable and reliable service than the traditional record labels' offering, could eventually dominate the music world.[86]

Although many newcomers are still to make a profit and seem somewhat overvalued in the current tech bubble landscape, it is these new growth players that might well attract interest from future LBO fund managers and see their cash flows – once these exist and become predictable – repackaged as tradable securities. Incumbents Universal, Sony and Warner must devise a sustainable revenue model or they might eventually get renamed the three music 'minnows' and be absorbed as nice add-ons by tech content-delivery specialists. Music retail chains like HMV, which opened its first store on London's busiest shopping avenue Oxford Street with great fanfare in 1921, have already vanished in many parts of the world. Few of these physical chains survived the advent of online distribution: American retailer Tower Records filed for Chapter 11 bankruptcy in 2006, while in the UK the main players Zavvi (ex-Virgin Megastores) and HMV were put into administration in 2008 and 2013 respectively. Will traditional music producers follow their example? Once upon a time offering cash-flow predictability, it is possible that, in a not-so-distant future, record labels will be remembered as relics of a bygone pre-internet era and disappear the EMI way.

PART FOUR
Repurchases or Relapse Buyouts: Seller's Remorse

T HE FIRST THREE PARTS OF THE BOOK HAVE ALREADY shown that, after 40 years of activity, LBOs have become truly diverse in their nature. All the ingredients are there to demonstrate that, on some transactions, PE firms have lost the plot. There is, however, no better illustration of the industry's whimsical dealmaking obsession than its increasing taste for repurchases – when a financial sponsor buys back a company that it had owned in the past, often quite recently. Seller's remorse, which I would also term the relapse syndrome, seems to happen with increasing frequency in the well-trodden American and European markets.

Like secondary buyouts, relapse buyouts (RBOs) are a by-product of the industry's stage of maturity. I am being facetious when I say that PE investors suffer from seller's remorse. The reality is far worse: some LBO fund managers have run out of ideas, become lazy or lost their competitive edge. Whatever the reasons behind RBOs, they cannot hide the perpetrators' desperation to appear busy and to earn fees by putting money to work.

Despite the increasing frequency of buybacks, it is unclear what their true economic impact and performance are. No one knows whether they are beneficial to LPs, or whether the latter should incorporate in their investment agreements a clause banning, curtailing or setting limits on such practice. Of course, there are plenty of examples where relapse buyouts not only go according to plan but exceed expectations. Still, the risks associated with these transactions are often overlooked by the financial sponsors because, as our case studies will show, investment executives feel that they know the assets extremely well, which enables them to outbid any interested party.

It would have been easy to include Frans Bonhomme in the section on secondary buyouts, or in the case studies related to quick flips. Equally, PHS belonged as much to the listing-delisting chapters of Part Five or to Part Two on asset-flipping. But both are very good examples of why repurchases are not such great bets. If, after having read the PHS and Frans Bonhomme cases, you are still unconvinced that RBOs are the product of overconfidence, feel free to jump directly to Chapter 12; the Seat Pagine Gialle story is sure to help you make up your mind.

CHAPTER 7
PHS – Washed-up

P HS IS WHAT IS ENIGMATICALLY CALLED A WORKPLACE
service provider. In short, it delivers the products and services that offer
support to an organisation. These activities are not just considered non-
core, they have in fact nothing to do with the clients' business, and yet they are
meant to increase workers' productivity, maximise efficiency, and reduce costs.
Workplace service providers deal with waste recycling and removal (such as used
syringes at a hospital), data scanning, storage and shredding (ever wondered
where the documents you discard end up?), crate rental and packaging, interior
and exterior landscaping (that's where the plants in your office come from),
testing and compliance (look at your employer's fire alarm system), laundry
equipment and workwear, water coolers, washroom services (think toilet roll
holders), and much more.

Under the name Tack Retail Consultants, PHS started life as a washroom
sanitary disposal provider on 14 August 1963. Founded by brothers Alfred and
George Tack, bit by bit, and organically, the British company expanded its line
of offering with soap dispensers, paper towel dispensers and hand dryers.

Primary and secondary buyout

Headquartered in the Welsh town of Caerphilly, 7.5 miles north of Cardiff,
Personnel Hygiene Services was the subject of a management buyout in October
1995 following the death of the founders. Investment company Electra Fleming
paid £42.9 million for the supplier of sanitary products, and supported the
group's external growth via the acquisition of several businesses, including
flooring specialist Stardust Mats in 1996 and plant service provider Interscape
two years later.[1]

In July 1999 PHS was sold for £215 million in a secondary buyout to
Charterhouse Development Capital, yielding over £120 million or six times cash-
on-cash returns to Electra. PHS had turned into the archetypal leveraged buyout
of the 1990s, consolidating the very fragmented office services industry while

creating considerable value for its PE backer through underlying performance enhancement – its operating profits had gone from £4.1 million to £12.1 million during Electra's holding period without much need for irresponsible leverage. Electra's returns had been helped by a positive multiple-arbitrage on exit: a business acquired for 10.5 times operating profits (that is, EBITA) in 1995 was sold at a 17.8 times multiple four years later.[2]

Charterhouse's SBO did not deviate in its strategy from the path taken under Electra's leadership. PHS kept on buying smaller rivals and expanding into new segments of the support services market. In October 1999 PHS paid £6.4 million for Jardinerie, a supplier of plants trading on London's junior Alternative Investment Market (AIM). The following year the group acquired the UK distribution rights of Waterlogic, a maker, installer and vendor of mains-fed water coolers.[3]

In June 2001, less than two years after taking over PHS, Charterhouse flipped the company on the London Stock Exchange for a market value of £414 million or 80p a share, cashing in £85 million in exchange for selling off most of its 84% stake. Despite the short holding period the PE firm had returned twice its original investment and retained a 12.7% stake in the listed entity (selling it a year later at 94p a share). Under Charterhouse's ownership PHS had upgraded its cash-generation potential, with operating margins rising from less than 20% to 27.5% over the previous two fiscal years; no doubt a sign that the group's senior executives were reaping the benefits of their vertical consolidation strategy, being able *inter alia* to cross-sell their washroom products, water coolers and flooring services to a diverse set of 82,500 customers.

Using the £236 million of proceeds to reduce its debt to £55 million, PHS's executive team continued its ambitious acquisition strategy, buying for instance the plumbed-in drinking water provider UK Water Group for £6.4 million and crate-rental specialist Teacrate for £15.3 million in 2002. In its 2001-02 fiscal year, the company bought businesses for a total £40 million, before spending £37.5 million to purchase 16 companies the following year, and over £61 million for 18 acquisitions in the year to 31 March 2004.[4] In 2003 it acquired washroom service providers Airstream and Johnson for £25 million and £13.7 million respectively, as well as waste management company Wastetech. And in 2004 it bought shredding company Securishred.

Despite this frenetic corporate activity, the group occasionally failed to beat analysts' expectations. In April 2003 its stock fell to 61.5p, or 23% below its IPO price of June 2001, because it announced that its 22% jump in profits would fall slightly below market consensus. And in October 2004 management disappointed investors once more by claiming that a change in product mix – read more lower-margin services as a proportion of total sales – and the introduction of customer service improvements had affected profitability. The stock duly fell 5% to 72p, or 10% below its introductory price.[5]

Irrespective of pricing pressure, PHS was hugely cash generative. It had a healthy balance sheet. Its management was disciplined in picking value-accretive acquisitions and, as a result, its market position had strengthened. It is worth pointing out at this stage that the business's performance was partly helped by trading issues encountered by its main rival, market leader Rentokil. More on that later. Apart from its stock performance, PHS was doing great. Too well, in fact, to be left alone by PE firms, constantly on the lookout for targets able to service piles of debt.

On 18 May 2005, JPMorgan Partners, the PE arm of the American bank, was reported to have approached the business support services group. Shares shot up 12% to 98p on the news.[6] To fulfil their fiduciary duties towards their shareholders, PHS's senior executives retained the services of investment bank Merrill Lynch to organise a formal auction. Within a month, a long list of private equity's nobility was rumoured to be looking at the asset, including US-headquartered Clayton Dubilier, British outfit BC Partners, and a name that would have been recognised as management's likely favourite: Charterhouse.

In its four years as a listed company, PHS had spent over £160 million in acquisitions, but as a consequence it held over £140 million of loans on its balance sheet. Because of the consolidation strategy followed by management, revenues had shot up from less than £100 million in the year to March 2001 to £190 million four years later, while operating margins had risen from 27.5% to 29.3%. Yet the company's share price had hardly moved over the period, sitting in the mid 80s ahead of the JPMorgan bid, compared to 80p on flotation. Its enterprise value had gone from £460 million at the time of IPO to £600 million pre-bid, hence the EV multiple had dropped from 17 times to 11 times operating earnings over the same period. In theory, this made PHS a prime candidate for a takeover.

Upon reporting its results for the financial year ended 31 March 2005, PHS had to confess that profitability erosion at its core hygiene division was enduring, with operating margins down from 45% to 43% year-on-year. Top-line growth for the entire group was still in the double digits, but at 13.6% it was at a much slower pace than the 18% recorded the previous year and 22% two years earlier. Perhaps the most striking was that the group's operating profits had displayed single-digit growth for the first time since the IPO – the previous five years had all registered increases of more than 20%.[7]

The information, though, did little to deter potential buyers. After a six-week auction process, on 8 July 2005 Charterhouse's 116.36 pence per share bid, including a final dividend, was victorious. Giving the business a market capitalisation of £600 million, Charterhouse was taking private its former portfolio company four years after selling it. Including debts of over £140 million, the enterprise value of £740 million granted the target an EBITDA multiple of 10.7 times. The LBO structure, predictably, was much different. It included £500 million of bank debt and a shareholder loan from Charterhouse. The latter controlled 80% of the company, with management holding the rest.[8] PHS's debt-to-equity ratio had moved up from 20/80 to 67/33. But it was just the beginning.

Charterhouse's relapse

The two years that followed the public-to-private transaction saw the cleaning-services group perform extremely well, owing to the robust growth of the British economy. Naturally, management persisted in spending a large chunk of its acquisition facility and spare cash to purchase smaller rivals. As a consequence, revenue grew by 19% in the year to March 2006 and by 22% the following year. The group's operating profit cash conversion ratio – a key performance metric used by management to highlight and monitor the cash-generating potential of the business – was consistently above 110%. Operating margins were maintained between 28% and 29%, somewhat lower than the 29% to 30.5% encountered between 2002 and 2004, but strong nonetheless.

On the back of this solid accomplishment, in the first half of 2007 Charterhouse turned to PHS's lenders to put in motion a dividend recap procedure, the first pillar of PE value maximisation. The timing, however, was quite unfortunate. The months of May and June saw debt markets cool down to such an extent that there were rumours that Charterhouse might have to scrap plans to take out a dividend because of difficulties securing the refinancing – the Credit Crunch was starting to have repercussions even on LBOs offering predictable cash flows.[9]

Even so, on 31 July 2007 the group successfully recapitalised its balance sheet, repaying bank debt totalling £687 million due under the old facilities, and £123.5 million of Charterhouse's shareholder loan notes. The new leverage ratio was a reflection of the times: bank debts now represented 75% of the capital structure. While the underwriters initially struggled to syndicate the new loan package, in October they relaunched a reduced £955 million deal with discounts in the range of 96.5 to 97.5 cents on the dollar.[10] Charterhouse managed to reduce its shareholder loan exposure from £333 million in the year ended March 2007 to £250 million as at 31 March 2008.[11] Having now recouped approximately half its initial investment, Charterhouse could look forward to making a tasty profit on the deal, especially because its loans were yielding a cumulative 15% annual interest rate. But things do not always work according to plan, no matter how well intentioned.

*   *   *

It is fair to say that PHS's July 2005 take-private had occurred at a full valuation, and its recapitalisation two years later did not allow any room for mishaps in the management's business plan. Yet, despite the unfavourable credit environment, PHS continued to do well for a while. In the 12 months to March 2009, turnover grew by another 16%, helping all the earnings yardsticks beat past records: both EBITDA and operating profit were up 12%. The fact that the group had purchased 18 smaller companies was beneficial, and it was quickly building a solid market position in a new segment: the testing and calibration of medical equipment. However, this M&A spree had cost £70 million and the group had been forced to draw down a large chunk of its acquisition facility.

Without further external funding, the following year saw a noticeable slowdown in corporate activity: just four companies were gobbled up for a total price tag of £14 million. Another factor behind this subdued dealmaking was the Great Recession, which had started to bite in the second half of 2008, after the collapse of Lehman Brothers and the ensuing financial crisis. The after-effect of this deceleration was instantaneous. When PHS issued its annual report for the year to March 2010, revenue and operating profit were flat. The management team's growth story was facing its first hurdle.

Oddly, it is with this sort of recent lacklustre performance that Charterhouse decided to put the business on the market. In January 2011 Goldman Sachs was retained to shop the cleaning service provider around at a £1.5 billion valuation, or 12 times EBITDA. What was amusing about this headline was not just that Charterhouse was trying to flog its portfolio company with a positive multiple-arbitrage (having taken the business off the quote for 10.7 times EBITDA four years earlier); it was that Goldman was reportedly offering a debt package worth six times EBITDA for a business carrying at the time the equivalent of 7.5 times in bank loans on its balance sheet. What the American bank was in effect admitting was that PHS was overleveraged.[12] This notion was not shaken by the fact that, when PHS's March 2011 year-end results came out, they exhibited single-digit growth for both sales and earnings. It was encouraging, but far from sufficient to attract bidders in a weak economic context: in 2010, the UK economy had grown at a respectable 1.9% rate, but the pace had slowed down noticeably in the second half of 2010 and first half of 2011.

Throughout 2011, Charterhouse and Goldman tried to find a buyer for the asset, but no one was prepared to take the plunge. The eurozone crisis, and in particular the risk that Greece might have to default on its sovereign debt, be asked to drop the euro and revert to its old currency the drachma, had seen international debt markets freeze once more. Several PE transactions had therefore collapsed or were postponed. It was also obvious that, in view of current trading, PHS had been grossly overpriced. So, in January 2012, the buyout firm did the right thing and reduced its asking price. Except that it only shaved off a measly £100 million.[13] Once again it was unrealistic, as the hygiene services group's annual results showed too well two months later. The group's underperformance had already forced the board of directors to introduce the internal restructuring of certain divisions, but that had proved insufficient to bring PHS back to health.

Shortly before the fiscal year end, in March 2012, after a 14-year tenure, Chief Executive Peter Cohen was defenestrated, taking the blame for a misbegotten buy-and-build strategy that had lost momentum and failed to deliver the sort of performance predictability indispensable to a company nursing a leverage of 7.3 times EBITDA and 8.9 times operating profit.[14] In the 12 months to March 2012, despite a 6% jump in revenue on the prior year, EBITDA had been flat while operating profit had dipped 2.7% – the first fall since PHS had abandoned its family-ownership structure in the 1990s. Keen to generate cash in any way possible, in February 2011 the debt-strapped office services group had even entered into a sale and leaseback agreement for its £3.6 million headquarters in South Wales.[15]

Sweeping changes

After the departure of its long-standing CEO – a 10% shareholder – PHS had to pause and reassess its options. A sale of the business was now compromised. In any case, trading continued to get worse, so Charterhouse needed to mull things over. The next 12 months followed a typical LBO restructuring blueprint: downward revaluation of assets, redundancies, and operational restructuring of certain activities. The management team, led by new Chief Exec Gareth Rhys Williams from May 2012 onwards,[16] also designed a new strategy, not so much focused on external growth – although bolt-on acquisitions in selected markets were still welcome – but on operating efficiency. The aim was to promote customer service and product innovation, reduce customer churn, and focus on cross-selling. Recently, the group had met a series of corporate scandals that had dangerously tarnished its image: the appalling customer service record at its waste collection and recycling divisions Wastetech and All Clear had led to an increase in customer attrition. An investigation by national broadcaster the BBC had even divulged that Wastetech had been embroiled in 92 court cases with customers claiming unfair treatment.[17]

In the 2013 fiscal year, the new management team announced that it had decided to tighten "acquisition procedures and hurdle rates". As the company stated when releasing its results:

> "For many years, PHS enjoyed an extended period of excellent financial performance and growth. However, the model which delivered this was not sustainable and, particularly as the market environment became more challenging, organic growth faltered. The greater pressures on cost that our industry has faced have been largely passed on to customers, at a time when we have also faced more competition, both on the level of service offered, and on pricing. In order to respond to this, the new management team has focussed on formulating a new strategy to deliver sustainable future growth."[18]

What this strategy entailed was finally to start running the group as one entity, if only to ensure that customers did not have to deal with as many sales forces or receive as many invoices as there were PHS units. Not surprisingly, given the number of acquisitions completed since the Electra days, the group had done a great job in consolidating the support services sector by building scale across customer segments (it had over 250,000 customers in 2011 compared to less than 85,000 ten years earlier) and product verticals.

However, PHS now operated across 17 service lines – from replica plants, washroom services, mats, shredding, and records management, to medical device testing, specialist waste services such as light bulbs and aerosols, and water coolers. Its management team had hardly taken time to pause and rationalise operations, derive synergies other than low-hanging fruit, and consider whether acquisitions were all value accretive to the same degree. For instance, the move into waste collection and disposal had forced a re-rating of the PHS stock. The group's primary hygiene activities were mid-40% operating-margin segments, while waste management generated EBITA margins in the mid 20s. The economic recession post-2008 had forced governments and businesses to tighten their purse strings, demanding price reductions from service providers like PHS. The group's traditional hygiene division had always been quite resilient to adverse economic conditions. But while hand dryers were needed in washrooms no matter how severe the recession, pot plants, document storage, welcome mats and waste recycling were products and services that customers could entirely do without, or skimp on.

PHS's waning financial and operational performance in its fiscal years to March 2012 and March 2013 had led to a rapid deterioration of its balance sheet, so in October 2012 the company agreed with its lenders an Amend and Extend (A&E) proposal in order to reschedule its bank facilities until 2016. In January 2013, bearing the blame for the messy financial position, John Skidmore, the finance director who had served under previous CEO Peter Cohen, was unceremoniously replaced.

Despite the new management team's initiatives, the company's performance had worsened. Embarrassingly, just six months after having reset its debt covenants and commitments, PHS was delivering worse results than anticipated. For the first time since its first MBO in 1995, the company recorded negative top-line growth, with revenue down 0.2% in the year ended 31 March 2013, or minus 1.5% when excluding acquisitions. EBITDA had dropped by 9% and operating profit by more than 13%. On top of a £70 million impairment charge – in part related to its All Clear clinical waste division, and because of issues at its Spanish and Irish units – exceptional restructuring costs totalled £19 million. Post-exceptionals, PHS had actually produced an operating loss. Most of the pain had come from the waste management division, where sales had decreased by nearly 6% and operating profit had halved. Net debt, including shareholder loan notes, had reached £1.44 billion, or 12.7 times EBITDA and 16.3 times operating profit. Bank borrowings alone sat at £930 million or 10.4 times operating profit. The group's financial position was getting extremely uncomfortable. Two months after the year end, Charterhouse was forced to pump in £13 million of cash to cure the group's debt-to-earning covenant. PHS was officially in distress, unable to pass its covenant tests.

While its investee company was crumbling under piles of debt, Charterhouse had not forgotten to charge its bog-standard 15% compound interest rate on the new equity tranche.[19] However, PHS, which had earned the buyout fund manager more than twice its money between 1999 and 2002, was not going to be such a success the second time around. In their 'going concern' statement that forms part of the annual report, the directors were able to confirm that, following the successful restructuring of the group's debt facilities and the resulting reduction in indebtedness, they were confident that the company would "have in place sufficient funding to enable it to continue trading".[20] But it was all too optimistic. As the saying goes, sometimes things must get worse before they get better.

The management team's various attempts to quickly return PHS to health proved unsuccessful. Throughout 2013 and the early part of 2014, trading deteriorated further. Rhys Williams had been recruited to put the business back on the growth track – his plan had been to triple the company over the following ten years.[21] What PHS needed, though, was a complete reorganisation. It had expanded too quickly: between 1998 and 2012, turnover had grown from less than £50 million to £420 million. It was time to focus on rationalisation and profit maximisation. And that called for a new leadership style and, more importantly, a very different capital structure; one not needlessly weighed down by debt.

At the March 2014 year end, revenue was down a further 0.5% (1.1% when excluding acquisitions). Earnings, though, had nose-dived: EBITDA was off 20% and EBITA 27.7%. Both were back to their 2006 levels, a year when sales had been about half those of 2014. Apart from the data storage division, all parts of the business were in retreat: profits in hygiene services had fallen by 10% while in the workplace unit (which included plants, crates and water coolers) and in waste management they had collapsed by a quarter and a third respectively. PHS had only closed two acquisitions that year, so the underlying organic performance could no longer be kept hidden.

In the summer of 2014 PHS's lenders and Charterhouse finalised their protracted discussions. Having breached its financial covenant in relation to its debt-to-earnings ratio for the testing periods ending on 5 January 2014, 30 March 2014 and 20 July 2014, it would not be an embellishment to say that the group urgently needed a financial restructuring. In early July, reports emerged that PHS had hired the services of investment bankers and restructuring experts Rothschild to find a buyer and help lenders work out how much the firm was worth ahead of debt-restructuring negotiations. For several months various credit fund managers had plotted to take control of the troubled cleaning service provider. The ineluctable handover occurred in September, when several distressed-debt investors, led by PE group KKR and including asset manager M&G and hedge funds Monarch, Anchorage and Halcyon, agreed to bring total bank debt down to £373.5 million.[22]

In exchange for writing off £560 million and turning the remaining debt into a PIK loan, the lenders were taking ownership of PHS. The latter had finally succumbed to common LBO-related ailments: a stretched capital structure, imperceptibly tightening covenant tests, and the relentless demands for continued profit growth. In an interview with the *Business in Wales* magazine in June 2013, Rhys Williams had declared that the £900 million of bank debts PHS held in its books were "totally manageable".[23] It turns out that they were not.

Partly because he had been appointed by the previous PE shareholder, and partly due to his profile as a growth-focused CEO, on 20 November 2014 Rhys Williams was removed by the lender-owners. For the second time in less than three years, PHS was changing CEO with the appointment of Justin Tydeman, an experienced operator with former chief exec and finance director roles whose docket certainly included profit and cash-flow improvements. Rhys Williams's ten-year growth plan had been short-lived. What PHS needed was an almost maniacal focus on the bottom line; not only so that the company could eventually repay its bank loans – given that they were of a payment-in-kind nature, they were only repayable when PHS got sold – but because this is what value creation is all about.

A question of value

It would be tempting to take the view that PHS was underrated by the market when Charterhouse delisted it in 2005. After all, its share value of 85p or so had hardly moved from its 80p introductory price of mid-2001. However, in a scenario only too frequent (refer to the case studies of Debenhams, DX, eDreams and Foxtons), it seems that the PE-backed IPO had been inflated. On 27 June 2001, its first day of trading, PHS had even seen its stock drop 5% below the 80p listing price. Charterhouse had already been forced to reduce the price to that level after potential institutional investors had called the 110p-to-150p suggested range excessive. Like so many overpriced PE-sponsored stock offerings, the 17 times operating earnings set in the summer of 2001 had eventually reverted to the mean.[24]

Is it possible that Charterhouse's multiple paid in July 2005 (13.6 times EBITA) had also been a tad expensive, especially because the £750 million headline price was more than two-thirds financed with debt? Back then, one of the equity analysts following the stock had claimed that a value of 110 pence per share would have been 'pushing things'.[25] With a 115p bid, Charterhouse had not been deterred. As explained in the case studies recounting take-privates (Caesars, DX, EMI and TXU), PE firms' tendency to consider that public markets are mispricing an asset often proves greatly misconstrued.

There were several reasons why PHS had never been much appreciated by the public markets. First, its double-digit growth was dependent on management's ability to find new acquisition targets. Otherwise, demand for sexy products and services like doormats, soap dispensers and waste recycling was determined by the economy. It should not therefore grow much faster than GDP. Though management's buying spree does not allow us to precisely assess organic growth in the early years, it is fair to assume that, aside from winning contracts from competitors when they came up for tender, the potential for revenue expansion was not significant. Upon reviewing PHS's annual reports during Charterhouse's ownership period, Figure 7.1 demonstrates that top-line growth between 2008 and 2014 was minimal when excluding acquisition-related revenue upswings.

Second, barriers to entry in the sector were low. Even if in the early noughties PHS boasted a renewal rate of more than 85% in its hygiene division, its poor track record with cross-selling meant that any contract renegotiation was likely to be price-driven, which could only impact margin. Third, as stated at the very start of this case study, workplace services are non-core. Hence they are frequently the first category of overheads to be cut when the going gets tough. On that basis, while PHS was certainly a very cash-generative company, the recurrence of its contracts was not as defendable as Charterhouse had imagined.

Figure 7.1: PHS's revenue growth (2008-14)

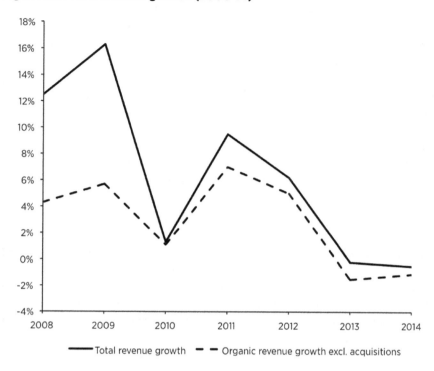

Source: Company accounts and author's analysis

Finally, the fact that 95% of customers only spent a few thousand pounds with PHS was, for a long time, seen as positive since the lack of customer concentration offered serious protection on the revenue front.[26] Unfortunately, the counterargument is that many of these small contracts were likely to be sub-scale, meaning low-margin or maybe loss-making. In business, the 80-20 rule applies on an eerily frequent basis: if management had developed the right data analytics tools, it would probably have concluded that 20% of its customers generated 80% of its earnings. Instead of bragging that it served 250,000 customers, PHS would then have concluded that it needed to scale down its operations and customer base instead of obstinately staying on the M&A trail.

In any case, if they felt (and at times publicly declared) that the stock price was undervaluing their company when it was trading on the stock exchange, neither the chief executive Peter Cohen nor his finance director John Skidmore hesitated in selling part of their shareholding below the IPO price of 80p in the years that followed the 2001 listing. In 2003 Skidmore sold part of his stake at 75 pence a share, while the following summer Cohen disposed of 800,000 shares at 78p.[27] These directors' dealings were clear indications that PHS might have been accurately valued by the public after all. When Charterhouse decided to bid 115p in July 2005, not only did it translate into an excessively high earnings multiple, it was also setting an all-time high for the shares, applying a 33% premium on the pre-bid price. By now the reader will not be surprised to hear that only weeks before PHS had received an approach from JPMorgan Partners, one of its European peers, Danish group ISS, had been delisted for £2.1 billion by Scandinavian buyout specialist EQT and US bank Goldman Sachs at a similar premium to that tabled by Charterhouse for the British washroom service provider.[28] The PHS transaction was merely an ersatz version of the ISS take-private.

If the group's valuation at the time of its public-to-private is open to debate, it is unquestionable that Charterhouse overvalued its portfolio company when it tried to sell it in early 2011. Between 2005 – the year when it had taken PHS private – and 2011, operating margins had dropped from over 29% to 26.5%. And yet Charterhouse had put PHS on the market at an EV of £1.5 billion, giving the support services business an EBITA multiple of 14.3 times. Not only did PHS's financial performance not warrant a positive multiple-arbitrage, but the macro-environment, swayed by the lingering financial crisis, the slouchy national economy and the eurozone sovereign debt conundrum, was far from conducive to such a premium.

Buy-and-build strategy

Essentially, until it fell under PE ownership in the mid-1990s, PHS had grown organically. It only started expanding by acquisitions when Electra backed a primary buyout of the business. We know that because PHS says so on its website. In that sense, the company underwent a traditional roll-up strategy; PE's second pillar of value creation described in Chapter 1. This approach continued during Charterhouse's SBO (1999-01) and went unabated when the group was quoted on the London Stock Exchange (2001-05) and after Charterhouse repurchased the business in 2005. However, this consolidation strategy was dependent on constant cash-flow gains or external funding.

As the financial markets and the economy were grinding to a halt post-Lehman, PHS had maxed out its bank credit, drawing down an extra £90 million of its acquisition facility in the year ended 31 March 2009, for instance, in order to finance £70 million worth of corporate activity that year. After purchasing 27 businesses in fiscal year 2008 and another 18 in the following 12 months, it could only rely on operating cash (that is, the cash generated from day-to-day trading). For that reason, its corporate activity and top-line growth slowed down dramatically. PHS made four acquisitions in 2010 and 15 in 2011. Its revenue growth rate went from 12.5% in 2008 and 16.3% in 2009 to 1.3% in 2010, 9.5% in 2011 and 6.2% the following financial year. But because many of these new acquisitions were of businesses generating lower margins than PHS's, profitability suffered. As shown in Figure 7.2, for the three fiscal years to March 2010, EBITA grew at 12.4%, 11.7% and 0.1%. If we took the effect of acquisitions out, earnings growth would obviously be slower, as evidenced by Figure 7.1. It would seem logical that, on that basis, PHS would have started feeling constrained by its loan covenants from 2011 onwards. It would partly explain why management launched a reorganisation and cost-cutting plan and Chief Executive Cohen was ousted in early 2012.

Figure 7.2: PHS's operating profit growth and margin (2000-14)

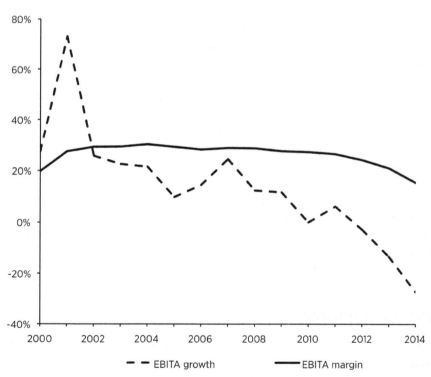

Source: Company accounts and author's analysis

One of the questions that springs to mind when going through this case study concerns the attitude of management in relation to acquisitions. It is understood that the management team leading Charterhouse's relapse buyout was keen to pursue its buy-and-build strategy in order to attempt to grow revenue, and more importantly earnings, with the aim of keeping pace with the accruing cost of the LBO debt. However, it is difficult to comprehend why, even when it became clear to all parties (management, Charterhouse, the lenders) in early 2012 that the debt commitments were impossible to meet, PHS's senior executives continued to make acquisitions. In the financial year 2013, even though they had declared that they were tightening acquisition procedures and hurdle rates, they still closed 13 deals, spending £20 million in the process. Instead of focusing exclusively on sorting out the legacy issues inherited from the Peter Cohen-John Skidmore era, Rhys Williams and his team kept on buying assets, even if small ones, further complicating their task of rationalising the group. After the A&E process of October 2012 and Charterhouse's equity cure of May 2013, they likely felt that they were out of trouble. They misjudged how dire the group's financial position truly was.

In any case, PHS's buyout owes its failure to the naïve view that a buy-and-build programme can keep on delivering profit uplifts indefinitely. When the group's performance faltered in the 2010 financial year, Charterhouse and PHS should have acknowledged that they needed to slow down and introduce profit-improvement measures. The issue with that approach is that it required a change in management style, and therefore, the appointment of a new management team with the necessary skills. Charterhouse's investment executives, who had sat on the board of the company for five years and had seen the same CEO deliver strong returns during their first LBO between 1999 and 2001, would have been reluctant to tell Peter Cohen that his time was up. The support services group had carried out over 100 acquisitions between 2007 and 2012. Between 2007 and 2014, while the UK was going through a financial crisis and an economic recession, approximately £300 million had been spent on bolt-on purchases. It is tempting to conclude that the money would have been better spent redeeming creditors' loans and reducing leverage ratios.

Debt commitments

Between 2007 and 2013, total debt net of cash had gone from ten times EBITDA to more than 12.7. The bank debt was not that complex, at least when compared to structures adopted by the vast majority of LBOs in the mid-noughties. The term loan was split into two tranches, all priced reasonably at Libor +2.25% to 3%, and the second lien had a 4.5% margin. Interest on Charterhouse's shareholder loan notes, however, accrued at an extortionate 15% per annum and was payable on redemption of the loans.[29] In the early noughties, most PE firm's shareholder loans had only yielded 8% to 10%. In an attempt to boost their IRRs without taking additional risk on the equity side, investors like Charterhouse had got into the very bad habit of taking the place of mezzanine providers by offering (more like imposing) a very expensive loan that they themselves underwrote. Because of that, PHS was facing an uphill battle to keep pace with financial commitments.

Figure 7.3: PHS's net bank debt* to EBITA and EBITDA multiples (2005-14)

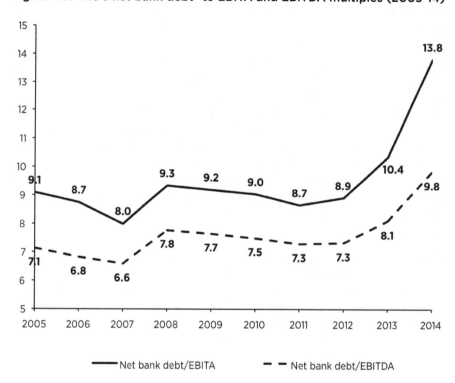

Note: * Excluding Charterhouse's shareholder loan notes. Source: Company accounts and author's analysis

Figure 7.3 highlights that despite the economic recession, PHS's net debt ratios remained high. When a company undergoes an LBO, it is committed to reducing its leverage gradually, with the aim of meeting covenant tests on a quarterly and yearly basis. Each quarter, PHS had to meet three financial covenants: debt-to-earnings, interest cover, and capital expenditure limit. With net-debt-to-EBITA and net-debt-to-EBITDA ratios consistently at or above nine times and 7.5 times in the period from March 2008 (the financial year when it carried out a refinancing) to March 2011, it appears that PHS's management was no longer able to increase profitability at a faster pace than its cost of debt.

Part of the reason why the leverage ratios were stuck at such high levels is the accruing interest cost, but most of the problem resides in the shortcomings inherent to a buy-and build strategy. Unless it is coupled with a thorough cost-management programme, it will eventually prove incapable of generating enough profitability uplift to keep up with the swelling cost of debt, in particular when acquisitions are funded with fresh loans as was the case at PHS.

Another way to demonstrate PHS's stretched capital structure is by adding Charterhouse's shareholder loan notes into our calculation of the group's net-debt-to-earnings ratios. Figure 7.4 illustrates a similar plateau between 2007 and 2011. But with earnings growth unable to progress as fast as the 15% compound interest rate charged on Charterhouse's loans, in 2012 leverage ratios headed up. From £250 million in the year ended 31 March 2008, these loans' book value had reached £460 million four years later – the £210 million difference entirely explained by accrued interest – pushing the total net debt multiple from 12.2 to 13.3 times EBITA over the same period. It is at that point that Charterhouse chose to remove the chief executive and to impose, a bit late in the day, an operational review.

Figure 7.4 also reveals that, had the lenders not taken over PHS in 2014, because of the compounding effect of interest commitments on Charterhouse's shareholder loans, total leverage multiples would have reached 23.3 times operating profit that year, instead of the actual 13.8 ratio (and 16.6 times EBITDA instead of 9.8). Once earnings fall or fail to grow fast enough, the impact of expensive debt can be felt very quickly indeed.

Figure 7.4: PHS's total net debt* to EBITA and EBITDA multiples (2005-14)

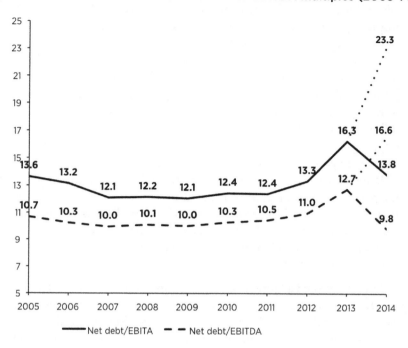

Note: * Including Charterhouse's shareholder loan notes. Source: Company accounts and author's analysis

The shortcomings of copycat strategies

To a certain extent, PHS's setbacks are reminiscent of those experienced by its main rival Rentokil. Throughout the 1990s, the latter led a far-reaching consolidation across several segments of the workplace service industry. Under the leadership of its hugely ambitious CEO Clive Thompson, Rentokil, which started life as a pest control company, primarily grew by external growth. Between 1992 and 1999 its turnover rose from £474 million to over £3 billion. The company's chief exec earned himself the nickname 'Mr 20%' for his consistency in delivering at least that much growth in profitability year after year. Between 1992 and the end of the decade, profits before tax had jumped from £122 million to over £540 million.

Sadly, as in the case of PHS, the Rentokil story was not to have a fairy-tale ending. In 2000 the company, by now operating in hygiene, security, tropical plants and conferencing as well as its original rat-catching activities, reported its first of a long series of profit warnings. Unfocused, the group had expanded into lower-margin activities like parcel delivery (for more on the subject, read Chapter 9 on DX, with Rentokil's courier business City Link operating in that very competitive sector) and had to rationalise its various divisions. The next few years turned desperate following more profit shortfalls, with Clive Thompson eventually stepping down in May 2004 from the conglomerate he had built and led for over 20 years – a sequence of events extraordinarily similar to those at PHS eight years later. In a last attempt to straighten things out, in 2005 the pest control group even considered an offer for PHS, but no rational party could outbid LBO investors in those days. Because Rentokil was a constituent of the FTSE 100, its downfall unfolded for all to witness: after a painful reorganisation, it was dropped from the prestigious stock market index in 2007.

PHS had followed a 'growth-by-acquisition' model similar to that of the much larger market leader. With the added subtlety that, when it was forced to hit the brake in the early noughties, Rentokil only held net debt totalling 2.5 to three times operating profits. In March 2013, PHS's bank debt-to-EBITA ratio was an uncomfortable 10.4 times. That is why Rentokil was able to take time reorganising, more or less successfully, its operations whereas PHS ended up hitting the wall, at least in terms of debt commitments, when it ran out of bolt-on targets to artificially boost revenue and profits. It serves to stress that buy-and-build strategies, a key ingredient in mid-market LBO recipes, can at times be over-egged. PHS's consolidation plans eventually ran out of steam. Figure 7.5 depicts how, over the years, revenue growth petered out.

Another factor could explain why the Charterhouse executives got it wrong on their relapse buyout. When owning PHS the first time around (1999-01), they would have observed that, in addition to being enormously cash-generative, the company's activities were relatively unaffected by the economic softness experienced in the aftermath of the dotcom crash. It seems they inaccurately concluded that the support services group could weather economic trouble. Unfortunately, several elements differed between the 1999-2001 SBO-cum-listing and the 2005 buyback-delisting.

Figure 7.5: PHS's revenue growth (2001-14)

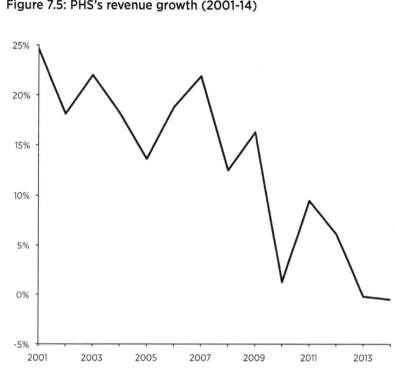

Source: Company accounts and author's analysis

For one thing, the Great Recession that took place post-Lehman was on a grander scale than the slowdown of the early noughties – even if a slump in business activity was widely anticipated, no one could have foreseen its full reverberation. It touched all sectors of the economy, including workplace service outsourcing like washroom dispensers, if only in terms of pricing. Secondly, during the early noughties PHS benefitted from the troubles its main rival Rentokil was facing. The group won a few important contracts with retailer Asda, Lloyds Bank and mobile phone operator Orange in 2002 alone. It is likely that some of these new customers were willing to trade down to a smaller supplier in the hope of getting better value for money. But the third and most striking distinction between the two periods is that, by the mid-noughties, PHS no longer operated just in the hygiene segment. As with Rentokil, its management had practically run out of targets to consolidate traditional core activities, so it started venturing elsewhere.

That diversification strategy was the reason why the group adopted the PHS brand, dropping the too restrictive Personnel Hygiene Services title. The change was not just cosmetic; it reflected the move into unrelated, though somewhat complementary, sectors like waste management, water coolers, crate rentals and office plants. While washroom services represented 70% of revenue and 80% of profits in 2003, five years later their contribution was just over half and less than two-thirds respectively.[30] This horizontal expansion (into adjacent services that could be cross-sold alongside hygiene products) got the company involved with lower-margin services, as discussed. But, disappointingly – and perhaps due to the fact that the group's senior executives were more focused on deal doing than operational management – in 2004 only 12% of customers used more than one PHS service or product, and nine years later that proportion was still only 25%.[31] The cross-selling strategy should have been pushed more aggressively.

As an aside, these newly acquired activities were also far from recession-proof, to put it mildly. The vast number of acquisitions managed to hide such underperformance for a while. That oversight cost Charterhouse and its LPs dearly.

Wiping the slate clean

Charterhouse performed admirably out of its 2002 vintage, Charterhouse Capital Partners VII, the €2.7 billion vehicle used to complete PHS's repurchase. That fund yielded an IRR of 37%, for a return multiple of 1.9 times cash on cash. This high IRR implied several dividend recaps and quick exits, such as the expedited sale of Coral Eurobet to gambling group Gala in 2005 after keeping it in portfolio for three years (see Chapter 2). But the eighth fund, raised in 2006, did not fare as well, affected as it was by the financial crisis. As at 31 March 2015, CCP VIII had generated a negative IRR of -0.55%. Much less than the unlevered annual return of 10% achieved by the FTSE 250 index between 2006 and the end of 2014.[32]

A search on Charterhouse's website for any reference to its PHS adventure would be fruitless. Charterhouse's RBO of the office support group brings too many bad memories to be worth disclosing. A business that the authoritative British PE house owned not once but twice has vanished from its marketing material. None of the three partners who sat on the board of PHS make any mention of their past involvement in their online profiles. It is as if the company, on which Charterhouse lost about £200 million, had never existed.[*]

And yet PHS is well and truly alive. As one of the UK's leading providers of workplace services, it was too busy trying to survive to properly celebrate its 50th birthday in 2013. It is slowly recovering from Charterhouse's second visit. But its new senior executives should not let their guard down. Pretty soon, it is likely that its unnatural assemblage of distressed investors will aim to sell the company to the highest bidder. The latter might well be another financial sponsor. Remember, PHS is highly cash generative. To prove the point, in January 2016 PHS's water cooler division was sold to Waterlogic, a water-dispensing system provider backed by PE firm Castik. It was the sixth transaction by the acquirer over the previous 12 months.[33] Co-heading the buy-and-build strategy at Waterlogic was its commercial CEO, one Peter Cohen, former chief exec of PHS. Old habits are hard to break.

[*]. Charterhouse website, 31 December 2015 – PHS employees and managers should not feel aggrieved. French fashion retailer Vivarte, a portfolio company that was bought in 2007 and fell out of Charterhouse's control in September 2014 through a €2.8 billion restructuring – France's largest ever debt-for-equity swap – also does not appear on Charterhouse's website.

CHAPTER 8
Frans Bonhomme – Down the Drain

Disclaimer: Always operating as a private company, Frans Bonhomme made few voluntary or mandatory public disclosures. Consequently, some of the information related in this case study has been pieced together from market research, the media, and statements by the company's owners and lenders. The author issues the customary caveats associated with the use of second- and third-hand information.

NEXT TIME YOU FLUSH THE TOILET, CONSIDER THAT THIS simple act is an important factor behind the economic and social progress experienced by the developed world over the past 200 years. The vast majority of countries were devoid of a proper sewerage system until the late 19th century. To dispose of their waste, people would frequently open doors or windows and throw the contents of a chamber pot or bucket onto the streets, adding human faeces to horse dung – remember that before cars were invented and people complained of their greenhouse effect, horses were the principal means of transportation and generated their fair share of environmental issues. It is easy to imagine that this situation led to the spread of illnesses, germs and viruses.

In most countries of Western Europe, it was in the second half of the 19th century that indoor bathrooms, sewage collection, mains drainage and systematic water treatment, including chlorination, were introduced. The impact this had on the death rate, population growth and general well-being cannot be overemphasised. Modern civilisation owes its prosperity to the fantastic gains made in hygiene, itself derived from better sewage disposal and treatment. If despite all the above arguments, evacuation mains still do not look all that appealing to you, you might not be working in private equity. Because if you are, you must be salivating at the mountain of cash flows that can be generated from distributing pipes and by-products indispensable to social well-being and future GDP growth.

Just one word: plastics

There is no question that the deployment of pipe networks is an integral part of our economies' development. However, the materials used in the early generation of pipes were metal-based. One in particular was, unbeknown to our ancestors, extremely harmful. Lead is a heavy metal that can be toxic to humans. When ingested, its worst effects are exerted on the central nervous system, but it can also reach red blood cells and the digestive system, provoking weight loss, vomiting, chronic fatigue and many other unpleasant side effects. Lead-poisoning can bring about grave growth and cognitive disorders in children. Contamination occurs when lead is dissolved in water, a pretty major occurrence when you are using lead pipes to transport and hold water, a technique used by civilisations as far back as the Roman Empire.

There are several materials that can be used to replace lead. Historically, the main ones were cast iron and copper. Although the latter is generally considered the best alternative because of its bactericidal properties – a fact apparently known since antiquity, when the material was used to treat illnesses or prevent infections – modern societies have taken a liking to plastic due to its affordability and malleability. It was in the 1950s that plastic gained widespread acceptance. Offering corrosion resistance, plastic requires less maintenance. Although in the early days plastic components had higher wear-and-tear rates and strength limitations, engineering improvements meant that, gradually, they outperformed metal across many industries. But the compelling argument in favour of plastic is that, in most applications, it is much cheaper than metal thanks to lower raw material, transportation, assembly and manufacturing costs. When market research indicates that up to 25% of freshwater is lost during transport from pipe leaks in distribution systems and in-house connections, using the most cost-effective technology is essential.

* * *

In France, the largest distributor of plastic tubing and fittings to the construction and public works markets and to local tradesmen is a company called Frans Bonhomme. Naturally, the latter doesn't just provide pipes to expel whatever people decide to throw down the bowl. Its products are used for water treatment, drainage and irrigation in applications as varied as gutters, sewers, plumbing, pumping, ventilation, heating, flooring equipment, sanitation, farming, public road networks, garbage dumping and quite a few others. Pipes are handy with water and waste, but they can prove equally as effective a tool for gas transportation and to protect telecommunication cables and electric wires. With 2,200 employees and an 800-strong sales force in 2015, Frans Bonhomme serves 200,000 corporate clients, from local authorities to home builders and infrastructure developers. The group has one of the widest product ranges on the scene and holds a 30% market share in France.

The company started as a trader and wholesaler of building materials in 1935. Its founder, Mr. Frans Bonhomme, had been in business for 20 years by the time he visited a trade fair in Milan and came across a product manufactured by Gresintex, one of his Italian competitors. Instead of using metal-based tubing and fittings, Gresintex supplied plastic ones. Frans Bonhomme negotiated the exclusive distribution rights of these products for the French market. After spending the following ten years growing organically by opening several wholesale depots, in 1965 Frans Bonhomme sold part of his company to Blanzy Ouest, a specialist in heating and air conditioning. The company continued to expand even after its founder retired and sold his remaining shares a few years later. By 1989 Blanzy Ouest became part of Sofical, a tobacco and transport business that belonged to Groupe Bolloré, and in 1992 Frans Bonhomme was moved to Bolloré's newly acquired freight unit and shipowner SCAC Delmas Vieljeux.[1]

For years, despite the various changes in ownership, the company, its management and employees lived a peaceful if uneventful existence in the sleepy French town of Joué-lès-Tours, situated in the outskirts of the mid-sized city of Tours, itself lying 240 kilometres southwest of Paris. It probably would have remained a run-of-the-mill business with reliable though unremarkable profitability if its owner had not decided to flog it. In need of cash to delever his industrial conglomerate, business tycoon Vincent Bolloré sold several of his group's divisions in 1994, including Frans Bonhomme, even though he had previously declared that he would not part with such a steady cash provider.

In December 1994, Fonds Partenaires Gestion, a subsidiary of French investment bank Lazard, took 49% of the pipe distributor alongside investment firm Gaz et Eaux (with 18%) and the local office of PE outfit Apax Partners (with 17%). The trio decided to finance a 1.15 billion French francs (FF) – about €180 million – management buyout of Frans Bonhomme, which by then employed 1,140 people across 107 outlets. The target had generated an EBIT of FF114 million on sales of FF1.4 billion in 1993. Sales had reached FF1.6 billion by the time the LBO was taking place, confirming that the company's double-digit revenue growth profile was as inviting as its profitability.[2] To make the move less painful, Bolloré was getting a decent multiple of ten times historical operating earnings, or 9.3 times 1994 EBIT. Debt funding for the LBO was simply structured, with FF730 million of senior facility, including a single 7.5-year amortising term loan tranche (priced at 1.75% over Libor) and a revolver, as well as FF150 million (€23 million) of mezzanine sourced from British mezz expert Intermediate Capital Group (ICG).[3] That translated into a leverage ratio below seven times EBIT.

Just like it had under the leadership of its original founder and its subsequent industrial owners, PE-backed Frans Bonhomme proved a solid growth machine, expanding its network of outlets and its revenues by two-fifths over the next five years. It is common in the PE world for the holding period not to exceed five years unless the underlying business is failing to perform. Thus, in late 1999 Fonds Partenaires, Apax, and Gaz et Eaux (by now renamed Azeo) put Frans Bonhomme back on the market. In February 2000 British firm Cinven led a €390 million secondary buyout in partnership with French buyout shops Suez Capital and PAI Management, BNP Paribas's direct investment arm. Cinven and PAI each held a third of the business while Suez's managed fund, Astorg, had a 17.9% stake, with management and other financial investors holding the rest.

Given the good performance of the underlying asset over the previous five years, the secondary buyout could afford to be a bit more imaginative on the capital structuring front. Senior debt totalled FF1.3 billion (close to €200 million), comprising a FF900 million seven-year amortising term loan A at 200 basis points over Euribor, a FF300 million eight-year term B at a 2.50% margin, and a FF100 million seven-year revolving credit facility at 2%. Acquisition debt had been provided and its syndication led by local bank Crédit Agricole Indosuez, while mezzanine financing of FF400 million (€61 million) had again come from ICG.[4] Leverage accounted for two-thirds of total financing. You can imagine that with an economy growing at 2% per annum over the ensuing three years the construction sector did well, which in turn underpinned Frans Bonhomme's expansion across the country. With group revenues growing by 25% in 2002 to reach €440 million, after just three years the financial backers were more than happy to consider an exit at the right price.

*   *   *

In September 2003, Apax France provided such an occasion by deciding to repurchase its previous portfolio company alongside American bank Goldman Sachs, the private equity divisions of British bank Barclays and French bank Crédit Lyonnais, local investment firm Quilvest, and General Electric's pension fund. Every institutional investor had heard of the PVC pipe distributor's unequalled ability to generate cash and seemed to want to join the banquet. Including this new set of shareholders, Frans Bonhomme had seen ten different financial institutions back its roll-out strategy in the past ten years. In a €520 million tertiary closed in December at an EBIT multiple of ten times, Apax was helping the previous financial shareholders, led by Cinven, bag a 2.5-time multiple on their three-year bet.[5]

With senior debt of €301 million syndicated by Goldman and Natexis, and mezzanine and junior PIK of €85.55 million arranged by Natexis as bookrunner, the tertiary buyout was on debt multiples of close to 5.7 times EBITDA and 7.5 times EBIT.[6] Leverage now represented three-quarters of the enterprise value. On many parameters, the target was getting stretched, but all parties seemed prepared to push the boundaries in order to get their share of the bounty. Goldman in particular had been generous with its time, acting as M&A adviser to the buying consortium while providing both debt and equity to make sure that its employees' time was rewarded with the suitable amount of fees and potential capital gains.[7] The American bank had also taken a chunk of the generously priced mezz for itself.[8] Thanks to the faith expressed by such backers, the lively story of the fast-expanding distributor could go on.

Frans Bonhomme had grown consistently for the past 20 years, and there seemed no reason for this to end. The fundamentals of its financial performance were tied to one key factor: by expanding its network of outlets across the country the company had addressed previously untapped demand, particularly in less densely populated areas, consolidated its market position vis-à-vis the competition, and grown in the greater Paris region, where the group had historically been weaker due to its provincial origins. Its scale and market share were strong barriers to entry. Importantly, Frans Bonhomme had strengthened its influence over many of its clients, such as the small local builders with limited bargaining power. Growth had also come from widening the range of products, for example with the introduction of protection equipment and boilers. Through its division CNCP Bordet, spread across the southern regions of France, the group was also present in subsegments like gardening and watering, which provided some diversification in revenue generation. For those reasons, margins and cash flows had consistently gone up, a vital ingredient for a successful leveraged buyout.

Within a year of the tertiary, the new PE consortium did a dividend recap and returned a significant percentage of its equity. The €80 million of subordinated convertible bonds initially subscribed by the financial sponsors had been prepaid, and so had half of the mezzanine. Led by Goldman and local bank Natexis and completed in December 2004, this recapitalisation had used €403 million of senior debt, adding a €90 million term loan D and a €30 million second-lien tranche, keeping only €48 million of the more expensive mezz.[9] As a consequence, despite making the capital structure more complex, the cost of debt had decreased. The refinancing had been made possible by solid and reliable cash flows, which confirmed Frans Bonhomme's reputation as having good credit among lenders.

Absence makes the heart grow fonder

In 2003 and 2004 sales had grown by 8% and 15% respectively while gross operating margin had reached 35% in both years thanks to the continued roll-out of the points-of-sale network. A bullish construction market had allowed Frans Bonhomme to raise prices. By the end of 2005 the number of depots exceeded 300, or twice the number four years earlier. Thanks to economies of scale, EBIT margins had risen steadily, going from less than 11% in 2003 to 12.6% the following year and were predicted to come within a hair's breadth of 13.5% for the 2005 financial year. With such stupendous achievements, two years after the tertiary buyout by the Apax-led consortium, it was time to think of getting out, for what is a better way to lift your IRR than to flip a business.

In a game of musical chairs, Cinven's Paris-based investment team pined for another pop at Frans Bonhomme in a quaternary buyout full of promises. The process was likely to be competitive. Only bidders with a unique angle and a deep understanding of the target's management team's motivations could pretend to fully price in the pipe wholesaler's growth potential. By the third week of October 2005, Cinven's executives held the victory in the hollow of their hands, taking the keys back from Apax and its co-investors. The French group's enhanced profitability guaranteed the prospect of high financial gearing.[10] Acquiring the target on a cash-free, debt-free basis for €893 million, or 10.76 times EBIT, and cheered up at the thought of repurchasing a company it had sold only two years earlier, Cinven was ready to shell out. Or so it claimed by promising to fund Frans Bonhomme's pan-European expansion, starting with Spain where, in July 2004, the group had acquired S.O.T. (Subministres a Òbres i Tennerys), a business with four outlets in Catalonia, just across the French border.

Through French acquisition vehicle Bonhom SAS, itself owned by Luxembourg-registered Bonhom Luxembourg & Co. SCA, which was controlled by funds managed by Cinven, the British buyout house was to take full advantage of the generosity of the debt markets. The senior loans arranged by Royal Bank of Scotland totalled €525 million, but no LBO debt package was complete without a good slab of subordinated notes, so €130 million of mezzanine had also been subscribed by an international syndicate of banks.[11] The 11-year mezzanine tranche was paying 4% cash over Euribor and 5% PIK notes.[12] Total leverage was just shy of three-quarters. In early 2006 RBS led the syndication alongside local banks Calyon and Natexis.[13] The senior debt included a €160 million term A loan with a seven-year maturity and a 2.25% margin on Euribor, a €100 million term B (eight-year, 2.75% margin), a €100 million term C (nine-year, 3.25%), and a €50 million term D (ten-year, 3.75%).

Wait, that's not all. There was also a €45 million second-lien facility described as term loan E (11-year, 5.50%), and a €70 million bridge loan (seven-year, 0.75%). Plus, the company could draw down on a €50 million acquisition facility (with the same margin as the term A) in case it decided to pursue its expansion in Spain or elsewhere. A €30 million revolver at 200 basis points over Euribor was also available to deal with occasional working capital requirements, as well as a €30 million borrowing base facility, the latter representing an amount that can be drawn against the company's asset base.[*] That was just for the senior debt. The €130 million mezz piece sat on top of it. Senior leverage was 5.45 times EBITDA; total leverage was 7.4 times.[14] In addition to bank debt, the balance sheet was being loaded with a classic shareholder loan.

It would be stating the obvious to say that the tubing wholesaler was not just extremely popular with LBO fund managers. It was also the darling of the leveraged banking community. Its quaternary buyout had contributed to the consolidation of the Royal Bank of Scotland's and Calyon's positions at the top of the league tables in France. Both had led more than €4 billion of LBO loan processes in 2005. Their nearest rival, BNP Paribas, was far behind in third place, with less than €3 billion to its credit.[15] Deals like Frans Bonhomme were very desirable, notwithstanding their swollen balance sheets.

One of the great advantages of the business was that it had very limited requirements in terms of capital investments; there was no need for a capex facility. In any given year, only 1% of sales were spent on capital expenditures. Over the past three years annual capex spend had been between €4 million and €5.5 million.[16] Launching a new outlet only cost €20,000 to €100,000, and since the company had opened approximately 30 new ones a year in the past three years, organic growth funding was easily doable without requiring external financing. It also meant that most of the cash flows generated could be used to service debt through a cash sweep or to pay a dividend if the lenders were so inclined. Although the market had become somewhat lax in terms of debt quantum and margins, some form of credit-risk management tool was still in place. Frans Bonhomme had to respect three sets of covenants: net debt-to-EBITDA, EBITDA-to-net interest expense; and cash flows-to-interest and principal repayments (the debt service coverage ratio). Few would have paid much attention to these at a time when the French distributor's operating performance was making it the darling of European LBO fund managers and lenders.

---

*. Note that borrowing base facilities are usually issued at a discount to the asset base. In this case, Frans Bonhomme could borrow 80% of the receivables used as collateral.

As with all the previous iterations, the main PE shareholder was not alone at the trough. Alongside Cinven, French insurer Axa had taken a 5.6% stake, and Goldman Sachs had elected to roll over some of its proceeds to keep a 3.36% holding, while management's ticket gave it about 4% of the business (see Figure 8.1). The investment by the (not so) new owners was partly in the form of a €145 million ten-year convertible bond accruing interest at a bountiful rate of 12% per annum.[17] It was a simple way for the new PE consortium (the fourth in a row) to generate a minimum return in case Frans Bonhomme struggled to deliver sufficient equity upside. But no one was really worried about such risk. The ink had not yet dried on the sale and purchase agreement when the portfolio company submitted another admirable set of returns for the 2005 financial year. Revenues were up 14% while operating earnings had risen by a fifth. Frans Bonhomme now had a network of 306 outlets, triple the number of 1993, while its workforce doubled over the same period. No doubt the company's steady performance and broader market presence were confidence boosters to the financial backers.

In the summer of 2006, the French company went through a capital-raising exercise to give its employees a once-in-a-lifetime opportunity to subscribe to up to €25 million worth of shares in Frans Bonhomme. It looked like management and Cinven were being generous, giving staff a chance to take part in the future capital gains that they were all certain to make. In recent years, a growing number of French LBOs had encouraged staff members to become shareholders alongside management and financial sponsors. The practice had been proactively encouraged in order to avoid any industrial action. In a country known for its tough trade unions and its wariness towards Anglo-Saxon capitalism, PE firms investing in France had taken fright when, in September 2005, the vast majority of tile manufacturer Terreal's 1,700 employees had gone on strike. Spread across 14 production facilities, the strikers had reacted to the recent quick flip of their company by PE groups Carlyle and Eurazeo in an €860 million secondary buyout to their peer LBO France, just two years after having purchased the business for €470 million. Eventually, Terreal's employees had received a one-off €500 bonus and a 1% salary increase – that's what the generosity of PE fund managers looks like.[18]

No doubt Frans Bonhomme's managers and the new owners wanted to avoid a similar scenario. So they were asking the 1,800 French employees if they wanted to invest alongside them. The €25 million that was expected to be raised was not to be reinvested in the company but to be used to repay a €20 million shareholder loan issued by Bonhom SAS and subscribed by Cinven. A further amount of €828,493 of the proceeds would also be employed to repay interest on these loans accrued as of 30 June 2006 at an annual rate of 8%.[19] In essence, by subscribing to the new share issue, Frans Bonhomme's employees were repaying Cinven's bridge loan, which had been made on 15 December upon closing its relapse buyout. The loan had been earmarked to fund the Bonhom Management entity at the same time as the rest of the group was being acquired. If fully subscribed, it would give Frans Bonhomme's employees 8% of Bonhom SAS's ordinary shares, as Figure 8.1 shows.

Figure 8.1: Frans Bonhomme's simplified group structure post-capital increase of June 2006

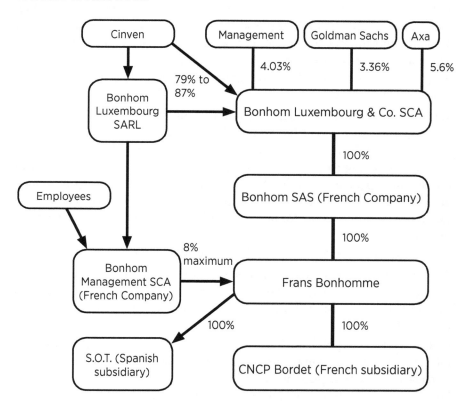

Source: Bonhom Management SCA capital increase prospectus

The calm before the storm

In 2006 Frans Bonhomme's top line expanded 15% to €711 million.[20] As it continued to open new outlets across France and Spain, the business was propelled by three main drivers: spending on equipment for civil works projects and by public entities; European Union regulations on water treatment, which tended to favour plastic substitution; and construction, maintenance, repair and improvement activity in general. As briefly touched upon, it was its geographic expansion that had brought to the group the benefits of economies of scale and propelled profit margins. Even though it served very large public entities such as the state-owned rail operator SNCF, telecom service provider France Télécom, and utilities Électricité de France and Gaz de France, the tubings wholesaler benefitted from low customer concentration. Frans Bonhomme's biggest client represented 5% of the group's turnover, while the top ten only generated 17% of sales.

With over 90,000 active clients, including many one-person plumbing and building businesses, Frans Bonhomme held enviable negotiating power over the majority of them.[21] The inability of local farmers, bricklayers, electricians and other building entrepreneurs to negotiate on price had made this sort of profitability upgrade easier. On the supply side, scale had also helped, though not to the same extent. The company dealt with about 300 suppliers, but the top five of them accounted for one-third of Frans Bonhomme's sourcing while the top 15 represented more than half of it. Clearly the strength of the business model was on the customer side and the fragmentation of the market.

With trading going well, what better way to celebrate than by upping the leverage! A refinancing seemed de rigueur to return money to Cinven and its LPs. In February 2007 RBS led the recap with a new debt package totalling €816 million, helping the mezz lenders to recoup their entire investment.[22] One year after its repurchase, Cinven had recovered 50% of its outlay. The fifth pillar of PE value creation (timing a quick repayment) was appearing in all its splendour. Little transpired about the terms of the new loan package, but we know that tranche B of the senior debt saw its pricing reduced from 2.75% to 2.125%,[23] so the other debt instruments certainly received similarly preferential treatment. The French distributor had seduced its banks once more. And the trust shown by the lenders was vindicated when, at the end of 2007, Frans Bonhomme reported a 15.7% increase in group sales. The Spanish operations had seen sales jump 160% thanks to the opening of many outlets across the country.[24] Leaning on a 27% share of its home market,[25] the pipe specialist had continued to build its position in Spain where it had created a new division the year before in order to expand beyond Catalonia, the region where it had earned a presence in 2004 with its purchase of S.O.T.

* * *

Frans Bonhomme served two main industries: construction and public works. Whereas the latter was more resilient to economic downturn given that government budgets, local and national, are frequently maintained to avoid social and political backlash, conversely the private construction sector is one of the first affected by recessions. The real estate market is very cyclical and, in a financial crisis, a squeeze on credit terms will have detrimental effects on small contractors like bricklayers and plumbers, and on housing starts and purchases.

In the first two years of the quaternary buyout, the company had increased its revenues by one-third, and its network of outlets had expanded by a fifth. As the year 2007 ended, it was facing its first real test. It was unclear what impact the Credit Crunch that had begun in the summer would have on customers, many of them highly susceptible to house- and infrastructure-financing. If banks were getting nervous, they would likely change the terms they would be prepared to lend on. The broader economy and consumer confidence would certainly be hit, with the traditional ripple effect on mortgage demand, house purchases and repairs ultimately hurting demand for pipes.

In the second quarter of 2008, French and Spanish GDP experienced a significant slowdown compared to recent quarters, with France recording a 0.5% contraction of its economy and Spain only growing by 0.1%. By comparison, in the first quarter of the year both had registered 0.5% growth rates. As in the rest of the developed world, the economic slump settled in during the second half of 2008: both national economies dropped off by nearly 2%.[26] The Great Recession had started. For the whole of 2008 Frans Bonhomme recorded €837 million in sales, just 1.8% up on the prior year.

The group's performance could be divided into two halves. The financial crisis gained momentum as the year progressed and was being felt by the group and its customers. In the last six months of the year, the economic slowdown had harmed trading both in France and Spain. In the latter, the group had closed four of its 40 outlets, while at home it had completed the implementation of existing projects but put future openings on hold.[27] Few at that stage considered the Frans Bonhomme situation to be particularly serious, even if the construction industry had experienced a major correction. Across the 27 countries of the European Union, in 2008 the number of building permits for residential buildings had collapsed by a quarter. In France, the correction had been less marked but was still noticeable at 17%. Spain, on the other hand, had witnessed a disastrous 57% fall.[28]

I started this case discussion by explaining how vital pipes are to our economies. Without them, our roads would be flooded, our privies would be blocked, and our pavements would be muddy. But the main specificity of products and services whose demand grows in tandem with the economy is that they suffer from recessions. In 2009 French GDP waned by 2.9% and purchases of new homes tumbled 8.7%. The production index of the national construction industry lost 6.1% after a more modest 0.9% decline in 2008.[29] Very much dependent on a healthy construction sector, in 2009 Frans Bonhomme's sales crashed 15% to €711 million. In fact, because the group had chosen to part with its non-core, no-growth division CNCP Bordet, the sales figure for the remaining activities was €683 million, a drop of 18.4% on the prior year, bringing Frans Bonhomme back to its 2006 trading level.[30] The recession had already wiped out three years' worth of growth.

After eight years with the group, six of them as chief executive, Michel Pic, 62, had chosen the early months of the Great Recession as his cue to retire.[31] In the summer of 2009 he had handed over the leadership of the group to outside candidate Caroline Grégoire Sainte Marie. The departing CEO had reportedly made seven times his equity between 2003 and 2005, the two years Apax's tertiary buyout had lasted, after having invested about €1 million at the outset.[32] Naturally Pic would have been asked to roll over part of his proceeds in late 2005 by the new owners Cinven, but no doubt a large proportion of his €7 million had been set aside for rainy days. And by mid-2009, it was bucketing down. Grégoire Sainte Marie was unlikely to repeat the performance but the question, as she took over, was not whether she could make a seven-fold return on equity, assuming she was remotely willing to take a punt on the troubled business by investing her own money. Rather, it was whether years of experience in the construction industry – she had recently been running the French and Belgian operations of Tarmac, a concrete products and aggregates group – would be enough to revitalise Frans Bonhomme.

When Frans Bonhomme's market had begun to suffer severely from the effects of the crisis in 2008, Cinven and management had acted to defend their investment. They had focused on controlling costs and maximising margins, chopping new outlet-opening projects, reducing inventories and capital expenditure, disposing of non-core assets to maintain positive cash generation and reduce debt, and entering into discussions with lenders to reset covenants.[33] The subsidiary CNCP Bordet had been sold in a management buyout backed by local investor Avenir Entreprises. With its focus on gardening and swimming pools, the division offered too few synergistic benefits, so a disposal certainly made sense to create liquidity (the small subsidiary was sold for more than €5 million) and to give its 157 employees a better chance to survive.

In Spain, Frans Bonhomme's performance had been disappointing. At first, management had built its presence there by aggressively increasing the density of its network. But the lack of economic growth and the poor creditworthiness of local businesses had forced the closure of non-profitable sites as well as a review of rental agreements. In 2009 Frans Bonhomme's revenues in that country had fallen by more than a fifth, so management had implemented a ruthless downsizing programme, closing 16 of the country's 40 depots and sacking 80 of the 300 employees. In a fractionally less desperate situation, the French operations had lost 15% of their top line.[34] The big unknown for the indebted business, its PE owners, lenders and recently appointed CEO pertained to the economic prospects in the two geographies it covered.

Plus ça change...

The chain reaction of the crisis had been acutely felt in the construction sector. On an annualised basis, new housing starts in France had gone from more than 450,000 in the second half of 2006 to less than 350,000 in the first quarter of 2010.[35] It looked like Frans Bonhomme would be stuck with Cinven for the long haul, and vice versa.

Most observers would have known that the change in CEO at the French wholesaler the year before was only the starting point of the corporate upheaval. Cinven and its co-investors Axa and Goldman were experienced enough to know that, in a period of recession, a leveraged buyout can turn into a distressed scenario. What this means is that debt restructuring soon makes its way to the top of the agenda, with the finance director becoming a whipping boy or a punching bag, depending on what sport takes your fancy. After nine years in the role of CFO, 56-year old Philippe Ringelstein was replaced in October 2010 by one of Cinven's own investment principals, Geoffroy Willaume. Three months earlier, the human resources and the information systems leadership functions had also been filled by new joiners.[36] Five years into its repurchase, Cinven was facing a very different situation. With the exception of the COO Jean-Louis Ott who had 40 years in the group, the entire senior executive team had now been revamped. Heads would keep rolling in the coming years.

The French economy expanded by 2% in 2010 but builders remained cautious. The construction production index was 5.5% down at the end of the year.[37] In a market showing no sign of growth, it now looked like extending the network of outlets was out of the question – the group had actually reduced its number of depots and distribution centres in Spain by almost two-fifths over the previous two years. In many parts of France the market had reached saturation. Even in the June 2006 prospectus to its employees, Frans Bonhomme's management had acknowledged that product penetration was already high.[38] Growth, if it came, would originate from renovation and replacement of existing pipes rather than from new construction. Any market share gain would likely be achieved at the expense of margins due to the need to be price-competitive.

With the construction sector in the doldrums, the company's full-year 2010 sales in its domestic market lost 2.1% to €618 million. Demand had been partly affected by industrial action across many sectors and regions of France in October of that year. The real trouble for the group had come from its sole foreign market. The Spanish economy had been flat in 2010, which was a massive improvement on the 3.6% contraction suffered in 2009, but it was not enough to stop the bleeding. Frans Bonhomme's revenues in that market decreased by 16.5% in 2010, and there was no indication that the tide would turn anytime soon. Irrespective of this disappointing foray abroad, management remained optimistic, indicating in the 2010 annual report that activity at home had started to pick up in the early part of 2011.

Indeed, the French economy pursued its ascent, registering a 1.1% growth rate in the first quarter of 2011. The construction and public works segment finally experienced a resurrection thanks to government plans to support demand through stimulus programmes and fiscal measures. Despite the newly improving economic context, for several months the company had been in negotiations with its lenders with the aim of amending its debt covenants; operating performance was just too far below budget for the group to be able to respect its contractual obligations. A new set of covenants was agreed on 15 April 2011. At the time, Chief Exec Grégoire Sainte Marie optimistically declared that the new terms would allow the group to "work in a secure financial environment".[39] But it did not take long for reality to hit back. In September the outside world had a rare glimpse of how dire the situation had become at the French company when asset manager Henderson Global Investors, one of Frans Bonhomme's lenders with a bearish view on the bond markets, decided to go through a fire sale of about three-quarters of its bond portfolio. It was then reported that Frans Bonhomme's bonds were trading in the mid 60s, more than a third below face value.[40]

In a routine typical of distressed businesses, management changes kept coming. After only two years in place Grégoire Sainte Marie was replaced, having tried without success to rekindle the group's prosperity. Eager to send a message that after years of cost control top-line growth was once again a priority, the freshly parachuted CEO, Dominique Masson, appointed a new commercial director as the year drew to a close.[41] There were reasons to be hopeful. For the whole of 2011 French GDP had risen by 2.1%, while building permits and new housing starts were up 12% and 10% respectively.[42] Frans Bonhomme had recovered some of its pep and recorded a 4% jump in group revenues to €686 million. The top line was still 18% below the 2008 level, but management and its backers were hoping that they had turned a corner.

The same could not be said about Spain, where sales had shrunk a quarter to €32.5 million and Frans Bonhomme had pursued outlet closures. With 23 points of sale at the end of December 2011, the Spanish business was a shadow of its former self. Three years earlier, sales had stretched to €66 million across 40 distribution depots.[43] The country's prolonged economic paralysis – Spain's GDP had lost more than 4% over the past three years – had made commercial and operational initiatives by Frans Bonhomme's management all but irrelevant.

Flushed down the tubes

Unfortunately for Cinven, management and the French group's creditors, the uptick in trading witnessed in 2011 was brief. After having tried its hand at economic stimulus, the French Government fell in line with many of its European counterparts by instituting austerity measures in the later part of 2011. In order to bridge public deficits, the government introduced a vast array of new taxes, going from a 'soda tax' increasing duties on sugary drinks to a higher levy on real-estate gains, all applicable from 1 January 2012. To cap it all, lending conditions were tightened by many banks still attempting to rebound from the financial crisis. The government's 'plan de relance' had given way to its 'plan de rigueur',[44] and the consequences for the French economy and SMEs like Frans Bonhomme would be far reaching.

For a start, GDP dipped 0.3% in the second quarter of 2012, followed by a similar correction during the third quarter.[45] France was experiencing a double-dip recession. The contraction of the construction sector was immediate, which brought demand for building materials to a new low, a situation that was becoming life-threatening for Frans Bonhomme. After more discussions with the group's creditors, Cinven was forced to inject €15 million into the business in order to keep ownership, reset the bank covenants and prevent an event of default. The lenders' coordinating committee had comprised many eminent banks and credit asset managers, including American investment firm Alcentra, European outfit Avoca, French bank Crédit Agricole, and British Government-owned Royal Bank of Scotland.[46] The market had been quite bumpy since 2008; Cinven's equity cure had helped negotiate another tricky corner.

Frans Bonhomme was far from safe, though. The previous year's economic recovery had not stayed the course, with France recording a meagre 0.2% growth rate for the whole of 2012. Likewise, the construction sector had fallen back into a deep sleep, and building permits for residential housing had collapsed 7.5% that year.[47] Accordingly, cycle-dependent Frans Bonhomme had gone into reverse and recorded a 5% drop in consolidated sales – the French division had shed 4% whereas Spanish revenues had surrendered a further 23.5%.[48]

Intoxicated with expensive LBO loans, the wholesaler had pursued its now customary management reshuffle, with the experienced COO Jean-Louis Ott leaving after 42 years with the group, and the director in charge of development and key accounts also departing by the end of 2012. The chief information officer appointed in 2010 would be replaced in March 2013. It was a hopeless situation. No matter who was in charge, the economic context made a rebound very unlikely.

By the end of 2012 it would be difficult even for a fervent supporter of LBOs to hold that the quaternary had generated much support for Frans Bonhomme's market leading position and future prospects. In the five years since 2008 the distributor's revenues had fallen by a fifth, its number of outlets in France had gone from 407 to 380, and the number of employees had dwindled by 10%. Despite the fact that the number of clients had risen from 120,000 to 200,000 over the period, it had not been sufficient to boost revenue. Equally, the cost-cutting measures in terms of headcount reduction and closures of wholesale depots – in Spain alone, the number of outlets had gone from 40 to 18 as sales in that country shrank 55% – had not been sufficient to avoid covenant breaches, hence the loan renegotiations in April 2011 and Cinven's equity cure in 2012.[49] And yet more pain was just around the corner.

*   *   *

Whereas the number of new housing starts in France had increased steadily throughout 2011 to reach a 400,000-to-450,000 range on a cumulative 12-month basis, unfortunately, by the first quarter of 2013, the numbers were back to 350,000, or the level registered at the worst stage of the Great Recession.[50] This double-dip of the French construction industry was behind Frans Bonhomme's poor trading in 2012. Under normal circumstances, the covenant reset of 2011 and the recapitalisation the following year would have been enough to get the business on an even keel. But these were not normal times: France and Spain were recording their worst economic performance in living memory. The problem is that even after all that toing and froing between shareholders and lenders, Frans Bonhomme was left with leverage unchanged at 9.3 times EBITDA. As it was, the French wholesaler had emerged from the financial crisis with a rotten balance sheet, so the company had little room to manoeuvre. But the final blow would not come from the economic context or from the competitive landscape, nor would it be explained by management error. An abrupt government decision was to seal the fate of Frans Bonhomme's fourth buyout.

In May 2013 the pipe distributor warned lenders that it would not make a debt payment following the introduction of a new French law that changed levies on employee shareholdings and profit-sharing. Management explained that the rule would lead to a one-time €10 million hit on cash flows, breaching the company's cash-sweep covenant. With a debt-to-EBITDA ratio of more than nine times and a looming event of default, Frans Bonhomme was looking down the wrong end of the barrel. About €45 million of its revolving line of credit and term loan fell due in 2014.[51] Negotiations with lenders had to resume. Promptly, talks centred on a debt-for-equity swap for approximately 70% of the €527 million outstanding LBO loan balance. In June 2013 multi-strategy asset managers Angelo Gordon and Centerbridge were reported to be buying Frans Bonhomme's loans from CLO players and banks on the secondary market at about 80 cents on the euro in anticipation of the equitisation process. By mid-July Centerbridge was believed to be holding over a third of the company's debt and was thereby in a position to block any restructuring proposal. Whereas some speculated that Cinven would be making a fresh equity injection of a size similar to the one it had made a year earlier, it seemed more likely that, through a consensual restructuring, the British PE firm was mentally preparing for a humbling exit, or a major dilution, as credit specialist Centerbridge was getting ready to pounce.[52]

Frans Bonhomme was witnessing the changing of the guard, the modern equivalent of hostile takeovers. Its PE backers were being evicted by a new breed of credit investors, a type of lender who, unlike Royal Bank of Scotland and Crédit Agricole, did not care much for 'relationship banking'. Outsiders recognised that a change of control was good news for the group's prospects of survival, and during November trading in Frans Bonhomme's senior loans edged up in the secondary market.[53] In late December 2013 Centerbridge became the French group's majority shareholder, with Angelo Gordon becoming a significant minority shareholder, leaving Cinven with a puny slice of the business. The group's debt was more than halved to less than €300 million, resulting in a reduction in finance costs and extended maturities. The lenders, including RBS, Crédit Agricole and Avenue Capital, agreed to reschedule the rest of the debt.[54] With just two years of presence in Europe under its belt, Centerbridge had closed another 'loan-to-own' deal that same month of December by taking the keys of German auto-repair group ATU from its owner KKR.[55] A new sheriff was in town, assuming the mantle of private investing.

In 2013 French GDP only rose 0.7%, not enough to motivate the construction industry. New residential housing was down 5% and public works off 4%. The production index of public works in the country was now a fifth below its level of 2008.[56] Frans Bonhomme's €616 million of consolidated revenues for 2013 were 5.5% lower than in the previous year, or more than a quarter down on 2008, as seen in Figure 8.2. In keeping with the trend witnessed ever since the start of the recession, activities in Spain had recorded the biggest fall, with sales ending 22% down year-on-year. The market environment remained alarming, but hopefully the financial restructuring would give Frans Bonhomme the room necessary to wait for a rebound.

Figure 8.2: Frans Bonhomme's revenue breakdown (2005-13)

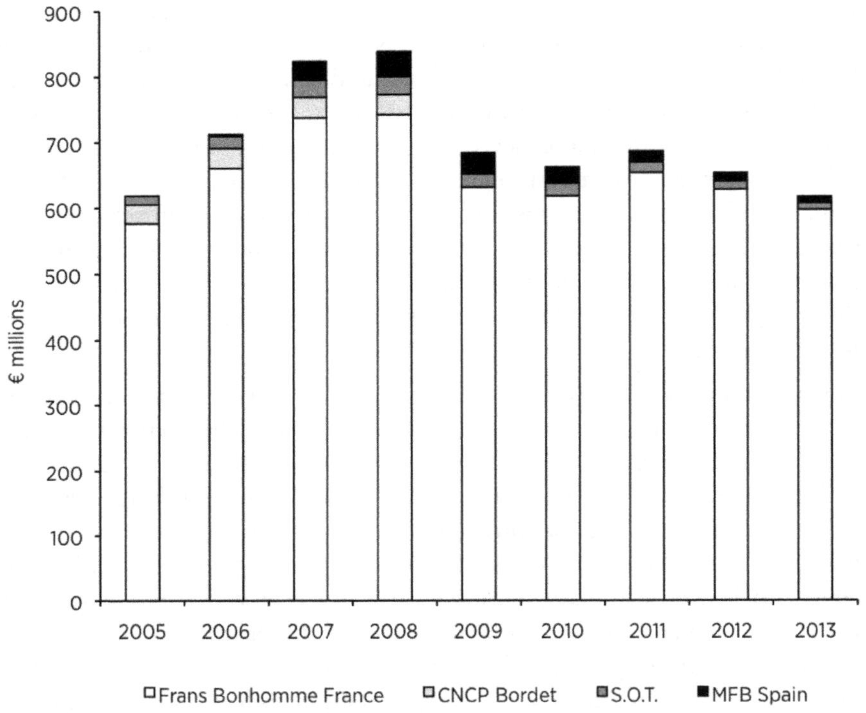

Source: Company filings

The limits of relapse buyouts

In January 2014 Centerbridge officially took control and Frans Bonhomme started contemplating a few more years of ownership by financial investors. The company was now worth about €500 million,[57] a 45% reduction on the value assigned by Cinven in December 2005. In an attempt to make the shareholding as broad-based as possible, you will recall that one of the requirements of the

June 2006 capital increase had been the participation of at least 400 of the group's employees; their investment was now officially well under water.

Over the past decade, Frans Bonhomme's valuation multiples had gone full circle. Figure 8.3 illustrates that, in 2014, Frans Bonhomme was on a similar EV-to-sales ratio to that of 1994 (0.81 vs. 0.75). Eventually, markets revert to the mean, so hopefully multiples will move closer to the 1.10-time turnover paid in 2000 and 2003 when Centerbridge is ready to exit. But the new owners are unlikely to get back to the 1.44 earnings multiple granted by Cinven in 2005. As management had cautioned at the time: "The level of EBITDA multiple found in the last sale of Frans Bonhomme Group may, in the future, experience corrections."[58]

Figure 8.3: Frans Bonhomme's valuation metrics (enterprise value and EV-to-sales)

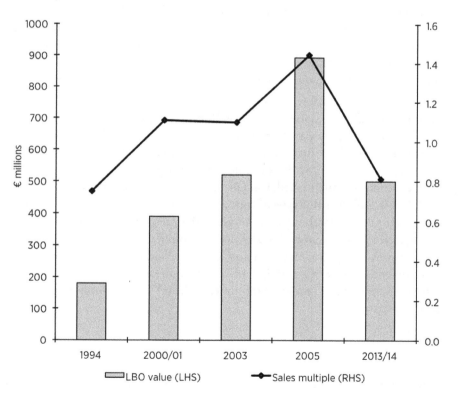

Source: Company filings and author's analysis

In July 2014, Cinven exited its investment in Frans Bonhomme, more than 8.5 years after completing its quaternary RBO.[59] It was left to Centerbridge to repair the damage done by 20 years of leveraged transactions. And one thing was for sure, the new majority shareholder would not get any help from the economy. In the first two quarters of 2014 French GDP dropped 0.2% and 0.1% respectively, experiencing a rarely seen triple-dip. Although the second half of the year showed an uptick in growth, it only served to cancel out the mini-recession of the first half. For the third year in a row Frans Bonhomme recorded a contraction of its top line, with its French activities trading 4.8% below the 2013 level. Still, at last the plastic-pipe distributor had addressed its bloated capital structure, which bought its management some time to solve the conundrum: how do you service LBO loans and meet financial covenants when your market is shrinking?

It was a brain-teaser that many managers of leveraged zombies were wrestling with. The year 2014 had been active in terms of French LBO distress, with fashion retailer Vivarte (owner of trendy brand Kookaï) and directories publisher Solocal (see Chapter 11) respectively going through a €2.8 billion and a €1.6 billion debt restructuring. By comparison, Frans Bonhomme's negotiations about its €570 million loan package had been the equivalent of holding small talks. But Cinven's French team had also been busy with another stressed asset.

In May 2007, weeks before the onslaught of the Credit Crunch started and only three months after recapitalising Frans Bonhomme, Cinven's Paris office had bought a 65% stake in pan-European women's fashion retailer Camaïeu, in a €1.5 billion SBO from Axa Private Equity, the same institution that had taken a minority stake in Frans Bonhomme's quaternary alongside Cinven. PE is a small community. Partly listed, Camaïeu spent the next four years as a leveraged PIPE (we will discuss this type of transaction in Part Six) before Cinven finally convinced public shareholders to let go of the prey. By December 2014, after having increased its number of stores almost twofold despite the Great Recession and Europe's barely growing economy, Camaïeu had been forced to re-engage with its lenders as its €1.2 billion LBO loans, already extended in mid-2012 and in February 2014, remained too much to bear.[60] Frans Bonhomme was in good company.

* * *

A new year called for a new management change. On 13 January 2015, it was announced that two months hence, Patrick Destang, a former senior executive at tile manufacturer Terreal (the same Terreal that we saw living through a strike in 2005, and that had since been taken over by its lenders in early 2013 as its

LBO debt proved cumbersome), would replace CEO Dominique Masson.[61] The latter, after four years at the helm, had not been able to breathe new life into the group – further evidence that management changes of corporate zombies do not necessarily deliver the desired recovery. Maybe Destang's experience at failed Terreal would have given him the tools to solve the aforementioned conundrum. In 2014, revenues for the French operations had reached €568 million whereas EBIT and net income had respectively fallen by a quarter and more than a third on the prior year.[62] On all financial performance parameters, Frans Bonhomme's results were back to their 2004 levels. If Destang had know-how, it would be put to good use.

In the spring of 2015, as it welcomed its fourth CEO in just ten years, Frans Bonhomme was still reeling from the combined effects of its ill-timed aggressive refinancing of February 2007 and the lacklustre economic context in France and Spain. One of the distributor's widely-quoted syndicated loans, its term loan B, traded at a discount to par, in the high 80s to low 90s,[63] indicating that the markets remained cautious on the group's ability to regain its footing. After so many years of tepid growth, Frans Bonhomme's core markets had forced its successive teams of senior managers to slow down expansion plans. Between 2001 and 2005 the group's number of outlets had doubled to 306 – a 19% compound annual growth rate. But by 2015 the group only managed 380 outlets, giving an annual increase of just 2% over the past decade.

The reason behind such a dramatic slowdown was three-fold. First, as discussed, the French economy had never fully recovered from the financial crisis. Second, Frans Bonhomme's network of outlets covered most parts of France so there remained few locations that could justify opening a workshop. Last, the fragmented building products distribution market was no longer so fragmented. Frans Bonhomme's key competitor – PUM Plastiques – had doubled its number of outlets to 205 during the previous ten years,[64] gaining market share in the process. Owned by global construction materials specialist Saint Gobain, PUM had benefitted from the healthy balance sheet of its parent, which was also Spain's market leader in tubing distribution. Frans Bonhomme's double-digit growth story had ended, as many tertiary and quaternary buyouts often do. The trick is not to be holding an uncomfortably large amount of debt in your books when that happens.

A rare find

The Frans Bonhomme situation is a showcase for the multiple facets of modern-day private equity. The company's ordeal was inflicted by familiar sins:

- **The application of huge leverage.** A business that had LBO loans worth 5.7 times EBITDA in 2003, during the Apax repurchase, was on 7.4 times during Cinven's repurchase only two years later, and on 9.3 times by 2012 as performance waned. Management could tell that it was getting a bit rich, stating during the capital-raising exercise of 2006:

  > "The LBO set up on 15 December 2005 [...] by Bonhom SAS is the fourth LBO on the Frans Bonhomme Group since 1994 and these transactions were successively conducted on the basis of enterprise values constantly increasing. Accordingly, these acquisitions resulted in refinancing through debt amounts that have been growing and are for the last LBO on EBITDA multiples higher than those found during previous operations."[65]

- **A rushed auction.** Estimating the value of a target is full of simplifications and approximations. In the case of Frans Bonhomme, the bidding process swayed the outcome, as the accelerated process did not allow Cinven to carefully assess the risks associated with a quaternary LBO. In its annual review 2011, Cinven admitted that when Apax et al. chose to sell in 2005, Cinven's executives were able to conclude the transaction quickly given their 'prior knowledge of the business and strong relationship with the management team'. Ten years later, it would appear that this intimate knowledge of the asset did not count for much and might have led to overconfidence in Cinven's ability to create value for its LPs.

- **A complex debt structure.** As we saw, from using a single tranche of term loan to finance the first LBO in 1994, the successive transactions invariably increased the complexity of the debt products employed, first by adding tranches to the senior debt (term B in 2000, term C for the tertiary in 2003, term D during the dividend recap of 2004, term E of second-lien during the relapse buyout of 2005), then by providing little add-ons such as acquisition facilities and borrowing base facilities. The company's strong cash conversion had been very enticing. The subsequent troupes of PE owners could not resist the temptation of trying their luck by stirring and muddling the capital structure, if only to see how far they could push it.

- **The company's growth strategy** began to falter, a common ailment of SBOs, as we saw in Chapter 2. Cinven's strategy was to continue rolling out the business by increasing the density of outlets in France and in Spain. As soon as the economic crisis hit, the business was so indebted that it could no longer afford to invest in its network.

Desperate to meet debt obligations, management and Cinven had to focus instead on cash-flow maximisation and deleveraging, including cost control and inventory reduction initiatives. Some would be quick to point out that, in a recession, it made no sense to continue to expand the number of outlets. But then, how does one explain that Frans Bonhomme's main rival PUM Plastiques pursued its roll-out strategy and increased its gain of market share?

To expand on the last point, it can be argued that thanks to tight monitoring exercised by Cinven and the appointment of a Cinven insider in the CFO position, Frans Bonhomme's sales productivity, pricing policy, network optimisation, customer relationship management, customer segmentation, and inventory optimisation were perfected during the period of ownership – although it could be argued that with the French group going through its fourth LBO in ten years, one wonders what the previous owners had been doing if most of these efficiency initiatives had not been already implemented to a great extent. Anyway, as the company was beginning to fray during the recession, incentivising the sales force could not reverse the trend, so cost savings had been indispensable.

In this instance, Cinven's turnaround approach had followed a blueprint adopted with another of its portfolio companies; one that also operated in the construction sector. In order to lift margins, Cinven had cut the workforce aggressively at Ahlsell. The latter, a leading distributor of heating and plumbing, electricals, and refrigeration products across the Nordic region, had suffered from the economic downturn, seeing revenues dwindle from 22 billion Swedish krona (SKr) in 2008 to SKr19.3 billion two years later. To adapt the cost structure, Cinven and management had reduced the number of employees at Ahlsell by about 15%.[66] At Frans Bonhomme, headcount reduction had been 12% from 2,500 to 2,200 between 2009 and 2012.[67] But whereas Cinven had managed to find an exit solution for Ahlsell by selling the business in a secondary to its British peer CVC in February 2012 – even yielding a surprisingly good 1.9-times investment multiple during the six-and-a-half-year holding period – no such lucky escape was to be achieved with Frans Bonhomme.[68] In October 2005, a PE professional had confidently stated about Frans Bonhomme: "This is a rare find. With it, we could do an endless series of LBOs."[69] Thankfully, the observer was spared public embarrassment by making this comment on condition of anonymity.

Reading the small print

Cinven hadn't shown much originality during its repurchase of the asset in 2005. Because Apax had done a repurchase and flipped it so easily, the Cinven executives had followed a classic aping strategy so prevalent in the PE world. Success, however, was dependent on a strong economic context. Between 1994 and 2005 France had seen its economy expand by 37%. After going through the early-1990s recession with the rest of Europe, the country experienced a long period of uninterrupted growth. A correction was in order. No one at Cinven seemed to appreciate that the period of growth would eventually end when, in 2005, it was decided to lard Frans Bonhomme's balance sheet with a huge loan package and to up the ante in a dividend recap 15 months later.

The first time it had owned Frans Bonhomme, between 2000 and 2003, Cinven had benefitted from an average annual GDP growth rate of 2% – the British firm made 2.5 times its investment on Frans Bonhomme that time around.[70] During the lightning tertiary, Apax, Barclays, Goldman and the rest of the consortium had also doubled their money as the French economy registered a 2.2% annual growth rate during those two years. In the first phase of Cinven's quaternary, Frans Bonhomme had benefitted from a booming credit-infused economy, with France growing 2.4% in each of 2006 and 2007. This is obviously the reason behind the refinancing that took place in 2007 – it enabled Cinven to return half its investment.[71]

Could it be that Cinven was just too happy to take its dividend in 2007 regardless of the possible consequences to the underlying asset, or did its fund managers not anticipate that Frans Bonhomme's trading would suffer whenever the debt frenzy ended? Between 2008 and 2013, the annualised GDP growth rate for France was 0.3%. Of course the new context was detrimental to trading and the pipe distributor could not generate sufficient cash flows to repay its loans. The fact that Frans Bonhomme's sales in 2013 were 26.5% below the 2008 figures had turned the former darling of financial sponsors and lenders into a cash-poor business. In keeping with PE custom, by the time it exited its investment in 2014 Cinven had replaced the entire management team it had backed in 2005. The CEO, the COO and the CFO had left. Only the Cinven dealmakers remained to tell the tale.

Cinven did extremely well out of its 2001 vintage (Cinven Fund III), yielding nearly 32% in net IRR as of 31 December 2014.[72] Going a long way in explaining the third fund's strong returns was the quick flip of Eutelsat, in which Cinven had acquired an 11% stake in December 2004 only to IPO the satellite operator 12 months later, returning 4.6 times its outlay when selling its position in December 2006.[73] Another expedited exit and great result had been bagged in April 2007 when disposing of German fashion retailer CBR after 2.5 years in portfolio, making Cinven a four-times multiple.[74] Out of the same fund, the PE house had also returned about three times its money on British car-park operator NCP, after just three years of ownership.[75] So the Frans Bonhomme RBO mishap had not hindered the third fund's glorious performance. Cinven's quixotic behaviour on that deal does not seem to have cost the firm much. It lost 50% of its original ticket, but was fully diversified.

If only Frans Bonhomme's employees who had participated in the mid-2006 capital increase could say the same about their investment. But they had been warned about the typical risks associated with LBOs. As with any investment decision, it often comes down to reading the small print. On page 28 of the 227-page prospectus distributed to all employees in June 2006, management had declared: "Given the size of the debt, a steady improvement in profitability is necessary to ensure a smooth repayment."[76] Quite.

PART FIVE
Listing, Delisting, Relisting: On a Fool's Errand

MONG ALL THE TRICKS AND ZEALOUS ACTIVITIES OF PE
investors, there is a fair amount of competition to determine which
one best embodies their tendency to run around in circles, adding very
little in the process. SBOs, where PE owners transact between themselves,
RBOs, where they repurchase companies they used to own, and even quick
flips could qualify for the crown. In my opinion, the winning prize has to go to
the pointless exercise of listing, delisting and relisting the same business, often
within a short period, which would tend to indicate that little has been done
to reconfigure the underlying company.

The argument often heard to justify the blossoming of leveraged buyouts since
the 1980s posits that privately held companies can achieve more than their
publicly listed counterparts because they do not suffer from various disruptions
emanating from the outside world, such as activist investors, equity analysts or
journalists having the audacity to ask uncomfortable questions to management.
Truly, if that is the case, it is difficult to comprehend the growing trend behind
PE-backed delisting-relisting transactions in a mindless carousel of public-
to-private transactions and IPOs. At the peak of the recent LBO bubble,
PTPs became very popular. Stock markets played the same role that carve-
outs of conglomerates did in the 1970s and 1980s: they became a rich source
of leveraged transactions. In 2006 alone, an estimated $460 billion of public
companies were taken private in the US. The hysteria was so great that late that
year Carlyle's David Rubenstein predicted that markets could soon witness a
$100 billion buyout.[1]

Limited research has been made on the topic, but several case studies in this
book serve to demonstrate that take-privates are far from universal successes. A
read through Chapters 5, 6 and 15, covering the TXU, EMI and Caesars buyouts
respectively, sums up the risk of assuming that public markets are undervaluing
an asset. It could explain why these deals tend to make up less than 5% of the
number of LBOs annually on a worldwide basis.[2]

But if delistings are risky, what should investors make of the opportunity
to invest in a business that is later relisted by the same PE owners? You will
remember the accelerated relisting of Celanese reviewed in Chapter 4 or the
IPO-take-private of PHS by Charterhouse in Chapter 7, but two other stories
will serve to point out the dangers of delisting-relistings. The first one is what
the industry would qualify as a small to medium-sized transaction. DX is a
postal group that operates in the UK and competes with former monopoly

Royal Mail. To state that the DX take-private and subsequent IPO failed to create value would be too kind. Our second example, Debenhams, is another case in point. Under the co-ownership of three PE firms, the department store chain got in trouble shortly after its relisting. Ten years later, it was still in survival mode.

CHAPTER 9
DX Group – Going Postal

B Y THE TIME POSTAL STRIKES STARTED ON 20 JANUARY 1971, post-war Britain had experienced a somewhat disappointing economic climate – at least when compared to continental European countries like France and Germany that had lived through a steadfast recovery and reconstruction in the wake of the Second World War. After two decades of lean times, British postal workers were feeling the pinch and they were demanding a 15% to 20% pay rise. The strikes, the first on a national scale in the history of the country's postal services, lasted seven weeks. With the state-owned monopoly out of service for so long, licensed and unlicensed private contractors emerged to fill the gap and provide local, national and international deliveries. The need for professional firms and other enterprises to be able to continue operating, even when the Post Office was forcefully closed for business, made corporate clients realise that alternative mail delivery operations needed to be introduced.

With origins dating back to 1516, when Henry VIII appointed a Master of the Posts to maintain the safe and orderly delivery of his missives across the kingdom, the General Post Office was later made available to the public by Charles I on 31 July 1635. At the time of the foregoing strikes, it had only recently changed its status from a government department to a corporation following the passing of the Post Office Act in 1969. Its influence on the lives of British people and businesses was undisputed. In addition to its universal mail service monopoly, it operated the country's telecommunication network and service, owned the National Giro bank, and ran a very sizeable parcel delivery unit. Although it would take another 35 years for the group to lose its mail distribution monopoly, its high-margin parcel business was soon to face competition. In the years that followed the 1971 strike, private courier service operators started to emerge to ensure delivery of high-value items. Their clients were often professionals, like lawyers and business consultants, keen to guarantee that their time-sensitive, mission-critical documents reached their intended destination. One of these new independent despatch service operators was named Document Exchange.

Set up in 1975, DX, as it would eventually be known, was formed as a lawyers' club to exchange legal documents.[1] Throughout the late 1970s and 1980s, DX's mainstream activity was in business-to-business document and parcel delivery. In September 1996 DX's parent company, Hays, expanded its business mail activities with the £65 million acquisition of Inkhold, the management buyout holding company of ICS, a business generating £3 million of operating earnings on £60 million of turnover. ICS (short for Insurance Courier Services) offered a range of early morning delivery services through a national depot network handling some 800,000 items a night. Its services and customer base were complementary to those of Hays Document Exchange, serving the insurance, travel, optical health and government sectors via the handling of goods like optical lenses, tickets and passports.[2]

To further expand its DX division, in September 2001 Hays obtained a licence from Britain's postal regulator Postcomm to deliver mail to business addresses.[3] When on 1 June 2002 the regulator also announced that private sector and foreign postal organisations could apply for a long-term licence to deliver bulk mail across the UK, Hays DX joined a long list of postulants that included UK Mail, a subsidiary of Business Post, the operator of the Dutch postal service TNT Post, and Deutsche Post, the German national postal monopoly. All confirmed that they would seek licences to deliver bulk mail from January 2003.[4] As it was due to partially lose its monopoly, the Post Office's mail delivery division had also gone through a name change and was henceforth to be known as Royal Mail.[*]

By March 2003, FTSE 100 conglomerate Hays could boast an annualised EBITA of more than £32 million on £130 million in sales. While margins of 25% were a lot more impressive than the massive losses incurred by its state-owned rival Royal Mail, earnings had nevertheless fallen 23% over the second half of 2001, partly because of DX's intense commercial tussle with Royal Mail. As a consequence, management stated its intention to sell off its mail and parcel division. In fact, Hays's management's goal was to dispose of three of its four activities and to retain the most promising: personnel and recruitment services. Despite the disappointing results, the group was not expected to find it difficult to dispose of its postal division, not least because since January DX was one of a handful of participants allowed to collect and deliver bulk mail. At the start of the year the regulator had opened up to competition the segment for large-

---

[*]. Originally, in 2001, the name Consignia was chosen as the new brand of the Post Office's delivery unit. In the face of public outcry (the British population has always held strong views about the Post Office, in part due to its universal mail service), the name was changed to Royal Mail a year later.

volume deliveries of more than 4,000 items – representing 30% of the UK's postal market.

In the months that followed the announcement that Hays was planning to restructure, a slew of potential buyers made approaches. First, management sold the archiving and business process outsourcing division for a bit more than £220 million. Then went the logistics activities, selling for £102 million in November 2003. Finally, DX was on the block, and analysts set an enterprise value of £250 million to £300 million for it.[5] Early on, UK Mail expressed interest in taking over its direct rival in order to bolster its position against state-controlled goliath Royal Mail. Other parties were soon rumoured to be lurking. In a public statement that betrayed the former monopoly's desperate intentions, Royal Mail stated: "We will continue to fight for every letter and push our competitors as hard as we can." It was ominous.[6]

Nevertheless, an unforeseen event would lend Hays support in its attempt to pretty up DX ahead of a disposal. Since the summer of 2003, Royal Mail and the postal unions had been at loggerheads. The national group was haemorrhaging – it had reported a £1.1 billion loss in the year to March 2002 – so its management had launched a three-year plan that involved boilerplate cost cuts and layoffs. The unions were not buying it, so they did what unions do: in October and November 2003 a series of wildcat strikes paralysed postal services in a few major cities.[7] It was easy to understand postal workers' anguish. According to management's rationalisation plans, daily deliveries were to be cut from two to one a day, the workforce was due to shrink by about 30,000, and 3,000 post offices were foreseen to be shut. Royal Mail employees could sense that these changes would alter working conditions, so thousands of them failed to turn up to work. Though disruptive, these actions lasted less than a week. But they gave Royal Mail's corporate clients a renewed desire to look for alternatives.

In December 2003, DX's former managing director Neil Tregarthen declared his interest in buying DX.[8] Keen to maximise value for the group's shareholders, Hays's management decided to take a different route by announcing that it would demerge and float DX, giving shareholders stakes in both Hays and DX. Hays's argument in favour of an IPO was that it would enable its shareholders to reap the full benefits of DX's performance improvements rather than see a private equity firm list the business itself at a later date.

DX's subscription-based services offered good downside protection and its commercial contracts' renewal rate exceeded 90%.[9] That kind of predictability made the business an attractive target for financial sponsors, with plenty of cash flows available to meet future loan obligations. Not surprisingly, several parties knocked at the door. Montagu Private Equity was mentioned; in June 2004 British LBO house HgCapital tabled a rumoured £250 million offer.

Potential trade buyers were circling too. In addition to the UK Mail/Business Post's already noted interest, in August 2004 former Dutch monopoly TNT – quite powerful in Britain with sales of £1.25 billion and 18,000 employees – was reported to be considering a bid.[10] But Hays's senior executives had set their view on a flotation, so all approaches were rebuffed.

Market introduction

DX employed 1,200 people and handled about 350 million items a year, including the exchange of documents for professional firms. While it claimed to be already Britain's leading private mail business thanks to its nationwide network, the management's plan was for volumes to increase by a further 100 million items over the following three to five years. The company's list of clients was prestigious, and its activities in overnight package delivery for small legal firms as well as bigger clients, including the Land Registry, the courts and the police, gave it a strong niche position. In the year to 30 June 2003 DX had generated sales of £129 million and made an operating profit of £33 million. At the very least, once public, such a profitable, highly cash generative business would offer potential investors a dividend yield. And it was in turnaround mode, so it was likely that anyone buying into the stock at the time of listing would see an uptick down the road.

The big upside, however, was in the promise of further deregulation. Two years after having seen 30% of its activities liberalised, Royal Mail still held a 99% share of the UK market. Regulator Postcomm and the British Government were planning to fully open up the £5 billion letter and parcel delivery market by January 2006 in order to give the former monopoly's rivals a real chance to shake up the industry.[11]

DX's main equivalent in the private sector was Business Post's UK Mail, which handled about 250 million items a year. Already listed on the London Stock Exchange, it had seen its shares rise 200% in the previous three years, indicating that the sector was greatly appreciated by institutional investors and the public.[12] The key unknown, though, was whether the mail activities would ever be profitable. DX's intention was to increase turnover from its regulated mail business from £2.8 million in the year to June 2003 to £6 million by June 2005. The aim was for that division to break even within 12 to 24 months following IPO.[13] In a sense, a public offering of DX Services had every reason to be well received. And so it proved to be.

On 1 November 2004, the company was introduced to the London Stock Exchange. Originally priced at 220 pence, it listed at 265p, for a market value of £230 million, and closed on its first day at 287 pence. It passed the 300p mark within ten days on bid speculations from Business Post. By January of the following year, the stock had reached 350 pence, before cooling down somewhat as no bid was forthcoming. With a 13% market share of the £700 million corporate mail segment, DX still had room to grow. And its decisions to issue its own stamps (previously one of Royal Mail's monopolistic activities) in March 2005 and, two months later, to establish its own blue pillar boxes to take business-to-business letters and packages in outlets of retailer Mail Boxes Etc. – in direct competition with Royal Mail's red drop boxes – showed how serious management's intentions were.[14]

However, it soon became clear that, despite the authorities' decision to fully liberalise the postal industry from January 2006, setting up a network capable of matching a much larger rival's capabilities would not be an easy feat. In September 2005 DX announced its maiden annual results as an independent company. Its operating profits were down 6% year-on-year to £31 million on sales of £130 million. While at the time the market felt that the business still warranted an enterprise value of about £370 million, in November DX issued its first profit warning, giving a belated explanation for the announcement three months earlier of the group chief executive's resignation, less than a year after leading DX to the stock exchange.[15] Unfortunately, actual results came up short of the downwardly revised forecast. In January 2006, the mail group reported a 12% fall in first-half operating profits due to a slowdown in the property market, a key industry serviced by the company's document-exchange division. Shares fell almost 17% to 287 pence on the day as the new CEO also blamed underperformance on rising costs. As could be expected, the finance director followed the previous chief exec out the door. Turning more realistic, the group announced its decision not to issue its own stamps after all.

Interestingly, DX was not the only party finding competition with a former state monopoly a challenge: its peer Business Post had seen its own boss Paul Carvell depart the previous month after two profits warnings. The sector, which had been cherished by the City until then, was suddenly being re-rated.[16] Observers pointed out that the competition of electronic communication and the need to offer a national or multiregional network put smaller players like DX and Business Post at a disadvantage. Regardless, by March 2006 DX was still valued above £325 million, including net debt of £70 million. Ignoring leverage, its market value translated into a fairly demanding 16 times prospective price-earnings ratio, but it was in fact gauged at a significant discount to its troubled rival Business Post's 21-times multiple.[17] And this rebate partly explains what happened next.

Market consolidation

Because its client list included blue-chip names like supermarket chain Tesco and optical retailer Vision Express, despite recent underperformance DX was still viewed by some as a desirable asset. It generated about two-thirds of its activity from predictable, cash-generative, time-critical document exchange – a service widely used by lawyers and estate agents. The question was whether the company would ever be able to compete head-on with larger players like Royal Mail, Deutsche Post and TNT in delivering parcels and letters.

Nonetheless, this big unknown did not deter one bidder. In June 2006 rumours started circulating that a private equity house had made an approach for the struggling independent postal company. On 4 July shares leapt 24% to an all-time high of 410 pence on confirmation that talks were taking place. Three days later, the identity of the bidder was disclosed: Candover, one of Britain's leading LBO shops, had offered 415p a share for DX, or a 26% premium on the pre-bid stock price, granting DX a market cap of £350 million, or an enterprise value of £420 million when including debt.

The PE investor was paying 20 times pre-tax earnings with the hope that it could extract significant synergies by merging DX with Secure Mail Services, a smaller rival delivering passports, cheque books, credit cards and other high-value items that Candover was acquiring at the same time from another buyout firm, Baring Private Equity. The plan was for the combined entity to be led by James Greenbury, the CEO of Secure Mail.[18] Upon announcing the delisting, Candover's deal leader, Senior Managing Director Marek Gumienny, explained the rationale for the move: "There are lots of opportunities. As deregulation comes in, it is all about being quick on your feet."[19] It was a confident view, but although the CEO of DX Services, Paul Kehoe, remained involved with the group in this capacity, he publicly showed a more prudent stance by saying that he was "taking no stake in the new business".[20] The merged entities, with £175 million in revenue and 1,840 employees, would presumably be more resilient in the face of their larger competitors. There was talk of a buy-and-build strategy and service improvement as key drivers behind the merger, in an attempt to take the fight to Royal Mail.

But the main refrain from analysts was that Candover was paying a full price for DX, a company that had recently experienced negative top-line growth in its core document-exchange activities and had gone through two profit warnings and a management transition since its public listing. On the face of it, it was difficult to comprehend why the mail company warranted a market capitalisation of £350 million compared to its £230 million value on IPO-day 20 months earlier. DX had registered no growth in the intervening period. It would not take long for events to corroborate the general feeling that Candover was overpaying. And although limited information was made public on the Secure Mail transaction, the few details that emerged made it clear that, on exit, Baring had made several multiples of its investment, with the prospect of further consideration subject to the achievement of certain milestones.[21]

Yet maybe new owner Candover was in luck after all. In June, July and October 2007, Royal Mail saw its service severely disrupted by another series of strikes. The dispute centred on modernisation plans, which Royal Mail said were required to remain competitive – two-fifths of business bulk mail had gone to the competition since the start of deregulation four years earlier. The unions believed that 40,000 jobs were at risk. Both sides eventually came to an agreement, though because 90% of small businesses exclusively used Royal Mail, industrial strife had cost the national postal group £100 million. On the back of this, independent mail operators had reported a 10% to 30% upswing in activity. DX Group's CEO Greenbury acknowledged that his company's sales had been boosted and that he would be able to double the top line within a few years thanks to deregulation. Other postal groups had also gained in confidence, with TNT undertaking full-scale trials of next-day door-to-door deliveries in various cities across the country in order to launch a complete rival service, including the use of its own postal delivery staff. Nevertheless, despite the disruption Royal Mail remained the dominant market participant: 97% of letter deliveries in the UK still went through its 'final-mile' postmen. DX was the only competitor providing doorstep service via its proprietary network.[22]

Market correction

Within a year, the entire postal industry experienced a true shock to the system. While the credit markets' jitters in the second half of 2007 were unlikely to upset growth noticeably, step by step the ensuing financial crisis led the economy towards a down-cycle. The Great Recession hit the industry hard, reducing demand for mail delivery services and encouraging clients to cut costs, via the increase of email usage when possible. Consequently, in the year to June 2008 DX Group registered sales of £174 million, showing no gain on the combined revenue generated two years earlier when DX and Secure Mail Services had merged.[23] Chief Exec Greenbury admitted defeat and departed at the start of the year.

At such a dire moment, DX would have needed a solid cash infusion to weather the storm and maintain its competitive advantage, at any rate in the document exchange and parcel delivery segments. But its PE backer was going through its own, mostly self-inflicted crisis. As the Credit Crunch was taking hold, Candover's senior executives had chosen to accelerate their investment timetable, closing expensive deals with inadequate due diligence and massive debt multiples. In the first seven months of 2008 alone, a period considered well past the buyout bubble peak, Candover had closed over £2.5 billion worth of transactions, not a mean feat for an investment firm frequently categorised as a 'mid-market' player and more used to deal sizes similar to DX's, in the half-billion-pound region. It wasn't just the new transactions that were puzzling. Some, carried out a few years back, like Gala Coral (see Chapter 2), were also losing their glitter.

In late March 2009 DX's stretched balance sheet became a public embarrassment when management had to admit that it had commenced talks with its lenders over relaxing its 31 March covenant test. While a source close to the company claimed that the company had no liquidity issue but was simply sustaining a market softening, the hiccup served to show that Candover's investee company was operating in a cyclical industry.[24] However, what had transpired earlier that month was that DX's situation was no temporary setback. Candover's parent company was listed on the London Stock Exchange, which forced it to issue an annual report. In its 2008 accounts issued on 2 March 2009, Candover Investments plc had decided to completely write-off DX's value in its books.

The equity invested in DX was now worth less than the face value of a second-class stamp. The buyout specialist had stated that the adjustment was a reflection of public market comparables, but it also admitted that the economic downturn had harmed DX's volumes, and hence sales and profitability. With fewer property transactions and lower credit-card issuance, the postal company's core document-exchange activity had been badly affected. Delisted three years earlier with the help of a £250 million loan package (not including the Secure Mail debt portion), it was finding life as a leveraged business hard work. Reports emerged regarding negotiations with the banks that could lead to significant dilution of Candover's equity stake.[25]

DX soon received some assistance from the usual corner. Two years after going through a six-month period of industrial action, Royal Mail faced yet another bunch of strikes in June and the fall. Management was keen to push its modernisation plan ahead, with or without the consent of the unions. Two waves of walkouts in October 2009 led to backlogs of 30 million and 50 million letters and parcels. It took until the following spring for the dispute to get resolved. All that upheaval had again benefited private operators, DX among them. Nevertheless, it was not sufficient to take Candover's portfolio company out of its debt nightmare.

Sorting out the mess

In April 2010, when announcing its decision to inject further cash into the company following long negotiations with DX's bankers, Candover reluctantly handed over a 49% stake in the mail group to the junior lenders in exchange for a full recapitalisation. It transpired that, in its fiscal year ended 30 June 2009, DX's EBITDA had fallen below £35 million, several millions less than expected by lenders. It was not only the covenant tests that were troublesome. With over £350 million of bank and shareholder loans remaining outstanding, the June 2009 leverage ratio had shot up to a stringent 9.2 times EBITDA – up from 6.6 times two years earlier. The consolidated balance sheet was displaying a net liability position of £70 million, and the profit and loss account had been impacted by an exceptional goodwill impairment of £237 million.[26] Reorganising the capital structure had become a necessity.

At the same time, the mail company took the opportunity to reveal one of private equity's favourite tricks: a management reshuffle. The group's CEO John Coghlan, who had taken the reins in February 2008, relinquished his position to Petar Cvetkovic, while a new chairman was also brought in to complete this thinly camouflaged refinancing-cum-secondary MBI.[27]

Candover and DX's lenders had thrown the company a lifeline, arranging a full (if complex) capital restructuring that included:

- Candover making a £15 million cash injection via the issue of a zero-coupon guaranteed loan, helping the troubled PE house retain a 51% stake.

- The extension of repayment dates on the existing senior debt facilities to 2014 for term loan A, 2016 for term loans B and C, and 2017 for term D, as well as a new set of looser banking covenants.

- The acquisition of DX's outstanding mezzanine debt facilities with a face value of £68.6 million by Candover, the mezzanine lenders and DX's management team, and the cessation of cash interest payments on the mezzanine.

- The write-off of DX's outstanding investor loan notes worth £86.9 million.

- The conversion of the existing preference shares and accrued dividends into deferred ordinary shares with a nominal value of £236.9 million.

As a consequence of the comprehensive refinancing, the postal group was left with total debts of about £200 million, or a still punchy 7.4 times EBITDA. Net of cash, though, the leverage multiple had been somewhat tamed, equating 6.1 times. The existing mezzanine facilities and investor loan notes were derecognised at 19 July 2010 and the new instruments were recognised at that date. The fair value attributed to both new instruments was assessed to be nil – in exchange for which the mezzanine holders had grabbed 49% of DX. When it came time to issue its 2010 annual report, Candover Investments plc acknowledged that it had injected further cash into the mail company but that its equity book value remained nil.[28]

The extent of this recapitalisation leaves no room for doubt: even as its sector was experiencing the full force of the economic downturn and fierce price competition from heavyweights Royal Mail and TNT, in the wake of the financial crisis DX had been restrained by its expensive financial gearing, unable to follow its original buy-and-build, innovation-focused strategy. Its management had sought to expand its national network of 350 parcel exchanges and 4500 private mail rooms and sorting offices, but the cost of servicing the debt was preventing a full-scale roll-out of local collection points.[29] Perhaps, via its balance-sheet restructuring, DX would get a second wind.

For Candover, though, there was no such lucky escape. Poor strategic, operational and investment decisions on the eve of the financial crisis eventually led to its dismantling. In August 2010, the investment group announced its intention to wind itself up. Making its break-up and wind-down processes official, in April 2011 publicly-listed Candover Investments plc announced the disposal of its subsidiary Candover Partners Limited's assets to Arle Capital, an independent partnership of former Candover executives that was to become the new manager for the 2001, 2005 and 2008 vintage funds, as well as DX's new owner.

With a somewhat easier to manage balance sheet, DX tried to insulate itself from Candover's woes and from the decline in traditional postal services by expanding its offering into courier services and logistics. It went on the acquisition trail and mustered up the courage to attack a new market segment: in March 2012, as a turnaround play, it bought for its net asset value Nightfreight, a poorly performing specialist in irregular-dimension and weight freight. Thanks to sufficient cash-flow improvement, during the year ended 30 June 2012 the group purchased some of its bank debt at a discount to par value: following an auction process, £5.9 million of debt was purchased for a cash cost of £4 million, realising a gain of £1.9 million for DX.[30] But if management truly wanted to rekindle the group's fortunes and turn the LBO page, a solution was required to sort out the bloated capital structure once and for all and provide shareholders with a clean exit.

Return to sender (market introduction – take 2)

Ever since Royal Mail had lost its monopoly, first on bulk mail delivery in 2002, then on the rest of the mail business in 2006, the topic of its privatisation had been high on the British Government's agenda. But several stumbling blocks had prevented such a move. First among them was the gigantic size of the postal group's pension liabilities. After years of public inquiries and parliamentary debates – a favourite occupation for British politicians – in 2012 it was finally agreed that, for Royal Mail to become a viable private enterprise, the best course of action was for its £28 billion of pension-related assets and £38 billion in liabilities to be transferred to the state. Other obstacles that were removed at the time included the separation of the retail activities of the Post Office from the rest of the group and the partial elimination of price controls. The latter enabled Royal Mail to charge higher 'final-mile' fees to parcel operators and, in March 2012, to hike the price of first-class stamps by 30% and of second-class stamps by 40%.[31]

After such profound reforms, the natural next step was for a sale of the business. Keen to maximise value for the taxpayer and encourage Royal Mail employees to become shareholders, the government opted for a public offering. Royal Mail's IPO took place on 11 October 2013. The aftermarket performance of the shares was so strong that it led to dogged criticism against public officials, and in particular Business Secretary Vince Cable. Observers claimed that the government had seriously undersold the company, short-changing the taxpayer in the process. Still, the most unexpected effect of this strong stock performance was that the markets had suddenly built an appetite for mail and parcel delivery businesses.[32] Sensing that the window of opportunity they had waited for was unlikely to last long, DX's management and its shareholders launched a sale process for their company. After more than seven years as owners, Candover and its reincarnation Arle had overstayed their welcome.

As it prepared to float on London's junior market AIM, DX had what could once again be described as a stretched balance sheet. With leverage up by 26% in the last three years to £210 million, its net-debt-to-EBITDA ratio had reached 6.4 by June 2013. Even based on the prospective 2014 EBITDA numbers, the debt multiple remained as high as 6.24 times. Recent revenue growth had been a paltry 2% while EBITDA was growing at less than 2.5% per annum. We could wonder why such a low-growth business was still saddled with so much debt despite undergoing a debt-for-equity swap.[33] In reality, if Candover and DX's lenders had not agreed to write down part of their loans back in 2010, the total debt value in 2013 would have been £383 million. Net of cash, the leverage multiple would have neared 10.7 times.

The real concern, though, was that a portion of that leverage was extremely costly. While the three tranches of the bank's term loans were vanilla instruments priced at Libor plus margins of 3% to 3.75%, and the mezzanine cost a less attractive, though still market standard, Libor +8.25%, the senior and junior subordinated loan notes (issued by Candover) were pricey. Their coupons rolled up at 15.25% and 15.50% interest annually. These interest expenses, although non-cash items, had the nasty effect of cancelling out operating income in both financial years to June 2012 and June 2013. But there was a simple solution to address this problem. Floating DX, and inviting institutions and the public to invest in the business, would help repay the loans and put an end to the financial burden.

On 27 February 2014, 9.5 years after having first been introduced to the stock exchange, the parcel and document exchange group was relisted at £1 per share with an enterprise value of £212 million. By raising £200 million from the market, DX was AIM's largest placement in eight years, a sign if one was needed that the markets had become bullish on postal businesses post-Royal Mail IPO. The enterprise multiple on last-12-months' EBITDA appeared reasonable at 6.3 times – even if the business had failed to show much growth in recent years.

Because it was quoted at a hefty discount to its peers Royal Mail and UK Mail and promised the distribution of generous dividends, DX saw its stock shoot up 30% on IPO day, closing at 130 pence a share. It was very reminiscent of the aftermarket uplift the group had experienced at the time of its first public listing in 2004, though back then bid speculations were used to justify the frothy stock performance. Anyhow, this time around the proceeds had been used to fully repay the LBO loans so net debt had been reduced to a lowly 0.35 times earnings, making DX's healthy balance sheet a strong plus given the challenge that competing against a giant like Royal Mail represented. The latter, with EBITDA surpassing £900 million (or 27 times DX's) and net assets of £2.4 billion – compared to DX's pre-admission net liabilities position – was likely to remain a formidable rival in the parcel and packet segment.[34]

Unusually, all of DX's shares held by financial investors had been floated – with management retaining a 3.6% stake.[35] Apparently, the company's institutional shareholders did not have the patience, or confidence, to hang around for a post-IPO exit. Arle-Candover had sold its entire 51% stake and booked a small gain over the business's residual written-down book value, but the £210 million valuation was a far cry from the combined £550 million-plus the buyout firm had paid to take the company off the stock market and merge it with Secure Mail back in 2006. Especially because, as noted, DX had diversified its revenue stream into courier and logistics services and made a string of acquisitions in the intervening period.

To get another sense of the extent of the transaction's underperformance and value destruction, the mail group's EBITDA for the year ended 30 June 2013 was 5% below its fiscal year 2009 earnings even though its top line was 80% larger. Put another way, EBITDA margins had halved to 11% over the previous four years. Between the time of its demerger from Hays in 2004 and its relisting ten years later, DX's valuation had declined from £275 million to £210 million.

When Candover had bid to delist DX in 2006, one analyst had explained that it was easy to see the attraction of the business from the PE house's perspective: a strong market position, high margins and very strong cash contribution that could support substantially higher levels of debt. In view of what happened under Candover's ownership, it was an erroneous opinion. The buyout firm had evidently overpaid for an ex-growth business, squandering more than £150 million of its LPs' capital in the process.

The public markets' sirens

DX's first 20 months of post-IPO performance could easily serve as exhibit A in a case against delisting/relisting treadmills and PE-backed stock offerings. A brief look at Figure 9.1 will convince the reader that something, somewhere, went badly wrong.

The first six months proceeded relatively smoothly. In fact, thanks to the market's sudden infatuation with anything remotely related to mail services, DX's stock price stayed above its introductory price. The interim results announcement of 24 March 2014 was received with much apathy, with the stock dipping 0.8% on the day, still up 25% on the 100-pence IPO price, on the news that revenues were up 3.2% and EBITDA was flat year-on-year.[36] When on 15 July management issued a trading update to inform the public that full-year numbers to 30 June were in line with expectations, the market's reaction was as riveting, with the share price losing 0.9% on the day, still a fifth up on the introductory price. Even on 29 September 2014, when the final 2013-14 financial-year results were revealed, the 2.1% increase in sales and the flat EBITDA failed to provoke much of a reaction. DX's stock was in fact up 1.6% on the day.[37] For a group trading on seven times EBITDA, it was a fairly lenient view. In the following few days, though, the market finally started to compute the significance of this situation.

DX was a no-growth business operating in a highly competitive market. What should have been factored in at the time of the IPO was about to be priced in several months later. In the four days following the full-year to June 2014 results, the share price shed 4.5%. The week after, it lost almost 8%, dipping below its introductory price for the first time since IPO during the trading session of Friday 10 October. After closing at 96.5 pence a share on 16 October, the stock would never again reach its IPO value. The market had reassessed the fundamentals of a business that, for the past seven years, had registered low single-digit organic growth at best, and seen its EBITDA margin shrink from 25% in 2007 to less than 11% in the year ended 30 June 2014. Settling in the 80p-to-90p range for most of the ensuing 12 months, the stock could have fooled investors into thinking that DX was the typical value play, offering a dividend yield north of 5% but limited upside in terms of stock appreciation. It would have been an ideal scenario for those who believe in the proper functioning of marketplaces. However, businesses that have underperformed for many years rarely turn out to be reliable blue-chip securities.

Figure 9.1: DX (Group) plc's share price from IPO (27 February 2014) to 31 December 2015

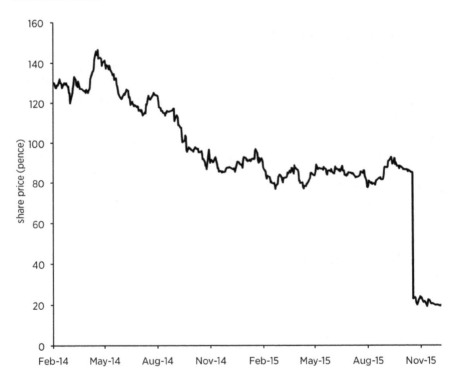

It took time for the outside world to recognise that DX should never have been listed in the first place; that it was not able to operate according to the rules set out by public markets, whereby quoted companies must be able to offer either regularity and stability (which attracts value investors) or strong upside potential (for growth investors). DX, it turns out, offered neither. Despite reporting in mid-February 2015 negative revenue growth of 5.6% and flat EBITDA in the six months to 31 December 2014, the company could consider itself lucky that its shares only lost 6.5% of their value in the following week. Within a month, the stock had shed 16%, sitting around 80p per share during most of the spring of 2015.

Since the group had consistently delivered lacklustre results, the market could have anticipated future disappointments. Instead, equity analysts all came up with reports announcing that with a stock 20% below its IPO price 12 months after the public offering, DX was a 'Buy'. On 21 September 2015 management made another results announcement, this time for the full year to June 2015, and once again results were down and EBITDA was flat. DX had become extremely predictable; it just wasn't the sort of consistency the market was looking for. And yet the stock started edging its way up from the low 80s to the high 80s. It was probably a sign of relief from the market, and so were the brokers' notes that reiterated their 'Buy' ratings and a consensus target price of 110 pence.[38]

By the time DX's management was ready to make its next announcement, the stock had settled into its mid-80s trading habit. But then, the company released a profit update on Friday 13 November 2015. That day, management admitted what any observer should have concluded long ago. It was facing a very tough market: first, its core, high-margin DX Exchange business, which handled business-to-business mail and documents, was experiencing a faster erosion of volumes than expected. Second, pricing pressure was ongoing and the difficulty of attracting delivery drivers had increased costs.[39] EBITDA had been flat for the past three reporting periods, but it looked like momentous earnings erosion was on the way. This time, the market did not factor in the update in an orderly fashion: DX's stock crashed by 73% on the day (see Figure 9.1), acting out its own Friday the 13th horror movie. Trading in the low-to-mid-20s for the rest of the year, or more than three-quarters below its IPO price, the formerly PE-backed group offered a few scary lessons to all parties involved.

Delisting-relistings assume that a previously underperforming public company will do better the second time around, once PE professionals have applied their expert operational and financial skills to the business. The DX chronicle, summed up in Table 9.1, shows that it is not a given. As we will see in Chapters 13 and 14, public investors are often on the wrong end of the IPO stick. There are simply too many parties aiming to make money out of the flotation – investment bankers, lawyers, brokers, consultants, not to mention the selling shareholders, who usually include management – that it is virtually impossible to obtain independent advice regarding the true worth of the business being floated. As Table 9.1 illustrates, it is easy to paint a rosy picture when trying to sell a business: DX delivered limited organic growth, but thanks to acquisitions made in recent years, its revenues were showing healthy progress in the past three years.

If investors had paid attention to several data points in the IPO prospectus, they would have known that the number of letters being delivered in the UK was on the decline, that parcel volumes had only risen by 3.7% per annum since 2008 and were forecast to grow at an even slower pace over the next ten years, that EBITDA margins had shrunk significantly in the previous three years (they were down markedly since 2007 but prospective investors were not given that information), and that organic revenue growth in the largest mail and packets division was 3% in the past three years.[40] On that basis, a 6.3 times EBITDA multiple looked full rather than reasonable.

Table 9.1: DX Group's financials (in £millions except for margins and ratios)

Year end 30 June	2007	2008	2009	2010	2011	2012	2013	2014 Post-IPO
Revenue	172.0*	173.6	170.4	164.9	164.0	206.6	305.7	312.0
EBITDA	43.5*	46.0*	34.6	27.9	27.1	30.9	32.9	33.7
EBITDA margin	25.3%	26.5%	20.3%	16.9%	16.5%	15.0%	10.8%	10.8%
Total net debt**	285.3	298.6	316.2	314.9	166.6	187.9	210.4	11.8
Net debt / EBITDA	6.56x	6.49x	9.14x	11.29x	6.15X	6.08x	6.40x	0.35x

Notes: * Estimates ** Including shareholder's subordinated loan notes, zero coupon loan notes, and mezzanine portion. Source: Company accounts and author's analysis

Failure to deliver

What are the reasons DX, a company that had such a promising future at the time of its float in late 2004, ended up being such a disappointing investment for Candover and the public shareholders post-relisting?

1. Winning market share away from a former monopoly is a very costly enterprise that requires cash availability for the long haul. A

precedent that should have been a warning to all newcomers was the liberalisation of the UK gas sector in the 1990s. It had taken many years for cash-rich foreign groups like German E.ON and French EDF to grab a meaningful share of the market against incumbent British Gas. The UK Government had taken a more proactive stance in the electricity and water sectors by breaking up the original monopoly into separate regional players. This had created bitter rivalry and several strong market participants had emerged, ensuring healthy competition.

Unfortunately for companies keen to enter the postal industry, because it was difficult to break down the Royal Mail into several local entities due to the necessity to provide a universal mail service through a seamlessly connected network, the government had little choice but to take a similar approach to that followed with the gas market deregulation, and to maintain the state monopoly. It was very likely that only large sector participants would have the capital base and expertise necessary to give Royal Mail a run for its money. Large new entrants such as DHL Global Mail (the UK arm of German monopoly operator Deutsche Post, which opened its first distribution centre outside London in April 2005 to compete with Royal Mail for business mail)[41] and TNT Post (renamed Whistl in 2014) also benefitted from a war chest generated in their home markets, so they could try to run a low-margin, slow-growth operation in the UK to build market share over many years. DX could ill-afford such luxury. Eventually, even Deutsche Post threw in the towel and sold its domestic operations DHL to Home Delivery Network in early 2010.

2. When the UK postal industry had been deregulated, commentators had pointed out that already deregulated foreign markets had seen incumbents cling on to their dominant market positions. In Sweden, ten years after the postal market was opened up in 1993, 94% of mail was still being delivered by state-owned monopoly Sweden Post. Five years after losing its monopoly in 1998, New Zealand Post still controlled 98% of the market. Displacing Royal Mail was likely to be a long drawn-out battle. For that, a solid cash balance was needed.[42]

3. Despite its history of costly inefficiencies, Royal Mail bounced back. From a loss of £200 million in 2003, the former state monopoly saw profits of £220 million in 2004 and £500 million a year later. It did not hurt that in early 2006 the government handed over a charitable £1.75 billion allowance to plug its pension deficit. Despite its hard-to-manage unionised workforce and its bulky universal service across the

country, the national postal group proved a formidable competitor once it got its cash-flow management in order. By the time it IPO'd in 2013, Royal Mail employed 150,000 people – a 50,000 headcount reduction over the previous decade – and generated annual free cash flows in excess of £330 million. Even if in 2009 it remained one of the least profitable postal groups in Europe, its performance was supported by regular government intervention in order to maintain the universal postal service and ensure the funding of an accounting pension deficit estimated at £8 billion in March 2010. In March 2012 the group's historic pension deficit was removed from its balance sheet and transferred to the state – all with the blessing of the European Commission; the sort of liability remission that is not easy to match for a small rival like DX.[43]

4. New entrants had also cherry-picked the lucrative packets and parcels market to compete with Royal Mail, which was left running the loss-making 'last-mile' activities on its own. The UK Government agreed to give the incumbent more freedom in its pricing and marketing policies as a quid pro quo for maintaining the cherished universal mail service across the country. In March 2012, a more lenient regulatory regime was introduced that reduced price controls from 60% to only 5% of Royal Mail's activities, giving the latter more bargaining power. Rivals UK Mail and DX, with tariffs set well below Royal Mail's in the early years of deregulation, saw their competitive advantage eroded as the government progressively removed most of the former state monopoly's price controls. When it floated in 2013, Royal Mail derived more than half of its revenues from the parcel division.[44]

5. Business mail accounted for four-fifths of the UK postal market, but for all of the profits (since the universal mail service was loss-making). Understandably, most new entrants tried to focus on the lucrative end of the industry. Fourteen companies had registered with Postcomm in late 2005 ahead of the full deregulation of the market.[45] This led to intense price competition in corporate post, packets and parcels – hence the collapse of next-day parcel carrier City Link in December 2014 and the decision by Whistl to suspend door-to-door post delivery in London and other major British cities in May 2015. The squeeze on margins arose because industry participants misjudged how low barriers to entry in the parcel delivery sector truly were. Small courier firms were able to hire freelance van drivers on zero-hour contracts (allowing companies to hire staff with no minimum guarantee of work) and focus on local parcel delivery jobs

that did not require a regional or national network. For years, these traditionally high-margin, time-critical missions had been the bread and butter of independent groups like DX and UK Mail.

6. Royal Mail had a well-established network across the UK. Much of the mail that was being collected and sorted by rival companies was then passed on to Royal Mail for 'last-mile' delivery. It gave the incumbent the ability to pick and choose where it wanted to compete and focus on retaining its most valuable business customers.

7. The main disruption of the postal market was not just the deregulation process, but the widespread adoption of electronic mail. For a company deriving two-thirds of its sales from document exchange between law firms and their clients, emails rather than other physical delivery firms were the real threat. Moreover, the Royal Mail strikes that took place in 2007 and 2009 made mail much less attractive and encouraged faster adoption of electronic delivery for bills and bank statements. Between 2005 and 2011 letter volumes per person dropped by 25% in the UK.[46] Because Royal Mail's traditional letter delivery activity was experiencing disruptive competition from paperless communication, it was natural for the former state monopoly to exploit its market dominance with the aim of growing its higher-margin parcel delivery division. Smaller actors, be they courier or next-day parcel delivery service providers like DX, were bound to suffer.

8. Another threat to Royal Mail and other postal groups in the medium to longer term is the emergence of online retailers (think Amazon) choosing to internalise their product delivery services in order to control costs and ensure quality and reliability all the way to the last mile – that certainly won't provide much support to DX's stock.

9. Until 2004 DX had been part of Hays, an entity that had once belonged to none other than Candover: between 1987 and 1989, the buyout shop had been Hays's controlling shareholder before listing the mini-conglomerate on the London Stock Exchange. Maybe its previous ownership of DX's parent company had made Candover overconfident as to its ability to make this investment a success – a point that we raised regarding RBOs in Part Four.

10. Taking companies off the stock exchange is far from a sure thing to make money. For a start, it assumes that public market investors do not know how to value a business – a dangerous assumption nowadays given the number of hedge fund managers having little else to do with their time but to act as price arbitrageurs – or that

the bidding party has a unique angle to generate value post-delisting. Unless the bidder has synergistic benefits or a master plan to generate significant upside post-delisting, it is unlikely that the target's performance once under LBO will justify the premium paid to take it off the quote. Candover assumed that by merging DX and Secure Mail it would derive adequate synergies. It probably did not justify the 26% premium paid for DX.

Candover and the lenders backing DX's buyout underestimated the ongoing changes in the UK postal market and the complexity of the regulatory landscape; they misjudged the impact that email adoption would have on corporate mail volumes; and they undervalued the importance for the government of ensuring the preservation of a universal mail service via a healthy, well-capitalised Royal Mail. While all other major mail and parcel operators, TNT, Deutsche Post and UK Mail could, to varying degrees, be accused of making similar mistakes, none had made the unforgivable error of piling a huge chunk of expensive loans on their books. The amount of debt used to fund the delisting was aggressive.

DX's cash flows ended up being far less predictable than thought. Operating in a market facing across-the-board deregulation, DX offered limited visibility on future growth and margin progression – prerequisites to managing an LBO successfully. Rivalry from Royal Mail and other participants caused price pressure, squeezing margins considerably. Leverage killed any hope that DX management would have had of building a competitive alternative to Royal Mail's offering. To boost its IRR, Candover relied on the second pillar of value creation: add-on acquisitions. Unable to pursue a buy-and-build plan, in part due to its own in-house funding crisis, the LBO house did not benefit from dividend recaps either during the post-2008 credit squeeze.

By the time Candover sold out, the public markets had gone through a reassessment of valuations. As a consequence the PE firm's returns suffered from negative multiple-arbitrage, with its exit multiple of about six times EBITDA a third below the one paid on entry, the result of greatly reduced profit margins and limited organic growth prospects. It is partly because of its mail services division's underperformance that Hays Group incurred an exceptional £600 million write-down in September 2003, ahead of its decision to spin off three of its four divisions. If a large conglomerate like Hays had taken the view that competing against Royal Mail would not be to the benefit of its shareholders, was it unreasonable to expect that, as a standalone, DX's struggle would continue unabated?

We should not downplay the effect that the Great Recession had on the sector. Between 2008 and 2010, sales in DX's core activity of document exchange lost 16%, while its courier division's sales declined 17%. But a thorough market due diligence would also have helped Candover and the lenders figure out that the sector was far from a safe bet. As observed, one of DX's private competitors was already publicly quoted. And FTSE 250 constituent UK Mail's stock performance in the months preceding Candover's decision to bid for DX had been truly abysmal. Following a sudden deterioration in trading, between mid-August 2005 and late February 2006 UK Mail's market cap had collapsed more than 55%, from 680 pence to 305 pence. It should have served as a warning.[47]

Born out of the 1970s postal strikes, DX failed to build the scale and cash hoard indispensable to compete against a state-sponsored rival. Despite the best efforts of four separate management teams and repeated Royal Mail strikes, DX got caught in a mindless listing-delisting-relisting circus, all within a ten-year stretch. As a business quoted on the illiquid, underwhelming and underperforming junior exchange AIM, the company is unlikely to ever have the firepower to become an appealing investment proposition for public investors. It had been allowed to survive as a niche participant, but troubles began because it did not stay out of the way of Royal Mail. With a stock down more than three-quarters below its introductory price two years after flotation, the document exchange specialist will attract dividend-seeking investors, until it gets acquired or gets competed away, only to be remembered as another PE-backed IPO gone sour.

CHAPTER 10
Debenhams – Debt Never Goes Out Of Fashion

ON 13 JANUARY 2015, THE SHARE PRICE OF DEBENHAMS PLC, one of Britain's largest chains of department stores, sank 8% to 69p as its chief executive Michael Sharp announced one more disappointing set of results. Ten days later, retail entrepreneur Mike Ashley – the owner of Sports Direct, the largest chain of sports shops in the country – staked out a claim for himself in the long-running saga of clothing retail consolidation by disclosing that he had agreed a put-option deal with American bank Goldman Sachs over a 10.5% interest in Debenhams. It instantly pushed his shareholding in the underperforming retailer above 16%.

Ashley, a billionaire often described as mercurial and industrious, had built up his position in Debenhams over the previous 12 months but was not forthcoming about his true intentions. Although Debenhams had been trialling Sports Direct concessions in two of its stores, the partnership was meant to be commercial, not financial.[1] Maybe it was a sign that things were about to get uncomfortable for Debenhams's senior management. Indeed, given the period of upheaval and the litany of setbacks experienced by the fashion retail chain over the previous decade, it was high time for change.

From shopkeeper to retail empire

The origins of Debenhams can be traced back to 1778, when Thomas Clark set up shop as a draper at 44 Wigmore Street, in central London. It was a period of prosperity for Britain. Although the United States had declared independence two years earlier, the reign of King George III – from 1760 to 1820 – would otherwise mark the emergence of the country as the leading power in Europe, politically (as Great Britain and Ireland joined forces to become the United Kingdom in 1801, and France was weakened by the Revolution of 1789 and the subsequent Napoleonic wars), economically (Britain led the Industrial

Revolution, notably with James Watt's steam engine), and culturally (thanks to the works of Jane Austen, Byron, Shelley and Keats, among others).

In December 1813, Clark and 19-year-old William Debenham became equal partners and worked from the same location, although eventually the shop was extended to the other side of Wigmore Street, one establishment being called Clark and Debenham, the other Debenham and Clark. By 1823 the two business associates had opened a small drapery business at 3 Promenade Rooms, Cheltenham, selling a selection of silks, muslins, shawls, gloves, lace and fancy goods. The new shop flourished. In 1837 Clark retired from the business and Debenham assumed two of his most trusted staff, William Pooley and John Smith, as partners, trading in both London and Cheltenham as Debenham, Pooley and Smith.

By 1840 the management of the Cheltenham branch was given to Clement Freebody, Debenham's brother-in-law. Around 1843 another branch shop was launched in Harrogate, North Yorkshire. Extended and refurbished premises opened in Cheltenham in October 1844. Pooley and Smith retired from the business in 1851 and a new partnership was formed that included William Debenham's son, also called William, and Clement Freebody: the business became known as Debenham, Son and Freebody. Eventually, in 1905 the business was incorporated as Debenhams Limited. That same year it opened its first department store. The group blossomed and grew through several acquisitions, including chic retailer Harvey Nichols in London's Knightsbridge in 1920.

In 1928, by which stage no family member remained involved in the running of the group, the business listed on the London Stock Exchange. Acquisitive growth remained a core feature of its strategy and proved so successful that, by 1950, Debenhams was the largest department store group in the UK, owning 84 companies and 110 stores, many of them retaining their individual identity. The business was turning into a very efficient retail empire, but the deal-obsessed 1980s would see it lose its independence. The economy, in Britain as elsewhere in the developed world, was living through a euphoric phase of mergers and acquisitions turbocharged by deregulation, privatisation of state-enterprises, and takeovers by corporate raiders.

By 1985, the year when it was the subject of a hostile takeover by its rival The Burton Group, Debenhams plc owned 67 department stores and served 12 million customers through its branded stores and subsidiaries. It had doubled its profits before tax in the previous two years to £40 million.[2] Not too keen to be bought out by a weaker performing rival considered of low prestige, and certain that they were to be booted if Burton won the bidding war, Debenhams's chairman and his senior executive team had mulled over the possibility of a management buyout.[3] In the end the Burton Group, which had generated pre-tax profits of £56 million on £416 million of sales in its previous fiscal year and was not therefore much bigger than Debenhams, prevailed with a bid slightly short of £600 million.[4] Bringing under its sway illustrious names like Harvey Nichols, dating back to 1831, toy shop Hamleys, founded in 1760, and footwear shopkeeper Lotus, established in 1759, Burton was erecting the largest clothing retail concern in the country.

Back in the public eye

Under Burton's ownership Debenhams repositioned itself by introducing its own merchandise in key product areas and increasing its portfolio of stores. But the acquisition was not a success from Debenhams's point of view as it had a better image and focus than the other multiple-store concepts run by the Burton Group. The recession of the early 1990s proved too much for a conglomerate that included more than ten separate fashion brands, from young formats Topshop and Topman to feminine fashion designer Dorothy Perkins.[5] In truth, there was little logic in keeping department stores within the same corporate umbrella as Burton's apparel chains. The main advantage of running emporiums like Debenhams is to be able to offer a wide range of competing brands, not just in clothing but also in areas like home furnishings and accessories, electronics and household appliances. Both sides of the Burton Group had diverging value propositions.

By 1998 management's decision to demerge Debenhams from the rest of the group was welcomed by investors. In late January of that year the business regained its independence.[6] Despite the excitement, the transition was painful: in the financial year of 1999, its first post-demerger, Debenhams recorded negative like-for-like sales growth and flat pre-tax earnings of £138 million. The following year to August 2000 also failed to impress, with like-for-like sales growth of 1.8% and profits before tax down to £130 million. In the face of such poor performance, the group's CEO Terry Green stepped down in September 2000 and trading director Belinda Earl was promoted to the top job. The day the move was announced, Debenhams shares closed down 17.5 pence at 182.5p, indicating that despite the substandard performance of the group under Green, investors viewed the new boss as an unknown quantity.[7]

Their anxiety was to prove misguided. Without delay, results improved, and in the following two years like-for-like sales grew 8% and 4.8%. Total sales, which included new store openings, had grown 1.2% on average in the last two years under Green's leadership. The first three reporting seasons under Earl saw sales climb by a compound annual rate of 9%. In the early days of 2003, the share price had recovered and exceeded 270 pence. Earl had demonstrated that she knew a thing or two about managing department stores. Drawn by the sight of such robust trading, LBO firms were ready to make approaches.

By the time interested parties were running the rule over Debenhams in the spring of 2003, the department-store operator had spent five years on the London Stock Exchange. During that time it had focused on growth via brand enhancement and retail positioning, store expansion and modernisation. It had implemented new initiatives, such as *Designers at Debenhams*, which had a turnover of more than £200 million and helped designers showcase their new creations in the retailer's stores. The group had improved advertising campaigns, product innovation and the overall shopping environment. It had also opened 19 new stores, and modernised 40 of them. Its product range had long been extended beyond clothing, with cosmetics, perfume, skincare, beauty accessories as well as electronics and furniture all part of its offering. Since the demerger, average annual like-for-like sales had grown by 3.4% despite the deterioration of economic conditions. When reporting interim results to 28 February 2003, the public company confirmed that it was in rude health, with pre-tax profits and sales up 4.8% and 5.8% year-on-year respectively.[8] Some opportunistic PE investors felt that they could do better.

Back in private hands

Reports first emerged on 12 May that British outfit Permira had approached Debenhams and was working with Chief Executive Earl and her finance director Matthew Roberts to take the company over at 425p per share. Permira's team had been given six weeks to carry out due diligence and, with an offer described as fully priced and the target's management team on its side, it looked like the bidder's pre-emptive move might not be matched. However, there were corporate governance concerns among shareholders regarding the close working relationship between Debenhams's top executives and the financial sponsor. [9] In light of the CEO and CFO's apparent conflicts of interest, the retail group's non-executive directors were swiftly encouraged to invite rival bids. It took until the end of June for two PE firms, pan-European CVC and its American peer Texas Pacific Group, to jointly make an approach and be granted access to the books.

While the two laggards were busy catching up, Permira completed due diligence and confirmed its £1.54 billion offer in late July, partnering with two giant financial groups: Blackstone and Goldman Sachs.[10] In order to maintain tension while it was negotiating final details with the Permira-led consortium, the Debenhams board did something that one cannot find in too many textbooks: it offered to pay up to £5 million of due diligence expenses incurred by the bidding duo formed by CVC and TPG. Given that the general retailer was already committed to paying Permira a break fee of £6 million if its board failed to recommend the latter's offer, and an even more generous £8.5 million break fee if Permira's bid was trumped by another party, it was becoming difficult to keep track of the target's contractual obligations.[11]

Yet the pledge to cover a portion of CVC and TPG's deal costs did the trick: it led Debenhams's public shareholders to hold out rather than tender their shares to Permira's consortium – by 28 August only 2.22% of the group's shareholders had accepted the 425p-a-share offer. This enabled management to report on 3 September sales figures up 8% for the year to 31 August 2003 (further validation that under the leadership of Belinda Earl the group was doing very well), and it gave sufficient time and incentive for CVC and TPG to table a proposal. On 12 September the competing duo bid 440p a share, valuing Debenhams at £1.6 billion.[12] Shortly afterwards, war ensued. Each consortium spent the rest of September and the first part of October trying to outflank one another. At one point it got so expensive that Goldman decided to drop out of Permira's team.[13]

Goldman's decision, in effect, handed victory to the other side. After a four-month process blending traits of courtship and warfare, in late October CVC's party, acting through a newco called Baroness Retail, secured the prize with a bid 20% higher than Permira's initial offer and 83% above 256.25p, the price at which the stock was quoted on 8 April, before rumours of a possible offer had surfaced.[14] The retailer was valued at more than £1.9 billion, or eight times EBITDA. CVC and TPG, by then in tow with the PE arm of American bank Merrill Lynch, took the department store chain off the exchange in December 2003, 190 years after Thomas Clark and William Debenham had partnered in their venture.

*   *   *

The public-to-private buyout had been led by CVC, the largest LBO fund manager in Europe based on the total value of deals done. It operated out of its London-headquarters with a network of 12 European offices. Recently, the firm had opened outposts in Asia, raising a $750 million fund in 2000 to invest there, and indicating that it had global aspirations. But the Debenhams take-private was decidedly British. One of CVC's London-based partners, Jonathan Feuer, had identified the opportunity and worked with a couple of corporate executives CVC was well acquainted with: Rob Templeman and Chris Woodhouse.

Since February 2003 these two individuals were respectively Chairman and Deputy Chairman of Halfords Group plc, a retailer of car maintenance parts and cycling products that CVC had purchased eight months earlier. Throughout the summer of 2003 the two executives had worked with Feuer to diligence

Debenhams and identify the main financial and operational parameters that would generate fast and sizable returns. It was not just one of the largest take-privates attempted in the country, it was also CVC's biggest UK buyout to date, so every effort had to be made ahead of the delisting to analyse the potential in value creation.

Feuer, a chartered accountant who had joined the firm from British bank Baring Brothers back in 1988, knew that the equity ticket was likely to be too large for his firm to finance on its own. Importantly, CVC had raised its €4.7 billion European Equity Partners III fund two years earlier, so it was in great shape to back the transaction. However, the equity portion was likely to exceed £600 million (or the equivalent of €900 million). As is common for PE funds, CVC's 2001 vintage was not allowed to invest more than 15% of its aggregate commitments in any one portfolio company. If the equity ticket was £600 million, it would represent 19% of CVC III's capital. Of course the firm could always reach out to its limited partners and request their written consent to waive that restriction. But if the transaction turned out to be a fiasco, it would be an expensive mistake that could jeopardise the firm's future. In the majority of scenarios when LBO houses are faced with this dilemma, they prefer to bring in co-investors. Thus, CVC had brought Texas Pacific Group and US bank Merrill Lynch into the picture.

PE-style value creation

Upon taking ownership of the department store group, the Baroness Retail troika replaced top executive Earl and her finance chief – who had both been rooting for Permira's bid – and appointed Templeman and Woodhouse to run the show. In the process, CVC released the pair from their Halfords duties. If that decision was swift, the new owners soon made clear that they were not willing to waste time in extracting value from the business, and the way they would milk Debenhams over the next few years would become casebook material on how to ruthlessly maximise returns. Let us revisit the many ways this was achieved.

First things first. Naturally, most of the purchase consideration was in the form of debt, with 70% of the £1.9 billion-to-£2 billion valuation financed with £696 million of senior loans, £325 million of high-yield bonds and £355 million of property financing.[15] It was a bit of a jump from the 7.5% of leverage the retail group was on prior to the take-private, but that's why it is a called a leveraged buyout. Eventually, the high-yield bond tranche would be scaled down due to insufficient demand, but debt would still top 70% of total capital, including a revolving credit facility of £125 million and the requisite capex line to open new stores and revamp existing ones.

The day after they took the retailer private, the new owners were in negotiations to sell and lease back up to 26 properties in a deal that could raise £450 million in cash.[16]After six months in control, in July 2004 they paid themselves a dividend of £80 million by amending the debt package, all because EBITDA had increased by £30 million to £270 million between the launch of the debt syndication and its completion. The funds had come from the issue of a £160 million add-on to the company's £275 million eight-year notes that had been placed only two months earlier. Leverage remained unchanged at very reasonable ratios of 3.6 times EBITDA for total net debt and of 2.4 times for senior net debt. In order to get such a quick payback agreed by the lenders, however, the deal sponsors offered the latter a carrot in the shape of a 25-basis-point incentive fee.

This unusually rapid refinancing was mainly the result of a three-year cost saving plan completed in just three months. In those three months alone, management had delivered £115 million in working-capital improvements and produced £45 million in cost reductions. The newly leveraged business had also made a £160 million profit from selling its freehold and long-term leasehold property interests to an affiliated company.[17] Eventually, the real impact of the sale and leaseback agreement would appear in the 2005 fiscal year, with the book value of tangible assets shrinking by £370 million on the prior year.

In order to energise the top line and generate cash, in early 2004 management offloaded £30 million of inventory that was sitting in warehouses. Management also invested in store expansion and line extension. Organic growth was anaemic, so in March 2005 Debenhams took ownership of eight stores from collapsed department store group Allders. Shortly afterwards, and approximately one year after closing the loan syndication process funding the take-private, management focused its attention on a £2.05 billion recapitalisation, with £1.75 billion in senior facilities and a £300 million second-lien piece, in order to pay CVC, TPG and Merrill another dividend: an extremely generous £800 million going straight into the financial sponsors' pockets. This time, leverage multiples were going up to reflect the credit markets' increasing generosity and laxity: total-net-debt-to-EBITDA stood at 5.6 times, while senior-net-debt-to-EBITDA reached 4.7 times.[18]

Thanks to a very aggressive cost-cutting programme, in particular by reducing head office staff by 12% in the first year, and by chopping down refurbishments by three-quarters as well as negotiating more favourable terms with suppliers or taking twice as long to pay them,[19] gross profits rose from £248 million in the 2003 fiscal year to £256 million the following year and £336 million in the year ended on 3 September 2005. Between 2003 and 2005, operating earnings had soared by a third. Thanks to this upswing in profitability, the retailer took full advantage of the debt markets' generosity by refinancing during the 2005 fiscal year, replacing its expensive deep discounted bonds, high-yield bonds and mortgage facility with cheaper senior term loans.[20]

Back in the public eye – take 2

With such strong performance uplift, in late 2005 the PE consortium decided to prepare the business for sale. Less than two years after having delisted it, CVC et al. were planning to unload it. They were not just trying to do a quick flip on the basis that Debenhams had the ability to deliver easy cash back; they were also fully aware that the economy was enjoying one of its regular bullish phases. The stock markets were booming – the FTSE 100 index had risen by almost 17% through 2005 – and the private equity sector had seen an increase of two-thirds in deal values in the previous 12 months. Who knew how long the bulls were going to stick around? Flipping this middle-of-the-range retailer would not only boost the internal rate of return, it would instantly crystallise the value of the quick fixes they had implemented during the two years of ownership. The idea was to relist Debenhams.

However, the disposal process was unlikely to be simple. Many of the institutional investors asked to take a look at the Debenhams IPO would be the same ones that had sold the company to the three PE owners in 2003. Most would be concerned about the profile of this investment. Debenhams was not a strong franchise and given the reputation of financial sponsors it was likely to be put back on the market at a full valuation. It had become a leasehold estate dependent on operating abilities rather than an asset play. The PE owners had squeezed an awful lot out of this business and it would be more difficult to achieve above-average earnings growth.[21]

Eventually, the float went ahead in early May 2006, helping the company raise £950 million. It was twice oversubscribed, mostly thanks to the fact that shares had been priced at the bottom of the indicative range: 195p. It gave Debenhams a market capitalisation of £1.675 billion. Combined with debt of £1.2 billion, the retailer had a total enterprise value of £2.875 billion, or over 12 times operating profits and 8.2 times EBITDA. The debt of £1.2 billion was net of £700 million raised from the IPO, which indicates that before its listing Debenhams had total net debt of £1.9 billion, or 8.3 times operating profits. Recall that the financial sponsors had bought the business for £1.9 billion with £1.3 billion of debt. Their original £600 million equity ticket had already been repaid through the refinancings previously mentioned. In fact, commentators speculated that, even before the IPO, the backers had taken home £1.3 billion.[22]

CVC, TPG and Merrill sold a 57% stake upon listing. Thanks to their previous dividend cash-outs and the £250 million they derived from the float, they were rumoured to have already made three times their money in less than 30 months. And they still held 35% of the shares. Chairman John Lovering, CEO Templeman and CFO Woodhouse, who held a combined, pre-IPO, 14% stake in the group, made estimated profits of £6 million, £9 million and £11 million respectively, and retained a holding worth about £60 million at the time of the listing.[23] All on a transaction that some had felt, back in late 2003, was fully valued and would require a lot of hard work. But they had pulled it through, and in normal circumstances, this is where our case study would end. This chapter, however, is all about understanding the impact of leverage on relisted businesses. That's where this chronicle becomes intriguing.

The importance of detail in retail

Debenhams's operating margin in the three years of activity ahead of its 2003 delisting was in the 11.5% ballpark. In the 12-month trading period to August 2006 – the year it was re-introduced to the London Stock Exchange – that number was unusually high: 14%. Well above its historical average, this margin had gone from 12% in 2003 to 13.5% in 2004 to 14.2% the following year. Whereas group turnover had risen by 6% a year over that period, the EBITA's annual rate of growth was 20%. Expanding profitability at a rate three times faster than revenue in the space of two fiscal years cannot represent a fundamental change in business model; it is necessarily derived from quick fixes. No business or industry can transform its operations in just 24 months to such an extent that it becomes a significantly more profitable concern. One way for a retailer to profoundly and permanently improve its margins would be to trade via an online platform or, at the very least, adopt a click-and-mortar model in order to significantly and permanently reduce its fixed cost base. But this sort of reconfiguration takes years, not months.

This should have set alarm bells ringing among potential investors. Institutions that were looking at Debenhams's listing prospectus should have asked two very elementary questions:

1.   What explains such a sudden rise in margins?

2.   Is it sustainable?

With the benefit of hindsight, the answer to the first question was delivered by the numerous press articles that came out in the two years after the relisting and that exposed drastic headcount reductions, delayed payments to, and discounts from, suppliers, without forgetting cutbacks in capex. But most institutions could have easily diligenced the business by speaking to the many senior employees who had left the company during the tenure of Lovering and Templeman. In 2004 alone, Debenhams had lost its design director, the head of the home division, and its menswear trading director to rivals. Many of them would have had a view on Debenhams's sudden upgrade in profitability.

As for the matter of sustainability, an anonymous quote in the *Financial Times* a year after the relisting of the company sums up the view of a private equity peer that the institutions that had invested in the IPO might have been fooled by the story sold to them by the financial owners and Debenhams's top executive team: "They tried to present it in the best possible light, that there was sustainability to what was being done [to Debenhams]...But that is what the market got wrong."[24]

In exiting, Debenhams's executives and the PE triumvirate were not just benefiting from a swiftly engineered operating profit upswing. Thanks to the credit bubble that had swamped the public markets in the intervening period, as they were reintroducing the company to the stock exchange 29 months later, the owners could use comparable quoted retailers as benchmarks to justify a higher multiple for Debenhams. Their PTP of the company had been achieved at a demanding 11 times multiple of operating earnings in late 2003. The May 2006 float was going for 12.1 times, but main peers Next and Marks & Spencer were respectively quoted at 12.6 times and 17 times.[25] This multiple-arbitrage was primarily market-driven, even if, in practice, punters could have been influenced by the fact that Debenhams had become a higher-margin business and were prepared to pay more for it.

In the months following the public placing, the group's management team maintained an ambitious growth strategy. In October 2006 Debenhams acquired nine Roches stores in Ireland to add to its three existing outlets in that country. For a total consideration of €29 million, half of which differed over a two-year period, the purchase added 500,000 sq ft to the group's selling space. Templeman soon announced plans to grow the business in part through overseas expansion, opening 70 stores outside the UK by 2010 in markets such as Russia, India, Romania, the Philippines, Cyprus and Malta.[26] In the 2007 financial year the company added 20 new stores out of a total estate of 142. It is during that time, while senior management was busy running the business, that reports started emerging about the group's stressed financial situation.

In early 2007, the lenders that had led the company's refinancing at the time of the IPO were said to still be sitting on most of their £1.2 billion of underwritten loans. The market had taken the view that the terms of the loans and the capital structure represented too risky an investment. After the float the share price had held steady, even climbing above 200p, but by early 2007 it was down 10%.[27] It was beginning its long downfall. On 17 April it surrendered 15% of its value following an 'unexpected' profit warning.[28] For good measure, in the summer and autumn, Baugur, an Icelandic investment firm specialised in retail that owned House of Fraser, one of Debenhams's smaller rivals, had acquired a 13.5% stake in the newly listed Debenhams.

After several profit warnings, the department-store chain disclosed that, for the fiscal year ended 1 September 2007, its gross and operating margins were down by more than a fifth on the prior year. Shortly before delivering these results, Templeman had commented to a journalist: "You have to keep it in perspective. We have had one bad season – are we fixing it? Yes."[29] Time would tell otherwise. In the meantime, because of the fall in the share price, Debenhams's enterprise value had collapsed from 8.2 times EBITDA upon IPO to 5.8 times in September 2007. By the end of December the stock was down nearly 60% from its listing price on rumours that the business was about to breach its debt covenants. That same month, Spanish asset manager Bestinver and Milestone Resources, an investment group linked to Dubai-based retailer Landmark, also notified the company that they respectively held 10% and 7% of the Debenhams shares. The vultures were smelling blood.

Sadly, for these opportunistic buyers, they were too early for the kill. From then on, things were only going to get worse for Debenhams, its managers, investors and lenders. As we now know, the summer of 2007 experienced a gradual but marked tightening of credit markets worldwide. First felt in the subprime segment of the US real estate sector, the Credit Crunch was about to demonstrate how an exceedingly leveraged company can fail to adapt to a changing financial and economic environment. As could be expected, the world economy went into a tailspin. After registering a negative move of 0.3% in 2008, British GDP crashed 4.3% the following year. It was one of the worst performances among the G8 countries. Even in the US, where the subprime crisis had originated, GDP had 'only' shrunk 2.8% in 2009. The Irish economy, which had been propped up by a property bubble not dissimilar to that of the US, had plummeted 2.6% in 2008 and 6.4% the following year.[30] Since the UK and Ireland accounted for about 90% of Debenhams's gross transaction value, this was to have a calamitous repercussion on trading.

Trouble in store

In the two years that followed the IPO, like-for-like sales fell. Down 5% in the year ended August 2007, they dropped a further 0.9% in the subsequent 12 months. In the annual report for the financial year of 2008 management tried to remain upbeat, but it was hard to hide the fact that prospects were dire. Between the year to 2 September 2006 and the 2008 fiscal year, operating profit had sunk by one-quarter. From a high of 14% in 2006, operating margins reached 9.6% two years later. Cash flows generated from operations tanked from £382 million in the 2005 fiscal year to £286 million in the 12 months to 30 August 2008.[31] The quick fixes carried out during the short period of private ownership were coming apart.

In February and March 2009, the world's stock markets reached their nadir, with the FTSE 100 index hitting a six-year low and the Dow Jones Industrial Average a 12-year low. Debenhams, however, had not waited for the rest of the market and had bottomed at almost 20p a share on 8 December 2008: about a tenth of the IPO price of May 2006. That day, leverage exceeded 92%. The few predators that had taken speculative positions throughout 2007 had indeed been a tad early. After a difficult early 2009, the company saw its share price reach 90p in March of that year, and despite some temporary up-and-down movements thereafter, that price soon became a fair reflection of the intrinsic, long-term value of the debt-filled, underperforming retailer.

Because of the Credit Crunch and its ramification in the various geographies where Debenhams operated, trading remained weak. The real concern for management and shareholders was that leverage was uncomfortably high. From £1.2 billion at the time of the relisting, net borrowings still totalled £1 billion or so at the end of August 2008. It was clear to all parties that Debenhams needed to find a solution. The very survival of the company and its 27,000 employees was at stake.

After making a £100 million amortisation repayment in May 2009, the retailer worked on rescheduling its debt pile. Like-for-like sales were on course to fall a further 3.6% in the year to 31 August 2009, so restructuring was a necessity. Given its profitability and cash-flow erosion, the group would not be able to meet future loan obligations. Crumbling under its financial liabilities, in June Debenhams revamped its balance sheet by raising over £320 million in fresh capital from public shareholders and by cancelling its dividend indefinitely. Accordingly, its net debt shrank by £404 million to a much more manageable £590 million.[32] Templeman was quick to declare that the placing removed "leverage off the agenda".[33] As the following 12 months would show, it was an optimistic view, but at least debt now accounted for just 45% of the group's capital structure.

Running for the door

Embarrassingly, at a time when management were asking public investors to put money in as part of the capital raise, in that same month of June 2009 CVC elected to sell most of its stake in the company.[34] Far from shelling out more cash as had first been conjectured, the PE investors were working on taking their chips off the table.[35] In fairness, CVC had held on much longer than co-investor

Merrill Lynch: the US bank had abruptly checked out back on 26 March 2008, thereby triggering a 17% fall in the share price on the day.[36] Sheepishly, the CVC representatives stepped down from the board of directors as the capital increase was taking place. Chairman John Lovering also announced his retirement from the board by March 2010, signalling the end of his financially rewarding ride.[37] By October 2009, for an additional gain of £100 million, the other backer of the December 2003 buyout, TPG, had sold its remaining 9% interest to hedge-fund manager Och-Ziff, bringing the incredibly profitable LBO to a close. With a reported gain of approximately £500 million, TPG had achieved a return multiple of nearly four times.[38]

It is striking that, at a time when Debenhams's surly band of creditors were threatening to take over the business and the incumbent PE owners were unwilling to ante up the dough, outside investors were prepared to step into this madness. You could not hope for more gullible and docile patsies. It surely serves as a great example of PE investors' negotiating powers and savage business acumen. Though, if further evidence were required that the interests of financial sponsors are at times at loggerheads with those of a portfolio company's management, employees and lenders, the situation encountered by Debenhams in the spring of 2009, when the world's entire financial system was shutting down, is a case in point. After having secured a solid multiple on their equity ticket, the financial sponsors were not just refusing to bail out their debt-strapped investee company; they were actually planning their escape.

If the PE backers were out of danger after an eventful six-year holding period, Debenhams was still reeling. In 2010 it again publicly acknowledged its inability to tackle its loan commitments. It completed another refinancing exercise via a £650 million credit facility in July of that year while cancelling its dividend once more. Thanks to the renegotiated terms, the annual interest cost was brought down from 7% to a more manageable 4.5%.[39] That summer, the general retail group was also reported to be in negotiations to arrange another sale and leaseback deal to unlock further value from its property portfolio.[40] Since its freehold property assets had shrunk from £346 million in 2004 to less than £50 million five years later, there was not much left to suck the business dry anyway.[41]

* * *

Finally, as their financial sponsors had fully exited and the damage done was set to remain for years to come, the senior executives who had been brought in to manage the buyout eight years earlier stepped down during the course of 2011 to let a new chief exec and a new finance director handle the fragile parcel from then on. First, in the summer Deputy Chief Executive Michael Sharp took over the top job from Templeman. Then, in November, Simon Herrick, an external candidate, was brought in to replace Woodhouse in the key financial management role. Operating results in the five years post-IPO had been lousy: total sales had gone from £1.7 billion in the fiscal year ended 2 September 2006 to £2.2 billion in the 2012 fiscal year, but operating profits had sunk from £238 million to £175 million over the same period. Operating margin had dived from 14% to less than 8%. About the only sign that the PE-appointed executives had positively reformed the company was that online sales, still only 2.1% of total revenues in 2009, had reached 6.7% two years later.

Otherwise, Figure 10.1 makes it abundantly clear that the general retailer's performance since its relisting had been below par, and the situation deteriorated further after the departure of the PE-backed executives. Following a disastrous Christmas 2013 trading period and the all too familiar profit warning on New Year's Eve, followed by a 12% share price drop, Finance Director Herrick left on 2 January 2014 shortly after his second-year anniversary.[42] As is often the case, the job of sorting out the consequences of an ill-considered LBO can be a lot more disheartening than first appeared. It would take six months for Debenhams to identify a replacement, and another six months for niche retailer Mothercare CFO Matt Smith to take up the unenviable finance function in January 2015. Given that operating margin had collapsed to less than 6% by that stage, the department store group could do with some motherly attention.

Nine years after its relisting, Debenhams was yet to recover from its buyout adventure. Group turnover continued to edge up, passing the £2.3 billion mark in 2014, but profitability faltered further, with operating earnings diving to £134 million in 2015, translating into a paltry 5.8% margin. As could be expected, one factor behind Debenhams's fall in profit margins was the surge in expenses related to property leases. Retaining ownership of its stores would have protected the group from future rent reviews and rises. Instead, from less than £60 million in 2003, property lease rentals had increased nearly six-fold to more than £340 million by 2015. One of the numerous gifts left behind by the buyout wizards. Another present, but one with much greater long-term consequences, was the significant reduction in capital expenditure. Representing £132 million of net cash outflows in the 2003 financial year, capex spend never exceeded that number until 2013. The capex-to-revenue ratio had plummeted from 9.2% to 5.8% during those ten years.[43]

Figure 10.1: Debenhams's operating performance (2002-15)

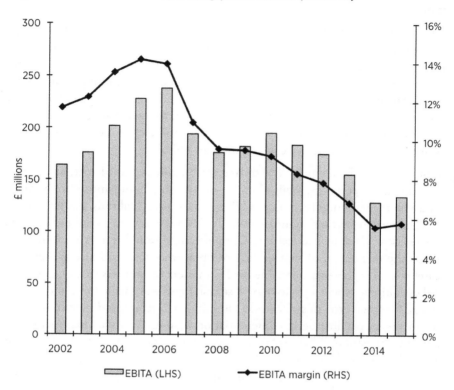

Source: Company accounts and author's analysis

Obsolete and outclassed

As it celebrated 200 years of expansion and tradition in fashion retail, in 1978 Debenhams incorporated a set of very prestigious brands and was a highly profitable fashion retail chain; perhaps too profitable to remain safe from the claws of free-market fanatics. In just three decades it suffered the ignominy of a delisting through a hostile takeover by the Burton Group (1985), the loss of its hold on premium brands Hamleys, Harvey Nichols and other cherished assets, a relisting through a demerger from the overextended and underperforming Burton Group (1998), a take-private through a leveraged buyout (2003), a quick-flip through another – this one blatantly overpriced – relisting (2006), followed by three profit warnings within 18 months of its stock market float,[44] and half a decade of multiple refinancing rounds in order to manage down its mountain of debt.

Sure, the company's PE-backed management team did not shy away from top-line growth and overseas expansion. It even took advantage of the economic maelstrom of 2009 to scoop up its British rival Principles's stock and brand out of administration as well as Danish department store group Magasin du Nord. However, if there is one constant in the world of fashion retail, it is that international build-up is fraught with obstacles. Many clothing retailers have stayed clear of it because differing fashion tastes and distribution channels from country to country can make localisation an ordeal.

Templeman, Debenhams's CEO during the buyout and until 2011, had gained considerable expertise in retail when he was running home improvement store group Homebase and distributor of bikes and car parts Halfords, but he was less familiar with the fashion industry until CVC brought him in to run Debenhams in late 2003. What he had learnt and implemented from his days at Homebase, under the ownership of that other LBO powerhouse Permira, was sale-and-leaseback arrangements to enable his PE masters to monetise assets, cost cuts and operational efficiency – to maximise cash flows and ensure prompt dividend recaps. Overseas growth strategies in clothing retail require a different mindset, one driven by product design differentiation, lean inventory management, and concept innovation. Whereas Spanish retail group Zara, for instance, had been established around these core values, Debenhams had inherited a traditional business model where managing information technology, fine-tuning short supply chains, juggling small and frequent shipments, eradicating bottlenecks through efficient outsourcing, and making late design decisions were never strategic differentiators.

As if the arrival of lower-cost, brick-and-mortar rivals was not enough of a challenge, while the company's balance sheet was being straddled with crippling debt, a new industry-reshaping phenomenon was taking hold: eCommerce. Debenhams's performance continues to be hampered by a fast-changing retail environment, and by the growing online shift in favour of pure plays like ASOS, Boohoo and Amazon's Zappos coupled with the adoption of flexible business models by low-priced, fast-fashion peers H&M, Next, Primark and Zara. A company that spends more time dealing with its lenders than with the changing taste of its price-conscious customers is likely to become as obsolete as last year's trend. Even if online channels accounted for 13.6% of sales in the 2015 financial year,[45] online players and pure clothing fast-fashion retailers had just experienced ten years of tremendous growth and stock market bliss. When, in December 2015, Debenhams's stock sat 60% below its listing price of May 2006, over the same period the shares of Next and Zara had seen their value go up almost five-fold, and those of online specialist ASOS were 33 times more valuable.

*   *   *

In management's defence, the economic context had been particularly gloomy ever since the Great Recession, and other major department store groups had also suffered during that period: food and fashion retailer Marks & Spencer had not registered any rise in sales in its general merchandise division between 2006 and 2015. Marks & Spencer's stock, down 20% over the period, had benefitted from the healthy performance of its grocery unit, but it would probably have suffered to the same extent without the premium food retail division.

Nevertheless, on most parameters the Debenhams of the 2015 winter season was worse off than its pre-LBO model. EBITDA margins had gone from 17% in the 2003 financial year to 10% in the 12 months to 29 August 2015. Annual growth in group turnover had dropped from over 6% in 2003 to 0.4% in 2015. Nor was cash flow upside quite as boundless as the IPO prospectus had made it out to be. Over the same 12-year periods, yearly operating cash flows had gone from £263 million to £236 million, even though group turnover was two-thirds higher in 2015 than in 2003.[46]

Besides, it was intriguing that management had spent so much effort building the group's top line when other players like Next had preferred to focus on earnings growth. Between 2006 and 2015 Debenhams had grown turnover by 36% whereas Next's 2015 revenues were only 29% higher. But at the operating profit level, Debenhams's 44% fall over the period was matched by a 73% jump at Next.

In summary, and despite claims made in the May 2006 listing prospectus about a "transformed business with a step change in profitability under current management",[47] we can safely state that, whatever improvements the financial sponsors and their executive buy-in team introduced between 2003 and 2006, these were not fundamental in nature since they did not translate into sustainable profit growth. If anything, structurally, after its delisting-relisting transaction, Debenhams seemed broken and out of touch with demand.

Value migration

Worth £2.8 billion at the time of its flotation, Debenhams saw its enterprise value more than halve in the ensuing nine years. Where did the money go? CVC, TPG and Merrill Lynch Global Private Equity might have the answer. The commonly held view is that they used all the tricks of the trade:

- Soon after the December 2003 PTP, they raised underlying performance via aggressive cost cuts and capex minimisation and generated one-off cash flows through sale and leaseback agreements: pillar number three of LBO value creation.

- During the two years of private ownership, they refinanced the business twice (PE's first value trigger).

- They had limited means to grow by acquisitions – pillar number two – but they still took control of some Allders stores and the Principles brand (arguably for very little since the over-indebted Debenhams was somewhat cash-strapped) once these rivals had entered administration. Even the 2006 acquisition of Irish stores Roches was partly funded through deferred consideration to make it as painless as possible from a liquidity standpoint.

- The financial sponsors benefited from a positive, even if modest, multiple-arbitrage on exit (pillar number four of any value-enhancement strategy). This partly contributed to the post-IPO stock plunge as most equity analysts soon took the view that the company was overpriced.

- Finally, their exit, even if partial, in May 2006 is a classic example of the use of speedy portfolio realisation to boost the IRR (the fifth value trigger).

When in August 2007 Debenhams was showing signs of weakness, its shares languishing 35% below the IPO price, in response to criticism Philippe Costeletos, the TPG partner behind the deal, called on investors to be patient: "We have been in for over three years and we can be patient and stay in for a long time. If people came in looking for a quick return they may be disappointed. The question is how patient they are."[48] TPG and its two co-investors are long gone; public investors are still patiently waiting, as Figure 10.2 demonstrates. The Debenhams stock has not come anywhere near its 195p listing price since early 2007.

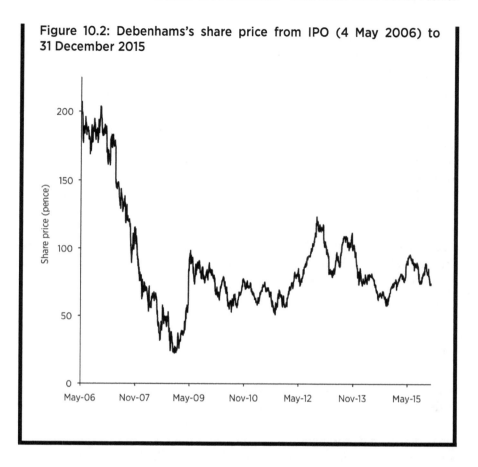

Figure 10.2: Debenhams's share price from IPO (4 May 2006) to 31 December 2015

Contrasting fortunes

After the financial crisis hit the buyout sector, the three financial sponsors faced their own challenges. In early 2009, with the entire American banking sector facing Judgement Day in the wake of Lehman Brothers's bankruptcy, subprime lender extraordinaire Merrill Lynch was forcefully absorbed by the boring but dependable financial group Bank of America. Merrill Lynch's private equity unit was merged with Bank of America's and spun off soon after.

CVC had raised a €4.1 billion tandem fund in 2007 followed quickly by a €10.75 billion fund in 2008, after having already raised €6 billion in 2005. Despite this glut of capital, the PE house delivered very decent returns: net IRRs of 6.4% from the 2007 vehicle and 10.4% out of the 2008 vintage, as of 31 December 2014. Over these eight and seven year periods, the FTSE 100 had generated total unlevered returns of 4.5% and 4.1%. Equally, CVC's 2005 vintage gave a 17.3% net IRR compared to 7% for the FTSE 100 and 6.5% for the FTSE Europe ex-UK index.[49] Unsurprisingly, given its strong performance, CVC closed a €10.9 billion fund in 2013, by far the largest European PE fund for that vintage.

As for TPG, it tried on several occasions between 2012 and 2014 to raise a megafund but the 3.5% IRR delivered on the 2006 global fund and the 11% yielded out of the following vintage of late 2008 (both yields shown as of 31 December 2014) somehow failed to convince enough LPs to chip in.[50] They would have earned more than 7.8% and at least 10% a year from the unlevered S&P 500 over the same nine and six-and-a-half-year holding periods, so maybe that's where LPs chose to invest instead. Eventually, in March 2015, TPG managed to hold a first close for its seventh flagship fund at $6.5 billion, then went back on the road, aiming to reach its target of $8 billion, with a hard cap of $10 billion – a target it finally hit in May 2016.[51] A bit of a letdown when compared to Texas Pacific Group Partners V's $15 billion commitments, to say nothing of TPG Partners VI's $19.8 billion. A read through the TXU (Chapter 5) and Caesars (Chapter 15) case studies will shed some light on TPG's particular situation.

* * *

There is one compelling argument that explains why Debenhams never recovered from its LBO. The management buy-in team had an unequivocal roadmap to follow: maximise short-term cash generation to accelerate equity redemption. Overvalued and levered up with reckless abandon, the target never had a chance. Starved of capex in a sector that requires constant store upgrades and concept innovation, Debenhams was doomed to begin a long and uncontrollable decline. Its fate was not helped by the healthy and ambitious UK expansion of foreign, family controlled and nurtured retailers H&M and Zara, as well as the compelling customer value-proposition initiated by pure online rivals. Shortly after Debenhams' float on the LSE by its owners, Bryan Roberts, an analyst at *Planet Retail*, compared the two periods when the British department store group was publicly listed:

> "It was successful compared to its peers when it was on the market the first time round. But when it exited private equity, it was swaddled with debt, its property had been sold and its performance was dismal."[52]

After years of hardship the department store group eventually weaned itself off most of its bank loans, but by early 2016 its image was ragged as it announced yet further management changes with the departures of both its chairman and its CEO. The group's weakened market position had made it a vulnerable target for corporate raiders. Is it so surprising that bargain-hunter Mike Ashley, famed for using a very lean and mean low-cost approach at his Sports Direct franchise, chose to take a closer look?

PART SIX
Private Investments in Public Equity: PIPE Dream or Nightmare?

PART SIX
Private Investor and Public
Company Director or Nightmare?

B Y NOW, THANKS TO THE VARIOUS IPOS AND TAKE-privates visited in previous chapters, you will have gathered that, despite their name tag, private equity investors regularly deal with the public markets. It is in part thanks to those interactions that information about LBOs is made public and that this book is possible. This consanguinity between the private and public worlds reaches its climax in what are termed private investments in public equity, or PIPEs. Because of this mixture of genres, the worst PE practices in terms of financial management, corporate governance and minority-shareholder protection can make their way into the public domain. The two following chapters will make this point explicit.

First, let's define what is meant by PIPE. This type of investment is made by an institution or a very wealthy individual into a publicly listed company. These transactions are common and not the exclusive hunting ground of LBO fund managers. Pension funds, hedge funds, banks, insurance companies and other financial institutions do PIPEs on a regular basis.

We must make a distinction between firms taking part in PIPEs for a minority stake in publicly quoted companies and the types of LBOs described in the following case studies. In the first instance, the institutions can at times buy stock at a discount to market value and do not leverage the portfolio operating company (termed OpCo) because they are minority investors, and the rest of the shareholders would be in a position to prevent them from exposing OpCo to such financial risk. In these minority-stake scenarios, the only leverage, if applied, sits at the HoldCo level, a newly formed investment holding company set up for the occasion. By contrast, you will see in the PagesJaunes and Seat Pagine Gialle stories that the OpCos were levered up because the financial sponsors took majority stakes in the target and managed to replace the shareholders' equity with LBO loans through the payment of a special dividend. This process is termed a debt push-down. More on that later.

The difference in outcome between the two types of scenarios can be huge. When OpCo faces deterioration in trading, it can easily stop paying dividends to its shareholders in order to preserve cash. In such a case, if OpCo is not financially geared the only trouble that its management team is exposed to is that the minority shareholder is unable to repay its own debt (due to the suspension in upstream dividend) and it turns into a distressed investor. That does not impact the performance of OpCo. In the second scenario, because the OpCo has subscribed to long-term debt, the financial risk is extremely high; the operating company gets into financial distress if its performance flags. When a PIPE is carried out through an LBO structure – in the case of PagesJaunes with both HoldCo and OpCo funded by debt – the situation can become desperate for management, lenders and public shareholders.

CHAPTER 11
PagesJaunes –
The French Disconnection

IN MAY 2005 BUYOUT GROUP 3I WAS REPORTED TO HAVE MADE over four times its investment in pan-European telephone directories company Yellow Brick Road. The British PE house and its American deal partner Veronis Suhler Stevenson sold the business to Australian bank Macquarie for €1.8 billion. The outcome surprised no one. The directories sector in Europe had gone through years of deal activity, most of it led by financial sponsors. Already in 1997, 3i had bought Thomson Directories, the UK's second largest yellow-pages publisher. Two years later, 3i sold a majority stake in an SBO to peers Apax and Advent. Despite stating its intention to take the company "on to its next stage of growth", lead investor Apax hadn't wasted too much time and effort trying to transform the target, choosing to flip it 12 months later to Italian group Seat Pagine Gialle.[1]

Thanks to its Thomson experience, in 2002 3i bought Fonecta of Finland. A year later, the same 3i clubbed together with Veronis Suhler to acquire De Telefoongids from Dutch telecom operator KPN. The two buyout shops then added Central European play Mediatel, lifting it from US telecom group Verizon. In March 2004, 3i and Veronis Suhler set up Yellow Brick Road to assemble those three assets, which, as aforementioned, they sold a year later to a consortium led by Macquarie Capital.[2] Given the unique talent that Apax showed in creating value at Thomson, within a year of selling the latter the British fund manager partnered with US counterpart Hicks Muse to acquire Yell, the largest business directory in the UK, owned until then by national telecom operator BT. Both PE owners then floated Yell 26 months later, kindly holding onto it twice as long as Apax had kept Thomson in its books.[3]

There were several reasons why directory businesses were popular targets among the PE community. The usual criterion of cash-flow generation was the main one. Thanks to EBITDA margins well in excess of 30%, yellow-pages publishers were able to service humungous piles of debt. Advertising spend in directories was predictable, generally increasing in line with consumption. Almost uniquely, these businesses were very resilient to economic downturns because classified ads were low-budget items compared to TV and radio commercials or advertising campaigns in newspapers. The other key factor that made them prime candidates for LBOs is that most of them operated in a monopolistic or oligopolistic environment. With few exceptions they were former state-owned operations, usually controlled through the national telecom service provider. When directory publishers were being privatised, governments did not bother to consider whether consumers were being served appropriately or even treated fairly. Thus, the huge cash flows these groups generated were derived from a strong market position – barriers to entry were significant, and customers were price-takers, unable to shop around for a better deal.

Governments had rarely run these businesses efficiently either, so they offered great opportunities for margin improvements via cost-cutting, cross-selling, and new product development. Many had been privatised in the 1990s or early noughties and had at once drawn the attention of LBO sponsors because, in addition to being cash-rich national monopolies, they represented a consolidation play. Since they had all been protected by their state owners, phone-directory publishers offered the possibility to follow a buy-and-build approach. The Yellow Brick Road three-way merger and Seat's acquisition of Thomson were examples of what was in store. All directories groups across Europe were being wooed for these compelling reasons. The potential upside was immense.

A prized asset

Surely, if Thomson, Yell and Yellow Brick Road had been such successes, a copycat approach was *de rigueur*. Now that these transactions had gone through and generated massively positive returns for their equity and debt sponsors, analysing business directory targets had become a box-ticking exercise. There was one problem though. As the PE industry was growing in stature and raising billions of dollars through fresh fundraising platforms, it was getting difficult to find relevant targets in the directory space. Most European groups had already gone through one or several iterations of LBOs. Opportunities in the sector were dwindling fast. One major player, though, hadn't yet had the pleasure of experiencing the joy of high indebtedness, quarterly or half-yearly financial covenant reporting, and board representation from self-assured private equity professionals. That business was one of the largest phone directory groups in Europe.

PagesJaunes (literally, 'Yellow Pages' in French) had emerged from the decision by France's Ministry of Posts, Telegraphs and Telephones, shortly after the Second World War, to transfer the *régie publicitaire* (advertising representation) business for the telephone directories of metropolitan France to the Office d'Annonces (ODA), a state-controlled entity. In 1998 Cogecom, a subsidiary of the country's communications monopoly France Télécom, acquired ODA. Two years later, ODA and France Télécom's directory activities, including PagesJaunes, a company incorporated on 12 January 1897, were transferred to the group's internet service provider Wanadoo ahead of the latter's IPO on the Paris bourse. In 2004 it was PagesJaunes's turn to commence trading on the Paris exchange via the flotation of 36.3% of its shares for a total market cap of €3.86 billion. France Télécom had retained a 62% stake in the directory group before placing a further 8% with institutional investors the following year.[4]

By the time PagesJaunes was being vaunted as an ideal buyout candidate, it was France's leading publisher of directories, both printed and online through the internet and the French national electronic network Minitel. Eight out of ten French people used its products. PagesJaunes's principal activity was the publication of listings for the general public and professionals, but it also provided website creation, hosting and advertising services, direct marketing, online access to databases and localisation services for businesses. In many of these activities, it had held a monopoly for years if not decades. Products for the general public included printed listings in France like the PagesJaunes directory, and l'Annuaire (the white pages equivalent). The group also owned QDQ, La Guía Util in Spain. Equivalent online directories were *pagesjaunes.fr*, PagesJaunes 3611, *QDQ.com*, and *mappy.com*, the latter being an online mapping service not dissimilar to Google Maps. International services included official directories in Lebanon, Editus in Luxembourg and Edicom in Morocco.

For professionals, the group published PagesPro registers in France and the Kompass industrial directories, which connected buyers and suppliers via an advanced classification system in France, Spain, Belgium and Luxembourg. The group published 358 editions of directories distributed in over 70 million copies. More than 575,000 professionals advertised in its printed PagesJaunes while 450,000 did so on the *PagesJaunes.fr* site.[5] In summary, the group was a diversified and international market leader. In 2003, local advertising in France was worth €3.8 billion, with directories representing 23% of the total. Internet-based spending only accounted for 4% of it.[6] With over €800 million in turnover that year, PagesJaunes alone accounted for 21% of the country's local advertising market. One in five euros spent on local ads in France was allocated to PagesJaunes.

After floating the business on Euronext Paris in the first week of July 2004, France Télécom should have been in no rush to dispose of its remaining stake – PagesJaunes's dividend yield for 2005 was a generous 4.5%.[7] Yet in early June 2006 the French communications group was reported to be eyeing an exit. It wasn't much of a surprise given that directories had for years been treated as non-core activities by major telecom operators. When reports of the auction process emerged, PagesJaunes was trading on 20 times projected 2006 earnings, valuing France Télécom's 54% holding at more than €3.45 billion. Not only was it debt-free, but the target had a cash reserve exceeding half a billion euros.[8] Like all other directory businesses, it was a cash cow. It just needed a new owner willing to milk it.

Bids were expected to come high for such a prime asset: PagesJaunes offered the stability of printed directories with the potential of online growth. The auction did not fail to attract the most ambitious of prospective trade and financial buyers. Local media-to-telecom conglomerate Vivendi had expressed an interest, but as the credit bubble kept inflating it looked like financial sponsors were not going to be outbid. The whole PE aristocracy was showing up for the occasion, with local outfits Eurazeo and PAI Partners mingling with the upper crust of British nobility Apax, BC Partners, Cinven, CVC and Permira, alongside the more enterprising Americans Carlyle, Texas Pacific Group and Goldman Sachs Capital Partners. Given the deal size, one obvious party to the feast was New York-headquartered KKR.[9] For weeks British joint bidders Apax and Cinven had been seen as sure winners, partly because since September 2004 they had owned VNU World Directories, a publisher present in seven countries. Both Apax and Cinven had a vast experience of the sector: they had been runners-up on the 2005 auction of Spain's TPI, for instance – unluckily, they had been outbid by Apax's former investee Yell. It was natural that they hold a certain competitive advantage. However, in the game of paying over the odds, another party was difficult to beat.

Coup de Foudre

Since its formation 30 years earlier, Kohlberg Kravis Roberts & Co had become known for its zippy deal-doing capabilities. Its core competency hinged on its ability to raise extreme levels of debt to fund the acquisition of cash-generative companies. While its track record had primarily been established in North America, including in the phone directories space – it was the owner of Canada's Yellow Pages between 2002 and 2004 – in recent years the investment powerhouse had grown its presence in Europe. Very particular about its selection criteria, KKR had searched for sizeable prey across the continent. The problem with the current auction process was that the target was in France.

For years the American buyout specialist had failed to make a name for itself in the notoriously US-wary country. Because of the image it had earned during the period of hostile takeovers of the late 1980s, KKR had never been particularly trusted or welcomed in France. For that reason, it had struggled to build a solid franchise there and had done relatively few deals in what was, in any given year, the fourth or fifth largest market for LBOs worldwide. This image had somewhat improved following KKR's purchase, alongside one of the country's most respected family investment groups Wendel, of electrical installation manufacturer Legrand four years earlier. Legrand had been a huge success for employees, management, lenders and PE owners alike. Keen to build on this episode, the buyout firm's combative, high-octane co-founder Henry Kravis himself had reportedly spent more time in the country, staying for long stretches at his Paris apartment in order to galvanise the French troops and show them how deals were done. To be sure, the goal was to do deals.

Given its size, the buyout of PagesJaunes, and in particular its full delisting if the buyer was able to effect a squeeze-out of minority shareholders, could not be orchestrated by a single party. Just like Apax and Cinven had joined forces, Goldman had chosen to bid jointly with local financial group Eurazeo, and British firm BC Partners with French peer PAI. Similarly KKR had reportedly allied forces with the PE arm of French insurer Axa.[10] Most of Europe's large-cap buyout fund managers seemed to be involved in the process. Final binding offers were due by mid-July. Shortly before the deadline, it transpired that KKR had switched bedfellow by joining Goldman, whose local ally Eurazeo had dropped out. The only trade bidder in the auction, Vivendi, also announced its decision to withdraw "primarily due to price considerations", leaving financial sponsors to battle it out.[11] PagesJaunes was set to become one of France's largest LBOs that year; the only remaining unknown was the identity of its future owners.

On the bid deadline of 17 July 2006, the directory group's share price reached €24.16, giving the business a market value in excess of €6.7 billion. Four days later, it was reported that the process had turned into a two-horse race: only Texas Pacific Group and KKR remained. Goldman Sachs, which acted as M&A adviser to the latter, was reported to have pulled out for the time being. On the same day of the deadline, however, in what was sure to impact the bidding price, PagesJaunes issued an embarrassing profit warning, indicating that because the French market for directory enquiries had been opened up to competition earlier that year, the group had recorded lower call volumes and higher-than-expected advertising expenditure. Consequently, management envisaged reporting revenue growth and operating margins at the bottom of the previously forecast range.[12] That would have made the bidding parties nervous.

If so, KKR failed to show it. And in view of what it was prepared to bid, its Texan rival no longer seemed a contender. With characteristic gusto, on 24 July KKR agreed to buy France Télécom's entire stake at €22 a share, for a total consideration of €3.3 billion. The seller could not have been more agreeable. After all, it was about to dispose of its holding in a maturing asset, operating in a fast-changing sector, at a top-of-the-range valuation: 13.7 times last-12-months EBITDA.[13]

In the middle of August, when customarily half of France is holidaying, KKR mandated a lender consortium, including bookrunners Bank of America, French bank Calyon, Deutsche Bank, Goldman Sachs, JPMorgan and Lehman Brothers, to assess the market's appetite for senior and subordinated loans to fund the deal.[14] After gaining official control of the France Télécom holding on 11 October 2006, KKR nominated its top man in Paris, Jacques Garaïalde, as PagesJaunes Groupe's chairman. A takeover bid was then launched for the remaining directories group's shares – about 44.3% held by public investors, the rest by PagesJaunes employees.[15]

The aim was to reach consent from enough shareholders to take the company off the quote. If a bidder fails to reach that level of support, it cannot delist the target. Bidders occasionally fail to take businesses private for that very reason, as minority stockholders can happily wait and see just in case the bidder feels obliged to raise its offer at a later stage. In France, the squeeze-out threshold is set at 95%, which makes public takeovers quite cumbersome and makes it expensive to persuade minorities to fold. Problem was, KKR had already paid a full price to acquire France Télécom's majority stake. Through a holding company called Médiannuaire, it was offering the same €22-per-share to the public, with a thoughtful €0.60 bonus as an incentive for the minority shareholders to hand over their shares in order to get to the 95% acceptance rate.

* * *

One of KKR's dilemmas was that its European Fund II, the European investment vehicle it was using to fund the equity portion of its PagesJaunes buyout, only held €4.5 billion in commitments. At best, the New York firm could invest €700 million of it in the French group without feeling overexposed to one single deal. However, if it did manage to squeeze out the minorities and take the business private, it was looking at a total EV in excess of €6.5 billion, making its equity exposure on this single position excessive. For that reason, the firm called upon its KKR Millennium Fund, a $6 billion vehicle raised four years earlier with a primary focus on North America, to invest alongside its European fund. It probably would have made sense for TPG and KKR to partner on the deal – they had unsuccessfully joined forces during the auctions for BT's directories business Yell in 2001 and for Seat Pagine Gialle (see Chapter 12) in 2003.[16] In the end though, what improved the odds of success for Henry Kravis's French colleagues was the decision by Goldman to reconsider its position and to invest on the equity side. By the time an offer for the minority shares was submitted to the French regulator, GS Capital Partners had taken a 20% stake in Médiannuaire, leaving KKR with 80% of the bidding vehicle.

On 24 October 2006 PagesJaunes concluded a financing arrangement with a syndicate comprising seven international banks for a maximum total of €2.35 billion. The sole purpose of the senior debt was to finance the exceptional dividend of €9 per share to be paid exactly a month later.[17] In PE parlance, the issue of LBO loans to pay out a dividend to the acquisition vehicle (in this case Médiannuaire) is called a debt push-down. It is a way of repaying the bridge financing provided by KKR and Goldman to acquire France Télécom's stake. Because the PagesJaunes share price had traded slightly above the €22-a-share Médiannuaire bid in the ensuing weeks, the view from the market was that there was room for further upside. So, by its 1 December deadline, Médiannuaire's takeover offer had only received acceptances from shareholders representing a very embarrassing 0.8% stake. Despite bidding more than 50% above the price the group had been floated at two years earlier, KKR and its deal partner had failed to seduce French investors and event-driven arbitrageurs. Their attempt at France's largest PE-backed public-to-private had turned into a trickier PIPE. Holding less than 55% of PagesJaunes, they nonetheless got cracking on doing what financial sponsors do best: leveraging a business till it bursts at the seams.

The new controlling shareholders chose to put debt both at the holding company level (Médiannuaire) and at the operating unit level (PagesJaunes Groupe), which is quite common in fully-fledged LBOs, not so much with PIPEs. What was not standard either, even for these frenzied times, was the amount of debt they decided to use to finance their purchase. The duo funded the LBO with the familiar accoutrement of high-yielding LBO loans. The group only had two maintenance covenants to report on: the net debt-to-gross operating profit ratio, and the interest coverage ratio (gross operating profit-to-net interest expense). At the HoldCo level, Médiannuaire had issued €1.24 billion of senior facilities split between a B tranche, a C tranche, a first-loss facility, and a revolver. In addition, a €210 million mezzanine was raised, yielding 4% cash and 4% payment in kind (accruing, rather than paid cash). The holding company's senior and mezzanine loans were facilitated by Deutsche Bank. Exceeding three times EBITDA, they were to be serviced via dividend payouts, using upstream flows of cash from the OpCo, PagesJaunes Groupe.[18] KKR's equity ticket in PagesJaunes Groupe was $787 million (about €640 million).[19] After accounting for Goldman's co-investment, the PE duet had glibly funded the deal with 75% of debt.

Due to the €9-a-share exceptional dividend paid in late November, €2.52 billion had flowed out of the business, forcing the French directory group into a net liability position (i.e., negative shareholders' equity) in excess of €2 billion.[20] It was a classic KKR-Goldman buyout. Figure 11.1 helps make sense of the post-PIPE organisation chart.

Figure 11.1: PagesJaunes Groupe's structure post-PIPE as at 31 December 2006

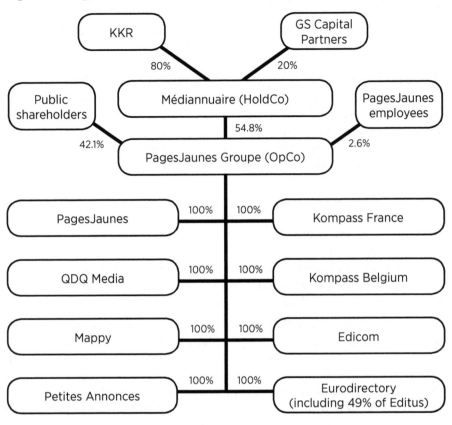

Source: Company accounts and author's analysis

When management reported full-year 2006 results, group revenue growth was at the lower end of the forecast range: 6% compared to almost 10% registered the previous year. No doubt this was partly due to the distraction bred by the ownership handover. Gross operating income (*marge brute opérationnelle*) had seen a 5% uplift compared to 14% the year before. The number of advertisers, both online and for the printed directories, had only experienced a marginal 2% rise. Gross operating margins, however, were a reassuring 44%; sufficiently high to entice lending institutions to subscribe to a few slices of debt.

From a lender's standpoint, due to its steady, recurring cash flows, PagesJaunes was seen as a safe credit. The customer renewal rate was 85%,[21] bringing high visibility to future cash production. As the lead debt arrangers were going through the syndication process in the early months of 2007, appetite for PagesJaunes loans was enormous. All tranches of the senior notes were reported to be 10 to 15 times oversubscribed, and the second-lien piece saw demand exceed supply 25 times over. It was love at first sight, for those inclined to French romance. Taking advantage of the situation, in February Médiannuaire used a reverse price flex[*], shrinking the margin to be earned by some of the senior HoldCo and OpCo tranches and on the second lien. The PE consortium also took more than €300 million, or 60%, off the mezzanine tranche and issued more of the cheap senior debt instead, saving a bundle on interest. And because the yield on the mezzanine was too good to give to third parties, the whole lot was allocated to Goldman's in-house mezzanine unit.

Given the enthusiasm of the lending community, Médiannuaire didn't need coaxing: it raised as much debt as the market would allow. When combining debt at both OpCo and HoldCo levels, the sponsors were arranging loans representing between 9.5 and ten times the company's historical EBITDA. When excluding revolvers, the debt multiple was a more 'reasonable' 7.5 to eight times. Since the leverage multiple of UK rival Yell was 5.4 following its acquisition of Telefonica's Spanish directories earlier that year, gunning for a ratio so much bulkier was showing nerves of steel. When the dust had settled, OpCo had €2.35 billion of loans on its books, comprising a medium-term senior loan of €1.95 billion and a revolving credit line of €400 million, while HoldCo's debt package totalled €1.65 billion with a €175 million revolver. Remember, the scene was taking place at the peak of the debt bubble, three months before the official start of the Credit Crunch.

A short honeymoon period

KKR had done its due diligence, the extent of which remains a matter of debate. The truth is, the directory sector was panting. The revenues of PagesJaunes's print division had recorded a marked slowdown in its growth rate from 5.4% in 2003 to 4% the following year, 3% in 2005 and 2.5% in the year of the PIPE. A gale of change was in the air: printed classifieds were gradually but surely losing market share to online propositions.

In their simplest form, phone directories are just a list of names and numbers. Data-mining and publishing are activities that lend themselves well to automation. With the advent of the information age and the internet, the collection and handling of data had greatly benefitted from the use of

---

[*]. Price flex – see Abbreviations and Lexicon.

algorithms, and if there was one company in the world that had mastered the art of targeted, fact-based advertising, it was Google, an eight-year-old Mountain View, California-based search engine and marketing platform promising to "provide unbiased, accurate and free access to information" to its users.

The point about free access, taken out of Google's Letters from the Founders in the April 2004 IPO prospectus, was the real threat to PagesJaunes's business model. Business directories had always been free to the public since the revenue model was advertising-based. Companies paid to feature prominently on the yellow pages by placing their advert according to parameters like the location on the page, the size of the ad (a full, half or quarter of a page), and black and white or colour text and images. Not only did online solutions offer greater flexibility at a lower cost, but they promised to provide result-driven analytics to marketers who, most of the time, had little means to assess how many eyeballs (to use the internet-specific expression) had viewed their adverts in a paper directory. By 2006, the only unique selling point that directory groups like PagesJaunes retained as a competitive advantage against online search engines was their knowledge of, and access to, local markets. But this key success factor was being eroded fast. Thanks to its obsession about data analytics and user experience, Google was building a global search engine capable of tweaking advertisements to adapt them to local demand.

KKR and Goldman were making two bets for the price of one. First, they believed that PagesJaunes would successfully transition from a paper-based advertising model to an online platform – but as we saw in the EMI case study, it is a considerable feat to achieve a business transformation when facing disruptive change. Second, given that PagesJaunes's main advertising customers were the self-employed as well as sole traders and small and medium-sized enterprises (SMEs), the financial sponsors were hoping that Google would not tailor its global advertising solutions to local tastes, thereby leaving the lion's share of classified ad budgets to yellow-pages publishers, the long-established local advertising experts.

This double-jeopardy situation did have some reason to it. In an increasingly globalised and connected world, business directories could grow in stature. However, the old paper format employed to distribute information was destined to be replaced by electronic data transfers. The benefit of this new digital data-processing system was twofold: lower costs and faster delivery. Printed directories like PagesJaunes were racing against the clock; they had to morph into online marketers. For that reason, in January 2007 the French group launched an online classified ads solution (*annoncesjaunes.fr*) based on the paper version *Petites Annonces*.[22] In 2006, already 72% of the group's advertisers used its online services, meaning that the share of customers choosing to advertise exclusively in print was just 28%. As for individual end-consumers, more than a quarter of them already used a combination of the group's printed and online directories.[23]

When the first year of trading under LBO came to a close, management was able to report strong results from the online unit, with revenue up 15% in 2007 as internet solutions (up 23%) replaced the traditional Minitel-based services (down 38%). The latter, an electronic service offering provided via France Telecom's fixed lines since the 1980s, was deliberately being phased out across the country, to be replaced by the World Wide Web. Minitel's revenue erosion was logical, expected and well compensated by internet adoption. The print division, however, had recorded another slowdown in growth, with the top line at the business directories only rising 0.3% whereas white pages revenues had fallen 2.2%. PagesJaunes Groupe's valuation parameters remained somewhat punchy, even if the Credit Crunch was starting to bite. By December 2007 the share price had faded 10% since the day of the PIPE, but the group's market cap was still €3.7 billion. When debt at OpCo level was added, total enterprise value stood at more than 11 times EBITDA. But once HoldCo's €1.5 billion loans were thrown into the mix, the value of the leveraged PIPE was 14.2 times earnings, for a business showing 5% annual growth in operating earnings.

* * *

As if it was not enough of a challenge for management to have to turn the 60-year-old phone directory publisher into a 21st century digital marketing service provider, the credit squeeze that had started in the summer of 2007 progressively swelled into a full-scale financial crisis. In the second quarter of 2008 the French economy slipped 0.5%, starting a recession from which it would not emerge until the third quarter of the following year.[24] Because PagesJaunes generated 98% of its activity in France, this was bad news. History has shown repeatedly that, when hard times hit, one of the first policies implemented by corporate executives is to cut advertising budgets. Rightly or wrongly, conventional wisdom posited that business directories were resilient to economic downturns. The main reason evoked by marketers was that classified ads were relatively low-budget items. That might have been true in the past, but this time, unfortunately, the Great Recession was served with a dose of disruptive change.

As remarked, online platforms offered a lower-cost, easy-to-monitor advertising medium. It was an attractive alternative for cost-conscious advertisers. I dwell on this issue because there is perhaps no better example of the substitution process the Great Recession provoked in the classifieds industry than the performance recorded by PagesJaunes in 2008. That year the French group's online activities grew by more than 17%. Revenue derived from the print yellow pages fell by 5.7%, experiencing the first reduction of a long series. Management were also forced to recognise €69 million of goodwill impairment related to QDQ Media due to the deteriorated situation of the Spanish market and a sharp slowdown in the activity of that subsidiary. Following the departure of approximately a fifth of QDQ Media's workforce, the group booked restructuring costs of €2.5 million that year.[25]

KKR chose to write down the value of its investment by more than two-thirds.[26] It was no doubt a mark-to-market requirement as, operationally, PagesJaunes was doing fairly well compared to its industry peers, closing 2008 with consolidated revenues and EBITDA up 3% and 6% respectively. The group was still the fourth largest in terms of internet audience in France.[27] The problem is that it was falling behind budget; never a good idea when dealing with a leveraged capital structure. The share price had mirrored the weakening performance and the market debacle by halving during 2008. By now, valuation parameters were making sense: PagesJaunes Groupe's valuation was less than 7.5 times EBITDA, in line with global comparables.[28] Though when including HoldCo's debt, KKR and Goldman were looking at an EV in excess of ten times earnings. They needed to act. In May 2009, after more than two years of underperformance against the management business plan, the company changed CEO, forcing Michel Datchary to step down after 13 years in charge. To replace him, the PE owners brought in Jean-Pierre Remy. While the press spoke of a strategic divergence between Datchary and Médiannuaire, the truth is that KKR had led the reshuffle to try to salvage its expensive French PIPE.[29]

The chairman of PagesJaunes and head of KKR France, Jacques Garaïalde, knew the incoming CEO well. When managing director at Carlyle Venture, Garaïalde had funded Remy's online corporate travel venture Egencia in 2000. Garaïalde had left Carlyle for KKR three years later, but was now keen to put in charge of PagesJaunes a trusted executive – and in particular one who knew a great deal about online business models, in order to implement the group's digital mutation. Remy had spent several years at US online travel agent Expedia after its acquisition of Egencia, so presumably his experience in web-based services was to prove useful. It was easy to understand the desperation of such a management substitution when looking at the group's capital structure. Because PagesJaunes's stock had fallen to around €6 per share in the first quarter of 2009, the group's market cap was €1.7 billion. Since PagesJaunes held €1.95 billion in net debt and Médiannuaire's debt was close to €1.5 billion, leverage had reached two-thirds of the financial sponsors' funding structure.

When releasing the first-half results on 23 July, management was relieved to declare that the group had eked out a 2% increase in revenue – online activity had recorded a very impressive 14% jump – and a respectable 6% gain in gross operating profit.[30] It was even more impressive when considering that the French economy had shrunk 1.7% over the same period. Despite the change in leadership, the group continued to face the vagaries of a weak economy. The second half of the year did not bring any reprieve, with advertising expenditures in the phone directory segment falling sharply. For the whole year, ad sales in printed listings dropped by 7.5%, while online classifieds were up 6%. The advertising market in France had experienced its worst fall in 50 years. The country's GDP had also crashed 2.9%, its biggest contraction since the Second World War.[31] It was a gruelling baptism of fire for the new chief executive. Proving its resilience, PagesJaunes's stock ended the year above its level of December 2008. Incomprehensibly, after a stormy year that had seen many of its European peers refinance their balance sheets – Italy's Seat Pagine Gialle, the UK's Yell and Sweden's Eniro had all gone through rights issues – PagesJaunes's EV multiples remained proudly high: 7.9 times at the OpCo level and 10.9 times EBITDA with Médiannuaire's debt.

Unimpressed, in early January 2010 Goldman's equity analysts chose to downgrade PagesJaunes from 'Neutral' to 'Sell', sending the latter's stock 3.6% lower to €7.51 on the day. To justify its decision of aligning the French group with sector laggards like Seat and Yell, the American bank cited the acceleration of print decline, Google Maps's apparent market share win, and the fact that PagesJaunes traded at a significant premium to its peers.[32] The note probably did not win the bank's analysts many friends internally, especially within the GS Capital Partners unit. A month later, however, the view expressed by Goldman's coverage team was shared by all analysts when PagesJaunes's management revealed the 2009 full-year results.

On an aggregated basis, the revenues of the print divisions were down 6.5% on the prior year, as average revenue per advertiser tumbled. The online activities, which had experienced double-digit growth for several years, grew at a corresponding 6.5% pace, but from a lower base. Unfortunately, sales from the international activities were not providing much solace, dropping by a fifth year-on-year. Consolidated group sales were down 2%, whereas EBITDA had fallen by 4%.[33] Arithmetically, the profit decline had led to an increase in debt-to-EBITDA ratio. As a consequence, the headroom against the leverage covenant had fallen from 30% to 19%.[34] PagesJaunes had handled as best it could the impact of the recession, but the digitalisation of its products and the growing adoption of the internet were proving insufficient to curb the disintegration of its traditional paper-based businesses.

At that point, the transition between print and digital gained momentum. Since coming on board in mid-2009, chief exec Remy had aimed to redesign the organisation. Needless to say the drive for efficiency had been traumatic: from 5,284 in the year 2008, the number of employees had been cut to 4,843 the following year, and 4,776 remained by the end of 2010. Redundancy and retrenchment plans in various units of the group, including PagesJaunes in France and QDQ in Spain, as well as the disposal in October 2009 of the Moroccan subsidiary Edicom, had contributed to the headcount reduction. Management had nonetheless tried to drive online growth by acquiring young start-ups like people finder 123people and traders' quote and estimate specialist keltravo.[35] But it was insufficient to compensate for the market correction: revenues for the entire printed-directory sector in France had faded a further 9.5% in 2010.[36] Naturally, PagesJaunes was not spared its fair share of pain. The print division suffered a double-digit plunge in revenue. The weak performance of the online unit seemed to indicate that Goldman's sector specialists had been spot on: PagesJaunes's digital inroads were losing pace. On a consolidated basis, its top line had lost 3% that year, though thanks to its downsizing efforts management had helped increase gross operating margins to 46% from 45.4% the year before.[37]

Without growing sales, however, the company was heading for trouble. The financial sponsors had piled a massive slab of debt on the books, with HoldCo requiring constant dividend payouts to cover debt commitments. In 2007 Médiannuaire had received €165.8 million in dividends from PagesJaunes, followed by €147.5 million in each of the next two years and €100 million in 2010. Yet, over the same period, operating cash flows had failed to make any progress, reaching €285 million in 2007, €320 million the following year, €284 million in 2009 and €292 million the year after. The group needed a significant increase in liquidity or it would not be in a position to meet its compounding debt obligations.

Directory assistance

The elaborate capital structure was beginning to show its drawbacks. To give management more time to transition toward a fully integrated print-to-online platform, in March 2011 Médiannuaire/HoldCo amended certain terms of its senior and mezzanine facilities. Over 90% of lenders agreed to extend the term loan B maturity by one year to 2015 in exchange for a 25 basis point consent fee. Further headroom was granted on the covenants. And creditors received a margin increase, the extent of which was contingent on whether they just consented to amend or also agreed to extend.[38] But HoldCo was not the only group entity needing a breather.

With PagesJaunes Groupe's net debt-to-operating-profit ratio at 3.48 times, giving a covenant headroom of only 11% in the quarter ended 31 March 2011, in April an amend-and-extend process was also initiated at the operating company level. The aim was to get the covenant relaxed and to push out maturities by two years from November 2013 to September 2015 on half of the term A loans – €960 million – in exchange for fees (20 basis points for consent, 50 bps for extending) and a doubling of the margin. The rest of the €1.95 billion A loan was split into two tranches with different margins but the same November 2013 maturity.

It was starting to look like proper financial engineering, especially when considering that, with its cash hoard dwindling and debt requirements throttling its growth plans, the company also launched a €350 million seven-year high-yield bond to pay down some of the existing term loan A2. Because it was not good enough to get lenders to voluntarily give the financial sponsors a second chance at making this overstretched LBO work, both Goldman Sachs and KKR got involved in the bond issuance in order to earn some well-deserved fees: the American investment bank acted as joint co-ordinator alongside Morgan Stanley, and KKR as joint bookrunner with French bank BNP Paribas.[39] With their investment increasingly looking like a complete write-off, the PE owners were hopelessly making up for it by generating extra fees.

Organic revenue growth was showing few signs of revival given France and Spain's economic weakness, so management made a couple of promising add-ons in the internet sector, purchasing property classifieds website A Vendre A Louer in April 2011 and a specialist of business appointments via the web, ClicRDV, the following month. At the half-year point, management revealed that the growth posted by the internet unit was still insufficient to compensate for the exodus of advertisers and pricing pressure in the print segment.[40] Things took a turn for the worse when, on 4 July 2011, management announced that the company would miss full-year revenue and profit targets. Luckily, the A&E negotiations had been completed before the trading update. How very convenient! The PagesJaunes stock sank 8.6% on the news, to €5.66 a share.[41] The stock went on losing value through the second half of the year, ending at €2.5 a share by late December, two-thirds down year-on-year. PagesJaunes's downhill spiral had gained strength in a year that had seen industrial action as management tried to reorganise the sales force to counteract weak trading. Total print activities had shed 9% and online sales were up 7% – more than half of revenues now originated from digital product streams – whereas other businesses, such as directory enquiry services by phone and text and marketing services, had lost a quarter of their top line.[42]

During an analyst presentation on 15 February 2012, where the group reported a dip in EBITDA for the third year in a row, management dropped a bombshell. Because its leverage only had 12.5% headroom against a freshly relaxed covenant of 4.3 times EBITDA, PagesJaunes was cancelling its 2011 dividend to preserve cash. Minority public shareholders were being penalised for KKR and Goldman's decision to fund the acquisition with too much debt five years earlier. To make matters worse, the stock dropped more than 12% on the day, down four-fifths since late 2006. Following the dividend suspension, Médiannuaire's debt was quoted at deeply distressed levels: 26 cents on the euro.[43] Valuation yardsticks were falling in line with the rest of the market, with OpCo's enterprise value at 5.6 times EBITDA (compared to 7.9 in late 2010). Even Médiannuaire's capital structure, while stubbornly high at 8.6 times EBITDA, was down from 10.8 in December 2010.

When it was publicly announced three months later that dividend payments would not resume until PagesJaunes's leverage fell below three times EBITDA, press reports were quick to point out the paradox: a group generating over €1 billion of revenues and an EBITDA margin above 40% was unable to pay dividends to its shareholders. As *Le Monde* newspaper volunteered, the explanation for such absurdity could be summed up in one word: debt.[44] The Paris-listed company needed to delever to improve its credit profile.

During that same month of May 2012, in the second A&E proposal in just over a year, OpCo offered to extend €640 million of existing term loan A1 maturities from 2013 to 2015, giving creditors the option to either extend the maturity on their claims fully in exchange for a partial repayment, a consent fee and a margin increase, or to receive a maximum repayment of 50% of their existing loans.[45] Contentiously, the proposal suggested by PagesJaunes was to include a new clause in the agreement that would stop even lenders that turned down the A&E request from selling their loans, as long as lenders holding two-thirds of the loan voted in its favour. It was a coercive way for management to get as many as possible of the tranche A1 lenders to agree to extend the loan's maturity.[46] War between the company and its lenders had officially started.

Two months later, Médiannuaire, now virtually in default given its inability to pay back debt due to the cessation of dividend payments from PagesJaunes (its sole source of cash), entered into restructuring talks with lenders. Management was trying to force a debt-for-equity swap at the HoldCo level. Under the proposal, KKR and Goldman would see their stake fall from 54.7% to about 20% post-restructuring.[47] But if they were going to cancel out their loans, many creditors clearly preferred to see the PE owners' combined stake completely erased.

To say that the French directory group was facing an uphill battle to survive barely hints at the scale of the matter. Though the OpCo had made net free cash flows of €58 million in the second quarter thanks to the suspension of the dividend, ugly rumours were circulating about the company's possible default. Because of the stock's collapse to €1.5 per share and the collateral effect on market capitalisation, by July 2012 combined leverage for HoldCo and OpCo stood at 90%. The last-12-month EBITDA was about €470 million, but net debt at OpCo was still €1.83 billion, or close to four times earnings. Leverage at HoldCo hadn't budged since it was all bullet[*] (€1.47 billion was redeemable upon exit), so debt-to-EBITDA was at 7.5 on a combined basis. It looked like management time was going to be filled for years to come with debt-related issues rather than strategic considerations. That could only be a good thing for PagesJaunes's online competitors.

In September 2012, the company's management finally received permission from more than half of its bondholders to appoint a *mandataire ad hoc*, a special mediator whose role is to report to the commercial court on the financial situation of a company and on the progress being made in negotiations between a company and its lenders. Part of many pre-insolvency procedures in France, the *mandataire ad hoc* can, in particular, request a standstill to creditors in order to ensure the solvency of the company during the mediation. It was a free option for management to protect the company against lenders who might otherwise wish to postpone the negotiations in the hope of seeing the company default on its loan obligations.

Two-thirds of lenders had already agreed to OpCo's debt extension since talks had started in May, agreeing to push the maturity from 2013 to 2015 in exchange for a partial repayment and a consent fee. But the company was targeting approval from 90% of them. To put pressure on the obstinately uncooperative lenders, management asked the President of the Commercial Court of Nanterre, in the outskirts of Paris, to appoint the urgently-needed mediator.[48] In view of the ongoing talks, Moody's chose to downgrade the company deeper into the speculative category. OpCo's 8.875% bond duly fell to 80, trading at a 20% discount 18 months after being issued.[49] Eventually, in mid-November 2012, PagesJaunes completed its A&E process, receiving enough support from its tranche A1 and revolver holders to extend the maturity by two years. Only €72 million of the €2.35 billion OpCo facilities remained due on the original November 2013 maturity.[50] Management had bought the company some welcome breathing space and the stock responded accordingly, gaining 46% in two trading days.

The following month, HoldCo also obtained an agreement regarding its €1.46 billion debt restructuring between its PE shareholders KKR and Goldman Sachs Capital Partners, two of its main creditors – Cerberus and Goldman Sachs Mezzanine Partners – and the working group formed by other lenders (representing 55% of Médiannuaire's total debt). The restructuring comprised two parts. Firstly, Médiannuaire would completely delever (meaning that its senior and mezzanine credit facilities would be removed). Lenders would be

---

*. Bullet loan – see Abbreviations and Lexicon.

partially reimbursed with PagesJaunes shares and cash, as well as through a conversion of the residual debt into Médiannuaire equity.

Secondly, Cerberus would become the main shareholder in the HoldCo. Médiannuaire's shareholders (Cerberus, Goldman Sachs and KKR) would enter into a lock-up agreement for their PagesJaunes shares, which would prevent them from selling for a short period. Certain governance terms – the appointment of three board members by Cerberus and two additional independent members – had also been included. The restructuring of Médiannuaire aimed to clarify the shareholding structure. Between mid-December 2012 and mid-January 2013, HoldCo obtained 90% of senior lender consent, whereby these creditors would recover about one-third of their claims and Médiannuaire would implement a debt/equity swap through a fast-track court procedure. Having received approval from all mezzanine lenders, the group was still seeking unanimous consent from senior lenders to avoid a *sauvegarde* court procedure – the closest process France has to America's Chapter 11.[51] If you think all this is impossible to follow, put yourself in the management's shoes.

Taking French leave

From a trading standpoint, at OpCo level the year 2012 had been brutal. The double-digit decline in print revenues was now deeply embedded. Because of the extent of the fall, consolidated sales had shed more than 3%. Group revenue had dived 11% in the period 2008-12. The stock had followed suit, going from €7 per share in late 2008 to less than €2 four years later. It had lost a third of its value in 2012 alone. The slump in sales stemmed in part from discontinued international businesses that management had considered non-core, and to a greater extent from the general gloom in printed products in France – revenues for the national market had sunk by 14% in 2012 after having lost 8% the previous year.[52] Over the four years to 2012, total advertising billings in the French printed telephone listings had collapsed by more than a third.

By December 2012, leverage had fallen slightly to 3.71 times EBITDA, but the headroom had got to within 7% of the maintenance covenant. To generate some indispensable liquidity and reduce its debt, in October the French group had sold most of its 49% stake in Luxembourg-based affiliate Editus. Elaborately avoiding the word default, the company confirmed at its February 2013 analyst presentation that a restructuring proposal had finally been approved at HoldCo level. After eight months of talks under the aegis of a *mandataire ad hoc*, all senior and mezzanine holders had consented.[53] As explained, the goal was for a complete clearing of HoldCo debt through a partial reimbursement in OpCo securities, with Médiannuaire retaining about 19% of the capital of

PagesJaunes Groupe – KKR and Goldman were becoming irrelevant minority shareholders.[54] After having spent two long years without any cash due to its subsidiary's suspension of dividends, HoldCo was soon to be debt-free. Yet, shortly after the February announcement, the group's 8.875% notes due 2018 were trading at 85-to-87 cents on the euro, down from 97 cents the month before: rating agency Fitch had chosen to downgrade the business due to the lack of short-term cash-flow stability and reduced profit guidance for the year.[55] To outsiders, the French directory publisher remained a risky credit.

The following month, it was revealed that KKR was rejigging its European investment team ahead of an upcoming fundraising in the region due to start at some stage in 2014. Jacques Garaïalde, who had served as chairman of OpCo's board of directors ever since KKR had taken control in October 2006, and Reinhard Gorenflos – a partner who had worked on the French directory deal alongside Garaïalde, had been a non-executive of PagesJaunes, and had also led the €1.45 billion investment in German auto-repair group ATU on which KKR would eventually lose half a billion euros of equity – were not to take part in the next European fund.[56] Now that it had lost control of the French company, KKR seemed determined to show its LPs that lessons had been learned, shortly after Goldman's deal leader Hugues Lepic had himself left the American bank and stepped down from the PagesJaunes board. The representatives of the two financial sponsors were out. Sadly for PagesJaunes's management, they were replaced by two of Cerberus's American executives: Steven Mayer, co-manager of the Global Private Equity activity and chairman of the investment committee of Cerberus, and Lee Millstein, chairman of the turnaround specialist's European activities, joined the board on 23 April 2013, the day of Garaïalde's resignation.

Post-restructuring, Médiannuaire – now controlled by Cerberus through its holding Promontoria, alongside minority holders Goldman and KKR – owned 18.5% of PagesJaunes's shares but 28.3% of voting rights.[57] Médiannuaire had double voting rights, as is allowed in France for companies that choose to grant such rights to shareholders. The rest of the lending syndicate held 35% of OpCo with 46% remaining listed on Euronext.

It didn't look like the change of control at the HoldCo would make much of a difference, though. To most observers, Cerberus and KKR were like tweedledum and tweedledee. With its double voting rights as well as three of the 11 board seats, Cerberus was able to control the proceedings at shareholders' general meetings and management board meetings. Some questioned whether it was proper corporate governance and in May 2013 Franco-American activist investor Guy Wyser-Pratte, a small minority PagesJaunes stockholder claiming to be pro-management, pushed for a new debt deal to give the directories group further breathing room, declaring: "We're on the side of management. They feel like they've gotten short shrift. They're in shackles with this debt."[58] Worried that

Cerberus – which also owned 53% of American directories group Yellow Pages after acquiring the stake from telecom giant AT&T in April 2012 – might try to get its hands on PagesJaunes surreptitiously, a month later Wyser-Pratte tried to obtain board representation and have Cerberus's double voting rights annulled. To no avail.[59] Figure 11.2 reveals that, in the meantime, the group's shareholding structure had become messier, the real giveaway of a failed LBO.

Figure 11.2: Solocal Group's organisation post-restructuring in June 2013

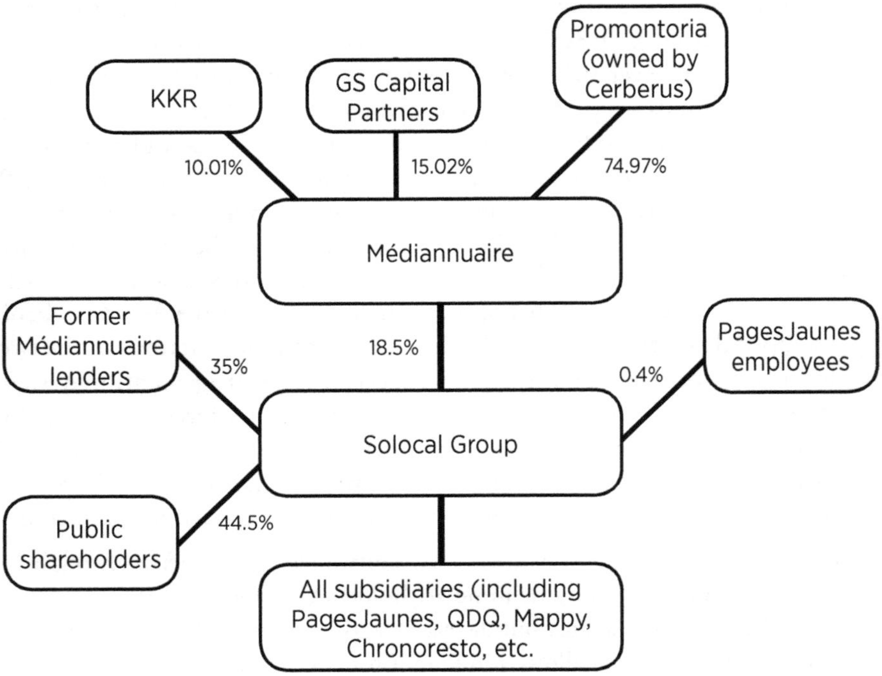

Source: Company accounts and author's analysis

Now that PagesJaunes's management was no longer under the thumb of unpredictable financial sponsors, it took the opportunity to go through a rebranding exercise. Choosing Solocal as the company's new name, the aim was to reflect the positioning as a local digital advertiser and content distributor, and the move away from traditional directories. The former brand had somewhat become meaningless in a group generating most of its revenue online. Managing 17 separate brands, Solocal launched Digital Plan 2015 and restructured its offering along five verticals to be able to compete head-on with specialist websites like online property agents or restaurant reservation platforms. Among other things, the move required a total reorganisation of the sales force.[60]

Management tried to make the most of a commercial agreement signed with Google in late September 2013, whereby clients would be able to buy ad space on Google sites through their contracts with Solocal's various brands, including PagesJaunes and Mappy. The US search engine had traditionally been the French group's main rival, but more than a third of traffic indirectly connected to Solocal's sites came from Google. Partnering for local advertising services was therefore seen as vital by management and shareholders alike, with the stock jumping 7% on the announcement.[61] But it was not sufficient to hide another set of poor results. On 13 November the company issued a profit warning, not just on its 2013 results but on the following year's as well, leading equity analysts to retain their 'Sell' rating. On the day, the stock lost one-sixth of its value as 13% of the free float changed hands.[62] PagesJaunes/Solocal had morphed into a yo-yo stock, with a marked bias to the downside.

After a few weeks reviewing the implications of the profit-warnings, on 23 December Moody's downgraded Solocal a notch closer to default due to concerns about September 2015 maturities (€1.2 billion of bank debt was due at that time) and a highly likely covenant breach in 2014.[63] With the end of the year nearing, management had a chance to assess the situation. Ongoing weak fundamentals throughout 2013 had seen full-year print revenue fall 17% to €345 million, and internet activity had only risen 1.6% to €633 million. Solocal was still a hybrid print-online play, though the group's conversion into a pure digital marketing platform was forging ahead. However, the changeover was as much due to the erosion of billings on the print side as to the expansion of web-based services. Because of the weak performance of the high-margin paper division, gross operating profit had continued its downfall, off 9% to €424 million.[64] Margins had lost more than 100 basis points. There was only one area of improvement. Thanks to better cash management, net debt had dropped to €1.58 billion vs. €1.74 billion the year before. Coupled with a smaller market cap, the reduced leverage gave an enterprise value a notch below 5.5 times EBITDA, the proper reflection of a low-growth depreciating asset.

Emergency call

Now that Médiannuaire's debt had been wiped out, in mid-February 2014 KKR officially conceded that it had entirely written off its investment,[65] and Solocal/OpCo announced its intention to launch an equity rights issue in order to delever, extend the maturity schedule through another A&E, and provide covenant relief, in particular for its net-debt maintenance covenant, which was getting uncomfortably close to a breach. As at 31 December 2013 the leverage ratio had reached 3.73 times EBITDA, conveniently 0.5% below the authorised limit.[66] With hardly any headroom left, OpCo was likely to soon trigger an event of default. The 8.875% secured bond due 2018, now the group's most subordinated debt portion following Médiannuaire's refinancing, reflected the gravity of the situation, trading at a 20% discount.

The issuance of fresh funds was contingent upon getting the green light from shareholders at an extraordinary general meeting to be held in April. If successful, the capital increase would enable Solocal to repay €400 million of term loans (specifically, tranches A3, A5, and B3 – it sounded like a battleship game, with no one able to predict the winner) and would include €361 million of preferential subscription rights open to existing institutional shareholders. In addition, €79 million of reserved capital with preferential rights was to be raised from a subset of institutions including credit funds Paulson, Amber Capital, and Praxient. Two existing shareholders, DNCA Finance and Edmond de Rothschild, were to subscribe pro rata. It was messy.

The rights issue was contingent on an A&E deal for the term loans, with the company seeking to extend at least 90% of loan maturities totalling €1.3 billion from September 2015 to March 2018, with an option to extend to 2020 if the €350 million senior secured bond due in June 2018 was refinanced with a longer maturity. Upon the announcement of the capital-raising process, credit rating specialist Fitch lowered its grade and placed it firmly in the 'substantial risk' category, given the uncertainty of the recapitalisation process.[67]

To make headway in the negotiations, in March 2014 management asked a court to appoint a *conciliateur*.[68] By mid-May, via a court-sanctioned accelerated *sauvegarde* procedure and with approval from its shareholders, Solocal managed to raise €440 million of fresh capital, which had a massively dilutive effect on the share price due to the issue of more than 700 million new shares: the stock went from €1.61 on Wednesday 14 May to open at €0.80 the following day. It was more bad news for those public shareholders who had not subscribed to the new issue. The company, on the other hand, was able to repay one-quarter of its €1.6 billion debt at par, reschedule loan maturities from 2015 to 2018 by gaining consent from more than two-thirds of its lenders, and set aside €40 million to invest in digital initiatives that could hopefully secure its future.[69]

A buyout signed in the summer of 2006 now had loans due 12 years later. Still, the move was bringing net debt-to-EBITDA below 4-to-1.[70] But it was all rather desperate. Five years after European peers Eniro, Seat and Yell had gone through rights issues, the French group was falling in line with the rest of the sector. Because at the time of the PIPE its online migration had been more advanced than other directory groups, Solocal had been more resilient, but the depressed operating performance coupled with the hammered stock price had eventually forced management to tackle the overstretched capital structure. The benefit of seeing the emergence of distressed companies like Solocal was that France, which did not have a US-style Chapter 11 procedure, was discovering a way of organising proactive consensual debt restructurings as a pre-insolvency, court-accredited process. These corporate zombies could do so by using the accelerated *sauvegarde* process to bind minority holdouts to a decision taken by a majority of creditors.

Between May and November 2014, as required by stock exchange regulation, Cerberus-controlled Promontoria notified the company every time it crossed a shareholder threshold. Falling below the 10% threshold by 19 May, the American firm owned less than 1% of Solocal's shares by 6 November.[71] At the end of December the French company's annual report revealed that Médiannuaire only held 0.4% of capital and voting rights. Seemingly keen to escape, Cerberus had seen vulture hedge funds, including Amber Capital and Paulson, gain access to the incomprehensibly cherished asset. By year end these two firms respectively held 6.6% and 5.9% of capital and voting rights in Solocal. While the latter had become the subject, through successive debt-for-equity swaps and a fresh capital injection, of a tactical game between financial institutions, public investors had seen the value of their shares plummet more than two-thirds between December 2012 and the same month of 2014. In the process they had learned a valuable lesson: when PE firms lose money on a PIPE, they usually drag the public along for the ride.

The successful refinancing gave all parties the chance to take stock. In the past two years, sales had faded 12%, with the 31.5% plunge in print activities far from being compensated by the weak 1.6% rise in the online division. Between 2007 and 2014 the number of advertisers on all of the group's platforms had fallen from 763,000 to less than 700,000, but 550,000 of the latter advertised online, up from 470,000 seven years before. From less than 30% of consolidated revenue in 2005, the internet accounted for 70% of activity nine years later. PagesJaunes could claim to have made great strides in its digital transition.

* * *

Solocal's management started 2015 with the firm intention of delivering on its Digital Plan, an initiative that was meant to complete the group's mutation into an online lead generator with a small, but vital for cross-selling, paper business on the side. After six years of uninterrupted revenue deterioration, management was promising growth for 2016 onwards. The 2014 results, out in

February 2015, showed that it would not be an easy task. Combined revenue had fallen 6.3% (missing management's guidance of minus 3% to minus 6%). Print activities were down 17% but, more worryingly, online revenue was flat on the prior year. For the first time since it had launched its internet activities, Solocal had not registered any growth in that division. EBITDA had tumbled more than a quarter and EBITDA margin had lost nine percentage points to 28.3%, its lowest level as a public company. Via the refinancing effort, debt had been reduced from €1.65 billion to less than €1.2 billion, but cash from operations had plummeted 84%.[72] The directory group had not just turned ex-growth; it was fast going ex-cash.

Figure 11.3: PagesJaunes/Solocal's share price (July 2004 – July 2015)

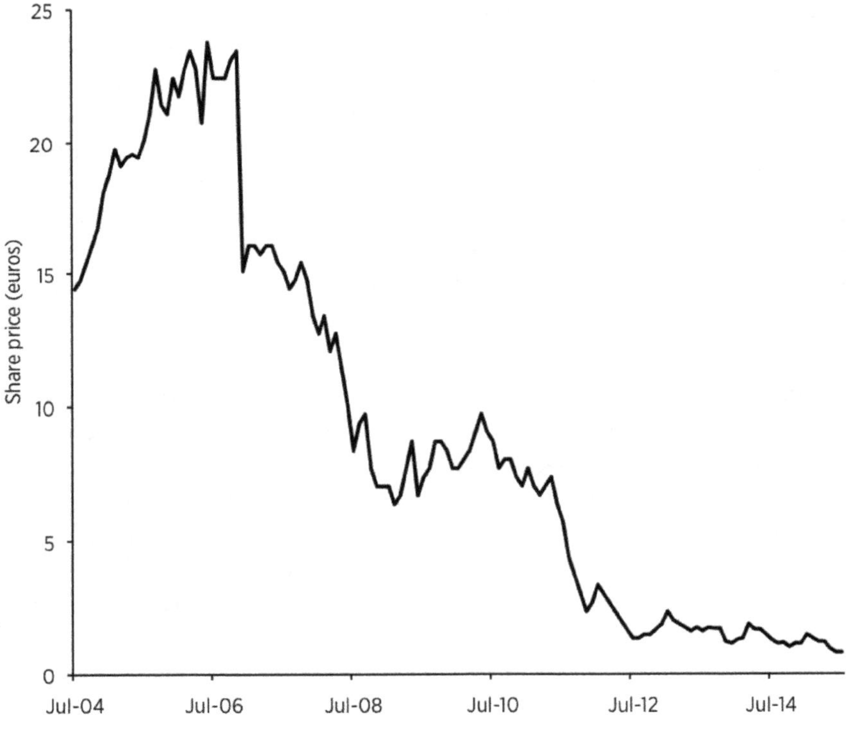

Note: The collapse in the share price from €23.40 on 23 November 2006 to €15.29 on the following day is due to the payment of a €9 exceptional dividend

Thankfully, negotiations with the lenders had given some breathing room, with the actual leverage ratio of 3.73 times gross operating earnings comfortably below the reset 4.5 times covenant.[73] It was gladly appreciated, because the half-year results for 2015, out on 21 July, revealed that top-line erosion in the print unit was accelerating (down 22% year-on-year). Consolidated revenue had shed 4% and EBITDA was down a fifth in that period. It was the group's worst display since going public 11 years earlier, a fact faithfully reflected in the stock's performance (Figure 11.3).

Cherchez la femme

KKR and Goldman got burnt on their PIPE of PagesJaunes. Their experience is not unique. Another case in France was the acquisition in 2007 by Wendel (KKR's former deal associate on the Legrand buyout) of a 17.5% stake in Europe's largest building material supplier, Saint Gobain, only to see the stock lose two-thirds of its value in the following 18 months. Similarly, French buyout shop PAI Partners's purchase in 2008 of a 22.6% stake in IT service provider Atos Origin saw the target's stock linger below PAI's entry price for the best part of four years.

These examples spotlight the root causes of what is often wrong with PIPEs:

- For a start, they do not offer PE firms what they cherish most: privacy. KKR and Goldman's problems with PagesJaunes were highly visible and freely commented upon. This is not the kind of situation financial sponsors relish.

- Second, by remaining public the target faces problems encountered by any publicly traded business: quarterly reporting; strict oversight from the stock exchange authorities; immediate sanction of the share price. This leaves no doubt as to the equity value of the business, since the market cap is assessed daily.

- Third, because of the rights held by minority shareholders, PE owners not fully in control of a business can face legal challenges from minority investors if the latter feel that their personal interests are negatively impacted by the PE owners. It is surprising that given the stiff indebtedness forced onto OpCo, which was 45% owned by public shareholders, no one chose to challenge Médiannuaire's actions in a court of law. The worst backlash Médiannuaire met was when minority activist Wyser-Pratte unsuccessfully tried to block Cerberus's power usurpation. Regarding this third point, the Seat Pagine Gialle scenario (see Chapter 12) shows buyout fund managers what sort of risks PIPEs expose them to.

The key difference, though, between the PagesJaunes buyout and the PIPEs of Saint Gobain and Atos is that neither Wendel nor PAI loaded the OpCo with debt. Thus, Saint Gobain and Atos were able to weather the economic crisis without needing to constantly negotiate A&E and refinancing processes with a herd of impatient lenders. In addition to the three issues raised above, a leveraged PIPE has the drawback of wasting valuable management time with lenders. In the case of PagesJaunes, it was all the more problematic that it was applied to a business facing tumultuous times.

Trouvez le zombi

Operating company PagesJaunes was expected to juggle almost €2 billion of senior loans. As Table 11.1 indicates, thanks to strong stock markets until 2008, the group's equity value was high enough to keep leverage ratios below 50%.

Table 11.1: PagesJaunes Groupe's (OpCo) capital structure ratios (2006-14)

Year end 31 Dec	OpCo net debt (€m)	OpCo market cap (equity value in €m)	OpCo net debt-to-EBITDA	OpCo debt-to-equity	OpCo leverage (debt-to-total capital)
2006	1,866	4,160	4.05	0.45	30%
2007	1,863	3,720	3.70	0.50	33%
2008	1,882	2,000	3.54	0.94	48%
2009	1,931	2,150	3.77	0.90	47%
2010	1,900	1,950	3.80	0.97	49%
2011	1,915	700	4.04	2.73	73%
2012	1,742	470	3.92	3.71	79%
2013	1,580	320	4.27	4.94	83%
2014	1,136	640	4.29	1.78	64%

Notes: EBITDA calculated to derive debt-to-EBITDA ratio rather than gross operating earnings used by management; Equity values are the market capitalisations while debt values are book values; Debt numbers exclude undrawn revolving facilities. Source: Company accounts and author's analysis

For public shareholders, until 2011 OpCo's leverage was reasonable, even below its peers' indebtedness. It was only from 2011 onward that debt represented more than one times equity and reached or exceeded three-quarters of OpCo's capital structure. For KKR and Goldman, what threw the ratios off the scale was Médiannuaire's debt. Figure 11.4 illustrates the picture when HoldCo's loans are added to the mix.

Figure 11.4: EBITDA ratios for Médiannuaire's debt and PagesJaunes's debt and equity (2006-14)

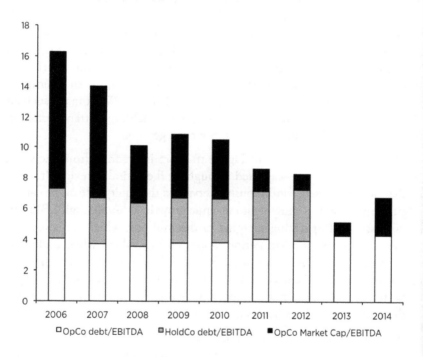

Notes: *EBITDA calculated to derive debt-to-EBITDA ratio rather than gross operating earnings used by management; Equity values are the market capitalisations while debt values are book values; Debt numbers exclude undrawn revolving facilities. Source: Company accounts and author's analysis*

At no point during the LBO, that is until KKR and Goldman were forced out of their control position in 2013, did HoldCo's net-debt-to-EBITDA ratio fall below six times. As early as 2008, consolidated leverage represented 168% of equity, or two-thirds of the capital structure. To fund their deal, the two PE groups were looking at the sort of gearing ratio usually associated with asset-rich project financing. But PagesJaunes's asset base was limited. Its total assets on 31 December 2006 were €850 million, half of which came from trade debtors. Tangible fixed assets had a €19 million book value. As remarked, after the €2.5 billion exceptional dividend of November 2006, PagesJaunes was showing a net-liability position in excess of €2 billion.

To put €1.95 billion of loans on the balance sheet of a business so asset-poor made the deal's success subject to expansive cash generation; especially when cash flows needed to be distributed upstream to serve HoldCo's €1.5 billion loan commitments. As we saw, the print side of PagesJaunes's activities was in slow wind-down mode, making cash flows somewhat unpredictable until the online conversion had been completed. Making the double-bet that PagesJaunes would succeed in transitioning from a traditional print model to an online marketing platform *and* that online platforms would fail to adapt their offering to local advertising needs was not unreasonable per se. What made such an investment outlandish was to ask the group to achieve its transformation with the added challenge of high financial gearing.

The most surprising part of Figure 11.4 certainly comes from the stock valuation PagesJaunes captured throughout the period in review. It seems that public markets continuously overvalued the equity side of the capital structure. A group showing no revenue growth, a double-digit EBITDA decrease, and operating margins in the mid 30s, when they exceeded 45% during the 2008-10 period, appeared overvalued when trading at 6.7 times EBITDA in late 2014. Most likely, investors were looking at Solocal's peers and considered that the French group was a more resilient performer, as Figure 11.5 proves by depicting revenue erosion at several directories publishers between 2006 and 2010.

It is important to point out that with LBOs, once the underlying company is unable to service its loans, it implies that the equity portion is close to worthless – and most likely that some or all of the subordinated debt will need to be written down as well. Despite CEO Jean-Pierre Remy's experience in online product delivery and the marked progress in transforming PagesJaunes/Solocal into a web-based advertiser, the operating company was bogged down by its leverage. A look at Figure 11.6 illustrates the pressure that tightening covenants can put a levered company under. From 30% at the time of the buyout, headroom had virtually disappeared six years later. As is often the case in LBOs that turn sour, financial sponsors are prompt to change management in the hope that the blame for the underperformance can be put on the incumbent team, when in reality the problem is due to a heavy debt load. PagesJaunes's experienced CEO, Michel Datchary, had already engaged the company in a well-conceived online transformation – internet revenues as a proportion of total group sales had gone from 21% in 2002 to more than 36% by the time KKR decided to oust Datchary in May 2009. In the first year after launching its online classifieds solution *annoncesjaunes.fr*, the group had already won 5,400 customers – proof that its digital strategy was full of promise.[74]

Figure 11.5: Revenue trend of various quoted European directory groups (2006 = base 100)

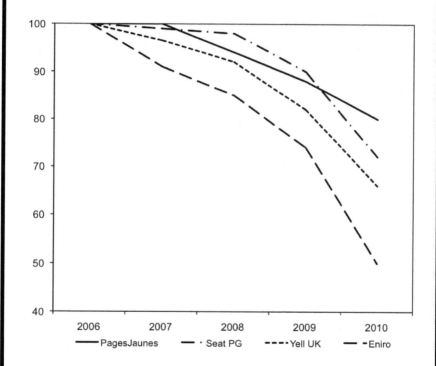

Source: PagesJaunes analyst presentation – 9 February 2011

Replacing Datchary with Remy was not necessarily a bad thing; it just was not going to solve the real issue. As noted in the EMI case study, a company attempting to transform its business model in the face of market disruption cannot do so without spending all its spare cash in innovation and operational restructuring. But what happened during the LBO period is that operating earnings were increasingly absorbed to service debt. During its time under LBO, the group experienced a net cash outflow in 2009, 2011, 2013 and 2014; annual net cash inflows never exceeded €42 million (in 2008).

Figure 11.6: PagesJaunes/Solocal's financial leverage and covenant headroom (2007-14)

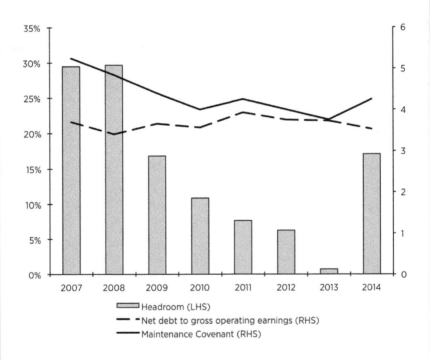

Source: Company accounts and author's analysis

Between 2007 and 2014, PagesJaunes paid €2.36 billion in debt-related obligations: interest repayments totalled €866 million while principal redemption reached €846 million. A staggering €650 million was related to dividend upstreaming to Médiannuaire, in order to repay HoldCo's loan interest during the years leading up to 2011 when PagesJaunes's management had been happy to oblige. By contrast, a company experiencing one of the most eventful periods in its history due to the digitalisation of its content and the sudden influx of competitors in a market on which it used to hold a monopoly, spent just €300 million in research and development (mainly in the form of software and equipment) and a paltry €70 million in acquisitions. When you consider that the group generated €8.7 billion in sales over the LBO period, investing annually less than €40 million in innovation (or less than 4% of revenue) and €9 million in external growth (less than 1% of revenue), when rivals Microsoft and Google allocated 13% of their top line to R&D, was not going to give PagesJaunes a proper shot at the digital revolution. Especially because, as is often the case with corporate integrations, some of these M&A deals failed to deliver. One such case was the March 2010 purchase of 123people: the online people search business was shut down four years later.

PagesJaunes was so cash-strapped that, between 2011 and 2014, it needed three amend-and-extend processes (ignoring the two A&Es at the HoldCo level) and a capital increase. Not surprisingly, the group did not have the wherewithal to invest in R&D on the same scale as online rivals. The business plan was a little too dependent on cash extraction for a largely uninspired copycat strategy. Today, even in France, Google is the most popular method for accessing maps online. The mapping products introduced by PagesJaunes were never performance-competitive with Google's, and the blame lies in part with the restricted R&D budget. To keep generating cash on a recurring basis, the group needed to redesign its business model.

A solid online business

I know what you're thinking: hindsight is 20/20. Maybe the trend was not so bleedingly obvious from the outset. Unfortunately, media sector research published at the time of the PagesJaunes LBO indicates that, by 2005-06, there was no longer any question that online B2C advertising, led by search engines Google (with a 57% market share in 2005), Yahoo! and Microsoft's MSN,[75] was slowly but surely eating away at printed classifieds and display revenue. With €320 million in online revenues in 2006, PagesJaunes itself was one of the biggest internet companies in France. When KKR got involved with the company, radical transformations of the business directory sector were well underway, stimulated by the still faltering attempts at digitalisation.

At first gradual, online substitution gathered pace throughout the noughties. Internet usage and adoption had seen marked differences between countries. Online access had had the most influence on the number of users and the time spent online. By 2006, while internet penetration in the UK and the US had reached 70%, in France it was still below 50%. The inflection point for internet penetration in France took place in 2007, the year following KKR's buyout of PagesJaunes. PagesJaunes's sharp underperformance from 2007 onwards can be attributed to a larger proportion of the French population getting internet access. Of course, this also benefitted PagesJaunes's efforts to build its online offering, but since 60% of revenue in 2007 and 2008 was derived from printed directories, increased internet penetration had the effect of boosting the performance of the group's online rivals. France was still behind the US and the UK in terms of online access, but it was only a matter of time before it caught up. What were to be the implications for PagesJaunes when that happened?

A look at American publishers, an exercise that any commercial due diligence adviser would have carried out ahead of the LBO, would have served as a warning. US telecom operator Verizon filed a registration form with the SEC on 7 July 2006 in preparation for the spin-offs of its print and internet yellow-pages publishing operations, a couple of weeks before KKR was reported to be in exclusivity with France Télécom. KKR's advisers would have looked at the data apprehensively. Verizon's directories had lost 12% of their sales over four years. Management had worked hard to preserve margins at the expense of staff costs. Reflecting the increasing tension between management and employees, a subsection of the unionised workforce had gone on strike for 14 weeks in October 2005. Naturally, Verizon Directories had seen electronic revenue increase, recording a 21% jump in 2004 and 19% the following year, for instance. Unfortunately printed products, which accounted for 94% of total revenue, had experienced an annual 5% fall in sales for these two years.[76] The trend was unmistakable: printed directories were losing ground and preserving margins would require aggressive cost-cutting, including layoffs, and heavy capex spend. Research from the US trade body for directories, the Yellow Pages Association, also demonstrated that the decline of directories in America had started several years before KKR and Goldman took a look at PagesJaunes.

For a while, the situation in France was more hopeful. At the time of the LBO, *pagesjaunes.fr* was second in search engines, with two out of five web users visiting the site compared to 78% adopting Google's services. The French site was the best established among European directories. In Spain and the UK, the online market share of directories was below 10%.[77] PagesJaunes was also the fourth most visited website in the country, behind Google, MSN and France Télécom's Wanadoo.[78] One of the main reasons why PagesJaunes had seen better online migration of its users than European peers is the fact that it had benefitted from the existence, since the 1980s, of the 'national web' service Minitel, a precursor to internet-based advertising models where digital ads featured prominently. Still, by 2003 the internet was already eating at Minitel's market share and Figure 11.7 demonstrates that it was altering PagesJaunes's online revenue performance.

Figure 11.7: Growth rate of PagesJaunes's French online revenues (2003-10)

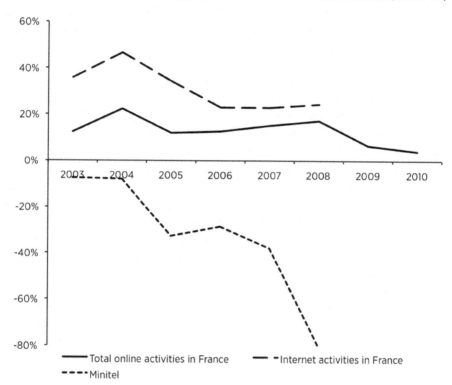

Source: Company accounts and author's analysis

It was not only online searches that were winning market share. The purpose of printed directories had always been to generate customer leads, which was the main reason why small and large business owners paid extra to feature in an otherwise user-unfriendly list of addresses and phone numbers. By the mid-noughties online classified ads had become all the rage. In the US, Craigslist celebrated its tenth birthday in 2005. It operated separate sites listing ads for bikes, jobs, apartments, you name it, in 120 cities in 25 countries.[79] And let's not forget eBay, a global platform connecting buyers and sellers directly and doing the product search for you. By 2005, eBay was also celebrating its tenth anniversary and it was serving 200 million registered users worldwide.[80] These were consumer-to-consumer sites, but they nonetheless gave sole traders direct access to local consumers, which in turn upset the revenue model of traditional yellow pages.

Beleaguered PagesJaunes had tried to boost growth through acquisitions, absorbing in 2011 A Vendre A Louer, ClicRDV and FineMedia (a local online editor), as well as 49% of Leadperformance, a specialist in sales outlet location on the internet. Eager to keep its internet strategy on the right track, in January 2013 management had acquired Chronoresto, a player in online meal delivery.[81] The French group had done a great job in the face of enormous upheaval in its core markets. Total revenue had fallen by 15% between 2006 and 2014, but management had profitably migrated the company online, with internet revenues representing more than two-thirds of the top line in 2014 compared to less than a third at the time of the LBO.

When you compare Solocal's performance to that of its British rival Yell, you fully appreciate how successful the French group's transformation truly was. The following anecdote, set across the English Channel, will demonstrate that PagesJaunes's management does deserve credit for steering the group's transformation. In February 2007 Yell was a FTSE 100 constituent with a market cap exceeding £6 billion. The group spent the next six years making acquisitions of printed directory businesses in the US and Latin America, failing to adapt to the online revolution despite announcing a "new transformation strategy" in 2011. Oddly renamed Hibu the following year in a revolutionary effort at rebranding, the company reported a loss of £2 billion in its 2013 fiscal year, before going through a debt/equity swap to get rid of bank loans of £2.3 billion in July of that year. All shareholders were wiped out. As it entered administration before delisting in late 2013 Hibu had a market cap of less than £30 million.[82]

Not so strong on paper

In 2005 the print products delivered by PagesJaunes had shown limited revenue growth, with business directories up less than 4% and its white pages presenting an increase of 0.1%.[83] When the PIPE was finalised in late 2006, the PagesJaunes's print activities had seen a slowdown in revenue growth in both business and personal directories for several years. In 2007 the unit had posted no growth. Thereafter annual revenue changes turned negative, going from minus 5% in 2008 to minus 10% in 2010. Post-2010, the rate of decline stepped up a gear, with the print division's sales registering a fall of 15% in 2012 and 17% in each of the two following years.

This trend is very common in businesses experiencing disruptive change. At first, the core activities see their growth slow down as the disruptive products (here, online classified advertising and data search) are only consumed by a minority of customers (early adopters). In a way not dissimilar to what we saw in the music sector (refer to Chapter 6 on EMI), as the new products become more competitive in terms of price and convenience, more consumers try them out and the pace of migration from old products (paper telephone directories or CDs) to new services (online directory or digital music downloads) accelerates until mass adoption of the modern technology makes the old products redundant or turns them into nice but not indispensable cross-selling add-ons.

KKR and Goldman no doubt knew about it, but they considered that the adoption of PagesJaunes's online solutions (its mapping product *mappy.fr*, its online classifieds service *annoncesjaunes.fr*, and its web-based directories *pagesjaunes.fr*) would compensate for the erosion of the mainstream division. However, there is one element of the puzzle that they critically failed to factor into their analysis. PagesJaunes held a quasi-exclusivity on the old activities of printed directories in France whereas, when it came to the internet, the French company was operating in a nascent, grab-all-you-can arena of perfect competition – the exact opposite of a monopoly.

With web-based solutions, consumers were free to shop around and to play one service provider against another. PagesJaunes's online activities were certain to meet fierce competition from local and international rivals. This made the transition all the more challenging: margins on online activities were, initially, lower than for print, and PagesJaunes's online revenue never completely replaced lost print ads since internet rivals took a big share of the digital market. Between 2007 and 2015, consolidated revenues lost almost one-quarter, going from €1.16 billion to €873 million, when the print division had shed two-quarters of its top line. Consolidated operating income had collapsed 70% from €489 million to €143 million. Competitive forces led operating margins into a downward spiral, from 42% in 2007 to 16% eight years later.[84]

Between 1977 and 2007 total advertising revenue derived from the printed directory sector in the US had grown from less than $2 billion to more than $14 billion.[85] Then it plateaued before going fast into reverse due to lower advertiser renewal rates, reduced advertiser spend and price discounting, all driven by the emergence of pure online classifieds. Eventually, mobile and social media advertising allowed for geolocalisation. What attracted advertisers to the likes of Facebook and YouTube was the ability to access a global audience while localising the content of their ads. Via Facebook Places, launched in 2010, the social website provides users with the ability to receive targeted advertising and friends' advice directly relevant to their location. While in 2014 Google chose to discontinue a similar product (called Latitude), after five years of underwhelming performance, geotargeting remains a key component of Google Maps.

Despite concerns about privacy, locally targeted advertising is growing fast. The real benefit of geolocalisation is that it offers advertisers the opportunity to learn about consumers' habits. A national champion like PagesJaunes, though well established in France and thereby among that country's corporate clients, does not offer economies of scale to global marketers. Pure online and mobile platforms provide location-targeted advertising as easily as old printed directories. So, as in the music industry we looked at in Chapter 6, PagesJaunes's core market was disrupted by new technologies. Tech firms, not incumbent yellow pages, led the new generation of local, classified advertising services.

Market disruption

At this point, it is worth contrasting PagesJaunes's relative failure to compete with online rivals to EMI's and other music majors' inability to react to digital piracy and downloads. It is legitimate to observe that Google had commodified the business directories' core characteristics the way music download platforms like Apple's iTunes had made the distribution of music seamless and cheaper. However, there are also key distinctions between the two scenarios that could explain why the physical directories were destined to be outclassed.

The business model of PagesJaunes and its foreign equivalents had always been country-centric. In fact, practically all had started as national monopolies protected by government regulation. Though they had benefitted from their exclusivity in producing national listings, unlike Google they had no international footprint. It is only in the late 1990s and early noughties, when globalisation took hold, that a few of them started consolidating across borders (e.g., Yellow Brick Road and VNU World Directories across Europe; Yell in the UK, Latin America and the US).

Not only was the directories' national monopoly a handicap, but producing physical telephone and address listings on an international stage would have proven very costly and highly impractical. The core business offered limited economies of scale. The advent of the internet changed the industry leaders' unique selling points. It was no longer as important to offer a paper-based, encyclopaedic list of businesses. Global footprint, accessibility (i.e., convenience of access) and seamless editing (meaning up-to-date content) were the new requirements. Web-based advertising platforms supplied these requirements at a fraction of the cost and did not have the burden of a legacy paper product. So, whereas EMI already had a worldwide presence and could have competed head-on with downloading platforms by offering its catalogue of artists online and on a global basis (as all record companies eventually and reluctantly did), the publishers of national yellow pages had no experience abroad and could only compete locally, serving SMEs, leaving the benefit of economies of scale typical of large, international accounts to global internet rivals.

Making the task of directory publishers well nigh impossible was the fragmentation of their industry. While music recording and publishing activities were 70% to 80% controlled by a handful of majors, which would (or should) have made their cooperation easier against the digital threat, the business directory market had as many players as there were countries – not to mention that some countries had several participants. Without a comprehensive global footprint already in place – without the existence of industry majors – the classifieds sector was vulnerable to internet-based globalisation.

Finally, the music market, although global in terms of production of acts, was heavily concentrated when it came to consumption. The five largest territories (the US, Japan, the UK, Germany and France) accounted for about three-quarters of music sales' total retail value. By contrast, the purchase and use of yellow pages were essentially local and therefore as fragmented as the supply side. Business directories stood very little chance of being able to conceive a product capable of vying with global digital platforms. By 2007, internet penetration for households in most developed countries exceeded 70%; a rate that was naturally much higher in the corporate world, making online searches for clients and suppliers convenient and accurate. Not only had internet access become ubiquitous, but online databases could also be updated in real time. Customers did not need to wait for the physical directory to be sent to them once a year to be informed about changes.

But globalisation and geolocalisation would never have been sufficient to compete with yellow pages. The principal source of competition from internet start-ups came from better classification of content. As for the company's name behind the disruptive breakthrough in online search technology, it is of course Google. Until the late 1990s, internet searches were going through a gateway called a web portal (such as Yahoo!) or a browser (like Netscape). Results were a disorganised amalgamation of more or less relevant facts. Because of the growing amount of data added to the World Wide Web and the increasing complexity of queries, it was becoming essential to bring order to the business of data queries. In 1998 Google launched its now famous algorithm, crawling and building an index of all web pages. The key success factor of Google's algorithm and of similar search discovery software developed by rivals is that they are able to perfect information gathering, organising and compartmentalising. This ability to learn from past queries and adapt searches accordingly is the reason behind the successful online migration of telephone listings and of their main monetised by-product: classified advertisements.

The loss of market share by printed directories accelerated during the Great Recession, but it started much earlier. By 2005 Google's advertising revenue had already topped $6 billion worldwide, up from less than $1 billion two years earlier. It exceeded $10 billion in 2006, derived primarily from the company's very popular AdWords product, a self-service programme enabling businesses to place text-based ads on Google. The search giant had created a user-friendly classified ads platform available not just to consumers receiving the yellow pages at home, but to all Google users worldwide. By 2006 AdWords – launched six years earlier – was no longer seen as a nice add-on to paper telephone directories; it was acknowledged as the future of classified ads, which explains why PagesJaunes had introduced *annoncesjaunes.fr* in early 2007.[86] When in 2009 the French group launched with much fanfare its 'vue du ciel' feature to allow *pagesjaunes.fr* users to get a satellite view of an address, it was five years late compared to the introduction of satellite photos on Google Maps and came several months after the latter's launch in France.[87]

Due to its limited R&D budget, PagesJaunes had been playing catch-up. Even the group's service Mappy added nothing extra to Google Maps, with the noticeable difference that the latter offered worldwide coverage. Tellingly, after years of resistance, in September 2013 Solocal finally partnered with its American archrival, offering Solocal customers access through AdWords, in a deal similar to those the French marketing group had already signed with Yahoo!, Microsoft and Facebook.[88] A traditionally monopolistic activity, directory publishing had been transformed by digitalisation. With the online revolution, classifieds became an industry where demand moved quickly while supply, supported by cash-rich print incumbents, proved sticky. The worst part is that the service offering derived from yellow pages got split into separate segments thanks to the flexibility provided by the internet. Local recommendation websites like Yelp, pay-per-click advertisers such as Google, and lead generators and data brokers like Experian forged their respective niches, leaving business directories looking austere and generic.

Not the best advertisement for PE performance

For KKR, PagesJaunes was just another road kill, even if the carcass was picked up by a strange army of ambulance chasers, starting with turnaround specialist Cerberus. Following Médiannuaire's loss of control to the benefit of vulture debt funds, PagesJaunes ended up with a market cap of €200 million for a total EV of €1.3 billion in late 2015, compared to €6 billion nine years earlier. It shouldn't therefore be a surprise to learn that the KKR European Fund II, closed in 2005 and partly invested in PagesJaunes, turned out to be a low-return vehicle. As of 31 December 2014, KKR's vehicle had achieved a 3.5% IRR, or

1.2 times the equity invested.[89] KKR's European performance lagged that of public stock indices. Over the ten-year period to December 2014, the French CAC40 returned 4.2% a year on a total return basis (with dividends reinvested), whereas the UK's FTSE 100 yielded 7%.[90] Sadly for KKR's limited partners, that fund had not granted them a minimum rate of return before KKR's executives were entitled to take their 20% share of the gains – the famous carried interest. Designed to compensate LPs for the longer holding period of PE investments, the hurdle rate is typically set at an industry standard of 8%, but KKR had not given its backers such a right due to its ability, historically, to generate higher returns than its peers. In view of the 2005 vintage's IRR, the firm's European Fund IV, raised in 2014 and 2015, was compelled to offer such a minimum performance target.[91] Live and learn.

KKR and Goldman Sachs should count their blessings as the situation could have been a lot worse had public investors accepted to be squeezed out in late 2006. Remember that the original goal was to purchase the whole company and take it private. Ignoring the public's 46% stake, the PagesJaunes deal totalled €3.3 billion, making it the third biggest buyout announced in France that year, well behind the €4.8 billion SBO of transmission and broadcasting tower specialist TDF, and a bit smaller than fashion retailer Vivarte's €3.5 billion.[92] When taking into account the minority stake, PagesJaunes's total EV exceeded €6 billion, which would have made it France's largest LBO but also the country's biggest failed buyout seven years later. That crown is now worn by British group Charterhouse and its ill-fated Vivarte, which fell under the control of creditors in 2014.[93]

In hindsight, of course, minority shareholders would have been better off selling out of PagesJaunes in November 2006. KKR and Goldman can thank the public for saving them and their LPs a tidy sum. But perhaps the most arresting fact about the PE duo's move to acquire PagesJaunes for more than 13.5 times EBITDA is that it had taken place three years after several European PE firms invested in a telephone directory group based across the Alps. Italy's Seat Pagine Gialle was already showing signs of fatigue by 2006 and is the subject of our next case study.

CHAPTER 12
Seat Pagine Gialle – The Italian Job

S EAT WAS BORN ON 23 MAY 1925 AS SOCIETÀ ANONIMA
Elenchi ufficiali per gli Abbonati al Telefono (literally 'public company
of official lists for telephone subscribers'). Over the preceding two years,
the Italian telecom network had been split between five separate companies
holding a monopoly in their respective regions. Each phone-book publisher
operated within one of the five regions. Seat, headquartered in Turin, published
its first directory the year after its creation, listing subscribers in the Piedmont
area. The 1950s saw the rise of Seat as a national provider, and by 1964 the
company had become the sole publisher of directories in Italy. Two years later
it issued its first *Pagine Gialle* (yellow pages). By then the group had become
integrated with all the telephone activities of STET (Società Torinese per
l'Esercizio Telefonico), a state agency controlling all assets related to satellite,
cable and fixed line communications in the country. For most of the 1970s
and 1980s, Seat consolidated its monopoly in the Italian market. Eventually,
it became incorporated within Telecom Italia, the national telephone operator
also controlled by STET.

As the latter and Telecom Italia were preparing to merge, in January 1997 Seat
gained its independence, listing on the Milan stock exchange. By October,
Seat's market capitalisation stood at €1.7 billion. To complete the company's
privatisation, a month later 61% of it was sold for 1.64 billion Italian lire (€850
million) to Ottobi, a consortium of investors led by De Agostini, one of the
main publishing houses in the country, alongside local PE firm Investitori
Associati, American LBO group Bain Capital, and British outfits BC Partners
and CVC.[1] The sale marked continental Europe's largest ever buyout. The
following year Ottobi merged with Seat and the combined entity was renamed
Seat Pagine Gialle.[2]

Excited by its newly found independence and suffering from an acute case of
internet-fever, management then got a bit sidetracked from the mainstream
activities, purchasing in 1999 the country's leading office supplies retail chain
Buffetti, web service firm Matrix, and internet service provider McLink.[3]
Having launched in 1998 *paginegialle.it*, the web version of its main product,

management followed suit with the white pages site *paginebianche.it*.[4] Thanks to this transformation into one of Italy's major internet portals, the publicly listed Seat Pagine Gialle saw its market cap reach €30 billion by March 2000 – its shares had risen 364% between 1 October 1999 and 29 March 2000. Its enterprise value exceeded 70 times EBITDA and 25 times sales.[5] The dotcom mania was at its peak.

What better way to top it all for Seat's financial investors than to sell the business? In February 2000 Telecom Italia's internet service provider Tin.it and Seat announced their intention to merge in a €50 billion transaction. Telecom Italia was preparing to regain control of a business it owned four years earlier at a valuation ten times higher.[6] Via this reverse takeover, the operator was creating the country's largest internet business. Since Telecom Italia was itself 55% owned by IT conglomerate Olivetti, Italy was seeing the creation of one of the largest technology groups in Europe, active in fixed line, mobile and online communications. It was all part of a craze for 'network convergence'.

Using its inflated currency – its share price – and while still under the temporary ownership of its financial sponsors, Seat continued its expansion through further M&A activity, acquiring German telephone service company Telegate in May 2000, absorbing three months later the UK's second largest yellow-pages publisher Thomson Directories, and also taking control of French data marketing company Consodata. Also in August, the Italian group announced its intention to purchase a controlling stake in the third-largest Italian TV broadcaster, TeleMonteCarlo (TMC).[7] In line with the market correction, Seat's stock tanked in the second half of 2000, going from a high of €7.4 a share in March to less than €2 by year end, well below the €4.2-per-share bid tabled by Telecom Italia.[8] But the merger with Tin.it went ahead anyway. In November 2000 Seat Pagine Gialle became part of Telecom Italia, helping the PE backers make more than 25 times their money on a three-year investment.[9] Their exit could not have been better timed, for Seat's visionary strategic plans soon dried up. With its share price down 80% since Telecom Italia had taken a controlling stake, in September 2001 Seat announced a €75 million net loss for the first six months of 2001.[10]

The hysteria demonstrated by Seat Pagine Gialle's senior execs in the days of the new-media revolution is fascinating, but enough already about the dotcom bubble and its predictable crash. What interests us is the group's odyssey in the next euphoric M&A period: the LBO bubble of the noughties.

A fistful of euros

As the internet sector lost part of its appeal, many of the tech and media conglomerates that had been constructed in earnest between 1998 and 2001 were disbanded with equal urgency. In March 2003 Telecom Italia announced its intention to spin off and sell the directories business from its subsidiary Seat in order to delever, and to raise cash to help finance the telecom operator's merger with Olivetti. The project provided for the demerger of Pagine Gialle, the directory assistance unit plus the business information activities, into a NewCo. The rest of the Seat group, including internet and TV activities, was to be separately listed. The damage carried out during the dotcom frenzy was about to be undone.

As part of the partial spin-off, Telecom Italia decided to keep the directories and business information division publicly listed. The NewCo was incorporated as a separate company on 1 August 2003, and three days later 37.5% was independently floated on the Borsa Italiana. Then, on 8 August, a controlling stake in the unit was sold to institutional investors. The winning bid had come from a bunch of financial sponsors. Called Silver S.p.A., the consortium included British buyout group Permira, alongside BC Partners, CVC and local shop Investitori – the last three well-acquainted with the target, as you will recall. Silver acquired Telecom Italia's 62.5% stake for a total consideration north of €3 billion.

The deal gave the target a total EV of €5.65 billion, including €0.5 billion of assumed debt.[11] It was Europe's biggest buyout to date.[12] The value represented 10.2 times 2002 EBITDA, or 9.4 times 2003 expected earnings. It was a generous price, but the target was a high-margin business. At any rate, the directory publisher was now back under the control of financial institutions. Naturally, the Seat transaction was meant to imitate LBOs done previously in the sector. Several European competitors had already been through their own buyouts, a fact that Seat's management knew since the Italian group had acquired Thomson Directories from Apax and Advent in the summer of 2000. Seat was hugely cash generative, producing EBITDA margins in excess of 40%. That called for some serious leverage. The plan was to issue a dividend in the new year to recapitalise the company and increase debt from half a billion to €4 billion.

In the meantime, the Silver consortium needed to make a compulsory tender offer for the minority stake they did not yet own. In September, Silver launched a public purchase offer (PPO) for the 37.5% listed on Borsa Italia. The offer was priced at €0.598 a share, the same price the PE investors had paid Telecom Italia for its majority stake.[13] The PPO was a disaster, with the PE owners only able to garner a further 0.02% of total outstanding shares. They could not squeeze out the minorities and take the business private. But in truth they had failed to show much enthusiasm in their attempt, and had even publicly admitted that their true intent was to keep the business partly listed (probably to avoid having to pay a premium and to facilitate their exit later on).[14]

The stock traded well above the bid price throughout the period, even exceeding €0.80 as the offer period expired. The minorities had factored in that the special dividend due to be paid out in early 2004 justified pushing the price 30% above the consortium's bid. As with the first LBO of 1997-2000, the PE investment holding was ultimately controlled by a Luxembourg-registered entity (Société des participations Silver), itself owned by BC Partners, CVC, Permira and Alfieri (the vehicle managed by Investitori).[15] Figure 12.1 helps to make sense of the corporate structure at the time of the buyout. [16]

Figure 12.1: Seat Pagine Gialle's group structure post-LBO (2003)

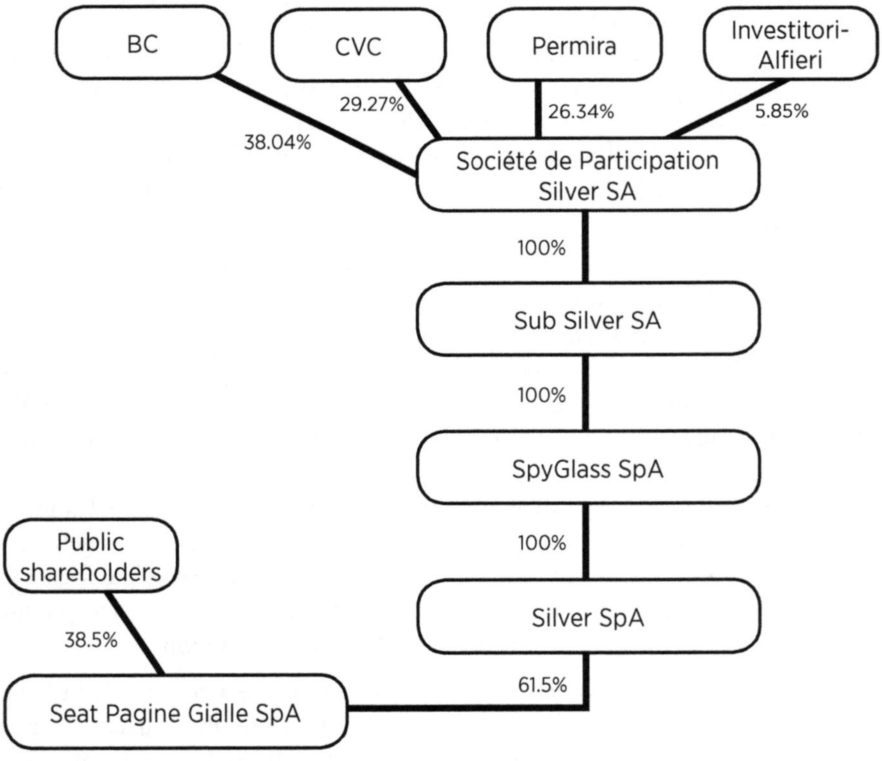

Source: Company accounts and author's analysis

The administrative board, set up in November 2003, included the usual senior executives, the group's chairman, Enrico Giliberti, and CEO Luca Majocchi, alongside three independent directors and eight PE executives, two for each buyout firm.[17] Executive and independent directors were vastly outnumbered by financial wizards. It was unusual from a corporate governance viewpoint. It would have made more sense for each financial sponsor only to have one board representative, maybe assisted by a board observer. But none of the PE backers wanted to be outshone by the others in the largest LBO in European history, so they had brought in the big guns, including CVC's co-founder Hardy McLain and Investitori's co-founder Dario Cossutta.

Management had the double misfortune of having to deal with a board full of PE representatives and to report on a quarterly basis to public shareholders and lenders. Presenting its Industrial Plan in late 2003, management confidently predicted, on a consolidated basis, a 5% to 6% annual sales growth rate and a 7% to 8% annual EBITDA increase for the 2003-06 period. Even the historically sleepy print operations in Italy were projected to grow sales at a 2% annual clip, with EBITDA up about 7% a year.[18]

Now that the proposed orderly take-private had turned instead into a cluttered PIPE, Silver tried to make the best of a bad situation. The equity sponsors needed Seat to issue a dividend in order to redeem the €2.2 billion bridge loan they had used to purchase Telecom Italia's stake.[19] Remember that we saw the same procedure in the PagesJaunes story; it is called a debt push-down. On 22 April 2004, a jumbo dividend totalling close to €3.6 billion was paid out to all stockholders via the proceeds of €2.75 billion of senior loans provided by Royal Bank of Scotland (RBS) – including term loans divided into three tranches with differing maturities and margins, as standard – and a €1.3 billion high-yield bond with an 8% coupon provided by Lighthouse International, a Luxembourg-based vehicle controlled by various lenders. The balance of the LBO loans was used to repay €528 million of existing debt. Seat was once again a respectable leveraged buyout.[20]

The stock normally adjusted as it went ex-dividend. To sustain the share price, management had indicated that it would pay €90 million to €100 million of annual dividends in the next few years, giving a yield of 4.5%.[21] The PIPE was going to test management's juggling skills, forcing it to play a balancing act to please financial sponsors, LBO lenders and public shareholders.

A difficult start

They had only been in charge a few weeks, but the new majority owners were already running the rule over Seat. And slashing costs was top of the agenda. Management was planning to implement a Restructuring Plan 2004-05. The jargon used to describe the planned reorganisation must have come straight from the latest management consulting handbooks, with goals including "proper dimensioning of the human resources deployed within the company", the "management of surplus labor, estimated at not more than 250 employees, through non-traumatic tools available under current labor laws" and "the restructuring of labor within the company through the consolidation and development of products as well as the modernization of processes."[22] In plain English, they were going to sack people who were deemed surplus to requirements.

Management and the financial sponsors were also keen to generate as much cash as quickly as possible. In March 2004 they sold the French operations of the Consodata subsidiary, followed by the German activities a month later.[23] In addition to the core yellow and white pages in Italy, they were keeping hold of the phone book activities in the UK (Thomson), the directory assistance business in Germany (Telegate), a French B2B directory (Eurédit/Europages), and business information in Italy (Consodata).

The leveraged PIPE, however, did not start on a strong note. The results for the first half of 2004 revealed that the Industrial Plan was going to be a challenge: Seat had only recorded a meagre 1% rise in EBITDA. Disappointingly, the top line had fallen by 2%. Now saddled with €4 billion of debt,[24] the company was under obligation to perform better. At the half-year point, the company also disclosed that the PE consortium, now called Sub Silver S.A. following a reorganisation at the HoldCo level, only held 50.14% of Seat, down from the 62.52% stake held shortly after launching its unsuccessful PPO a year earlier.[25] At the same time that they were benefitting from a special dividend to leverage the target, through a private placement the PE backers had passed on a fifth of their combined stake, or 12.4% of the company's share capital, to American bank Lehman Brothers for $990 million in proceeds. Lehman had then resold the entire stake to institutional investors.[26] Such a quick sale could do no harm to the financial sponsors' IRR.

In November 2004, CVC's Pietro Giovanni Masera joined the board, replacing his colleague Hardy McLain. The waltz of board members had started and would rise to a crescendo over time. That same month, anticipating that the Industrial Plan presented the year before was not going to work, management demonstrated its unique skills in moving the goal posts by presenting a Strategic Plan for the period 2005-07. The year 2005 was forecast to see revenue grow by 4% to 5% (though only 0.8% to 1.3% in print) and EBITDA rise by up to 2% as investment was made to support future growth. The plan's next two years were projected to see growth of more than 5% in both revenue and earnings.

These were ambitious targets for a group that had registered in the first three-quarters of 2004 a 1% revenue increase. Management rightly pointed out that Seat held the leading position in the highly fragmented and still underdeveloped market of SME advertising. While correctly establishing that new entrants such as search engines were still at an early stage of development, the senior executive team appeared a bit naïve when stating that Seat faced a window of opportunity to invigorate its competitive position in Italy.[27] If anything, its mainstream activity, printed directories, was a declining asset that was fast losing market share to online rivals not encumbered with the dated print business model.

Full-year 2004 numbers showed that the half-year incident was not a fluke. Seat was falling behind the Industrial Plan's projections: revenue had shed 3%, whereas gross operating profit and EBITDA were only up 0.8% and 1.5% respectively, compared to increases of more than 8% the year before. In the Italian division, online and voice revenues had risen by 12% and 8%, but the bulk of the business, yellow and white pages, had only shown marginal upward movement. This sort of performance was never going to help the business meet its debt covenants and obligations. Seventeen months into the PIPE, Seat's management was in danger of losing the confidence of its PE backers and lenders. During 2004 the stock had fallen sharply on the Milan exchange to end at about €0.30, a quarter down on the ex-div price set in late April. And yet the distressing fact was that, with a market cap of €2.6 billion and net debt of €3.9 billion (6.4 times EBITDA), the group was assigned an EV-to-EBITDA multiple of 10.6 times at the end of December.[28] Thanks to the very generous stock valuation, leverage remained manageable at 60% of enterprise value.

*   *   *

With Italy representing more than 72% of group revenues and 87% of EBITDA, Seat was much exposed to that country's economic situation.[29] After being practically flat the year before, in 2004 Italian GDP had grown at a languid rate of 1.6%.[30] The other major European economies where the group was present, France, Germany and the UK, had offered marginal support. The fragile economy was putting pressure on advertising spend for SMEs; Seat's key clients. Because of this, the company had underperformed the Mibtel, the Milan exchange's main index. Thomson's and Telegate's performances were the most troublesome. Number two directory publisher in the UK, Thomson was not growing and its EBITDA halved during the first half of 2005. Telegate, the second largest directory assistance group in Germany, with a third of the market behind Deutsche Telekom, registered revenue erosion, although a programme of cost efficiency in its call centres pushed EBITDA up by a fifth. More realistic than at the time of the LBO, senior management now predicted a 2.5% to 3.5%

EBITDA growth rate for 2005.[31] Even if management argued that its Strategic Plan was back-end loaded, with economic conditions worse than expected the full-year 2005 results were likely to fall further behind.

Ever since subscribing to its €4 billion LBO loans the company had nevertheless demonstrated why it was such a strong buyout candidate. In January 2005 it made a €50 million voluntary prepayment pro rata on all the debt facilities. Two months later it prepaid €84 million of its term A2 loan. Then, in June 2005 senior debt was successfully renegotiated to take advantage of lower prevailing interest rates. Seat's management and financial sponsors benefitted from the generosity of the credit markets by refinancing the loans, replacing the €2.27 billion remaining balance with a bigger quantum of €2.53 billion, split between a term A of €1.93 billion (at Euribor +1.91%) and a term B of €590 million (at Euribor +2.41%).[32]

It was a great improvement on the original senior debt deal, which had been split into three tranches: €1.25 billion of term A2 at a 2.415% margin, and terms B and C of €742 million each at 2.915% and 3.415% margins respectively.[33] Tranche A1, denominated in sterling and issued by the Thomson subsidiary, had been eliminated. Fourteen months after the LBO, and despite performing behind plan, the hugely profitable directories publisher convinced Royal Bank of Scotland to increase the leverage at a lower cost.

Nonetheless, the full-year 2005 figures showed that the leveraged group was struggling. Both revenue and gross operating profit were up just 1%. Management missed its own EBITDA growth forecast, delivering a 2% increase instead of the promised 2.5%-to-3.5%. The strange thing is that the enterprise value had gone up more than 6% during the year, so that the group's valuation now equated an even more demanding 11 times EBITDA. There was some good news, though. Because Seat was so profitable – its operating free cash flows exceeded €600 million in both 2004 and 2005 – it was able to easily absorb the cost of debt. Over €260 million worth of interest was paid during the year.[34] In addition, the deleveraging process was well underway. Between December 2004 and December 2005 net debt was reduced by close to €300 million – net-debt-to-EBITDA was now 5.8 times. And thanks to the surprising upbeat mood of the market, the stock price rose by more than one-quarter in 2005, bringing leverage down significantly to 52.6%.

* * *

With a 90% share of Italy's directory publishing market and more than 20% of the SME advertising market,[35] Seat was seemingly ideally positioned to gain a stronghold in internet penetration. The key to success, however, lay in innovation. The group's creaky infrastructure and antiquated sales structure needed to be revamped in order to provide customers with online functionalities, the sales force with an automated IT platform, and users with better direct-marketing offerings. That's not me talking. I am pulling this from the many management presentations and reports issued at the time. The goal was to turn Seat's agents from mere sales people to consultants, so a new sales organisation was put in place in January 2006.

Beyond the jargon, what the new "value-based" sales approach, "customer-satisfaction management practices" and "product innovation and improvement" programme aimed to achieve was to convert Seat's traditional publishing model into a web-based advertising platform. Sales and profits were suffering due to growth in online classifieds, which weakened print advertising demand. Only half of the 14-to-74-year-old population used yellow pages, and just two-thirds of internet users also flipped through paper directories.[36] Although it was seen at the time as an opportunity for cross-selling, it was also an indication that yellow pages readership was falling. It would take more than a newly retrained sales force to make Seat a leader in online advertising.

Continuing to tackle its debt, the company made €100 million of voluntary prepayments in January 2006.[37] And because of the June 2005 refinancing, its cost of debt fell to 5.9%, compared to 6.7% in the first quarter of 2005.[38] It was well needed as the management's efforts to put the business back on a stronger growth path were proving expensive. During 2006 Seat incurred one-off launch costs and investments because the Italian and French directory assistance markets were liberalised, as well as €5.4 million of reorganisation costs in the implementation of a new sales structure based on dedicated sales channels.

But the reorganisation did not translate into better results. By the end of the year, instead of showing progress, EBITDA had fallen by 2%, well below the projections of 5% growth. The business seemed in free fall despite management's reassuring words that product and sales innovations were paying dividends. Though it was emphasised that the white-pages unit had been shored up by new full-colour editions, it sounded quite gimmicky. Trying to give the situation a positive spin, management called 2006 the turning point of its three-year effort (2005-07) "to transform Seat into a multi-media directory player",[39] claiming that the turnaround of print, which accounted for three-quarters of the Italian activities and half of consolidated turnover, was well underway.[40]

Only time would tell whether management's pledge that colour printing was a "killer-app" was wishful thinking. What was undisputable was that print directories had lost 9% in turnover since 2003. In 2006 operating free cash flows had shrunk 9% on the prior year, falling below €550 million for the first time since 2003. Yet management had used some of this liquidity to reduce net debt by more than €200 million.[41] Sitting at 5.6 times EBITDA, indebtedness remained uncomfortably high, although thanks to another incomprehensibly strong year in the stock market, Seat had seen its leverage fall to less than half of the capital base. Enterprise value now sat at 11.7 times EBITDA, its highest level since the PIPE, and an abnormal multiple given that the group's gross operating profit had shed 3% in the past two years while EBITDA was flat.

No dolce vita

What explained the shareholders' optimism was the group's dominant position in Italy. Besides its quasi-monopoly in print directories, Seat ended 2006 with a 30% market share of Italy's €430 million online ad market. Perhaps more encouragingly, unlike the leading position it held in France and the UK, Google was only the fourth most visited site in Italy behind Yahoo!, MSN and Seat's three online properties *paginegialle.it*, *paginebianche.it* and *tuttocitta.it*.[42] In other words, Seat remained competitive. However, the way this situation was interpreted by management – and a large portion of the financial community – was mistaken. The group's sustainability was not due to management's successful transformation exercise. It was explained by Italy's surprisingly low internet penetration. In France, Germany and the UK (three foreign markets where Seat operated), 47%, 72% and 69% respectively of households had an internet connection at the end of 2006. In Italy, the proportion was 38%.[43] Oddly, it was thanks to Seat's former owner Telecom Italia's limited capex spend to provide faster internet broadband to the population that the directory publisher's market dominance was preserved and that pure internet rivals were relatively slow at making their mark.

Regardless, the strength of Seat, as acknowledged by most equity analysts at the time, was its cash flows, even if it typically traded at a 10% to 15% discount to its peers.[44] Management was certainly keen to prove them right. In February 2007, it prepaid €104 million of senior debt and, to boost investor confidence, the following month management announced that the dividend payout would rise by 39% year-on-year.[45] These were the signs of a bullish management team, for only a healthy company could afford to prepay debt and increase dividends while undergoing a fundamental restructuring of its business model.

On 11 May 2007, management made one of its favourite presentations, introducing a new Strategic Plan for the 2008-10 period. With the 2005-07 objectives proving wide of the mark, you would think that the top brass had learnt its lesson. Between 2003 and 2006 the group's revenue and EBITDA had grown respectively by 2% and 0.6% a year. But Chairman Giliberti and CEO Majocchi, still in place despite four years of significant underperformance against their plan, were not willing to be humble. Their projections to 2010 included a 4.5% to 5.5% annualised revenue growth rate at group level, and a 5.5% to 6.5% rise in the Italian activities thanks to double-digit growth online and high single-digit growth in the voice business. As for EBITDA, it was predicted to grow by up to 5%. With the first-quarter results of 2007 already in, management forecast that group EBITDA would swell by 10% to 12% for the whole year. These were wildly aggressive projections.[46] Reactions from equity analysts ranged from incredulity to dismay. To some, it was nothing more than a rollover of the miscarried 2005-07 plan.[47]

The reason behind such ambitious targets was made plainly clear when, ten days later, reports emerged that the four financial sponsors had appointed investment bank Lehman Brothers to explore "a wide range of potential financial and strategic options to maximise the value."[48] They wanted out, and a propitiously released bullish strategic plan for the coming three years was a sure way to arouse interest from potential buyers.

Marketwise, the timing could not have been better. First, media assets were extremely popular targets. French publisher PagesJaunes was acquired by KKR a few months earlier. Pan-European group VNU World Directories, backed by Apax and Cinven, had just completed a covenant-lite refinancing. Between 2005 and 2007, over €14 billion of LBO loans were to be issued by European yellow-pages publishers.[49] Second, Seat's home market was booming. In the first half of 2007, Italy recorded its largest LBO activity ever in value terms, closing €1.5 billion in buyout investments, more than three times the level recorded during the same period of 2006. The number of deals was also up by a quarter.[50] The buyout industry was reaching the apex of a four-year bubble. Getting out of Seat now, after years of underperformance against budget, would be ideal.

But it wouldn't be easy. With a prospective 2007 debt-to-EBITDA ratio of 5.1, the company's indebtedness was above that of European peers: Yell's leverage was at five times, PagesJaunes's at 4.2 times, Eniro's at 3.6 times.[51] Analysts rightly pointed out that the situation made these players unlikely bidders for Seat since it would further increase their leverage at a time when the credit markets were making it harder to shift LBO loans. Speculation was common regarding a possible break-up, especially because the non-Italian assets were lower-margin activities. In addition, BC, CVC, Investitori and Permira were really unlucky. As they started scouring the market, press reports revealed that two hedge funds managed by US bank Bear Stearns, and made up of bonds backed by subprime mortgages, had to be shut down, in a move that the *Wall Street Journal* declared was emblematic of the widening fallout from America's housing downturn.[52] It was late June 2007 and the Credit Crunch had officially started.

Equity analysts had run their own estimates of what the financial sponsors' IRR on Seat was likely to be. In the end, these speculations were all for nothing.

Although the four financial owners were at one point rumoured to be in advanced talks with Blackstone and the PE arm of Merrill Lynch, they failed to reach an agreement.[53] In October, after five months spent looking at exit options, Seat's PE quartet publicly acknowledged that it would not go ahead with the sale process given the prevailing conditions. The credit squeeze had tempered the market's enthusiasm for underperforming assets, even cash-generative ones.

* * *

As is all too common after a sale process has flopped, the financial sponsors officially reiterated their confidence in Seat's management and the 2008-10 business plan. Within three months, however, they would have rued their bad luck as the 2007 annual results became one more let-down. The uncertain international climate was putting advertisers in a conservative mood. Group sales fell marginally by half a percentage point, but all foreign operations recorded strong revenue drops. Because they had lost their footing the previous year, earnings had always been expected to increase. But the management's projections of a 10% growth rate in EBITDA had been misguided. Instead, earnings were up 6%. Still, it was the best performance since the group had fallen under PE control, with EBITDA margin reaching its highest point of 44.7%.[54] Using more of its operating cash to pay down debt, the company saw its net debt fall to five times EBITDA. Yet because Seat's stock had started to factor in the stubborn underperformance and lost two-fifths of its value in the second half of the year, leverage had risen to 57%. Despite the stock market dip, based on disclosures made by SVG Capital, Permira's cornerstone LP, as at 31 December 2007 Seat's PE owners were still valuing the Italian company at 1.5 times the initial investment.[55] They might have failed to sell the business during the year, but they remained buoyant.

Such optimism, though, was unfounded. On 18 March 2008 CEO Majocchi presented to investors the 2007 annual results and his 2008 guidance. He was met with disbelief. Not only was 2007 significantly below budget, but because of the credit market conditions and one-off investments required for future growth, EBITDA would be 6% lower in 2008, before predictably turning around the following year. In order to preserve cash and focus on debt repayment, the 2008 dividend was cancelled.[56] In recent months the financial community had already acknowledged the fact that Seat's enduring weak performance betrayed a deeper malaise. The business was structurally flawed.

Seeking a remedy, management tried to accelerate the group's online migration, not only by launching new products but also through external growth. The year 2007 had seen the €45 million acquisition of online business directory Klicktel to speed up the development of Telegate's online offering. Also in Germany, the group had acquired B2B supplier search website Wer Liefert Was. Although these moves fitted well with Seat's transformation strategy, crucially they could not produce the cash needed to address Seat's main threat: its indebtedness. Accordingly, in the first three months of 2008, Seat's stock pursued its brisk decline, shedding another half of its value. Only six months after shelving their exit plans, the PE owners were looking at an enterprise value a third lower than the one at which they had considered selling the business. By early April the market cap stood at €1.1 billion, compared to €2.5 billion at 2007 year end.[57] Four years after coming on board, significant value had been destroyed. It was time to introduce a management reshuffle.

In June, Massimo Cristofori became the new CFO,[58] replacing Maurizia Squinzi who had been finance director ever since the LBO loans were raised in 2004. Someone had to take the blame for the persistent underperformance, and it certainly wasn't going to be the chairman and CEO, both supposedly in charge of strategy. At least, not yet. When management presented the half-year 2008 figures, there were very few bright spots. Revenues at the core print business were down 3%. The online yellow pages had only grown 3%, which was not that surprising given that internet penetration in Italy remained perversely below 45%. International revenues had fallen off a cliff: Thomson had lost a fifth of its business and France's Europages two-fifths. Both had seen their EBITDA turn into a loss. Given the above, it was lucky that consolidated EBITDA was just 5% lower.

To obtain more flexibility under the senior facility, on 23 December the company revealed that it had reached an agreement with the Royal Bank of Scotland on the revision of the financial covenants. The company and its main lender okayed the guidelines of a freshly updated Business Plan 2009-11 and resolved to propose to the shareholders a reverse stock split of ordinary and savings shares (the latter being non-voting with perpetual dividend) and a share capital increase for a maximum amount of €200 million.[59] The fact that the company was considering raising fresh capital gave further indication that the weak operating results were starting to disrupt the financial position. Of course, it would have been easier to dispose of a non-core asset like Thomson, but in the prevailing market conditions, it was all but impossible to find a buyer. Anyway, it sounded like management was finally addressing the capital structure's inadequacies.

Fresh equity was indispensable because throughout the year the stock market had punished management's bungled digital transformation strategy. At the end of December 2008 Seat's shares stood at €0.06, an astonishing drop of three-quarters over the past 12 months. The stock was worth a tenth of the price paid by the PE consortium five years earlier. Mathematically, this had brought leverage to 86%, even if thanks to the company's peerless ability to produce cash – €545 million of operating cash had flowed in during the year – net debt had fallen by another €200 million to nearly €3 billion.[60] When reporting its own results, Permira's investor SVG Capital admitted that it had written down its equity in Seat to less than half its book value.[61] The PE backers were now looking at a paper loss.

RBS agreed to widen the headroom for the four covenants the Italian group had to abide by – the transaction had taken place before the crazy cov-lite deals of 2007, so Seat still had to respect stringent contractual obligations in relation to total-net-debt-to-EBITDA, senior-net-debt-to-EBITDA, net interest cover, and capex. In exchange, the Scottish bank received a €9 million amendment fee and a 75 basis point increase in margin. The lender had added another request that was a warning to all public shareholders who had stuck by the group despite it all: Seat would not be allowed to distribute dividends until the net-debt-to-EBITDA ratio remained above 4.[62] These new terms were the true signs of a troubled borrower. Facing so many debt-related costs and a battered share price, the company certainly needed to refill its equity coffers.

PIPE II

Following the downward trend in EBITDA generation and the uncertainty surrounding the ongoing execution of the online strategy, on 13 January 2009 rating agency Moody's decided to downgrade Seat's senior debt from speculative Ba3 to highly speculative B1. At the same time, Lighthouse's bond was also moved a notch further down the highly speculative category.[63] A rights issue was announced, but before it was to take place management wanted to do a bit of housekeeping. On 26 January 2009, a resolution was passed by a shareholders' extraordinary general meeting to regroup the company's capital. The number of ordinary shares and savings shares was to be reduced. As a footnote to the procedure, Seat decided that the par value of the shares would also be eliminated, as agreed during their talks with RBS.

It was an important decision. Par value, also known as nominal value, is the amount at which a share is issued. Legally, a company cannot redeem shares below such value. By removing it, Seat's management was admitting that it could not guarantee that there was any value left in the shares. Consequently, management was not prepared to commit the company to repaying these shares at any minimum price. A look at the stock's performance since the IPO (Figure 12.2) provides justification enough for management's prudence. In the days preceding the capital regrouping, Seat's stock traded at approximately €0.05.

Figure 12.2: Seat Pagine Gialle's share price from August 2003 (IPO) to January 2009

Note: The collapse in the share price from €0.80 to less than €0.40 in 2004 is due to the payment of a €0.43 exceptional dividend on 15 April of that year

On 9 February 2009, the regrouping came into effect at a ratio of one new share for every 200 shares outstanding.[64] On that same day the company announced that CEO Luca Majocchi was leaving,[65] finally taking responsibility for his inability to reset Seat onto a growth path. Now seemed as good a time as any to present the updated Industrial Plan for the period 2009-11, so 11 days later, as a farewell gift Majocchi revealed the preliminary 2008 results before warning the audience that 2009 would be another tough year. As usual the plan was back-end loaded, with the last two years of the forecast period promising to see a strong turnaround as payback for past R&D investments. Majocchi concluded with the optimistic line: "in 2011, Seat's solid operating performance is expected to allow the company to refinance its outstanding debt." But Seat had raised its LBO debt in 2004, so lenders were unlikely to wait until 2011 to figure out whether the company would be able to redeem its loans.

The full-year 2008 results showed why conversations with RBS and the chief exec's departure had been imperative. Group revenues and EBITDA had tumbled 5% and 6% respectively.[66] It was the worst performance since the PIPE and a sure sign – the third or fourth one – that the transformation strategy had misfired. Recognising that fact, and because of the economic context, management decided to book €130 million of goodwill impairment, €100 million of it related to Thomson and €25 million to Europages. The question was: could anyone turn the business around?

Within two months of announcing his departure, Majocchi had been replaced. New CEO Alberto Cappellini, a consumer goods expert having worked for many years at American personal care specialist Kimberly Clark, was an odd choice to lead a company experiencing significant technological upheaval in its core markets. This view was reinforced when the new boss presented the half-year results to investors on 5 August 2009. The Italian unit's revenues and EBITDA were down more than 7% year-on-year, whereas the international division's had recorded double-digit falls. Seat's obsolescence was accelerating, with the print unit's sales losing 15% in that six-month period.[67]

The important part, nonetheless, was that on 30 April the group had successfully completed its share-capital increase. The €200 million of proceeds were used to partially pay down the term A tranche in exchange for loosening the covenants. However, the rights issue was very dilutive to those public shareholders who had not taken part, granting 226 new shares for five old ones to the parties that injected fresh equity. Among the existing PE backers, only BC Partners refused to participate, taking the view that Seat was not in an ascending trend and that investing in this round would just be putting good money after bad. That left CVC, Permira and Investitori in charge of a rejuvenated board of directors (see Figure 12.3).[68] The three investors hoped that the cash injection would resuscitate their portfolio company.

Although it was good news that management convinced the market to provide further funding, because proceeds had been used to repay debt rather than invest in the poorly performing business, the move did not bode well for future growth. As the PIPE entered stage two without one of its original backers (BC had reportedly handed its holding to CVC), the group's balance sheet remained severely stretched, with leverage still above 85%. The clear benefit of the talks with RBS is that the company was no longer constrained by its covenants. In the third quarter of 2009, both its net leverage of 4.95 times and senior debt of 2.68 times EBITDA benefitted from a 21% cushion on the covenants, while headroom on the net cash interest cover was close to 25%.[69] Because of the financial crisis, Seat had not been alone in finding its leverage difficult to manage. In the second half of the year, yellow-pages publisher Truvo (f.k.a. VNU World Directories) had given its shareholders Apax and Cinven a few sleepless nights. Present in a hotchpotch of seven countries, namely Belgium, the Netherlands, Ireland, Portugal, Romania, Puerto Rico and South Africa, Truvo had undergone a very aggressive refinancing in 2007. Two years later, its leverage stood at 12 times EBITDA.[70]

Figure 12.3: Seat Pagine Gialle's group structure post-refinancing of 2009 (PIPE II)

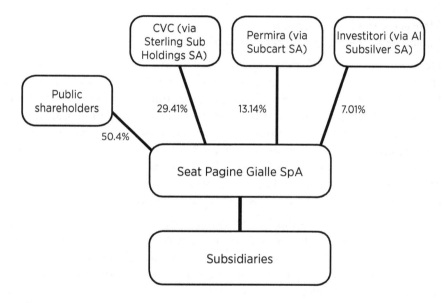

Source: Company accounts and author's analysis

The wheels had well and truly come off in 2009. Seat's revenue, gross operating profit and EBITDA were all off more than one-tenth year-on-year. Which was not surprising since the Italian economy had declined 5.5%.[71] Online trade now represented a fifth of the Italian division's revenues, but it was as much a result of the fast growth of web-based activity (up 13%) as of the equally quick attrition of print (down 8.5%). The economic recession was having a big impact, with the Italian advertising sector losing altitude fast. In 2009 the traditional local advertising segment had contracted by a quarter whereas the more promising local online advertising market had only risen by 6%.

In Italy, internet penetration was still hovering around 50%, but in the UK three-quarters of households had online access, which created tougher competition from pure online advertising platforms. Cost reduction remained a priority at troubled Thomson Directories, where the number of employees had fallen by 28% in two years. Thomson's 2009 revenues and EBITDA were down a third and two-fifths on the prior year. Accordingly, another €80 million of that division's goodwill had been written off, and €3 million of exceptional costs had been incurred to restructure the business. To promote customer retention across the group, management introduced web consultants to support the sales force, and multimedia print-online-voice packages to encourage cross-selling. Product innovation was also helping users track leads. A new Head of Transformation Management was to be hired in 2010 to run the new "multimedia organisation". Maybe he or she could help tune down the jargon.

Despite management's frantic prepayment of loans to try to keep lenders at bay (€300 million was repaid during the year),[72] net debt edged up to 5.24 times EBITDA. With the share price yielding another third of its value during 2009, leverage ended the year not far from 90% of the capital structure. Seat was in a parlous state. Permira's lead investor SVG wrote down its investment further, from 45 cents on the euro at the end of 2008 to less than 25 cents a year later.[73] With an outstanding balance of €950 million, the tranche A of Seat's senior loan was due to be fully repaid by June 2012. Given recent trading and profitability, the group would never be in a position to meet that commitment.

By the same token, it would be impossible for the company to find a buyer willing to pay a price that would cover the two term loans (including €465 million for tranche B due June 2013), the €1.3 billion Lighthouse bond, and the €250 million of asset-backed securities. Management therefore sought approval from its creditors to refinance. In early January 2010, 95% of lenders consented to the issuance of a new secured bond ranging from €500 million to €1 billion. The proceeds were to be used to redeem part of the term A (for the first €650 million raised) and part of the B tranche (if more was raised). It would have been easier for RBS to reschedule its own loans in exchange for a consent fee and higher margins, but the bank had been bailed out by the British Government the year before – it was desperate to reduce exposure to LBO loans, hence its decision to cut and run. The search for new lenders was on. Later that month, Seat announced that it had attracted demand for €550 million of 10.5% senior secured notes due 2017. It had not reached its €650 million target due to weak demand. The net proceeds were used to clear term A's 2010 and 2011 tranches.[74] It still left intact the small matter of the 2012 maturity wall. For now it would have to be ignored, but with troubled RBS as key lender Seat was not going to get much support. The British taxpayers wouldn't have rated the survival of Italy's main directories group a top priority.

* * *

On the strategy front, Seat was still working on its digital transformation. In its results presentation for the first half of 2010, management proudly remarked that online already represented one-third of revenues in Italy, but the jump in internet activity was overshadowed by the fall in print sales, which were down another quarter year-on-year.[75] International operations declined further, with Thomson's revenues down 17%, Telegate's down 13% and Europages's off a third. The combined international EBITDA had almost halved. At that rate, the group could soon hit the wall. And so management launched a €40 million cost-saving programme and also elected to reduce capex – not a great move for a group desperate to rebuild its top line, but a necessity if Seat wanted to service its debt.

In that respect, throughout 2010 management showed that it was keen to tackle its bloated capital structure. In July it repaid €50 million of its asset-backed securities due January 2014 by using cash. Then, in October it raised another €200 million of 10.5% secured bonds, bringing the total under this facility to €750 million (remember that it had consent from its lenders to raise up to €1 billion of longer-dated loans).[76] Despite such efforts, on 29 November 2010, to reflect the structural decline in the print-directory segment, the high leverage, and the refinancing risk of loans due from 2012 onwards, Moody's downgraded Seat and the Lighthouse bond further.[77] The credit agency was not rating Seat's chances of survival highly. And the market seemed to agree – the unsecured Lighthouse bonds were quoted at 38 cents on the euro by December.[78]

The full-year results would not alleviate matters. When the 2010 annual results emerged, they confirmed that the recapitalisation exercise had temporarily addressed the precariousness of the group's financial position, but the persistently weak operating results underscored the fact that Seat's problems were more fundamental: its business model was no longer adapted to market demand. Consolidated revenues had plummeted by more than 8%, and so had EBITDA; they now respectively sat one-quarter and one-fifth below their 2003 levels. Print sales had again suffered a double-digit dip, proof that the lower online penetration in Italy did not protect Seat's mainstream activities. Cost reduction remained a priority. The group was three-quarters of the way into its cost-cutting target of €40 million. Group-wide, 1,200 employees, including project workers and trainees, had been let go that year. Management had little choice but to write off goodwill by an additional €680 million. Via this impairment, one-fifth of Seat's Italian core business was expunged.

With operating cash flows just above €410 million and interest payments nearing €200 million, the group had only been able to repay €100 million of its loans, keeping net debt in line with the prior year.[79] Due to lower earnings, the debt-to-EBITDA ratio had gone up noticeably to 5.65. And because the stock had nose-dived, finishing the year at almost half the value it traded at in December 2009, leverage topped 94% by the end of 2010. Eighteen months after re-injecting equity into the business, the trio of CVC, Permira and Investitori was looking at a 90% write-down. Given its deflated stock, Seat traded at an EV-to-EBITDA of six times – less than the total leverage ratio it was on at the outset of its buyout six years earlier.

An offer no one could refuse

In early 2011 the company revealed that its chairman and its CEO had been mandated by the board to identify potential alternatives to heal the capital structure. Seat was once again planning to enter a refinancing process. After a brief respite the group had resumed its gliding descent into the markets' hell of penny stocks, its price settling below 10 cents per share with unshakable determination. The last few months had seen the sector pummelled after disastrous outcomes for several participants: Apax and Cinven's Truvo had put its US operations under Chapter 11 bankruptcy protection in June 2010, and Macquarie's European Directories had spent most of 2010 in negotiations to restructure €2.1 billion of LBO loans.[80]

Seat wasn't in a better situation. Its recently introduced multimedia package seemed to be accelerating the decline in print revenue. Although this was meant to be compensated by an increase in annual revenue per advertiser (ARPA), the latter actually dropped from €1800 in the third quarter of 2010 to €1100 in the second quarter of 2011.[81] The advertising downturn provoked by the Great Recession affected both print and online media. Consolidated revenues for the first half of 2011 saw further deterioration in all divisions. Group EBITDA shed 8% in the same period. Seat had reached the stage its management and PE backers had dreaded. The trading deterioration over the past four years had turned the business into a zombie. It was time to negotiate an orderly handover – one that would see the financial sponsors relinquish ownership of the distressed asset in exchange for meaningful deleveraging.

In March 2011, the Italian group appointed restructuring advisers Rothschild to consider various options in order to stabilise its long-term financial structure. After formalising a technical waiver with its senior lender RBS, in August management began negotiations with the Lighthouse unsecured noteholders via the proposal of a debt-for-equity swap.[82] However, the move needed the consent of all the parties that had a stake in the business. In all likelihood conversations would be long-winded. Creditors were spread across numerous legal jurisdictions including Italy, Luxembourg, the UK and the US. By October the Lighthouse notes were quoted at 16 cents on the euro and were rated one grade above default by both Moody's and Standard & Poor's.[83] To call them 'junk' would have been disrespectful to junk bonds.

Talks were ongoing, but to step up the pressure Seat missed the €52 million coupon payment of the unsecured notes due on 31 October. After failing to pay up within the 30-day grace period, the group saw Moody's downgrade it to the agency's second lowest classification, and the Lighthouse bonds to the bottom category.[84] The implications of this default could, in principle, be far reaching. RBS and the secured bondholders could gain control of Seat, with Lighthouse left with nothing. Alternatively, the Lighthouse bondholders could convert their debt into equity if RBS and the other secured lenders agreed to amend and extend their facilities. No matter, the coming weeks would determine Seat's future.

When the first restructuring deadline at the end of October failed to deliver an agreement, the timetable was amended to end on 30 November 2011. Because RBS had little incentive to agree to Lighthouse's debt/equity swap, since under management's proposal it would bestow €100 million of longer-dated Lighthouse notes secured status and thereby dilute RBS's collateral, the 30 November deadline came and went. Under the proposal, secured bondholders would see their collateral diluted, making the talks even more protracted. On paper, it was clear that RBS had the stronger hand: one-third of its debt was coming up for repayment in 2012 and the rest was due by 2013.[85] The event of default on the Lighthouse bonds would practically grant the British bank the right to gain equity control. But the bank was not in the business of owning companies – in truth, it was not in the business of doing much these days, other than trying to delever its own balance sheet crippled with bad loans, not just related to LBOs but also to residential mortgages; the result of poor risk management in the years leading to the Credit Crunch.

Third-quarter results did not strengthen management's position, with EBITDA down 27% on the year-ago quarter, bringing the net leverage ratio to the brink of the 6.35-times EBITDA covenant.[86] The task was not made easier by the fact that consent was required from parties with conflicting agendas. The PE shareholders were trying to retain some form of ownership, even if tiny, while RBS and the secured lenders were reluctant to give up on their asset-backed guarantees.

As for the investors in the Lighthouse consortium, they were in an awkward position: the default on the October interest gave them the right to appoint an administrator, but doing so would instantly give ownership of the company to the first-priority lender RBS and the secured bondholders, with little left for Lighthouse investors despite a complete write-off of their bonds. They were being asked to agree to a lock-up period, whereby they could not sell the equity granted in exchange for writing off their loans. Three-quarters of unsecured Lighthouse noteholders had to consent before Seat would agree to make the €52 million late payment.

Finally, the proposed financial restructuring had to be ratified by a majority of each category of stakeholders: the shareholders, RBS, and the secured bondholders. As usual in multi-party talks, it was hectic. After missing the 30 November deadline, the discussions were supposed to end by 14 December.[87] The parties did not reach an accord by mid-December, so the deadline was deferred again, this time to 16 January of the following year. All parties felt that they had a card to play, even the PE shareholders who probably should have realised by now that the game was up. Sure enough, the 16 January 2012 deadline – the fourth of a very tense round of negotiations – was also missed.[88]

* * *

The New Year saw the introduction of the latest Strategic Plan to the investment community, although management decided not to apply this overused term, preferring to speak of "strategic guidelines" with projections to 2013 and further out to 2015. By now a variety of factors indicated that Italian GDP would contract in 2012. Preliminary data on 2011 showed that the advertising market had fallen by 3% that year. This was not the sort of macro context Seat needed to turn its fortunes around. And it explains why financial projections were a lot more grounded than in the past, with management now simply aiming to stabilise EBITDA around the €340 million mark by 2013 before edging back up to €380 million two years later (once more it was back-end loaded). These were humbling figures when considering that annual earnings had exceeded €600 million during the 2003-08 period.

In terms of strategy, the goal was to make Seat Italy's leading "local internet company", just like the group had, for many decades, held the leadership position in the print classifieds world. However, to operate a monopoly in yellow pages is one thing, to lead the online classified ad world is quite another. On the web, Seat was just another player in a fast-changing market. New products were regularly being introduced by nimble, pure online advertising platforms. Seat was not considered an internet pioneer. Which is why the strategic plan unveiled by Chief Exec Cappellini put so much emphasis on innovation. The word came up 17 times in the 20-page document. In its eagerness to appear avant-garde, management was overdoing it, even speaking of the need "to continue to innovate in product innovation". Yet there was no mistaking the group's true intentions: it wanted to remain a strong Italian advertising service provider, even if this focus on the home market meant that the international activities were henceforth considered non-core.[89] The group would have been willing to dispose of them had any buyer presented itself. Until then, Seat had to sort out its capital structure.

To increase the pressure on the uncooperative lenders, Seat's management decided not to proceed with the coupon payment on its senior secured bonds due on 31 January 2012. The company's executives were getting pretty good at brinkmanship. In response, within a week of the non-payment Standard & Poor's dropped its long-term corporate rating of Seat to its lowest possible grade. The agency aligned the group's senior secured bonds to the same rating,[90] making them the junkiest of junk bonds. It was not much of a surprise. The interest payments and debt amortisation requirements on Seat's secured bank debt and subordinated notes, due in late 2011, had already been delayed. In effect, Seat had admitted that it could no longer meet its debt obligations, whether related to term loans, secured bonds or unsecured ones. The company's liquidity profile had weakened in line with its earnings. The rating agency was adopting the view held by public markets, which had punished the group by hammering its stock down two-thirds in 2011 – it was only marginally worse than what European peers Yell (-63.5%) and PagesJaunes (-58.8%) had witnessed.[91]

Negotiations between a corporate zombie's stakeholders have much in common with wars of attrition. After more than six months of proposals and counterproposals, on 7 March 2012 the PE owners got their comeuppance. All parties came to the following agreement: Lighthouse was to write off its unsecured bonds, except for €65 million to be converted into a secured instrument. Lighthouse and Seat were to merge, retaining the name Seat Pagine Gialle post-merger. Although Seat was incorporating the bondholders' consortium, from an accounting perspective it was a reverse takeover: the Lighthouse investors would receive most of Seat's equity. Tranches A and B of RBS's loans were to be consolidated and extended by three years in exchange for a higher margin and a covenant reset.

In spite of the restructuring, on Seat's balance sheet €600 million of RBS senior loans (half of them due 2016) and over €800 million of senior secured bonds due 2017 were still looming large.[92] So it looked like another refinancing would be necessary in the not so distant future. That is unless Seat's management was able to resurrect the group, which in view of the full-year 2011 performance was unlikely – the operational and financial deterioration of the previous four years had gone on with vigour, pushing group revenues and EBITDA down 7.5% and 11% respectively. EBITDA margin had toppled below 40% for the first time since the August 2003 buyout. Net debt had risen on the prior year, also a first since the financial sponsors took position at the helm. The double blow jacked up the net leverage ratio to 7.4 times EBITDA.

Understandably, due to the persistent earnings and liquidity erosion, Seat had written down its asset book value further. Almost €700 million of goodwill impairment was crystallised in December 2011, with Seat's Italian activities losing another quarter of their value, Telegate shedding one-fifth, and Thomson apparently worth 40% of its 2010 value.[93] Because of the high indebtedness, at the end of 2011 Seat's enterprise value was an abnormally high 7.5 times EBITDA. Compared to Yell's five times-plus ratio, it certainly looked toppy. But that was based on the book value of the loans. Since all of the Italian group's debt tranches traded at significant discounts – as at 30 March 2012, Lighthouse bonds were worth 10 cents on the euro, secured bonds 68 cents on the euro, and the RBS term loans 73 cents on the euro – the marked-to-market EV was a more realistic 3.1 times EBITDA. Yell's marked-to-market multiple was 1.8, so at least the outside world had pared down its expectations on the sector.[94]

But if such distressed ratios were depressing, another piece of news reminded everyone of the human cost of corporate crises. In late March, two weeks after saving the company from an all-too-certain collapse by concluding the financial restructuring, CEO Cappellini, aged 52, unexpectedly suffered a heart attack.[95] The company lost its leader but had earned another chance at successfully transforming itself into a digital publisher and advertiser.

As at 30 April 2012, with the capital restructuring yet to be finalised, both Moody's and Standard & Poor's respectively gave Seat's corporate credit their second lowest and lowest grades. The reason behind such cataclysmic ratings can be found in Seat's 2011 financial accounts. As at 31 December 2011, over €1.83 billion of financial debts were due within 12 months. In summary, to use the relevant accounting term, the Italian group was not a going concern. However, because the company was in active discussions with its lenders and putting the finishing touches to their agreement, the board of directors considered that "the current restructuring transaction is likely to be completed in a reasonable timeframe such as to allow for the long-term financial stabilisation."[96] It would take a few more weeks for the group's rescue to get sorted.

Seat was about to join a long list of Italian companies that had fallen into the hands of their creditors in recent years. In April 2009 Candover-controlled yacht maker Ferretti had seen banks Mediobanca and RBS (small world!) replace the financial sponsor after the secondary buyout proved unable to service its €1.1 billion debt.[97] Global Garden Products, a lawn-mower manufacturer headquartered near Venice, and also an SBO, had been seized by lenders from its British owner 3i in March 2010. Leverage had reached 18.5 times EBITDA after the business had under-delivered.[98]

Divorce Italian style

In early September, the junior lenders took over the business in what was characterised by management as "one of the most important and complex debt restructuring transactions ever carried out in Italy."[99] Following the merger with Lighthouse, effective on 31 August 2012, Seat PG had seen the number of ordinary shares jump from 1,927 billion to 16,066 billion,[100] the second major dilution for existing public shareholders after the rights issue of April 2009. It had the effect of Zimbabwe's hyper-inflation, shrinking the public's share of Seat's economic value (assuming there was any of it left) by a factor of eight without offering any compensation. Post-merger, the Lighthouse investors became the majority shareholders, accounting for 88% of the group's equity. These investors, including hedge fund managers Anchorage, Owl Creek, Sothic and Monarch, were in the unenviable position of owning shares in a business that had limited prospect of survival.

Figure 12.4: Seat Pagine Gialle's group structure in October 2012 (PIPE III)

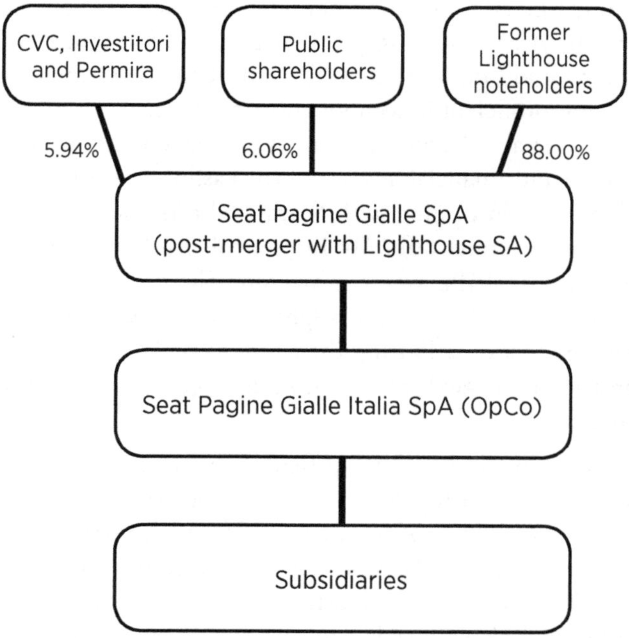

Source: Company accounts and author's analysis

Figure 12.4 shows that, alongside the former Lighthouse bondholders, the PE trio retained a small stake, and so did public shareholders. If the Lighthouse bonds were worth 10% of face value ahead of the merger (nearing €130 million), Seat's ordinary shares held less value – market capitalisation totalled €77 million as at 31 December 2012 – and as little upside. Still, the debt straightjacket had been loosened for now.

A new OpCo (emanating from the hive-down of Seat's assets to Seat Pagine Gialle Italia S.p.A. in order to provide security to senior lenders) called for a new executive team and a new board. By now Seat's directors, shareholders and lenders should have gotten the hint that the group's inability to meet budget in the previous eight years had something to do with the migration of advertisers to the internet, and that bringing in skills in web-based advertising was somewhat urgent. If so, they did not show it by appointing as new CEO Vincenzo Santelia, a former executive at Anglo-Dutch consumer goods conglomerate Unilever, and more recently director at consulting firm Bain & Company.

Joining the board on 26 October as the third chief executive since the buyout,[101] Santelia had strong expertise in the media sector, but he had no prior experience in running online advertisers or in transforming a traditional publisher into a tech-enabled marketer. Similarly, a new chairman was brought in to replace Enrico Giliberti. After nine long years of underperformance Giliberti was making way for Guido de Vivo, an old hand of the investment world who, though he was not proficient in technology or media, had extensive knowledge of the financial sector after having acted as CEO of investment firm Mittel, bank Credito Milanese and financial advisory firm Pasfin. At least his background would be relevant when dealing with Seat's creditors and financial investors. Anyway, lenders were now officially in control. And they must have been praying that this third PIPE would work out. The performance of PIPE II, spanning the period April 2009 (post-rights issue) to October 2012, had been as mediocre as the first one. During their second period of ownership, CVC, Investitori and Permira saw Seat's stock shed more than 95% of its value, as Figure 12.5 illustrates.

A change in ownership and leadership frequently gives the opportunity to be bluntly honest about a business's prospects. In the 2012 annual report, Seat's new management was keen to distance itself from the previous PE owners, explaining that the latter had "performed a leveraged buyout of the company in 2003, which has had a deep and lasting effect on the company's fate." The Italian economy had experienced a double-dip recession, shrinking 2.3% in 2012,[102] but the year-long financial restructuring process had also been a huge distraction for Seat's executive team and can certainly explain why consolidated revenues and EBITDA had fallen by one-sixth and one-fifth respectively. Both performance indicators had registered their worst annual change ever. All parts of the group were in agony: revenues from the Italian print activities were off by one-third, online advertising was down by 7% and voice advertising by one-quarter. Internationally, revenues had decreased by 6% at Thomson, 16% at Telegate and 8% at Europages. There wasn't any division redeeming the others. At €318 million, operating free cash flow was half its 2004 level. The year 2012 experienced further deterioration of the subscriber churn rate. Averaging 17% in 2006-07, churn had risen to about 20% in 2009-11 before reaching 24% in 2012. Customers were heading for the door in their droves.[103]

Figure 12.5: Seat Pagine Gialle's stock performance during PIPE II

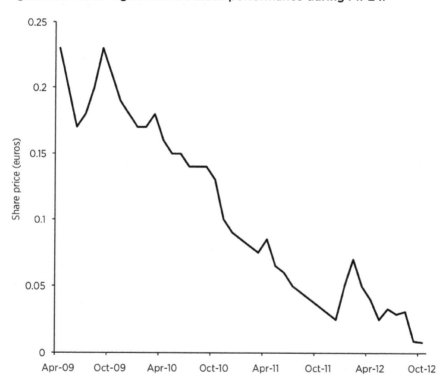

Unremarkably, the new chairman and his freshly appointed CEO chose to recognise further asset impairment. This time, €1.84 billion of goodwill and other intangible assets were erased from the company's books, including half a billion euros of marketing databases, patents and licences. About €1.1 billion were related to Seat's Italian activities. The latter's asset value had gone from

€3.2 billion in December 2009 to €723 million three years later.[104] The real concern was that operating performance kept getting worse even though PIPE III remained severely leveraged. Although 95% of Lighthouse bonds had been written off, the RBS term loans and the secured bonds remained intact. At the end of 2012, €1.53 billion of debt remained on the books. With EBITDA at its all-time low, leverage was already creeping up, getting to 4.5 times earnings on 31 December. The tanking share price meant that debt represented 94.5% of total capital at that date.

Naturally, when reporting the group's abysmal stock performance, management was keen to point out that many of its rivals had experienced an equally tough time, citing as example Hibu (f.k.a. Yell), which had seen its share price plunge 90.5% that year.[105] The school of thought that there is safety in numbers was followed only too well. But it no longer passed muster with the dissatisfied minority shareholders who, in January 2013, filed a motion for the judicial attachment and seizure of Seat's corporate assets. At long last, minorities were fighting back.

On 28 January, less than five months after completing its drawn-out debt restructuring and appointing a new board, Seat announced that it would not pay €42 million of semi-annual interest due on the senior secured notes the following day as it assessed whether its newly concocted business plan was viable with the Italian economy doing worse than expected.[106] The price of the bonds slumped by a third. Without hesitation Moody's downgraded the Italian group's €750 million senior secured bonds due 2017 and €65 million senior secured stub bonds due 2017 two notches to the third worst grade on the agency's rating scale. With a grace period of 30 days, the Italian group was not yet officially in default, but Seat's management had already admitted that the group was not in a position to cover the €200 million of principal and interest payments falling due in 2013.[107] A week later, Moody's downgraded the group to its second lowest possible rating. The same day, Seat applied for admission to the 'composition with creditors' procedure with the Turin Court, aiming to submit a proposal to lenders.[108] The Italian group was back on the ropes, its stock firmly below €0.002 (yes, the decimal point is in the right place), down 40% on the news.[109]

While the newish management team was working on a newish restructuring plan, having been granted 120 days by the court for doing so, in March 2013 the senior secured bonds were trading at 22 cents on the euro – a scenario eerily similar to the one faced by the subordinated Lighthouse bonds the previous year. Management's ambition was to halve the debt once more, bringing it down to €750 million, an amount that it hoped to be able to service despite the very challenging environment. According to market research experts Nielsen, advertising spend in Italy had tumbled 21% year-on-year during the fourth quarter of 2012.[110] When releasing the 2012 annual report, management humbly stated:

> "The last 18 months [...] may be considered the most troubled period in the long history of Seat Pagine Gialle."[111]

But more trouble was brewing. On 3 July 2013 the Italian group released a statement from independent auditors PricewaterhouseCoopers in which the latter explained that, because of the ongoing 'composition with creditors' procedure and the fact that Seat had incurred a €1 billion loss in 2012, the audit firm could not express an opinion on the consolidated 2012 financial statements.[112] This was a major blow, but with a share price already in the doldrums the statement's impact was somewhat limited. Further problems soon accumulated. On 19 August Seat announced that its British operations had been put in administration. Under the supervision of administrators Grant Thornton, a new owner had to be found for Thomson Directories,[113] which after years of poor results had lost its number two market position to BT's Phone Book. Not only had Thomson suffered from the online migration of classified advertising, but it had been notified that it faced a £48 million pension fund liability. It was time to hive off this toxic business unit.[114]

* * *

Endless negotiations with financial backers, whether PE owners or lenders, tend to wear down the finance team of many a portfolio company. Seat's was no exception. On 29 October 2013, CFO Massimo Cristofori left the distressed publisher and was replaced by Andrea Servo,[115] who became Seat Pagine Gialle's fourth finance director in ten years. Servo had been with the Italian group since 2000, first as tax manager, then as group chief accounting and tax officer.[116] As he was celebrating the completion of his 13th year at the company, this very courageous man was taking on a big challenge: sorting out Seat's capital structure once and for all. To cap another dreadful year, on 2 December Moody's downgraded Seat to its lowest possible rating, to reflect the view that the financial restructuring would result in creditor losses exceeding 70%. The agency also acknowledged that Seat was in default on all its long-term debt obligations. Then the rating specialist announced that it would not issue further notes on the company.[117] Just like equity analysts had stopped reporting on Seat months earlier, Moody's was no longer interested in covering this corporate zombie. Later that month, the bankruptcy section of the Court of Turin admitted the 'composition with creditors' procedure, allowing business continuity while negotiations went ahead. The court proceedings were supposed to last most of 2014, with one ultimate goal: to hand over ownership to the lenders.

The incoming chairman and the CEO blamed the 2012 results on the time spent by their predecessors negotiating with creditors. With another round of talks under court supervision, the group was unlikely to report first-rate results for 2013. Yet no one could have expected the results delivered that year. The ground had caved in at the print division: in 2013, the ARPA had sunk to €429 from €648 two years earlier. What must have made investors and lenders wonder whether Seat had any chance of survival was the fact that the online activities had also experienced steady deterioration since 2011, with ARPA down 10% and the number of unique customers 18% lower.[118] Advertisers were moving away from yellow pages, whether online or in print, preferring to market their wares across other platforms. Over the years the successive management teams had not remained idle. They scaled down the group wherever possible, curtailing in particular the use of external consultants. The reduction in printed publications led to lower costs of materials driven by a fall in paper consumption. Next came further layoffs, bringing the total headcount from 6,000 in 2009 to 4,000 in December 2012, then to half that a year later.[119] However, the deterioration of trading had outpaced all efficiency-improvement programmes.

The new sales organisation, including assigning the sales force between media consultants, web masters and back-office staff, had not borne fruit. Full-year group revenues had fallen by a quarter, but because of the significant proportion of fixed costs, EBITDA had crashed 60% to less than €230 million. EBITDA margin had broken another record: at 17.8%, it was less than half that of 2012. It was also much lower than the 43% forecast presented in January 2012 by the late CEO Cappellini.[120] As a reminder, these were the results of a company handling €1.5 billion of covenanted LBO loans. All Italian activities, including the previously vaunted online division, continued to record a strong decline. The blame for this disastrous set of results was put squarely on the national advertising market, which had apparently lost 12% year-on-year. Seat's performance certainly had not received any support from the macroeconomic environment: Italian GDP flagged further, down 1.9% on the prior year. The last bit of goodwill was written off. No more goodwill remained in the accounts, compared to a book value of €3.7 billion back in 2007.[121]

Understandably, the shareholders had run for the exit, dumping the stock to a rock-bottom €0.0017, giving the company a market cap of €30 million at the end of 2013. Despite the mid-2012 write-off of Lighthouse bonds, the Italian publisher remained ridiculously overleveraged, with debt accounting for more than 90% of the capital base, as Figure 12.6 indicates. Net debt stood at 16.3 times EBITDA by year end. There now was no question that the remaining bank debt commitments could not be met. The conclusion was self-evident: Seat needed to restructure.

Figure 12.6: Seat Pagine Gialle's leverage (2003-13)

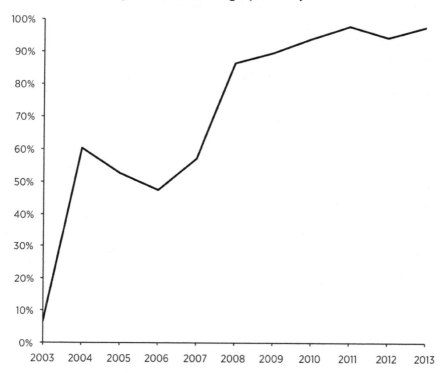

Source: Company accounts and author's analysis

Cost-cutting initiatives continued throughout 2014 while the capital restructuring exercise was ongoing. A reduction of the number of senior managers had started in 2013 and the goal was to achieve a 40% cull across the group. In February 2014, management signed an agreement with the trade unions whereby the number of working days for the year would be 10% below 2013. A voluntary reduction in salaries, ranging from 5% to 25%, was also asked of management for a period of one year. The number of top level executives was reduced from 11 to four.[122]

Strictly business

In its attempt to save something from the wreckage, Seat's management prepared a resentful move rarely seen in the world of leveraged buyouts. One that could well inspire executive teams and stockholders of other PE-backed businesses. On 4 March 2014 the company held an ordinary shareholders' meeting that few at BC Partners, CVC, Investitori and Permira will ever forget. That day Seat Pagine Gialle's board submitted a motion proposing to commence a legal action for liability against the company's directors who held office from 8 August 2003 to 21 October 2012,[123] the period during which the financial sponsors controlled the board. The recommendation put the responsibility of Seat's financial distress squarely on the shoulders of the previous directors, including former chairman Enrico Giliberti and CEO Luca Majocchi. The motion was approved by a majority of shareholders. Things were getting personal.

On 1 April 2014 management presented to investors its brand-new business plan, the fifth in the past ten years. For 2014-18 the senior team predicted that trading would bottom out in 2016 after a low point of €409 million in group revenue and about €15 million in EBITDA for 2015. Yes, €15 million, compared to the €600 million-plus recorded a decade earlier. Because their predecessors had been such poor forecasters, the current executives would certainly have found it difficult to convince their audience. On 24 February, Standard & Poor's had even followed the example of Moody's by withdrawing its ratings.[124] The credit agency would never report on Seat again.

The company was on its last legs. Circling the carcass was Dmail Group, a small listed eCommerce and publishing company that had seen its share price divided by three on the Borsa Italiana in as many years. Nevertheless, in May its management made a cheeky offer to the board of Seat, proposing to pay €46 million in cash to unsecured creditors and do a share swap with the directory publisher. A month earlier, Dmail had decided to go ahead with a €15 million capital increase as part of its own debt restructuring plan. It was quite an embarrassment for a company once as prestigious as Seat to be publicly linked to a loss-making, €50-million-revenue business with a market cap of €8 million.[125] This is how low LBOs can fall when they cannot service their debt. Despite Dmail's offer being revised upward to €60 million in early June,[126] Seat's directors refused to contemplate a merger with the bidder.[127] The numbers did not make sense.

In 2014 Italian GDP had recorded its first increase in three years, admittedly with a very modest 0.2% movement, but the national advertising market was still down 2.5% year-on-year.[128] Following two years of operational reorganisation, unit disposals, cost cuts and lay-offs, by the end of 2014 Seat's staff numbers had dwindled a further 5%: seven out of ten employees had left since 2006.[129] The important thing, though, was that, after a 25-month process, on 17 December 2014 Seat Pagine Gialle finally announced that the restructuring would take place and would include a share capital reduction. It was to be followed by the issue of 6.41 trillion new shares (yes, trillion!) for a total of €20 million – that is a nanovalue of €0.000031 per share – and by a reverse stock split (the second since the regrouping of early 2009) to bring the number of shares to a more manageable (it's all relative) 64.27 billion.[130]

Stepping away from the mindboggling figures, the conclusion of the new capital reorganisation was that the secured creditors ended up with 99.75% of the business, with two of them, Avenue Capital and GoldenTree, holding more than half of Seat's stock, while holders of the RBS senior loans seized 44.75%. Ten years after having raised €4 billion in loans to finance its LBO, Seat Pagine Gialle was, at long last, debt-free. As for the public shareholders who had made the mistake of sticking around, after two massively dilutive restructurings they were practically stock-free. With shares trading at €0.0022 each, the group had a market cap slightly above €185 million at year end. Because of a positive cash balance of more than €70 million in the accounts, the group's EV was actually €115 million, or 3.5 times EBITDA,[131] compared to the €5.65 billion and ten times EBITDA granted by BC, CVC, Investitori and Permira 11 years earlier.

Not only was the group relieved of its bank loans, but it was also drawing a line under the whole LBO episode. It is in that same month of December 2014 that Chairman de Vivo and CEO Santelia called for an ordinary shareholders' meeting to be held the following month to approve a proposed settlement received from the former directors against whom legal action had been brought. On 26 November these former board members in office during the period of PE ownership had submitted an offer to amicably settle all disputes pertaining to the acts contested, for a total of €30 million. According to press reports, the company had made claims for damages of €1.5 billion to €2.4 billion. While the proposal by the former directors was a pittance compared to the amount of value destroyed or the damages sought, it gave Seat a chance to leave the LBO adventure behind once and for all.[132]

Back to square one

On 2 January 2015, the group issued a press release stating that de Vivo had resigned "due to differences in opinion on the management of the transitional phase."[133] The departing chairman's view was that, with the completion of the debt write-off and the successful legal action brought against the previous board members, his job at Seat was done and the incoming shareholders should appoint a new board.[134] While he had a point, it looked like the new owners were not planning to hang around for too long anyway, so they nominated CEO Santelia to take on the group's chairmanship.

Later that month, no doubt grudgingly, the group's shareholders approved the €30 million settlement submitted by the company's former board members.

Two-thirds of that amount had been paid by insurance companies as part of a directors' and officers' liability cover, and despite the fact that former Chief Exec Luca Majocchi had reportedly left the company in 2009 with a severance package of €10 million.[135] The agreement ended the possibility of future retaliation from Seat Pagine Gialle, its new managers and shareholders, but it was time to move on.

To that effect, on 12 March 2015 Seat's management made the familiar presentation to the investor community, releasing the full-year 2014 results and reporting for the first time since successfully and fully ridding the group of its LBO debt. On the front page of the presentation document, management had typed the words: "MISSION ACCOMPLISHED". Embossed with red ink, the proclamation relayed the executive team's deep relief and proud sense of achievement. However, it could not hide the disastrous results of the past year. In 2014 Seat had suffered a decline in revenues of 19%, pushing EBITDA down by two-thirds despite the significant cost savings introduced earlier in the year. Margin had now fallen to 8%, five times lower than during the mid-noughties, as illustrated in Figure 12.7. Although management had stopped providing a breakdown of earnings between the print division and the online activities, it is likely that the paper directories had recorded their first operating loss, in another sign that traditional yellow pages belonged to the past.

On 21 May 2015, Avenue and GoldenTree agreed to sell their combined 54.34% in Seat to internet company Italiaonline. Managing web portals and controlled by Egyptian businessman Naguib Sawiris, Italiaonline aimed to create a group active in digital advertising and internet services for SMEs. Celebrating its 90th birthday, Seat was losing its independence, courtesy of 11 years under the ownership of financiers who had bitten off more than they could chew. The proposed combination was compelling, bringing together the directory publisher's 6.7 million monthly unique users and 15 million users at Italiaonline. Although the latter had only generated sales of €95 million in 2014, its EBITDA of €34 million exceeded Seat's.[136]

Figure 12.7: Seat PG's revenues, gross operating margins and EBITDA margins (2003-14)

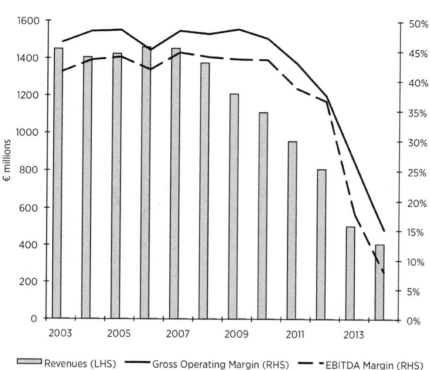

Source: Company accounts and author's analysis

At any rate, Italiaonline's deal proposal made a lot more sense than the one submitted by Dmail the year before. In the month of June 2015 the latter filed for its own admission to the procedure of 'composition with creditors'. It later transpired that, for the full-year 2014, the eCommerce specialist had recorded a 10% fall in revenue and its net loss had widened to €14 million. How the management of such a weak business – Dmail had recorded a loss for each of the previous six financial years – could have contemplated taking over an equally troubled group like Seat is incomprehensible.[137] What is undeniable, though, is that PIPE III had been as much a disaster as the first two editions, as Figure 12.8 demonstrates.

Figure 12.8: Seat Pagine Gialle's market capitalisation and share price (January 2013 to July 2015)

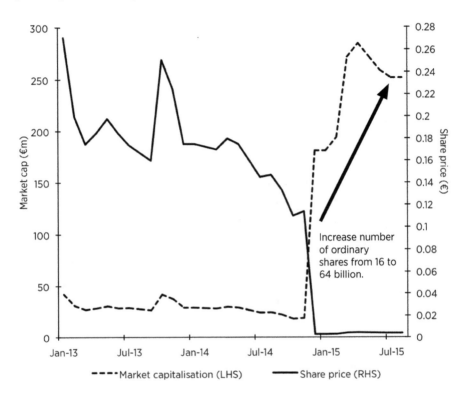

Source: Company filings

Putting an end to PIPE III, on 24 September the board of directors approved the not-so-generous €0.0039 cum-dividend mandatory public tender offer submitted by Italiaonline.[138] And two weeks later Italiaonline's CEO Antonio Converti became the official Managing Director of Seat Pagine Gialle.[139] The latter was seeing its fourth chief executive in 12 years, but its digital transition was almost complete. In 2000, it had merged with Telecom Italia's internet unit Tin.it. Fifteen years later the group was back where the hype had started, in the online arena, ready to ditch the past and face the future.

Lost in translation

Seat Pagine Gialle went from being Italy's third largest media company by advertising revenue in 2006 to not making it into the top five by the time it had fallen under the control of Italiaonline.[140] In October 2015, business-directory website *piaginegialle.it* was only the 67th most visited in Italy, whereas it ranked 30th in December 2004. White-pages site *paginebianche.it* was 102nd (compared to 12th at the end of 2004), while the more recent *tuttocitta.it* was 449th.[141]

Above everything else, Seat's story is one of poor strategy execution. From the outset, senior executives presented one Industrial Plan or Strategic Plan after another, and a Restructuring Plan for 2004-05 was followed by others in 2009 and 2010. Management speech was embarrassingly nebulous and consultant-like, referring to "deep, meaningful, relevant and rich proprietary content", "hyper local positioning" or "product innovation roadmap". For too long the group's leadership remained delusional about the real prospects of traditional yellow pages.

The Italian publisher owned strong assets, key among them its brand and the consumer and advertiser database. Yet management did not acknowledge early enough the need to aggressively migrate these assets to the web. In its 2008-10 plan, management confidently asserted: "Seat's print business will continue to be solid as risk of cannibalization by [the] internet is low given cultural divide and an already high penetration." It is easy for us to judge in retrospect. However, given that revenues coming from the print division had dwindled from €890 million in 2002 to €755 million five years later, the trend was already showing. Consider that in February 2015 management made the most of the launch of a new product, issued at a cost 15% to 20% cheaper than previous versions. What was this new product? The combination of the yellow and white pages into one product: a single printed directory.[142] That year no one could deny that innovation budgets would have been better spent on web-based solutions. It is tough for management teams to let go of legacy products, especially when the latter have generated billions of euros of cash flows over the years.

There were several reasons why the trend in print revenues was only going one way. A look at a market with much higher internet penetration like the US would have removed any doubt. In 2007 already three-quarters of American households had access to the web. Even when keeping in mind cultural differences, much of what was happening there was likely to have a similar impact in Italy as internet penetration caught up with America's. That same year Google Trends was already showing a gradual but steady decline in searches for the words "yellow pages", indicating that the drop in print revenues was not just due to a migration of classified ads to the net, but might well mean that consumer interest was moving away from directory-specific websites as well, and a new generation of users was browsing ads exclusively online rather than in a phone book. That year, over in the US, two companies were experiencing robust growth in the number of online searches at the same time that yellow-pages sites were falling down the search tables: their names were Google Maps and Yelp, two pure online providers of local advertising services.[143]

Another factor also pointed towards the likely persistent degeneration of traditional print directories: although consumers valued the convenience of phone listings, advertisers had long hated the yellow pages' monopolistic and price-setting behaviours. The internet gave businesses an alternative, and it was doing so at a much lower cost. With the exception of local repairmen and emergency services, placing local classified ads in yellow pages no longer made sense when a small enterprise could, with a cheaper online advert, broadcast its message to an entire region or country.

The final argument to make against Seat management's view of an eventual turnaround of the print division is the one made in the PagesJaunes scenario regarding the disruptive nature of the web. It is evident that none of the senior executives running the Italian group was familiar with the idea of disruptive change. It is incomprehensible that a company that had become one of Italy's main technology concerns during the dotcom era would fail to spot the real threat that internet competitors represented. The fact is that the internet-savvy Seat of 2000 had been split into two separate entities: directories and business information on one side and the pure technology services on the other. The internet expertise had been lost during the move.

There is another explanation behind management's failure to grasp the urgency of rushing the group into online services. By 2014 internet penetration in Italy remained the lowest among western European countries. At 62%, it was in fact lower than in many eastern European countries like Poland, Hungary and Slovakia, where two-thirds, three-quarters and four-fifths of the population had web access respectively.[144]

The blame for such slow adoption can be assigned to a combination of factors, but the fact that Italy had one of the slowest connections in the eurozone goes a long way in providing an answer.[145] Consumers were not keen to subscribe to an internet service provider if it meant getting a poor service. In 2013 ADSL remained by far the most common technology to access the web in Italy, whereas many western countries had prioritised cable and fibre technologies to provide more bandwidth. Italy's pedestrian broadband speed put the country 45th globally.[146] As a direct consequence, the use of technology was very low. In 2013-14, less than 55% of Italians used a computer and just over 57% accessed the internet.[147] In the US, 84% of households owned a PC while 74% of households used the internet. As discussed earlier, in the early years of the PIPE this low internet penetration and the slow pace of deploying the internet nationwide served to protect Seat's print division. The trade-off was that Seat's online sales did not grow as quickly as expected, which in turn hindered the group's transformation plans.

* * *

Still, just because Italy was somewhat Luddite, this does not fully explain why Seat's management failed to implement its digital strategy. Other reasons are specific to the group's operations and organisation. One is related to pricing and cost structure. Web advertising solutions had a lower price point than Seat's traditional print products, so for the group's sales force (and to a great extent for its leadership team too), it was natural to prioritise the print business. In 2005, 82% of the group's Italian directory activities were paper-based. By 2010 the print division in Italy still accounted for 54% of the classified ad activities. Again, because of low internet penetration and lower margins earned from digital solutions, it would have been difficult for management to phase out the high-margin mainstream print business more quickly.

And yet the only way for the business to become a leading online classified advertising platform would have been to spend all its efforts and spare cash on its internet unit. By 2014 Seat's digital proposition was not competitive with the likes of Google, which is a factor behind the 25% fall in digital revenues between 2010 and 2014. Seat's problems were exacerbated by an advertising downturn in Italy in 2012-14. New entrants, some pure web players, meant that Seat was losing pricing power. Therefore, senior management chose to be cautious. Migrating online too quickly risked cannibalising the print activities further and making the cost structure unjustifiable. The headcount was slashed by 40% between 2006 and 2012. It was difficult for management to cut back the core business at a faster pace without getting serious pushback internally. As it turns out, throughout the period of the LBO, discussions between Seat's management and trade unions were often prolonged and fiery.

The second operational factor behind the group's inability to retain its leadership when transitioning from print to digital is related to the lag in reaction time that is common from corporate executives who fail to identify disruptive change. Without setting up a separate, independent unit, management was unlikely to carry out the digital transformation successfully. As we saw in our previous case study, in Europe PagesJaunes/Solocal is the only participant that seems to have adapted its model to the new digital proposition, and it certainly owes its relative success to the existence of the Minitel, an electronic network that had operated in France since the 1980s and gave PagesJaunes the opportunity to design digital adverts before they were even given that name.

The real costs of a leveraged PIPE

From the LBO's early days to the ownership handover of 2012, Seat shelled out €1.6 billion in loan interest and €1.7 billion in principal repayments. This €3.3 billion would have been better spent in innovative products, building an online platform, and maybe completing acquisitions of leading internet advertising businesses. Instead, about €280 million (or 2.7% of revenue) was devoted to intangible asset acquisitions – a loose proxy for research & development – during those eight years of PE ownership.[148] Two chairmen, three CEOs and four finance directors later (confirmation that CFOs tend to take the blame when buyouts miscarry, even when the reason behind the underperformance is strategy-related), the leveraged PIPE had floundered helplessly in part because, as for PagesJaunes, it did not give the underlying company the means to invest in innovation.

Wayward economic statistics and market signals made it hard to bet on research, but investing such a small proportion of dwindling revenues was a costly mistake. Google was spending 13% of sales in R&D at that time, so it was a lost cause for Seat to try to compete with a sliver of Google's budget. Seat's mapping business TuttoCittà Maps was introduced in 2012,[149] a full seven years after the creation of Google Maps and four years after the latter's introduction to the Italian market. It is a tall order to convince clients to switch from a strongly-performing and leading product they have been using for years to a replica version that brings little additional functionality.

Because of the leveraged structure, management had not delivered on its promise made in early 2004 to pay €90 million to €100 million of annual dividends, for a yield of 4.5%. In reality, after paying out €45 million and €62 million in 2006 and 2007 respectively, generating a third of the promised yield, Seat paid dividends of less than €4 million in each of the ensuing four years.[150] As is common in LBOs, dividend payouts were capped by debt covenants.[151] Between 2004 and 2008, a minimum of 70% of Seat's annual operating cash flows were sucked out of the group to repay debt principal and interest.

What was not spent on debt-related matters went into capex and tax. In 2009 and 2011, the ratio of debt repayments-to-cash flows exceeded

100%, meaning that management was drawing from the group's positive cash balance. It is another sign that, when push comes to shove, the interest of financial sponsors and lenders always comes first, no matter how good management's intentions are. It is best for public investors to stay clear of leveraged PIPEs – approximately 300,000 of them were believed to have been burnt on the Seat Pagine Gialle epic. A reported 40,000 filed a petition to the company and the Italian financial markets authority Consob to complain that they had not been included in the proceedings during the various ownership changes.[152]

Figure 12.9: Seat Pagine Gialle's debt- and equity-to-EBITDA multiples (2003-14)

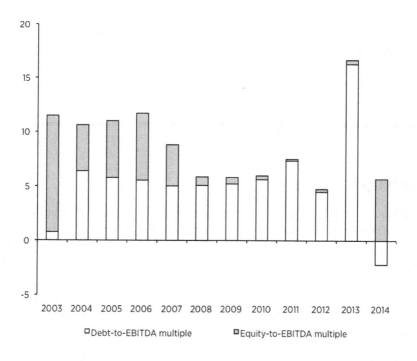

Notes: The debt numbers are at book value whereas equity is derived from the market capitalisation. If market quotes were used for the various loans, debt multiples would be much lower. The combination of debt and equity multiples gives the total EV multiple. The year 2014 shows net cash position. Source: Company accounts and author's analysis

By applying debt of nearly 6.5 times EBITDA, the financial sponsors led Seat onto a long stretch of underinvestment. Of course, this is a common principle of LBOs, especially when the target is seen as a cash cow: most of its spare liquidity is to be used to service bank loans. Unfortunately, unbeknown to management and the PE backers, the group was about to face the onslaught of new technologies, a major development in a sector that had witnessed no real innovation since Seat had seen the light in 1925. As pure online rivals changed the rules of the game, Seat spent the best part of eight years refereeing lengthy battles between its owners and its lenders.

When you add to these factors the Great Recession, the Italian economy's double-dip recession and the advertising downturn, it is all credit to the resilience of monopolistic, cash-rich businesses like phone directories that it took the Italian publisher so long to seek court protection and force creditors to cancel their loans. As Figure 12.9 highlights, the full equitisation of the LBO loans could not have been delayed further. By the end of 2013, the debt-to-EBITDA ratio topped 16 times. Like PagesJaunes, Seat had been a slow bleed. Its high indebtedness turned it into a zombie, going from one recapitalisation to the next.

Turning the page

The Seat story tells us more about modern capitalism than any authority on the subject ever will. The saga behind Seat Pagine Gialle's first LBO in 1997-2000 led to many books and newspaper articles on the subject. There were rumours of impropriety and insider dealing in the period leading to the disposal, but no charges were ever brought. In the end, the scandal was mostly based on the fact that the financial investors had made a fortune without paying much tax on their gains since they had invested through Luxembourg-based entities.[153] Nothing new there.

The buyout of the 2003-14 period spawned its own barrage of reports and enquiries. Seat II, as BC Partners calls it on its website, broke all records at the time of its completion. It was the largest buyout in Europe and the biggest PIPE ever in Italy; and the Lighthouse high-yield bond was the biggest euro-denominated issue to date.[154] If the Silver consortium had managed to exit in 2007 as originally intended, it would have been remembered as a huge success. Instead, via three separate PIPEs and the chaotic exits of successive institutional investors, it turned into the country's most visible LBO failure. The most damaging element of Seat's indebtedness was the series of restructuring talks it held with its creditors. When rumours emerged in 2011 that discussions were stalling and the company might well end up in administration,[155] it encouraged advertisers to take their business elsewhere. This kind of ramification is hard to pinpoint. All we know is that, between 2003 and 2012, the PE-backed publisher had seen revenues and EBITDA halve.

The Great Recession and the emergence of online substitution demonstrated that the success of BC Partners, CVC and Investitori during their first buyout of Seat Pagine Gialle was not so much due to superior investment skill but rather to fortunate timing. Investitori had made close to 28 times its outlay in the 1997 LBO through Investitori Associati II, a €60 million investment vehicle. In its 2003 relapse buyout it used its third fund, a €400 million mid-cap vehicle raised three years earlier. Seat was that vintage's last investment. In 2004 Investitori Associati IV was closed with €700 million of capital. In April 2013 it was reported that Investitori had given up trying to raise a fifth fund.[156] The performance of the fourth vehicle explains why. As at 31 March 2015, more than ten years after being raised, Investitori Associati IV had generated a negative IRR of 10%.[157] While Seat certainly hurt the third fund's returns, fund IV also fell way short of expectations. The team who had worked on Seat had been purged – with the noticeable exception of the deal lead, Investitori's co-founder Dario Cossutta – but it was not enough to reassure LPs.

Investitori's three British co-investors were more fortunate, primarily because their international activities gave them a chance to diversify away the country-specific risk – not that it will help them to rebuild their reputation in Italy. BC opted out of Seat when the 2009 refinancing required an equity cure, losing a sizeable chunk of capital in the process. In fact, the fund manager had been good at cutting its losses in Italy. In December 2007 it had crystallised a €150-to-€200 million loss on its investment in Mark IV, an underperforming Italian manufacturer of engineering systems it had acquired seven years earlier.[158] In 2010, BC closed its Milan office. With its poor economic record, Italy had lost its appeal. Regardless of its performance on Italian deals, and despite generating an IRR of just 4% on the 2005 vintage BC European Capital VIII, in February 2012 the firm completed the fundraising of its ninth fund by hitting the €6.5 billion cap, a decent upgrade on the €5.5 billion raised seven years earlier. Had LPs invested in the FTSE 100 index between 2005 and early 2015, they would have yielded an unlevered 7% annual return (with dividends reinvested). The broader FTSE Europe ex-UK index returned an annual 6.5% during those ten years. LPs should have stuck to the more liquid public markets. Some still elected to give BC the benefit of the doubt by investing in the ninth fund.[159]

Having made the mistake of piling on further exposure in 2009 by injecting fresh equity, CVC saw its Italian executives involved on the Seat deal seek fortune elsewhere. But thanks to its global presence and robust performance in other jurisdictions, the firm raised a €10.9 billion fund in 2013. It also helped that its 2007 and 2008 vintages showed very respectable performances when benchmarked against leading stock indices. The €4.1 billion tandem of 2007 yielded 6.4% annually and the following year's €10.75 billion vehicle netted a 10.4% IRR, both as of 31 December 2014. Over these eight and seven-year periods, the FTSE 100 generated yearly returns of 4.5% and 4.1%. As for CVC's 2005 vintage, its 17.3% IRR was vastly superior to BC Partners's 4%.

Seat Pagine Gialle is not included in Permira's list of past transactions.[160] How a €3 billion transaction could have vanished from the firm's track record is hard to explain, but as we saw in the Gala Coral quaternary (Chapter 2), Permira tends to omit failures from its deal log. This practice is not in line with the industry's disclosure guidelines introduced in the UK in 2007. Since christened the Private Equity Reporting Group, it does not look like this monitoring panel is having much influence on the industry's power players. But LPs do and Permira's mistakes before and during the financial crisis explain why it took two years for the group to close Permira V in June 2014. At €5.3 billion, the new fund was less than half the amount raised in 2006, even though the firm had attempted to eradicate all trace of its Seat experience after the departure of the four Italian employees who had sat at some stage on the board of the yellow-pages publisher. The net IRR of 6.3% generated by Permira's fourth fund compares to a 5.5% unlevered annual return from the FTSE 100 during the same nine years,[161] but the Gala Coral and Seat PG stories would have worried some LPs.

No doubt the most damning fact against the PE quartet's deeds came in the legal action taken by Seat in 2014. The early 2015 settlement enabled the financial sponsors to move on without admitting any responsibility or guilt, but their worst practices had been exposed. In February 2015, a columnist from the prestigious newspaper *Corriere della Sera* raised the suggestion that the publisher's former directors had got off lightly. In addition to financial damages, the journalist had advocated that, in Italy, directors found guilty of fraudulent bankruptcies and financial and economic crimes should be handed jail terms. He had chosen the Seat Pagine Gialle buyout as the main example to support his thesis. As part of an ongoing investigation, by November of that year Italian prosecutors decided precautionarily to ban from office for a period of 12 months the 11 directors, including the PE representatives, who had sat on Seat's board at the time of the 2004 extraordinary €3.5 billion-plus dividend.[162] The debt push-down had seemed such a good idea back then.

PART SEVEN
PE-backed IPOs:
The Search for a Patsy

ACCORDING TO DATA RELEASED BY RESEARCHERS PitchBook in February 2015, PE-backed public offerings accounted for 44% of all IPOs globally in 2014, their highest share during the period covered, 2006 to 2014. They accounted for 39% of IPO proceeds that year, also the highest point over the same nine year stretch.[1]

The proportion of PE-backed businesses exited via IPO is contingent on the level of development of stock markets. In the US and the UK, floats represent a higher percentage of PE portfolio realisations than in countries with less advanced public markets. The ability of financial sponsors to exit via an IPO also depends on the state of the economy and the degree of anxiety in the markets. One year IPOs can represent a big chunk of PE realisations, while they can completely disappear the following year. For instance, in the US, in 2006 and 2013 IPOs accounted for 15% of PE exits in value terms; in 2008, they represented less than 5% of the total.[2] In the UK in recent years, stock market listings as a percentage of PE exits ranged from zero in 2008 to 14% in 2013.[3]

The wide range of research papers that have been issued on PE-backed IPOs is frustratingly contradictory. Many pundits posit that such offerings produce lower returns than non-PE-backed ones; other scholars assert the opposite.[4] There are problems with such studies. First, their samples are usually small. Second, PE-backed IPOs have increased in popularity so they were a lot more prevalent in the late 1990s and in the noughties than in the 1980s and early 1990s. It might well be that we need more time to judge the recent batch of listings. As more PE-backed companies floated in the noughties and since, the quality is likely to have suffered. Third, it would appear that, although PE-backed listings outperform other types of listings in the short term (three to six months post-IPO), they tend to underperform, sometimes significantly, in the longer term. Whatever merits one assigns to research on the subject, my inclination is not to agree with one side or the other. I am more interested in showcasing the broader market implications of such transactions.

Inevitably, as you are about to read, the main victim of these listings is the public; more specifically, retail investors. Institutional investors often have little alternative but to take part in new stock issues. The reasons are several, but one in particular that can be baffling is that asset managers running index trackers or sector-specific funds have to get their allocation of new stock offerings. Our two examples, eDreams and Foxtons, managed to float partly because asset managers running an index product (e.g., IBEX Medium or FTSE 250) or a travel- or real-estate-focused fund must take a stake, even if minimal. Irrespective of whether they are fully diversified or not, in view of the next two case studies, investors would be well advised to be very selective and to take into account the following facts about PE-backed initial public offerings:

- The company being floated often remains overleveraged, which could lead to more volatility than in other IPOs.

- A large quantity of shares might need to be sold in the secondary market by the PE firm(s) once the lock-up period has expired. This is known as the post-IPO overhang. A financial sponsor is never willingly a long-term investor; it is more often than not an opportunistic speculator. It will sell as soon as it sees a good time to dispose of its stock (for instance, when the stock is to go down due to upcoming disappointing results – the sort of information a PE investor will be made aware of in advance if sitting on the board of directors). This will negatively impact the share price, in particular if the size of the block being sold is meaningful.

- The post-IPO price can be manipulated by institutional investors 'stagging' the stock in the aftermarket. Stagging means reselling/flipping the shares once trading has begun, taking advantage of the hype that can surround an IPO. Shares are bought at the offer price and sold once the stock has gone through its 'pop'. Financial sponsors are pretty good at lining up institutional investors, probably because like them they emanate from Wall Street and the City.

- The corporate executives who have run the buyout alongside the PE firm(s) have usually made a bundle during the float and are therefore thinking of an early retirement or spending time on the beach rather than continuing to manage the business.

- Ambitious plans stated during the pre-IPO roadshow are rarely met, probably because they are marketing gimmicks to lure in the patsy.

- The main argument against participating in such IPOs is that they will usually be fully priced. No financial sponsor wants to be accused by its LPs of having left money on the table. An LBO fund manager's duty is to maximise value for the limited partners. Naturally, many of these listings perform adequately, but it is almost despite the overpricing at the time of the IPO.

It was a challenge to pick two examples out of a vast sample of failures. What the case studies will underline is that investors in PE-backed listings are very much alone in this dangerous game and cannot rely on anyone to root for their interest. All other parties – the selling LBO sponsor, the management team and the bankers coordinating the float – are strongly incentivised to overprice it, even if it leads to long-term after-market underperformance. As the two following chapters will demonstrate, PE-backed IPOs are not for the fainthearted, a message that might already have come across in the Debenhams, DX and Hertz stories.

CHAPTER 13
eDreams – Reality Fights Back

THE YEAR 2000 WILL FOREVER BE REMEMBERED AS ONE when technology took centre stage. Before it had even started it promised to be an eventful year. A computer flaw dating back to the early days of programming was believed to represent a real threat to an increasingly digitised world when, on the first day of 2000, computers and electronic devices run by them, using only two digits to denote the year in dates, would be unable to distinguish between 1900 and 2000. By sending inaccurate data they would force planes and satellites to come crashing down, trains to revert to the steam engine (presumably), banks to start paying you in century-old currency, and nuclear plants to explode according to their respective time zone in a macabre finale. The Y2K bug, a.k.a. the Millennium bug, was to end civilisation as we knew it. The prevailing paranoia led millions of businesses to spend a fortune on IT experts in the years leading up to the fateful day to ensure that they would still be able to handle customer orders and run their factories. An estimated $300 billion was spent worldwide (almost half of it in the United States) on upgrades to be Y2K-compliant. On New Year's Day, with the exception of a few minor incidents, the drama was disappointingly underwhelming. A much bigger news item, and one that the world hardly seemed to notice, was the resignation the day before of Russian President Boris Yeltsin, who was handing over power to his Prime Minister, Vladimir Putin.

Technology remained the buzzword in the first months of 2000 as the Nasdaq continued its steep climb thanks to the internet mania that had enthralled America and parts of Europe for half a decade. In 1999 the tech-heavy stock index had climbed more than 85% to end the year at 4069. By 10 March 2000, the index was closing at 5048, a brisk 24% increase in just 70 days. Every corporation that wanted to be noticed and avoid seeing its share price fall by the wayside had to reposition its business model as an internet-centric outfit, a dotcom as they were called. The new paradigm (remember the consulting jargon of the times?) promised that e-tailers, eCommerce marketplaces and P2P platforms (that's peer-to-peer or person-to-person, not public-to-private) would take over the global economy. In fact, the 'e' designation wasn't just used to coin new industries. Companies, starting with American auctioneer eBay and online broker E*Trade, sought premium branding by adding the shortened 'electronic' prefix. In Europe the craze was more subdued, but one Spanish company then seeing the light would outlive many start-ups launched at the time.

Launch

In February 1999, two marketing professionals who had worked together in the San Francisco Bay Area at web browser pioneer Netscape had the idea of setting up eDreams as a new travel website. Javier Pérez-Tenessa de Block, aged 32, and James Hare, 31, had known each other since their days at Stanford University, where they had obtained their MBAs in 1997. Immersed in the Silicon Valley internet ecosystem, they witnessed the emergence of online travel specialists, including Expedia, a website launched in 1996 as part of computer giant Microsoft's MSN division before being spun off as a publicly traded entity. Backed by €30 million of funding raised in two rounds – one in 1999, the other in 2000 – from venture capitalists Doll, Apax, Atlas Venture and 3i, the eDreams website launched in early 2000. It aimed to reproduce part of Expedia's offering in Europe. From day one Expedia had allowed consumers to make air, car, and hotel reservations online and to browse a library of multimedia travel guides. Despite being a start-up with more limited means, Barcelona, Spain-headquartered eDreams had ambitious goals. Within months of its formation it had established websites in Italy and Britain.[1]

The idea certainly was not original. By that stage dozens of similar holiday and travel specialist websites had emerged in Europe, such as Degriftour in France, Tiss in Germany, and eBookers and Lastminute in England, just to name a few. Aerospace engineer and windsurfing instructor Pérez-Tenessa and Harvard alumnus and former tour guide Hare were positioning their venture differently. Employing the services of hundreds of "Dreamguides" based around the world, they offered online expert advice on faraway destinations and adventures. Their site also sold upmarket package holidays on behalf of tour operators, with a niche inclination for unusual, aspirational or hard-to-find holidays.[2] Chaired by Pedro de Esteban – another Stanford MBA graduate with various executive roles as Managing Partner for turnaround specialist Inversiones Novae and chairman and CEO of Spanish tour operator Grupo Experto – eDreams was the sort of online service provider that managed to look like a travel agent and a trip adviser without actually being either.

The chief functionality of the website was to aggregate information from diverse sources and present it in a uniform way to facilitate decision making for consumers. Called a web portal, it was like many websites in the early days of the internet: America Online, Microsoft Network, and Yahoo! were the quintessential web portals, offering access to generic news and information. Thus, eDreams and other travel portals were offering services that were not only low value-adding, but for which demand was limited due to the low web usage back then. As a case in point, in 2000 eDreams recorded €8 million worth of bookings.[3] That same year, internet penetration in Spain, Italy and the UK – the three countries where eDreams operated a website – was 13%, 23%, and 27% respectively.[4] Given Spain's poor internet adoption, it is not surprising that the founders chose to expand abroad from the outset. Whether it was due to the founders' drive or their visionary belief in the eventual widespread embracing of internet services, after a stuttering beginning the Spanish upstart managed to make a place for itself in the very crowded European online travel market.

Liftoff

Eventually the company turned into a travel search engine, a.k.a. an online travel agency (OTA); an aggregator of flight tickets sold by airlines and brick-and-mortar travel agencies. The information appearing on the company's websites was sourced from what is called a global distribution system (GDS), a central reservation system used by airlines and, over time, by train operators, hotel groups and other companies of the travel sector like cruise liners, car leasing companies and, naturally, travel agencies. American groups Galileo and Sabre, at the outset backed by United Airlines and American Airlines respectively, were two of the largest reservation systems in the world. But in November 2000, eDreams agreed with Amadeus, a Spanish GDS owned by several European airlines, to give eDreams's users access to the best available fares from 500 airlines worldwide.[5] With an almost exclusive focus on flights, the Barcelona-based travel group worked on consolidating its leadership in Italy and Spain, and pursuing its international development. By 2004, eDreams was handling €70 million worth of bookings, not far from nine times the level recorded in its first year of operation.[6]

Thanks to increasing internet penetration and the adoption of online flight reservations, the next two years saw the company record solid top-line expansion. It enabled its VC backers to sell out their holdings to American growth investment firm TA Associates for €153 million in November 2006. TA financed the deal with senior loans from Belgian bank Fortis and subordinated debt from TA's own funds. The deal left the two co-founders with a 45% stake.[7] By that stage, half of the Spanish population had web access. Thus, online flight reservations continued to win market share from traditional travel agencies: in 2006, eDreams recorded €300 million of bookings, and two of its key local competitors, Rumbo and Atrápalo, billed €200 million and €100 million respectively.[8]

Between its launch in 1999 and its buyout by TA seven years later, eDreams had become the leading online booking group in southern Europe, having sold hotels, flights and package holidays to more than six million customers over that period. Building on this, in 2007 the Spanish group expanded its international franchise by launching operations in Portugal, France and Germany. That year it recorded a 50% increase in bookings to €445 million, becoming the second largest travel agent in Spain behind brick-and-mortar leader Viajes El Corte Inglés.[9] In October, press reports alleged that TA Associates was planning to flip the business by selling its stake to a trade or financial investor, or by introducing eDreams to the stock exchange at a rumoured €345 million valuation.[10] But the Credit Crunch and the ensuing market jitters sabotaged the PE firm's exit plans.

Despite the volatile context, online travel continued to do well. The sector's strong fundamentals also lifted the performance of eDreams's Spanish rivals during 2007, with Atrápalo's bookings reaching €160 million, 60% up on the prior year. And Orizonia, one of the country's leading tour operators, acquired travel website Viajar.com.[11] To build its capabilities in the fast-moving OTA space, in January 2008 Orizonia also bought 50% of Rumbo, creating a major national champion in the travel sector since the two groups had combined bookings of €3 billion. As part of the transaction Rumbo absorbed Viajar.com.[12] It formed a serious rival to eDreams.

But the overwhelming success of online travel agencies was bothering some market participants. In August 2008, for instance, low-cost airline Ryanair decided to launch legal action against online flight booking platforms, including Swiss-based Bravofly and Germany's V-Tours, arguing that their activities were illegal. The Irish operator was keen to regain control of its ticket sales at a time when the economic recession was increasing competitive pressure between airlines. In Spain it threatened to cancel bookings made through the three main "unauthorised ticket tout" websites Atrápalo, eDreams and Rumbo because of the hidden mark-ups they levied on passengers, protesting that these intermediaries were merely adding cost to the end-consumer.

To many, it was an attempt by Ryanair to avoid seeing its fares compared to other airlines. Regardless of the motivations behind the move, it was the first time that an airline had expressed opposition to the online aggregator business model.[13] It would not be the last. Notwithstanding the pushback the OTA sector was suddenly getting from one of Europe's major airlines, the year 2008 saw eDreams record €607 million in bookings (36% up year-on-year), €65.4 million in revenue margin (defined as revenue net of commissions paid to agencies) and €13.3 million in EBITDA.[14] That same year, local rivals Atrápalo and Logitravel billed €165 million and €60 million respectively, while UK-based Lastminute invoiced €200 million in Spain alone.[15] The sector had gained acceptance from the consumer.

Cruise control

In the first quarter of 2009, the economic situation in Spain, and to a similar extent across Europe, was truly troubling. As a consequence of the financial crisis and the ensuing Great Recession, eDreams's home market saw its GDP tumble 1.6% in the first three months of the year, and it officially entered recession after recording a fall of 1% in the last quarter of 2008. Unemployment now exceeded 17% – it had been below 8% in the second quarter of 2007. Spain's unemployed population topped four million, more than double the number seen at the end of 2007.[16] All of eDreams's overseas markets were also in recession. Since 80% of the group's bookings were from consumers – with the rest coming from the corporate sector, primarily small and medium-sized enterprises – the economic downturn and its repercussions on tourism were forecast to leave a mark on the company's growth.[17]

Understandably, for the whole of 2009 eDreams reported a meagre 7% increase in bookings. Rumbo's, Atrápalo's and Logitravel's billings were up as well, but their growth had been equally affected. Badly hurt by the downturn – in 2009, GDP had shrunk 3.6% in Spain, 2.9% in France, 5.5% in Italy, 4.3% in the UK, 5.6% in Germany and 3% in Portugal – and by intense rivalry in its home market, eDreams had been forced to drop its prices by 17%. It had, however, benefitted from a presence in 14 markets, its international activities recording a 35% jump in sales during the year.[18] And thanks to economies of scale, the group had recorded a 14% increase in revenue margin, to €74.6 million, and €16.5 million of EBITDA, up 24% year-on-year.[19]

In regard to the ongoing tussle with Ryanair, in January 2010 a Barcelona tribunal found in favour of eDreams and its rival Atrápalo in their fight against the Irish airline, giving the two online aggregators the right to sell Ryanair tickets through their websites.[20] And the good news kept coming for the Spanish travel group and its owner TA Associates. Several European countries, with the noticeable exception of Spain, emerged from recession in the second half of 2009.

As the first six months of 2010 confirmed a much rosier business climate, in July, in a deal comprised between €250 million and €300 million, British buyout group Permira made an approach to take a 75% stake in eDreams, partly funded with €117 million of loans arranged by Swiss bank UBS, including €46 million of six-year term A loan, paying a margin of 4.50% over Euribor, and the same quantum of seven-year term B loan paying 500 basis points over Euribor.[21] Donning the structure of a proper leveraged buyout, eDreams was celebrating the tenth anniversary of its formation in style, valued at an EBITDA multiple of 11 to 12 times. Permira had pre-empted the competition, directly approaching the Spanish company shortly after losing an auction for eDreams's French counterpart GO Voyages. The latter had been sold two months earlier to French investment firm Axa Private Equity.[22] After losing that battle, Permira's investment team had run the rule over the sector's main players and chosen eDreams, with entrenched positions in Spain, Italy and Portugal, as the most obvious LBO candidate given its cash generation, organic growth and sector consolidation potential.[23]

Figure 13.1: eDreams's gross bookings (2004-10)

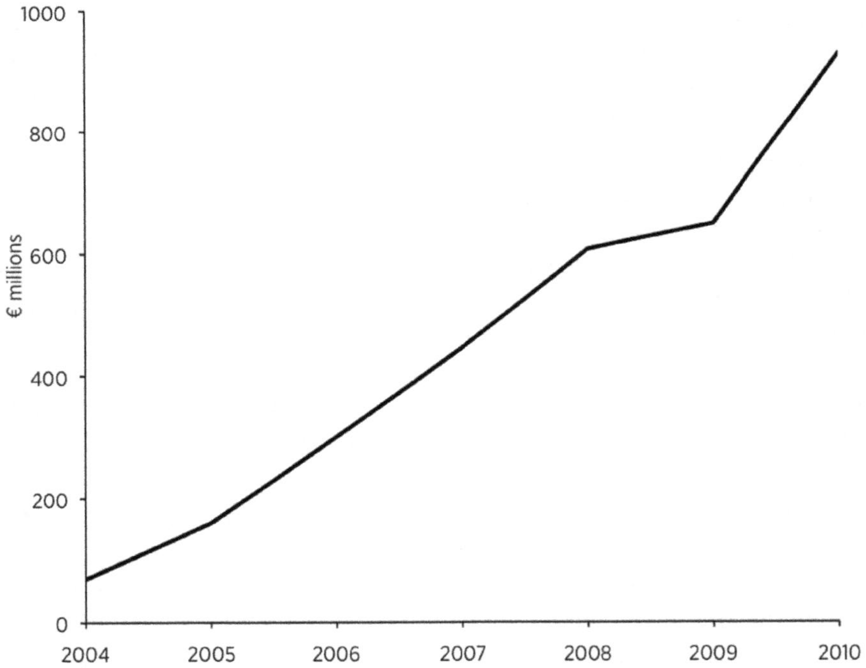

Source: Company filings and press releases

The year ended with Spain's unemployment rate exceeding 20%.[24] Key markets France and Portugal had also seen their jobless rate hit 9.3% and 10.8%

respectively in 2010.[25] Despite its already large size and the weak economy in the Mediterranean region, thanks to its geographic diversification eDreams experienced a 43% jump in bookings, invoicing €928 million of transactions for the whole of 2010, netting itself a revenue margin of €100 million and an EBITDA of €24 million, up one-third and 47% respectively on the 2009 numbers.[26] As illustrated by Figure 13.1, the group's performance in recent years, including its expansion into international markets, translated into robust and steady growth in gross bookings. In 2010, online travel bookings in Spain grew 8.7% to reach €7 billion,[27] implying a market share in excess of 13% for the group. It was easy to understand the potential Permira saw in the business, though other OTAs had also benefitted from the general trend in online service adoption, with Logitravel's bookings, for instance, reaching €198 million in 2010, a 115% leap on the prior year.[28]

Long-haul consolidation

In the past five years, the European online travel market had grown at more than 20% per annum and was predicted to expand further as consumers continued to shop online.[29] But it remained a very fragmented sector. Consolidation had been on the agenda for some time. Given the relatively small size of all the participants, especially compared to their American peers, the OTA space was ripe for the kind of pan-European buy-and-build strategy that private equity professionals are so keen on. In February 2011, eDreams's new owner Permira partnered with French investment fund Axa Private Equity – 58% shareholder of number one French online travel operator GO Voyages since May of the previous year – to acquire British rival Opodo, an online agency present in France, Germany and the UK, and owned by Amadeus, the reservation service provider. The Opodo buyout was to give instant access to the more mature Scandinavian markets, where the British operator held a leading presence through its subsidiary Travellink.

Paying €450 million, or about 11 times Opodo's last-12-months EBITDA, Permira and Axa saw off competition from American behemoths Expedia and Orbitz as well as Spanish tour operator Orizonia. The plan was to combine eDreams and GO Voyages with the target, thereby creating the largest European OTA in the flight segment and the fourth in the world in terms of gross bookings, to take advantage of further migration of travel reservations via the web. In Scandinavian countries, for instance, where internet penetration neared or exceeded 90%, almost 60% of trips were already being booked online. The trend was expected to win over other European markets, thus growth prospects were underpinned by relatively low levels of online penetration in the core markets of southern Europe. The potential for further geographic expansion and moves into non-flight business areas was another rationale behind the merger.[30]

Now employing 1,200 employees in 27 countries, the group rebranded itself ODIGEO. On a pro forma basis, for the 12 months ended 31 December 2010 the three combined entities generated €432 million in revenue, over €300 million in revenue margin, and recurring EBITDA and operating profit of €106 million and €68 million respectively.[31] They made a formidable market leader. For tax-planning purposes, ODIGEO's registered offices were moved from Barcelona to tax shelter Luxembourg. Permira's Luxgoal and Axa's Axeurope invested through LuxGEO Parent and LuxGEO GP (a 'double Luxco' structure, in legal jargon).

As often with the modern-day game of value maximisation, it was all becoming hopelessly complicated; eDreams was officially leaving the world of growth financing and entering the one of structured LBOs. To finance the Opodo acquisition, ODIGEO borrowed, through one of its newly created Luxembourg-based entities, Geo Travel Finance, €340 million equally split between term A (six-year amortising) and term B (seven-year bullet) loans, priced at Euribor +450 and +500 basis points respectively. In April 2011, the group also issued €175 million of 10.375% eight-year-non-call senior notes, in the first ever European eCommerce high-yield bond. The total net leverage of the transaction was 4.7 times EBITDA.[32]

The growth and market consolidation stories coupled with the positive trend in favour of online migration of travel bookings proved strong arguments for convincing investors. Adding to the debt pile, on 30 June Permira and Axa decided to subscribe to a €117.7 million convertible bond accruing interest at a generous annual rate of 9.875%. Given that this interest did not have any cash impact and with the promising growth prospects of the merged entities, the two PE owners were making sure to earn their fair share of the upside. By the end of 2011, ODIGEO's combined bookings totalled €3.5 billion (up 5% in the year) via 12 million customers across 28 countries.[33] It was the classically potent result of a PE-backed buy-and-build approach. The pan-European OTA was now a major player in a sector that continued to experience positive fundamental indicators.

Nevertheless, the bankruptcy on 27 January 2012 of Spain's fourth largest airline operator Spanair, a flagship of the regional Government of Catalonia, reminded everyone that the sputtering national economy was hurting the travel sector. Unemployment in Spain, ODIGEO's second largest market, reached 24%, or more than 5.6 million people, in the first quarter of 2012.[34] And yet ODIGEO generated €423.5 million in revenue and recurring EBITDA of €95.4 million, for a very respectable 30% EBITDA margin, in the fiscal year ended 31 March 2012. Following the Opodo acquisition and the merger with GO Voyages, France had turned into the biggest market for the group, accounting for two-fifths of bookings and 47% of revenue margin in that same fiscal year.[35]

In August, Sicily's low-cost airline Wind Jet followed Spanair's example by ceasing all activities after talks of a possible acquisition by Italy's flag carrier Alitalia failed.[36] As the Great Recession overstayed its welcome, European airline bankruptcies in 2012 included Malev in Hungary, Spanair and Mint Airways in Spain, Climber Sterling, City Airline, Skyways and Air Finland in Scandinavia, Cirrus Airlines in Germany, and Czech Connect and OLT Express in Central Europe. Although ODIGEO was well diversified and could weather the collapse of minor airlines, unfortunately Europe's economic slump was not going away. In 2012, ODIGEO's main market, France, had not provided much of a boost to the group's activities, with GDP growing at 0.2%. That same year Italy had seen GDP fall by 2.8%, while its unemployment rate had hit 11.4%. Portugal's economy had shrunk 4%, pushing the country's unemployment rate above 15%. The Spanish economy had plunged a further 2.1%. With unemployment reaching 6.2 million people, or more than 26% of the working population, in the first quarter of 2013, it would be stating the obvious to say that Spain was facing its worst social, economic and political crisis since the adoption of democracy upon the death of dictator General Franco in 1975.

The raw violence of the crisis had not just led to the collapse of airlines. In February 2013, leading Spanish tour operator Orizonia, with a click-and-mortar business model, became insolvent. The whole of southern Europe witnessed a double-dip recession, provoking political stalemate in the eurozone. Germany was only doing marginally better, recording a paltry 0.4% GDP growth rate in 2012. The UK, another important market following the Opodo acquisition the year before, reported the highest growth rate of the lot, at a seething 0.7%.[37] Despite the dire economic landscape, in the fiscal year ended 31 March 2013 the group generated 8.7 million bookings, revenue margin of €373 million and EBITDA of €108 million. Though still recording earnings growth, EBITDA margins had fallen from 29.5% in the 2012 fiscal year to 29.1% in the following period.[38]

Final approach

Two months before fiscal year end, in January 2013, through its Luxembourg-based subsidiary Geo Debt Finance, eDreams ODIGEO issued a €325 million, 7.5%, five-year bond. The issuance was reportedly four times oversubscribed, proving how safe a credit the group was considered to be.[39] The proceeds were used to prepay a big chunk of the term loans A and B issued to finance the Opodo acquisition.[40] Though more expensive than the old term loans, the bond had the benefit of removing most of the group's maintenance covenants, which had recently been tightening. The new offering led rating agency Standard & Poor's to upgrade the online travel group.[41] Alongside the new bonds, the group signed a larger super-senior revolving credit facility of €130 million. Thanks to the accompanying improvement in liquidity, in October 2013 ODIGEO acquired for €13.5 million travel search engine Liligo from French railway monopoly SNCF, the first acquisition since the three-way merger orchestrated in early 2011.[42]

Although the pan-European consolidation play had not been as vigorous as Permira, Axa and ODIGEO's management had promised at the time of the Opodo acquisition, by late 2013 the economic recovery in some of the group's major markets, including the UK, Sweden, Norway, France and Germany, was well established. Southern Europe, however, continued to suffer. The Italian and Portuguese economies were 1.7% and 1.6% smaller by the end of 2013. After years of negative growth, Spain had seen its GDP fall a further 1.2%, reverting to the level generated seven years earlier. Boosted by a massive property bubble and immeasurable generosity from the European Union, the Spanish economy had grown at an annual clip of 3% or more between 1997 and 2007. The financial crisis had closed the liquidity tap, leading the country into its own economic depression. The impact on local consumers and businesses was far-reaching. The country experienced a negative net migration of population in 2011 for the first time since 1990. And in 2013 its population even shrank.[43] Thankfully for eDreams, its management was ambitious to expand abroad.

Coming around in the second half of 2013, Spain's GDP was forecast to grow in 2014. As is often the case, the recovery had a positive effect on the stock markets. Between May 2012 and the early weeks of 2014, the Madrid Stock Exchange's chief index, the IBEX 35, shot up 70%. It was time for our PE protagonists to head for the door. On 14 January 2014, rumours emerged that the travel group was looking at a public offering to take place on the Madrid exchange later in the year.[44] On 6 March, ODIGEO publicly confirmed plans for an IPO on the Spanish bolsa, to be jointly coordinated by Deutsche Bank and JPMorgan with the support of mid-market bank Jefferies. With five brands – eDreams, GO Voyages, Opodo, Travellink and Liligo – the group had become a leading player among aggregators. Despite a still sluggish European economy, management was able to sell a growth story thanks to its diversification across 42 countries. Its offering prospectus emphasised that its revenue margin had risen by more than 16% in the nine months to 31 December 2013, while recurring EBITDA had grown 10%.[45]

On 8 April, in what was Spain's biggest IPO in three years, eDreams ODIGEO went public at €10.25 a share, giving it a market capitalisation of €1.075 billion.[46] With net debt of €442 million, the group's EV was just north of €1.5 billion, the equivalent of 12.8 times EBITDA, implying a positive multiple-arbitrage on the Opodo transaction closed three years earlier. Due to strong demand for the first IPO of 2014 on the Madrid exchange, 35% of the share capital was allotted to the public. Permira sold a third of its stake, bringing it down from 48.5% to 31.4%. Its co-investor Axa PE, renamed Ardian in September 2013, shaved its holding by the same portion, retaining 20.1% of the newly floated company. Employees and members of the senior management team, including CEO and co-founder Pérez-Tenessa, also disposed of a third of their shares. Alongside the 32 million shares sold by the existing shareholders, the company issued new shares to raise fresh capital, planning to use the €50 million proceeds of the public offering to partly repay its 2009 high-yield note. And it converted its €155 million of outstanding shareholder loans into equity.[47] Though more than 15 million shares, or 14.7% of total capital, changed hands on the first trading session, the stock fell 4.3% on a day when the broader IBEX 35 index surrendered 1.2%.[48]

As noted, the timing of the float was not random. The previous week the Madrid main index had hit its highest level since May 2011. After two years of recession, Spain was seeing the green shoots of recovery. As promised, on 30 April eDreams ODIGEO announced that by the end of May it would redeem €46 million of its €175 million 10.375% senior notes due 2019 (the high-yield bond raised in the spring of 2011).[49]

Crash landing

On 14 May 2014, the three banks that had sponsored the IPO issued their first recommendations on the group. Both lead-coordinators Deutsche Bank and JPMorgan timidly chose to put a hold on the stock with targets of €10.50 and €11.30 respectively, whereas Jefferies rated it a buy with a target price of €13.50.[50] The previous day eDreams ODIGEO shares had closed at €11.23. Then, on Friday 20 June, management presented its latest set of figures to the investment community, proudly emphasising that bookings in the year to 31 March 2014 were up 12% year-on-year, while revenue margin had risen 15% and EBITDA was up 8%.

Unfortunately, either due to poor communication skills on eDreams's management's part or because of the high price-earnings ratio the company was trading on, the market was looking for any indication of weakness in the growth story the company had sold ahead of the IPO. Thus, the only message that equity analysts seemed to hear during the presentation was that, during the last quarter of the fiscal year (the three months ended 31 March 2014), the company had experienced growth of only 4% on the same quarter of the previous year. Management expressed that it was due to stronger competition in its core markets.[51] The stock shed 10% on the day. The following week, eDreams's stock snapped, losing 35% to €5.75 on Monday 23 April. JPMorgan dropped its target price to €10 a share on the news.

The colossal share-price drop led management to release a statement the next day, explaining that there had been "a misunderstanding of the implications that the change in the competitive landscape" would have on the group, and that the business model was underlain by "solid fundamentals".[52] The move seemed to work as the stock recovered 8.7% on the day, although Deutsche Bank's analysts decided to reduce their target price to €8.40 regardless. But the shorts were soon back in action, bringing the stock to a close of €5.39 on Friday 27 April, down a third in one week and 47.5% since the flotation two-and-a-half months earlier. The ensuing two weeks failed to bring much calm, and by 10 July the stock had reached €3.63, two-thirds down in just one month. The market cap of the group had fallen to €380 million. With net debt of €440 million, the EV now equated to a more reasonable seven times EBITDA – compared to the 12.8 times offered to public investors three months earlier.

To some it would have seemed like an overreaction by the markets. Sadly the second half of 2014 was not to bring any respite. On 31 July 2014, Irish low-cost airline Ryanair won a temporary injunction against eDreams, preventing the online travel service company from advertising that it offered the "guaranteed best price on all flights" on its German website eDreams.de. That was deemed untrue since eDreams added charges on top of Ryanair's fares.[53] On 4 August, as ODIGEO marked four months on the stock exchange, one of the two lead IPO sponsors, Deutsche Bank, chose to drop its target price to €5.40 – a serious adjustment compared to its previous €8.40-a-share recommendation, and rather less than the €10.25 at which the German bank had helped introduce the travel group to the stock market.[54]

On 29 August, ODIGEO released its highly anticipated financial statements for the three-month period ended 30 June. They showed that the markets and equity analysts had been right to lose their nerve: for the first post-IPO quarterly results, revenue was down 6% year-on-year whereas operating profit was more than a quarter lower. EBITDA margin had sunk from 31% the year before to 21%.[55] The online travel group's shares duly dived 25.6% on the day to €3.14 a pop, almost 70% down since the float. And Deutsche Bank's analysts did not need to be asked twice, obligingly issuing on the same day their latest 'Hold' guidance with a target price of €3.40.[56]

Contrary to what naturalists will tell you, bears usually move in packs. Piling on the pressure, on 5 September rating agency Standard & Poor's decided to issue a bearish note, grading the travel group's 2019 high-yield notes a CCC+, its first notch in the little envied 'substantial risks' category. That same day, rival credit agency Moody's also changed the group's outlook from positive to stable.[57] Both agencies had rated the company a 'very speculative credit' even before its IPO due to ODIGEO's leverage; a geographic concentration in southern Europe and France; and industry risks, including value chain disintermediation from airlines or other third-parties. But things had become worse since. Leverage, for a start, now stood at more than 50% of the capital structure as a consequence of the stock collapse – the net-debt-to-EBITDA ratio had been below 30% on flotation day. And as the quarterly results to June showed too well, eDreams had gone ex-growth at the time when its management and PE owners had been preparing their exit.

It was not a great start for the newly quoted group, but it was about to get awkward for all parties involved. On Friday 24 October, now a bit more than six months after its IPO, the company confirmed that some ticket sales had been halted. Iberia and British Airways had decided to withdraw tickets from several of the company's websites, in particular in France and Spain, as their commercial negotiations with ODIGEO regarding price transparency had hit a roadblock. The share price of the online travel group lost more than 59% on the day to €1.02 – a fall worthy of the dotcom crash days of 2000. Trading had to be suspended by the CNMV, the Spanish stock exchange regulator.[58] The stock now stood 90% below its listing price. The company's high-yield notes fell by 57% on the same day.

Yet it was a temporary glitch. No doubt realising that a group trading on a public stock exchange cannot afford to play hardball with suppliers, especially when those have the bargaining power of international airlines, ODIGEO's management agreed to clearly state the full cost, including fees, of tickets sold on its sites. The 10.375% bonds almost fully recovered the following trading day when the two airlines reinstated their tickets, and so did the stock, up 50% on Monday 27 October, after having been re-admitted by the market authorities.[59] Though eDreams condemned the two airlines' behaviour as a trick to negotiate better terms in their ongoing discussions, on Tuesday 28 October low-cost airline Ryanair opportunistically chose to pile on the pressure by backing British Airways and Iberia's view of the online travel agency's evasive pricing practices.[60]

ODIGEO hardly had time to clear one hurdle before another presented itself. On 25 November, its management presented the first-half (to September 2014) results, showing that bookings were down 1% on the prior year, revenue margin was up 2.4% but had fallen 1% in the flight division, which accounted for four-fifths of the group's revenue margin. In its three core markets, namely France, Spain and Italy, the group had failed to grow revenue margin. Consolidated EBITDA sat at €46 million, from €62 million in the previous year's first half, keeping margin stubbornly around 21%. The decline was attributed to a number of factors including higher merchant costs, changes to a Google algorithm resulting in higher acquisition costs per booking, as well as higher call centre costs – just about everything under the Spanish sun was seemingly to blame.

It was now evident that the growth story much vaunted at the time of the IPO had been misleading. With very little room to fall further, the stock only shed 5.75% on the day of the announcement to close at €1.64, granting ODIGEO a market capitalisation of €170 million and an enterprise value of half a billion euros, two-thirds down from its listing day. Struggling to keep pace with the group's worsening performance and its stock's dip, equity analysts issued their now standard downgrades, with JPMorgan recommending the stock at €4 a share on 26 November while Jefferies issued a more pessimist target of €2.35 two days later.[61] Sensing trouble, on 1 December Moody's decided to change its outlook again, moving from stable to negative. Justifying its stance, the agency stated that eDreams ODIGEO's results presentation had showed a double-digit plunge in earnings for the second quarter in a row.[62]

Emergency procedures

The following year did not start well for the Spanish group as, on 8 January 2015, the Court of Hamburg issued a judgement preventing eDreams from using a subdomain that included the Ryanair name (ryanair.edreams.de).[63] It was just part of the Irish low-cost airline's ongoing battle against screenscrapers across Europe. After a disastrous second half of 2014, ODIGEO's board of directors and controlling PE shareholders Permira and Ardian knew that they needed to make some drastic changes if they wanted to rebuild their reputation. So, on 26 January 2015, they went through a well-needed management substitution, elevating COO Dana Dunne to the CEO position as co-founder Pérez-Tenessa took a humbling bow after 15 years at the helm. A former chief exec of AOL Europe and chief commercial officer of low-cost airline easyJet, Dunne had joined three years earlier to bring some discipline to the group's fast-expanding operations.[64] Through some deft manoeuvring and a bit of luck, perhaps the new boss could put the business back on the right path.

Due to the significant underperformance against budget, the group's financial position was becoming an issue – the leverage ratio was creeping up as earnings wore away. Within a month of Dunne's promotion, the company issued its results for the quarter ended 31 December 2014, confirming that growth had become marginal in the core flight activity and in the main southern European countries, where it generated most of its trade. EBITDA was down 27% year-on-year, pushing margin to a record low of 19%.[65] As problems never arise in isolation, now that the group was stuck with its 'double Luxco' structure for the foreseeable future, given that its PE owners could not possibly sell their equity stakes at the prevailing discounted market price, ODIGEO's management started getting involved in organisational matters rather than strategic ones. The Luxembourg-based tax structure that had been set up upon the formation of ODIGEO in early 2011 was due to provoke a tax leakage of €4.5 million per year. So, in the second week of March, the group obtained consent to amend restrictive covenants related to its 7.5% senior secured notes due 2018 and the 10.375% senior notes due 2019.

To give itself more room to manoeuvre, make potential acquisitions, and lead a well-needed restructuring, or to use management's own terminology "to improve the tax efficiency of certain of the intra-group financing arrangements", ODIGEO received approval from the lender group to loosen its covenant of the net debt cover (net-debt-to-EBITDA ratio) from 5.50-to-1 to 6.00-to-1 for the period ending 31 December 2015.[66] Strategic vision had been replaced with operational and tax restructuring. The next set of financial results showed why it was needed.

On 22 June 2015, the company released its full-year numbers. More than 16 million customers and 9.7 million bookings had been served in the year ended 31 March 2015, the group had recorded €436 million of revenue margin – up 1.7% on the prior year – but only €90 million of adjusted EBITDA, down by a quarter year-on-year. EBITDA margin had fallen to less than 21%, its lowest full-year figure since the merger, and a full 10% below the margin achieved in the year ended 31 March 2012, as Figure 13.2 demonstrates. Following the slump in earnings, leverage had risen to 3.63 times from 2.98 times at the previous year end. Revenue margin for its core 'flight' business was flat on the previous year. Growth had come entirely from car rentals, cruises and hotel reservations.[67]

The change in leadership earlier in the year had given management an opportunity to come clean about the desperate situation, admitting what the markets already knew: the business wasn't worth what they had been told. ODIGEO booked goodwill impairment totalling €149 million and wrote €29 million off the GO Voyages brand, almost half of the French entity's brand book value. The exceptional amortisation of goodwill had been recorded to acknowledge that the core markets of France and Italy and the other large European markets of Germany, the Nordics and the UK did not offer the sort of growth prospects previously expected. Reporting a negative EBIT of €125 million compared to a positive €44 million the previous year, management could only watch as the shorts made a comeback, beating down the stock.[68] Shares of the afflicted group lost 11.3% on the day of the announcement, closing at €2.75. Equity analysts faithfully did what they do best, acknowledging reality by reducing their target price to €3.80 at JPMorgan and €2.90 at Deutsche Bank.[69]

Within a year of its stock offering, ODIGEO had suffered more bad news than during its entire 15-year history. After announcing one set of weak results after another, the PE-controlled travel group had introduced the typical management changes. But it would take months if not years to regain trust from the markets. Management had been chippy when the stock had flopped following the first post-IPO investor presentation. But the markets had read the script perfectly, punishing management and the financial sponsors via extreme share price volatility for having overpromised and under-delivered.

Figure 13.2: eDreams ODIGEO's performance in financial years ended 31 March 2012 to 2015

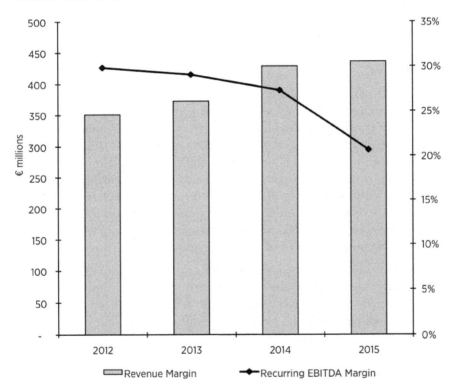

Source: Company accounts and author's analysis

Great trips start with great prices

eDreams ODIGEO flamed out shortly after its IPO, but it shouldn't have been such a surprise for those who had done their due diligence. It is true that the group had built a reputation as a growth company, riding the wave of online migration for flight bookings throughout the noughties. But several factors had severely weakened the organic growth potential of the business:

1. eDreams and its dotcom era companions had been formidable disrupters to the travel agency sector, and eventually to the entire holiday reservations value chain. By 2012 the share of online travel agencies already exceeded 50% of the Spanish market according to ODIGEO's own estimates,[70] and about 40% of gross bookings across Europe,[71] therefore the future pace of revenue gains would logically taper off.

2. The fantastic growth engine of online migration had slowed down because, by 2013-14, in many western and northern European countries already two-thirds of consumers were buying their airline tickets online – in 2006, only 15% of air travellers in the southern European markets were doing so.[72]

3. Over time airlines fought back, either through legal means like Ryanair, or by developing their own websites and international alliances (such as SkyTeam or Oneworld), to encourage passengers to book directly with them (tickets booked through online screenscrapers often did not earn frequent traveller rewards).

4. Many travellers using screenscrapers had negative experiences with these websites and chose to book directly with the airlines or through traditional travel agents.

5. eDreams already had a dominant position in some of its core markets. In Spain and Italy, it reportedly held a 36% market share in December 2011.[73] Further expansion was likely to come at the expense of profitability due to pricing pressure.

6. As management admitted when it announced its first post-IPO results, competition had become ferocious, putting pressure on growth and margins. It wasn't just airlines and traditional agencies that competed directly but new sites called 'metasearch engines', providing internet users with fare aggregation on a broader scale, including in their search not just airlines but all the screenscrapers as well. An estimated

40% of millennials were using metasearch to source their travel.[74] It was one of the motivations behind ODIGEO's purchase of Liligo in 2013, the latter having metasearch capabilities. In addition, the three big American rivals (Expedia, Orbitz and Priceline) had leveraged their robust market position across the Atlantic to fight a price war in Europe; they had driven the consolidation game, with Priceline buying metasearch Kayak for $1.8 billion in November 2012, Expedia taking over metasearch Trivago for $632 million in early 2013 and even gobbling up Orbitz for $1.34 billion in February 2015. The latter already owned eBookers, a key competitor of eDreams in Europe. Closer to home, in recent years Bravofly had matched eDreams's consolidation efforts by incorporating Italian OTA Volagratis, Spain's Rumbo and Viajar.com, and the UK's Lastminute under one roof. Thus, when eDreams commenced trading on the Madrid exchange, the online travel sector had become much more competitive and external growth opportunities less compelling.

7. Management was a bit unfortunate in its choice of geographic focus. The three core economies representing more than 60% of ODIGEO's revenue, namely France, Spain and Italy, had been on a downhill slope ever since the financial crisis. Other regions like the UK, Germany and Nordics offered better prospects but were not able to compensate for the drag exercised by the southern European region.

For all these reasons, a business that had grown at triple-digit rates during its early-stage phase – when backed by venture capitalists – and at a double-digit pace when under the ownership of TA Associates (from 2006 to 2010), was only growing at low single-digit numbers after its merger with GO Voyages and Opodo. This is what the public was buying at the time of the IPO: a low-growth business.

* * *

The information on eDreams's recent performance included in the April 2014 IPO prospectus was so strangely reported that it was enough to befuddle the typical stock dabbler. The consolidated numbers for the year to 31 March 2012 only included nine months of Opodo's results. So when the group was showing in its listing document gross bookings up 13% and revenue margin and EBITDA both up 17% year-on-year in the 12 months to March 2013, that statement was not comparing like with like. Instead, what could be gathered by reading pages 71 to 74 of the prospectus is that, in the year to March 2013, on an aggregated basis (i.e., including all acquired entities for a full year of operation, as one should), gross bookings had only grown 2.8%, while revenue, revenue margin and recurring EBITDA had risen 1.4%, 6.3% and 1%. The prospectus meekly spoke of "limitations on comparability" to justify the puzzling statements.

Figure 13.3: eDreams ODIGEO's share price from IPO (8 April 2014) to 31 December 2015

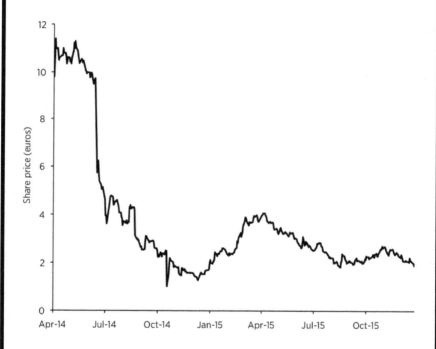

Going back to the point about the limited upside at ODIGEO, according to the same offering memorandum revenue growth for the nine months ended 31 December 2013 (the most recent period of reporting before the IPO) had been nil when compared to the same period of the previous year, operating profit was down 10% on the prior year, and net cash from operating activities had seen an outflow of €13 million compared to an inflow of €16 million in the April-to-December 2012 period. Recurring EBITDA margin had fallen from 30% in the last three-quarters of calendar year 2012 to 28.5% in the same period of 2013 – it would sink to 27.5% by March 2014 and 20% a year later. These were not trends typically associated with fast-growth enterprises, and an enterprise value of 12.8 times EBITDA on IPO day failed to reflect that fact. As often in PE-backed flotations, prospects for the underlying business had been exaggerated. The travel company's advertising slogan used to read: "Great trips start with great prices." That would explain why the public investor's journey turned sour very quickly. They certainly hadn't got a bargain when they made the fatal mistake of buying eDreams ODIGEO shares. As Figure 13.3 shows, they paid the price in more ways than one.

When a duck is actually a duck

Any sector that uses intermediaries, where a direct connection between supplier and user would do perfectly, often comes under fire. No doubt, travel agencies had for many years played a key role to make sure that tourists, for a fee, were given a chance to compare fares between airlines and between hotels. In the process, it is equally certain that many intermediaries took advantage of the imperfect information distribution to charge a premium for their service. When the internet provided newcomers with the opportunity to offer flight and hotel comparison very efficiently without having to spend much time with the consumer, giving instant (and almost complete) information on the products available, it was progress. Unfortunately, the way the data was compiled soon raised issues among airlines. The British Airways/Iberia incident so soon after ODIGEO's IPO may look like bad luck, but eDreams (and its online peers) had been wrestling with the airlines for years.

I have mentioned the case of Ryanair because the Irish airline was the most vocal in its opposition to what it splendidly dubbed 'screenscrapers'. The latter crawled through airline websites using automated software programmes and resold flight tickets to the consumer. Although the process still gave the airlines full face value for the tickets sold that way, it did two things that infuriated the likes of Ryanair: it gave screenscrapers a chance to charge a handling fee that often increased the cost of a ticket by 10% to 15%, thereby hurting the traveller. But more importantly, by seeing their customers use third-party websites, airlines were losing the direct relationship with passengers – for some airlines two out of five bookings come from scrapers.[75] It restricted the ability to market directly and to encourage frequent travellers to use their airline rather than the competition.

Ryanair litigated across most jurisdictions where it operated, including against various sites of the eDreams ODIGEO group. Rival low-cost airline easyJet grumbled about the loss of control over the sales channel and argued that, once ancillary fees were added, the discounts applied by aggregators were fictitious

– in June 2013 it called on regulators to stop eDreams using misleading tactics to win customers. Even flag carriers had been in a tug of war with these OTAs. Spanish national airline Iberia complained about their unfair practices and Air France took eDreams to the Paris commercial court to make it stop its crafty practices. In May 2015, Delta Airlines unilaterally withdrew its data from several third-party booking sites.[76]

But that's looking at it from the airlines' point of view. What about travellers, how did they fare when booking through eDreams, any of the group's other websites, or OTAs in general? A look through any travel blog gives an idea of the lack of customer-service culture among many of these intermediaries. It is easy to understand why the airlines were not fans of online aggregators: it was adding an intermediate stage to the supply chain. However, for the consumer, in principle using scrapers allowed the widest possible search to compare in one place hundreds of fares to the same destination. In addition, it provided options for hotel stays, car hire and travel insurance products. For sites like eDreams, although flights accounted for 80% of revenue, these cross-selling opportunities were high-margin items. Thus, the websites offered convenience at a cost. Unfortunately, over the years too many travellers appear to have experienced a fair amount of bad luck, from double-charging to ancillary fees to the lack of terms and conditions normally associated with flight and hotel reservations as far as cancellations and delays were concerned. All of ODIGEO's sites – eDreams, GO Voyages, Opodo and Travellink – faced countless complaints on travel forums and were warned against by the website TripAdvisor, a very popular resource among travellers.[77]

The moral of this story is that when a company mishandles its suppliers (the airlines) and allegedly rips off its customers (the travellers), only a very brave person (or one using other people's money) would choose to invest in such a company without fear of being hurt in the process. Public shareholders must feel aggrieved, but they have themselves to blame. As the saying goes: if it looks like a duck, walks/swims/quacks like a duck, then it's a duck!

Running out of runway

There is further evidence that, although the financial sponsors and management were trying very hard to sell a growth story, facts spoke louder than words.

IPOs are usually a way for corporations to raise fresh capital in order to fund expansion projects or acquisitions. It is one of the most effective means to call upon growth funds. As we saw, ODIGEO's public stock offering intended to raise €50 million in fresh capital. A *Bloomberg* article assumed that the capital was to be used to make further acquisitions.[78] Instead, the company spent more than 90% of the capital raised to pay down part of its loans due 2019. Approximately 25.5 million of the 36.7 million shares made available to the public were sold by the two financial sponsors and another 6.5 million was sold by ODIGEO's management and employees. Thus, the float was a liquidity event for the owners, it was not to raise money to finance growth. After four years in charge, the PE firms wanted out, and because the business was already on its tertiary buyout and was a market leader, it was unlikely to provide the type of buy-and-build opportunity attractive to other financial sponsors. An IPO was the ideal way to offload a business offering single-digit growth prospects (at best). Naturally, prospective investors should have paid more attention to the small print – a recommendation that can also be made to users of online travel agencies' services.

With more than 16 million customers in 44 countries worldwide in late 2015, the group had established itself as a strong participant in many parts of the world. Observers might therefore suggest that there were little growth opportunities left and that it would have been fruitless for management to raise significant cash since there were few acquisition opportunities left. There are counterarguments to this view.

First, ODIGEO derived 80% of its sales from airline tickets. This compares with 8% at Expedia and 28% at Orbitz. Based on bookings and revenue, ODIGEO was a tenth of Expedia's size.[79] So there definitely was room for growth. It just wasn't in the flight division, where the Spanish group focused its international expansion, but in hotels, car rentals, cruises, trains, buses, and even insurance products. In fact, the non-flight activities were the only ones showing organic growth with the group in the 2014 and 2015 fiscal years. Second, although ODIGEO had a meaningful presence in Europe, its competitive position in the rest of the world was weak. It would therefore have been logical for the public offering to bring in fresh capital to acquire strong local brands in large emerging and developed markets. Instead, eDreams organically launched sites in Russia and Japan in 2014 and 2015 respectively. Third, the travel group had a focus on consumers. Corporate clients, though more demanding, frequently offer higher-margin prospects. Raising significant funding through the IPO could have helped to finance a more professional, service-oriented organisation.

This seeming lack of acquisitive ambition on the part of ODIGEO's management might have been due to a common shortcoming of founder-led companies. While a visionary founder is great to run a start-up through its growth phase, if necessary by flouting regulations and archaic business practices, there comes a time when the company is established and must respect the stakeholders on which its very success depends: suppliers, customers and regulators. At that stage, the mature company needs an operator, someone capable of handling large, complex acquisitions, processes and systems; someone like Dunne who had worked in an executive position at airline easyJet before joining ODIGEO as COO.

By 2014 the group's operations had all the characteristics of a mature business, following with uncanny regularity the 80/20 rule so common in established organisations – 80% of revenue margin came from 20% of the online travel company's websites; 80% of revenue margin came from flights (one of five main product categories alongside hotels, cars, cruises and holidays); 80% of revenue was derived from consumers and 20% from corporate clients; and based on the geographic revenue breakdown, 20% of the countries covered accounted for 80% to 90% of the top line.[80] If the company publicly disclosed the proportion of sales derived from the top 20% of the 60,000 flight routes and 440 airlines it served, the rule would probably also have applied.[81] Again, this is a hallmark of maturing companies; most start-ups only have one or two products and cover one or two markets; they therefore derive not far from 100% of turnover from one category. A business following the 80/20 rule needs an operator, a controller, a manager; an early-stage enterprise needs a visionary, an innovator, a networker, a motivator. Dunne's appointment was in the natural order of things. It is in the ordinary course of business for founders eventually to step down.

When two come along at once

As observed, the Switzerland-based Bravofly Rumbo Group followed a similar market consolidation approach to ODIGEO's. By 2013 it boasted over €1 billion in gross bookings, 4.5 million passengers, €123 million in revenues and €23 million in EBITDA. Strangely enough, in a classic parody, within one week of ODIGEO's float, Bravofly elected to list on the SIX Swiss Exchange.

Priced at CHF48 a share for a total EV of CHF700 million (€575 million), Bravofly started life as a public company on 15 April 2014 at a stratospheric 25 times EBITDA multiple. Even if the full-year 2013 EBITDA of €6.5 million for its recently acquired French metasearch site Jetcost had been included, the EBITDA multiple at the time of IPO would have reached 19.6 times.[82] Here is what happened to the group's share price shortly after the float: within a week it was down 10%; after two months and a bit it had lost a quarter of its value; a week after that it was down 35%; and after three-and-a-half months it had halved. After four months, it had lost 60%, while after six months it was two-thirds off. Even its $120 million acquisition of the troubled British OTA Lastminute, in early 2015, failed to inspire the public markets. When the consolidated business, renamed Lastminute.com Group, issued its 2014 financial results in late March 2015, EBITDA was down 7% on the prior year.[83] With a share price sitting at CHF16, an implied market cap of €185 million and an enterprise value of €96 million, the Swiss company now sanctioned a bargain-basement multiple below five times EBITDA. As Figure 13.4 illustrates, the Lastminute.com Group only fared marginally better than eDreams ODIGEO.

Figure 13.4: eDreams's and Bravofly's indexed share prices from 15 April 2014 to 31 December 2015

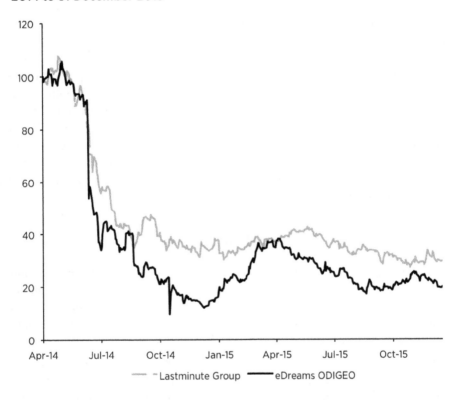

It could be seen as a vindication that financial sponsors are not the only ones who overvalue their portfolio companies on exit. While undoubtedly true, in the case of the Bravofly/Lastminute.com Group, one of the key shareholders was one of eDreams ODIGEO's own PE owners, Ardian. The latter had been an investor since July 2010, providing funding in 2012 for Bravofly's acquisition of Rumbo, one of eDreams's main rivals in Spain. Given their hapless situation, maybe the two largest OTA groups in Europe could eventually devise a merger of equals.

Emergency evacuation

ODIGEO recorded one of the most spectacular post-IPO crashes of a PE-backed company. Its public stock offering had been the largest in Spain in three years, since the listing of Bankia, the country's fourth largest lender, in July 2011. Back then, Bankia had the very bad idea of seeking a €4 billion listing on the Madrid Stock Exchange despite its weak fundamentals and overexposure to the Spanish real estate sector. Apparently, international appetite had been so lukewarm for the float of that financial institution – formed the year before via the merger of seven savings banks – that 98% of the shares were sold to domestic investors. By May of the following year, the Spanish Government had been forced to bail out and partly nationalise Bankia through a €20 billion recapitalisation, or the equivalent of 2% of Spain's GDP. In the process, Bankia restated its 2011 financial results from a net profit of €309 million to a net loss of €3 billion (no doubt due to a rounding error). A year after commencing trading on the Madrid exchange, the bank's stock was more than 80% down.[84]

So it is fair to claim that ODIGEO's float in the spring of 2014 could be considered a fresh attempt to rebuild public confidence in the stock markets. Entrusting PE firms with such a task was probably a wee bit naïve. It was reportedly the first ever IPO of an internet start-up in Spain. Of direct significance to the group's individual shareholders is that the PE owners and management had also seen the value of their equity tumble, but based on the number of shares they had disposed of in the offering, Permira and Ardian had already drawn proceeds of €159 million and €102 million respectively, co-founder and CEO Pérez-Tenessa had bagged €9.83 million (in addition to the takings received for his shares sold at the time of the Permira LBO), while other senior managers had taken home over €6.5 million.[85] They could all very well sell the remaining shares at a deep discount to the IPO price and come out on top. The only move that could save the day for the online travel group's public shareholders would be a bid from Expedia or another competitor. Whether they will be prepared to pay the €10.25 a share at which the group was floated is another story.

All things considered, financially the outcome wasn't too bad for Permira and Ardian and their track record in Spain. But the British investment firm and the French secondary specialist could consider themselves lucky, as Spain is not a country where PE investors are highly regarded, nor their brash practices readily accepted. For proof, consider the decision in December 2014 by the bankruptcy administrators of tour operator Orizonia to declare the latter's owners, including its 55% shareholder The Carlyle Group, responsible for the demise of the travel specialist. Alongside British mezzanine expert Intermediate Capital Group (with a 5% stake) and local outfit, 36% owner Vista Capital, Carlyle controlled

Orizonia until its collapse in February 2013, at which point the financial sponsors elected to pull the plug on the business, unable to rearrange the capital structure or find a buyer for the debt-laden company.

Carlyle and Vista – the PE unit of national bank Santander – had bought Orizonia in 2006 for around €850 million from Spanish hotel, airline and tour operator Iberostar. Financed with 81.5% of LBO loans, the target included three divisions: wholesale travel company Iberojet, travel agent Viajes Iberia and airline Iberworld. With Spain sustaining one of the fiercest economic recessions in its history in the aftermath of the Credit Crunch – the country's GDP per capita lost 18.5% between 2008 and 2012 – tourism and leisure had become discretionary spending for consumers (unless you could save a bundle by booking online through eDreams, naturally).

It couldn't be argued that the deal champion did not know the travel sector given that his name was Pedro de Esteban, the head of Carlyle in Spain since joining the firm in April 2001 and, as you might recall, a former chairman of eDreams during its start-up days. Another member of Carlyle's deal team was Alex Wagenberg, a former CFO of eDreams. The two of them knew the tourism industry inside out. The problem is that Orizonia, the largest tour operator in the country with 5,000 employees and 8 million customers, had racked up €476 million in debt-related interest expenses between 2006 and the year before it was put to rest. With cumulative operating income of only €234 million over the same period, Orizonia had nowhere to hide but behind bankruptcy administrators. It was those same administrators who declared the PE owners' responsibility in the group's insolvency, and requested that Vista, ICG and Carlyle pay €159 million in indemnity to those employees who lost their jobs as part of the liquidation process.[86] By comparison, the eDreams ODIGEO adventure was a pleasure cruise, at least for its PE backers.

CHAPTER 14
Foxtons – Timing the Market

I N 1981, AFTER WORKING FOR EIGHT YEARS AS AN ESTATE agent, Jonathan Hunt, aged 28, set up shop in the then run-down but charming neighbourhood of Notting Hill, central London. To give it a distinctive cachet, Hunt named his business Foxtons, after the village of Foxton in Cambridgeshire, 60 miles north of London.[1] Located near Notting Hill Gate tube station, the agency traded from a former pasta restaurant in the royal borough of Kensington and Chelsea, one of the most affluent and fashionable areas of the British capital, focusing at the time exclusively on property sales, a higher-margin service than lettings. These were the early years of Thatcher's Government, when entrepreneurship and initiative were the new buzzwords. But the country was also experiencing a deep recession. Times were difficult for all sectors of the economy; property was no exception. Hunt compensated by offering temporary discounts on commissions and working more aggressively and longer hours than the competition: a surprisingly easy feat in the indolent, sleepy world of property brokerage of the times.

Benefitting from the economic recovery finally taking hold, over the ensuing five years Foxtons opened two more agencies, in the London districts of Fulham and South Kensington. Determined to set himself apart by opening weekends and evenings, and by charging sellers a 3% fee – double many of his rivals' rates – Hunt earned a reputation for getting sellers a better price than his competitors could. Despite a temporary blip during the early 1990s recession, the company continued to expand. Hunt was careful to select locations in better-off neighbourhoods. By the late 1990s, he had established outposts in areas favoured by the young professionals and well-heeled families: Chiswick, Putney, Hampstead, St John's Wood, Islington and Park Lane were on the list.

With the noughties starting as strong as the 1990s had ended, expansion continued, together with a noticeable effort to make Foxtons a premium brand in the traditionally fragmented, undifferentiated universe of estate agents. In 2001, Hunt introduced the first branded cars, driven around town by his devoted sales and lettings staff (the Foxtons Minis, as they became known), and the following year he launched the concept of café-style branches. Both ideas would be widely and unashamedly copied by rivals. With such strong expansion and focus on high-end niches, Foxtons blossomed. In the fiscal year 2005, it turned over £72 million and delivered pre-tax profits of £13 million.

For sale

The reputation of property brokers is analogous across the world, no matter what country you happen to live in. Untrustworthy, sharp-suited, sharp-elbowed profiteers who are after a quick-buck are some of the kinder words you can find in the press and consumer surveys. In Britain, their underhand tactics go from flyboarding (placing 'for sale' and 'for let' signs outside houses that are not actually available as a mean of cheap advertising), to Chinese whispers (information such as lower-end offers that never get delivered to the vendor if the agent feels he or she can make more money from a higher offer even if it takes several weeks or months to achieve), to gazumping (when a seller's agent accepts an oral offer of the asking price from one potential purchaser, but then welcomes a higher bid from another, or simply raises the price at the last minute when the interested buyer has already incurred survey costs or legal fees). In a trade where, in many countries, a professional qualification is not required to set up shop and, more broadly, consumer protection is an oxymoron (how else could you explain the noughties subprime bubble in the US?), there is only one way to succeed: you have to abide by the industry's sole commandment, which states that 'a sale is a sale'.

In this context, Foxtons understandably had its fair share of controversy over the years. Its robust sales techniques soon caught the attention of journalists (who themselves know a thing or two about pushy behaviour). One particular gripe expressed against Foxtons was its close relationship with mortgage broker Alexander Hall, also owned by Jon Hunt. A BBC undercover programme aired in 2006 alleged that the company used confidential information gleaned from Alexander Hall to find out the financial status of buyers.[2] Despite the polemic, by early 2007 Foxtons had 19 offices in London and one in neighbouring Surrey. It employed 1,300 people and was seen as a prominent and dominant player in the most profitable real-estate market in Britain: London. Thanks to a big push in mortgage financing from all major lenders since the mid-1990s, the UK had experienced 13 years of uninterrupted economic growth; house prices, on which estate agents like Foxtons charge their commissions, had gone through the roof. Between January 1995 and March 2007, residential property prices in the British capital had risen at a compound annual growth rate of 11%.[3]

In the months preceding the 2005 general election campaign, Chancellor of the Exchequer (later Prime Minister) Gordon Brown boasted that under his stewardship the country had experienced the longest period of prosperity for 200 years. By now house prices in London, and in pretty much every part of the world, were defying gravity. Understandably, Foxtons had thrived in this bullish environment. In 2006 its turnover exceeded £104 million, representing a growth rate of more than 40% on the prior year. Revenues almost quadrupled between 1999 and 2006, as shown on Figure 14.1.[4] In the past three years, EBIT margins had recovered well from their slump after the dotcom crash and from the increase in operating expenses incurred to open new branches. Hunt, a man who knew a great deal about economic cycles, after having managed to scrape through the early 1980s and early 1990s recessions and property slumps, decided that he wanted to cash in while the going was still good. In early 2007, he put a sale sign outside his own business and waited for prospective buyers.

Figure 14.1: Foxtons's turnover and EBIT margin (1999-2006)

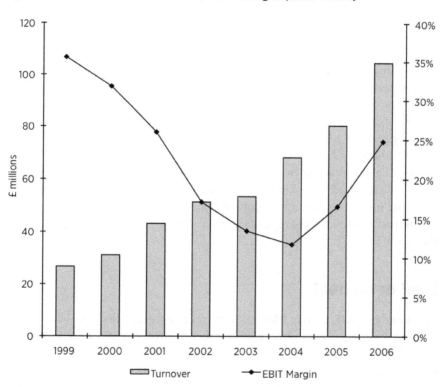

Source: Company accounts and author's analysis

There were reports that Hunt's advisers Credit Suisse were running a dual-track process by drumming up interest in the IPO market, but in an environment where the availability of bank debt had gone mainstream, this manoeuvre was seen as the best way to flush out potential bidders. Promptly, the shortlist of parties included three financial sponsors: American outfit TA Associates and two of Britain's largest players, 3i and BC Partners.[5]

BC Partners was born in 1986 as Baring Capital Investors, one of British merchant bank Baring's numerous venture capital activities. When Barings Bank collapsed in 1995 following fraudulent investments by Nick Leeson, one of its traders in Singapore, the bank's activities were spun off and Baring Capital was renamed BC Partners, not least to avoid being tarnished by the reputation that the Baring name had earned from the Leeson scandal. By the time its investment team was sniffing around Foxtons ten years later, BC had become specialised in very large transactions and was under the chairmanship of Simon Palley, a former management consultant and investment banker who had earned his MBA from the Wharton School. BC Partners was one of the most active PE investors in Europe, and its latest vintage BC European Capital VIII had filled up in 2005 with over €5.5 billion.

Recent investments included Intelsat, the world's premier provider of fixed satellite services with an enterprise value of $16.6 billion, Brenntag (a German chemicals distributor with revenue of €6 billion), Spain's travel distribution system operator Amadeus (mentioned in Chapter 13), valued at €4.3 billion, leisure products provider Dometic of Sweden, with sales of SEK 7 billion, Picard Surgelés in France, bought for €1.3 billion, Italy's business directory Seat Pagine Gialle (reviewed in Chapter 12), worth €5.65 billion, and Germany's Unity Media, a cable provider to millions of households.[6] Observers pointed out that, for these guys, a £50 million equity ticket to back Foxtons's buyout was pocket money: about 1% of their latest vintage. Was it even worth leaving the house for it?

Deal or no deal

Apparently, it was. In late May 2007 it was announced that BC had won the auction, tabling a rumoured performance-contingent bid of £360 million to £390 million, and making Hunt a very rich man. Controlling over 90% of the company he had founded 26 years earlier, he was walking away with £300 million, plus a £50 million shareholder loan repayable based on future performance. At the time, most commentators believed that if Hunt, a well-plugged-in property entrepreneur, was selling, it was likely a sign that house prices had peaked. A strong argument supporting this view was that on 10

May, 12 days before BC Partners signed the deal, the Bank of England had raised interest rates another 25 basis points to 5.50% and was rumoured to be considering another 25 bps increase at its next monetary policy meeting. The further central bank rates rose, the more pressure house prices would come under due to the rising cost of a mortgage. Also, the average value of a London property had multiplied by a factor of 3.5, from £91,947 to £321,380, over the last 12 years.[7] Wasn't a correction overdue?

Unbeknown to BC and the two mandated lead arrangers in charge of the deal's debt finance, Bank of America and Japan's Mizuho, a storm was brewing in the international banking markets, and first and foremost in the US property sector. Since 2000, through a process called securitisation, a vast number of illiquid assets (in particular mortgages) had been transformed into tradable securities. Termed residential mortgage-backed securities (RMBS) and commercial mortgage-backed securities (CMBS), these instruments' value had grown from less than $500 billion in 2000 to $2 trillion six years later. At the peak of the cycle, RMBS accounted for more than half of securitisation values worldwide.[8] But by mid-2007 the syndication process, on which the securitisation market depended, was becoming clogged up. The reason was simple: in the last few years, the quality of the securitised products issued by all major American mortgage brokers and lenders had seriously deteriorated. As in any gold rush, seeing that they could make more money on the commissions they were charging than on the gains they would make if they held onto these assets, brokers and lenders focused their attention on packaging new structured products (including non-prime ones) and on syndicating them to third parties. Given the sheer volume of new RMBS and CMBS issues, the syndication market was overwhelmed, and no longer able to absorb such large quantities of low-quality securities.

It is in this febrile climate that, in early July 2007, the two lenders to Foxtons's LBO went out with £170 million of senior debt and £70 million of mezzanine with the aim to syndicate these loans, a normal procedure for any leveraged transaction. However, the level of saturation in the US syndication markets was having ramifications worldwide. On 9 August, French bank BNP Paribas decided to freeze (that is, halt withdrawals from) three of its funds exposed to the US subprime mortgage market. The bank was unable to price the funds due to a sudden lack of liquidity.[9] That day the Credit Crunch took on a life of its own. Banks across the globe refused to put any more loans on their books. An immediate casualty of this tremor was British bank Northern Rock. A member of the FTSE 100 index and the third largest mortgage underwriter in the UK, the Newcastle-headquartered lender was a heavy user of securitisation for its mortgage book. Now unable to resell its loans to third parties, it was running out of liquidity. It had to be bailed out by the Bank of England on 14 September 2007.

With such upheaval in the debt markets, and despite the fairly reasonable debt-to-equity ratio of two-thirds/one-third, Bank of America and Mizuho got stuck with most of the Foxtons senior and mezzanine tranches.[10] If BC had managed to limit its exposure by only putting in the equivalent of 15% of Foxtons's enterprise value – the rest of the equity, as stated, was through a £50 million vendor loan from Hunt – the debt side of the deal appeared a tad aggressive at ten times trailing EBIT, especially given the intrinsic cyclicality of the property sector.

Home wrecked home

The next few months made it unquestionable that BC Partners had got its timing woefully wrong, quickly earning itself the nickname 'Bloody Crazy' Partners.[11] As the debt markets were getting squeezed, all the major developed economies, including Britain, experienced a dramatic slowdown.

Initially, the credit squeeze had a disastrous impact on the entire mortgage sector and, quite logically, on property transactions and prices, be it in the US, the UK or the rest of Europe. As we now know thanks to numerous official reports on the matter, one of the key explanations behind the US property market's rapid growth during the late 1990s and first half of the noughties is that the quality of mortgages had been lowered significantly in order to sate Wall Street's appetite for more tradable securities. In 2002 and 2003, the mortgage denial rate in the US had fallen to only 14% for conventional home purchase loans, half that of 1999.[12] As a consequence, total annual mortgage originations had swollen by a factor of 2.5 between 2000 and 2005, to reach $2.9 trillion. From 2002 to 2006, subprime mortgages (those with a high credit risk) underwritten in the US had trebled to $600 billion. Their share of total mortgage originations in the country had gone from 7.4% to 23.5%. These were the seeds of a true bubble: from 1995 to 2003 US house prices had risen by 91%. Boosted by low federal funds rates, the surge in subprime lending and the general endorsement of the securitisation process, home values had jumped a further 36% between early 2004 and their April 2006 peak.[13]

The bloodbath was likely to be extensive. Nevertheless, Foxtons's trading was not greatly shaped by the UK or world economy and property market. Primarily active in London, only the capital's local economy was likely to have a meaningful effect on its performance. On that front, the news wasn't good either. By January 2008, house transactions in the capital were down 39% year-on-year.[14] What would be the ramifications for Foxtons and its PE backer? A correction had been expected. With home prices up by double digits each year over the previous decade, it was common knowledge that household incomes had not grown anywhere near that number, so property values had been inflated by a steep increase in mortgage underwriting and the influx of foreign money in more recent years. What no one knew was how severe the market U-turn would be.

By March 2008, Foxtons's debt was trading at 50 pence on the pound.[15] Many property brokers across Britain were closing or scaling down. In June, Humberts, an agency based in the southeast of England and quoted on London's junior stock exchange AIM, suspended trading after its shares had dived 96%. It filed for bankruptcy that month. If anything, the housing market collapse was accelerating. By the summer, the much larger Savills, employing 17,000 people worldwide (4,000 of them in London), saw transactional volumes dip 45% on the prior year: its stock had lost 60% over 12 months. In August, Foxtons's mezzanine tranches were changing hands at 35 pence on the pound, indicating that few believed the company could continue to service its debt. Halifax Estate Agents were on track to close one-quarter of their branches while another competitor, Countrywide[*], which had gone through its own £1 billion LBO backed by US investor Apollo at the peak of the credit boom, was forecast to generate in 2008 half the revenue recorded the previous year; it had even started rolling up some of its loan interest payments to lighten the debt load.[16]

In this dire setting, only one year after the completion of the Foxtons LBO, Rothschild's restructuring experts were called in to look at strategic options and assess whether the group was in a position to meet onerous debt payments that totalled £26 million a year – equivalent to Foxtons's operating profits two years earlier. Unsurprisingly, trading and profitability had suffered since then. Property sales were down 50% to 70% in the first 12 months of trading post-LBO.[17] Another factor making the company's situation dicey is that, one year before selling his business, Jon Hunt had done a sale and leaseback on Foxtons's offices. Left with only £3 million worth of freehold property, the estate agency could not offer any meaningful asset-backed security to its lenders.[18] Eventually, in that summer of 2008 underwriters Bank of America and Mizuho hired their own adviser, British restructuring boutique Close Brothers. By the end of the year, as widely anticipated, Foxtons breached its loan covenants, and BC wrote down its investment to zero.[19]

The international picture was unremittingly gloomy. Between June 2006 and the first quarter of 2009 house prices in America had tumbled by a third.[20] In Britain, property sale volumes were down, though lettings were holding firmly across the country, including London. Since sales were a higher-margin activity, lettings were never going to fully compensate for the loss of activity. And sales

---

[*]. British estate agent Countrywide should not be confused with the American mortgage lender of the same name that got into trouble during the 2008 financial crisis. They are two distinct companies.

were getting hammered on two fronts: while transactions were down more than 50% in 2008, house prices had also nosedived. Between the first quarter of 2008 and the same period of 2009, London property values had fallen by 15%.[21] Foxtons, like all estate agents, charged a commission on the transaction value. As volumes and prices were both dropping, the impact on the company's revenue was magnified.

Discussions between BC Partners and the lending syndicate stalled for most of 2009. The PE house was reluctant to put more cash into the business unless Bank of America and Mizuho agreed to write off a £60 million-to-£90 million portion of their £260 million debt.[22] While entitled to do so following Foxtons's repeated covenant breaches, the lenders seemed hesitant to take ownership of the estate agent. As the two sides nursed an alternative plan, the British economy's distress intensified: GDP fell by 2.4% in the first quarter of 2009; a 4.9% drop over the previous 12 months. According to official figures, between the peak of the property cycle in mid-2007 and its trough two years later, residential home transactions in London as well as in the rest of England dived between 50% and two-thirds.[23]

The bottom had fallen out of the housing market. After a lengthy game of chicken with BC, in December 2009 Foxtons's bankers finally stepped in to claim over half of the firm via a debt-for-equity swap, writing their £300 million of loans and unpaid interest down to £120 million. The PE house retained a 31% minority stake in exchange for an additional £50 million cash injection. Management sat on a performance-related 12.5% holding.[24] As for Jon Hunt, he had to forfeit the £50 million shareholder loan he had granted BC as an incentive to sign the original LBO. Still, in all likelihood he was content to be moving on. By any performance measure, he had done well for himself. Across the table, BC had seen its 85% holding shrink, but it was better than the alternative: losing total ownership.

Back in October, Foxtons's precarious financial situation had made it impossible for its directors to file annual accounts with Companies House as is a requirement for all UK businesses to do within nine months of any tax year end.[25] As part of the filing, management needed to confirm that, in their view, the business was a going concern and would not default within 12 months. Without an undertaking from its debt-holders that they would not call on their loans as they were entitled to do, thereby risking to put the company in administration, Foxtons had waited till December to get clarity on its immediate future. And what a future it would turn out to be!

Home is where the heart is

By surrendering its majority stake in Foxtons, BC Partners was losing partial control of its ill-timed investment. Luckily, the combined equity ticket of £100 million was small-fry for BC. All its recent buyouts had been much larger, so the estate agency was on the small side and would not move the needle when assessing the LBO shop's overall performance. But given the timing of the purchase, it could still tarnish BC's image as a savvy investor. It was now clear that it had bought Foxtons at the height of the market.

To make matters worse, BC's chairman Simon Palley had abruptly left the firm in September 2007 – only four months after the Foxtons deal – amongst rumours that he disagreed with the seven other managing partners over the firm's leadership style.[26] Although at the time all parties had downplayed the rift, by 2010 Palley was to become chairman of PE firm Centerbridge Partners Europe, proving that despite his 17-year tenure at BC, he was not done with the sector just yet. Things could in fact have been worse for BC Partners. In view of his London success, in 1999 Hunt had started trading in the US, where seven offices in New York, New Jersey and Connecticut offered a discounted service to local realtors. By September 2007, Foxtons US had folded due to huge losses, liquidity concerns, and a sharp decline in the East Coast's home sales market.[27] Had the American offices been packaged together with the British business, it is likely that the LBO would have ended there and then.

Michael Brown, who had been appointed CEO upon Foxtons's acquisition by BC, was familiar with situations where the odds are somewhat stacked against you. Before joining Foxtons as chief operating officer in 2002, he had been European general counsel and COO of now infamous US energy trader Enron. Facing an equally challenging situation at the estate agent, Brown spent most of 2009 and 2010 lowering costs, shedding 300 jobs in 2009 alone. Growth plans had been put on hold. Brown also pushed the business hard to take advantage of resilient activity for lettings. While house sales had represented two-thirds of turnover in the go-go years, lettings accounted for half of revenue by 2010. But it was not just cost-cutting and strategic recalibration that would eventually enable Brown to turn the business around. Unexpectedly, the London market proved more resilient than the rest of the UK, not in terms of transactions or mortgage underwriting, which throughout 2010-12 remained obstinately 40% to 50% below the 2006 peak, but as far as valuations were concerned. Between April 2009 – the official nadir of the house price fall in the British capital – and December 2010, house values rose 13.5%. In 2011 they nudged up another 1%.[28]

As transaction values picked up, Brown took the initiative and opened new branches. Starting 2010 with a leaner headcount of 1,000, he recognised that his competitors' retrenchment or bankruptcies gave Foxtons the opportunity to expand at lower cost by taking over their leases and redundant staff. The number of branches reached 27 by September 2010 and 31 a year later – up from 24 in late 2009.[29] There was a simple explanation behind Brown's optimistic stance: since the second half of 2009 financial performance had perked up dramatically. The gain in house prices helped Foxtons to increase revenues by 15% in 2009 (not bad considering they had collapsed by one-quarter the previous year) and 5% in 2010. But the real impact was felt on the bottom line.

The reduction in overheads significantly improved the firm's operating leverage, with earnings jumping from breakeven in 2008 to £35 million 12 months later and a less exceptional but still respectable £31.5 million in 2010.[30] Thanks to a very thorough reorganisation exercise, Brown had made the company even more profitable than before the property crash. With house prices marginally up in 2011, Foxtons managed to record £32 million in operating profits and a 13% increase in turnover to £116 million. To keep generating cash and pay its debt down, management had not shied away from the usual PE-inspired cash-generative practices: that year, Foxtons's accounts let on that a £2 million sale-and-leaseback deal had been carried out on the group's fleet of 890 Mini Coopers.

With the business back on a firmer footing and the recovery of the housing market underway, BC Partners started discussions with Bank of America and Mizuho with the aim of buying back their equity stakes in Foxtons. Any investment firm would have told BC to dream on. But one characteristic of leveraged bankers is that they do not regard owning a majority holding in any business as a core activity (unless they run a captive fund, as we saw with Merrill Lynch Private Equity in the Debenhams case). Thus, even though divesting their equity in an estate agency at such an early stage of the housing market recovery could be considered somewhat untimely, in March 2012 both lenders agreed to sell their controlling stakes back to BC. For the latter it would prove a well-timed move, especially because published reports would later disclose that the arrangement had valued the company at a very reasonable £250 million.[31] By buying the lenders out, the LBO firm built its holding back up from 31% to 75%.

* * *

By 2012, home sales volumes had recovered slightly, but they remained 40% below the average volumes achieved during the period leading to the Credit Crunch. Again, to an estate agent almost exclusively targeting the prime and highly sought-after London region, property prices were more relevant. London and Surrey were certainly not the most affected by the subprime crisis. Their properties were respectively Britain's most expensive and third most expensive.[32]

Between the first quarter of 2009 and the same period of 2012, London's home values had risen by 20%. By comparison, price increases across Britain had not exceeded 10%. Most of the price movements recorded in the country-wide index had in reality been fed by the large upward shift in London values. In some parts of Britain, such as Yorkshire and Scotland, values were virtually flat.[33]

The brisk turnaround of the London property market and Foxtons's concomitant revival so soon after the outbreak of the financial crisis can be explained by a number of factors. One in particular helped the company and BC Partners to find salvation: the lowest interest rates in the Bank of England's 320-year history. Kept permanently low, they became Foxtons's guardian angel. When interest rates go down, the respective expected returns of all financial products, from stocks to corporate bonds, and from treasuries to property, tend to fall in unison. As investors look for higher-return assets like equities and real estate, these assets' valuations rise and their yields drop. Few would have predicted that, after reaching an all-time low of 0.5% in March 2009, the central bank rate would stay there for more than seven years, thereby protecting heavily mortgaged households and propping up house prices somewhat artificially.

Other factors played an important role. Foxtons's exclusive focus on super-affluent London was a blessing. Quite naturally for a financial centre that at times embodied all that is wrong with free markets, the capital city remained a haven for über-rich, non-domiciled tax exiles aiming to hide from their respective country's tax authorities, without having to pay taxes in the UK either on money earned from abroad. Business people and expatriates were equally keen to stash their savings in a relatively safer asset class when stock markets had once again turned out to be so unreliable. Research data revealed that most of the property-buying in the years post-financial crisis was being done by foreigners. The latter accounted for half to three-quarters of central London home purchases.[34] With a sweet spot for homes worth £200,000 to £1.2 million-plus, Foxtons was well positioned to capitalise on the bonanza.

Still, the year 2012 turned out to be one of transition for the London economy, and while house prices rose 4.9% that year, Foxtons's growth came primarily from the resilience of its lettings activities, which throughout the financial crisis consistently represented over half of its business. That year, turnover from lettings was up 5.5%, whereas sales revenue increased marginally by 1%. But BC Partners was not prepared to hang around too long before cashing in. It had been caught with its pants down once; the last thing it wanted was to lose its shirt next. By early 2013, the PE firm started planning its exit. Despite the tiny equity ticket at stake, Foxtons had gradually become an embarrassing investment. It was time to flog it. In March 2013, one of the estate agent's key rivals, Countrywide, had publicly listed after having undergone its own debt-for-equity exchange to the benefit of distressed specialists Oaktree and

Alchemy.[35] The float had been well received. Countrywide's stock had risen 13.5% on the first day.

It looked like the IPO window was opening up after years of remaining inaccessible. In 2011 and 2012, the number of IPOs taking place on the London Stock Exchange had fallen by one-fifth and 12% respectively. But in the fourth quarter of 2012, 22 companies had been introduced on the LSE, up from 14 the previous quarter. Thanks to the recovering British economy the pipeline for new floats looked stronger. BC was advised to take advantage of the upward trend. In June 2013, 15 months after winning back control of the asset, the buyout house appointed not one but three advisers to plan an introduction later in the year. On the face of it, it would not be an easy sale, even for a typically assertive estate agent. Between 2010 and 2012, the company's revenue had risen annually by 8%, but earnings had been flat, indicating that additional operating expenses had been incurred in order to generate top-line growth. Confirming that fact, public records would eventually point out that, after remaining steady between 2007 and 2009, the number of branches had reached 42 by June 2013, a doubling since the May 2007 buyout.[36]

Building capability had remained top of the agenda for CEO Brown, in spite of all the drama he had faced with his shareholders and lenders. This expansion was a clear sign that management and BC Partners were trying to drum up activity in the run-up to the listing. In the same vein, press reports emerged in the summer preceding the stock offering that, in order to gain market share, Foxtons had reintroduced 0% commission on homes it sold for three months in some of its newly opened London branches.[37]

That summer, London house prices sat 7% above their February 2008 level, the highest point reached before the financial crisis. Unlike in the US, Ireland, Spain and many other overpriced property markets, prices in London had never experienced much of a reversal, and house-hunting was now back with a vengeance. Foxtons continued to prosper: total revenue for the first six months of 2013 was up 10.5% year-on-year, and because property sales were finally doing much better than lettings (up 13% vs. 7%), the situation had translated into a 20% jump in operating earnings. Much of the boost in Foxtons's trading was also attributed to the British Government's schemes to kick-start house purchases, such as Funding for Lending, launched in July 2012, and the Help to Buy equity loan programme, spearheaded a year later, under which the state-subsidised mortgages by guaranteeing a portion to the bank, allowing borrowers to buy houses with as little as 5% down payment. Some at the time compared such schemes to state-sponsored subprime lending.[38]

Home run

After a smooth roadshow, the float was priced on 20 September 2013. The timing could hardly have been better: the month of July had recorded the biggest rise in house prices since 2006.[39] BC managed to offload a sizeable chunk of its stake in the company, reducing its holding from 75% to 22.3%. At a top-of-the-range 230 pence a share, the business had a frothy valuation of £650 million, or a forward price-earnings ratio of 18 times 2014 estimates. The company had been marketed as a prime asset due to its exclusive positioning in the well-to-do London and Surrey areas. It had benefitted from the surge in housing transactions and prices in central London but was trading at a 9% premium to its more geographically diverse peer Countrywide. Interestingly, and as a cautionary tale for retail investors, Foxtons was being marketed at a higher multiple than the already generous 15 times headline bid tabled by BC back in 2007. After such a roller coaster, the LBO house was getting a positive multiple-arbitrage!

The selling shareholders were raising a reported £390 million. Taking into account £55 million used to fully repay outstanding loans, BC yielded twice its total investment.[40] The financial sponsor's investment team, which in the early months of the subprime crisis admitted that the acquisition had been a mistake and internally referred to the portfolio company as the "F-word",[41] had shown its mettle. As for Chief Exec Brown, he was also making a few bob by halving his stake in the company to 8.8%. The lenders Bank of America and Mizuho had had a lucky escape. It is unlikely that in late 2009, when they had taken control of Foxtons, they could have foreseen that the property broker would recover so promptly and that they would recoup their money. No British bank had been willing to lend money to finance the buyout of Foxtons back in 2007, because all of them – Barclays, HBOS and Royal Bank of Scotland – had extensive high-street mortgage lending activities and were fully aware that the UK property market was overheating. Bank of America and Mizuho, both keen (some would say desperate) to gain market share in the trendy buyout sector, had fought over getting a piece of the action. As their loans had been fully repaid by the time Foxtons listed, they had somewhat preserved their reputations, a feat that would have seemed all but impossible four years earlier.

Following a vertiginous 74% ascent in the five months that followed the float, Foxtons's stock started a gradual but determined correction. Sadly for the punters who had bought in on the IPO marketing spiel (the issue had been seven times oversubscribed), the sagging share price was not helped by the announcement in early April 2014 that Michael Brown, who had made £52 million through the IPO, was taking compassionate leave, nor by a follow-on press release three months later that he had in fact decided to step down as CEO for personal reasons.[42] It was unfortunate. As recently as 11 March, as a result of exceptionally strong results during its 2013 fiscal year – and no doubt in a bid to entice investors and help to support the share price – Foxtons had announced the payment of a special dividend in addition to its final dividend. Four months later, it repeated the trick alongside the payment of its interim dividend.[43] In both cases, BC obviously benefitted from these special payouts, only to sell off on each occasion a meaningful portion of its holding shortly thereafter. Once again, BC's timing was impeccable. But the firm's follow-on disposals in May and September of that year, bringing its stake in the estate agent down from over 22% to 7%, did nothing to shore up confidence amongst public investors.

All the same, the killer blow came on 23 October 2014, just 13 months after the company's listing, when Foxtons announced a profit warning triggered by a "sharp and recent" slowdown in demand. In reality, mortgage approvals had experienced a slowdown since April, following the introduction by the UK's financial regulator of a stricter mortgage test for lenders. With an uncertain General Election looming, the second half of 2014 had also started to experience a slump in property values. Several political parties, from the Liberal Democrats to Labour to the Scottish National Party, had publicly voiced their intention, if elected, to introduce a mansion tax on properties worth north of £2 million. As most expensive properties, and certainly those above the £2 million tag, were located in London, Foxtons was a collateral victim. Its share price fell two-thirds from more than 400 pence on 28 February 2014 to less than 145 pence on 19 November of the same year.

As predictably as a London bus is soon followed by another, a second profit warning was issued in late January 2015. Swinging wildly in the first half of 2015, in the summer the stock stubbornly sat in a narrow range, within striking distance of its introductory price. When the uncertainty related to the General Election had cleared in early May and the pro-market Tories had unexpectedly won an outright majority, Foxtons's stock had shot up to 285 pence by the end of that month. The threat of a Labour or Liberal Democrat Government and the introduction of a mansion tax had suppressed activity in Britain's housing market since the start of the year. With those risks removed, investor sentiment had recovered.

Once more timing its exit perfectly, BC Partners racked up more than £53 million by selling its remaining 7% holding on 3 June 2015, four days after cashing in £1 million in special and final dividends. The sale marked the end of an eventful eight-year investment. The PE group had made cash-on-cash returns of more than three times. Between the IPO proceeds, the follow-on stake sales, the interim, final and special dividends, it was a conservative estimate. The British LBO firm had even bought Foxtons's loans at a discount in the secondary market after they had been savaged during the financial crisis. The move had helped BC to make up for part of its earlier losses.[44]

The archetype of exit timing

Reviewing the post-flotation timetable shows why it is not always a good idea to invest in a PE-backed IPO:

20 September 2013	Foxtons floats about 60% of its shares, at 18 times forward net earnings.
28 January 2014	Foxtons appoints Credit Suisse and Numis as joint corporate brokers. Both were bookrunners and sponsors alongside Canaccord on the IPO.
28 February 2014	The post-IPO pop peaks at 402.20 pence a share during the trading session.
7 March 2014	Numis rates Foxtons an 'Add' and mentions that the company might pay a special dividend.[45]
11 March 2014	Foxtons announces final and special dividends thanks to strong full year 2013 figures.
7 April 2014	CEO Michael Brown takes compassionate leave. In the following five trading days, the share price loses 9%.
30 April 2014	Shares go ex-div for both the final (1.70p a share) and special (3.74p) dividends. BC makes £3.4 million.
1 May 2014	BC Partners offloads 22 million shares at 312 pence per share or a 7.8% stake worth £68.6 million, retaining 14.5% of Foxtons.[46] The stock falls by more than 3% on the news. Ahead of the placing, Canaccord Genuity, one of the three lead banks co-managing Foxtons's IPO six months earlier, had issued a 'Buy' recommendation.
3 June 2014	The company announces that Brown is not coming back (though he remains involved as non-exec at the company's request). The share price drops 9.2% in two days. Both Numis and Canaccord issue positive notes regarding the handover to the company's COO.
8 July 2014	Credit Suisse issues a broker's note with an 'Outperform' recommendation on the stock.

27 August 2014	The company admits that, due to stricter mortgage rules and growing expectations of a rise in interest rates, housing demand will be slower in the second half of the year. Still, management proposes to pay an interim and a special dividend. Shares slip 13% in two days to 255 pence. Credit Suisse and Numis reduce their earnings forecasts but maintain their 'Buy' rating.
3 September 2014	Shares go ex-div for both the interim (1.77p a share) and special (2.77p) dividends. BC makes £1.85 million.
5 September 2014	BC Partners sells off a 7% stake (around half its remaining holding), via an accelerated book-build placing by Credit Suisse and Numis (them again), at a reported 232 pence for £47.6 million.[47] Stock sheds 4.5% on the day to close at 230 pence, its introductory price.
1 October 2014	BC's Stefano Quadrio Curzio steps down from the board of Foxtons. The share price hits 219 pence.
23 October 2014	The company issues a profit warning, blaming political and economic uncertainty in Britain and Europe. Canaccord Genuity downgrades the stock for the first time. The stock loses nearly one-fifth of its value to 165p, almost 30% down on its IPO price.[48]
19 November 2014	The post-IPO flop reaches its nadir at 142.70 pence a share during the trading session.
27 January 2015	Foxtons issues a second profit warning, explaining that residential sales were down 12% and commissions down 25.7% in the previous trading quarter. Instead of a forecast £57 million EBITDA and £50 million recorded the prior year, the property broker is now expecting £46 million.[49]
30 April 2015	Shares go ex-div for both the final (3.17p a share) and special (1.99p) dividends. BC earns £1 million on 29 May.[50]

| 3 June 2015 | BC sells its remaining 7% holding for more than £53 million. Stock loses 4.2% on the day to close at 270.2 pence.[51] |

The reason why BC was able to time these moves so impeccably is because its representative, Stefano Quadrio Curzio[*], was still on the board of Foxtons. He would eventually step down, but not before helping his employer time two follow-on sales with canny precision. Importantly, he would leave before Foxtons's first profit warning in October 2014. Yet another example of an IPO that would turn out to the benefit of the selling financial sponsor and to the detriment of the buyers: the public. Timing markets isn't an exact science. In the case of its investment in Foxtons, BC Partners got it wrong on the way in, but was meticulous when the time came to exit. The PE firm had lost credibility when the financial crisis had reached its zenith, but BC had rewritten the rules of smart investing: you can actually buy high, sell low, then repurchase low and resell high. BC certainly was the patsy in 2007. It found a greater fool in 2013 and 2014.

Home and dry

With over 50 branches in mid-2015, Foxtons was in better shape than at the onset of the financial crisis – if only because its balance sheet was now debt-free. But it had been sold to the public at a full earnings multiple of 13.1 times its 2013 EBITDA. When it reported full-year 2014 adjusted earnings of £46.2 million in March 2015 – well below the £57.2 million which analysts had pencilled in – its growth story looked a tad overhyped. By then its EV-to-EBITDA multiple also stood higher than at the time of listing, at 14 times.

With a stock fluctuating widely and somewhat arbitrarily throughout the summer of 2015, in a range of plus-to-minus 10% of the 230 pence listing price – affected as it was by the startling retirement of the PE-backed CEO, the well-timed follow-on stake reductions by BC Partners and a couple of profit warnings

---

[*]. The month of September 2014 was a busy one for Quadrio Curzio. That month, UK mobile phone retailer Phones4u, a BC Partners investee with 5,500 employees where Quadrio Curzio was chairman of the board, collapsed into administration after its two largest clients, Vodafone and EE, cancelled their contracts. It later transpired that BC had more than recouped its original £154 million equity via a dividend recap carried out twelve months earlier.

in the first two years following the flotation – Foxtons's new incarnation might not be remembered as PE's finest hour. But what brought the final blow to the public's confidence was yet another disappointing trading update, this one on 22 October 2015, letting shareholders know that the economic recovery was taking longer to translate into more housing transactions and that group turnover had risen by 1.6% while EBITDA had shed 5.6% in the first nine months of the year.[52] That day, Foxtons's stock lost more than 7%, and within a month it was one-quarter below its introductory price of September 2013, as seen in Figure 14.2.

Figure 14.2: Foxtons's share price from IPO (20 September 2013) to 31 December 2015

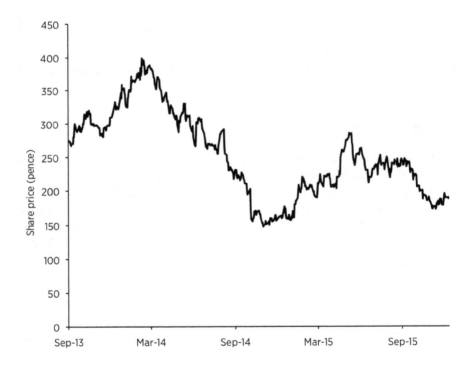

Operating results pre- and post-listing demonstrate that, far from having become a reliable growth business, the estate agent is as erratic as one would expect a housing market participant to be. While top line grew 35% between 2010 and 2013 thanks to Britain's recovery from the Great Recession and new branch openings, the upturn subsided. Adverse government policies on property taxes and non-domiciled investors as well as the timid behaviour of mortgage lenders affected both revenues and profitability, as illustrated in Figure 14.3. This kind of uncertainty and volatility was eventually priced in, but it took two long years for the market to adjust, forcing Foxtons off the FTSE 250 index in December 2015.

Figure 14.3: Foxtons's revenues and EBITDA margin pre- and post-IPO (2010-15)

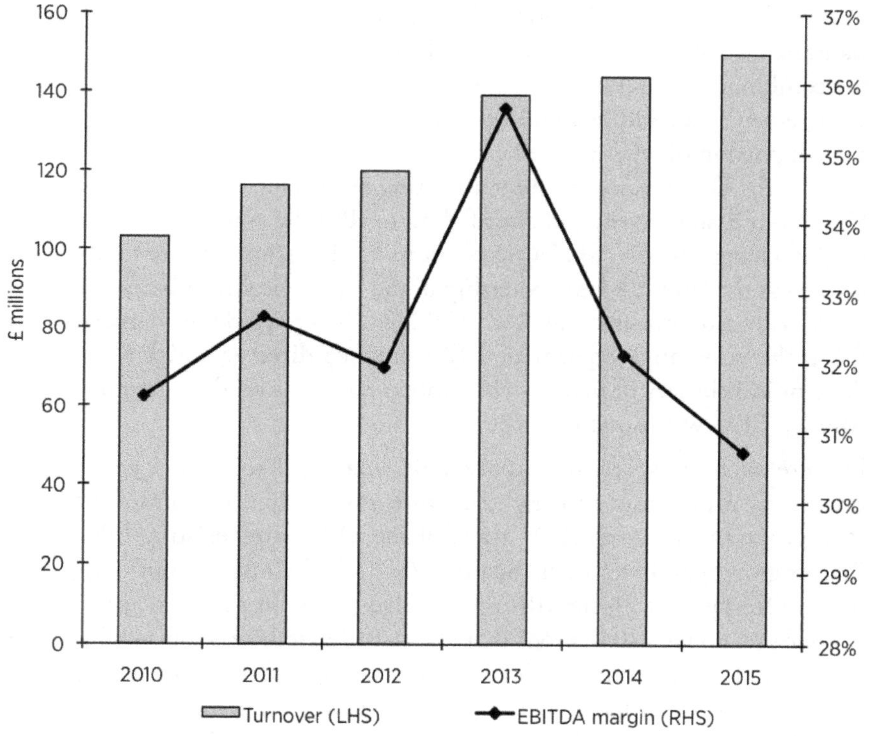

Source: Company accounts

Home alone

When the reduction in credit availability had spread post-2008, BC Partners had regrouped and scaled down its international network by closing its Milan and Geneva offices. Like many of its peers it had lost control of some high-profile investments made at or near the peak of the bubble. In September 2009, via a debt restructuring, Sweden's Dometic – a secondary buyout inherited from Scandinavian investment group EQT four years earlier – was grabbed by its lending syndicate led by Japanese bank Mizuho (obviously keen to work with BC Partners) as the supplier of mini-bars and fridges could not cope with its $800 million loan package.[53] It is in that same year, as we saw in Chapter 12, that BC opted out of its portfolio asset Seat Pagine Gialle, when a refinancing imposed by the company's lenders required an equity cure. BC Partners had squandered a whopping lump of equity in the process.

And in early 2012, British gym chain Fitness First, employing 13,000 and claiming 1.2 million members worldwide, was taken over by its lenders through the combination of a £550 million debt/equity swap and a company voluntary arrangement – an administrative procedure that allowed the business to settle a small portion of what it owed creditors and which saw it shed half of its 140 gyms in the UK. Seven years after acquiring Fitness First for £835 million in an SBO from rival Cinven, and after failing to IPO the company on Singapore's stock exchange in 2011, BC Partners lost its battle against vulture fund Oaktree Capital as the latter yanked ownership of the largest health club operator in the world. Advised once again by Rothschild, BC had purged senior management, firing the company's chairman, CEO, finance director and UK managing director in February of that year, but chopping senior heads had come too late. Another SBO was biting the dust.

Despite such conspicuous setbacks, BC managed to raise a new vintage, closing its ninth fund in early 2012 with €6.5 billion of commitments, up 13% on the previous vehicle.[54] Some of the LBO firm's existing LPs, like the Washington State Investment Board (WSIB), had chosen to opt out, perhaps not thrilled by the 5.7% net IRR they received between 2005 and 2011 from BC European Capital VIII – proof that although Foxtons was too small to have a detrimental (eventually beneficial) impact on that fund's performance, other portfolio companies had failed to deliver.[55] If LPs had invested their capital in the FTSE 100, their total unlevered annual return over the same seven years would have been 5.9%, with the added benefit of better liquidity derived from public markets. On the same basis, the mid-cap FTSE 250 index would have yielded an average 8.4% a year. It is easy to understand WSIB's decision. Even so, the weak performance of BC Partners's eighth fund had not deterred other LPs, with Californian pension fund CalSTRS happily pledging $280 million to the BC European Capital IX vehicle, although the amount was markedly less than the $610 million invested in the previous fund.[56] CalSTRS might have applied the adage: past performance is not necessarily indicative of future results. An optimistic view that Foxtons's public investors will be keen to adopt.

PART EIGHT
Asset-Stripping: Modern-day Creative Destruction

N O REVIEW OF THE PE FUND MANAGERS' TOOLBOX IS complete without a case study on the ancestral industry practice of asset-stripping. While controversial, selling divisions or activities of a group can sometimes be part of a healthy restructuring. Few readers of Chapter 6 will contest the fact that music major EMI was overdue a rationalisation. Its rivals Universal and Warner had already gone through such a process by the time Terra Firma came on to the scene. Part Eight, however, is more interested in the type of asset-stripping made necessary by the actions of the financial sponsors rather than by the intrinsic weaknesses of the corporation being acquired. Notwithstanding what free-market activists will claim, carving out divisions or sacking employees in droves cannot be only a matter of operating efficiency. There is an ethical angle to such an approach to corporate and financial management.

LBO firms' reputation as asset-strippers dates from the 1980s, the age of the corporate raiders when 'friendly' takeovers could be the source of public embarrassment. Better to go hostile, as the slash-and-burn tactics adopted by KKR in its acquisitions of Beatrice Companies in 1985 and food and tobacco giant RJR Nabisco in 1988 demonstrated by making front-page news. Back then, financial sponsors benefitted from a deconglomeration phase, which offered many spin-off opportunities from large, unfocused and inefficient corporations. When KKR took it over, Beatrice operated in dairy products, luggage manufacturing, water treatment, beverages and many other unrelated activities from bottling operations to car rentals. KKR spent years disposing of Beatrice's units piecemeal.

Nowadays, such low-hanging fruit of corporate restructuring are few and far between. Thus, as our next case study on Caesars Entertainment will prove, LBO enthusiasts have to be a lot more ingenious.

CHAPTER 15
Caesars Entertainment – PE's Version of Strip Poker

VISITORS TO RENO, NEVADA, CAN BE PRONE TO THE occasional physical activity. The city sits in a high desert at the foot of the Sierra Nevada and attracts accomplished skiers and keen mountain climbers. Many local residents are the outdoorsy type, with a passion for cycling, trekking, fishing, or hunting. And any self-declared fanatical triathlete knows that Lake Tahoe, a freshwater expanse located at an altitude of almost 1,900 metres, 38 miles south of Reno, is home to one of the most challenging Ironman triathlons in the world.

Nevada is not a place just known for its pursuit of healthy outdoor exercise. Reno, like all major cities in the state, is famous for its casinos. It was there, in the 1930s, that a gambling operation was founded under the brand Harrah's. On 30 October 1937, the company's founder William Harrah, a 26-year-old who had started his activities at Venice Beach, California, opened a bingo parlour in Reno. Nevada had legalised casino gambling six years earlier while California considered games of chance illegal. Launching in a more welcoming jurisdiction was a logical step. While this first Reno venue only lasted a few weeks, Harrah was more successful the following year when he opened another parlour closer to the city's main gambling neighbourhood. Quickly, though, Bill Harrah turned to casinos, opening his Harrah's Club in 1946. Given how hard the Depression years had been for all, Harrah applied the very novel idea, at least among casino operators, of customer service, aiming not to rip off his visitors but to encourage them to return. Trading perked up. In 1955 Harrah built a casino on the south shores of Lake Tahoe, busing punters from all over California to ensure that the winter season, usually confined to skiing, would remain active.

Harrah was not the most disciplined operational manager and frequently used his business's cash flows to finance his lavish lifestyle. In need for funds, the company publicly listed in 1971, joining the New York Stock Exchange two years later. Eighteen months after Bill Harrah's death in June 1978, the company was sold to hotel operator Holiday Inn. After regaining its independence in 1995,

Harrah's expanded organically and through acquisitions into new locales, with Las Vegas becoming a focus of its development over the ensuing decade.

The big game-changer occurred in mid-2004, when the group announced the $9.4 billion acquisition of rival Caesars Entertainment to create the world's largest gambling company. Closing on 13 June 2005, this transaction was funded mostly with Harrah's common stock and an additional $1.9 billion in cash, adding 15 casinos to Harrah's portfolio of more than 20.[1] Restricting Harrah's to its humble beginnings would therefore only tell half the story. Today, several years after its merger with Caesars, the gambling group claims to be the world's most geographically diversified casino-entertainment company. With 68,000 employees, over 100 million visits a year, $8.5 billion in total net revenues, more than 56,000 slot machines and 3,500 table games worldwide, there is no question that it is a serious player in the sector. Having gained such influence in an industry that has no shortage of critiques due to the concern surrounding people's addiction to gambling, the company also pays particular attention to its impact on the community and, for many years now, its management has spared no effort to emphasise the importance of responsible gaming, including via a Code of Commitment that spells out its policy in terms of staff training and law enforcement.

Birds of a feather

Aside from their often-chronicled connections with organised crime, money laundering and prostitution, casinos are famed for being cash cows, extremely profitable businesses. In fact, very few industries offer higher predictable, recurring cash flows. Return on assets is particularly strong, due to the fast customer replacement ratio (a typical visitor parts with his or her cash within a few hours before another takes over) and high equipment usage (casinos are ordinarily open 24/7, all year long). Besides, casino operators have a huge benefit over other venue operators: they hold a licence that, until the internet started disrupting the status quo, often constituted an unassailable barrier to entry. Other industries have one or two criteria in common with casinos' business model; very few hold them all. For instance, no-frills airlines like Southwest and Ryanair have high equipment usage thanks to efficient turnarounds of their aircraft. Unfortunately, passengers cannot be replaced part-way through the flight and, due to environmental and safety regulations, planes cannot be flown 24/7. Similarly, retail shops can benefit from high customer walkthrough, but rarely operate around the clock.

Perhaps the most valuable aspect of modern-day casinos is their almost compulsive use of information management tools. Operators have taken the habit of collecting data on all aspects of customer experience within their establishments. They can track a punter's gambling preferences, eating pattern, show attendance and number of room stays. Well before retailers or even most airlines started introducing them, loyalty cards were central to casino groups' customer-relationship management processes. Given the high customer churn – many visitors are casual gamblers – identifying the 'regulars' is a vital skill. Data-mining can help determine the customer's future cash streams and lifetime value. In turn, a casino can decide how much to spend on a visitor. Harrah's marketing strategy in that area, through its Total Rewards loyalty programme, explains why it derived 71.5% of its revenues from gaming in 2006 (the rest coming from lodging, entertainment, food and beverage) whereas its rival MGM Mirage only drew 40% of revenues from it.[2] Because of their local oligopolies, great cash generation, intimate customer knowledge, and lofty return on assets, casinos can deliver tremendous investment returns to their owners. Which explains why they are prime candidates for LBOs, as seen in Chapter 2.

Harrah's and Caesars spent the best part of 2005 ironing out the details of their merger. After receiving approval from their respective stockholders on 11 March 2005, they went through a comprehensive post-integration programme. Both companies generated $4 billion of revenues a year and had shown double-digit growth in 2004. Harrah's 17% operating margins, though, were much better than Caesars's 10%. For that reason, Harrah's CEO Gary Loveman was to become the combined group's chairman. There was no ambiguity as to which company was acquiring the other.[3] On the dealmaking front, it was unlikely that the combined entity would be sitting idle for long. Times were propitious for M&A. The US economy was in the midst of a credit bubble. Debt was cheap, readily available, and it increasingly came with few strings attached. More than happy to borrow in order to fund his consolidation strategy, on 23 December 2005 Loveman led his fast-expanding company through the acquisition of the Imperial Palace in Las Vegas, in a deal worth $370 million. It was the perfect way to end a game-changing year.

But the debt balloon had not only helped corporate activity. It had supported the microcosm of LBOs. For the previous three years, PE firms had raised capital in quantities never seen before. In 2005 alone, the industry had raised over $350 billion globally. That same year had seen $300 billion-worth of buyouts completed worldwide. The following year LBO transaction value was to reach $700 billion.[4] Few companies could now be deemed outside the remit of private equity. Recent months had seen household names like retailer Toys "R" Us, car rental operator Hertz (see Chapter 3), and film studio Metro-Goldwyn-Mayer get gobbled up in multibillion-dollar buyouts. No target was off-limits; especially not corporations like Harrah's that were intent on leading the consolidation game by themselves. LBO gurus considered that sort of attitude as creeping on their turf.

Due to its public exposure, the Harrah's-Caesars combination was drawing interest from the PE community. Eventually, the inevitable happened. A couple of LBO specialists, Apollo and Texas Pacific Group, started having conversations with Loveman, helping him to grasp all that he could achieve if only he would accede to increase leverage well above the pitiful 45% Harrah's capital structure was endowed with at the time. Loveman himself was looking for ways to raise the intrinsic value of his gambling group, which he considered unappreciated compared to other property-rich sectors like hotel management.[5]

After months of conversations, on 2 October 2006 Apollo and TPG offered $81 per share, $15.1 billion, to take Harrah's off the New York Stock Exchange. It was a 21% premium to the recent share price, but everyone knew that Harrah's and Caesars were still in the process of merging, so significant synergistic benefits were yet to be factored into the stock. After a brief reality check, nine days later the two bidders raised their proposal to $83.50 a share.[6] The following months saw the usual press rumours about other parties taking a look at the asset. The third largest casino operator in the country, Pennsylvania-based Penn National Gaming, partnered with hedge fund D.E. Shaw to make an approach, which forced Apollo and its stablemate to raise their price once again. In early December they reviewed their valuation models and came back with an improved $87-a-share bid. But other prospective buyers were still not deterred. So on 19 December 2006, the PE duet tabled a recommended $17.1 billion offer, or $90 a share – 35% higher than Harrah's closing price on 29 September – plus the assumption of about $10.7 billion of debt.[7] The deal was sealed as chairman and CEO Loveman gave the go-ahead. Still, now that their offer had been recommended by Harrah's board, Apollo and TPG had to apply for gambling licences in every state where the target operated; a strenuous process that could take up to 18 months.

Predictably, in a world of uninspired replica dealmaking, soon after management's decision to sell out to Apollo and TPG a bevy of bids sprang up in the sector. In June 2007, an attempt by investment firms Fortress and Centerbridge to take Penn National Gaming private for $6.1 billion fell through. Two months later, the Dubai Government's holding Dubai World agreed to spend up to $5.2 billion in the second largest American casino operator, MGM Mirage, for a 9.5% stake in the group and half of MGM's CityCenter project, a 76-acre Las Vegas development of hotels, condos and retail outlets due to open in 2009. At some point in the first half of 2007 even beleaguered gambling group Trump Entertainment had been rumoured to be in bid discussions.[8]

* * *

At the time of making their approach for Harrah's, Apollo and TPG were already members of the private equity elite. They prided themselves on the pithiness of their investment style. Their combined buying power exceeded $25 billion for LBO transactions. This sort of influence brings a sentiment of invincibility. Apollo had been set up in 1990 by Leon Black, a Harvard Business School graduate who had led Drexel Burnham Lambert's M&A group through that institution's eventful period of the late 1980s. Unlike most other investment banks at the time, Drexel was known for its aggressive attitude as a lender, always ready to advise and fund its clients' hostile takeovers, in particular with what came to be called 'junk bonds'. The bank had, for instance, supported dealmaking machine KKR's multibillion-dollar bid for RJR Nabisco in 1988. After Drexel's collapse into bankruptcy in February 1990 following the indictment for insider trading of several of its employees, including bond specialist Michael Milken and Managing Director Dennis Levine – one of Black's colleagues in the M&A department – the bank's staff had no choice but to seek refuge elsewhere. Having worked on the advisory side of so many LBOs, Black elected to enter the investment world, co-founding Apollo that same year alongside former Drexel colleagues Josh Harris and Marc Rowan, among others. As it was contemplating Harrah's public-to-private in late 2006, Apollo had $24.5 billion under management, having raised its sixth LBO fund the year before, closing at $10.1 billion.

While Black's firm had been established in the world's capital of mergers and acquisitions, New York City, Texas Pacific Group proudly gave away its unusual location (at least when it comes to financial services) by including its state of origin in its name. Though since shortened to TPG, there is no question in everyone's mind that the Fort Worth-headquartered investment firm is not part of the East Coast tribe, and the fact that it operates in a state better known for oil exploration and livestock farming ought to give it added panache. The type of transactions that the firm got involved in from the outset were also deeply influenced by its main co-founder, Harvard Law School graduate David Bonderman. A former bankruptcy and antitrust lawyer at Washington, D.C. law firm Arnold & Porter, before establishing TPG Bonderman had, like his co-founders James Coulter and Bill Price, held operational roles in large corporations, a rare occurrence in the PE arena, where most professionals are simply deal doers.

The catalyst for the formation of Texas Pacific Group was the decision in April 1993 to buy bankrupt Continental Airlines for a song and put it back on its feet. The firm's focus on complex transactions, industries undergoing change, turnarounds and restructurings made it stick out in a sector more concerned with headline-grabbing acquisitions. Yet TPG did occasionally participate in traditional buyouts. Harrah's take-private was one of them. Only five weeks after announcing its joint bid for the casino giant, TPG had closed its largest flagship buyout fund to date: a monstrous $15.4 billion investment vehicle. Like Apollo, TPG was ready to put its firepower to work.

Betting the ranch

On 28 January 2008, after successfully clearing regulatory and licensing hurdles, in the fourth-biggest LBO on record, Harrah's acquisition went ahead in an all-cash transaction valued at $30.7 billion, including the assumption of $12.4 billion of debt and the incurrence of $1 billion of acquisition costs. The company's stockholders had approved the deal during a special meeting on 5 April the previous year, though the gambling licence applications had taken some time as expected. The Credit Crunch had derailed several high-profile LBOs since mid-2007, but the Harrah's deal was not subject to financing conditions, implying that the underwriting banks had entered into a contractual commitment at the time of the bid, in December 2006, and could not walk away without incurring severe financial penalties, maybe even a lawsuit. In truth, the casino operator had performed very well in 2007, recording revenue growth of 12% and property EBITDA[*] margins of more than 26%. Harrah's management had been busy selling off non-performing or non-core assets, which had helped push profitability. As a consequence, its total-debt-to-EBITDA ratio sat at a very respectable 4.4 times.[9]

Under LBO, things were bound to differ slightly. At a total EV of $30 billion, multiples were 10.5 times property EBITDA and 14.8 times operating profit on the last-12-month financials. Debt multiples were also toppy. With a proposed structure including $7.25 billion in term loans, a $2 billion revolver, and $6.5 billion in CMBS (commercial mortgage-backed securities, a type of secured debt), to which a $6.75 billion of unsecured bonds (yielding 10.75%) was added for good measure, Harrah's would be carrying leverage worth 8.2 times EBITDA and 11.5 times operating earnings.[10] Thanks to $6 billion of equity injection – Apollo and TPG had each spent $1.325 billion with co-investors in tow – leverage stood at almost 80%.[11] To reflect the prevailing credit bubble, the financing structure was also somewhat cryptic, with a list of debt instruments too long to reproduce here, including several term loans with different margins and maturities, senior notes due 2016 and senior PIK toggle notes due 2018.[**]

---

*. Property EBITDA is a profitability yardstick commonly used in real estate and other property-rich sectors.
**. Toggle meaning that, in order to free up liquidity, Harrah's had the option to defer any interest payment by agreeing to pay an increased coupon in the future.

In addition to the previously discussed CMBS line earning 4.2% and maturing in 2013, over ten tranches of unsecured senior notes and subordinated senior notes yielding varying interest rates and with maturities spreading from 2009 to 2017 were issued. The PE owners did not want to be left out, so their preferred stocks accrued dividends at an annual rate of 15%.

Perhaps unsurprisingly, given that Moody's and Standard & Poor's were giving all the debt slices a speculative grade, the banks backing the deal found it laborious to place a majority of the $20 billion-plus debt into the portfolios of institutional investors. Apollo and TPG used a series of underwriters, including Deutsche Bank, Bank of America, JPMorgan and Credit Suisse, to market the financing on a multi-city investor roadshow across the country. There was limited appetite for the transaction. The high-yield bonds came down 10% within hours of trading due to concerns around the risk profile. The debt markets were questioning the deal structure from day one.

Figure 15.1 illustrates that it was an unusual structure – though pretty conventional in the world of asset-rich transactions. A property company (PropCo) was created alongside the legacy structure of the operating company (OpCo). As part of the reorganisation, eight key casinos – three in Las Vegas: Harrah's, Rio, Flamingo; three in Lake Tahoe: Harrah's, Harveys, Bill's; and two in Atlantic City: Harrah's and Showboat – were moved to PropCo to be used as security for the CMBS line. There was to be no direct upstreaming or downstreaming of cash between OpCo and PropCo, as can be seen from the diagram. Both were meant to trade separately and feed directly to the holding company (HoldCo) Harrah's Entertainment. What it meant in practice is that both group companies held casinos that were competing for visitors.[12]

On the equity side, Harrah's was in good hands. All of the group's voting stock was held by Hamlet Holding, a company controlled by representatives of Apollo and TPG. Each buyout firm had three senior executives holding around 17% of Hamlet. And these executives were none other than Apollo's three co-founders, Leon Black, Joshua Harris and Marc Rowan, and two of TPG's co-founders, David Bonderman and James Coulter, alongside one of the Texan firm's senior partners, Jonathan Coslet. With so much brain power looking after the investment, how could anything go wrong?

Figure 15.1: Harrah's group structure at the time of January 2008 LBO

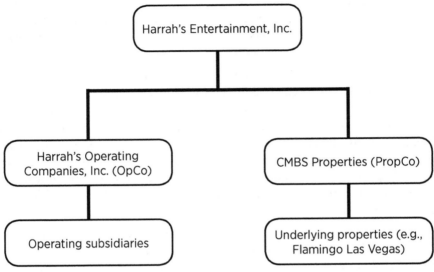

Source: Company filings

*   *   *

The debt syndication, actually, did not go according to plan. In February 2008, press reports emerged with some bad news. Over half of the debt package, $14 billion to be precise, could not find enough buyers, forcing the underwriters to delay the process.[13] The latter were still trying to flog large portions of the loans when first-quarter results for 2008 were released in May. Disclosing revenues and EBITDA down 6% and 7% respectively, OpCo was quickly falling behind budget. Though PropCo was doing better due to the quality of its casino portfolio, Harrah's operating company did not fare well over the following quarters, making debt syndication impossible for the subordinated tranches.

The effects of the Credit Crunch were being felt by consumers, who were scaling back their casino spending in the face of broader economic uncertainty. The introduction the year before of smoking bans and legislation in various jurisdictions where Harrah's operated – London, England, Atlantic City and Illinois – harmed financial performance. The pace of earnings erosion grew unabated throughout 2008 and affected the group's credit quality. By the fourth quarter, rating agencies were labelling Harrah's a 'substantial risk'. Only ten months after the buyout, some of OpCo's senior notes were trading at less than 30 cents on the dollar. The high-yield bond scourge was in full view.

So the two PE owners did what could be expected of them: they bullied the bondholders into accepting a private exchange of their old debt for new notes worth half as much and maturing at a later date. In addition, the lenders were to be paid a nominal cash amount. Few holders of the 2010 and 2011 notes tendered to the unappetising offer: only $2.2 billion of OpCo's old loans were removed in December 2008, reducing OpCo's total debt by about $900 million, or half a turn of leverage. It was not going to lift the company's prospects in a meaningful way. Neither would the news, a month later, that the gambling group was facing a lawsuit – the first of a long series – when two bondholders alleged that the coercive swap wrongly impaired their rights.[14] Regardless, the year end was approaching and it was time to focus on the group's annual performance.

Playing a poor hand well

When consolidated numbers for 2008 came out, they showed a material drop in revenues (minus 6%) and a much more pronounced property EBITDA fall of 15%. Performance had worsened in the second half of the year. Financial results of the post-LBO period, from 28 January to 31 December, included $5.5 billion in pre-tax charges for impairment of goodwill and other intangible assets.[15] On the first anniversary of the LBO, the dilemma facing Apollo and its co-investor was no longer how to make Harrah's a two-times return type of investment; it was how to avoid default. Leverage multiples had shot up to more than 9.5 times property EBITDA and 13.4 times operating earnings (pre-exceptionals, naturally).

The Harrah's situation was alarming. And because the credit binge was well and truly over, Apollo and TPG were also nursing losses in other parts of their respective portfolios. Housewares retailer Linens 'n Things, a company that Apollo had taken private in early 2006, had filed for bankruptcy in May 2008 as one of the first victims of the Credit Crunch. Weighed down by its debt, TPG-owned aluminium company Aleris had seen volumes tumble 40% in 2008 and had no alternative but to file for Chapter 11 in February 2009, less than three years after it was delisted by the Texan PE group. Ironically, one of the distressed-debt investors in that transaction was none other than TPG's partner in crime on the Harrah's LBO: Apollo. In fact, the crisis had already been merciless on TPG. In late September 2008, the firm had lost $1.35 billion on an investment in troubled Washington Mutual when federal regulators seized the bank and forced it into the arms of JPMorgan Chase.[16]

And it looked like the two LBO groups' gamble on casinos was not paying off either. Desperate for liquidity, in March 2009 Harrah's launched another tender offer to exchange its remaining old bond notes for new ones. This time around, the offer was more successful. Reluctant bondholders had realised that, without further liquidity runway, the casino operator was toast, as it would be unable to meet its debt commitments over the coming two years. Harrah's managed to exchange $3.65 billion of new 10%, second-priority, senior secured notes due 2018 for $5.5 billion of its existing debt due between 2010 and 2018. The two offers helped the company amend and extend about two-thirds of its legacy bonds.[17]

These moves did not sit comfortably with a good many lenders to the company. Yet the situation for the creditors was about to get worse. Only three months later, Harrah's OpCo offered close to $1.4 billion of 11.25% senior secured notes due 2017. Proceeds from the issuance were used to pay a portion of OpCo's outstanding term loans and revolver. The deal also gave Harrah's a chance to extend debt duration. In the first half of 2009, via the bond exchange and the new offering, the group had successfully cut its long-term debt by more than 16% to $19.3 billion.[18] But that wasn't the end of it: in September the company issued another slice of 11.25% senior secured notes due 2017, this time worth $720 million. Amazingly, these two new tranches were excluded from the senior leverage covenant, meaning that these noteholders had no covenant protection. A month later, to buy itself some time, Harrah's carried yet another tender offer for certain of its existing debt securities with maturities in 2010 and 2011. It could appear surprising that lenders were prepared to relinquish part of their principal at a discount while receiving in exchange loans with later maturity and no covenant. The answer can be found in Harrah's operating performance.

By early 2009, with the worst economic environment in a generation, casino attendance was no longer 'front of mind', as marketers would say. A typically discretionary expenditure for consumers, gambling is like any entertainment activity: when the going gets tough, people do without. Other than true addicts, few would dare visit a roulette table when facing the prospect of unemployment. What had to happen happened: casino gaming groups started to drop like mayflies at the end of a busy day. On 28 July 2009, Colony Capital-backed Station Casinos, headquartered in Las Vegas, Nevada, filed for Chapter 11 protection. As part of its November 2007 $8.8 billion take-private, the operator had taken on too much balance-sheet risk and needed to scale down its steep leverage. In a sad note appended to this corporate drama, Frank Fertitta Jr., the founder of Station Casinos, died from heart complications less than a month after the Chapter 11 filing. Six months earlier, Atlantic City-based Trump Entertainment had entered bankruptcy for the third time in its history, leading its larger-than-life founder and chairman Donald Trump to resign.

Trump's group itself followed closely the footsteps of smaller operator Las Vegas Tropicana, which had filed the year before.[19]

It turns out that gambling is not recession-proof after all. The soggy economy had a devastating impact on casino attendance. In 2009, American GDP dropped by 2.8%. Accordingly, the downturn hit Harrah's hard, wiping out 12% of its top line that year. Over the previous 12 months, management had implemented a restructuring plan, generating substantial efficiency gains by scaling down the number of rooms by 14% and pushing room occupancy by 15%. Nevertheless, adjusted EBITDA was off 23% in the fourth quarter and down 9% for the whole year. So Loveman and his team had spent the year trying to sort out Harrah's bloated balance sheet. Thanks to bond exchange offers and fresh debt issuances, the casino group recorded $5 billion in pre-tax gains on early extinguishments of debt.[20]

To summarise, the main reason behind OpCo's bondholders' acceptance to exchanging their notes with maturities of 2010 and 2011 for ones with later maturities is that the company would have been otherwise unable to meet its short-term debt commitments. In case of default, the holders of term loans would be repaid first, with subordinated lenders only paid afterwards on further asset liquidations, assuming there was any residual value by that stage. It just wasn't worth taking the risk.

OpCo wasn't doing great, but PropCo was facing its own financial pressures. Due to the property company's 20% EBITDA fall in 2009, the $6.5 billion CMBS tranche was expected to deliver a leverage ratio of more than 10.7 times (up from 7.3 in the first quarter of 2008). In anticipation, in November management used $237 million of cash to buy CMBS lines on the secondary market at a purchase price of 25 cents on the dollar. With the remaining $5.55 billion of CMBS, the year-end debt-to-EBITDA multiple at PropCo read a more reasonable, albeit still worrisome, 9.2 times. On the operational front, after taking such a heavy blow in the period ended 31 December 2009, management had no alternative but to recognise at the consolidated level (i.e., OpCo's and PropCo's combined results) $1.6 billion in pre-tax charges for impairment of goodwill and other intangible assets, and $112 million in pre-tax charges for write-downs. The year had been eventful and Harrah's senior executives had done their utmost to salvage the situation by cutting leverage and costs – 11,000 employees had been let go.[21] They would get many more opportunities to demonstrate their restructuring skills.

If the environment was challenging for the overleveraged group, it also created opportunities. Management chose to open the throttle with fresh acquisitions. The following year started with the announcement on 19 February that the group had completed the purchase of the Planet Hollywood in Vegas, giving

Harrah's seven contiguous resorts on the east side of the Las Vegas Strip. Like so many other casino groups, the target had flirted with bankruptcy in the previous summer. Local regulator Nevada Gaming Control Board had approved Harrah's bid on the understanding that the latter would acquire $306 million in Planet Hollywood debt at a deeply discounted price, and would assume the remaining $554 million debt. That was another half a billion dollars' worth of loans added to Harrah's books. Only three months later, on 25 May 2010, the fast-expanding group entered into a new agreement to buy the assets of Thistledown Racetrack, a thoroughbred racing facility located in Cleveland, Ohio.[22] Both transactions appeared to indicate that management was hoping to ride the cyclical upturn and benefit from it by acquiring recovering assets on the cheap.

* * *

Among the various parties jumping at the chance to buy Harrah's debt at a bargain price was event-driven hedge fund manager Paulson & Co. Keen to convert its bond holdings into equity as a way to gain negotiating power when dealing with the two fickle PE owners, Paulson took the unusual view that it was better off owning equity – an instrument ranking behind any debt in case of default – rather than unsecured senior notes. In August 2010, Harrah's announced the registration of stock held by the hedge fund manager as part of a debt-for-equity swap completed in June. In the exchange, which wiped out roughly $1.1 billion of debt and enabled the gambling group to further optimise its balance sheet, Paulson received a 9.9% equity stake, worth $470 million.[23]

In parallel, Harrah's two majority PE owners had spent the best part of the previous two years buying up their investee's second-lien debt on the secondary market. In early 2009 they had purchased, at greatly reduced prices, loans with a face value of $2 billion. While TPG had apparently lost appetite half-way through the exercise, later that year Apollo had kept on betting that the casino operator would recover. At the same time that Paulson was swapping its debt for equity, in an attempt to consolidate their ownership Apollo and TPG were trading in $408 million of notes for equity representing 5.6% of the company.[24]

Armed with an – arguably inflated – equity value of about $4.7 billion (derived from the valuation ascribed to the Paulson stake), in October 2010 the casino operator announced its intention to float and to raise $575 million in the process. A month later, it also filed a placement prospectus to help Paulson dispose of its stockholding if and when needed. According to the company's annual report, the hedge fund manager exchanged $835 million of 5.625% senior notes due 2015, 6.5% senior notes due 2016 and 5.75% senior notes due 2017, together with $283 million of notes previously acquired, for voting common stock at an exchange ratio of ten shares per $1000 of notes tendered. Upon listing, the group was to be valued at a 10% discount to the price initially paid by Apollo and TPG. But the implied $27 billion EV, at 14 times EBITDA, was universally described as 'rich', particularly when compared with the 10.5 times paid at the time of the LBO. When you consider that Harrah's main rival, MGM Resorts, had seen its stock fall 85% over the same period, the lunacy of the proposed public stock price takes its full meaning. It was obvious that the original $6 billion equity contribution was not worth 75 cents on the dollar. By the end of November, the unrealistic IPO was aborted.[25]

For reasons that were never made clear other than via management's claim that it gave the group a luxury connotation, during the same month of November Harrah's went through an imperial name change, to be from now on known as Caesars. While management kept busy with acquisitions and seemingly inconsequential branding matters, the gambling group's indebtedness remained problematic. Negotiations with lenders had taken place throughout the year. On 5 March 2010, PropCo had agreed with its CMBS lenders to amend the terms of the financing, extend the maturity of the loans by two years to February 2015, and repurchase tranches using excess cash flow from the eight CMBS trading entities at marked-down prices of 30 to 50 cents on the dollar. The group had purchased $124 million face value of the CMBS loans for $37 million in September, and $191 million face value for $96 million in December, reducing the CMBS outstanding value to $5.2 billion. In April OpCo had issued $750 million of 12.75% senior secured notes due 2018 and used the proceeds to redeem existing notes – thereby extinguishing $217 million face value of shorter-dated bonds.[26] It was difficult to follow.

With the balance-sheet restructuring and A&E agreements, the group had sorted its short-term liquidity crunch, but it had erected a very big debt wall for 2015: over half its debt maturities now fell that year. The immediate concern, however, was related to operating performance. The dimensions of the debacle became evident when the company released its latest figures. For full-year 2010, EBITDA had taken another dive to $1.9 billion, down 14% on the prior year. Despite management's many attempts to reduce it, total leverage now exceeded 12 times. Nevertheless, recent quarters had seen trading pick up on the back of higher hotel occupancy, visitor counts and convention space bookings, so there was renewed hope that Caesars, serving both the leisure and business traveller, could expect a stronger set of figures in 2011. It was high time: between 2007 and 2010, the group's average daily hotel rate had plunged from $109 a room to $86, and average spending per customer lodging on site had taken a hit from $191 to $158.[27]

Carrying Caesars and Caesars's misfortune

If there was any improvement in trading, it proved marginal and short-lived. The first quarter of 2011, though strong in Las Vegas, continued to see revenue deterioration in far-flung operations in Louisiana, Mississippi, Iowa, Missouri, Illinois and Indiana. Because leverage remained a thorn on the group's side, another A&E process was launched in May, aiming to postpone the term loan maturity from 2015 to 2018 for a 1.25% rise in margin. As with the previous amendments, management and the PE backers were asking the lenders to bear the brunt of the group's underperformance and liquidity issues. However, their offensive practices no longer found favour with most creditors. Only $815 million worth of the $5.8 billion term loans due 2015 were extended to 2018. As for the CMBS loans, just $158 million of them were repurchased on the secondary market in March and April 2011, leading the group to recognise a $48 million gain on early extinguishment of debt.[28]

Management did its best to position the group on a growth trajectory, acquiring Boston-based horse-racing track operator Sterling Suffolk Racecourse in March 2011 and a social games developer in Israel two months later. The trading uplift in Vegas strengthened throughout the year but was simply not enough to compensate for weak demand in other parts of the group. In particular, in August, performance on the East Coast was badly affected by Hurricane Irene, which forced the uninsured closure of Atlantic City casinos and led to an 8% fall in third-quarter revenues in that territory. Beside these localised setbacks, underperformance had been general and practically relentless ever since the buyout. In the face of consumer retrenchment, the last four financial years had seen annual operating cash flows take a beating, falling from $530 million in 2008 to about $120 million in 2011. No relief had been forthcoming from the group's operations.

Meanwhile, Caesars's sole maintenance covenant (the senior secured leverage ratio) kept working its way up, reaching 4.32 times by the end of 2011, getting ever closer to its covenant of 4.75-to-1, despite the fact that it excluded over $2.4 billion of various debt instruments. Three other covenants, however, had been conclusively breached. The fixed charge coverage ratio (EBITDA-to-fixed-charges) had to match or exceed two times; the first-priority secured-debt-to-EBITDA ratio had to remain below or equal to 4.5-to-1, and the consolidated leverage ratio (total-debt-to-EBITDA) had to be below or at 7.25 times. As of 31 December 2011, the first-priority secured leverage and consolidated debt ratios reached 5.80 and 11.15 times respectively, while earnings were insufficient to cover fixed charges. These three were not maintenance covenants, meaning that non-compliance did not constitute a default, but their breach indicated that (in case anyone doubted it) the casino operator's indebtedness was unsustainable.

And things were only going to get worse: as of 31 December 2011, $11.1 billion of Caesars's loans were still scheduled to mature in 2015. The debt wall remained impossibly tall. What the annual report also let on was that, although the company was disclosing only $19.8 billion of long-term debt in its balance sheet, its full liabilities, including estimated interest payments of $8.1 billion, exceeded $30.5 billion that year.[29] But the PE backers and management could not be accused of appearing discouraged. As their fourth year of ownership drew to a close, they were once again rumoured to be eyeing an IPO, alongside their fourth A&E. If at first you don't succeed…

On 7 February 2012, the gambling group filed to sell 1.8 million shares in a public offering. With a combined 70.1% holding, the PE duo agreed to a nine-month lockup period, but Paulson, for whom the IPO had been engineered to provide liquidity as part of its debt-for-equity exchange, was free to sell a portion of its 9.9% stake.[30] At the top of the proposed price range, or $9 a share, Caesars Entertainment Corporation (CEC) was to be worth $20 billion – an almost reasonable ten times last-12-months EBITDA, if you ignore the fact that the indebted casino operator was priced at a steeper multiple than its less risky peer MGM Resorts. As of 31 December 2011, Caesars had net debt of $18.5 billion, so the stockholders reckoned that their equity was worth $1.5 billion, or three-quarters below face value.[31] The headline price was also a quarter below the $27 billion suggested 14 months earlier. Desperate to sort out the stretched capital structure, management, Apollo and TPG had tempered their expectations. The group's structure (Figure 15.2) had been rejigged ahead of the listing to separate some subsidiaries such as the online division Caesars Interactive Entertainment (CIE) from the rest of the operating companies (Caesars Entertainment Operating Company, or CEOC), but it did not look too different from the original Harrah's structure.

In one of the most bizarre transactions in stock market history, a $20 billion business was going through a $16 million stock offering. Given the small proceeds generated from it, the IPO had no material impact on the company's financial position. Only 2% of the shares were sold on the day, with a further 17% of common stock – including that owned by Goldman Sachs, Deutsche Bank and Paulson – allowed to transfer once the group was publicly traded. Jumping 71% on its Nasdaq debut, CEC was granted a market cap of more than $1.9 billion.[32] Having such a small float made little sense. The limited liquidity and the prospect of volatility, partly caused by the huge debt overhang, made owning the stock a very risky bet. The weak performance of the group's activities in the Midwest and the Gulf Coast was a drag. So was the fact that, with fewer new markets opening for development in the coming years, competition in existing markets was due to intensify.

Figure 15.2: Caesars's group structure upon CEOC's listing (February 2012)

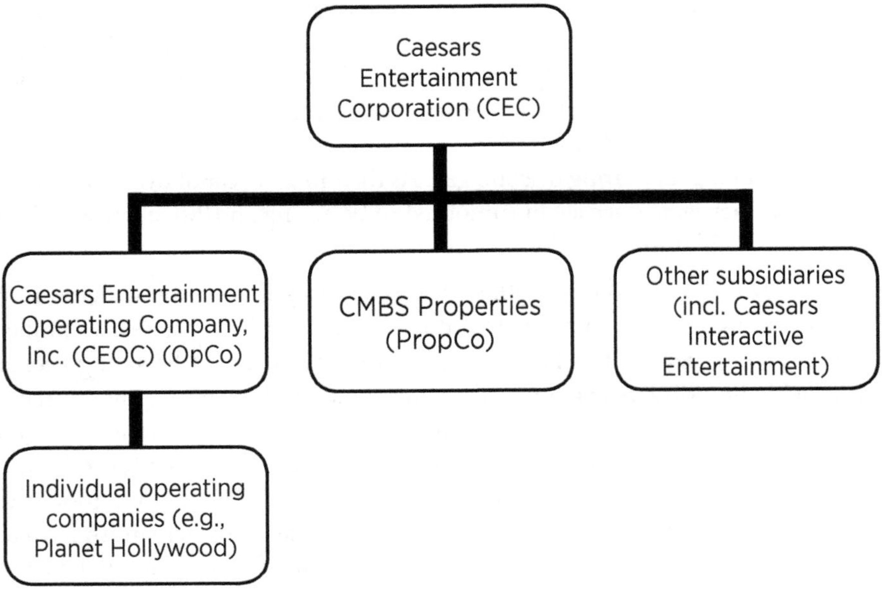

Source: Company filings

But the IPO prospectus pointed out upside opportunities, which sort of helped to make a compelling equity story. For a start, there was the potential legalisation of online gaming. Prior to the Unlawful Internet Gambling Enforcement Act, passed in 2006, and the subsequent ban on internet gambling, experts had estimated that the US online poker industry generated $1.5 billion in revenues a year. With Caesars Interactive Entertainment, the group's division that owned the World Series of Poker brand, management was confident that the company would become a major online player once internet poker was legalised. The timing, though, was uncertain. Until then, management's main strategy was to harden its Vegas leadership, which had recorded steady progress through 2011 and the start of 2012. To compensate for the lack of traction in other regions, the executive team was proposing to close down the least performing assets (in the previous two years it had liquidated one of its London Clubs properties and closed Bill's Casino in Lake Tahoe) and implement efficiency and cost-saving programmes. Yet without a permanent pickup in casino attendance, Caesars's liquidity problems would not be solved. According to the US Bureau Economic Analysis, between early 2008 and early 2010 casino gaming spending had dropped by 10%.[33] The Great Recession had seen Nevada slot machines' revenues suffer a 20% to 25% slide across counties between the first quarter of 2007 and the same period of 2012.[34]

Regardless of the positive news derived from the company's IPO, on 26 March 2012 rating agency Moody's downgraded $11.5 billion of Caesars's debt.[35] And it was justifiable. Operating trends were not improving. To offset the persistently poor trading, management spent most of 2012 launching initiatives to pay down debt and promote liquidity, as exhibited in the following (non-exhaustive) inventory:

- Group property Chester Downs issued $330 million of 9.25% senior secured notes due 2020, using part of the proceeds to repay existing term loans.

- $3.8 billion of term loans saw their maturity extended from 2015 to 2018, bringing down the book value of the tranche due 2015 from $5 billion to $1 billion.

- $367 million of CMBS loans were purchased for $229 million, for a gain of $135 million.

- Offerings of $1.25 billion of 8.5% senior secured notes and $1.5 billion of 9% senior secured notes due 2020 were completed for CEOC.

- Harrah's St. Louis casino was sold to Penn National Gaming for $610 million.

After two years of mild recovery, Caesars's managers would have been forgiven for thinking that the worst was behind them. But there was no getting around the fact that Apollo and TPG had massively overpaid to begin with. It showed in the 2012 annual report. That year, impairment charges of $1.1 billion, comprised of $195 million concerning goodwill, $209 million for trademarks and $33 million related to gaming rights, as well as $180 million related to a previously halted development project in Biloxi, Mississippi, were revealed. Perhaps as an appropriate metaphor, fourth-quarter trading had been badly undermined by Hurricane Sandy, a storm that had hit the East Coast in October and was behind a $450 million impairment for an Atlantic City property. After two years of positive earnings, the group was back into the red, disclosing a loss of $320 million for 2012.

Caesars remained in a precarious position as the maturity wall of 2015 got closer. Due to the management's balance-sheet restructuring efforts throughout the year, a large portion of the wall had now been moved three years forward to 2018. That year, over $9 billion of debt was due. Few of the concerned parties believed that Caesars would still be operating with over $20 billion of debt by then. As of 31 December 2012, CEOC's sole maintenance covenant, the senior secured leverage ratio, read 4.44, ever so close to the allowed 4.75-to-1 limit.[36]

Total leverage, though, exceeded 90% and had reached 10.6 times EBITDA.[37] Luckily, it was uncovenanted.

Stripping Caesars

By now it would be normal to assume that 2013 would be a repeat of 2012, with subdued operating performance coupled with more refinancing projects. But things were about to get nasty for the gambling group's lenders. The PE owners' coerciveness and inventiveness were to reach a degree of malevolence rarely witnessed in an industry not known for its high-principled ways.

First, the year 2013 started with another revolving credit facility conversion into term loans due 2018. This transaction only concerned $134 million-worth of loans so would not alter the group's financial position. What mattered for the lenders was the creation in late 2012 of a new entity, confidently named Caesars Growth Venture Partners. In the words of management, CGVP was to be "a growth oriented vehicle focused on projects complementary to Caesars Entertainment Corporation's existing properties". It was to "improve the group's liquidity and credit profile, enhance its distribution network and provide additional support for potential new ventures". Could it be that, after years of poor trading and repeat A&Es, Apollo and TPG had found a way to clear the casino operator's financial chokepoint?

Hardly. All the PE managers had in mind was a transfer of assets – key among them Planet Hollywood, an investment in a casino project under development in Baltimore, Maryland, and shares in the online division Caesars Interactive Entertainment (CIE) – together with about $1.1 billion of senior notes. Net-net, it had no impact on operating performance. As some put it, it was akin to rearranging deckchairs on the Titanic. But it was spreading assets and liabilities across entities, thereby diluting the bondholders' authority. Or looking at it the other way round, it was giving the LBO backers more clout in the now inevitable upcoming round of negotiations with lenders. The creditors had been positively radiant with naïvety. They genuinely thought that their loans gave them some sort of entitlement. The two equity investors were there to prove them otherwise.

In the end, the 'Venture' part was dropped to leave the slicker CGP, but another entity was created to make sure that the financial sponsors retained control and to dilute the influence of OpCo's public stockholders and creditors. Formed on 25 February 2013, Caesars Acquisition Company (CAC) was to own a minority stake in CGP but hold 100% of voting rights in that company. In turn the majority of CAC's common stock was to be owned by Apollo and TPG, with the rest to be listed on Nasdaq, separately from CEOC (OpCo). What this means is that the two PE owners would control CGP via CAC even though they would hold a minority stake in the newfangled growth enterprise. The sole raison d'être of CAC was to own 100% of CGP's voting rights. That entity had no other purpose. It was a clear attempt by the private equity duo to control what CGP was allowed to do. Once assets (and liabilities) were transferred from CEOC to CGP, the lenders to the group could make no claim on the assets in the event that CEOC defaulted on its loans and filed for bankruptcy.

To clarify, all the assets being transferred were not being used as security for any of the group's existing loans, so the financial sponsors could, at least in principle, transfer such unrestricted assets out of OpCo's group of companies. But the implications were that while the indebted operating company was mitigating liquidity risks, it was also foregoing future cash flows. Pointedly, the public stockholders who had made the mistake of trusting management and the PE backers by buying up shares via the IPO back in February 2012, somewhat on the premise that Caesars was ideally positioned to benefit from the upcoming legalisation of internet gambling, were losing partial ownership of the online activities run by Caesars Interactive Entertainment (CIE) since the newly created CAC (in which public investors held no stock) owned 42% of CIE through its CGP affiliate. All this assumes that public investors were even able to follow what was happening.

Creditors were no longer the only victims of the group's property shuffles. The equity interests in, and 50% of the management fees to be derived from, Planet Hollywood and the Baltimore project were valued at a combined $360 million, plus the assumption of $513 million of outstanding secured loan related to Planet Hollywood. CIE was valued at $525 million, giving CGP's portfolio a total value of $1.3 billion after a few minor adjustments.[38] The two controlling shareholders could not be accused of being callous. They granted CEC the right to buy back Caesars Growth Partners three years hence. If Caesars met certain minimum liquidity thresholds, it could exercise the right, guaranteeing Apollo and TPG a minimum IRR of 10.5% and a maximum of 25%.[39] It was ingenious. An updated organisation structure for Caesars is shown in Figure 15.3.

The casino operator continued to repurchase CMBS loans (the only remaining sizeable chunk of debt maturing in 2015) and spent over $250 million to that end in the second quarter of 2013. But management had a bigger plan. Bear with me, but it is necessary to add that the group structure was made even more complex in September 2013 when Caesars Entertainment Resort Properties (CERP) was formed to take on the CMBS loans and lead a refinancing that saw the old loans retired and three new tranches issued: a $1 billion 8%, first-priority, senior secured notes due 2020; a $1.15 billion 11%, second-priority, senior secured notes due 2021; and a first lien in the form of $2.5 billion senior secured term loans. When the dust settled, as of 31 December 2013 Caesars had reduced the book value of the CMBS loans by $500 million by buying them at a discount, furthermore improving the group's liquidity and maturity profile.

Figure 15.3: Caesars's group structure in February 2013

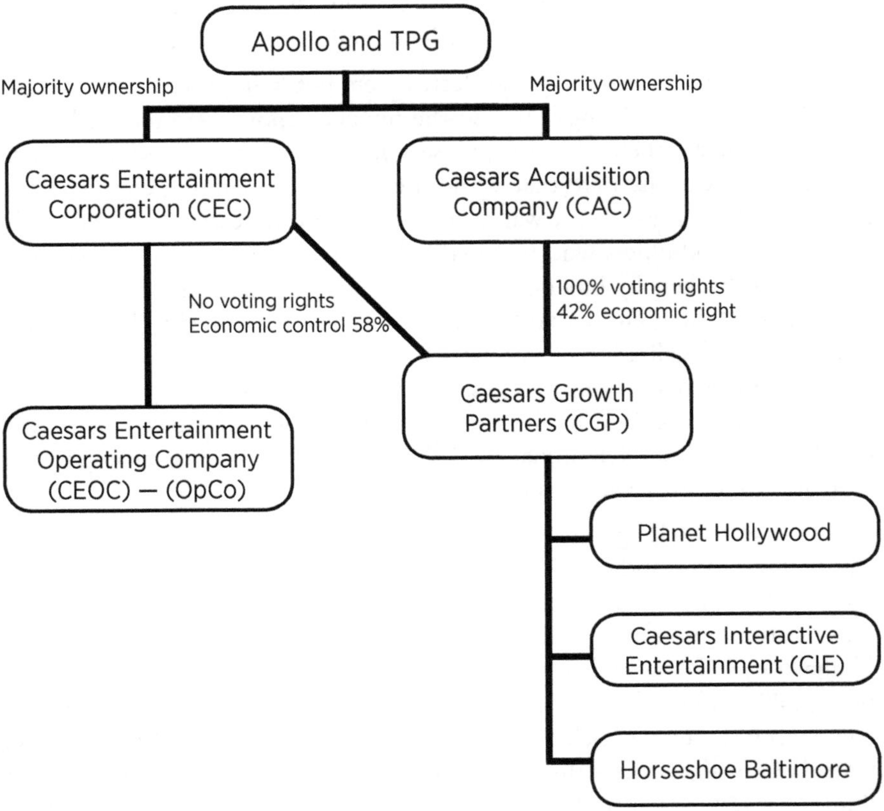

```
                    ┌─────────────────────────┐
                    │      Apollo and TPG      │
                    └─────────────────────────┘
   Majority ownership                    Majority ownership

┌─────────────────────────┐      ┌─────────────────────────┐
│  Caesars Entertainment   │      │    Caesars Acquisition   │
│     Corporation (CEC)    │      │       Company (CAC)      │
└─────────────────────────┘      └─────────────────────────┘

              No voting rights          100% voting rights
              Economic control 58%      42% economic right

                          ┌─────────────────────────┐
                          │     Caesars Growth       │
                          │     Partners (CGP)       │
                          └─────────────────────────┘

┌─────────────────────────┐          ┌─────────────────────────┐
│  Caesars Entertainment   │          │     Planet Hollywood     │
│   Operating Company      │          └─────────────────────────┘
│   (CEOC) — (OpCo)        │
└─────────────────────────┘          ┌─────────────────────────┐
                                     │   Caesars Interactive    │
                                     │   Entertainment (CIE)    │
                                     └─────────────────────────┘

                                     ┌─────────────────────────┐
                                     │   Horseshoe Baltimore    │
                                     └─────────────────────────┘
```

Source: Company filings

With so much activity on the financing and structuring front, it would be easy to forget that management was supposed to be running a business. Sadly, 2013 was not the year of the long-awaited return of the gambling masses. Revenues ended up flat on the prior year and property EBITDA was down 6%. The third quarter bucked the trend but had not compensated for an abysmal first quarter, which was a period affected by adverse weather conditions.

To make the year complete, on 31 December 2013 the downtrodden casino group had to recognise further asset write-downs for a grand total of $3.1 billion. The impairment was driven by charges totalling $2.4 billion in the Atlantic Coast region due to continued weakness in customer visits, resulting largely from intense regional competition. Operating cash flows had pursued their descent into oblivion. From a positive $30 million in 2012 they had turned negative, reaching minus $110 million a year later. The sharpness of the slide raised worries that Caesars might collapse before long. While pundits opined that Apollo and TPG's ultimate objective throughout their mystifyingly circuitous restructuring process was to avoid bankruptcy, by 31 December 2013 CEOC's senior secured leverage ratio had edged up to 4.52 times. The key maintenance covenant remained below the 4.75-to-1 limit. However, this feat had only been achieved by receiving agreement from the lenders to modify the calculation of the ratio for purposes of the maintenance test to exclude the $1.5 billion notes issued in February 2013.[40]

Divide and conquer

With two entities separately listed on Nasdaq (CEC since February 2012 and CAC since November 2013), two further subsidiaries (CERP and CGP) created to manage properties outside the remit of the main operating company, and 31 separate tranches of debt on its consolidated balance sheet, the Caesars Group started 2014 with a level of complexity that was not just baffling to the specialist press; it raised questions about what economic value PE investors as renowned as Apollo and TPG, the third and fifth largest alternative investment managers in the world respectively, could pretend to promote. Negotiations with Caesars's creditors were in constant danger of collapsing. The gambling group was no longer run to retain its market leadership or to contribute to the community where it operated (as proudly asserted on its website). Its PE backers, never short of ideas, cleverly contrived one new plan after another with the sole aim of retaining possession of the business, while management's sole mission had seemingly become to help them achieve this goal. The risk, as perceived by outsiders, was that this process could end up siphoning out the key cash-rich assets, leaving a lifeless shell behind.

Aiming to restructure the group further, Apollo and TPG appointed investment bank Lazard in February 2014. Rumours had it that the bank's role was to advise CAC, the controlling entity of the growth vehicle CGP.[41] A month later, it became clear what they had been working on. Through a newly-created entity unimaginatively called Caesars Growth Properties Holdings (CGPH), Caesars Growth Partners was to acquire from CEOC four casinos for a total of $2.2 billion (inclusive of debt) as well as a financial stake in the management fee stream for all of those properties. A rough estimate of the EBITDA multiple paid on these assets was 8.2 times: a bargain. In addition, the Planet Hollywood casino was being incorporated into CGPH. The transactions were financed by issuing two new debt instruments: a $1.1 billion term loan due 2021 and a $675 million high-yield note due 2022. Leverage on the new CGP structure sat at about six times, particularly attractive when compared to CEOC's 17.5 times.[42]

In anticipation of the deterioration of the operating company's various debt cover ratios, in late March credit agency Moody's piled on the pressure as it downgraded CEOC further and assigned a negative outlook rating.[43] Foreseeing that the OpCo might face growing liquidity issues, in May 2014 management and the two LBO sponsors devised yet another way to protect their equity interests in CERP and CGP by establishing a new company (the fifth in only 15 months) called Caesars Enterprise Services (CES). The latter was to be "granted a non-exclusive, irrevocable, worldwide, royalty-free license in and to all intellectual property owned or used by" CEOC and a couple of other divisions until then acting as caretakers of the group's intellectual property (IP). In summary, this reengineering exercise meant that the Caesars Group, and above all its key division CEOC, were relinquishing control of licences and IP to CES, the latter to be partly owned by CERP and CGPH, two entities that had just earned their independence from Caesars Entertainment Corporation in the previous year and were now getting their hands on management and licensing rights for assets not even under their control.

As the financial sponsors continued to act in ways adverse to the interest of creditors (that's putting it kindly), during that same month of May the gambling group faced claims from some of its lenders alleging fraudulent conveyance, a legal term literally meaning that the property transfers orchestrated in favour of CGP were unlawful. In view of the repercussion that these manoeuvres were having on the junior lenders' rights, CEOC's second-lien bonds traded at 40 to 45 cents on the dollar.[44] While creditors and the company locked horns throughout the summer over whether or not events of default had occurred, uncertainty gripped the company as a covenant breach seemed imminent. The only material maintenance covenant in the OpCo's credit agreement was the senior secured leverage covenant already mentioned, which promulgated that net debt could not exceed 4.75 times EBITDA. Because the company was allowed to exclude some loans for the purpose of calculating this ratio (in particular its first-lien bonds, but also the two tranches of secured notes raised in 2009), it had avoided a breach all along. If the LBO had not been agreed in the halcyon days of the debt bubble, that kind of covenant-lightness would not have been applied in the credit agreement and Harrah's/Caesars would have defaulted long ago. In the first quarter of 2014 the ratio had reached 4.6, compared to the pro forma 3.73 estimated by management.[45] Something had to be done.

To pre-empt an unavoidable breach, in July Caesars amended its credit facilities to modify the maintenance covenant and increase the ratio from 4.75-to-1 to 7.25-to-1. Likewise, to give itself sufficient headroom, the group excluded any incremental term loans incurred after 31 March 2014 from the definition. To make things even more impossible to track, management then chose to set different ratios for each division. So CERP had a maximum ratio of eight times and delivered 6.3 on 31 December 2014, while CGPH could not exceed six times and managed 3.1 on the same date. Other individual properties, such as the Horseshoe Baltimore and the Cromwell, had their own credit facility agreement setting maintenance covenants.[46] The CEOC's covenant would certainly have been breached by year end, but it was no longer possible to monitor. It was pure genius on the part of the PE sponsors.

Knowing that their allegations of default could take months to prove, the bondholders decided to press state regulators to reject the applications made by Caesars to transfer its assets from the operating company (CEOC) to the property holding CGPH. Their requests were denied, mostly because spreading the ownership of local casinos across a larger number of legal entities was perceived by state officials as an efficient way to keep some of them active in case of bankruptcy by one of the parent companies. Given the well-known financial weakness of CEOC, its bondholders were poorly positioned to argue otherwise. Having failed to convince the regulators, the bondholders were left with one last weapon: legal action.

On 4 August 2014, the bank Wilmington Savings Fund Society, in its capacity as indenture trustee for one of the second-priority senior secured notes (read, second-lien bonds), filed a lawsuit against the company and its directors alleging "claims for breach of contract, intentional and constructive fraudulent transfer, breach of fiduciary duty, aiding and abetting breach of fiduciary duty, and corporate waste." The outcome of the highly unusual asset transactions had been the de facto creation of a 'Good Caesars' and a 'Bad Caesars'. The bank, representing more than 50% of the noteholders – among them big-name hedge fund managers Appaloosa, Canyon Partners and Oaktree – wasn't just seeking damages. It also wanted certain of these transactions, the earliest of them dating back to 2010, to be declared void and for the recipients of the assets to return them to CEOC. The suit alleged that the operating division was insolvent when its parent company forced it to give up some of its most valuable assets, spotlighting in particular Caesars's interactive gambling unit, the Planet Hollywood casino in Vegas and Harrah's New Orleans. It was the latter's disposal that, according to the noteholders, constituted an event of default. Because the default had not been cured within 60 days of the notice given to the company, the lawsuit was the logical next step.[47]

*　*　*

To prove that it would not be outdone in the game of wasting money on legal fees, two days later Caesars filed its own lawsuit against more than 30 bondholders, including Appaloosa, Canyon, Oaktree and restructuring virtuoso Elliott, asserting that they were preventing the company from restructuring its debt. The casino operator accused some of the lenders of "disruptive appearances before gaming regulators" and "a baseless default notice" as well as having an ulterior motive in seeing that the group defaulted rather than survived.[48] Sabre-rattling had officially started between Caesars's shareholders and creditors, and the company's management kept ploughing ahead with the incessant capital restructuring, issuing another tranche of term loans (worth \$1.7 billion) due 2018.

Sadly for Caesars, Wilmington's lawsuit was emulated by other creditors. On 3 September 2014, a group of lenders holding the senior notes due 2015 and 2016, including hedge fund MeehanCombs, advisory firm Chicago Fundamental, and PE manager Trilogy Capital, filed a suit alleging that their rights had been infringed through backroom deals between Caesars and some noteholders. A month earlier, the gambling group had apparently paid par – 100 cents on the dollar – for \$155 million of notes held by some (not all) of the noteholders. The value assigned to the notes was more than double the prevailing market price for the debt. In exchange, CEOC's parent company's guarantee of principal and interest payments for all the remaining notes held by other investors had been removed from the notes' governing documents. Changes could be made to the note terms if holders owning at least 51% agreed to them, and Caesars had approached just the right proportion of investors to reach that threshold.[49]

By now all parties knew that CEOC's capital structure was unsustainable. It had been left with most of its debt while unrestricted assets had been siphoned off. On 11 November 2014, a *Bloomberg* article uncovered the existence of an arrangement between Caesars and its first-lien creditors that would see OpCo placed under Chapter 11 protection as early as 14 January 2015.[50] Heading inexorably towards bankruptcy, the group found itself confronted to a third legal action, this one filed on 25 November by UMB Bank, the indenture trustee and holder of CEOC's 8.5% senior secured notes due 2020. In a 207-page document, the company and its board members were rebuked for "unimaginably brazen corporate looting and abuse." The plaintiff also alleged that OpCo had been robbed of "more than \$4 billion in value and counting" through fraudulent asset transfers "without any legitimate commercial justification", and that when the company's management and PE owners had vindicated the series of manoeuvres as part of an inexorable deleveraging exercise, in fact CEOC's leverage had dramatically increased under their stewardship. In its request for redress, UMB was asking the court to declare the operating company insolvent and for a receiver to be appointed.[51] Four days before filing, eager to square accounts with the group's owners and management, UMB had served CEOC with a default notice on the $1.25 billion in notes.

In an attempt to increase the pressure during its protracted talks with the second-lien bondholders (the lenders represented by Wilmington Bank), Caesars decided not to pay them the $225 million coupon owed on 15 December. It had 30 days to pay before provoking an event of default, leading to instantaneous bankruptcy. Because of the ongoing litigation and CEOC's technical insolvency, management had taken the view that paying the interest due on that date would have hindered its restructuring efforts. Or perhaps it was just settling scores. To end an unforgettable year, CEOC saw its debt downgraded another notch by Moody's to the rating agency's second worst speculative grade, Ca.[52]

Despite the prevailing chaos, the most surprising decision was yet to come. To prolong the game, if that is what it was, management, Apollo and TPG proposed to merge CEC and CAC. No, this is not a typo. After creating CAC in 2013 in order to acquire assets from CEOC (the main OpCo of CEC, as per Figure 15.3) and supposedly focus on growth opportunities via CGP, the best idea they could come up with was to reunite the two entities that had just gone through 18 months of cash and asset-swapping. It would be tempting to conclude that the group would be back to square one. But do not forget that, in the meantime, the two PE owners had done two things: grant themselves exclusive voting rights on CGP strategic decisions, and move cash-generative assets out of CEOC towards the independent CGP and away from the grasp of OpCo's creditors. But the corporate reorganisation programme could not hide the operational reality. After a disappointing 2013, the year ending 31 December 2014 delivered further mediocrity: group EBITDA was down 10% on flat revenue. Impairment charges of $1 billion were booked. Goodwill impairment alone totalled $695 million. Bankruptcy might turn out to be the group's salvation after all.[53]

The die is cast

The year 2015 started with reports that a bankruptcy of dead broke CEOC was imminent. In anticipation, in December the operating company's first-lien noteholders had agreed with senior secured holders of several CEOC notes to support a restructuring that would split the business into two separate units, a real-estate investment trust (REITs pay little or no corporate income tax because they distribute most profits to their shareholders) and a management company running the properties. The arrangement would see Apollo and TPG lose ownership, eliminate $10 billion of OpCo's $18.4 billion debt and cut annual interest payouts by 75%.[54] The operating company's $2 billion-plus annual interest charge had handicapped the group's financial performance ever since the January 2008 LBO, thus shaving so much of the annual debt expense was throwing a lifeline to the business.

Still, it was not enough and a full capital restructuring was needed, so under that first-lien agreement, Caesars had agreed to place CEOC in bankruptcy by 20 January. Shareholders and creditors had spent months trying to outsmart each other, but in the end, there was just one victim. Steadfast in adversity, Caesars's operating company filed a voluntary petition for bankruptcy protection in Chicago, Illinois on 15 January 2015, starting a Chapter 11 reorganisation and hoping to give management time to devise a rescue plan while the lenders and PE owners became wedged into a mindless internecine feud. The reality is that the decision to file had not been as free-willed as it appeared. Three days earlier, a group of second-lien noteholders owed more than $4 billion, including the inveterate Appaloosa and Oaktree, had sought an involuntary petition to force CEOC into bankruptcy in Wilmington, Delaware.[55] The different choice in venue, Illinois vs. Delaware, could affect the ability of Caesars's lenders to pursue their various litigations.

The casino operator stated in its 'voluntary' petition that it had received the support of more than 80% of the first-lien noteholders, a sign that the most secured creditors were more than happy to give the group a chance to restructure, confident that their claims on CEOC's assets were still valid.[56] The two PE owners were determined to play both ends against the middle. The proposed bankruptcy reorganisation could enable first-lien creditors to recoup 92% of their loans while junior lenders would take home no more than $549 million for their $5.24 billion in second-lien notes.[57] Second-priority lenders knew that with so many assets re-assigned to independent entities within CAC, their case was less than straightforward, as the updated organisation chart (Figure 15.4) illustrates.

But if Caesars's management and PE backers thought that the bankruptcy protection given to CEOC also applied to them, they were in for a surprise. The success of the financial restructuring was dependent on getting support from CEOC's parent company (Nasdaq-listed CEC) and on the ability to continue to run the rest of the group unencumbered. Within ten days of the Chapter 11 petition, yet another group of lenders, including Silver Point Capital, the world's largest asset manager BlackRock, and the world's largest PE group Blackstone's credit management unit GSO Capital, asked a judge to bar the casino company from handing out fees to obtain votes in favour of the reorganisation.

Figure 15.4: Caesars's group structure upon CEOC's Chapter 11 filing in January 2015

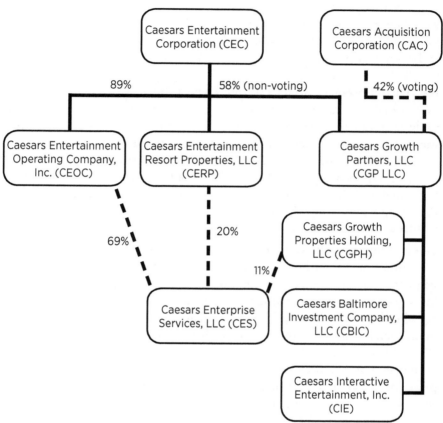

Source: Company filings

The plaintiffs claimed that they had been offered a $150 million consent fee to back CEOC's proposed refinancing, along with opportunities to buy new convertible notes worth $150 million issued by the healthier parent company (CEC) and take cash from the bankrupt OpCo.[58] A similar accusation, regarding inducements totalling $206 million, had been made by Appaloosa ahead of Caesars's bankruptcy filing.[59] The aim of the ongoing legal action by the various groups of lenders was to block CEOC's restructuring, knowing full well that, if it was allowed to take place, their loans' discounted value would crystallise – junior bonds were trading at about 14 cents on the dollar. But they received a boost when, five days earlier, a judge had ruled that Caesars's intra-group asset transfers in recent years had violated federal law.[60]

On 4 February 2015, Caesars announced that its harried chief exec Loveman would be stepping down in the summer and remain involved as chairman of CEC and CEOC.[61] After 17 years with the group, seven of them under LBO, and a stressful period of oft-recurring balance-sheet restructurings, now that CEOC had entered bankruptcy protection, Loveman fancied a well-deserved rest. His replacement, Mark Frissora, knew a thing or two about managing over-geared companies after having spent eight years at Hertz (see Chapter 3). Only 12 months before, Loveman had confidently declared that bankruptcy was not an option, essentially because the group didn't have any significant debt maturities until 2018.[62] But lenders had lost patience. The numerous restructuring shenanigans orchestrated for the best part of the last three years had convinced them that no one at Caesars was looking after their interests. Provoking a bankruptcy via a variety of lawsuits was their only option to prevent further asset-stripping.

The months that followed CEOC's bankruptcy filing were eventful, with a core group of defiant bondholders refusing to settle. Under pressure, on 15 February Caesars agreed to file a motion for a judge to appoint an examiner to investigate pre-bankruptcy insider dealings at the company – a similar request had already been filed by Appaloosa on 12 January. The appointment took place on 23 March, with the former Weil Gotshal partner and Watergate prosecutor Richard Davis entrusted with the chore.[63] In mid-June, UMB hit Caesars with an updated $6.3 billion lawsuit, seeking damages equal to the outstanding principal and interest and blocking the group's restructuring efforts.[64] After three years of almost permanent corporate reorganisation, management was now seemingly spending more time in court than in the office.

But it is time to leave Caesars at the mercy of its belligerent financial sponsors and creditors, turning itself into what *Forbes* magazine would later dub "a billionaire battleground".[65] Their bickering and the probing from bankruptcy lawyers and judges, though riveting and representing interesting precedents for deal-hungry LBO managers and lenders, are not what this review is about. Asset-stripping is what concerns us.

Render to Apollo what is Caesars's

In the years leading up to Caesars's collapse, the PE owners had used every trick in the book – they had practically written their own book – to delay the bankruptcy in order to give the economic recovery sufficient time to boost casino attendance. Their single-minded intention, or rather obsession, was to retain control of their investment. Observers and litigious lenders claimed that, with that sole goal in mind, Apollo and TPG had diverted ("plundered" was the term they used) the most valuable assets away from CEOC. A table (reproduced as Table 15.1) in Caesars Entertainment Corporation's 2014 financial accounts, and reporting EBITDA by entity, helps to illustrate their point.

Table 15.1: Caesars Group's property EBITDA by entity

	Years ended 31 December			Change	
	2014	2013	2012	2014 vs. 2013	2013 vs. 2012
	$m	$m	$m	%	%
CEOC	816	1,063	1,310	-23.2%	-18.9%
CERP	520	530	517	-1.9%	2.5%
CGP casinos	265	248	260	6.9%	-4.6%
CIE	84	62	46	35.5%	34.8%
Parent / other	4	-26	-105	115.4%	75.2%
Total	1,689	1,877	2,028	-10.0%	-7.4%

Source: Caesars Entertainment Corporation. Form 10-K for the fiscal year ended 31 December 2014

While CEOC was being gutted of very profitable casinos, the allocation of loans across the group had likewise become somewhat skewed in favour of the equity owners and their new creation, CGP. Based on data released in the group's annual report, leverage ratios as of 31 December 2014 read 19.7 times EBITDA for CEOC, 9.2 times for CERP and a measly 6.7 times for CGP. No wonder bondholders chose to take the matter to court. These transactions should have helped to re-equitise the group, but none of them took place on an arm's-length basis. The PE owners' seeming lack of respect for the company's creditors had seen the latter lose any claim on assets that had been transferred by one of the group entities (CEOC), which lenders partly controlled through various guarantees and security pledges, to another subsidiary (CGP) on which they had no influence. A large chunk of the debt, however, had been left behind with CEOC, as Table 15.2 exhibits. Since neither CERP nor CGP had filed for bankruptcy, it appears that Apollo and TPG were set to retain part ownership of two healthy, growing, profitable, reasonably-levered units.

Table 15.2: Caesars Group – summary of debt by financing structure (in $millions)

	Face value	Book value	Book value
	December 31, 2014		December 31, 2013
CEOC	18,371	16,100	15,783
CERP	4,832	4,774	4,611
CGP	2,386	2,326	721
CEC	13	13	—
Total debt	25,602	23,213	21,115
Current portion of long-term debt	(18,049)	(15,779)	(197)
Long-term debt	7,553	7,434	20,918

Source: Caesars Entertainment Corporation. Form 10-K for the fiscal year ended 31 December 2014

Many commentators were perplexed by the attitude adopted by Apollo and TPG as Caesars was leisurely heading for default (and ultimately bankruptcy). But the idea of setting up a good company (GoodCo) to help a corporation survive was not a novice concept. It is part of the toolkit of any restructuring enthusiast – a way to masquerade asset-stripping as value preservation and enable parts of a group to keep operating while the least performing units prepare for bankruptcy. This concept of GoodCo/BadCo was not dissimilar to the approach used by many a government when bailing out institutions during the financial crisis of 2008. The American authorities set up a Good Bank and a Bad Bank within Lehman Brothers, and the British Government followed the same approach in order to restructure Northern Rock, the country's third largest lender bailed out in September 2007.

So, if state officials were allowed to conduct themselves that way, why couldn't PE investors follow the same path? For one key reason: government interventions during the financial crisis had been imperative in order to limit the systemic risks associated with the failure of such large financial institutions, a sort of force majeure argument that Lehman's and Northern Rock's creditors were unlikely to dispute. Seeking the latter's consent was superfluous as the reorganisation was carried out for the public weal. Apollo and TPG could not apply the same logic with CEOC's bondholders, so they bullied their way through a coercive restructuring.

The sad part is that private equity as practised in this case seems almost exclusively focused on financial engineering to generate returns, and by doing so Apollo and TPG were dragging corporate executives down a dangerous path. CEO Loveman and his team spent as much energy managing the group's capital structure as they did running day-to-day operations, if not more. As the Great Recession and the quiescent economy that ensued led to a permanent reduction in casino attendance, Caesars was unable to grow into its capital structure. The PE investors' contemptuous response was to drain the corporation of valuable and profitable assets with a view of protecting their own interests, irrespective of their obligations vis-à-vis Caesars's creditors.

It is not known what the various credit agreements between the group and its lenders state, but the sale of material assets of a distressed company, allegedly "below fair value" if we believe the claims made by the suing parties, to affiliated interests in the equity control group at the expense of creditors is not a common practice. For the simple reason that it is usually disallowed. In bankruptcy, owners typically walk away empty-handed unless there is money left after paying creditors in full. By setting up separate subsidiaries beyond the reach of these creditors, the two PE investors were diverting a whole chunk of the asset base to their benefit.

According to some estimates, by the time it filed for Chapter 11 Caesars had lost half of its enterprise value. The matter-of-fact accounts relayed in the creditors' lawsuits give an insight into the kind of vigorous and uniquely unpleasant practices employed by today's LBO fund managers to extract value, almost at any cost. In their respective lawsuits, Wilmington and UMB griped about the varied transgressions allegedly committed. A non-exhaustive list included the transfer of trademarks in August 2010; the transfer of interactive gaming operations by CEOC to CEC for little or no consideration in 2011 (two years later ascribed a value by CEC of as much as $779 million); the relocation in September 2013 of two CEOC Las Vegas properties to CERP; and, as already reported, in October 2013 the transfer of Planet Hollywood and the Baltimore project to CGP followed in March 2014 by the sale to the same entity of four more CEOC properties. The "looting" saw intellectual property, including the Total Rewards customer loyalty programme, re-assigned for no consideration. UMB also denounced that the May 2014 $1.75 billion issuance of new term loans had been structured "to require CEOC to use a quarter of the proceeds to purchase $427 million of unmatured, unsecured CEOC notes from [...] CGP for more than 100 cents on the dollar, a premium so substantial that it implies a negative yield." The group structure had been altered beyond recognition and included the sale of 5% in CEOC to undisclosed parties, also in May 2014, as shown in Figure 15.5.[66]

Apollo and TPG proved very imaginative in the way they extracted value, giving a new definition to economist Joseph Schumpeter's concept of creative destruction. But all is not lost, as this case study describes an instructive omnishambles from which regulators, legislators, investors and lenders can all draw valuable lessons:

- Do not expect PE investors to abide by contractual obligations towards lenders. Financial sponsors are only accountable (according to Apollo's public statements) to their limited partners. This naturally raises far-reaching questions regarding the type of capitalism we want to foster in the aftermath of the biggest financial crisis since the 1930s.

- LPs can decide for themselves whether their capital is being managed appropriately. If they want to invest in private equity because they are keen to support the economy and social cohesion, then deals like the buyout of Harrah's do not fulfil that goal.

- Once the dust has settled, CEOC has left Chapter 11 and the court rulings have been served, the behaviour of Apollo and its sidekick TPG will either be seen as a clever act of moneymaking prowess (for equity preservation) or a sordid, modern way of defrauding creditors. In the latter case, it might lead to more profound changes in regulation than the ones introduced so far post-financial crisis.

- Finally, in view of the way their peers were treated during Caesars's glorious reorganisation, LBO lenders will need to decide whether investing in junior debt is now too risky and requires a much punchier coupon, whether it is worth taking the risk of working with buyout fund managers, or even if they should avoid certain PE groups because of their track record.

Figure 15.5: Caesars's group structure in August 2014

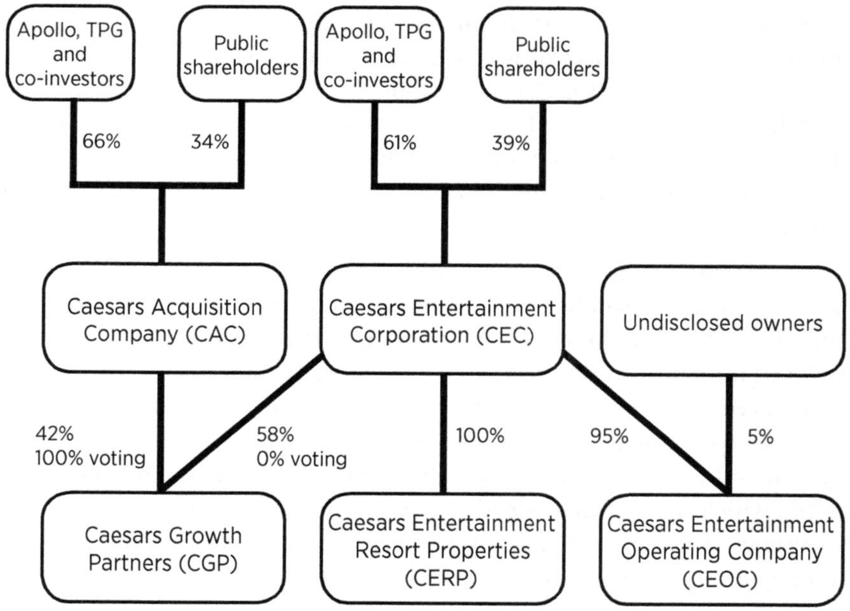

Source: Wilmington Savings Fund Society lawsuit filing document dated 4 August 2014

The fall of Caesars

Management, Apollo and TPG waited in vain for the return of the gambling public. Between 2007 and 2013 Caesars's home market, Nevada, had seen gambling revenues dip from $6.8 billion to $6.5 billion, but the biggest corrections had come from the two other major states that accounted for the second and third largest share of the group's activity: gambling revenues for the states of New Jersey and Mississippi were 43% and a quarter off their peaks respectively. The Great Recession had been followed by an enduring coma.

What had hurt incumbents like Caesars was the proliferation of casinos across the country, taking market share away from established operators and creating a saturation problem even as the broader economy remained sluggish. Desperate to increase tax revenues, local authorities in several states had chosen to expand their gambling offering: Maryland and Ohio had approved their first casinos in 2008 and 2009, while Massachusetts and New York had followed suit in 2011 and 2013 respectively.[67] In this context, financial results at Caesars had failed to deliver on budget but the group's long-term debt had pursued its ascent (as Figure 15.6 demonstrates) despite repeated attempts by the two financial sponsors to purchase slices of it at a discount on the secondary markets. For the best part of the LBO, Caesars's liabilities were one-quarter to one-third larger than its assets, not just because of its combined $20 billion in long-term loans, but also due to the amount of contractual debt obligations that had been accumulated: capitalised interest payments exceeded or approached $10 billion in most years between 2008 and 2013.

Harrah's had paid eight times forward EBITDA when gobbling up Caesars in mid-2005. With $4.2 billion of existing debt, Caesars's capital structure was then levered at less than 45%.[68] At the time of their merger, the two entities employed a total of 95,000 people. After ten years under LBO, the business had reduced its headcount by a third. Despite managing nine of the most strategically positioned Las Vegas casinos, generating 29% of the Strip's revenues in 2009, and being the most geographically diversified gambling operator in the US, which should have helped to weather the downturn better than most, its leverage of 11.5 times operating profit and 80% of total capital made the gambling group a basket case straight from the get-go.[69]

Socked by growing loan commitments, within months Caesars had turned into a zombie. Worse, from vindicating the largest enterprise value of the sector in 2006, by the time its CEOC division filed for Chapter 11 nine years later, the group had been overtaken by Las Vegas Sands (with a breathtaking $55 billion EV), MGM Resorts ($23 billion) and Wynn Resorts ($22 billion). Caesars was then valued at $15 billion. Its three larger rivals also suffered from a sluggish home market, but they had capitalised on their overseas operations, maintaining leverage below 50% at the same time. Macau, the biggest gambling market in Asia, where Caesars's three main American competitors operated, delivered a welcome respite from weak demand in many US regions. Las Vegas Sands, in particular, controlled the world's largest casino: spread across 546,000 square feet, the Venetian Macao operates 3,000 gaming machines, 870 tables and poker games, 24 restaurants and bars, and 3,000 hotel rooms. MGM's biggest venue is also located there: its Grand Macao is just short of 222,000 square feet. It is the seventh largest casino in the world and accounted for a large proportion of its owner's earnings growth in recent years, helping group EBITDA grow 62% in the first quarter of 2012, for instance, when all US properties experienced a drop in earnings. Wynn's Macau venue is a smaller affair, with 1,270 gaming machines and 600 rooms spanning 100,000 square feet, but it is also a strong contributor to Wynn Resorts's operating profits.[70]

Figure 15.6: Caesars's consolidated long-term debt (2007-14)

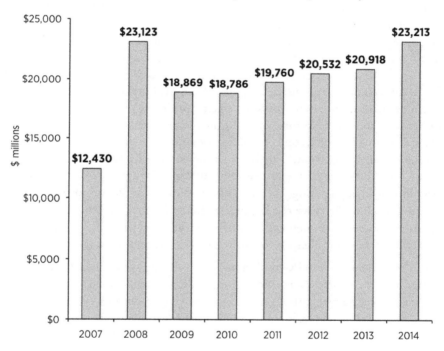

Source: Caesars Entertainment Corp annual reports. Note: long-term debt as at 31 December 2014 was shown as $7.4 billion in the accounts since $15.8 billion of the loans were due within one year. The debt remained due as CEOC filed for bankruptcy.

Caesars never managed to get a licence in the Chinese city, in the face of opposition from the local government. It threw in the towel in October 2012, choosing instead, in November of the following year, to dispose of a land concession it owned in the city.[71] The group's lack of strategic ambition was exacerbated by troubles at home as a result of competition from new entrants, leading to a move away from the least performing assets, including the disposals of Harrah's St. Louis casino in November 2012 and of the Claridge Hotel Tower in February 2014, and the closure of Atlantic City-based Showboat in the summer of 2014.

I came, I saw, I surrendered ownership

For the two PE investors, the transaction will hopefully lead to some valuable changes. Both investors prided themselves on being contrarian, a claim made by Apollo in its March 2011 listing prospectus, and by TPG on its website when describing its investment philosophy. In their Harrah's buyout, they were wrong to go against the grain and would have been well advised to peruse the target's Code of Commitment on responsible gaming. But unlike their counterparts at TPG, Apollo's executives did not shy away from the limelight after the gambling operator's bankruptcy, making several statements in the press that their fiduciary duties were to their investors (the LPs), not to anyone else. Wharton alumnus Marc Rowan – as noted, one of Apollo's co-founders – was leading the charge on the restructuring front. A member of the boards of CEC and CAC, he was quoted in a June 2015 *Fortune* magazine article as saying: "I'll never shy away from financial engineering," before adding "People can like or not Apollo, but we are tenacious, [...] we dig in, and we try to fix the problems."[72] As Julius Caesar once declared: "men willingly believe what they wish to".[73] Some lenders argued that these problems were created by the PE owners in the first place.

There is evidence that TPG took a back seat during what turned out to be a period of very controversial intra-group transactions. Apollo's approach, by contrast, was to actively seek ever more creative ways to preserve equity value. One clue that would explain Apollo's uncompromising behaviour during the reorganisation process of 2010 to 2014 is that the PE group is a hugely experienced distressed investor. In a prospectus issued for its own IPO in 2011, the firm bragged about its "unique set of skills" in "establishing flexible capital structures with long-term debt maturities and few, if any, financial maintenance covenants." Its executives often took position on the debt side of a transaction, so they thought more like debt providers than long-term equity backers. They were not a conventional source of capital, they were bottom fishers. The afflicted situation Caesars was in suited their investment style. Their mind worked best in situations where incremental tweaking rather than grand expansion plans created value.

For that reason Apollo (with TPG in tow) had made side bets in Caesars's debt when loans started trading at significant discounts. By early 2014 credit analysts had started speculating that the bondholders in CEOC would be offered a debt-for-equity swap either in the Nasdaq-listed CEC or in CEOC itself. But the PE owners had no intention of relinquishing any part of their stockholding in exchange for a partial debt write-down. To do so would have revealed signs of weakness. Worse, they could stand accused of not acting in the interest of their LPs, the ultimate insult for any self-assured LBO fund manager. This point was made clear by one of Apollo's representatives, Charles Zehren, in a statement reproduced by the *Wall Street Journal* ten days before CEOC's voluntary bankruptcy filing:

> "Large, complex transactions involve tough negotiations and Apollo takes its fiduciary responsibility for its funds very seriously, [...] as such, we will aggressively protect our investments and defend our companies using all the tools available to us, which greatly differentiates us from our peers."[74]

All along, creditors had been looking for a square deal, but Apollo and TPG didn't see it that way. In that respect, the outcome of the UMB v. Caesars and Wilmington v. Caesars lawsuits was widely regarded as crucial. The casino operator's aggressive and creative financial engineering practices were likely to inspire other PE groups to disregard the rights of LBO lenders, which would in turn have repercussions on future relationships between financial sponsors and banks, and the way transactions get structured.

One entertaining anecdote perhaps illustrates the contention that PE owners do care more about their own interests than the well-being of the portfolio companies they aggressively lever up. TPG's co-founder David Bonderman's 70th birthday bash, held in Las Vegas on Saturday 17 November 2012, could serve as appendix A. First reported in the *New York Times*, this celebration took place at the Wynn Las Vegas, a hotel located on the Strip, a five-minute cab ride from other feted high-end venues like Caesars Palace, Paris Las Vegas, Flamingo, and Harrah's Las Vegas, all part of troubled Caesars's collection of assets. The press rightly wondered why Bonderman would be prepared to spend, according to *Fortune* magazine, a rumoured $7 million to $8 million with one of his investee company's main rivals at a time when Caesars was down to its last cent.[75] Maybe the relationship between the casino operator and its Texan owner had become strained, which would explain a Caesars executive's comments relayed in that same *Fortune* article: "It was so demotivating to the people that work here that our principal owner is going to have this big event somewhere else." Could it be that the billionaire did not want Caesars's staff to witness firsthand the decadence of the country's upper class? Perhaps it was simply because the Wynn resort boasted on its website that it offered the ultimate party destination.

In other ways, Apollo and TPG were typical financial sponsors. When it came to dividend-yielding stocks, we saw that they were happy to charge 15% per annum, accruing 'income' year in, year out. Since Caesars could not quite afford such a heavy cash burden, preferred dividends kept accumulating, reaching $300 million by December 2008, $650 million the following year end, and $717 million by February 2010, at which point the two investors finally decided to cancel all accrued dividends and to convert their preferred stock into common stock.[76]

Naturally, Caesars's PE investors decided to raise follow-on funds years after the financial crisis of 2008. In part thanks to its widely reported efforts to turn the desperate Caesars situation to its benefit, in January 2014 Apollo announced the closing of its eighth investment fund, with $17.5 billion from outside investors and $880 million of its staff's money.[77] The firm convinced its investors that its approach to investing offered the right kind of risk/reward profile. Three years earlier, the firm had even managed to pull off its own IPO. By contrast, TPG struggled to get its fundraising plans off the ground. Having launched its campaign in early 2014, it only hit its $10 billion hard cap in the spring of 2016,[78] not specifically because of the investment in Harrah's, although it could hardly have helped, but due to a collection of poorly considered moves, including the hereinbefore reviewed TXU case study (see Chapter 5) and the already discussed failures of Aleris and of Washington Mutual, a West Coast bank bailed out only six months after TPG's investment.

A look at our two protagonists' performance sheds some well-needed light on why LPs treated them differently. Both Apollo's and TPG's vintage funds that invested in Harrah's saw their returns badly impacted. As of 31 December 2014, the two 2006 investment vehicles, Apollo Investment Fund VI and TPG Partners V, modestly displayed net IRRs of +9.5% and +3.5% respectively. Not great when compared to the target 8% hurdle rate, or with the 7% achieved by the unlevered S&P 500 index returns (including dividends) between January 2007 and December 2014.[79] The contrast between the two funds makes Apollo look good.

In truth, this exercise should also include the returns achieved by both firms on their purchases of Caesars's debt on the secondary market. In 2009, for instance, they had bought second-lien notes for 37 cents on the dollar.[80] In addition, in 2008 both had raised even larger vehicles than the previous vintages: Apollo Investment Fund VII and TPG Partners VI had received $14.7 billion and $19.8 billion in commitments respectively. By 31 March 2015, Apollo VII presented a net IRR of 25% whereas TPG VI's lagged well behind at 11%. Had their LPs invested in the S&P 500 between 1 January 2009 and 31 March 2015 they would have yielded 17.7% a year (including dividends reinvested), or 26% with a leverage ratio of 50%. To quote Shakespeare: "men at some time are masters of their fates."[81]

PART NINE
Trick or Treat

EPILOGUE
Sheriffs and Cowboys

"You start with a given: free enterprise is the engine of our society; communism is pretty much down the drain and proven so; and there doesn't appear to be anything else that can compare to a free society based on a market economy. Nothing can touch that system — not unless leadership and management get selfish or lazy."[1]

Sam Walton, Wal-Mart founder

PRIVATE EQUITY HAS A FUTURE; IT JUST NEEDS TO BE markedly different from its past. At the outset, LBOs won plaudits for playing a central role in cleansing economies of underperforming businesses, stripping them of non-core assets, slashing overheads, refocusing their strategies. Yet the infatuation has worn off, for a troubling pattern has emerged. Every once in a while, the sector gets carried away, throwing caution to the wind by structuring acquisitions without applying adequate risk management or common sense. The use of leverage in PE deals emulates the pattern of any substance abuse. It often proves difficult to take oneself off the sauce. Unless the patient is strong willed and decides to check into rehab, changing destructive habits sometimes requires the intervention of social workers. In the case of LBOs, third parties will need to step in to restrict the most provocative practices applied by some, not all, of the industry's worst offenders.

Zombie, or not zombie: that is the question

When they first arrived on the scene in the 1970s, buyouts instantly became one of the most important drivers of corporate restructuring in America, and progressively in Europe. Some, rather absurdly, saw private equity as the bridge between the traditional corporate culture, some of it family-owned, often portrayed as antiquated in its financial management style, and the ultimate stage of post-modern capitalism, the take-no-prisoner, dog-eat-dog Darwinist approach that frequently prevailed in the decade leading up to the financial crisis. Over time, as the case studies in this book demonstrate, the PE firms' aggressive methods in terms of financial engineering, value extraction, and makeshift restructuring produced their own lethal side effects that crippled the corporate landscape. If there is one consistent message that comes to light from the reviewed case studies and Table A, it is that excessive leverage, two-thirds of total capital and above, just does not sit well with many businesses.

Table A: Capital structure parameters of the case studies

	Leverage ratio (debt-to-total EV)	Comments
Caesars	80% in 2008	Leverage reached 90% soon after the LBO and never fell until the Chapter 11 filing in 2015.
Celanese	83% upon delisting in 2005	Leverage was managed through A&Es once the company was publicly listed.
Debenhams	70% upon delisting in 2003	Leverage dropped to 40% at the time of the IPO in 2006, then exceeded 80% in 2008 before falling thereafter.
DX	Two-thirds upon delisting in 2006	Leverage was no longer a problem by the time the company was publicly listed.
eDreams	Three-quarters in Permira's SBO in 2010	The IPO brought leverage down to 30% in April 2014 but leverage then rose to two-thirds by late 2014.
EMI	Over three-quarters in 2007 delisting	Equity became worthless shortly after the LBO, which was confirmed when Citi gained full ownership in 2011.
Foxtons	Two-thirds upon LBO in 2007	Leverage was no longer a problem by the time the company was publicly listed.
Frans Bonhomme	Three-quarters in quaternary of 2005	Leverage exceeded 75% after the dividend recap of 2007.
Gala Coral	Two-thirds in quaternary of 2005	Leverage shot up to nearly 100% after equity was deemed worthless by Permira's and Candover's LPs in 2009.
Hertz	84% in delisting of 2005	Leverage went below 70% after the IPO, then back up to 86% in late 2008, and fell gradually thereafter.

	Leverage ratio (debt-to-total EV)	Comments
PagesJaunes	Less than 50% in 2006 due to the PIPE	By 2011 leverage exceeded 80%. Eventually, creditors took over.
PHS	Two-thirds in delisting of 2005	Refinanced in 2007 to reach 75%.
Seat Pagine Gialle	60% in 2004	Leverage reached 90% in 2009 and 98% in 2011 and 2013.
TXU	79% in delisting of 2007	By 2011 equity had lost 90% of its value, so leverage was at 98%. It never fell until Chapter 11 filing in 2014.

The LBO boom of the noughties will be remembered for many new tricks, but one unintended consequence and palpable legacy of the exorbitant debt packages raised during that period will be the emergence of corporate zombies, the embodiment if ever there was one of PE's lethal potential. When pushed to extremes, leveraged buyouts have the potential to do more harm than good over a prolonged period. Our case subjects were once prestigious companies. Some are now synonymous with brinkmanship between investors and creditors that battle for control over these corpses. The Caesars, Celanese, EMI and TXU deals show that it has become all too frequent for LBO lenders and financial sponsors to use their contractual rights on the underlying assets as a way to fight it out in court, without regard to what years of legal wrangling do to the indebted corporations.

For those curious to ascertain how it feels to be a corporate executive sitting like a lame duck while creditors and PE owners vie for the assets of a company you have worked painstakingly to build over the years, consider the following words from Neil Goulden, at the time still chairman of the largest British gambling operator, Gala Coral:

> "At one stage, the mezz lenders accused me of being in the pocket of the private equity players. The senior lenders accused me of being a mezz poodle. And my private equity players accused me of being too close to the senior lenders. My view on that was I had to be doing it about right because everyone seemed to hate me."[2]

A mere mortal would turn schizophrenic at less. Quite a few of these investee companies, riven by years of war between investors and creditors, serve as exhibits in the case against the sector. Industry insiders pledge that these cases remain exceptions, but the reason why mid-sized buyouts like DX, eDreams, Foxtons, Frans Bonhomme and PHS were included in this book is to demonstrate that, contrary to the argument commonly offered, the sector's extravagance is not confined to the 'mega' end of the deal spectrum. Which is not necessarily all that surprising, since no one running a buyout fund has ever received formal training. Instead, they were all expected to learn on the job, adopting a trial-and-error approach that showed its limits in 2008. As TPG's co-founder David Bonderman once put it himself, the PE approach can be described as "catch as catch can".[3] We saw where it led TPG.

Leverage is now part of Wall Street lore. It is firmly entrenched as a way for fund managers to make money with minimum personal risk but maximum reward. The corrosive use of debt is a factor that contributed, in the years leading up to and since the Credit Crunch, to the loss of faith in the free-market model by a large chunk of the public. With the private equity industry and the whole capitalist system so much under the influence of debt, little long-term value can be shared among all the participants. PE investors' obsession with leverage can be shockingly short-sighted. Their ingenuity is admirable, the impact of their practices questionable. Debt usage must somehow be reined in, through stricter regulation if necessary.

Hopefully the cases illustrated in this book provided more than just a jolly good tour of what not to do when heading a multibillion-dollar fund. Somewhere in there is a salutary moral lesson about the devastating mess that one can expect when applying Wall Street's favourite, hastily-measured blend of greed, callousness and indifference. It is indecent to suck any spare cash out of a well-run corporation in order to upstream dividends for the sole purpose of enriching a small number of investors. It is conceited to assert that any behaviour, no matter how vile towards third parties (lenders, employees, suppliers or tax authorities), is acceptable as long as it serves the interest of LPs (and of GPs, of course) – in what world can one behave unscrupulously towards the majority in order to serve a privileged minority? It is immoral to incentivise senior corporate executives to cut costs and headcount for short-term gains, notwithstanding the long-term damage it does to the over-indebted investee company – why is it okay to lever up perfectly viable, cash-rich enterprises in the hope of making extraordinary gains but not to suffer any consequences when these businesses get hurt or destroyed in the process?

The crucible of regulation

In the past, as the case studies prove, private equity operated with relatively few checks and balances. Yet the main question, which has been left partly unanswered many years post-financial crisis, is how governments and supervisory bodies should act.

There is much confusion among free-enterprise advocates following the increasing regulatory and political pressure exercised over the financial services and banking sectors since 2008. Some issued cataclysmic predictions with respect to our way of life if we aimed to stifle entrepreneurship. No government or regulator anywhere in the Western world is considering introducing limits on entrepreneurship, innovation and business financing – except in cases where such financial engineering and exotic and toxic products are used to dabble with other people's money without much care for the broader social, economic and political consequences. Supporting free enterprise is one thing, letting financial wizards gamble with people's savings and retirement funds is another. As we saw in several of our examples, via quick flips and dividend recapitalisations the intention of many PE owners is no longer to fund the underlying companies' development. Rather, it often seems that their guiding principle is to suck every ounce of spare cash out of their investees and to redistribute it to their LPs as fast as possible (not forgetting to levy a fee in-between).

Equally, there is little logic in toughening up the regulatory framework for commercial and investment banks if central banks and other agencies let shadow lending and equity investing grow unsupervised. In the wake of the financial crisis, guidance from US regulators tried to dissuade American banks from arranging LBO loans exceeding six times EBITDA. By early 2014, already 40% of LBOs carried at least that much leverage.[4] That's the problem with guidelines – they do not have to be adhered to. Interestingly, that restriction does not even apply to non-bank lenders.

After 2010, American banks were also compelled by the Volcker Rule to pull out of most proprietary speculative activities like alternative investments in hedge funds and private equity. This is a commendable approach as it protects commercial banking from risky investments, but unfortunately the number of self-regulated private debt funds has mushroomed. And the latter do not have to comply with many of the new rules. Understandably, they have beefed up their market share and are predicted to continue doing so. Some are even bringing under the same roof private debt and private equity activities, which generates conflicts of interest. With its growing size, the alternative asset management industry increasingly creates the moral hazard that has plagued banking for so long. As Table A above illustrates, it seems that restricting leverage multiples, like US regulators have suggested, would be a way to avoid excessive risk-taking. Whether debt is limited to a multiple of earnings or a percentage of total capital (60% seems a reasonable compromise), guidelines on leverage restrictions will need to become law if regulators are serious about reform.

All the evidence also suggests that private equity and private debt fund managers will not voluntarily offer to submit themselves to further disclosures. In 2007, as the credit bubble was unwinding and the first LBOs were showing signs of stress, in the UK Sir David Walker was commissioned by the industry itself to produce guidelines for disclosure and transparency. Some of the recommendations concerned the need to report on portfolio companies' performance and prospects. Many of the sector's grandees, including CVC and BC Partners, never bothered to issue an annual report as was recommended by the Walker guidelines. Permira and Apax both stopped publishing such a review in 2012. Instead, they stated that the information released online was plenty enough. If so, why did Permira remove from its website's investment section any reference to the Gala Coral and Seat Pagine Gialle transactions – at the time the second largest LBO in Britain and the largest in Italy respectively? So much for transparency! We saw that Charterhouse followed a similar path by erasing PHS and Vivarte from its log of realised investments. By choosing to omit their failures when advertising their credentials, these investors give outsiders a very incomplete picture of their true capabilities. Stricter rules around disclosures must be introduced.

Arguably, the biggest challenge to capitalism in the early part of the 21st century is to maintain a steady flow of liquidity in the global financial system in order to support the market economy while making sure that this same liquidity does not find itself redirected in unreasonable proportions towards the coffers of the '1%' wealthiest section of the population, as seems to have occurred during the LBO bubble. Prohibiting predatory interest rates like the 15%-plus charged by some financial sponsors (refer to the Caesars, PHS and DX cases) would be a start. By charging such high coupons, PE firms no longer seem willing to take equity risk. They would rather take the place of junior lenders. Yet another proof that they have turned into rent-seekers. No one interested in the long-term viability of our economies can be in favour of a system that operates according to the mainstream principle of enriching a tiny minority to the detriment of the vast majority, but in essence this is what modern capitalism has become, and private equity is one of its most stark embodiments.

The crusade for disintermediation

If there is one constant of the capitalist model, it is that every generation has its lot of takeover artists. The 1890s witnessed the emergence of the almighty trusts, the 1920s and 1930s saw vertical integration become fashionable, while conglomerates became ubiquitous during the 1960s and 1970s. Since the 1980s, leveraged buyouts have grown in stature and become one of the most efficient modern methods of profit making. In North America and some European countries, buyouts can account for half or more of yearly M&A transactions.

But the unconvincing track record of many PE firms may have signalled a shift away from traditional LBO houses to the benefit of other investors. Recent trends show that buyout shops are being squeezed out of some lucrative deals, many of these transactions using the same financial engineering techniques implemented by PE firms over the last 30 years. Sizeable LPs have decided to disintermediate the investment process. Family offices and pension funds are likely to steal market share from traditionally fee-hungry GPs. In emerging markets, sovereign wealth funds are choosing local solutions to keep control of the decision-making process and save on the raft of expenses usually extracted by traditional fund managers. Because of the financial sponsors' extravagant practices, limited partners will gradually upstage general partners, eating away at the latter's market share and margins. Some LPs will insist on tighter supervision, others on more co-investment opportunities; others, finally, will continue to build in-house skills to go direct.

Corporate executives' do-it-yourself temptation

Executives working for PE-backed companies can be blunt about how much value they believe modern-day LBO specialists bring to the table. When commenting on the secondary buyout that Charterhouse completed for his betting-shop chain Coral Eurobet, finance director Mick Mariscotti opined:

> "It is not a question of Charterhouse thinking it is bringing anything to the business. This is very much a management buyout: Charterhouse have seen our business plan and they are backing it."[5]

Going forward, CEOs and other members of the C-suite are likely to exercise more caution when dealing with financial sponsors, primarily because an increasing number of executives are mistreated, blamed for operational and financial underperformance and subsequently replaced, even in the numerous cases when failure is due to the inordinate leverage stacked on their company's balance sheet by PE backers. At exasperatingly frequent intervals, management under LBO will be asked to meet a covenant test, recalibrate a budget to take into account a more aggressive cost-cutting strategy, or prepare a special cash-flow forecast to assess the potential for special dividend recap. For a finance director, that does not leave much time for proper financial strategy.

It is rumoured that up to three-quarters of senior executives present at the outset of an LBO get replaced during the holding period. CEOs and CFOs are particularly exposed, as we saw in the Debenhams, EMI, PagesJaunes and Seat Pagine Gialle scenarios. So it makes a lot of sense for corporate executives to ask themselves a simple question: could they complete an MBO without the hassle and the aggravation of having to deal with aggressive, overconfident and greedy PE investors who only care about one thing: to extract as much value as imaginable (you might have noted that their imagination appears limitless) in as short a time as possible, without much consideration for the long-term consequences on the business.

Some might express scepticism that lenders will ever be willing to transact directly with corporate clients when it comes to complex LBO transactions. However, once you consider the way PE firms behaved towards lenders during the financial crisis, either suing them (EMI) or allegedly breaching contractual obligations (Caesars), debt providers should welcome the opportunity to initiate closer relationships with corporations keen to prioritise the long-term viability of the underlying business over short-term speculation.

Creditors at the gate

Banks and other traditional lenders have experienced a liquidity squeeze due to tougher in-house monitoring and stricter regulation (compliance departments have all expanded). As discussed, the consequence has been the emergence of non-bank lenders. If one ignores the PE groups' own private debt units, independent credit specialists, many of them aggressive hedge funds with little time for relationship banking, are likely to play a 'regulatory' role by punishing excessive leverage. Independent debt fund managers will not be as open to repetitive A&Es that allow borrowers to chip away at maturity walls, and will be more inclined to take control of, and run, zombie companies themselves. They might welcome higher-yielding bonds as part of a temporary refinancing, especially if they see a way through a debt-for-equity swap, but they are active investors more willing to take charge of an asset.

As we saw in several of our case studies, buyouts frequently became lender-led. In the cases of EMI, Gala Coral, PagesJaunes and Seat, the existing lenders simply converted their debt holdings into equity. In other cases, like Frans Bonhomme, aggressive lenders bought the distressed loans at a discount on the secondary market with the aim of inviting themselves to the negotiating table. Centerbridge and Angelo Gordon bought 'loans-to-own' from CLOs, then squeezed Cinven to a small minority position. It was also the approach taken by several private debt and hedge fund managers in the case of TXU and Oncor. This sort of market-driven regulation often has more weight than government initiatives or the use of judges, mediators and *mandataires ad hoc* as referees or peacemakers. What is troubling when going through some of the cases is how often traditional lenders seem content to let PE firms retain control of assets they have mismanaged for several years. In the future, creditors need to step in, if only to avoid more Caesars-type scenarios becoming a common affair – it is clear that some financial sponsors are more than happy to ride roughshod over their responsibilities towards lenders in order to preserve their LPs' interests.

New beginning

One of the main conclusions that can be drawn from this book is that not all sectors are suitable for LBO transactions. Traditionally, PE investing had always specifically excluded industries deemed highly speculative, those too volatile or overly regulated. Unfortunately, some PE specialists became overconfident and decided to use high leverage in parts of the economy that everyone knew were cyclical (retail and estate agents among them) or exposed to constant changes in licensing rules (like gambling operators). The EMI, PagesJaunes and Seat scenarios also serve to demonstrate that LBO managers must be able to identify early on risks related to disruptive innovation. At present, most are ill-equipped to do so.

The buyout industry's unique selling points will continue to give its participants a competitive advantage over alternatives like corporate buyers and public markets. PE firms can deliver speedy deal closure thanks to readily available cash, a network of long established connections with key lenders, and a strong expertise in due diligence and financial structuring. Besides, unlike corporate mergers, bids from financial sponsors do not usually need to endure lengthy antitrust reviews. For that reason alone, sellers looking for immediacy and certainty – that was the situation at Hertz and EMI – should be willing to accept a slightly lower price from fund managers not factoring synergistic benefits into their offer. Being private likewise provides, in principle, the investee company with more freedom to fund multi-year projects without being overly concerned with quarterly results (that is, until management realises that quarterly loan covenants are almost as draconian). All these arguments will remain valid going forward, but the destructive practices of private equity portrayed in these case studies will have to stop or be stopped.

Wal-Mart founder Sam Walton adds the following comment to the selected passage quoted at the start of this conclusion:

> "In the future, free enterprise is going to have to be done well – which means it benefits the workers, the stockholders, the communities, and, of course, management, which must adopt a philosophy of servant leadership."

As touched upon in this book's introduction, many sector pundits assert that PE is a net creator of economic value, a faithful supporter of social progress. Our case studies have shown that it can also be harmful and deadly, frequently letting portfolio companies drift without moorings. In the wrong hands, because of its heavy reliance on leverage, private equity can be unfair and brutal. When using debt in disproportionate amounts, the penalty for being wrong is total or partial loss of ownership, usually to the creditors' benefit. Sometimes it even leads to bankruptcy, with unquantifiable consequences for the investee.

Some of the masterminds featured in our case studies are part of the industry's top brass, which goes to show that no one is safe from the occasional slip-up. In view of their recent track record, the financiers leading the charge at the most influential LBO firms have undoubtedly failed the 'Sam Walton test'. They certainly do not seem to have drawn appropriate conclusions from their mistakes. The rules of free competition dictate that the authors of such failures should take the hint that their investment skills are shaky and retire, retrain or be forced out. Years after leading their firms astray, many of the sector's lead protagonists are still very much in charge.

Who knows whether these 21st century financial gurus will ever be able to restore credibility among the institutions giving them money to invest and among the corporate executives they must partner with to generate top-quartile returns. If LBO professionals prove unable to self-medicate and control their most preposterous behaviours, other market participants and public officials will need to step in or the whole fabric of our capitalist societies will self-destruct.

What will likely happen is that the market will find a solution to the GPs' current abuse of power. Because one thing is for certain: if lenders, limited partners, corporate executives, legislators and regulators refuse to wear the sheriff's badge, financial sponsors will continue to behave like cowboys. Capitalism belongs to all of us, not to anyone in particular, and certainly not to a small minority, no matter how rich and powerful. At present, it feels like our economic system has been highjacked by a bunch of single-minded financiers who, because they fail to use black boxes to redress amateurish practices, represent a growing systemic risk. Without proper protection against soulless and unrestrained greed, shadow capitalism could well be heading for a crisis on the scale witnessed by the banking sector in 2008.

Acknowledgements

The idea of writing this book came to me during various conversations with business students and industry professionals. I am grateful to the many anonymous contributors without whom it would have been impossible to go to the source of the matter and to the reasons behind the events described therein. Many students and professional acquaintances offered valuable suggestions about making the topic more understandable to non-specialists.

I would like to thank the following institutions for permission to reproduce copyright material: the US Energy Information Administration, and the Recording Industry Association of America. The case studies draw extensively from public records, newspapers, magazines and research material. Sources are credited accordingly in the endnotes.

My publishers Harriman House were very supportive during the editing process. My thanks go to Craig Pearce, Stephen Eckett and their team for skilfully and kindly guiding me throughout. All errors and omissions are involuntary and my own.

About the author

Sebastien Canderle was educated in France and the United States. He has more than 20 years of experience in the consulting and financial sectors in New York and London, including as an investor for various private equity firms. He is also the author of *Private Equity's Public Distress*, a book covering the impact of the financial crisis of 2008 on the buyout industry, and has been a contributor to several financial blogs as well as a business school lecturer in private equity. He is a fellow of the Institute of Chartered Accountants in England and Wales and received his MBA from the Wharton School.

Endnotes

Introduction

1. *The Life of Reason*, Volume 1, by George Santayana (1905).
2. *Why are Buyouts Levered? The Financial Structure of Private Equity Funds*, U. Axelson, P. Strömberg, M.S. Weisbach.
3. *Private Equity International* magazine, September 2015; *Global Private Equity Report 2016*, Bain & Co.
4. As expertly analysed by Eileen Appelbaum and Rosemary Batt in their book *Private Equity at Work* (2014).
5. *Financial Intermediaries in the United States: Development and Impact on Firms and Employment Relations*, E. Appelbaum, R. Batt, and J.E. Lee, Center for Economic and Policy Research, Working Paper, August 2012; *Implications of Financial Capitalism for Employment Relations Research: Evidence from Breach of Trust and Implicit Contracts in Private Equity Buyouts*, E. Appelbaum, R. Batt, I. Clark, Center for Economic and Policy Research, July 2012; *A Primer on Private Equity at Work: Management, Employment, and Sustainability*, E. Appelbaum, R. Batt, Center for Economic and Policy Research, February 2012; *Private Equity Performance and Liquidity Risk*, F. Franzoni, E. Nowak and L. Phalippou, Swiss Finance Institute, 17 June 2010; *Private Equity, Public Loss?*, P. Morris, Centre for the Study of Financial Innovation, July 2010; *Ownership matters: private equity and the political division of ownership*, Erturk et al., Organization, 2010; *The Buyout of America: How Private Equity Will Cause the Next Great Credit Crisis*, Josh Kosnan, November 2009; *The growing crisis in private equity: binding regulation and an action plan are needed*, Sigurt Vitols, ETUI Policy Brief, Issue 3/2009; *Data collection study on the impact of private equity, hedge and sovereign funds on industrial change in Europe*, Eckhard Voss, Sig Vitols, Peter Wilke, Jakob Haves, European Economic and Social Committee, Hamburg, June 2009; *Labour and the Locusts: Private Equity's Impact on the Economy and the Labour Market*, British German Trades Union Forum, Conference Report, 2008; *Losing the battles but winning the war: the case of UK Private Equity Industry and mediated scandal of summer 2007*, J. Montgomerie, A. Leaver, and A. Nilsson, CRESC, The University of Manchester, August 2008.

Chapter 1

1. Academy of Achievement – Stephen Schwarzman interview, 20 June 1999.
2. S&P Capital IQ Leveraged Commentary and Data, Sober Look, 12 September 2014; Pitchbook, US Middle Market Report 2015 Annual.
3. Thomson Reuters, Dealogic data from Les Echos, 8 December 2014; S&P Capital IQ Leveraged Commentary and Data from *Financial Times* article, 4 May 2015.

Part One

1. Pitchbook, PE Exits and Company Inventory, 1H15.
2. Preqin, 20 December 2013.
3. *Daily Telegraph*, 8 Februrary 2003.

Chapter 2

1. *news.bbc.co.uk*
2. *Financial Times*, 19 September 1996; *Sunday Times*, 8 December 1996; *Guardian*, 7 February 1997.
3. *Times*, 1 December 1997.
4. The National Archives, UK Government.
5. *CityAM*, 11 October 2012.
6. Wikipedia.
7. *Telegraph*, 1 November 2005.
8. *Independent*, 24 September 1998.
9. *Times*, 24 October 1980 and 10 January 1981.
10. *Daily Telegraph*, 5 December 1996 and 16 October 2012; *Independent*, 23 September 2006.
11. *Financial Times*, 3 January 1998.
12. *Independent*, 24 September 1998.
13. *Financial Times*, 23 December 1998.
14. *Financial Times*, 7 July 1998.
15. *Times*, 13 March 2000; *Independent*, 13 March 2000.
16. *Times*, 10 November 2001.
17. *Evening Standard*, 26 March 2002.
18. *Independent*, 16 July 2001; *Daily Telegraph*, 18 July 2001.
19. *Times*, 13 July 2002.
20. *Times*, 3 December 2002.
21. *Sunday Times*, 2 February 2003.
22. *Daily Telegraph*, 24 January 2003.
23. *Times*, 23 January 2003.
24. *Times*, 25 January 2003; *Daily Telegraph*, 8 February 2003.
25. *Times*, 8 February 2003.
26. *Birmingham Post*, 8 February 2003.
27. *Independent*, 29 July 2003; *Times*, 6 September 2003.
28. *Daily Telegraph*, 15 June 2004.
29. *Financial Times*, 17 December 2004.
30. Permira press release, 1 August 2005.
31. *Sunday Times*, 17 and 31 October 2004.
32. *GlobalCapital*, 28 February 2003; Candover Investment Plc, Annual Report 2004; *International Financing Review* 1571 – 19 to 25 February 2005.
33. Candover Investments Plc, Annual Report 2005.
34. *Times*, 26 May 2000.
35. *Sunday Telegraph*, 14 January 2001.
36. *Independent*, 28 January 2001; *Sunday Telegraph*, 4 Februrary 2001.
37. *Financial Times*, 13 July 2001.
38. *Scotsman*, 30 May 2002.
39. *Guardian*, 3 August 2002; *Sunday Times*, 27 April 2008.
40. *Sunday Times*, 27 June 2004; *Mail on Sunday*, 18 July 2004.
41. *Evening Standard*, 5 February 2004; *Financial Times*, 1 December 2004.
42. *Journal*, 12 November 2003.

43. *Sunday Times*, 26 June 2005.
44. *Financial Times*, 1 December 2004.
45. *Daily Telegraph*, 1 August 2005; *Financial Times*, 1 August 2005.
46. *Times*, 1 August 2005.
47. *Sunday Times*, 26 June 2005.
48. *news.bbc.co.uk*, 22 December 1998.
49. *Sunday Times*, 2 July 2006.
50. *thisismoney.co.uk*, 7 October 2005; *Sunday Times*, 27 April 2008 and 26 April 2009.
51. Gala Coral Group Limited – Annual Report 2006.
52. Gala Coral Group Limited – Annual Report 2007.
53. *Guardian*, 10 November 2007.
54. *Times*, 8 February 2008.
55. *Daily Mail*, 15 December 2007.
56. *Sunday Times*, 2 March 2008.
57. *Daily Telegraph*, 12 September 2008; Gala Coral Group Limited – Annual Report 2008.
58. *International Financing Review* 1794 – 1 to 7 August 2009.
59. Gala Electric Casinos Limited – Annual Report 2009.
60. *Daily Telegraph*, 15 June 2009; *Daily Mail*, 16 June 2009.
61. *Observer*, 26 July 2009.
62. *Sunday Times*, 4 October 2009.
63. *Daily Telegraph*, 21 November 2009; *Sunday Telegraph*, 6 December 2009.
64. *Times*, 13 March 2010; *Daily Telegraph*, 22 June and 19 July 2010.
65. Gala Electric Casinos Limited – Annual Report 2009.
66. Moody's Investors Service, 12 July 2010.
67. Gala Coral Group Limited – Annual Report 2010.
68. *Financial Times*, 29 January 2009.
69. *Daily Telegraph*, 19 July 2010.
70. Written evidence submitted by the Gala Coral Group – Culture, Media and Sport Committee – Select Committee Publications, *www.parliament.uk*
71. Moody's Investors Service, 2 December 2011.
72. *CityAM*, 11 October 2012.
73. *Times*, 14 December 2013.
74. *Times*, 24 March and 5 April 2014.
75. M&G Investments – Press release 22 December 2014.
76. *Evening Standard*, 18 November 2015.
77. Moody's Investors Service, 27 March 2015; *Financial Times*, 24 July 2015; *CreditSights*, 27 July 2015.
78. Sky News, 26 October 2015.
79. *Guardian*, 17 May and 28 June 1990.
80. *Times*, 16 December 1997.
81. *Financial Times*, 5 March 2009.
82. Washington State Investment Board – Portfolio Overview by Strategy as of 31 December 2012.
83. CalPERS – Private Equity Program Fund Performance Review as of 31 December 2013.
84. Based on EBIT of £309.9 million and EBITDA of £401.8 million. Source: Gala Coral Annual Report 2007.
85. *Journal*, 7 December 2004.
86. Based on EBIT of £40 million. Source: *The Belfast News Letter*, 23 December 1998.

Part Two

1. For information on the post-IPO performance of LBOs involved in quick flips, see *The Oxford Handbook of Private Equity*, by Douglas Cumming, 2012; *EDHEC-Risk Institute – Giants at the Gate: On the Cross-Section of Private Equity Investment Returns*, F. Lopez-de-Silanes, L. Phalippou, O. Gottschalg, January 2011; NBER – *The Performance of Reverse LBOs*, J. Cao and J. Lerner, October 2006.
2. *Are buyout sponsors market timers of RLBOs?*, J. Cao, August 2007.

Chapter 3

1. *Auto Rental News*, Fact Book 2015.
2. Hertz website; *Los Angeles Times*, 8 February 1985; *Chicago Tribune*, 10 February 1985; *Automotive Fleet*, March 1985; *Times*, 15 July 2006.
3. *New York Times*, 18 June 1985.
4. *Los Angeles Times*, 3 October 1987 and 3 May 1989; *The Spokesman-Review*, 23 June 1988; *Chicago Tribune*, 9 August 1988.
5. *New York Times*, 15 February 1994 and 15 April 1994.
6. The Hertz Corporation – Form 10-K for the fiscal year ended 31 December 2004.
7. *Motortrader.com*, 21 April 2005; *Times*, 21 April 2005.
8. *USA Today*, 4 January 2005; *Autoweek.com*, 4 January 2006.
9. *Buyouts Magazine* data used in Bank of America presentation, 2007; Dealogic data from *Washington Post* article, 21 December 2011.
10. The Hertz Corporation – Forms 10-K for the fiscal years ended 31 December 2003 and 31 December 2004.
11. *Wall Street Journal*, 6 May 2005.
12. *Times*, 26 July 2005.
13. *New York Times*, 9 September 2005; *Wall Street Journal*, 13 September 2005; Hertz Global Holdings, Inc. – Form 10-K for the fiscal year ended 31 December 2006.
14. The Carlyle Group L.P. – Form S-1, 10 January 2012.
15. *Financial Times*, 15 December 2015.
16. *International Financing Review* 1601– 17 to 23 September 2005, and 1609 – 12 to 18 November 2005; Hertz Global Holdings, Inc. – Form 10-K for the fiscal year ended 31 December 2006.
17. *Washington Post*, 7 November 2005.
18. Hertz Global Holdings, Inc. – Form S-1, As filed with the Securities and Exchange Commission on July 14, 2006; *New York Times Dealbook*, 14 July 2006.
19. Hertz Global Holdings, Inc. – Form S-1, As filed with the Securities and Exchange Commission on July 14, 2006; *Financial Times*, 14 July 2006.
20. MarketWatch, 15 November 2006; *Times*, 17 November 2006; Hertz Global Holdings, Inc. – Form 10-K for the fiscal year ended 31 December 2006.
21. Hertz Global Holdings, Inc. – Form 10-K for the fiscal year ended 31 December 2006.
22. *Financial Times*, 29 December 2006.
23. *BusinessWeek*, 6 August 2006.
24. MarketWatch, 15 November 2006.
25. Hertz Global Holdings, Inc. – Forms 10-Q for the periods ended 31 March, 30 June and 30 September 2006.
26. Hertz Global Holdings, Inc. – Form 10-K for the fiscal year ended 31 December 2006; Avis Budget Group – Form 10-K for the fiscal year ended 31 December 2006.
27. Hertz Global Holdings, Inc. – Form 10-K for the fiscal year ended 31 December 2007.
28. Service Employees International Union – Behind the Buyouts, Inside the world of private equity, April 2007.

29. Hertz Global Holdings, Inc. – Form 10-K for the fiscal year ended 31 December 2007.

30. *Financial Times*, 30 March 2007; Enterprise Rent-A-Car press release, 1 August 2007.

31. *Washington Post*, 31 October 2007; *Financial Times*, 1 November 2007.

32. Hertz Global Holdings, Inc. – Form 10-K for the fiscal year ended 31 December 2007.

33. *Ibid.*

34. Hertz Global Holdings, Inc. – Analyst meeting presentation, 28 May 2008.

35. Hertz Global Holdings, Inc. – Form 10-Q for the period ended 30 September 2008.

36. OECD quarterly national accounts data.

37. Avis Budget Group – Form 10-K for the fiscal year ended 31 December 2008.

38. Hertz Global Holdings, Inc. – Form 10-K for the fiscal year ended 31 December 2008.

39. Avis Budget Group – Form 10-K for the fiscal year ended 31 December 2008; Avis Budget Group – Letter to shareholders, 21 April 2009.

40. The Hertz Corporation – Form 10-Q for the quarterly period ended 31 March 2009.

41. *Edmunds.com*, 5 January 2009; CNN, 1 June 2009; *Guardian*, 2 June 2009; *The Economist*, 4 June 2009.

42. *International Financing Review* 1784 – 23 to 29 May 2009.

43. Hertz Global Holdings, Inc. – Form 10-K for the fiscal year ended 31 December 2009.

44. The Hertz Corporation – Form 10-Q for the quarterly period ended 30 June 2009.

45. World Bank data.

46. International Air Transport Association press release, 27 January 2010.

47. Hertz Global Holdings, Inc. – Form 10-K for the fiscal year ended 31 December 2009.

48. *International Financing Review* 1804 – 10 to 16 October 2009.

49. Avis Budget Group – Letter to shareholders, 1 April 2010.

50. Hertz press release, 9 April 2009.

51. PEHub, 8 April 2009; Hertz press release, 17 August 2009.

52. Hertz Global Holdings, Inc. – Form 10-K for the fiscal year ended 31 December 2009.

53. Reuters, 28 July 2010; *International Financing Review*, 7 October 2010; *Wall Street Journal*, 22 August 2011; Bloomberg, 7 October 2010 and 27 August 2012.

54. Hertz Global Holdings, Inc. – Form S-1, As filed with the Securities and Exchange Commission on 14 July 2006 and Form 10-K for the fiscal year ended 31 December 2010.

55. Hertz Global Holdings, Inc. – Form 10-K for the fiscal year ended 31 December 2010.

56. Hertz Global Holdings, Inc. – Form 10-K for the fiscal year ended 31 December 2011.

57. Hertz Global Holdings, Inc. – Form 10-Q for the quarterly period ended 31 March 2011.

58. *Wall Street Journal*, 22 August 2011.

59. *International Financing Review* 1902 – 24 to 30 September 2011; Bloomberg, 27 August 2012.

60. *New York Times*, 17 July 2011.

61. Hertz Global Holdings, Inc. – Form 10-Q for the quarterly period ended 30 June 2012.

62. *International Financing Review* 1923 – 3 to 9 March 2012.

63. Dollar Thrifty Automotive Group, Inc. – Form 10-K for the fiscal year ended 31 December 2011; Bloomberg, 27 August 2012; Hertz Global Holdings, Inc. – Form 10-K for the fiscal year ended 31 December 2012.

64. Hertz Global Holdings, Inc. – Form 10-K for the fiscal year ended 31 December 2012.

65. Bureau of Transportation Statistics press release, 4 April 2013; National Bureau of Economic Research, US Business Cycle Expansions and Contractions.

66. World Bank data.

67. Hertz Global Holdings, Inc. – Form 10-K for the fiscal year ended 31 December 2012.

68. *International Financing Review* 1974 – 9 to 15 March 2013.

69. Reuters, 7 May 2013; Clayton, Dubilier & Rice press release, 9 May 2013.

70. Hertz Global Holdings, Inc. press release, 16 April 2013; MarketWatch, 17 April 2013.

71. Hertz Global Holdings, Inc. – Form 10-K for the fiscal year ended 31 December 2013.

72. *Ibid.*

73. The Hertz Corporation – Form 10-K for the fiscal year ended 31 December 2004; Hertz Global Holdings, Inc. – Form 10-K for the fiscal year ended 31 December 2014.

74. Hertz Global Holdings, Inc. – Form 10-K for the fiscal year ended 31 December 2011.

75. Hertz Global Holdings, Inc. – Form 10-K for the fiscal year ended 31 December 2006.

76. *Sunday Times*, 2 July 2006.

77. Bloomberg, 27 August 2012.

78. *New York Times*, 7 January 2013.

79. Hertz Global Holdings, Inc. – Forms 10-K for the fiscal years ended 31 December 2007 and 2009.

80. *Financial Times*, 3 January 2006 ; *zonebourse.com*, 9 March 2006.

81. Europcar Groupe – Prospectus visé par l'Autorité des marchés financiers, note d'opération, 24 June 2015; market capitalisation from Boursorama website.

82. Europcar press release, 13 November 2006.

83. The Hertz Corporation – Form 10-K for the fiscal year ended 31 December 2004; Hertz Global Holdings, Inc. – Form 10-K for the fiscal year ended 31 December 2014.

84. Hertz Global Holdings, Inc. – Form 10-K for the fiscal years ended 31 December 2007 to 2014.

85. *International Financing Review* 2025 – 22 to 28 March 2014.

86. Reuters, 7 June and 8 September 2014; *Financial Times*, 20 August 2014.

87. Hertz Global Holdings, Inc. – Form 10-K for the fiscal year ended 31 December 2014.

88. Hertz Global Holdings, Inc. – Form 10-Q for the quarterly period ended 30 September 2015.

89. MarketWatch data.

90. Return multiple based on cash outflows of $2.3 billion invested at the outset and $200 million of common stock acquired in May 2009.

91. Bloomberg, 15 May 2014.

92. CalSTRS – Private Equity Portfolio Performance as of 31 December 2014.

93. CalPERS – Private Equity Program Fund Performance Review as of 31 December 2014.

94. MarketWatch, 17 March 2005; *Financial Times*, 17 March 2005.

95. *International Financing Review* 1553 – 2 to 9 October 2004.

96. *International Financing Review*, 5 February 2005.

Chapter 4

1. Blackstone press release, 16 December 2003; *Independent*, 17 December 2003; *ICIS Chemical Business*, 19 December 2003; *Manager Magazin*, 2 April 2004.

2. Celanese website; Celanese Corporation – Form 10-K for the fiscal year ended 31 December 2011.

3. Celanese AG Prospectus, 25 October 1999; *International Financing Review* 1307 – 30 October to 6 November 1999.

4. *International Financing Review* 1515 – 10 to 16 January 2004; *International Financing Review* 1525 – 20 to 26 March 2004; *International Financing Review* 1533 – 15 to 21 May 2004.

5. The Blackstone Group – IPO prospectus dated 21 June 2007.

6. Bloomberg, 8 December 2003; Blackstone press releases, 19 November 2002, 4 September 2003 and 16 December 2003.

7. *Manager Magazin*, 14 March 2004; Blackstone press release, 1 April 2004.

8. *International Financing Review* 1534 – 22 to 28 May 2004.

9. Blackstone press release, 3 August 2004.

10. ICIS News, 28 June 2004; *International Financing Review* 1540 – 3 to 9 July 2004.

11. *International Financing Review* 1540 – 3 to 9 July 2004; *International Financing Review* 1552 – 25 September to 1 October 2004; Celanese Corporation – Form 10-K for the fiscal year ended 31 December 2006.

12. Celanese website; Blackstone press release, 23 November 2004.

13. *ICIS Chemical Business*, 19 December 2003.

14. *Financial Times*, 5 November 2004; *Manager Magazin*, 5 November 2004.

15. Celanese Corporation – IPO prospectus dated 26 January 2005; *Forbes*, 11 February 2005; *Fortune*, 13 June 2005; Celanese Corporation – Form 10-K for the fiscal year ended 31 December 2006.

16. Blackstone press release, 16 December 2003.

17. *International Financing Review* 1565 – 8 to 14 January 2005; Celanese Corporation – Form 10-K for the fiscal year ended 31 December 2006.

18. Blackstone press release, 3 January 2005.

19. Paulson & Co. Inc. – Counter-Resolution for Celanese AG Annual General Meeting on May 19, 2005 in Oberhausen; *ICIS Chemical Business*, 20 May 2005; *Manager Magazin*, 22 May 2005; *Forbes*, 20 June 2005.

20. Celanese Corporation – Form 10-K for the fiscal year ended 31 December 2006.

21. *Dallas Business Journal*, 19 and 22 August 2005.

22. *International Financing Review* 1609 – 12 to 18 November 2005; *International Financing Review* 1610 – 19 to 25 November 2005; Blackstone press release, 15 December 2005; *International Financing Review* 1614 – 17 December 2005 to 6 January 2006.

23. *International Financing Review* 1633 – 13 to 19 May 2006; Celanese Corporation – Form 10-K for the fiscal year ended 31 December 2006.

24. *International Financing Review* 1659 – 11 to 17 November 2006.

25. Celanese Corporation – Form 10-K for the fiscal year ended 31 December 2007.

26. Celanese Corporation – Form S-1 Prospectus dated November 3, 2005; Celanese Corporation – Form 10-K for the fiscal year ended 31 December 2006.

27. Celanese Corporation – Prospectus supplement dated May 15, 2007; *International Financing Review* 1674 – 10 to 16 March 2007 and 1684 – 19 to 25 May 2007.

28. *Financial Times*, 17 December 2003.

29. *Forbes*, 20 June 2005.

30. Blackstone press release, 13 July 2005.

31. *Forbes*, 11 February 2005.

32. *International Financing Review* 1536 – 5 to 11 June 2004.

33. Paulson & Co. Inc. – Counter-Resolution for Celanese AG Annual General Meeting on May 19, 2005 in Oberhausen; Celanese Corporation – Form 10-K for the fiscal year ended 31 December 2006.

34. *Forbes*, 11 February 2005; *Fortune*, 13 June 2005.

35. *Manager Magazin*, 26 February 2004; *International Financing Review* 1565 – 8 to 14 January 2005.

36. Celanese Corporation, 2006 Annual Report.

37. Celanese Corporation – Prospectus dated 20 January 2005; Celanese Corporation – Form 10-K for the fiscal year ended 31 December 2005.

38. Paulson & Co. Inc. – Counter-Resolution for Celanese AG Annual General Meeting on 19 May 2005 in Oberhausen.

39. *International Financing Review* 1610 – 19 to 25 November 2005.

40. Celanese Corporation – Form 10-K for the fiscal years ended 31 December 2006 to 2014.

41. Spiegel Online, 12 June 2007.

42. Translated from SPD Tradition und Fortschritt, Start der Programmdebatte, January 2005: "Wir müssen denjenigen Unternehmern, die die Zukunftsfähigkeit ihrer Unternehmen und die Interessen ihrer Arbeitnehmer im Blick haben, helfen gegen die verantwortungslosen Heuschreckenschwärme, die im Vierteljahrestakt Erfolg messen, Substanz absaugen und Unternehmen kaputtgehen lassen, wenn sie sie abgefressen haben."

43. CalPERS – Private Equity Program Fund Performance Review as of 31 December 2014.

Part Three

1. *Guardian*, 24 March 2015. Source: Bureau of Aircraft Accident Archives (BAAA).

Chapter 5

1. Based on State Electricity Profiles 2006, Energy Information Administration, 21 November 2007, and on TXU Corp. – Form 10-K for the fiscal years ended 31 December 2004 to 2006.
2. *Times*, 26 January 2006.
3. TXU Merger Investor Presentation, Executive Summary, August 2007.
4. Bloomberg, 21 July 2004; *New York Times*, 3 October 2005; MarketWatch, 3 October 2005; *Wall Street Journal*, 3 October 2005.
5. Goldman Sachs 1999 IPO prospectus and 2007 Annual Report.
6. *Wall Street Journal*, 31 October 2006.
7. KKR press release, 26 February 2007; Bloomberg, 26 February 2007; Reuters, 26 February 2007; KKR & CO. L.P. – Form S-1 filed on 3 July 2007.
8. Energy Information Administration.
9. TXU Merger Investor Presentation, Executive Summary, August 2007.
10. *Financial Times*, 1 March 2007.
11. Reuters, 1 May 2007; TXU Merger Investor Presentation, Executive Summary, August 2007.
12. *International Financing Review* 1708 – 3 to 9 November 2007.
13. *International Financing Review* 1707 – 27 October to 2 November 2007.
14. CNBC, 3 December 2007; *New York Times*, 3 December 2007.
15. TXU Merger Investor Presentation – Executive Summary, August 2007; Energy Future Holdings, Q4 08 Investor Call, 3 March 2009.
16. Energy Future Holdings Corp. – Form 10-K for the fiscal year ended 31 December 2007.
17. *Ibid.*
18. Energy Future Holdings Corp. – Form 10-Q for the quarterly period ended 30 June 2008; Energy Future Holdings Corp. – Form 10-K for the fiscal year ended 31 December 2007.
19. Bloomberg, 6 May 2008.
20. Energy Future Competitive Holdings Company – Form 10-K for the fiscal year ended 31 December 2008.
21. Energy Future Holdings Corp. – Form 10-K for the fiscal year ended 31 December 2008.
22. US Bureau of Economic Analysis.
23. US Energy Information Administration.
24. *International Financing Review* 1757 – 25 to 31 October 2008.
25. Moody's Investors Service, 3 August 2009.
26. CreditSights, 6 October 2009; Energy Future Holdings Corp. – Form 10-K for the fiscal year ended 31 December 2009; KKR & Co. L.P. – Form 10-K for the fiscal year ended 31 December 2010.
27. Moody's Investors Service, 11 October 2010.
28. Bloomberg, 26 August 2010; KKR & Co. L.P. – Form 10-K for the fiscal year ended 31 December 2010.
29. Moody's Investors Service, 27 February 2011; *International Financing Review* 1873 – 5 to 11 March 2011; CreditSights, 3 April 2011.
30. *International Financing Review* 1879 – 16 to 22 April 2011; Energy Future Competitive Holdings Company – Form 10-K for the fiscal year ended 31 December 2011.
31. Potomac Economics – 2011 State of the Market Report for the ERCOT Wholesale Electricity Markets, July 2012.
32. Energy Information Administration, Annual Energy Review 2011.
33. *Historic Opportunities from the Shale Gas Revolution*, KKR Report, November 2012.

34. KKR press release, 25 January 2011; *Oil & Gas Financial Journal*, January 2012.

35. *New York Times*, 28 February 2012.

36. Bloomberg, 19 January 2012.

37. *New York Times*, 28 February 2012.

38. Oncor Electric Delivery Company LLC – Form 10-Q for the quarterly period ended 31 March 2012.

39. Moody's Investors Service, 9 August 2012.

40. Energy Future Competitive Holdings Company – Form 10-K for the fiscal year ended 31 December 2012.

41. Bloomberg, 25 February 2013.

42. Energy Future Competitive Holdings Company – Form 10-K for the fiscal year ended 31 December 2012.

43. Energy Future Holdings Corp. and Energy Future Competitive Holdings – Form 8-K dated 4 January 2013.

44. Energy Future Competitive Holdings – Forms 10-Q and 10-K for the fiscal year ended 31 December 2013.

45. CreditSights, 5 November 2013.

46. *Forbes*, 15 October 2013; *International Financing Review* 2006 –19 to 25 October 2013.

47. Moody's Investors Service, 28 August 2013.

48. *Financial Times*, 24 April 2014.

49. *Financial Times*, 12 March 2014.

50. *International Financing Review* 2027 – 5 to 11 April 2014; *Financial Times*, 24 April 2014.

51. *International Financing Review* 1937 – 9 to 15 June 2012.

52. TXU Annual Reports 2002 and 2006; Energy Future Competitive Holdings Company LLC – Form 10-K for the fiscal year ended 31 December 2013.

53. Oncor Electric Delivery Company LLC – Forms 10-K for the fiscal years ended 31 December 2008 to 31 December 2014; Energy Future Holdings Corp. – Form 10-K for the fiscal year ended 31 December 2008.

54. Oncor Electric Delivery Company LLC – Form 10-K for the fiscal year ended 31 December 2008.

55. Berkshire Hathaway Inc. – Shareholder letters 25 February 2012 and 28 February 2014.

56. Natural Gas Year-In-Review 2007, Energy Information Administration, Office Of Oil and Gas, March 2008.

57. TXU Corp. – Form 10-Q for the quarterly period ended 31 March 2007.

58. TXU Merger Investor Presentation, Executive Summary, August 2007.

59. CreditSights, 20 August 2008.

60. TXU Corp. – Form 10-K for the fiscal year ended 31 December 2003.

61. *International Financing Review* 1873 – 5 to 11 March 2011.

62. *International Financing Review* 2001 – 14 to 20 September 2013.

63. Reuters, 16 May 2014.

64. *International Financing Review* 2039 – 28 June to 4 July 2014.

65. TXU Merger Investor Presentation, Executive Summary, August 2007.

66. For more detail on the LTCM story, read *Hedge Funds and the Collapse of Long-Term Capital Management*, Franklin R. Edwards, Journal of Economic Perspectives, Volume 13, Number 2, Spring 1999; *Lessons from the collapse of hedge fund Long-Term Capital Management*, David Shirreff, 2000; *When Genius Failed: The Rise and Fall of Long-Term Capital Management*, by Roger Lowenstein (2001).

67. *The Economist*, 4 August 2012.

68. CalPERS – Private Equity Program Fund Performance Review as of 31 December 2014; Oregon Public Employees Retirement Fund – Private Equity Portfolio as of 31 March 2015.

69. Samson Resources Corporation – Form 10-K for the fiscal year ended 31 December 2014; *Wall Street Journal*, 17 December 2014, 26 February 2015 and 14 August 2015; Samson

Resources, Year-end 2014 Conference Call presentation, Supplemental Materials, 1 April 2015; *New York Post*, 1 June 2015.

70. Goldman Sachs 2014 Annual Report.

Chapter 6

1. Recording Industry Association of America (RIAA).

2. Digital Music Reports, IFPI – 2004.

3. *New York Times*, 26 November 2008; Recording Industry Association of America (RIAA); Wikipedia.

4. CNNMoney, 25 April 2013.

5. *Guardian*, 24 April 2007.

6. *New York Times*, 10 January 2010; *Daily Telegraph*, 28 September 2010.

7. *news.bbc.co.uk*, 19 November 2003.

8. *news.bbc.co.uk*, 3 May 2006; *Sunday Telegraph*, 7 May 2006; *Times*, 29 June 2006.

9. IFPI 2005 Annual Report.

10. *Guardian*, 7 February 2005; *Birmingham Post*, 29 June 2006; *Guardian*, 15 December 2006; *Daily Telegraph*, 15 February 2007; *Times*, 3 March 2007; *Birmingham Post*, 19 July 2007.

11. *Sunday Times*, 6 May 2007.

12. *International Financing Review* 1682 – 5 to 11 May 2007.

13. *Daily Telegraph*, 7 May 2001.

14. *Guardian*, 1 February 2011.

15. Terra Firma website.

16. Based on EBITA of £150.5 million and EBITDA of £174 million in financial year ended 31 March 2007 – Source: EMI Annual Report 2007; *Financial Times*, 21 May 2007.

17. Terra Firma Annual Review 2007.

18. Dow Jones International News, 14 July 2008.

19. Musicweek, 14 Sept 2007; *Guy Hands, Citigroup and the fight for EMI*, Reuters, 11 June 2010.

20. *Daily Telegraph*, 3 August 2007.

21. *Guardian*, 2 August 2007.

22. Maltby Capital Limited, Directors' report and consolidated financial statements for the year ended 31 March 2008.

23. *Times*, 7 August 2007.

24. *Guardian*, 18 August 2007.

25. *Financial Times*, 29 August 2007.

26. *Guardian*, 29 August 2007; *Financial Times*, 13 November 2007.

27. *New York Post*, 29 October 2007; *Daily Telegraph*, 30 October 2007; *Financial Times*, 29 November 2007; *Daily Telegraph*, 15 January 2008.

28. *thisismoney.co.uk*, 15 October 2001; *Guardian*, 13 January 2007; *Daily Telegraph*, 15 February 2007; *Guardian*, 30 August 2007 and 3 November 2007; *Times*, 29 November 2007; *Independent*, 30 November 2007.

29. *Daily Telegraph*, 9 January 2008; Wadsworth profile from *musictank.co.uk*; *Evening Standard*, 11 January 2008; *Times*, 16 January 2008; *Birmingham Post*, 1 February 2008; *Financial Times*, 24 April 2009.

30. Maltby Capital Limited, Directors' report and consolidated financial statements for the year ended 31 March 2008.

31. *Sunday Times*, 13 January 2008; *Independent*, 15 January 2008; *Sunday Telegraph*, 18 May 2008; *Financial Times*, 25 October 2008.

32. BBC News, 15 January 2008.

33. CNET, 1 April 2008; *Financial Times*, 2 April 2008 and 16 April 2008; *Hypebot.com*, 16 April 2008.

34. *Financial Times*, 3 December 2008; Maltby Capital Limited – Directors' report and consolidated financial statements for the year ended 31 March 2009.

35. *Daily Telegraph*, 17 January 2009.

36. *Financial Times*, 4 February 2010.

37. *Financial Times*, 17 March 2009.

38. The other investee company was reported to be Irish aircraft leasing company AWAS. Terra Firma – Annual Review 2008; *Financial Times*, 2 March 2009; Reuters, 3 March 2009; *Wall Street Journal*, 4 March 2009.

39. *Financial Times*, 16 July 2009; *International Financing Review* 1792 – 18 to 24 July 2009.

40. *Financial Times*, 16 November 2009; Terra Firma – Annual Review 2009.

41. *Sunday Telegraph*, 13 December 2009; *Independent*, 14 December 2009.

42. *Daily Telegraph*, 17 November 2009; *Financial Times*, 17 and 18 December 2009; *Guardian*, 20 December 2009; *Sunday Times*, 21 March 2010; *Financial Times*, 31 March 2010.

43. Maltby Capital Limited – Consolidated financial statements, 31 March 2009 and 31 March 2010.

44. *Ibid.*

45. *Financial Times*, 10 March 2010.

46. *Sunday Times*, 11 and 18 April 2010; *Times*, 21 April 2010 and 8 May 2010.

47. *Guardian*, 12 May 2010; *International Financing Review* 1833 – 15 to 21 May 2010.

48. *Financial Times*, 18 June 2010; Maltby Capital Limited – Directors' report and consolidated financial statements for the 18-month period ended 30 September 2011.

49. *Financial Times*, 17 August 2010.

50. *Independent*, 14 December 2009; *MoneyWeek*, 24 December 2009; *Daily Telegraph*, 19 October 2010; *Guardian*, 4 and 5 November 2010; *Wall Street Journal*, 5 November 2010; *International Financing Review* 1858 – 6 to 12 November 2010.

51. *Financial Times*, 1 February 2011 and 17 March 2011; *Independent*, 2 February 2011; *Sunday Times*, 6 February 2011; *International Financing Review* 1870 – 12 to 18 February 2011; Terra Firma – Annual Review 2010.

52. *Financial Times*, 11 January 2011.

53. *Daily Telegraph*, 12 November 2011; *Washington Post*, 29 June 2012; *New York Times*, 29 June 2012; *Guardian*, 21 September 2012; *New York Times*, 21 September 2012 and 7 February 2013; Warmer Music Group, 1 July 2013 press release; *Financial Times*, 9 July 2013; Vivendi Annual Report 2014.

54. *Daily Telegraph*, 1 December 2007.

55. *Sunday Times*, 27 May 2007; Maltby Capital – Consolidated financial statements for year to 31 March 2010.

56. Recording Industry Association of America (RIAA).

57. International Federation of the Phonographic Industry (IFPI).

58. Valuation at time of IPO stated in *The Rise and Fall of EMI Records*, Brian Southall (2012).

59. Vivendi Universal Annual Report 2003; Vivendi Annual Report 2007; Universal Music Group website; Warner Music – Forms 10-K for the fiscal years ended 30 September 2005 and 2007.

60. EBITA multiple calculated on the basis of £2.1 billion of net debt upon acquisition and an EBITA for the year ended 31 March 2007 of £150 million (source: EMI Annual Report 2007).

61. Vivendi Annual Report for the year ended 31 December 2007; Universal Music Group investor presentation, June 2008 (Vivendi website).

62. *universalmusic.com*

63. Tech Guru Daily, 31 July 2007.

64. *data.worldbank.org*

65. *Sunday Times* and *Sunday Telegraph*, 7 October 2007; *Business Insider*, 10 October 2007; *Times*, 1 and 14 December 2007; *Observer*, 2 December 2007.

66. *Financial Times*, 7 July 2008.

67. Recording Industry Association of America (RIAA) website.

68. CNNMoney, 25 April 2013.

69. International Federation of the Phonographic Industry (IFPI) – Digital Music Report 2009.

70. *Variety*, 7 September 2010.

71. *Guardian*, 11 November 2011.

72. *Guardian*, 22 April 2010; BBC News, 9 November 2010; *Financial Times*, 21 October 2011.

73. *Sunday Times*, 16 July 2006; *Daily Telegraph*, 22 May 2007; *Irish Times*, 15 January 2008; *Financial Times*, 3 December 2008 and 18 December 2009; *Independent*, 28 September 2010; *GQ Magazine*, 2 February 2011.

74. *Completemusicupdate.com*, 6 March 2013.

75. Oregon Public Employees Retirement Fund – Private Equity Portfolio as of 31 March 2015.

76. EMI Annual Reports for the years ended 31 March 2002, 2003 and 2004; Vivendi Universal, 2003 Consolidated Financial Results; *Times*, 18 September 2009.

77. Bloomberg BusinessWeek, 18 December 2009.

78. Digital Music Nation, BPI – 2013; Digital Music Reports, IFPI – 2013 and 2015.

79. *Guardian*, 10 June 2008; *Allthingsd.com*, 23 March 2009; *hypebot.com*, 9 August 2009.

80. *Financial Times*, 24 March 2009.

81. *Daily Telegraph*, 28 February 2008; *Financial Times*, 8 December 2008, 8 September 2010 and 23 September 2011.

82. *Forbes*, 6 June 2005; Service Employees International Union – Behind the Buyouts, Inside the world of private equity, April 2007.

83. World Entertainment News Network, 21 April 2008.

84. HgCapital website; *Financial Times*, 15 April 2008; *Times*, 17 April 2008.

85. *Sunday Telegraph*, 18 May 2008; *Financial Times*, 7 September 2010.

86. *Los Angeles Times*, 26 January 2010; *Financial Times*, 6 November 2013 and 11 and 23 June 2015; *Business Insider*, 10 April 2015; The Street, 13 April 2015; Reuters, 22 September 2015; Billboard, 16 October 2015.

Chapter 7

1. *Times*, 30 October 1995; PHS website.

2. *Financial Times*, 10 July 1999; *Times*, 30 October 1995 and 10 July 1999.

3. *Times*, 27 October 1999; PHS website.

4. *Independent*, 28 June 2001 and 13 June 2002; *Financial Times*, 28 June 2001, 2 January 2002 and 6 June 2003; *Western Mail*, 10 April 2002; *Daily Telegraph*, 16 June 2004.

5. *Financial Times*, 4 April 2003 and 9 October 2004.

6. *Financial Times*, 18 May 2005; *Times*, 18 May 2005.

7. *Financial Times*, 15 June 2005; *Times*, 15 June 2005.

8. Multiple based on an EBITDA of c. £70 million in financial year ended 31 March 2005; *Financial Times*, 8 July 2005; *Daily Telegraph*, 8 July 2005; PHS Group Holdings Limited – Full year results 2013.

9. *Sunday Times*, 29 July 2007.

10. *Financial Times*, 29 October 2007.

11. PHS Group Holdings Limited – Annual Report for the year ended 31 March 2008.

12. *Sunday Telegraph*, 23 January 2011.

13. *Sunday Telegraph*, 15 January 2012.

14. *Sunday Telegraph*, 13 May 2012; PHS Group Holdings – Annual Report for the year ended 31 March 2012.

15. *Western Mail*, 16 February 2011.

16. *Western Mail*, 17 May 2012.

17. BBC Radio 4, 9 May 2012; BBC News, 11 May 2012.

18. PHS Group Holdings Limited – Full year results 2013.

19. PHS Group Holdings Limited – Annual Report for the year ended 31 March 2013.
20. PHS Group Limited – Annual Report for the year ended 31 March 2014.
21. *Western Mail*, 19 June 2013.
22. PHS Group Limited – Annual Report for the year ended 31 March 2014; *Daily Telegraph*, 7 July 2014; *Sunday Times*, 7 September 2014.
23. *Western Mail*, 18 June 2013.
24. *Independent*, 28 June 2001.
25. *Daily Telegraph*, 1 June 2005.
26. *Daily Telegraph*, 16 June 2004.
27. *Sunday Times*, 18 July 2004.
28. *Daily Telegraph*, 30 March 2005; *Times*, 8 July 2005; *Investors Chronicle*, 15 July 2005.
29. PHS Group – Annual Review and Audited Financial Statements 2013.
30. *Financial Times*, 4 April 2003; PHS Group Holdings Limited – Annual Report for the year ended 31 March 2008.
31. *Daily Telegraph*, 16 June 2004; PHS Group Holdings Limited – Full year results 2013.
32. CalSTRS – Private Equity Portfolio Performance as of 31 March 2015.
33. Waterlogic press release, 13 January 2016.

Chapter 8

1. *Le Monde*, 30 September 1989; Frans Bonhomme – Annual Report 2008.
2. *Libération*, 22 December 1994; *Le Monde*, 23 December 1994.
3. *International Financing Review* 1063 – 7 to 14 January 1995; Intermediate Capital Group PLC – Annual Report for the year to 31 January 1995; *Acquisitions Monthly*, 1 July 2003; *Le Monde*, 24 October 2005.
4. BNP Paribas press release, 1 February 2000; *GlobalCapital*, 17 March 2000; *The Treasurer*, September 2000.
5. Equistone website, December 2003; *Le Monde*, 24 October 2005; Bonhom Management prospectus, 5 June 2006 ; Frans Bonhomme – Annual Report 2008; Cinven – Annual Review 2011.
6. *International Financing Review* 1514 – 13 December 2003 to 9 January 2004; *GlobalCapital*, 27 June 2004; *Acquisitions Monthly*, 1 January and 1 March 2004; Bonhom Management prospectus, 5 June 2006.
7. *Financial News*, 26 June 2003.
8. *International Financing Review* 1500 – 6 to 12 September 2003.
9. AltAssets, 13 December 2004; *GlobalCapital*, 17 December 2004; *International Financing Review* 1563 – 11 to 17 December 2004; Quilvest – Annual Report 2004; Bonhom Management prospectus, 5 June 2006.
10. *Le Monde*, 21 October 2005; AltAssets, 21 October 2005; Equistone website, December 2005.
11. Bonhom Management prospectus, 5 June 2006.
12. *EuroWeek*, 27 January 2006.
13. *Acquisitions Monthly*, 1 February 2006.
14. *GlobalCapital*, 27 January 2006; *International Financing Review* 1618 – 28 January to 3 February 2006; Bonhom Management prospectus, 5 June 2006.
15. *Les Echos*, 22 February 2006.
16. Bonhom Management prospectus, 5 June 2006.
17. *Ibid.*
18. *Les Echos Capital Finance*, 24 October 2006.
19. Bonhom Management prospectus, 5 June 2006.
20. Frans Bonhomme – Annual Report 2008.
21. Bonhom Management prospectus, 5 June 2006.

22. *Private Equity Magazine*, June 2007; Euromezzanine website; Bloomberg, 7 June 2013.

23. Based on data from LSTA/Thomson Reuters Mark-to-Market Pricing – The Week's Biggest Winners, 22 November 2013.

24. Frans Bonhomme – Annual Report 2008.

25. Cinven – Annual Review 2007.

26. OECD quarterly national accounts data.

27. Frans Bonhomme – Annual Report 2008.

28. Insee – Tableaux de l'Economie Française, édition 2010, Industrie – Construction.

29. World Bank data; Insee data.

30. Frans Bonhomme – Annual Report 2009.

31. *Ibid.*

32. *Le Monde*, 7 February 2006.

33. Cinven – Annual Review 2010.

34. Frans Bonhomme – Annual Reports 2008 and 2009; *Les Echos*, 23 March 2010.

35. Commissariat Général du Développement Durable – Observation et Statistiques, Construction de Logements, February 2014.

36. Frans Bonhomme – Annual Report 2010.

37. Insee data.

38. Bonhom Management prospectus, 5 June 2006.

39. Frans Bonhomme – Annual Report 2010.

40. *International Financing Review* 1902 – 24 to 30 September 2011.

41. Frans Bonhomme – Annual Report 2011.

42. World Bank data; Insee data.

43. Frans Bonhomme – Annual Reports 2008 and 2011.

44. *La Tribune*, 8 September 2011; *L'Express*, 5 October 2011; *Le Monde*, 21 October 2011; Francetvinfo, 27 October 2011; *Le Figaro*, 3 October 2012.

45. OECD quarterly national accounts data.

46. Standard & Poor's LCD Daily – Europe, 14 May 2013; Bloomberg, 7 June 2013.

47. Insee – Tableaux de l'Economie Française, édition 2014, Industrie – Construction.

48. Frans Bonhomme – Annual Report 2012.

49. Frans Bonhomme – Annual Reports 2008 and 2012.

50. Commissariat Général du Développement Durable – Observation et Statistiques, Construction de Logements, February 2014.

51. Standard & Poor's LCD Daily – Europe, 14 May 2013; *International Financing Review* 1984 – 18 to 24 May 2013; Bloomberg, 7 June 2013; Reuters, 26 July 2013.

52. Standard & Poor's LCD Daily – Europe, 14 May 2013; Bloomberg, 7 June 2013; *International Financing Review* 1992 – 13 to 19 July 2013; Reuters, 26 July 2013.

53. LSTA/Thomson Reuters Mark-to-Market Pricing – The Week's Biggest Winners, 22 November 2013.

54. *Les Echos*, 9 December 2013; Willkie Farr & Gallagher press release, 17 December 2013; *Magazine des Affaires*, edition 2013.

55. *Financial Times*, 29 December 2013.

56. World Bank data; Euler Hermes Economic Research, 26 March 2014.

57. Oloryn Partners presentation document, 2014.

58. Bonhom Management prospectus, Autorité des Marchés Financiers, 5 June 2006.

59. Cinven website.

60. Reuters, 25 May 2012; Cinven – Annual Review 2013; *Les Echos*, 4 August 2014; Bloomberg, 12 December 2014.

61. *Batiactu.com*, 13 January 2015.

62. Les Echos bilans.

63. LSTA/Thomson Reuters Mark-to-Market Pricing – The Week's Biggest Winners, 13 February 2015, 13 March 2015 and 31 July 2015.

64. PUM Plastiques website.

65. Bonhom Management prospectus, Autorité des Marchés Financiers, 5 June 2006.
66. Cinven – Annual Reviews 2008 and 2010.
67. Frans Bonhomme – Annual Reports 2009 and 2012.
68. Cinven press release, 29 February 2012 and Annual Review 2011.
69. Translated from *Le Monde*, 24 October 2005: "C'est une perle rare. Avec elle, on pourrait enchaîner les LBO sans fin."
70. Cinven – Annual Review 2011.
71. *Ibid.*
72. Washington State Investment Board – Portfolio Overview by Strategy as of 31 December 2014.
73. AltAssets, 3 December 2004; Cinven press releases, 29 November 2005 and 5 December 2006; RWB Newsportal, 5 December 2006.
74. Cinven – Annual Review 2011.
75. Unquote, 14 July 2005.
76. Bonhom Management prospectus, Autorité des Marchés Financiers, 5 June 2006.

Part Five

1. *The Globe* and *Mail*, 27 April 2007.
2. PitchBook, 24 July 2015.

Chapter 9

1. *Sunday Times*, 2 August 2009.
2. *Independent*, 3 September 1996.
3. *Independent*, 19 March 2002.
4. *Times*, 1 June 2002.
5. *Financial Times*, 11 December 2003; *Times*, 8 September 2004.
6. *Guardian*, 5 March 2003 and 31 August 2003.
7. *Guardian*, 30 October 2003.
8. *Financial Times*, 11 December 2003.
9. *Daily Telegraph*, 2 November 2004.
10. *Sunday Times*, 6 June 2004; *Guardian*, 12 August 2004.
11. *Guardian*, 4 June 2004; *Sunday Times*, 6 June 2004; *Independent*, 21 September 2004.
12. *Financial Times*, 28 October 2004; *Western Daily Press*, 31 December 2005.
13. *Times*, 2 November 2004.
14. *Times*, 9 March 2005; *Financial Times*, 16 May 2005.
15. *Independent*, 17 August 2005; *Investors Chronicle*, 16 September 2005; *Daily Telegraph*, 12 November 2005.
16. *Financial Times*, 7 January 2006; *Guardian*, 7 January 2006.
17. *Investors Chronicle*, 13 January and 10 March 2006.
18. *Daily Telegraph*, 7 July 2006.
19. *Express*, 7 July 2006.
20. *Financial Times*, 7 July 2006.
21. *Secondarylink.com*, 12 September 2006.
22. *Financial Times*, 7 and 8 June 2007 and 5 October 2007; *Scotsman*, 20 June 2007; *Guardian*, 29 June and 16 July 2007; *Sunday Telegraph*, 14 October 2007.
23. *Sunday Times*, 11 October 2009.
24. *Independent on Sunday*, 29 March 2009.
25. Candover Investments plc – Report and accounts 2008; *Sunday Times*, 2 August 2009.
26. DX Group Limited – Report and financial statements for the year ended 30 June 2009.
27. *Daily Telegraph*, 13 April 2010; *Financial Times*, 14 April 2010.

28. Candover Investments plc – Report and accounts 2010; DX Group Limited – Report and financial statements for the year ended 30 June 2010; DX (Group) plc – Admission to AIM prospectus, 21 February 2014.

29. *Independent on Sunday*, 3 January 2010; *Financial Times*, 19 February 2010.

30. DX (Group) plc – Admission to AIM prospectus, 21 February 2014.

31. BBC News, 27 March 2012; *Independent*, 14 November 2012.

32. *Independent*, 12 October 2013.

33. Multiples based on net debt, EBITDA and revenue figures provided by DX (Group) plc's Full Year Results Presentation for the year ended 30 June 2014.

34. The IPO was priced at £1 a share, for 200.5 million shares, plus net debt of £12, according to DX (Group) plc's Full Year Results Presentation for the year ended 30 June 2014; Royal Mail plc IPO prospectus and Annual Report and Financial Statements 2013-14; *Independent*, 24 February 2014; *Times*, 28 February 2014.

35. *Times*, 22 February 2014.

36. *Investegate.co.uk* RNS, 24 March 2014.

37. *Investegate.co.uk* RNS, 29 September 2014.

38. DX (Group) plc – Preliminary results for the year to 30 June 2015, 21 September 2015.

39. DX (Group) plc – Trading Update, 13 November 2015.

40. DX (Group) plc – Admission to AIM prospectus, 21 February 2014.

41. *Financial Times*, 21 April 2005.

42. *Herald* and *Sunday Herald*, 8 January 2006.

43. *Financial Times*, 16 May 2005; *Times*, 31 May 2006; Richard Hooper's reports – Modernise or decline, December 2008 – Saving the Royal Mail's universal postal service in the digital age, September 2010; Royal Mail plc – IPO prospectus, 27 September 2013.

44. Royal Mail plc – IPO prospectus, 27 September 2013; *Investors Chronicle*, 11 April 2014.

45. *Western Daily Press*, 31 December 2005.

46. The outlook for UK mail volumes to 2023 – PwC, 15 July 2013.

47. DX Group Limited – Reports and financial statements for the years ended 30 June 2008 and 2010; *Times*, 14 October 2005 and 15 November 2005; Hargreaves Lansdown chart performance.

Chapter 10

1. *Financial Times*, 20 June 2014.

2. *Times*, 8 June 1985, and 5 and 13 July 1985.

3. *Times*, 13 May 1985.

4. *Times*, 14 November 1984.

5. Historical facts were taken from various sources, including Debenhams's website and Annual Reports, the *debenham.org.uk* and Arcadia Group websites, and *housefraserarchive.ac.uk*, to name a few.

6. *Financial Times*, 23 January 1998.

7. BBC News, 13 September 2000.

8. *Guardian*, 16 April 2003.

9. *Evening Mail*, 12 May 2003; *Financial Times*, 13 and 14 May 2003.

10. *Times*, 30 July 2003.

11. *Independent*, 29 July 2003.

12. *Birmingham Post*, 28 August 2003; *Financial Times*, 3 and 12 September 2003.

13. *Daily Telegraph*, 21 October 2003.

14. *Sunday Telegraph*, 5 October 2003; *Financial Times*, 24 October 2003.

15. *International Financing Review* 1508 – 1 to 7 November 2003.

16. *Times*, 5 December 2003.

17. *International Financing Review* 1529 – 17 to 23 April 2004; *GlobalCapital*, 21 May 2004; *Daily Telegraph*, 28 July 2004; *International Financing Review* 1544 – 31 July to 6 August 2004.
18. *International Financing Review* 1582 – 7 to 14 May 2005.
19. *Financial Times*, 6 August 2007.
20. Debenhams plc – IPO prospectus, May 2006.
21. *Sunday Telegraph*, 23 April 2006.
22. *Sunday Times*, 22 January 2006.
23. *Herald*, 21 April 2006; *Independent*, 4 May 2006; *GlobalCapital*, 5 May 2006; *Financial Times*, 6 August 2007.
24. *Financial Times*, 6 August 2007.
25. *GlobalCapital*, 5 May 2006.
26. Debenhams plc press release, 8 August 2006; *Management Today*, 1 February 2007; Debenhams Annual Report 2007.
27. *International Financing Review* 1640 – 1 to 7 July 2006; *Sunday Telegraph*, 21 January 2007.
28. *Daily Telegraph*, 18 April 2007.
29. *Financial Times*, 6 August 2007.
30. GDP data from the World Bank.
31. Debenhams plc – Annual Reports 2005, 2006, 2007 and 2008.
32. Debenhams plc – Annual Report 2009.
33. *Daily Telegraph*, 5 June 2009.
34. *Guardian*, 5 June 2009.
35. *Observer*, 4 January 2009.
36. *Times*, 27 March 2008.
37. *GlobalCapital*, 5 June 2009; Debenhams plc – Annual Report 2009.
38. *Times*, 28 October 2009; *Real Deals*, 19 November 2009.
39. Debenhams plc – Annual Report 2010.
40. *Independent*, 5 August 2010.
41. The company entered a sale-and-lease agreement during its 2011 fiscal year, retaining virtually no freehold on its books (based on Annual Reports of 2011 to 2014).
42. *Financial Times*, 2 January 2014; *Independent*, 2 January 2014.
43. Debenhams plc – IPO prospectus, May 2006; Debenhams plc – Annual Report 2013.
44. *Observer*, 4 January 2009.
45. Debenhams plc – Annual Report 2015.
46. Debenhams plc – IPO prospectus, May 2006; Debenhams plc – Annual Report 2015.
47. Debenhams plc – IPO prospectus, May 2006.
48. *Financial Times*, 6 August 2007.
49. CalPERS – Private Equity Program Fund Performance Review as of 31 December 2014; FTSE Group – FTSE 100 index and FTSE Europe ex UK index, 30 September 2015.
50. CalPERS – Private Equity Program Fund Performance Review as of 31 December 2014.
51. *Fortune*, 2 March 2015; Bloomberg, 9 May 2016.
52. *Guardian*, 18 April 2007.

Chapter 11

1. *Independent*, 31 July 1999; *Daily Telegraph*, 2 August 2000.
2. 3i Case Studies 2005; *Daily Telegraph*, 16 May 2005; Bloomberg, 14 October 2005; 3i Investor lunch presentation, New York – 3 March 2006.
3. *Sunday Times*, 24 April 2005.
4. PagesJaunes Groupe results, document de référence 2004.
5. PagesJaunes S.A. – IPO prospectus, international edition dated 7 July 2004; PagesJaunes Groupe – Analyst presentation for 2006 annual results, 16 February 2007.

6. PagesJaunes Groupe – Document de référence 2004, data compiled by market expert France Pub.

7. PagesJaunes Groupe – Assemblée générale mixte, 19 April 2006.

8. PagesJaunes Groupe – Consolidated financial statements as at 31 December 2005; *Financial Times*, 7 June 2006.

9. *Guardian*, 16 June 2006; *Sunday Telegraph*, 18 June 2006; *International Financing Review* 1639 – 24 to 30 June 2006.

10. *Times*, 29 June 2006.

11. *Financial Times*, 18 July 2006.

12. *Financial Times*, 21 July 2006; *Times*, 21 July 2006.

13. *Financial Times*, 24 and 25 July 2006; *International Financing Review* 1644 – 29 July to 4 August 2006.

14. *International Financing Review* 1647 – 19 to 25 August 2006.

15. PagesJaunes Groupe – Document de référence 2004.

16. *Birmingham Post*, 6 April 2001; *Financial Times*, 12 June 2003.

17. PagesJaunes Groupe – Document de référence 2006.

18. *International Financing Review* 1666 – 13 to 19 January 2007.

19. KKR & CO. L.P. – Form S-1 filed on 3 July 2007.

20. PagesJaunes Groupe – Document de référence 2006.

21. PagesJaunes Groupe – Analyst presentation for 2006 annual results, 16 February 2007.

22. PagesJaunes Groupe – Report on Operations, Consolidated Financial Statements as at 31 December 2006 and Annual Financial Report at 31 December 2007.

23. PagesJaunes Groupe – Analyst presentation for 2006 annual results, 16 February 2007.

24. OECD quarterly national accounts data.

25. PagesJaunes Groupe – Document de référence 2008.

26. *Financial Times*, 2 December 2008.

27. PagesJaunes Groupe – Consolidated financial information at 31 December 2008; KKR Private Equity Investors, L.P. – Final transcript of earnings conference call, 2 March 2009.

28. Value Investors Club, 9 April 2009.

29. *Le Figaro*, 19 May 2009.

30. PagesJaunes Groupe – Half-year financial report as at 30 June 2009, Board of directors 23 July 2009.

31. IREP/France Pub – Le Marché Publicitaire Français en 2009; Groningen Growth and Development Centre, University of Groningen – GDP database.

32. Goldman Sachs – Europe Media: Publishing, 6 January 2010.

33. PagesJaunes Groupe – Consolidated financial information at 31 December 2009.

34. PagesJaunes Groupe – Analyst presentation for 2009 annual results, 19 February 2010.

35. PagesJaunes Groupe – Documents de référence 2009 and 2010.

36. IREP/France Pub – Le Marché Publicitaire Français en 2010.

37. PagesJaunes Groupe – Annual results 2010 – Analyst presentation, 9 February 2011.

38. *International Financing Review* 1874 – 12 to 18 March 2011; *GlobalCapital*, 25 March 2011.

39. *International Financing Review* 1878 – 9 to 15 April 2011; *GlobalCapital*, 15 April 2011 and 9 May 2011; *International Financing Review* 1882 – 7 to 13 May 2011.

40. PagesJaunes Groupe – Half-year financial report as at 30 June 2011, Board of directors 26 July 2011.

41. *Financial Times*, 5 July 2011; Google share data.

42. PagesJaunes Groupe – Consolidated financial information as at 31 December 2011.

43. Bloomberg, 15 February 2012; PagesJaunes Groupe – Analyst presentation for 2011 annual results, 15 February 2012; *International Financing Review*, 15 February 2012.

44. *Le Monde*, 29 May 2012.

45. *International Financing Review*, 28 May 2012.

46. *International Financing Review* 1943 – 21 to 27 July 2012.

47. *International Financing Review*, 17 July 2012; *GlobalCapital*, 17 and 27 July 2012.

48. *GlobalCapital*, 17 and 28 September 2012; International Financing Review, 1952 – 22 to 28 September 2012 and *International Financing Review*, 26 September 2012; *GlobalCapital*, 13 November 2012.

49. Moody's Investors Service, 20 September 2012; *International Financing Review* 1955 – 13 to 19 October 2012.

50. Reuters, 13 November 2012; *International Financing Review* 1962 – 1 to 7 December 2012.

51. Standard & Poor's LCD Daily – Europe, 12 December 2012; *International Financing Review*, 12 December 2012; *GlobalCapital*, 12 and 14 December 2012; *International Financing Review* 1967 – 19 to 25 January 2013.

52. IREP/France Pub – Le Marché Publicitaire Français en 2013; IREP/France Pub – Le Marché Publicitaire Français en 2011.

53. PagesJaunes Groupe – Document de référence 2012.

54. PagesJaunes Groupe – Consolidated financial information as of 31 December 2012.

55. PagesJaunes Groupe – Analyst presentation for 2012 annual results, 13 February 2013; LCD Daily – Europe, 13 February 2013; Dow Jones, 20 February 2013; Reuters, 20 February 2013.

56. *Financial Times*, 3 March 2013 and 5 December 2013.

57. Investir, 5 June 2013; Solocal Group – Document de référence 2013.

58. Reuters, 13 May 2013.

59. Dow Jones, 15 May 2013, 6 and 7 June 2013; *L'Opinion*, 28 and 30 May 2013; Reuters, 5 June 2013.

60. *Les Echos*, 30 August 2013.

61. *Le Figaro*, 25 September 2013; Reuters, 25 September 2013.

62. *Le Figaro*, 13 November 2013; Dow Jones, 13 November 2013.

63. Moody's Investors Service, 23 December 2013; Dow Jones, 23 December 2013.

64. Solocal Group – Document de référence 2013.

65. KKR & Co. L.P. – Form 10-K for the fiscal year ended 31 December 2013.

66. Solocal Group – Analyst presentation for 2013 annual results, 13 February 2014.

67. Reuters, 14 February 2014; *GlobalCapital*, 14 February 2014 and 14 May 2014; *International Financing Review* 2020 – 15 to 21 February 2014; *International Financing Review* 2033 – 17 to 23 May 2014.

68. Dow Jones, 4 March 2013; *International Financing Review* 2023 – 8 to 14 March 2014.

69. Reuters, 9 and 23 April 2014; Dow Jones, 25 March and 23 April 2014; *Les Echos*, 2 June 2014; *International Financing Review* 2037 – 14 to 20 June 2014; *Le Revenue*, 14 January 2015.

70. Based on net debt and EBITDA data in Solocal Group – Document de référence 2014.

71. Dow Jones, 23 May 2014; Solocal Group press release, 19 November 2014.

72. Solocal Group press release, 20 June 2014; Solocal Group – Consolidated financial information as at 31 December 2014; IREP/France Pub – Le Marché Publicitaire Français en 2014.

73. Solocal Group – Analyst presentation for 2014 annual results, 10 February 2015.

74. PagesJaunes Groupe – Document de référence 2007.

75. ZDNet, 26 September 2005.

76. Verizon Directories Disposition Corporation – Form 10-K dated 7 July 2006.

77. PagesJaunes Groupe – Analyst presentation for 2006 annual results, 16 February 2007.

78. Weeko Etude PagesJaunes, February 2010.

79. *Time*, 20 June 2005.

80. eBay 2006 Annual Report.

81. PagesJaunes Groupe – Documents de référence 2011 and 2012.

82. *Daily Telegraph*, 25 July 2013; *Financial Times*, 25 July 2013; *Guardian*, 25 July 2013.

83. PagesJaunes Groupe – Consolidated financial statements as at 31 December 2004 and 2005.

84. PagesJaunes Groupe – Document de référence 2007; Solocal Group – Consolidated financial information as at 31 December 2015.

85. *Searchengineland.com* – Data from the Wireline Competition Bureau of the Federal Communications Commission; *emarketer.com* – Data from Citigroup Investment Research, March 2006 and eMarketer calculations.
86. Google Inc. – IPO prospectus dated 29 April 2004 and Forms 10-K for the fiscal years ended 31 December 2005 and 2006.
87. Google Annual Report 2005; *Commentcamarche.fr*, 5 May 2009.
88. Dow Jones, 30 September 2013.
89. CalPERS, Private Equity Program Fund Performance Review, as of 31 December 2014.
90. Amundi ETF CAC 40 UCITS; FTSE Group, FTSE 100 index, 30 September 2015.
91. Bloomberg, 4 November 2014.
92. *International Financing Review* 1647 – 19 to 25 August 2006; Investir, 24 February – 2 March 2007.
93. *Les Echos*, 4 August 2014.

Chapter 12

1. Deutsche Bank, Seat broker's note, 1 August 2003.
2. Presentation by Lorenzo Pellicioli, President and CEO of Seat, Welcome to the Yellow Economy, Università degli Studi di Torino, 8 June 2001; Il Fatto Quotidiano, 5 February 2013.
3. *Wall Street Journal*, 27 December 1999; Intermonte Securities, Seat/Tin.It broker's note, 7 March 2000.
4. Seat Pagine Gialle website.
5. Intermonte Securities, Seat/Tin.It broker's note, 7 March 2000; *Financial Times*, 21 March 2000.
6. *Financial Times*, 12 February 2000 and 9 June 2000; *Wall Street Journal*, 15 March 2000.
7. *Sunday Times*, 28 May 2000; *Financial Times*, 6 July and 14 August 2000; *Daily Telegraph*, 2 August 2000; *Guardian*, 11 August 2000.
8. *Financial Times*, 24 May 2000 and 5 January 2001.
9. *La Republicca*, 6 August 2012; Bloomberg, 6 August 2012.
10. *Financial Times*, 13 September 2001.
11. Corriere della Sera, 13 June 2003; Deutsche Bank – Seat broker's note, 1 August 2003; Seat Pagine Gialle – Annual Report 2003; Mediobanca, Seat broker's note, 31 July 2003; Seat Pagine Gialle – Presentation to the Financial Community, 29 March 2004.
12. *Financial Times*, 12 June 2003.
13. Mediobanca, Seat broker's note, 2 September 2003; Seat Pagine Gialle – Annual Report 2003.
14. Corriere della Sera, 12 June 2003.
15. *Wall Street Italia*, 9 August 2003.
16. Seat Pagine Gialle – Presentation to the Financial Community, 29 March 2004.
17. Seat Pagine Gialle – Annual Report 2003.
18. Banca Akros, Seat broker's note, 3 December 2003; Lehman Brothers, Seat broker's note, 27 January 2004; Caboto, Seat broker's note, 8 April 2004.
19. Banca Akros, Seat broker's note, 22 October 2003.
20. Caboto, Seat broker's note, 8 April 2004.
21. Banca Akros, Seat broker's note, 21 May 2004.
22. Seat Pagine Gialle – Annual Report 2003.
23. Seat Pagine Gialle – Quarterly report as of 31 March 2004.
24. Seat Pagine Gialle – First-half report as of 31 March 2004.
25. Seat Pagine Gialle – Annual Report 2003; Seat Pagine Gialle – First-half report as of 30 March 2004.
26. Total Telecom, 7, 14 and 20 April 2004.
27. Seat Pagine Gialle – Strategic Plan 2005-2007, 29 November 2004.

28. Seat Pagine Gialle – Annual Report 2004; Seat Pagine Gialle – Investor presentation, 16 March 2005.

29. Seat Pagine Gialle – Strategic Plan 2005-2007, 29 November 2004.

30. World Bank data.

31. Lehman Brothers, Seat broker's note, 12 May 2005.

32. Seat Pagine Gialle – Annual Report 2005; Seat Pagine Gialle – Investor presentation, 22 March 2006.

33. Seat Pagine Gialle – 3Q 2004 Results investor presentation, 9 November 2004.

34. Seat Pagine Gialle – Annual Report 2005; Seat Pagine Gialle – Investor presentation, 22 March 2006.

35. Cazenove, Seat broker's note, 21 February 2006.

36. Euromobiliare, Seat broker's note, 1 February 2006.

37. Seat Pagine Gialle – Investor presentation, 22 March 2006.

38. Seat Pagine Gialle – 1st Quarter 2006 Results investor presentation, 12 May 2006.

39. Seat Pagine Gialle – Annual Results 2006 investor presentation, 13 March 2007.

40. Lehman Brothers, Seat broker's note, 14 March 2007; Goldman Sachs, Seat broker's note, 14 March 2007.

41. Seat Pagine Gialle – Annual Report 2006.

42. Bear Stearns, Seat broker's note, 5 October 2007.

43. World Bank data.

44. UBS, Seat broker's note, 16 March 2005; CA Cheuvreux, Seat broker's note, 19 October 2006.

45. Seat Pagine Gialle – Annual Results 2006 investor presentation, 13 March 2007.

46. Seat Pagine Gialle – Strategic Plan 2008-2010, 11 May 2007.

47. Kepler, Seat broker's note, 24 May 2007.

48. Banca Akros, Seat broker's note, 22 May 2007; Goldman Sachs, Seat broker's note, 1 June 2007.

49. *Financial Times*, 27 May 2007 and 5 February 2010.

50. Associazione Italiana del Private Equity e Venture Capital (AIFI) – The Italian Private Equity and Venture Capital market, first semester 2007.

51. Banca Akros, Seat broker's note, 22 May 2007.

52. *Wall Street Journal*, 20 June 2007.

53. *Financial Times*, 2 December 2008.

54. Seat Pagine Gialle – Annual Report 2007.

55. SVG Capital plc – Annual Report 2007.

56. Seat Pagine Gialle – Annual Results 2007 and Outlook 2008 investor presentation, 19 March 2008.

57. Seat Pagine Gialle – Annual Report 2007; Citi, Seat broker's note, 7 April 2008.

58. Massimo Cristofori LinkedIn account.

59. *Financial Times*, 2 December 2008; Seat Pagine Gialle – Press release, 23 December 2008.

60. Seat Pagine Gialle – Annual Report 2008.

61. SVG Capital plc – Interim report 2008 and Annual Report 2008; *Financial Times*, 2 December 2008.

62. Seat Pagine Gialle – Press release, 23 December 2008.

63. Moody's Investors Service, 13 January 2009.

64. Seat Pagine Gialle – Annual Report 2009.

65. Seat Pagine Gialle – Press release, 9 February 2009.

66. Seat Pagine Gialle – Annual Report 2008.

67. Seat Pagine Gialle – First Half 2009 Results investor presentation, 5 August 2009.

68. Seat Pagine Gialle – Annual Report 2009; *Handbook on International Corporate Governance: Country Analyses*, edited by Christine Mallin (2011).

69. CreditSights, 17 January 2010.

70. *Financial Times*, 5 February 2010.

71. World Bank data.
72. Seat Pagine Gialle – Annual Report 2009; Seat Pagine Gialle – Annual Results 2009 and Outlook 2010 investor presentation, 16 March 2010.
73. SVG Capital plc – Annual Reports 2008 and 2009.
74. CreditSights, 24 January 2010.
75. Seat Pagine Gialle – First Half 2010 Results investor presentation, 4 August 2010.
76. CreditSights, 4 August and 10 November 2010.
77. Moody's Investors Services, 29 November 2010.
78. CreditSights, 12 December 2010.
79. Seat Pagine Gialle – Annual Report 2010.
80. *Financial Times*, 17 May 2010; *Sunday Times*, 4 July 2010; *Times*, 20 September 2010.
81. Seat Pagine Gialle – Nine months 2010 results, 10 November 2010; Seat Pagine Gialle – First Half 2011 Results, 30 August 2011.
82. Il Sole 24 Ore, 1 May 2011; *Financial Times*, 24 May 2011; Seat Pagine Gialle – Annual Report 2011.
83. Il Sole 24 Ore, 1 May 2011; CreditSights, 25 October 2011.
84. Moody's Investors Service, Global Credit Research, 2 December 2011.
85. Seat Pagine Gialle – Annual Results 2011 investor presentation, 2 May 2012.
86. CreditSights, 9 November 11.
87. CreditSights, 30 November 2011; *Financial Times*, 8 December 2011.
88. CreditSights, 20 January 2012.
89. Seat Pagine Gialle – Strategic Guidelines 2011-2013 and 2015 Projections Update, 18 January 2012.
90. Standard & Poor's – Global Credit Portal, RatingsDirect, 7 February 2012.
91. Seat Pagine Gialle – Annual Report 2011.
92. Seat Pagine Gialle – Annual Results 2011 investor presentation, 2 May 2012, and Annual Report 2011.
93. Seat Pagine Gialle – Annual Report 2011.
94. CreditSights, 17 April and 24 August 2012.
95. Reuters, 25 March 2012.
96. Seat Pagine Gialle – Annual Report 2011.
97. *Financial Times*, 8 April 2009.
98. AltAssets, 5 March 2010; Paul Hastings presentation – *Italian restructurings, distressed debt and M&A opportunities*, 24 June 2010.
99. Seat Pagine Gialle – Press release, 6 September 2012.
100. Seat Pagine Gialle – Annual Report 2012.
101. Seat Pagine Gialle – Press release, 26 October 2012; Vincenzo Santelia LinkedIn account.
102. World Bank data.
103. Seat Pagine Gialle – Full-Year 2010, 2011 and 2012 Results investor presentations.
104. Seat Pagine Gialle – Annual Reports 2009 and 2012.
105. Seat Pagine Gialle – Annual Report 2012.
106. Seat Pagine Gialle – Press release, 28 January 2013.
107. Moody's Investors Service, 30 January 2013; *Financial Times*, 5 February 2013; Standard & Poor's, LCD Daily Europe, 13 February 2013; *International Financing Review*, 20 February 2013.
108. Moody's Investors Service, 7 February 2013.
109. *Il Fatto Quotidiano*, 5 February 2013; *Il Sole 24 Ore*, 9 February 2013.
110. CreditSights, 15 March 2013.
111. Seat Pagine Gialle – Annual Report 2012.
112. Seat Pagine Gialle – Press release, 3 July 2013; PricewaterhouseCoopers, letter to the shareholders of Seat Pagine Gialle, 3 July 2013.
113. Seat Pagine Gialle – Press release, 19 August 2013.
114. BBC News, 27 November 2013.

115. Seat Pagine Gialle – Annual Report 2013.

116. Andrea Servo LinkedIn profile.

117. Moody's Investors Service, 2 December 2013.

118. Seat Pagine Gialle – Full year 2013 results and first outlook on 2014 investor presentation, 1 April 2014.

119. Seat Pagine Gialle – Annual Reports 2009, 2012 and 2013.

120. Seat Pagine Gialle – Strategic Guidelines 2011-2013 and 2015 Projections Update, 18 January 2012.

121. Seat Pagine Gialle – Annual Reports 2007 and 2013.

122. Seat Pagine Gialle – Full year 2013 results and first outlook on 2014 investor presentation, 1 April 2014.

123. Seat Pagine Gialle – Report on Corporate Governance, 1 April 2014 and press release, 7 April 2014.

124. Seat Pagine Gialle – Annual Report 2014.

125. Reuters, 8 May 2014 and 30 September 2015.

126. Corriere della Sera, 10 June 2014.

127. Seat Pagine Gialle – Press releases, 20 May 2014 and 12 June 2014.

128. Seat Pagine Gialle – First Half 2015 Results investor presentation, 5 August 2015.

129. Seat Pagine Gialle – Annual Reports 2006 and 2014.

130. Seat Pagine Gialle – Press release, 17 December 2014.

131. *Il Sole 24 Ore*, 3 October 2014 and 23 December 2014; *Corriere della Sera*, 26 December 2014; Seat Pagine Gialle – Annual Report 2014.

132. *Il Fatto Quotidiano*, 5 July 2014; Seat Pagine Gialle – Press releases, 26 November and 22 December 2014; *Corriere della Sera*, 26 December 2014 and 20 February 2015; *Il Sole 24 Ore*, 4 January 2015; *La Repubblica*, 4 January 2015.

133. Seat Pagine Gialle – Press release, 2 January 2015; *La Repubblica*, 4 January 2015; *Il Sole 24 Ore*, 4 January 2015.

134. *Il Sole 24 Ore*, 4 January 2015.

135. *Il Fatto Quotidiano*, 5 July 2014; Reuters, 27 January and 10 February 2015; *Corriere della Sera*, 20 February 2015.

136. Seat Pagine Gialle – Press release, 26 May 2015; First Half 2015 Results presentation, 5 August 2015.

137. Intermonte – Dmail broker's note, 25 April 2012; Dmail Group S.p.A. Half-year Report at 30 June 2012, 27 August 2012; Reuters, 17 and 24 June 2015 and 30 September 2015.

138. Reuters, 24 September 2015.

139. Seat Pagine Gialle – Press release, 8 October 2015; Reuters, 8 October 2015.

140. Seat Pagine Gialle – Strategic Plan 2008-2010 investor presentation, 11 May 2007; report *I nuovi padroni della pubblicità*, Libertà di Stampa, Diritto all'informazione, March 2014.

141. Alexa, December 2004 and 24 October 2015.

142. *Il Sole 24 Ore*, 20 February 2015.

143. Google Trends: *Yellow Pages Will Be Toast In Four Years*, Chris Silver Smith, Search Engine Land, 24 September 2007.

144. World Bank data.

145. Netindex; Wikipedia.

146. ZDNet, 23 September 2013.

147. Istat, Citizens and the ICTs, 18 December 2014; United States Census Bureau, Computer and Internet Access in the United States: 2013, Issued November 2014.

148. Seat Pagine Gialle – Annual Reports 2004 to 2011.

149. Seat website.

150. Seat Pagine Gialle – Annual Reports 2006 and 2007.

151. Cazenove, Seat broker's note, 21 February 2006.

152. *La Repubblica*, 4 January 2015.

153. Bloomberg, 6 August 2012; La Repubblica, 6 August 2012.

154. *Financial Times*, 13 April 2004.
155. Il Sole 24 Ore, 21 July 2011; *Financial Times*, 1 November 2011.
156. Investitori Associati website; Breakingviews, *Permutation*, Quentin Webb 26 April 2013.
157. California State Teachers' Retirement System – Private Equity Portfolio Performance as of 31 March 2015.
158. *Financial Times*, 28 January 2008; Bloomberg, 29 January 2008.
159. California State Teachers' Retirement System – Private Equity Portfolio Performance as of 31 March 2015; FTSE Group – FTSE 100 index, 30 September 2015 and FTSE Europe ex UK index, 30 September 2015.
160. Permira website, 15 October 2015.
161. CalPERS – Private Equity Program Fund Performance Review as of 31 December 2014.
162. *Corriere della Sera*, 20 February and 10 November 2015.

Part Seven

1. PitchBook, PE Exits and Company Inventory, 1H15.
2. PitchBook, US PE Breakdown, 2Q15.
3. Centre for Management Buyout Research.
4. On the argument that postulates PE-backed IPOs' underperformance, read *Underpricing and Long-Term Performance of Private-Equity Backed IPOs compared to Non-Private-Equity Backed IPOs*, by Sylvain Bourrat and Guillaume Wolff, June 2013; and *Private Equity IPOs Are Being Beaten by Others* in *Wall Street Journal*, 3 June 2014. On the opposite side of the argument, asserting that PE-backed IPOs offer better returns, read *The Performance of Private Equity-backed IPOs*, by Mario Levis, December 2010.

Chapter 13

1. *Expansión*, 10 February 2010; *Sunday Times*, 11 June 2000 and 2 July 2000; *Financial Times*, 14 November 2000; Expedia website.
2. LinkedIn website; *Times*, 2 August 2000.
3. *Expansión*, 10 February 2010.
4. World Bank data.
5. Breaking Travel News, 27 November 2000.
6. *Expansión*, 18 October 2004.
7. *Real Deals*, 16 November 2006; *Financial Times*, 18 October 2007; *Expansión*, 19 October 2007 and 19 February 2008.
8. *Expansión*, 8 November 2007 and 13 August 2009.
9. *Expansión*, 19 February 2008 and 13 August 2008.
10. *Financial Times*, 18 October 2007; *GlobalCapital*, 26 October 2007.
11. *Expansión*, 13 August 2009.
12. Carlyle press release, 28 January 2008.
13. *Expansión*, 11-14 and 23 August 2008; *Times*, 13 August 2008; *Edinburgh Evening News*, 26 August 2008; *Birmingham Post*, 27 August 2008 and 3 September 2008.
14. *Expansión*, 10 February 2010; Geo Travel Finance S.C.A. €175,000,000 10.375% Senior Notes due 2019 offering circular, 28 June 2011.
15. *Expansión*, 13 August 2009 and 20 April 2010.
16. OECD quarterly national accounts data; Instituto Nacional de Estadística – Encuesta de Población Activa (EPA), 24 April 2014.
17. *Expansión*, 24 November 2009.
18. *Expansión*, 20 April 2010.
19. Geo Travel Finance S.C.A. €175,000,000 10.375% Senior Notes due 2019 offering circular, 28 June 2011.

20. *Expansión*, 4 January 2010.

21. *Financial Times*, 27 July 2010; *Expansión*, 27 and 29 July 2010; *International Financing Review* 1859 – 13 to 19 November 2010.

22. *Financial Times*, 18 May 2010.

23. Permira, Annual review 2010.

24. Instituto Nacional de Estadística – Encuesta de Población Activa (EPA), 24 April 2014; World Bank data.

25. World Bank data.

26. *Expansión*, 29 June 2011; Geo Travel Finance S.C.A. €175,000,000 10.375% Senior Notes due 2019 offering circular, 28 June 2011.

27. *Expansión*, 8 August 2011.

28. *Expansión*, 24 March 2011.

29. Permira, Annual review 2010.

30. Permira, Annual review 2010; *Expansión*, 9 February 2011 and 21 May 2012; *Times*, 10 February 2011; *GlobalCapital*, 11 April 2011; Moody's Investors Service, 12 April 2011 and 17 January 2012; eDreams press kit, July 2013; eDreams ODIGEO press kit, 2015.

31. Geo Travel Finance S.C.A. €175,000,000 10.375% Senior Notes due 2019 offering circular, 28 June 2011.

32. *GlobalCapital*, 11 and 18 April 2011; *International Financing Review* 1879 – 16 to 22 April 2011; Geo Travel Finance S.C.A. €175,000,000 10.375% Senior Notes due 2019 offering circular, 28 June 2011; Geo Travel Finance S.C.A. and Subsidiaries – Consolidated financial statements and notes for the year ended 31 March 2012.

33. *Expansión*, 1 December 2011.

34. Instituto Nacional de Estadística – Encuesta de Población Activa (EPA), 24 April 2014 ; World Bank data.

35. eDreams ODIGEO offering memorandum, 3 April 2014.

36. *centreforaviation.com*

37. OECD quarterly national accounts data; Trading Economics; Instituto Nacional de Estadística – Encuesta de Población Activa (EPA), 24 April 2014.

38. eDreams ODIGEO offering memorandum dated 3 April 2014.

39. Expansión, 24 January 2013; *GlobalCapital*, 25 January 2013.

40. eDreams ODIGEO offering memorandum, 3 April 2014; eDreams ODIGEO, consolidated financial statements for 31 March 2014.

41. Standard & Poor's, 21 January 2013.

42. *GlobalCapital*, 25 January 2013; eDreams ODIGEO, consolidated financial statements for 31 March 2014.

43. Eurostat; Instituto Nacional de Estadística; *www.spanishpropertyinsight.com*.

44. *Financial Times*, 14 January 2014; Bloomberg, 14 January 2014.

45. *International Financing Review* 2023 – 8 to 14 March 2014; eDreams ODIGEO offering memorandum, 3 April 2014.

46. *Expansión*, 7 and 8 April 2014.

47. Standard & Poor's Ratings Services, 20 March 2014; *GlobalCapital*, 3 April 2014.

48. Reuters, 2 April 2014; eDreams ODIGEO offering memorandum, 3 April 2014; *Agence France Press*, 8 April 2014; *International Financing Review* 2028 – 12 to 18 April 2014.

49. eDreams ODIGEO press release, 30 April 2014.

50. *Expansión*, 14 May 2014.

51. eDreams ODIGEO investor presentation for the year ended 31 March 2014.

52. *Expansión*, 23 and 24 June 2014; eDreams ODIGEO press release, 24 June 2014.

53. *Travelmole.com*, 31 July 2014; *Argophilia.com*, 1 August 2014.

54. *Expansión* website.

55. eDreams ODIGEO – Condensed Interim Consolidated Financial Statements for the three-month period ended 30 June 2014; eDreams ODIGEO results presentation for the period ended 30 June 2014.

56. *Expansión* website.
57. Standard & Poor's Ratings Services report on Geo Travel Finance SCA Luxembourg, 5 September 2014; Moody's Investors Service, 5 September 2014.
58. *Wall Street Journal*, 24 October 2014; *Expansión*, 24 October 2014.
59. *Bolsamania.com*, 24 and 27 October 2014; *Expansión*, 25 October 2014; Bloomberg, 21 November 2014.
60. *Expansión*, 28 October 2014.
61. *Expansión* website.
62. eDreams ODIGEO investor presentation for the period ended 30 September 2014; *Expansión*, 25 November 2014; Moody's Investors Service, 1 December 2014.
63. *Independent.ie*, 8 January 2015; *Irish Times*, 8 January 2015.
64. *Expansión*, 26 January 2015.
65. eDreams ODIGEO investor presentations for period to 31 December 2014 and year to 31 March 2015.
66. Geo Debt Finance and Geo Travel Finance – Consent solicitation announcements, 24 February and 10 March 2015; *Expansión*, 11 March 2015; eDreams ODIGEO investor presentation for the year ended 31 March 2015.
67. eDreams ODIGEO investor presentation for the year ended 31 March 2015; *CityAM*, 23 June 2015.
68. eDreams ODIGEO Annual Report for the year ended 31 March 2015.
69. *Expansión* website.
70. *Expansión*, 1 December 2011.
71. Geo Travel Finance S.C.A. – Annual Report 2012.
72. *Financial Times*, 18 October 2007.
73. eDreams press kit, July 2013.
74. *Trimetric.net* – Travel Analytics Blog, Metasearch – Threat or Opportunity for Travel Suppliers?
75. *eyefortravel.com*, 7 July 2014.
76. *Telegraph*, 5 June 2013; *Expansión*, 9 August 2013; *roadwarriorvoices.com*, 20 May 2015.
77. *Wall Street Journal*, 28 January 2015.
78. Bloomberg, 7 March 2014.
79. *Wall Street Journal*, 28 January 2015.
80. eDreams ODIGEO investor presentation, first half results as of 30 September 2014.
81. Number of routes and airlines taken from *Expansión* article dated 26 May 2015.
82. Based on data in Bravofly Rumbo Group intention to float press release dated 19 March 2014 and on Bravofly Rumbo Group 2013 Annual Report; Bloomberg, 15 April 2014.
83. Bravofly Rumbo Group 2014 consolidated financial statements.
84. *The Economist*, 30 June 2011; *Financial Times*, 25 May 2012; *Expansión*, 25 May 2012.
85. Based on data in eDreams ODIGEO offering memorandum, 3 April 2014.
86. *Expansión*, 17 August 2010; *El Confidencial*, 10 October 2012; Reuters, 6 November 2012; *economiadigital.es*, 20 February 2013; *Cinco Días*, 24 December 2014; *El Mundo*, 5 January 2015; *Hosteltur.com*, 23 July 2010 and 6 February 2015.

Chapter 14

1. *Evening Standard*, 22 May 2007.
2. BBC News, 21 March 2006.
3. House Price Index, Land Registry, December 2014.
4. Companies House filings.
5. *Daily Telegraph*, 8 March 2007.
6. BC Partners website.
7. House Price Index, Land Registry, December 2014.

8. Thomson Reuters.

9. Bloomberg 9 August 2007; *Financial Times*, 9 August 2007.

10. *International Financing Review* 1691 – 7 to 13 July 2007; *Financial Times*, 25 August 2007.

11. *Evening Standard*, 7 December 2007.

12. Federal Financial Institutions Examination Council – Press release, 26 July 2004.

13. Statista; Financial Crisis Inquiry Commission – The Financial Crisis Inquiry report, 25 February 2011.

14. *Financial Times*, 14 June, 2008 – Source: Land Registry.

15. *Times*, 25 March 2008.

16. *Sunday Telegraph*, 15 June 2008; *Daily Telegraph*, 6 August 2008.

17. *Financial Times*, 12 September 2008.

18. *Evening Standard*, 11 Februrary 2009; *Financial Times*, 14 June 2008.

19. *International Financing Review* 1765 – 10 to 16 January 2009; *Evening Standard*, 20 September 2013.

20. Case-Shiller Home Price Index.

21. *The Economist*; Office for National Statistics; Reuters, 20 September 2013. Source: Land Registry.

22. *Evening Standard*, 16 April 2009.

23. HMRC, National Statistics – Annual UK Property Transaction Statistics; Foxtons IPO prospectus.

24. *Daily Telegraph*, 9 January 2010; *Sunday Times*, 4 September 2011; *International Financing Review* 24 September 2013.

25. *Mail on Sunday*, 29 November 2009.

26. *Financial Times*, 21 September 2007.

27. Bloomberg, 27 September 2007.

28. Land Registry.

29. *Times*, 24 January 2010; *CityAM*, 13 September 2010; *Sunday Times*, 4 September 2011.

30. Companies House filings.

31. *Sunday Times*, 18 March 2012.

32. Land Registry – House Price Index, December 2014.

33. Land Registry and Office for National Statistics.

34. *Financial Times*, 3 August 2013; British Property Federation – *Who buys new homes in London and why?*, February 2014.

35. *Financial Times*, 19 February 2010.

36. Foxtons IPO prospectus; Foxtons Interim Report for the six months to 30 June 2014.

37. *Financial Times*, 6 June 2013.

38. *International Financing Review*, 24 September 2013.

39. *Independent on Sunday*, 1 September 2013.

40. *Daily Telegraph*, 20 September 13; *International Financing Review* 2001 – 14 to 20 September 2013.

41. *Independent*, 27 August 2013.

42. *Guardian*, 3 June and 20 August 2014; Reuters 20 September 2013 and 7 April 2014.

43. *Financial Times*, 11 March and 27 August 2014.

44. *Financial Times*, 22 March 2013.

45. *Interactive Investor*, 7 March 2014.

46. Reuters, 1 May 2014; *Times*, 2 May 2014.

47. *Financial Times*, 5 September 2014; *Evening Standard*, 5 September 2014.

48. *Times*, 24 October 2014; *thisismoney.co.uk*, 23 October 2014.

49. *thisismoney.co.uk*, 27 January 2015.

50. Foxtons Group plc – Interim results for the half year ended 30 June 2015.

51. Property Industry Eye, 5 June 2015.

52. Foxtons Group plc – Third quarter of 2015 trading update, 22 October 2015.

53. *GlobalCapital*, 11 September 2009.

54. BC Partners press release, 21 February 2012.
55. Washington State Investment Board – Portfolio Overview by Strategy as of 31 December 2011.
56. CalSTRS – Private Equity Portfolio Performance as of 30 September 2013.

Chapter 15

1. *Gambling in America: An Encyclopedia of History, Issues, and Society*, William N. Thompson (2001); *Wall Street Journal*, 15 January 2015; CNN Money, 15 July 2004; NBC News, 15 July 2004; Harrah's Entertainment, Inc. – SEC filing, 19 July 2004; Harrah's Entertainment, Inc. – Form 10-K for the year ended 31 December 2005.
2. *Integrated marketing communications strategy: An examination of Harrah's Entertainment, Inc.*, Michael Mehling, University of Nevada, Las Vegas (Fall 2007).
3. Harrah's Entertainment, Inc. – Form S-4 dated 24 January 2005.
4. Bain & Company – Global Private Equity Report, 2012.
5. *Fortune*, 15 June 2015.
6. *Financial Times*, 3 October 2006; CreditSights, 12 October 2006; Bloomberg, 19 December 2006.
7. *Financial Times*, 29 November 2006; *Wall Street Journal*, 15 December 2006; Bloomberg, 19 December 2006; Harrah's Entertainment, Inc. – Form 10-K for the fiscal year ended 31 December 2006.
8. *USA Today*, 15 June 2007; MarketWatch, 2 July 2007; Reuters, 22 August 2007.
9. Harrah's Entertainment, Inc. – Form 10-K for the fiscal years ended 31 December 2007 and 2008.
10. Including c. $4 billion of legacy senior unsecured but excluding $2 billion undrawn revolver. Based on full-year 2007 earnings figures.
11. Harrah's Entertainment, Inc. – Form 10-K for the fiscal year ended 31 December 2008; *Wall Street Journal*, 25 October 2010.
12. *Las Vegas Review Journal*, 29 January 2008; CreditSights, 1 February 2008; Harrah's Entertainment, Inc. – Form 10-K for the fiscal year ended 31 December 2008.
13. *Financial Times*, 4 February 2008.
14. Harrah's Entertainment, Inc. – Forms 10-Q and 10-K for the fiscal year ended 31 December 2008; Moody's Investors Service, 20 November 2008.
15. Harrah's Entertainment, Inc. – Form 10-K for the fiscal year ended 31 December 2008.
16. Bloomberg, 2 May 2008 and 13 February 2009; *New York Times Dealbook*, 9 April 2008, 29 September 2008 and 2 March 2009; *Wall Street Journal*, 26 September 2008; Aleris website.
17. Harrah's Entertainment, Inc. – Form 10-K for the fiscal year ended 31 December 2009.
18. Bloomberg, 23 October 2009; Harrah's Entertainment, Inc. – Form 10-K for the fiscal year ended 31 December 2009.
19. *Wall Street Journal*, 29 July 2009; *International Financing Review* 1794 – 1 to 7 August 2009.
20. GDP data from World Bank; Harrah's Entertainment, Inc. – Form 10-K for the year fiscal ended 31 December 2009; Harrah's 2010 Investor Presentation.
21. Harrah's Entertainment, Inc. – Form 10-K for the fiscal year ended 31 December 2009.
22. Harrah's Entertainment, Inc. – Form 10-K for the fiscal year ended 31 December 2009; *Las Vegas Sun*, 3 February 2010.
23. *International Financing Review* 1856 – 23 to 29 October 2010; *Wall Street Journal*, 25 October 2010.
24. New York Post, 4 November 2009; Bloomberg 4 June 2010.
25. CreditSights, 19 October 2010; *Wall Street Journal*, 25 October 2010; Harrah's/Caesars Placement prospectus – SEC filing amendment No 4 to form S-1, 22 November 2010; Caesars Entertainment Corporation – Form 10-K for the fiscal year ended 31 December 2010.

26. Caesars Entertainment Corporation – Form 10-K for the fiscal year ended 31 December 2010.

27. Caesars placement prospectus – SEC filing amendment No 4 to form S-1, 22 November 2010; Caesars Entertainment Corp. – Form 10-K for the fiscal year ended 31 December 2010; CreditSights, 28 February 2011.

28. Caesars Entertainment Corporation – Form 10-K for the fiscal year ended 31 December 2011.

29. *Ibid.*

30. *International Financing Review* 1919 – 4 to 10 February 2012.

31. Breakingviews, 7 February 2012.

32. Bloomberg, 8 February 2012.

33. *Bloombergbriefs.com*

34. Gaming and the Great Recession, An Overview of Gambling Trends and the Oregon Lottery Outlook, Josh Lehner, State of Oregon, 27 February 2013.

35. Moody's Investors Service, 26 March 2012.

36. Caesars Entertainment Corporation – Form 10-K for the fiscal year ended 31 December 2012.

37. *International Financing Review* 1981 – 27 April to 3 May 2013.

38. Caesars Acquisition Company – Form 8-K filed on October 24, 2013 and Form 10-K for the fiscal year ended 31 December 2013.

39. *International Financing Review* 1981 – 27 April to 3 May 2013.

40. Caesars Entertainment Corporation – Forms 10-K for the fiscal years ended 31 December 2013 and 2014.

41. *Las Vegas Review Journal*, 11 February 2014.

42. CreditSights, 27 March 2014; Internal Financing Review, 30 April 2014; Caesars Entertainment Corporation – Form 10-K for the fiscal year ended 31 December 2014; Caesars Acquisition Company – Form 10-K for the fiscal year ended 31 December 2014.

43. Moody's Investors Service, 28 March 2014.

44. *International Financing Review* 2032 – 10 to 16 May 2014.

45. CreditSights, 11 May 2014.

46. Caesars Entertainment Corporation – Form 10-K for the fiscal year ended 31 December 2014.

47. *New York Post*, 17 June 2014; Wilmington Savings Fund Society, FSB lawsuit document filed in the court of Chancery of the state of Delaware, 4 August 2014; Caesars Entertainment Corporation – Form 10-K for the fiscal year ended 31 December 2014.

48. *Las Vegas Review Journal*, 5 August 2014; Bloomberg, 6 August 2014; Law360, 3 September 2014.

49. Law360, 3 September 2014 and 4 December 2014; *New York Times*, 13 September 2014.

50. Bloomberg, 11 November 2014.

51. UMB lawsuit document filed in the court of Chancery of the state of Delaware, 25 November 2014.

52. Moody's Investors Service, 16 December 2014; *International Financing Review*, 17 December 2014; Bloomberg, 12 January 2015.

53. Caesars Entertainment Corporation – Form 10-K for the fiscal year ended 31 December 2014.

54. Law360, 13 January 2015; *Wall Street Journal*, 15 January 2015.

55. Bloomberg, 12 and 13 January 2015.

56. Caesars Entertainment Operating Co. – Press release, 15 January 2015.

57. Bloomberg, 19 January 2015.

58. Law360, 23 January 2015; Bloomberg, 24 January 2015.

59. Bloomberg, 13 January 2015.

60. Bloomberg, 19 January 2015.

61. Caesars Entertainment Corporation – Form 8-K, 4 February 2015.

62. *Las Vegas Review Journal*, 11 February 2014.
63. Bloomberg, 12 January 2015; CreditSights, 15 February 2015; *Wall Street Journal*, 23 March 2015.
64. Reuters, 16 June 2015; Bloomberg, 16 June 2015.
65. *Forbes*, 22 July 2015.
66. Wilmington Savings Fund Society, FSB lawsuit document filed in the court of Chancery of the state of Delaware, 4 August 2014; UMB lawsuit document filed in the court of Chancery of the state of Delaware, 25 November 2014.
67. *Bloomberg Businessweek*, 3 April 2014.
68. CNN Money, 15 July 2004.
69. Harrah's 2010 Investor Presentation.
70. MarketWatch data; MarketWatch, 30 July 2012; Bloomberg, the 20 biggest casinos.
71. Bloomberg, 3 October 2012; *Wall Street Journal*, 30 October 2012; Caesars Entertainment Corporation – Form 10-K for the fiscal year ended 31 December 2013.
72. *Fortune*, 15 June 2015 magazine issue.
73. *The Gallic Wars*, Book III, Chapter 18, Julius Caesar.
74. *Wall Street Journal*, 5 January 2015.
75. *New York Times*, 19 November 2012; *Fortune*, 5 June 2015.
76. Harrah's Entertainment, Inc. – Form 10-K for the fiscal year ended 31 December 2008; Caesars Entertainment Corporation – Form 10-K for the fiscal year ended 31 December 2010.
77. Apollo Global Management press release, 9 January 2014.
78. Bloomberg, 9 May 2016.
79. CalPERS PE performance reports as of 31 December 2010 and 31 December 2014.
80. *Private Equity at Work: When Wall Street Manages Main Street*, Eileen Appelbaum, Rosemary Batt (2014).
81. William Shakespeare, *Julius Caesar*.

Epilogue

1. *Sam Walton: Made in America*, by Sam Walton with John Huey (1993).
2. *Daily Telegraph*, 19 July 2010.
3. *The Harbus*, 2 February 2004.
4. *Wall Street Journal*, 20 May 2014; *Financial Times*, 22 June 2015.
5. *Guardian*, 3 August 2002.

Index

Ingram Content Group UK Ltd.
Milton Keynes UK
UKHW021028030423
419491UK00006B/144